Year	Gross Domestic Product in 1987 Dollars (billions)	Personal Consumption Expenditures in 1987 Dollars (billions)	Government Purchases in 1987 Dollars (billions)	Gross Private Domestic Investment in 1987 Dollars (billions)	Exports in 1987 Dollars (billions)	Imports in 1987 Dollars (billions)	Treasury Bill Interest Rate	U.S. Dollar (1973 = 100)	Federal Budget Surplus (+) or Deficit (−) (billions)	Money Supply (December) (billions) M₁	M₂
1959	1,931.3	1,178.9	477.8	296.4	73.8	95.6	3.405	—	−2.6	140.0	297.8
1960	1,973.2	1,210.8	479.2	290.8	88.4	96.1	2.928	—	3.5	140.7	312.4
1961	2,025.6	1,238.4	503.3	289.4	89.9	95.3	2.378	—	−2.6	145.2	335.5
1962	2,129.8	1,293.3	525.9	321.2	95.0	105.5	2.778	—	−3.4	147.9	362.7
1963	2,218.0	1,341.9	538.7	343.3	101.8	107.7	3.157	—	1.1	153.4	393.3
1964	2,343.3	1,417.2	551.7	371.8	115.4	112.9	3.549	—	−2.6	160.4	424.8
1965	2,473.5	1,497.0	569.9	413.0	118.1	124.5	3.954	—	1.3	167.9	459.4
1966	2,622.3	1,573.8	628.5	438.0	125.7	143.7	4.881	—	−1.4	172.1	480.0
1967	2,690.3	1,622.4	673.0	418.6	130.0	153.7	4.321	120.0	−12.7	183.3	524.4
1968	2,801.0	1,707.5	691.0	440.1	140.2	177.7	5.339	122.1	−4.7	197.5	566.4
1969	2,877.1	1,771.2	686.1	461.3	147.8	189.2	6.677	122.4	8.5	204.0	589.6
1970	2,875.8	1,813.5	667.8	429.7	161.3	196.4	6.458	121.1	−13.3	214.5	628.1
1971	2,965.1	1,873.7	655.8	481.5	161.9	207.8	4.348	117.8	−21.7	228.4	712.7
1972	3,107.1	1,978.4	653.0	532.2	173.7	230.2	4.071	109.1	−17.3	249.3	805.2
1973	3,268.6	2,066.7	644.2	591.7	210.3	244.4	7.041	99.1	−6.6	262.9	861.0
1974	3,248.1	2,053.8	655.4	543.0	234.4	238.4	7.886	101.4	−11.6	274.4	908.6
1975	3,221.7	2,097.5	663.5	437.6	232.9	209.8	5.838	98.5	−69.4	287.6	1,023.3
1976	3,380.8	2,207.3	659.2	520.6	243.4	249.7	4.989	105.7	−52.9	306.4	1,163.7
1977	3,533.2	2,296.6	664.1	600.4	246.9	274.7	5.265	103.4	−42.4	331.3	1,286.7
1978	3,703.5	2,391.8	677.0	664.6	270.2	300.1	7.221	92.4	−28.1	358.4	1,389.0
1979	3,796.8	2,448.4	689.3	669.7	293.5	304.1	10.041	88.1	−15.7	382.8	1,497.1
1980	3,776.3	2,447.1	704.2	594.4	320.5	289.9	11.506	87.4	−60.1	408.8	1,629.8
1981	3,843.1	2,476.9	713.2	631.1	326.1	304.1	14.029	103.4	−58.8	436.4	1,793.3
1982	3,760.3	2,503.7	723.6	540.5	296.7	304.1	10.686	116.6	−135.5	474.4	1,952.9
1983	3,906.6	2,619.4	743.8	599.5	285.9	342.1	8.63	125.3	−180.1	521.2	2,186.3
1984	4,148.5	2,746.1	766.9	757.5	305.7	427.7	9.58	138.2	−166.9	552.2	2,374.7
1985	4,279.8	2,865.8	813.4	745.9	309.2	454.6	7.48	143.0	−181.4	619.9	2,569.7
1986	4,404.5	2,969.1	855.4	735.1	329.6	484.7	5.98	112.2	−201.0	724.3	2,811.6
1987	4,540.0	3,052.2	881.5	749.3	364.0	507.1	5.82	96.9	−151.8	749.7	2,910.1
1988	4,718.6	3,162.4	886.8	773.4	421.6	525.7	6.69	92.7	−136.6	786.4	3,069.0
1989	4,836.9	3,223.1	900.4	789.2	469.2	544.9	8.12	98.6	−124.2	793.6	3,223.1
1990	4,884.9	3,262.6	929.1	744.5	505.7	557.0	7.51	89.1	−165.3	825.4	3,327.8
1991	4,848.4	3,256.7	936.7	672.6	539.6	557.2	5.42	89.8	−210.4	896.7	3,425.4
1992	4,883.0	3,273.0	939.0	719.0	570.0	618.0	3.45	86.6	−303.0	892.0	1,019.0

MICROECONOMICS

MICROECONOMICS

Paul R. Gregory
University of Houston

Roy J. Ruffin
University of Houston

HarperCollins*College*Publishers

To Elizabeth Gregory and Blanche Ruffin

Senior Acquisitions Editor: Bruce Kaplan
Project Coordination and Text Design: York Production Services
Cover Design: Ed Smith Design
Production Manager: Kewal Sharma
Compositor: York Production Services
Printer and Binder: R. R. Donnelley and Sons Company
Cover Printer: Lehigh Press

Microeconomics

Library of Congress Cataloging-in-Publication Data

Gregory, Paul R.
    Microeconomics / Paul R. Gregory, Roy J. Ruffin.
        p.   cm.
    Includes indexes.
    ISBN 0-673-99044-3
    1. Microeconomics.   I. Ruffin, Roy.   II. Title.
HB172.G774   1993
338.5—dc20   93-35763
                                                 CIP

9 8 7 6 5 4 3 2 1

CONTENTS IN BRIEF

CONTENTS

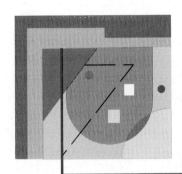

PART ONE

THE BUILDING BLOCKS OF ECONOMICS 1

APPENDIX 1   Reading Graphs 18

CHAPTER 2   The Price System 29

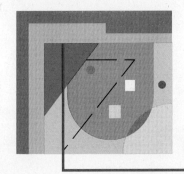

PART TWO

MICROECONOMICS AND THE PRODUCT MARKETS 89

CHAPTER 9   Perfect Competition   179

CHAPTER 10   Monopoly   201

CHAPTER 11   Oligopoly and Monopolistic Competition   219

CHAPTER 12   Regulation, Deregulation, and Antitrust   239

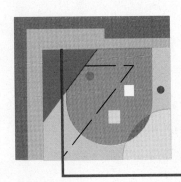

PART THREE

FACTOR MARKETS 271

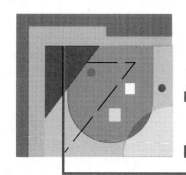

PART FOUR

ISSUES IN ECONOMICS 359

Microeconomics reflects our conviction that principles of economics texts have become too long and encyclopedic. *Microeconomics* is meant to teach students the most important economic principles—not *every* principle and its qualifications—and how these concepts can be applied to the real world in which we live. We have sought to provide a nontechnical, modern, policy-oriented text that can be covered in the normal-length course.

Microeconomics meets three basic needs of first-time students of economics. First, it teaches the core theory of economics in an up-to-date format. Second, it addresses the key economic policy issues of the day, from pollution control and poverty to information costs and international competition. Third, it teaches students to apply economics to the real world. Each chapter contains two or more real-world applications of theory to practice.

The emphasis on policy is achieved through a structural innovation. Each chapter begins with a "policy focus" to illustrate the policy issues that the chapter addresses. Each chapter ends with a "policy example" that applies the material of the chapter to a selected policy issue. This structure reinforces the importance of policy. This strengthens the student's interest in such policy issues as health-care reform and assistance to the former Soviet Union.

The "Doing Economics" sections at the end of each chapter, written by Jeffrey Parker of Reed College, challenge students to apply what they have learned in the chapter to a small project. The assignment poses an economic question and tells the student how and where to gather the information necessary to complete the assignment. In this way, students can test concepts they have learned and round out their understanding.

ORGANIZATION

Microeconomics is organized into four parts. Part One (Chapters 1–4) introduces the building blocks of economics that should be learned before proceeding to the study of microeconomics. These chapters discuss scarcity, opportunity costs, the production-possibilities frontier, the law of comparative advantage, the price system, the laws of supply and demand, and the role of government. An appendix to Chapter 1 explains how to read graphs.

Part Two begins with a study of the product markets (Chapters 5–13). Chapter 5 teaches price elasticities of demand and supply as well as income and cross-price elasticities of demand. Chapter 6 presents demand and utility (with an appendix on indifference curves for instructors desiring to give a more rigorous treatment). Business firms are studied in Chapter 7. Chapter 8 explains how costs and productivity are related. The standard market models—perfect competition, monopoly, oligopoly, and monopolist competition are covered in Chapters 9–11. The problems of antitrust and agriculture conclude Part Two.

Factor markets are taught as a five-chapter unit in Part Three (Chapters 14–18). Chapter 14 presents a theoretical overview of the workings of factor markets, and Chapters 15–17 focus on particular markets. Chapter 18 considers the determinants of income distribution.

Part Four is a two-chapter unit dealing with the broad issues of environmental economics (Chapter 19) and international trade (Chapter 20).

SUGGESTIONS FOR COURSE PLANNING

This book is intended for the microeconomics part of the two-semester sequence in economics that is traditionally taught as a first- or second-year college course. The instructor teaching a quarter course in microeconomics can build a course around the chapters listed below.

Introduction

1. What Is Economics?
2. The Price System
3. Supply and Demand
4. Government and the Economy

Microeconomics

5. Elasticity of Demand and Supply
6. Demand and Utility
8. Costs and Productivity
9. Perfect Competition
10. Monopoly
14. Factor Markets
15. Labor Markets

SUPPLEMENTS

This book's supplements include an *Instructor's Manual, Study Guide,* and *Test Bank* (available in both print and computer form for the IBM-PC and compatibles).

The *Instructor's Manual,* prepared by Henry Thompson of Auburn University, is a valuable teaching aid because it supplies the instructor with examples and real-world illustrations in addition to those in the text. A chapter outline gives a brief overview of the material; it assists the instructor in preparing lecture outlines and in seeing the logical development of the chapter. Each chapter contains teaching hints designed to bring economic concepts to the student level, key points, examples, short-answer questions and problems, and answers to questions and problems in the text.

The *Study Guide,* prepared by Jeffrey Parker of Reed College, contains an extensive review section for each chapter/appendix. The "Key Graphs" subsection features important in-text graphs, along with a detailed explanation of the meaning of each. "Key Equations" takes important in-text equations and links the symbolic representation to the verbal explanation. "Preparing Yourself for This Chapter" informs students of prior theories or chapters that should be reviewed to better understand the chapter at hand. "Foundations for Future Chapters" indicates what material in the present chapter will be built upon in future chapters. Multiple-choice problems, true/false questions, essay questions, and more advanced challenge problems all teach as well as test. Full solutions are available.

The *Test Bank* contains 2,200 questions, mainly multiple choice, and some short-answer questions.

ACKNOWLEDGMENTS

We are deeply indebted to our colleagues at the University of Houston who had to bear with us in the writing of this book. Joel Sailors helped us with a number of the examples. John Antel, Richard Bean, Thomas Mayor, Irwin Collier, Janet Kohlhase, and David Papell gave us valuable advice on many pedagogical points. To Gary Smith of Pomona College, Calvin Siebert of the University of Iowa, and Allan Meltzer of Carnegie-Mellon University we are particularly grateful for sharing with us their vast knowledge of macroeconomic issues.

The following people from across the country reviewed the manuscript in various stages of preparation. To them it is impossible to express the depth of our appreciation for their suggestions and contributions.

Wesley F. Booth	San Antonio College
Gary Burbridge	Grand Rapids Junior College
Louis P. Cain	Loyola University, Chicago
John F. Dahlquist	College of Alameda
Jan L. Dauve	University of Missouri-Columbia
Bernard Davis	Morehead State University
Gregg E. Davis	Marshall University
Donald H. Farness	Oregon State University
Martin G. Giesbrecht	Economics Associates
Robert Charles Graham	The University of North Carolina, Charlotte
Cole Gustafson	North Dakota State University
Judy Hoagland	Roane State Community College
Keith R. Leeseberg	Manatee Community College
George A. Loughran, Jr.	San Jacinto College North
Robert Metts	University of Nevada, Reno
Michael S. Miller	DePaul University
Ravindra Parashar	Saint Mary's College
Timothy Payne	Shoreline Community College
Doug Pressel	Cochise College
Ronald Schuelke	Santa Rosa Junior College
B. Ted Stecker	North Hennepin Community College
Robert W. Thomas	Iowa State University

Paul R. Gregory
Roy J. Ruffin

Many students find economics a difficult subject because economics cannot be mastered through memorization. Economics relies on economic theories to explain real-world occurrences—such as why people buy less when prices rise or why increased government taxation may increase unemployment. An economic theory is simply a logical explanation of how the facts fit together in a particular way. If the theory were not logical, or if the theory failed to be confirmed by real-world facts, it would be readily discarded by economists.

The successful student will be the one who learns that economics is built upon a number of fairly simple and easy-to-understand propositions. These propositions and assumptions—that businesses seek to maximize profits or that consumers base their expenditure decisions on disposable income—form the building blocks upon which economics is based. These propositions are typically little more than common sense. If a major building block is missing, however, the whole structure can fall apart. To prevent the student from overlooking or forgetting a critical building block, we frequently engage in pedagogical review. In other words, when a new proposition is added to a theoretical structure, the underlying propositions are briefly reviewed.

Economics—like other academic disciplines—has its own vocabulary. Unlike the physical sciences, however, where the student is encountering terms for the first time, much of the vocabulary of economics—terms such as *efficiency, capital, stock, labor*—has a common usage that is already familiar to the student. Economists, however, use the vocabulary of economics in a very exact way, and often the common usage of a term is not the same as the economic usage. In this book, each key term appears in boldface type where it is first discussed in text. Immediately following the paragraph where the term first appears in boldface type, the formal, economic definition of the term is set off in color. At the end of each chapter is a list of all the key terms that have been boldfaced and given formal definitions in that chapter; a glossary at the end of the book contains all the definitions of key terms and gives the chapter number in which the term was defined.

Economics attempts to explain in a logical manner how the facts bind together. Modern developments have occurred because established theories were not doing a good job of explaining the world around us. Fortunately, the major building blocks of modern theory—that people attempt to anticipate the future, that rising prices motivate wealth holders to spend less, that people and businesses gather information and make decisions in a rational manner—rely on commonsense logic.

Economics is valuable only if it explains the real world. Economics should be able to answer very specific questions like: Why are there three major domestic producers of automobiles and hundreds or even thousands of producers of textiles? Why is there a positive association between the growth of the money supply and inflation? Why does the United States export computers and corn to the rest of the world? Why do restaurants rope off space during less busy hours? If Iowa corn land is the best land for growing corn, why is corn also grown in Texas while some land stands idle in Iowa? Why do interest rates rise when people expect the inflation rate to increase? What is the impact of the well-publicized government deficit? The successful student will be able to apply the knowledge he or she gains of real-world economic behavior to explain any number of events that have already occurred or are yet to occur.

In writing this book, we have made a conscious effort to present arguments and evidence on both sides of every economic controversy. We attempt to make a case for each distinct viewpoint, even if it would be more interesting and less complicated to come out strongly in one camp. We believe it is best to allow the student to keep an open mind at this very early stage in the study of economics.

This book contains a number of important learning aids.

1. The *Learning Objectives* that precede each chapter provide a brief overview of the important points to be learned in that chapter.
2. *Definitions* are set off in color following the paragraphs in which key terms are introduced in context.
3. *Key Ideas*—important economic principles or conclusions—appear in the margins.
4. *Boxed Examples* allow the student to appreciate how economic concepts apply in real-world settings, without disrupting the flow of the text, and supplement the numerous examples already found in the text discussions.
5. A *Chapter Summary* of the main points of each chapter is found at the end of each chapter.
6. *Key Terms* that were defined in color in the chapter are listed at the end of each chapter.
7. *Questions and Problems* that test the reader's understanding of the chapter following each chapter.
8. A *Glossary*—containing definitions of all key terms defined in color in chapters and listed in chapter "Key Terms" sections—appears at the end of the book. Each entry contains the complete economic definition as well as the number of the chapter where the term was first defined.
9. A thorough *Index* catalogs the names, concepts, terms, and topics covered in the book.
10. The *Doing Economics* sections are end-of-chapter assignments and projects concerning the theoretical material in that chapter.

MICROECONOMICS

The Building Blocks
of Economics

P A R T   O N E

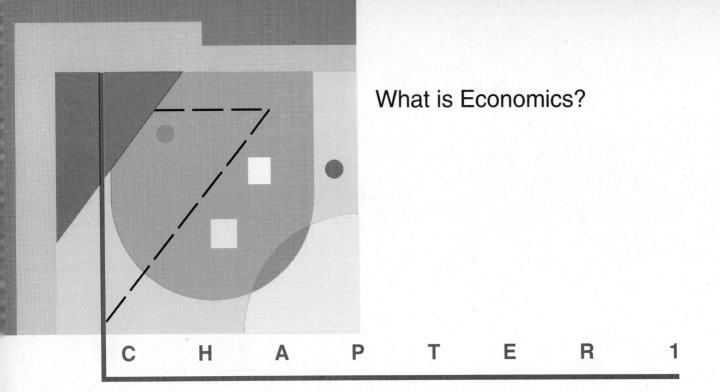

What is Economics?

C H A P T E R   1

Common expressions often reveal important truths. The expression, "There's no such thing as a free lunch," reveals a fundamental truth about economics. People are constantly being told there is indeed such a thing as a "free lunch." Unscrupulous companies promise unsuspecting small investors a "guaranteed" doubling of their money in one year. Tourists in vacation spots are promised a "free dinner and show" by peddlers of local condominium projects. Politicians promise unwitting voters that they can build new superhighways and have the best public health system in the world without an increase in taxes.

　Everyone yearns for a "free lunch," but economics explains it doesn't exist. Goods are scarce; resources are scarce. If we want more of one thing, we must give up something of another. If the government wishes to enact one spending program, society must sacrifice something else. If we want the "free lunch and show" from the condominium salesperson, we must sit through irritating sales pitches and be pestered by annoying telephone calls for the next month. Small investors who expect a guaranteed doubling of their money find either that the investment is a fraud or that the chance of the money doubling is remote.

　This chapter is about scarcity and choice, and why scarcity rules out free lunches. An understanding that there are no free lunches, and why, provides an important guide to policy. Later in this chapter, we apply the principles of scarcity and choice to explain why providing good medical care for all citizens, despite the claims of politicians and various interest groups, cannot be done on a "free lunch" basis. Each public policy must be examined in terms of its costs and benefits.

After studying this chapter, you will be able to:

- Define scarcity and how scarcity dictates hard choices.
- Understand the definition of economics as the study of how scarce resources are allocated among competing ends.
- Explain opportunity costs and how are they measured.
- Understand the shape of the production-possibilities frontier and how it can be used to show efficiency.
- Understand the use of the *ceteris paribus* assumption.
- Clearly differentiate between microeconomics and macroeconomics.
- See why most disagreements are in the area of normative economics and not positive economics.
- Understand the principle of unintended consequences.

SCARCITY AND CHOICE

The Law of Scarcity

Scarcity is the most important fact of economics. If there were no scarcity, there would be no need to study economics. As Nobel Laureate George Stigler notes: "Scarcity is the economist's equivalent of the law of conservation of matter." There is scarcity because society's virtually unlimited wants exceed the economy's ability to meet these wants.

> Scarcity exists when the goods and services that people want exceed the ability of the economy to produce those goods and services.

If we were to add up everyone's wants, it quickly would be apparent that not all wants could be met. One person's list of wants might include a different luxury car for each day of the week, a 10-bedroom and 7-bath home in the best part of town, a 15-room ski lodge, a full household staff, a private jet, several ounces of the best Russian caviar per week, a glass of the best champagne at every meal, a 20-carat diamond ring—the list could go on and on for pages. The only limits are time, imagination, and appetite. If we added together everyone's wish lists, the total number of luxury cars desired might equal 100 million per year; the total weight of Russian caviar might be 10 tons per week; the total number of household workers desired might be 50 million; people might want 100 million ski lodges. Wants are for all practical purpose unlimited.

The economy could not conceivably produce enough goods and services to meet all these wants. There is not enough land for 100 million ski lodges; virtually the entire adult population would have to become household workers; there are not enough skilled engineers and craftspersons to build the millions of luxury autos; the Caspian Sea would not yield the desired tonnage of Russian caviar per week.

The imbalance between wants and ability to meet wants is present at all times and in all places. This imbalance is such an important fact of economic life that we call it the **law of scarcity**.

> The **law of scarcity** states that the wants of every society exceed its ability to satisfy those wants.

It is impossible to escape the law of scarcity. A rich country like the United States faces scarcity just as a poor country like India does. The difference between the United States and India is in the urgency of their economic problem: Indians face so much scarcity that starvation is commonplace; most Americans face far less scarcity.

Scarcity and Allocation

We all have to make tough economic choices. Some are monumental; some are trivial. What kind of education is best for us and our children? How much should we save for retirement? Should we invest our money in stocks, bonds, real estate, or precious metals? What kind of jobs do we want? What should we do when we lose our jobs? Should we look for new jobs or should we wait to be recalled to our old jobs? Should we buy an expensive sports car and have less money for other things? Should we rent or buy a house? Should we go to a movie or eat at a restaurant?

The law of scarcity says that there will never be enough to meet everyone's wants. This means that someone or something must decide who is to get society's scarce goods. The task of allocating the goods and services that could be produced with society's resources among all the people who want them is not easy. Some wants could be met, but an even larger number would have to be denied.

There are different ways of deciding who gets what. Each of these ways is a possible means of allocating resources. One allocation system would be a lottery where only the lucky lottery winner would get the scarce good, such as a luxury car. Another allocation system would give luxury cars only to those who offer something in return—such as home repair or money. A third allocation system would be to let public officials decide who is to get luxury cars. (See Example 1.)

ECONOMIC SYSTEMS

The **economic system** is responsible for managing the allocation problem. Societies need an orderly system of allocating resources. The alternative is a breakdown in the social order as people fight among themselves for scarce goods.

> An **economic system** is the set of arrangements that a society uses to allocate scarce goods.

The two major alternative economic systems are **capitalism** and **socialism.** This book is primarily about capitalist or market economies. The next chapter explains how market economies use prices to deal with scarcity and choice. A later chapter discusses how planned socialist economies deal with scarcity and choice.

> **Capitalism** is an economic system in which the factors of production are privately owned and resource allocation decisions are made by private markets.

EXAMPLE 1

Opportunity Cost and Orbital Slots in Outer Space

Most people think of outer space as a limitless frontier. It would seem that there would be plenty of outer space in which to place the communications satellites that circle the globe. In fact, orbital slots for communications satellites are a scarce resource. The best place to put communications satellites is in a ring 22,300 miles above the equator. Satellites in this ring remain fixed relative to the point directly below on earth and are able to provide relay communications 24 hours per day.

Only a limited number of satellites can be placed in this ring at any point in time. If satellites get too close, they interfere with each other's signals, and their communications capabilities are diminished. Many communications firms would like to place their satellites in this ring, but all the slots are taken. Orbital slots are a scarce resource because the number communications firms want far exceeds the number available. Each satellite has an opportunity cost. Its presence means that another satellite cannot occupy its orbital slot.

Later chapters will show that scarce goods usually command a positive price. One economist estimates that communications companies might be willing to pay one billion dollars per year for a satellite in a prime orbital slot.

SOURCE: Timothy Tregarthen, "Outer Space: The Scarce Frontier," *The Margin,* Volume 3, No. 1 (September 1987), pp. 8–9.

Socialism is an economic system in which land and capital are owned by the state and the use of these resources is determined by the state.

The most important examples of socialism have been the former Union of Soviet Socialist Republics (USSR) and the People's Republic of China. Socialist leaders promised that their system would outlast capitalism. But the opposite has occurred. Socialism worked so poorly in the USSR that in 1991 the Soviet Union dramatically broke up into numerous separate republics, such as Russia, Latvia, and many others. All of the republics now have the goal of converting from socialism to capitalism; they are currently in the process of making this difficult transition. Socialism ran into similar difficulties in the People's Republic of China, but instead of a dramatic revolution, as in the USSR, the Chinese economy has been slowly converting from socialism to capitalism since 1979.

Unlike the examples of socialism, the laboratories of capitalism have flourished. The developing Asian countries of Hong Kong, Singapore, South Korea, and Taiwan—called the "four tigers" by some—have followed highly capitalistic policies. These countries have been so successful that other developing countries around the world are trying to use them as role models.

OPPORTUNITY COSTS

Scarcity requires that choices be made because not all wishes can be met. Scarcity means that when one person obtains more of a commodity, someone else will get less of it. Scarcity also means that when I buy one good, I cannot buy as much of other goods. Choice means that some alternatives must be forgone.

A sacrificed opportunity is called an **opportunity cost** because the economic cost of any choice is that which must be sacrificed in order to make that choice.

> The **opportunity cost** of a particular action is the value of the next best alternative.

If a person buys a new stereo, the next best alternative (its opportunity cost) might be new clothes, a television, or a video recorder. Because the person chose the car, he or she sacrificed these other things. The loss of the next best alternative is the true cost of the car. If the government increases defense spending, the opportunity cost is the next best government program that had to be sacrificed to make the funds available. If a business uses its fleet of trucks to deliver its own goods, it passes up the opportunity to rent these trucks to other businesses. If I study an extra three hours for tomorrow's exam, the opportunity cost is the next best use of that study time.

The law of scarcity implies that our economic choices involve sacrifices—opportunity costs cannot be avoided.

Every choice involving the allocation of scarce resources involves opportunity costs. Economic actions (decisions on what to buy, how to produce, what to sell at what price) are based on their opportunity cost. As we shall see, opportunity costs are a cornerstone of economic analysis.

RESOURCES

Economies face the law of scarcity because resources are limited compared to wants. The limitation of *resources* is the fundamental source of scarcity.

Resources are the natural resources (land, mineral deposits, oxygen), the capital equipment (plants, machinery, inventories), and the human resources (workers with different skills, qualifications, ambitions, managerial talents) that are used as *inputs* to produce scarce goods and services. Productive resources are also called **factors of production**. These resources determine how much output a society can produce. Because the factors of production are limited, society's ability to produce output is limited. The limitation of resources is the fundamental source of scarcity.

> The **factors of production** are the **resources** used to produce goods and services. They can be divided into three categories—land, labor, and capital.

When economists speak of capital, they mean physical capital goods—buildings, computers, trucks, plants. This concept is distinct from *financial capital.* Physical capital and financial capital are related. Financial capital is needed to purchase physical capital; financial capital represents the ownership's claims to physical capital. The owner of 1,000 shares of General Motors (GM) owns financial capital. But GM owns many automobile manufacturing plants and has a huge inventory of cars and trucks in various stages of completion. The owner of the financial shares indirectly owns GM's physical capital.

Aside from physical capital, which results from investing in machines, there is also *human capital,* which results from people making investments in themselves. People go to school to become lawyers, engineers, doctors, mechanics, and plumbers; they learn on the job to become even better at their chosen occupation. Through education and on-the-job training, the productive capacity of individuals is increased.

DEFINITION OF ECONOMICS

There are a number of definitions of economics. Despite differences, they all focus on the basic ingredients of economics—scarcity, choice, allocation, and resources. **Economics** studies how society allocates its scarce resources among all of the competing uses for those resources. It recognizes that different societies use different economic systems to allocate scarce resources, but it emphasizes that all societies—be they capitalist or communist—must grapple with the same problem.

> **Economics** is the study of how *scarce resources* are *allocated* among *competing ends*.

The following chapters will explain how land, labor, and capital resources are directed by market prices to produce the goods and services desired by consumers. We shall consider how resources are allocated, the purposes to which they are put, and how effectively this is done by market economies.

THE PRODUCTION-POSSIBILITIES FRONTIER

Economists use models to explain the economy. A *model* shows how different factors or variables fit together. These models portray the world in a simplified fashion, yet they illustrate and explain economic principles powerfully. The **production-possibilities factor *(PPF)*** is a useful analytical model for illustrating scarcity, choice, and opportunity costs.

> The **production-possibilities frontier** *(PPF)* shows the alternative combinations of different goods and services that a society can produce given its available resources and its technical know-how.

Suppose an economy produces only two types of goods: cars and space shuttles. The table in Exhibit 1 shows the number of space shuttles and cars that this hypothetical economy can produce with its limited supply of factors of production and its acquired technical knowledge. The graph gives a pictorial representation of the accompanying table.

What do these numbers mean? Think of the economy as having resources that can be used for either space shuttles or cars. If our hypothetical economy chose to be at point *a*, it would be producing no cars and a *maximum* of 18 space shuttles from the factors of production available. At point *f* the economy would be producing no space shuttles and a *maximum* of 5,000 cars. Point *c* shows that if 2,000 cars are produced, the maximum number of space shuttles that can be produced is 15. Each intermediate point on the *PPF* between *a* and *f* represents a different combination of space shuttles and cars that could be produced using the same resources and technology.

Our hypothetical economy is capable of producing output combinations *a* through *f*. The economy is unable to produce output combination *g* (17 space shuttles and 3,000 cars) because *g* requires more resources than the economy has available. Point *h* is an attainable combination because it lies inside the frontier. The economy can produce any combination of outputs on or inside the *PPF*. (See Example 2.)

EXHIBIT 1   The Production-Possibilities Frontier (PPF)

a. *PPF* Graph

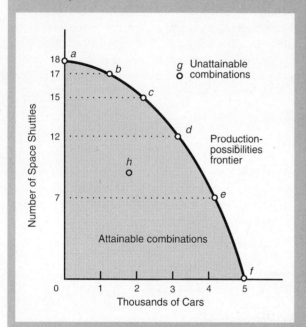

b. Production-Possibilities Schedule

Combination	Cars (thousands)	Space Shuttles	Opportunity Cost of Cars (number of space shuttles)
a	0	18	0
b	1	17	1
c	2	15	2
d	3	12	3
e	4	7	5
f	5	0	7

The *PPF* shows the combination of outputs of two goods that can be produced from society's resources when these resources are utilized to their maximum potential. Point *a* shows that if 18 space shuttles are produced, no car production is possible. Point *f* shows that if no space shuttles are produced, a maximum of 5,000 cars can be produced. Point *d* shows that if 3,000 cars are produced, a maximum of 12 space shuttles can be produced. Point *g* is above society's *PPF*. With its available resources, the economy cannot produce 17 space shuttles and 3,000 cars. Points like *h* inside the *PPF* represent an inefficient use of the society's resources.

The Law of Increasing Costs

The production-possibilities frontier is curved like a bow; it is not a straight line. Why? The economic cost of any action is the loss of the next best opportunity. In our example, the economy produces only two goods. The opportunity cost of increasing the production of one good is the amount of the other good that must be sacrificed. In this case, the opportunity cost of cars is simply the space shuttle production that must be sacrificed.

At *a* the economy is producing 18 space shuttles and no cars. The opportunity cost of increasing the production of cars from zero to 1,000 is the 1 space shuttle that must be sacrificed in the move from *a* to *b*. The opportunity cost of 1,000 more cars (moving from *b* to *c*) is 2 space shuttles. The opportunity cost of the fifth thousand of cars (moving from *e* to *f*) is much higher, 7 space shuttles. The number of space shuttles that must be given up at each level to increase car production is given in the last column of the table in Exhibit 1. The opportunity cost per thousand of car production rises with the production of cars, which is consistent with the **law of increasing costs.**

The **law of increasing costs** states that as more of a particular commodity is produced, its opportunity cost per unit will increase.

EXAMPLE 2

Hawaiian Pineapples and the Production-Possibilities Frontier

In our daily lives, we rarely see that the economy must sacrifice some of one good to produce more of another. On a two-dimensional diagram in which the economy produces only two goods, this is obvious. In real life, where we encounter millions of distinct goods, it is rarely apparent that the economy must trade off goods because resources are limited.

The small Hawaiian island of Lanai provides a rare direct insight into the principle of the production-possibilities frontier. As a small island economy. Lanai cannot produce everything. Its land mass is limited; its population is limited.

Until 1992, Lanai was renowned as the home of Dole Pineapple. The moist, fertile, volcanic soil of Lanai had proven ideal for pineapple production for more than a century, and Lanai Dole pineapples were known throughout the world. Yet, as the tourism industry spread from Oahu and Maui to Lanai, more money was to be made by building hotels and condominiums than by growing pineapples. Lanai could not produce more tourism services without producing fewer pineapples. As tourism expanded, workers were drawn from the Dole fields and plants into hotel and restaurant services. Land was switched from plantations to golf courses. Resources shifted from the declining industry to the rising industry, and Dole closed its historic pineapple operations in 1992.

The law of increasing costs is responsible for the bowed-out shape of the *PPF*. Suppose our hypothetical economy produced only cars. Its arch-rival plans to land a person on Mars by the end of the century. To respond to this challenge, our hypothetical economy must suddenly increase its production of space shuttles. The amount of resources available to the economy is not altered by the declaration of a space race, so the increased space shuttle production must be at the expense of cars. The economy must move along its *PPF* in the direction of more shuttle production.

At low levels of shuttle production, the opportunity cost of a unit of shuttle production will be relatively low. Some factors of production will be suited to producing both space shuttles and cars; they can be shifted from cars to space shuttles without raising opportunity cost. As space shuttle production increases further, resources suited to car production but not to space shuttle production (some assembly line workers, perhaps) must be diverted into shuttle production. As resources are increasingly used that are poorly suited for shuttle production, the extra shuttle output gained from shifting these resources falls. The opportunity cost of a space shuttle (the number of cars sacrificed) will rise, as the law of increasing costs would require.

Efficiency

The *PPF* shows the combination of goods an economy is capable of producing when its limited resources are utilized to their maximum potential. Whether an economy actually operates on its production-possibilities frontier depends on whether the economy utilizes its resources with maximum **efficiency**.

In Exhibit 1, if the economy produces output combinations that lie on the

PPF, the economy is said to be *efficient*. When an economy is operating on its *PPF*, it cannot increase the production of one good without reducing the production of another good. If the economy operates at points inside the *PPF*, such as *h*, it is *inefficient* because more space shuttles could be produced without cutting back on the other good.

> **Efficiency** results when no resources are unemployed and when no resources are misallocated.

The production-possibilities frontier shows the limits of what an economy can produce or consume without additional resources or new technology.

If workers are unemployed or if productive machines stand idle, the economy is not operating on its *PPF* because some resources are not being employed. If these idle resources were used, more of one good could be produced without reducing the production of other goods. *Misallocated resources* are resources that are used but not to their best advantage. For example, if a surgeon works as a ditchdigger, if cotton is planted on Iowa corn land, or if bananas are grown in Alaska, resources are misallocated. Again, if resource misallocations are removed, more of one good could be produced without sacrificing the production of other goods.

The Ceteris Paribus or "Other Things Equal" Assumption

The *PPF* illustrates the choice of outputs open to an economy operating with a *given supply of resources and a fixed technology*. The *PPF* in Exhibit 1 is drawn for a given amount of resources and a given technology. The *PPF* in effect asks the question: If the economy produces more space shuttles, how many cars would have to be sacrificed *if this were the only thing that changed in the economy?* The practice of asking what would happen if one thing changed and all other things remained the same is the **ceteris paribus** assumption.

> The *ceteris paribus* assumption (meaning "all other things equal") considers the effects of a change in one factor assuming that all other relevant factors remain the same.

The *ceteris paribus* conditions for the *PPF* are that technology and the quantities of the various resources are constant at every point along the curve. Holding these factors constant means that any change in auto production must be at the expense of space shuttle production. However, it may be possible to produce more of both cars and space shuttles if more resources become available or if an improved technology allows the economy to produce more cars or space shuttles from the same resources. In Exhibit 2, the *PPF* of Exhibit 1 is labeled as *XX*. It shows the trade-off between cars and space shuttles *with given resources and given technology*.

Ceteris paribus is a tool used frequently in economic analysis. It allows us to concentrate attention on one single factor at a time and hence to make sense of complicated processes.

As time passes, however, resources grow and technology improves. With more resources and better technology, the economy is capable of producing more cars along with the same number of space shuttles (or more space shuttles along with the same number of cars). The change in resources and technology has caused the production-possibilities frontier to shift out to the right (from *XX* to *YY*). The outward shift of the *PPF* illustrates the process of economic growth, studied in a later chapter.

EXHIBIT 2   Shifts in the *PPF* and the *Ceteris Paribus* Assumption

The production-possibilities frontier labeled *XX* is for the amount of resources and technology given in Exhibit 1. Movements along this *PPF* show what happens if more of one good is produced and there is no change in resources or technology. The *PPF* labeled *YY* shows that the *PPF* shifts to the right when resources increase and technology improves.

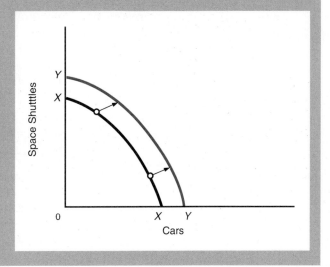

MICROECONOMICS AND MACROECONOMICS

Economics is divided into two main branches, *microeconomics* and *macroeconomics*. Microeconomics and macroeconomics deal with the economy from different vantage points.

Microeconomics

Microeconomics focuses on the individual participants in the economy: the producers, workers, employers, and consumers. In everyday economic life, things are bought and sold, people decide where and how many hours to work. Business managers decide what to produce and how to organize this production. These activities result in transactions that take place in markets where buyers and sellers come together.

> **Microeconomics** studies the economic decision-making of firms and individuals in markets; it is the study of the economy in the small.

Because it deals with economic decisions made in a market setting, microeconomics studies how all the buyers and sellers in particular markets (such as the market for wheat, or the market for cars, or the market for local residential real estate) come together to make transactions. Microeconomics studies how business firms operate under different competitive conditions in different types of markets and how the combined actions of buyers and sellers determine prices in specific markets. Microeconomics studies households as earners of wages, interest, rent, and profit and, accordingly, studies the distribution of income. Microeconomics studies all kinds of transactions.

Macroeconomics

Instead of analyzing prices, outputs, and transactions in individual markets, **macroeconomics** studies the production of the entire economy. Macroeconomics studies the *general* price level (rather than individual prices), the national employment rate, government spending, the federal deficit, interest rates, and the nation's money supply.

> **Macroeconomics** is the study of the economy in the large. Rather than dealing with individual markets and individual consumers and producers, macroeconomics examines the economy as a whole.

Because macroeconomics studies the economy as a whole, measures of total economic activity are required. Macroeconomic *aggregates,* such as gross domestic product, the consumer price index, the unemployment rate, and the government surplus and deficit, are used to determine macroeconomic outcomes. These measures are called *aggregates* because they add together (or aggregate) individual microeconomic components.

Just as microeconomics studies the relationships between individual participants in the economy, macroeconomics studies relationships between aggregate measures. What are the determinants of inflation? What is the relationship between inflation and interest rates? What are the effects of government deficits on prices and interest rates? What is the relationship between the money supply and inflation?

Microeconomics and macroeconomics share common ground. Macroeconomists study the behavior of persons and individual businesses to shed light on a number of key macroeconomic issues. How does inflation affect the output decisions of businesses and the job searches of unemployed individuals? How are individual saving decisions affected by government debt? How do individuals and businesses form expectations of inflation, and how are interest rates and inflation affected when these expectations change?

POSITIVE AND NORMATIVE ECONOMICS

Economists have the unfair reputation of being unable to agree on anything. People joke about getting "six different answers from five economists." While those in other sciences disagree, their disagreements are less visible. Theoretical physicists have long disagreed about the physical nature of the universe, but this scientific controversy is little understood by the public. Economic disputes, however, quickly receive public attention. Everyone is interested in economic questions: Will inflation accelerate? Will I lose my job? Will interest rates fall?

The amount of disagreement among economists differs depending on whether issues of *positive economics* or *normative economics* are involved.

Positive Economics

Positive economics studies how the economy works. It avoids the question of how the economy *should* work.

> **Positive economics** is the study of *what is* in the economy.

Economists generally agree on matters of positive economics. They agree that rising prices reduce consumption (*ceteris paribus*), that rising income will have predictable effects on consumer purchases, that wage and price controls cause shortages, that tariffs and quotas raise prices to consumers, and that minimum-wage laws increase unemployment among youth and unskilled workers. The easiest matters on which to achieve agreement involve the microeconomic relationships that actually prevail in an economy.

The areas of disagreement in positive economics tend to be concentrated in macroeconomics. Economists disagree on the causes of inflation and unemployment, on the relationship between deficits and unemployment, and on the role of government in fighting inflation and unemployment. It is not surprising that economics has not resolved these issues. The economy is a complex organism, comprised of millions of individuals, hundreds of thousands of business firms, and thousands of local, state, and federal government offices. Collective economic actions are difficult to analyze. Emotions are volatile; expectations can change overnight; relationships held last year no longer hold today; it is costly and difficult to collect up-to-date economic facts. Many economic events are random and unpredictable. Economists are not to be blamed for the complexity of these problems.

Normative Economics

Economists do disagree—often strongly—about **normative economics.**

> **Normative economics** is the study of *what ought to be* in the economy.

Economists disagree on whether we should have more unemployment or more inflation; over whether income taxes should be lowered for the middle class, the rich, or the poor; over job programs; over government-subsidized health programs. These disagreements are only partly over "what is"; opponents in a debate may agree on what will happen if Program A is chosen over Program B, but they may disagree sharply over their personal evaluation of the desirability of those consequences. Disputes over "what ought to be" are often the foundation for why economists disagree.

Normative economics always involves some concern over an economic problem—perhaps people think that there is too much inflation, too much poverty, too much unemployment, or inadequate medical care. In democracies, there is usually some pressure to pass a piece of legislation designed to correct the problem, but economic problems are not easy to solve. Normative economists must pay attention to the **principle of unintended consequences,** according to which the ultimate effects of economic or social policies may be different from the apparent or intended effects. Indeed, the "cure" can sometimes be worse than the "disease."

> The **principle of unintended consequences** holds that policies may have ultimate or actual effects that differ from the intended or apparent effects.

Numerous economic policies have unintended consequences. Rent control can cause housing shortages; unemployment benefits can increase unemployment; raises in the minimum wage can hurt the poor by eliminating jobs; welfare checks given to poor mothers can break up families; free housing for the homeless can hurt other poor people; taxing the goods rich people buy also taxes those who serve the

Why There Is No Free Lunch in Medical Care

Everyone agrees that people should have good medical care. It is not fair that some people get better medical care than others. This complaint is particularly prominent during political campaigns when the different candidates and parties try to persuade voters that their plan is better than others. Most often it is "fee-for-service" medicine that is criticized. If people have to pay to get medical service, those who can't afford it will be excluded.

If everyone agrees that everyone should have access to good medical care, why can't we simply do it?

Let's consider the options. One option would be for medical services to be free of charge. The government simply pays through tax dollars. Anyone who wants medical care can have it. In effect, medical care appears to be a "free lunch" in this situation. Although people typically do not relish going to doctors or to hospitals, the amount of medical care that people would want if it were free would far exceed the limited numbers of doctors, nurses, and medications available. Medical resources are scarce. As long as people want more than is available, someone must do without. Either those willing to stand in line the longest get the service or those with special connections get the service. The government may wish to set rules and standards (such as excluding the elderly or terminally ill) to limit the number of people receiving free medical care.

Another option might be for the government to mandate compulsory health insurance so that the insurance company pays health expenses. Even more appealing: Why don't we let the employer "pay" by requiring all businesses to pay for employee health insurance?

The appearance of the free lunch is deceiving. If the employer has to pay the employee's health insurance, hiring becomes more expensive, and the employer would cut back on the payroll. Many small businesses would not be started. People would be thrown out of work, and wages would fall. What appears to be a "free lunch" has been paid for by employees in the form of fewer jobs and lower wages. Moreover, if people knew that the insurance company had to pay the medical bill, they again would demand more medical resources than are available, and the insurance company, not the government, would have to establish rules concerning what kinds of medical treatments are insured and which are not. All of these reactions are examples of the law of unintended consequences explained in this chapter.

Why is it important to understand the principle that "there is no such thing as a free lunch"? In our everyday lives, we must carefully analyze what things really cost, either directly or indirectly. In our political lives, we must be wary of the promises of politicians that they can give us something for nothing. All private and public policies must be examined in terms of their true costs and benefits.

rich; equal pay for men and women can result in fewer jobs for women; bank deposit insurance to protect consumers can encourage bankers to act irresponsibly; medical insurance for some can lead to an explosion of medical costs for everyone; safety legislation for workers can lower their wages; and making cigarette advertising illegal can raise the profits of cigarette producers.

Economists can make important contributions to sound economic policy. It is one thing to identify a problem. The principle of unintended consequences tells us that the development of a sound economic policy requires creating private incentives that are consistent with the ultimate goal. For example, economists have suggested that we deal with pollution by setting up a market for pollution rights, or that we address the failure of public schools by giving students vouchers that can be used to purchase education from any private or public school.

Each of the following chapters contains a biographical sketch of one of the great economists of the past. Economists are a varied lot. Most are professors, but some have been stockbrokers, preachers, or journalists. They are interesting because their ideas affect the way we live. John Maynard Keynes, a great economist and one of economics' most fascinating personalities, once explained how the ideas of economists become widely applied.

". . . the ideas of economists . . . , both when they are right and when they are wrong, are more powerful than is commonly understood. Indeed the world is ruled by little else. Practical men, who believe themselves to be quite exempt from any intellectual influences, are usually the slaves of some defunct economist. Madmen in authority, who hear voices in the air, are distilling their frenzy from some academic scribbler of a few years back. I am sure that the power of vested interests is vastly exaggerated compared with the gradual encroachment of ideas. Not, indeed, immediately, but after a certain interval; for in the field of economic . . . philosophy there are not many who are influenced by new theories after they are twenty-five or thirty years of age, so that the ideas which civil servants and politicians and even agitators apply to current events are not likely to be the newest. But soon or late, it is ideas, not vested interests, which are dangerous for good or evil."

SOURCE: John Maynard Keynes, *The General Theory of Employment, Interest, and Money* (New York: Harcourt Brace and Jovanovich, 1936), pp. 383–84.

How the price system allocates scarce resources and the workings of a market economy will be discussed in the next chapter.

Chapter Summary

The most important point to learn from this chapter is: The law of scarcity means that people's wants cannot be fully satisfied from limited resources and that any choice of any scarce good involves sacrificed opportunities. That is, there is no free lunch.

1. Wants are unlimited; there will never be enough resources to meet unlimited wants. Scarcity dictates that choices be made among alternatives. The economic system allocates scarce resources.

2. Economics is the study of how scarce resources are allocated among competing ends. The ultimate source of scarcity is the limited supply of resources. The factors of production are land, labor, and capital.

3. The opportunity cost of any choice is the next best alternative that was sacrificed to make the choice.

4. The production-possibilities frontier *(PPF)* shows the maximum combinations of goods that an economy is able to produce from its limited resources when these resources are utilized to their maximum potential and for a given state of technical knowledge. If societies are efficient, they will operate on the production-possibilities frontier. The law of increasing costs says that as more of one commodity is produced at the expense of others, its opportunity cost will increase. The two sources of economic inefficiency are unemployed resources and misallocated resources.

5. Economists study how one factor affects another by considering what would happen if all other things remained the same. This is the *ceteris paribus* assumption.

6. Microeconomics studies the economy in the small. Macroeconomics studies the economy in the large.

7. Most disputes in economics are about normative economics (what ought to be) rather than about positive economics (what is). Policies often have unintended consequences because they create private incentives inconsistent with the ultimate goal.

Key Terms

scarcity (p. 3)
law of scarcity (p. 3)
economic system (p. 4)
opportunity cost (p. 5)
capitalism (p. 4)
socialism (p. 4)
factors of production (p. 6)
economics (p. 7)
production-possibilities frontier *(PPF)* (p. 7)

law of increasing costs (p. 8)
efficiency (p. 9)
ceteris paribus (p. 10)
microeconomics (p. 11)
macroeconomics (p. 12)
positive economics (p. 12)
normative economics (p. 13)
principle of unintended consequences (p. 13)

Questions and Problems

1. "The fundamental nature of economics has changed. Today, we worry about buying VCRs or compact disks; yesterday we worried about where our next meal was coming from." Evaluate.

2. This chapter argues that scarcity results from the fact that resources are limited. Does it follow that scarcity will be eliminated as resources increase?

3. Henry spends all of his extra money on compact disks. They cost $15 each. If Henry must spend $45 for a new tire, what is his opportunity cost measured in terms of sacrificed compact disks?

4. Because I bought a new stereo today, I am no longer able to buy a new TV set. Is the TV set my opportunity cost?

5. If higher TV prices mean that people will want to buy fewer TV sets, explain how the *ceteris paribus* assumption might be used to clarify this statement.

6. What are *ceteris paribus* conditions that apply to the production-possibility frontier?

7. Consider the data in Table A on a hypothetical economy's production-possibilities frontier *(PPF)*.
   a. Graph the *PPF*.
   b. Does the *PPF* have the expected shape?
   c. Calculate the opportunity cost of cars in terms of space shuttles. Calculate the opportunity cost of space shuttles in terms of cars. Do your results illustrate the law of increasing costs?
   d. If this economy produced 700 cars and 3 space shuttles, what would you conclude about how this economy is solving the *how* problem?

e. If this economy at some later date produced 700 cars and 12 space shuttles, what would you conclude?

TABLE A

Number of Cars	Number of Space Shuttles
800	0
700	4
500	10
300	14
100	16
0	16.25

8. In a hypothetical economy that produces only two goods, how would opportunity costs be defined? In a real-world economy that produces millions of goods and services, how would the opportunity cost of buying one good be defined?

9. One economist believes that higher interest rates lead to higher inflation. Another believes that inflation can be reduced by raising interest rates. Is this a disgreement over normative or positive economics? Why or why not?

10. Which of the following topics would fall under macroeconomics? Which under microeconomics? Explain why in each case.
   a. The price of fish.
   b. The effect of the stock market on the economy.
   c. Employment in the computer industry.
   d. The general price level.

e. The national unemployment rate.

f. The price of cars.

g. The number of new plants built in the United States.

11. Economists would be more likely to agree on the answers to which of the following questions? Why?

a. Should tax rates be lowered for the rich?

b. What would be the effects on economic output of a lowering of tax rates for the rich?

c. What would be the effects of an increase in the price of VCRs on purchases of VCRs?

d. Should government expenditures on defense be reduced?

e. What would be the effects of an increase in military spending on employment?

12. Why are economic policies difficult to design?

Doing Economics

Suppose that you have an economics test and a test in another subject next Monday. What would it mean for your study time to be scarce in this context? Suppose that your study time is, in fact, scarce. How could you represent the tradeoff between studying for economics and studying for the other subject on a production-possibilities frontier? (Hint: Make sure that you draw the frontier in terms of the outputs of your studying, not the input of time.) What shape would this *PPF* have? Why?

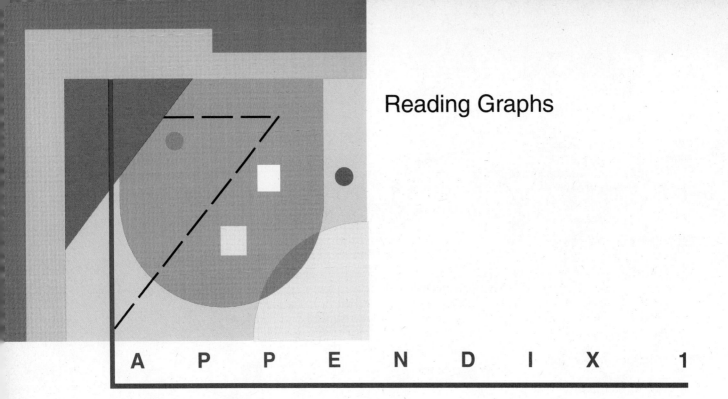

Reading Graphs

APPENDIX FOCUS   Graphs are an important tool in learning economics. In this appendix you will learn how to work with graphs. Topics covered are graph construction, positive and negative relationships, dependent and independent variables, and the concept of slope for both linear and curvilinear relationships. This appendix shows how slopes are used to find the maximum and minimum values, and it explains how to calculate the areas of rectangles. The use of scatter diagrams to view positive and negative relationships in real data is also discussed.

After studying this appendix, you will be able to:

■ Understand positive and negative relationships.

■ Determine the slopes of linear and curvilinear relationships.

■ Understand how to read scatter diagrams.

■ Know how to calculate the areas of rectangles.

THE VALUE OF GRAPHS

Economics makes extensive use of graphs. A graph is simply a visual scheme for picturing the quantitative relationship between two different variables. Not only can a graph display a great deal of data, a graph can efficiently describe the quantitative relationship that exists between the variables. As the Chinese proverb says, "a picture is worth a thousand words."

Positive and Negative Relationships

Graphs can show whether there is a **positive** (or **direct**) **relationship** or a **negative** (or **inverse**) **relationship** between two variables.

A positive (or direct) relationship exists between two variables if an increase in the value of one variable is associated with an *increase* in the value of the other variable.

When two variables are positively related the graph of the relationship is an upward-sloping curve.

For example, an increase in the *horsepower* of a car's engine will increase the *maximum speed* of the automobile (holding other factors, such as the weight of the car, constant). Panel (a) of Exhibit 1 depicts this relationship in a graph. The *vertical axis* measures the maximum speed of the car from the 0 point (called the *origin*); the *horizontal axis* measures the horsepower of the engine. When horsepower is 0 (the engine is broken down), the maximum speed the car can attain is obviously 0; when horsepower is 300, the maximum speed is 100 miles per hour. Intermediate values of horsepower (between 0 and 300) can be graphed. When a line is drawn through all these points, the resulting curved line describes the effect of horsepower on maximum speed. Since the picture is a line that goes from low to high speeds as horsepower increases, it is an example of an *upward-sloping curve*.

A negative (or inverse) relationship exists between two variables if an increase in the value of one variable is associated with a *reduction* in the value of the other variable.

When two variables are negatively related the graph of the relationship is a downward-sloping curve.

For example, as the *horsepower* of that automobile increases, the *gas mileage* (for given driving conditions) will fall (again, other things equal). In panel (b), horsepower is still measured on the horizontal axis, but now gas mileage is measured on the vertical axis. Since the picture is a curve going from high to low values of gas mileage as horsepower increases, it is an example of a *downward-sloping curve*.

EXHIBIT 1   Positive and Negative Relationships

a. A Positive Relationship   **b. A Negative Relationship**

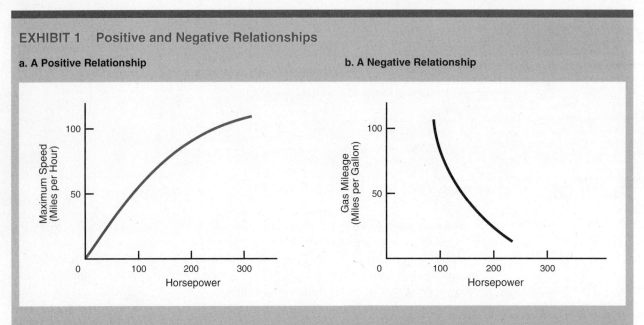

Panel (a) shows a positive relationship. As the horizontal variable (horsepower) increases, the value of the vertical variable (maximum speed) increases. The curve rises from left to right. Panel (b) shows a negative relationship. As the horizontal variable (horsepower) increases, the vertical variable (mileage) decreases. The curve falls from left to right.

Graphs Show Relationships and Display Data Efficiently

Panel (a) of Exhibit 2 shows a graph drawn from data shown in panel (b). The numbers in the table describe the quantitative relationship between *minutes of typing* and *number of pages typed*. The quantitative relationship between minutes and pages is that every 5 minutes of typing will produce 1 page of manuscript. Thus, 5 minutes produces 1 page, 15 minutes produces 3 pages, and so on. Zero minutes will, of course, produce 0 pages.

Each pair of numbers is plotted at the intersection of the vertical line that corresponds to that value of *X* and the horizontal line that corresponds to that value of *Y*. Point *a* shows that 5 minutes of typing produces 1 page. Point *c* shows that 15 minutes of typing produces 3 pages, and so on. Points *a, b, c, d,* and *e* completely describe the data in the table.

The first advantage of graphs over tables is that it is easier to see the relationship between two variables in a graph than in a table. Graphs provide an immediate visual understanding of the quantitative relationship between the two variables just by observing the plot of points. Since the points in this case move upward from left to right, we know that there is a *positive relationship* between the variables. This may not seem to be a great advantage for this simple and obvious case. However, if the data in the table had not been arranged in ascending order, it would have taken a while to figure out that the relationship was positive.

The second advantage of graphs over tables is that large quantities of data can be represented more efficiently in a graph. Suppose that in addition to the table, we had data for the number of pages that could be typed at all kinds of intermediate values of typing time: 6 minutes, 13 minutes, 24 minutes and 25 seconds. A large table would be required to report all these numbers. In a graph, however, the intermediate values can be represented simply by connecting points *a, b, c, d,* and *e* with a line.

EXHIBIT 2   Advantages of Graphs over Tables

a. Graph of Pages Typed per Minute

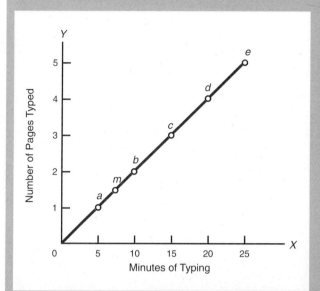

b. Table of Pages Typed per Minute

	Minutes of Typing (*X* axis)	Number of Pages Typed (*Y* axis)
	0	0
a	5	1
b	10	2
c	15	3
d	20	4
e	25	5

The graph reproduces the data in the table. Point *a* shows that 5 minutes of typing produces 1 typed page, *b* shows that 10 minutes of typing produces 2 typed pages, and so on. Graphs have two advantages over tables. First, the upward-sloping line drawn through *a, b, c, d,* and *e* shows clearly that the relationship between minutes of typing and number of pages typed is positive. Second, graphs suggest intermediate values. The points between *a, b, c, d,* and *e* (such as *m*) suggest the number of pages typed for amounts of typing time between the 5-minute intervals.

Shifts in Graphs

The relationship between minutes of typing and number of pages typed is graphed in Exhibit 2. The relationship can change, however, if other factors that affect typing speed change. Assume that Exhibit 2 shows minutes and pages typed on a manual typewriter. If the typist works with a high-speed electric typewriter, a different relationship will emerge. With the electric typewriter, the typist can type 2 pages every 5 minutes instead of one. Both relationships are graphed in Exhibit 3, which shows that if factors that affect speed of typing change (the quality of the typewriter), the relationship between minutes and pages can shift. Economists work frequently with relationships that shift, so it is important to understand shifts in graphs.

UNDERSTANDING SLOPE

The relationship between two variables is represented by a curve's **slope**. Many central concepts of economics require an understanding of slope.

Straight Lines

The slope reflects the response of one variable to changes in another. Consider the typing example. Every 5 minutes of typing on a manual typewriter produces 1

EXHIBIT 3   Shifts in Relationships

The curve *abcde* shows the relationship between minutes of typing and pages typed using a manual typewriter. The new (higher) curve *fghij* shows the relationship between minutes of typing and pages typed with an electric type-writer. As a consequence of the change from a manual to an electric typewriter, the relationship has shifted upward.

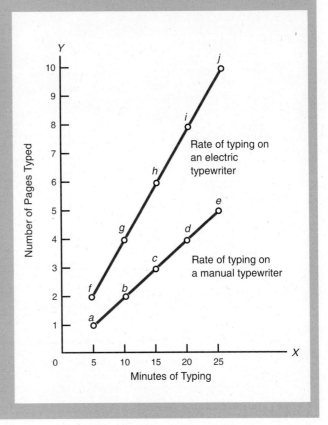

page; equivalently, every minute of typing produces 1/5th of a page. As we shall demonstrate below, the slope of the line *abcde* is 1/5th of a page of typing per minute.

The **slope** of a straight line is the ratio of the rise (or fall) in *Y* (measured on the vertical axis) over the run in *X* (measured on the horizontal axis).

A positive value of the slope signifies a positive relationship between the two variables. *A negative value of the slope signifies a negative relationship* between the two variables.

To understand slope more precisely, consider in panel (a) of Exhibit 4 the straight-line relationship between the two variables X and Y. When $X = 5$, $Y = 3$; when $X = 7$, $Y = 6$. Suppose now that variable X is allowed to *run* (to change horizontally) from 5 units to 7 units. When this happens variable Y *rises* (increases vertically) from 3 units to 6 units.

The slope of the line in panel (a) is:

$$\frac{\text{Rise in } Y}{\text{Run in } X} = \frac{3}{2} = 1.5.$$

This formula works for negative relationships as well. In panel (b) of Exhibit 4, when X runs from 5 to 7, Y *falls* 4 units to 1 unit, or rises by −3 units. Thus, the slope is:

EXHIBIT 4 Positive and Negative Slope

a. Positive Slope

b. Negative Slope

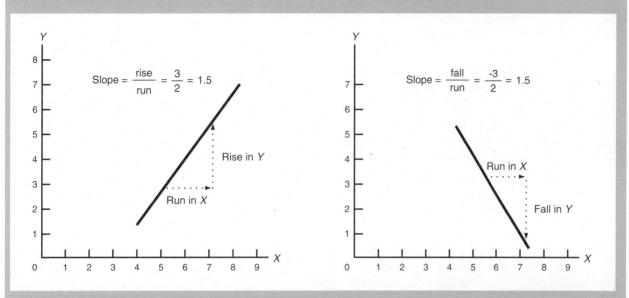

Positive slope is measured by the ratio of the rise in Y over the run in X. In panel (a), Y rises by 3 and X runs by 2, and the slope is 1.5. Negative slope is measured by the ratio of the fall in Y over the run in X. In panel (b), the fall in Y is –3, in the run in X is 2, and the slope is –1.5.

$$\frac{\text{Rise in } Y}{\text{Run in } X} = \frac{-3}{2} = 1.5.$$

If ΔY (delta Y) stands for the change in the value of Y and ΔX (delta X) stands for the change in the value of X,

$$\text{Slope} = \frac{\Delta Y}{\Delta X}.$$

This formula holds for positive or negative relationships.

Let us return to the typing example. What slope expresses the relationship between minutes of typing and number of pages? When minutes increase by 5 units ($\Delta X = 5$), pages increase by one unit ($\Delta Y = 1$). The slope is therefore $\Delta Y/\Delta X = 1/5$.

In Exhibits 2, 3, and 4, the points are connected by straight lines. Such relationships are called *linear relationships*. The inquisitive reader will wonder how slope is measured when the relationship between X and Y is *curvilinear*.

Curvilinear Relationships

A curvilinear example is given in Exhibit 5. When X runs from 2 units to 4 units ($\Delta X = 2$), Y rises by 2 units ($\Delta Y = 2$); thus, between a and b the slope is 2/2 = 1. Between a and c, however, X runs from 2 to 6 ($\Delta X = 4$), Y rises by 3 units ($\Delta Y = 3$), and the slope is 3/4. In the curvilinear case, the value of the slope depends on how far X is allowed to run. Between b and c, the slope is 1/2. The slope changes

EXHIBIT 5   Tangents and Slopes of Curvilinear Relationships

The ratio of the rise over the run yields a slope of 1 from *a* to *b* but a slope of 3/4 from *a* to *c*. From *b* to *c*, the slope is 1/2. To compute the slope at point *a*, the slope of the tangent to *a* is calculated. The value of the slope of the tangent is 3/2.

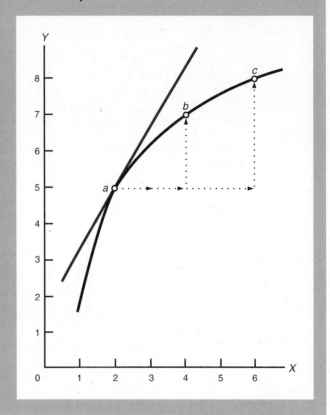

as one moves along a curvilinear relationship. In the linear case, the value of the slope will *not* depend on how far X runs because the slope is constant and does not change as one moves from point to point.

There is no single slope of a curvilinear relationship and no single method of measuring slopes. The slope can be measured between two points (say, between *a* and *b* or between *b* and *c*) or at a particular point (say, at point *a*). Insofar as the measurement of the slope between points depends on the length of the run, a uniform standard must be adopted to avoid confusion. This standard is the use of *tangents* to determine the slope at a point on a curvilinear relationship.

To calculate the slope at *a*, let the run of X be "infinitesimally small," rather than a discrete number of units such as 1/2, 2, 4, or whatever. An infinitesimally small change is difficult to conceive, but the graphic result of such a change can be captured simply by drawing a **tangent** to point *a*.

A **tangent** is a straight line that touches the curve at only one point.

The **slope** of a curvilinear relationship at a particular point is the slope of the straight line tangent to the curve at that point.

If the curve is really curved at *a*, there is only one straight line that just barely touches *a* and only *a*. Any other line (a magnifying glass may be required to verify this) will cut the curve at two points or none. The tangent to *a* is drawn as a straight line in Exhibit 5.

The slope of the tangent at *a* is measured by dividing the rise by the run.

EXHIBIT 6　Maximum and Minimum Points

a. Y Is Maximized When Slope Is Zero　　　　　　　**b. Y Is Minimized When Slope Is Zero**

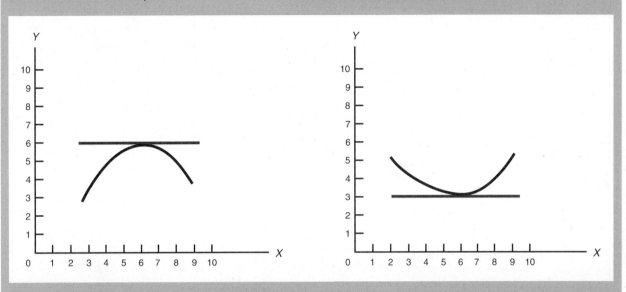

Some curvilinear relationships change directions. Notice that in panel (a), when the curve changes direction at $X = 6$, the corresponding value of Y is maximized. In panel (b), when $X = 6$, Y is minimized. In either case, the slope equals zero at the maximum or minimum value.

Because the tangent is a straight line, the length of the run does not matter. For a run from 2 to 4 ($\Delta X = 2$), the rise (ΔY) equals 3 (from 5 to 8). Thus, the slope of the tangent is 3/2 or 1.5.

Exhibit 6 shows two curvilinear relationships that have distinct high points or low points. In panel (a), the relationship between X and Y is positive for values of X less than 6 units and negative for values of X more than 6 units. The exact opposite holds for panel (b). The relationship is negative for values of X less than 6 and positive for X greater than 6. Notice that at the point where the slope changes from positive to negative (or vice versa), the slope of the curve will be exactly 0; the tangent at point $X = 6$ for both curves is a horizontal straight line that neither rises nor falls as X changes.

When a curvilinear relationship has a zero slope, the value of Y reaches either a high point, as in panel (a), or a low point, as in panel (b), at the X value where slope is zero.

Maximum and minimum values of relationships—as when a firm maximizes profits or minimizes costs—are of great importance in economics. Suppose, for example, that X in panel (a) represents the 1993 production of automobiles by General Motors (in units of 1 million) and that the variable Y represents GM's profits from automobile production (in billions of dollars). According to this diagram, GM should settle on $X = 6$ million units of automobile production because GM's profits would be higher at $X = 6$ than at any other production level.

Suppose that in panel (b), Y measures GM's costs of producing an automobile while X still measures automobile production. Production costs per automobile are at a minimum at $X = 6$. In other words, GM will produce cars at the lowest cost per car if GM produces 6 million cars.

Scatter Diagrams

The **scatter diagram** is a statistical tool frequently used to examine whether a positive or negative relationship exists between two variables. Statisticians have more powerful and exact tools to measure relationships, but the scatter diagram shown in Exhibit 7 is a simple analytical instrument.

> A **scatter diagram** consists of a number of separate points, each of which plots the value of one variable (measured along the horizontal axis) against a value of another variable (measured along the vertical axis) for a specific time interval.

In Exhibit 7, mortgage interest rates are measured along the horizontal axis, and new housing starts (the number of new homes on which construction has started) are measured along the vertical axis. Each dot on the scatter diagram shows the combination of mortgage rate and number of housing starts for a particular year. Because mortgage rates are plotted against housing starts for the years 1970 to 1986, there are 17 dots on this particular scatter diagram (each labeled by year). The pattern of dots on a scatter diagram provides convenient visual information about the relationship between the two variables. If the dots tend to concentrate in a pattern where low mortgage rates accompany high housing starts and high mortgage rates accompany low housing starts, then the scatter diagram suggests a *negative relationship* between mortgage rates and housing starts. A negative relationship is indicated by a generally declining pattern of dots from left to right. If the relationship were positive, there would be a generally rising pattern of dots from left to right. If there were no relationship, the dots would be distributed randomly on the scatter diagram.

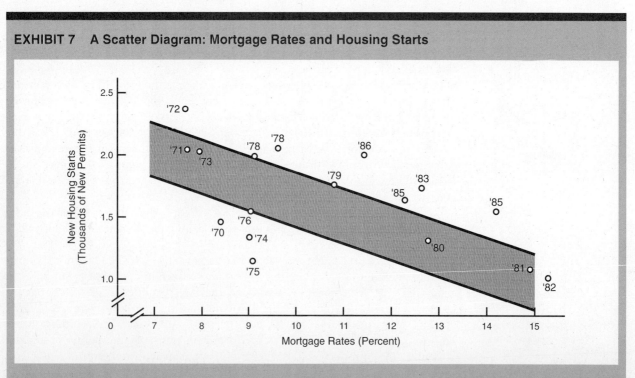

EXHIBIT 7   A Scatter Diagram: Mortgage Rates and Housing Starts

The generally falling pattern of dots suggests that there is a negative relationship between these two variables. The fact that not all dots lie on a single line suggests that other factors besides the independent variable (mortgage rates) affect the dependent variable (housing starts).

SOURCE: *Economic Report of the President*

EXHIBIT 8   Areas of Rectangles

The area of the rectangle *abcd* is calculated by multiplying its height (*ad*, or equivalently, *bc*) by its width (*ab*, or equivalently, *dc*). The height equals $4 and the width equals 8 units; therefore, the area of the rectangle equals $32. As the text explains, $32 is the amount of this firm's profits.

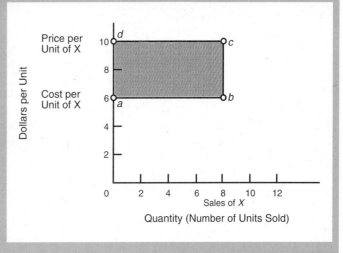

Exhibit 7 shows what appears to be a negative relationship between mortgage rates and housing starts. We have inserted a broad, negatively sloped band that traces out the general pattern of declining dots. This negative pattern indicated by the scatter diagram is not surprising. Most people would expect the number of houses being built to drop when the cost of borrowing to buy a home rises. The fact that all the dots do not lie neatly on a single negatively sloped line suggests that factors other than mortgage rates also affect housing starts.

AREAS OF RECTANGLES

In economics, it is important to understand areas of rectangles. Exhibit 8 shows how to calculate the area of a rectangle using a common economic example. It shows a firm selling 8 units of its product for a price of $10 while it costs $6 per unit to produce the product. How much profit is the firm earning? The firm's profit is the area of the rectangle *abcd*. To calculate the area of a rectangle, the height of the rectangle (*ad* or *bc*, or $10 − $6 = $4 per unit) must be multiplied by the width of the rectangle (*ab* or *dc*, or 8 units). Multiplication shows that the area of the rectangle is $4 per unit times 8 units equals $32 of total profit. If the good sells for $10 and costs $6 per unit, profit per unit is $4. The firm sells 8 units for a total profit of $32.

Appendix Summary

1. Graphs effectively present positive and negative relationships between two variables. A positive relationship exists between two variables if an increase in one

is associated with an *increase* in the other; a negative relationship exists between two variables if an increase in one is associated with a *decrease* in the other.

2. Graphs have two advantages over tables: the relationship between the variables is easier to see, and graphs can accommodate large amounts of data more efficiently.

3. For a straight-line curve, the slope of the curve is the ratio of the rise in *Y* over the run in *X*. The slope of a curvilinear relationship at a particular point is the slope of the straight line tangent to the curve at that point. When a curve changes slope from positive to negative as the *X* values increase, the value of *Y* reaches a *maximum* when the slope of the curve is zero; when a curve changes slope from negative to positive as the *X* values increase, the value of *Y* reaches a *minimum* when the slope of the curve is zero. Scatter diagrams are useful tools for examining data for positive or negative relationships between two variables.

4. The area of a rectangle is calculated by multiplying its height by its width.

Key Terms

positive (or direct) relationship (p. 19)
negative (or inverse) relationship (p. 19)
slope (p. 21)

tangent (p. 24)
scatter diagram (p. 26)

Questions and Problems

1. Graph the following data:
   X: 0   1   2   3
   Y: 10 20 30 40
   a. What is the slope?
   b. Is the slope in going from 0 to 1 different from the slope going from 2 to 3?
   c. Is this a linear or curvilinear relationship?

2. As income falls, people spend less on cars. Is the graph of this relationship positively or negatively sloped?

3. As the price of a good falls, people buy more of it. Is the graph of the relationship positively or negatively sloped?

FIGURE A

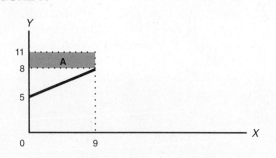

4. Answer the following questions using Figure A.
   a. What is the slope?
   b. What is area A (shaded area)?

5. Prepare two scatter diagrams relating the inflation rate to each of the other two variables from the data in Table A. In your opinion, do these diagrams reveal any positive or negative relationships?

TABLE A

	Inflation Rate	Unemployment Rate	Interest Rate
1980	9.5	7.0	11.5
1981	10.0	7.5	14.0
1982	6.2	9.5	10.7
1983	4.1	9.5	8.6
1984	4.4	7.4	9.6
1985	3.7	7.1	7.5
1986	2.6	6.9	6.0
1987	3.2	6.1	5.8
1988	3.9	5.4	6.7
1989	4.3	5.2	8.1
1990	4.2	5.4	7.5

SOURCE: *Economic Report of the President*

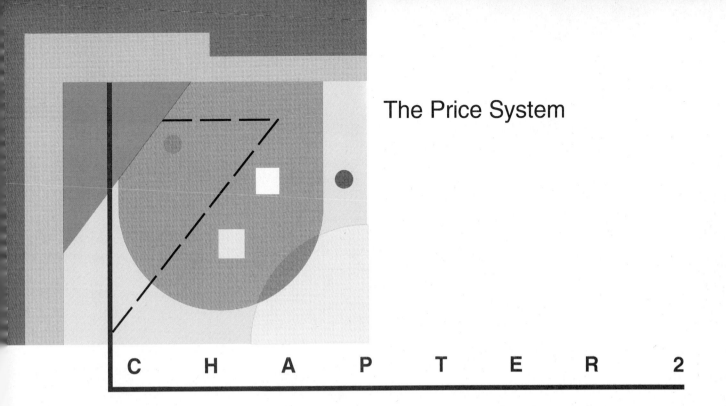

The Price System

C H A P T E R 2

CHAPTER FOCUS   We experience a daily wonder that has become so routine as to go unnoticed. The things that we wish to buy are waiting for us in stores, shops, and supermarkets. Residents of cities that manufacture only automobiles or power tools find that their stores are amply stocked not only with cars and power tools but also with products of every description. These things happen without direction from officials or bureaucrats. Adam Smith, the father of modern economics, described this phenomenon as *the invisible hand.*

Although the workings of the price system are routine to us, the leaderships of the newly emerging capitalist countries in the former Soviet Union remain skeptical. After decades of decision-making from above, they do not know if the price system can be trusted to coordinate economic decisions. Does not someone "upstairs" really have to decide? How can the price system ensure that people will have fuel to heat their homes and drive their cars, computers for their homes and offices, and even pencils for lecture notes and messages?

The price system coordinates the decisions of millions of consumers and producers without direction from above. Producers need not know much about their buyers. Buyers need not know how producers make the product. Moreover, producers themselves need not even understand the extraordinary chain of events required to make their product. The common wooden pencil requires the felling of trees, their milling by specialized equipment in faraway lands, the mining of graphite in Sri Lanka for the lead, and the production of rapeseed oil in the Dutch West Indies for the eraser. No single person in this chain need understand the entire chain. The decisions of all the people involved from the felling of the trees to the packaging of the pencils are coordinated by the price system.

After studying this chapter, you will be able to:

- See how the economy is a circular flow of goods and money from consumers to firms.
- Understand how solving the economic problem for any economy involves answering three questions: What? How? and For Whom?
- Know the difference between relative prices and money prices.
- Appreciate how relative prices guide decisions through the principle of substitution.
- See the importance of property rights in solving the economic problem.
- Understand how the price system coordinates economic activity and solves the economic problem.
- Explain the determinants of specialization and the role of money.
- Understand how transaction and information costs affect specialization and exchange.

THE CIRCULAR FLOW OF ECONOMIC ACTIVITY

Economic activity is circular. Consumers buy goods with the incomes they earn by furnishing labor, land, and capital to the business firms that produce the goods they buy. The dollars that households spend come back to them in the form of income from selling the services of their factors of production. A starting point for understanding how the price system works is to examine a **circular-flow diagram** of economic activity.

> The **circular-flow diagram** summarizes the flows of goods and services from producers to households and the flows of the factors of production from households to business firms.

Exhibit 1 illustrates the circular flow of economic activity. The flows from households to firms and from firms to households are regulated by two markets: the market for goods and services and the market for the factors of production. The circular-flow diagram consists of two circles. The outer circle shows the *physical flows* of goods and services and of productive factors. The inner circle shows the *flows of money expenditures* on goods and services and on productive factors. The physical flows and the money flows go in opposite directions. When households buy goods and services, physical goods flow to the households, but the sales receipts flow to the business sector. When workers supply labor to business firms, productive factors flow to the business sector, but the wage income flows to the household sector.

There are two pairs of supply and demand transactions in the circular flow:

1. The supply and demand for consumer goods are mediated by the market for goods and services.
2. The supply and demand for factors of production are mediated by the market for the factors of production.

THE ECONOMIC PROBLEM

Every society faces the **economic problem** of how to allocate scarce resources among competing ends. Three questions must be answered: *What* products will be produced? *How* will they be produced? *For whom* will they be produced?

EXHIBIT 1   The Circular Flow of Economic Activity

Economic activity is circular. The outside circle describes the flow of physical goods and services and productive factors through the system: business furnishes goods to households, which furnish land, labor, and capital to business. The inside circle describes the flow of dollars: households provide dollar sales to business, whose costs become incomes to households. These two circles flow in opposite directions.

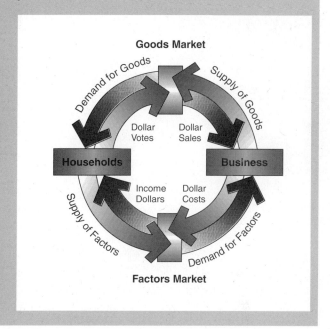

The **economic problem** is how to allocate scarce resources among competing ends.

What?

Should society devote its limited resources to producing civilian or military goods, luxuries or necessities, goods for immediate consumption or goods that increase the stock of capital (plant and equipment, housing, roads, and so forth)? Should small or large cars be produced, or should buses and subways be produced instead of cars? Should the military concentrate on strategic or conventional forces?

How?

Once the decision is made on what to produce, society must determine what combinations of the factors of production will be used. Will coal, petroleum, or nuclear power be used to produce electricity? Will bulldozers or workers with shovels dig dams? Should automobile tires be made from natural or synthetic rubber? Should tried-and-true production methods be replaced by new technology?

For Whom?

Will society's output be divided equally, or will claims to society's output be unequal? Will differences in wealth be allowed to pass from one generation to the next? What role will government play in determining *for whom?* Should government intercede to change the way the economy is distributing its output?

Adam Smith (1723–1790)

Adam Smith, the founder of modern economics, was born in Kirkaldy, Scotland, in 1723. He became Professor of Moral Philosophy at the University of Edinburgh in 1753. He was the prototype of the absent-minded professor, so engrossed in his thoughts that he sometimes forgot where he was. Smith lectured on ethics and published *The Theory of Moral Sentiments* in 1759—a book that brought him much fame but little fortune. The book argued that morals were the result of sympathy rather than self-interest.

At the time of Adam Smith, governments were active in granting monopolies and controlling foreign trade. In 1764, Smith had the good luck to have the time required to develop his thoughts on economics. Because of his reputation, he received an appointment as the tutor of a young Duke. He spent the next three years in France, where he discussed economic issues with leading French intellectuals and began a book on economics. Finally, in 1776, he published *An Inquiry into the Nature of Causes of the Wealth of Nations,* usually called *The Wealth of Nations.* One of the greatest books ever written, it brought Smith lasting fame.

Smith's great idea was that private greed may be a public virtue. He wrote:

> It is not from the benevolence of the butcher, the brewer, or the baker, that we expect our dinner, but from their regard to their own interest. We address ourselves, not to their humanity but to their self-love, and never talk to them of our own necessities but of their advantages

The self-interest of individuals leads them to specialize in those activities that maximize their own gain. In so doing, the nation as a whole experiences the greatest improvement in the productive powers of its labor force. The degree of specialization—or what Smith called the division of labor—is the consequence of the propensity of humans to engage in bargaining and exchange of one good or service for another. Smith has been regarded as the patron saint of capitalism. He argued that a system of free enterprise can solve the economic problems of society better than government monopolies and regulations.

RELATIVE PRICES AND MONEY PRICES

This chapter explains how a market economy, working through the price system, coordinates the millions of economic activities that enter the circular flow to solve the problems of what, how, and for whom. We begin our tour of the price system with the concept of relative prices.

Prices in the Land of Markkas

Suppose you find yourself in a strange land where the hospitable natives welcome you with a gift of local currency called the *markka.* Being in a hurry to eat breakfast, you locate a diner and order coffee, which costs 400 markkas. Is coffee cheap or expensive? Is the price high or low? You have no idea. Given the information you have at this point, the price of 400 markkas is meaningless.

How do you discover whether the price of coffee is high or low? You have to gather more information. The menu lists the price of a soft drink as 1,200 markkas, and another customer tells you that the typical worker earns something like 24,000 markkas per hour. Now you decide that coffee is cheap by reasoning: "Back home I pay $0.50 for a cup of coffee and $0.50 for a soft drink, and I earn $10.00 an hour. At home, an hour's work will purchase 20 soft drinks or 20 cups of coffee. But here an hour of work will purchase 20 soft drinks and 60 cups of coffee." This example delivers an important lesson: A money price in isolation from other money prices is meaningless. What is important is how a particular money price stands relative to other money prices.

CALCULATING RELATIVE PRICES

A **relative price** indicates how one price stands in relation to other prices. A relative price is quite different from a **money price**. In the above example, coffee sells for 400 markkas and soft drinks for 1,200 markkas. Three cups of coffee is the relative price of a soft drink, and one-third of a soft drink is the relative price of coffee. If coffee and soft drinks had both sold for 400 markkas, then the relative price of a soft drink would have been one cup of coffee.

> A relative price is a price expressed in terms of other commodities.

> A money price is a price expressed in monetary units (such as dollars, francs, etc.).

As these examples show, relative prices can be expressed in terms of anything. The relative price of a soft drink can be expressed in terms of cups of coffee, cups of tea, hours of work, number of T-shirts, or anything else that has a money price. If the price of apples is $0.50 per pound and the price of bananas is $0.25 per pound, the relative price of one pound of apples is two pounds of bananas. Conversely, one pound of bananas cost 0.5 pound of apples. If potatoes are $.10 per pound, the relative price of one pound of apples can also be expressed as five pounds of potatoes.

Money prices are meaningful when they are compared to prices of related goods. For example, as the price of electricity rises relative to the price of natural gas, it pays people to substitute gas heat for electrical heat. If pork prices rise relative to beef prices, it pays people to substitute beef for pork. If coffee prices rise relative to tea prices, people will substitute some tea consumption for coffee consumption.

As the relative price of a good falls, people tend to substitute that good for other goods.

Relative prices play a prominent role in answering the economic questions of *what, how,* and *for whom.* Money prices do not. Relative prices signal to buyers and sellers what goods are cheap or expensive. *Buying and selling decisions are made on the basis of relative prices.* If the relative price of one good rises, buyers substitute other goods whose relative prices are lower.

The emphasis on relative prices does not mean that money prices are unimportant. Money prices are important in macroeconomics. *Inflation* is defined as a general increase in money prices. Even in the case of inflation, money prices are not considered in isolation. Instead, the level of money prices today is compared to the level of money prices yesterday. Ultimately, this is also a form of relative price.

THE PRINCIPLE OF SUBSTITUTION

Relative prices are important because of the **principle of substitution**.

> The **principle of substitution** states that as the relative price of a product rises people will substitute another product to satisfy their demand.

Virtually no good is fully protected from the competition of substitutes. Aluminum competes with steel, coal with oil, electricity with natural gas, labor with machines, movies with TV, one brand of toothpaste with another, and so on. The only goods impervious to substitutes are such things as certain minimal quantities of water, salt, or food and certain life-saving medications, such as insulin.

To say that there is a substitute for every good does not mean that there is an *equally good* substitute for every good. One mouthwash is a close substitute for another mouthwash; a television show is a good substitute for a movie; apartments may be good substitutes for private homes. However, carrier pigeons are a poor substitute for telephone service. Costly insulation may be a poor substitute for fuel oil; public transportation may be a poor substitute for the private car in sprawling cities; steel is a poor substitute for aluminum in the production of jet aircraft.

Relative prices signal to consumers that substitutions are advantageous. If the price of one good rises relative to its substitutes, consumers will tend to switch to the relatively cheaper substitute. Substitutions are being made all around us. As the relative price of crude oil rises, utilities switch from oil to coal; retailers use fewer neon lights and hire more sales personnel. When the relative price of coffee increases, people consume more tea; when beef prices rise, the consumption of poultry and fish products increases. There is no single recipe for producing a cake, a bushel of wheat, a car, comfort, recreation, or happiness. (See Example 1.)

PROPERTY RIGHTS

Relative prices provide information to buyers and sellers on what goods are cheap and what goods are expensive. Substitutions depend on relative prices. The manner in which buyers and sellers act on relative-price information depends on **property rights**.

> **Property rights** are the rights of an owner to use and exchange property.

The individual owner of private property (whether it be land, a house, a horse, a truck, a wheat crop, or a can of peaches) has the legal freedom (the right) to sell that property at terms that are mutually agreed upon between the buyer and the seller. Normally, when property is sold, the buyer and the seller agree on a dollar price.

The legal system protects private-property rights. It protects private property from theft, damage, and unauthorized use and defines where property rights reside. An owner of private property usually has the right to use the property to the owner's best advantage and to sell the property at the best price possible. Most societies, however, place some restrictions on the use of private property. Deed restrictions, zoning, and licensing restrict the property owner's exercise of private property rights.

EXAMPLE 1

The Decline of IBM and the Principle of Substitution

This chapter teaches that when the price of one good rises, people substitute other goods that meet the same need. IBM, or "Big Blue," as it is called, has become an unexpected victim of the principle of substitution.

Since its rise to dominance of the computer industry in the late 1950s and early 1960s, IBM was the envy of all industry. Its markets grew every year; it employed the best salespersons who showed remarkable loyalty to the company. IBM stock became the favorite of Wall Street. No stock portfolio was complete without some shares of IBM. IBM's dominance of the computer industry became so strong that the Justice Department even charged it with monopolization of the computer industry in the 1970s.

As the 1990s progress, the luster appears to be wearing off IBM. IBM's share of the computer market is eroding. People are no longer rushing to buy IBM personal computers. Instead they are buying computers from companies with the unfamiliar names of Leading Edge, Eagle, Epson, and Macintosh. People are even buying "generic" IBM-compatible computers from companies that few have heard of.

Whereas in the 1970s and 1980s, people were reluctant to buy untested computers manufactured by unknown companies, in the 1990s people have come to realize that, with existing technology, a generic IBM-compatible computer can perform the same services as an IBM personal computer but at a lower price. Like wheat and corn, the personal computer market is becoming a generic market in which one computer brand is viewed as a good substitute for another, even if that other brand is made by IBM.

Owners of private property will be guided by relative prices in making decisions. The private owner of an oil refinery will use the relative prices of gasoline, fuel oils, and kerosene to determine how much of each petroleum product to refine and will look at the relative prices of imported and domestic crude oil to determine whether to use domestic or imported crude.

The private owner of labor (that is, the individual worker) will look at the relative wage rates in different occupations to determine where to seek employment. The private owner of farmland will look at the relative prices of agricultural products to determine what mix of crops to plant.

THE PRICE SYSTEM AS A COORDINATING MECHANISM

An economy consists of millions of consumers and hundreds of thousands of enterprises, and virtually every member of society owns some labor, land, or capital resources. Each participant makes economic decisions to promote his or her self-interest. What coordinates the decisions of all these people and businesses? What prevents the economy from collapsing when all these decisions clash? If all participants are looking out for themselves, will not the end result be chaos? Is it not necessary to have someone or something in charge?

The Invisible Hand

Adam Smith (see Gallery of Economists) described how the price system solves economic problems efficiently without conscious direction:

Every individual endeavors to employ his capital so that its produce may be of greatest value. He generally neither intends to promote the public interest, nor knows how much he is promoting it. He intends only his own security, only his own gain. And he is led by an invisible hand *to promote an end which was no part of his intention. By pursuing his own interest he frequently promotes that of society more effectively than when he really intends to promote it.[1]*

Smith's "invisible hand" works through the **price system**. A modern economy produces millions of commodities and services, each of which has a money price. These millions of money prices form millions of relative prices that inform buyers and sellers what goods are abundant and what goods are in short supply. If prices are set in free markets, the relative prices that emerge reflect the true economic scarcities of each good.

> The **price system** coordinates economic decisions by allowing people with property rights to resources to trade freely, buying and selling at whatever relative prices emerge in the marketplace.

Equilibrium

Each participant makes buying and selling decisions on the basis of relative prices. The family decides how to spend its income; the worker decides where and how much to work; the factory manager decides what inputs to use and what outputs to produce. Insofar as all these decisions on what to buy and sell are being made individually in isolation, what is to guarantee that there will be enough steel, bananas, foreign cars, janitorial services, steel workers, copper, and lumber for homes? What is to ensure that there will not be too much of one good and too little of another? Is Adam Smith's invisible hand powerful enough to prevent shortage and surplus?

Consider what would happen if U.S. automobile producers decide to produce more cars than buyers want to buy *at the price asked by the automobile producers.* The automobile manufacturers will be made aware of this fact, not by a directive from the government, but by the simple fact of too many unsold cars. Dealers must pay their bills and cannot live from unsold cars; therefore, they must sell the cars at lower prices. As the money price of cars falls, its relative price tends to fall, and customers begin to substitute automobiles for European vacations, home computers, or remodeled kitchens. The decline in the relative price of automobiles signals automobile manufacturers to produce fewer cars. Eventually, a balance between the number of cars people are prepared to buy (the demand) and the number offered for sale (the supply) will be struck, and the corresponding price is called an **equilibrium price**.

> The **equilibrium price** of a good or service is that price at which the amount of the good people are prepared to buy equals the amount offered for sale.

HOW THE PRICE SYSTEM DECIDES WHAT, HOW, AND FOR WHOM

The price system solves the *what, how,* and *for whom* problems without conscious direction. No single participant in the economy needs to see the big picture; each participant need only know the relative prices of the goods and services of

[1]Adam Smith, *The Wealth of Nations,* ed. Edwin Cannon (New York; Modern Library, 1937), p. 423.

immediate interest to that person. No single person or governmental organization is required to be concerned about the economy as a whole. No single person needs *all* the information available to the economy. The millions of individual economic decisions made daily are coordinated by the price system.

Consider an economy in which all property is privately owned and owners can freely use their property rights. Prices are set freely in markets. Each individual owns certain quantities of resources—land, labor, capital—that are sold or rented to business firms that produce the goods and services people want. Everything is sold at a price agreeable to the buyer and seller.

What the economy produces is determined by *dollar votes* cast by consumers for different goods and services and by the dollar costs of producing these goods and services. When consumers choose to buy a particular good or service, they are casting a dollar vote that communicates their demand for that good or service. Consumers, in casting their dollar votes, determine what will be produced. If no dollar votes are cast for a particular product, it will not be produced. If enough dollar votes are cast for a product relative to its cost of production, it will be produced. Just what quantities will be produced will be determined by prices. A higher price for any product signals to firms that greater profits can be made by increasing production. To illustrate, if consumers want more wheat, they will bid up wheat prices. In turn, the higher wheat prices will encourage farmers to grow more wheat.

How goods are produced is determined by business firms who seek to utilize their land, labor, and capital resources as economically as possible. Business firms produce those outputs that receive high dollar votes by combining resources in the least costly way. Business firms follow the principle of substitution. If the relative price of land is increased, farmers will use less land and more tractors and labor to work the land more intensively. If the relative price of farm labor increases, farmers will use less labor and more tractors and land. If the relative price of business travel rises, businesses will travel less and make more long-distance telephone calls. If the relative price of long-distance calls increases, businesses will telephone less and use more business travel. If business firms fail to reduce their costs through the use of the best available techniques and the best combination of the factors of production, the competition of other firms may drive them out of business.

For whom is determined by the dollar values the market assigns to resources owned by each separate household in the economy. The distribution of income between rich and poor reflects the prices paid for each resource and the distribution of ownership claims to scarce labor, land, and capital. People who own large quantities of land or capital will have a correspondingly large claim on the goods and services produced by the economy; those who are fortunate enough to provide high-priced labor services (doctors, lawyers, gifted athletes) will similarly receive a large share of the total output. At the other extreme, the poor are those who own few resources and furnish low-priced labor services to the market. (See Example 2.)

The invisible hand that solves the what, how, and for whom questions works through the setting of free market prices.

SPECIALIZATION

The price system automatically encourages the factors of production to specialize in those activities that they do better than others. Specialization raises efficiency and allows economies to produce ever larger output from their available inputs.

Specialization and Exchange

Suppose a single sailor were stranded on a remote island with no other human beings around—a modern Robinson Crusoe. While the sailor would have to

The Invisible Hand: The Paradox of Progress

As the U.S. economy entered the 1990s, Adam Smith's invisible hand brought about stunning downsizing in America's best-known companies. General Motors cut its labor force 74,000, Sears 83,000 employees, 25,000 at IBM, and 27,000 at Boeing. Such layoffs are big news and frightening to the average person.

But the invisible hand creates as well as destroys. While Sears downsized, Wal-Mart added 260,000 jobs; while IBM cut back, Microsoft, Intel, and Dell Computer expanded. General Motors shrank, but some 29,000 Americans were employed at new jobs with Honda, Toyota, Nissan, and other new Japanese plants built in the U.S.

Every day jobs are created and destroyed. In the short run, the process seems cruel. But in the long run, it is key to economic progress. In 1900, for example, 40 out of every 100 Americans worked in farms. Today, only 3 out of 100 need be farmworkers, while the remaining 97 out of 100 workers are involved in new homes, computers, pharmaceuticals, appliances, movies, video games, and many other goods and services.

Joseph Schumpeter called this process "creative destruction." In 1920, there were over 2 million railroad employees, now there are but 230,000. In 1900 only 51,000 workers repaired electronic equipment; today, 711,000 people do such work on much more advanced equipment. There are hardly any blacksmiths, boilermakers, or milliners today; but there are plenty of engineers, auto mechanics, and truck, bus, or taxi drivers.

The entire process is led by the invisible hand. Most people fear the process because it leads to lost jobs. Politicians sometimes want to freeze old jobs through government intervention. As pointed out in the 1992 annual report of the Federal Reserve Bank of Dallas: "History demonstrates the futility of saving jobs. For instance, it's hard to miss the absurdity of a well-intentioned program that 100 years ago might have aimed to keep blacksmiths and harness makers employed. As recently as 70 years ago, the United States had 10 million registered passenger cars but 20.5 million horses. Had our ancestors been able to freeze jobs, the United States would be stuck in the horse-and-buggy era."

SOURCE: "The Churn: The Paradox of Progress," Federal Reserve Bank of Dallas, 1992 Annual Report. Joseph Schumpter, *Capitalism, Socialism and Democracy,* 3d ed. New York: Harper and Brothers, 1950.

---

constantly make decisions about whether to make fish nets or fish hooks or whether to sleep or break coconuts, the economy of the desert island would lack many features of a modern economic system. The sailor would not be *specialized;* he would have to be a jack-of-all-trades. He would produce only those things that he wanted to consume, and he would not use *money.* He would still have to solve the problems of *what* and *how.* The *for whom* problem would be easy. Everything he produced would be for himself He could solve *what* and *how* without explicit relative prices, property rights, or markets.

In the modern economy, it is somewhat unsettling to think about the degree to which people are specialized. A typical household consumes thousands of articles; yet the principal breadwinner of the household may specialize in aligning suspension components on an automobile production line. In short, everyone in our economy (except hermits) is dependent on the efforts of others. We produce one or two things; we consume many things.

Specialization gives rise to exchange. Indeed, the exchange of one thing for another thing is the reverse side of the coin of specialization. If people consumed only those things they produced, there would be no trade and no need for money. Money, trade, exchange, and specialization are all characteristics of a complicated economy. Specialization means that people will produce more of particular goods than they consume and that these surpluses will be exchanged for other goods that they want.

Specialization and Productivity

Productivity increases when more output is produced from the same amount of productive resources. Specialization raises the productivity of the economy and raises incomes through economies of scale and by allowing resources to be used according to their comparative advantage.

Economies of Scale. Productivity can be raised by specialization to achieve **economies of scale**.

> Economies of scale are present when large volumes of output can be produced more cheaply than small volumes of output.

Economies of scale are achieved by concentrating certain resources in specific tasks. A worker spending all day typing and another worker spending all day sweeping floors can get more done than both spending half-days on each job. Individuals who focus on one task learn their jobs better and don't waste time switching from job to job. More cars can be produced by investing heavily in an elaborate assembly line that will produce millions of cars more cheaply than a few.

Comparative Advantage. Specialization allows resources, which have different characteristics, to be allocated to their best use, thereby raising their productivity and giving them higher income. People, land, and capital all come in different varieties. Some people are agile seven-footers; others are small and slow. Some people take easily to math and computers; others are frightened by numbers and technology. Some land is moist; other land is dry. Some land is hilly; other land is flat.

Because the factors of production have different characteristics and qualities, specialization offers opportunities for productivity advances. Economists refer to the best employment of a resource as its *comparative advantage*. The agile seven-footer has a comparative advantage in basketball; the fast-talker as a sales representative; the math whiz as a computer specialist. Land with high moisture content is best used in corn production; land with a relatively low moisture content is best used in wheat production.

Comparative advantage is not the same thing as an *absolute advantage*. It is possible that the agile seven-footer may also be the fastest typist. The math whiz may be the best salesperson. Particular farm acreage may be better suited to growing both wheat and corn than other farm acreage. Some people are poorly suited to just about everything in the sense that at every task they are less efficient than other people. How are comparative advantages determined in these more complicated cases?

In 1817, the English economist, David Ricardo, formulated the **law of comparative advantage**.

> The **law of comparative advantage** states that it is better for people to specialize in those activities in which their advantages over other people are greatest or in which their disadvantages compared to others are the smallest.

The easiest way to see this principle at work is to examine two extreme cases. Suppose that you can do any and every job better than anyone else. What would you, as such a superior person, do? You would not want to be a jack-of-all trades because it is likely that your *margin* of superiority will be greater in one occupation than in another. The job in which your margin of superiority over others is *the greatest* is the job you will do because it will give you the highest income.

Now examine the other extreme. Suppose there is no person in the community to whom you are superior *in any job;* you are less productive than any other person in the community in every occupation. What would you do in such an unfortunate situation? The job in which your disadvantage compared to others is the smallest would be the job that maximizes your income.

A mediocre computer programmer could possibly be the best clerk in the local supermarket. The clerks in the local supermarket may not be able to stock shelves and work a cash register as well as the computer programmer, but they have a *comparative advantage* in that occupation. An attorney may be the fastest typist in town, yet the attorney is better off preparing deeds than typing deeds. An engineering major may have verbal skills that exceed those of an English major, but his or her comparative advantage is in engineering.

The law of comparative advantage is nothing more than the principle that people should engage in those activities where their income is maximized. The price system encourages the factors of production to work according to their comparative advantage. For example, Sally can earn $1,000 a month as a bricklayer and $2,000 a month as a computer programmer. Joe can earn $500 a month as a bricklayer and $400 a month as a computer programmer. Sally is better than Joe at either bricklaying or programming. However, Sally should devote her time to computer programming and Joe to bricklaying. Each maximizes his or her income by devoting his or her energies to that task that maximizes income. Sally is 5 times better as a programmer, and only 2 times better as a bricklayer. Joe is disadvantaged at everything, but his least disadvantage is in bricklaying.

Everybody, from the best to the worst, has a comparative advantage in some job or line of work.

International Trade. The law of comparative advantage applies to people *and* countries. Both people and countries have one thing in common: Just as one person cannot transfer his or her talents to another, one country cannot transfer its people, climate, or natural resources to another country.

Each person has inborn "resources," such as intelligence, looks, manual dexterity, verbal skills, and mathematical skills. So do countries. The resource profile of the United States is quite different from that of South Korea. The United States is rich in capital and scientific personnel. South Korea has an industrious work force. A country's resources are best committed to those activities for which its advantages are the largest or its disadvantages are the smallest. America's largest advantages are in the production of high-technology goods, such as airplanes, and in agricultural products, such as wheat. South Korea's least disadvantages are in the production of such goods as TV sets and clothing. We say that South Korea has the "least disadvantage" because American workers produce TVs and clothing at higher levels of productivity than South Korean workers. The American productivity advantage is much higher in aircraft manufacturing and wheat farming than in TV and clothing manufacturing.

Just as people specialize in those activities in which they have a comparative advantage, so do countries specialize. Countries specialize and exchange, just as people specialize and exchange. The farmer exports wheat in return for manufactured goods. The United States exports aircraft and wheat in return for TV sets and clothing.

Specialization and Money

Money arises because people are specialized and do not produce everything they need. Money is useful because it reduces the cost of transacting with others. *Barter* is a system of exchange where products are traded for other products rather than for money. In barter, for example, it would be necessary for a barefoot baker to meet with a hungry shoemaker. In other words, a successful barter deal requires that the two traders have matching wants. In barter, successful trades require a double coincidence of wants.

Money is useful precisely because double coincidences of wants are rare. Money enables any person to trade with anyone else in a complicated economy. The form money takes differs from society to society. Money in a simple society will be quite different from money in a complicated society. In simple societies, things like fish hooks, sharks' teeth, beads, or cows have been used as money. In modern societies, money is issued and regulated by government, and money may (gold coins) or may not (paper money) have an intrinsic value of its own.

> **Money** is anything that is widely accepted in exchange for goods and services.

It is likely that if one form of money were abolished (by law), some other form would arise to serve as money. It is not necessary to pay the costs of barter.

TRANSACTION COSTS AND INFORMATION COSTS

People exchange goods and services because of specialization. One of the largest impediments to exchange is the existence of **transaction costs**. It is costly to bring buyers and sellers together. Some examples are the cost of transportation, the cost of negotiation, the cost of property-rights enforcement, government taxes and regulations, and the cost of acquiring information.

> **Transaction costs** are the costs associated with bringing buyers and sellers together and include the costs of negotiation, transportation, information, taxes, and government regulation.

A major part of the cost of making a transaction between a buyer and a seller is the **information costs** associated with searching for and acquiring economic information about prices and products. The buyer and seller must first find each other and then agree on the price and other terms of the contract. Knowledge of the existence and location of a willing buyer is valuable information to the seller, just as knowledge of a willing seller is valuable information to the buyer. Without this information, economic transactions cannot take place.

> **Information costs** are the costs of acquiring information on prices and products and include the costs of shopping, advertising, telephoning, and inspecting goods.

Buying and selling houses vividly illustrates the importance of transaction and information costs. Houses are not a homogeneous product, such as wheat or steel or sugar. Matching up buyers and sellers is a time-consuming process. Each buyer

EXAMPLE 3

How Transaction Costs Limit Exchange: Return Airline Tickets

The airlines often offer discounted round-trip fares that are cheaper than unrestricted one-way fares. Discounted round-trip fares have a number of restrictions (such as weekend travel or staying over a Saturday) that most passengers cannot meet. Because it is cheaper, many passengers buy round-trip tickets, fly one way, and let the return ticket go unused. Why don't ticket-holders simply sell their return tickets to people who can use them? There are any number of people who would welcome the opportunity to fly cheap from city A to city B.

High transaction costs explain why this opportunity for exchange is seldom utilized. Passengers with return tickets must use time and money resources to locate people willing to travel on the scheduled return date. If the return ticket is from Kansas City to St. Louis, the transaction costs of arranging a successful exchange would be too high relative to the benefits to the transacting parties. If the return ticket is from Honolulu to New York, the advantages of getting a cheap ticket may be high enough to outweigh the transaction costs.

In fact, Honolulu newspapers are full of personal advertisements offering to sell cheap return tickets to the mainland. The Kansas City newspapers, on the other hand, have virtually no ads offering cheap return tickets.

---

may have to inspect dozens of houses, and each seller may have to wait months or even years before finding a willing buyer. It is quite conceivable that for any given house, there are many people who would be more than willing to pay the seller's price. But finding them is another matter. It is so difficult that people often remain in an undesirable house for years. In a world of zero transaction costs, houses could presumably be sold instantly at the highest possible price! Obviously, it is the cost of transacting that makes the business of being a real estate agent a highly profitable occupation for those with a knack for matching potential buyers with potential sellers. (See Example 3.)

Because information is costly, each person specializes in certain types of information. Chemical engineers may know a great deal about producing plastics but may know little about building houses. The produce clerks know a great deal about displaying lettuce or apples but little about how they are grown. Homemakers know a great deal about the prices of groceries in their town but little about the prices of industrial machinery. Industrial-purchasing agents know more about machinery prices than about grocery prices. Some people—the industrial purchasing agent, the realtor, the stockmarket broker—make a profession of specializing in information, but their knowledge is limited to very specific areas. As the Chapter Focus explained, no one person knows how to make even a pencil from start to finish.

The role of scarce information in the economy is fundamental. Friedrich von Hayek, a Nobel laureate in economics, was one of the first to emphasize the way in which economies process and utilize information about prices and products. To Hayek, the principal problem of economics is "how to secure the best use of resources known to any member of society, for ends whose relative importance only those individuals know."[2]

---

[2]F. A. Hayek, "The Use of Knowledge in Society," *American Economic Review* 35 (1945): 510–30.

The Limits of the Invisible Hand

The same comment applies the invisible hand as to democracy: "Although democracy is a flawed system, mankind has yet to invent a superior system of government." Although there may be flaws in the workings of the price system, no one has yet to discover a superior means of allocating scarce resources. The collapse of the major alternative—the communist command economy—bears eloquent testimony to this point.

The fact that the invisible hand works well does not mean it works well in all cases. The most important policy issues in economics hinge on those instances when the invisible hand should not be used. Later chapters will show that, when the producer has a monopoly, the invisible hand may not provide the "best" result and that there are goods, called public goods, that private markets do not supply efficiently. The major policy question in macroeconomics is whether the invisible hand can provide an appropriate level of output and employment for the economy as a whole or whether some form of government guidance is required.

Societies are constantly exploring the limits to the invisible hand. Activities that had previously been the preserve of government allocation are no longer "off limits" for the invisible hand. The 1980s saw the advent of the private prison and the increasing use of private firms in garbage collection and waste disposal.

In the 1990s, private firms became involved in the business of managing welfare programs, an area that had been exclusively handled by government offices. Firms like MAXIMUS, Inc., America Works, and Lockheed IMS manage welfare training and disbursement programs in California, New York, and Colorado. Although private companies account for a small portion of the nation's massive $30 billion annual welfare bill, they promise to help more clients for less by using better computer programs, more flexible staff, and less bureaucracy. Some studies show that the use of private firms can cut welfare costs by half. Private firms are paid only if they are successful, while the government welfare bureaucracy must be paid no matter what.

Policy makers must choose what goods and services should be provided by the invisible hand and which by administrative and bureaucratic decisions. The choice between private or public provision of welfare administration is only one example. Others are the proposed "privatization" of public schools and the use of market principles to deal with pollution rights.

SOURCE: Jay Mathews, "Taking Welfare Private," *Newsweek*, June 29, 1992, p. 44.

How is the economy to utilize knowledge about product prices, qualities, and locations that is not available to any one person or institution in its entirety? Hayek's answer is that the price system allows specialization in information that is specific to each person's particular circumstances of time and place. People can acquire only the knowledge about those things that they need to know. By allowing people to be paid for their scarce information, the price system economizes on information costs. The auto mechanic does not have to learn nuclear physics, and the physicist does not have to know how to repair a car.

This chapter has described in general terms how scarce resources are allocated by the price system and has explained the organization of property rights. Equilibrium prices are like an invisible hand that coordinates the decisions of many different persons. The next chapter examines the detailed workings of supply and demand in an individual market and answers the questions: How is the equilibrium price set? What causes equilibrium prices to increase or decrease?

Chapter Summary

The most important point to learn from this chapter is: The price system can act like an invisible hand to guide people to do what is best for society even though people are looking out only for themselves.

1. The circular-flow diagram summarizes the flows of goods and services from producers to households and the flows of factors of production from households to producers.

2. Relative prices guide the economic decisions of individuals and businesses. They signal to buyers and sellers what substitutions to make.

3. The principle of substitution states that no single good is irreplaceable. Users substitute one good for another in response to changes in relative prices.

4. Property can be owned by private persons, by the state, or by combinations of the two.

5. The "invisible hand" analogy, originated by Adam Smith in 1776, describes how a price system can allow individuals to pursue their self-interest and yet provide an orderly, efficient economic system that functions without centralized direction. If too much of a product is produced, its relative price will fall. If too little of a product is produced, its relative price will rise. The balance of supply and demand is called an equilibrium. The *what* problem is solved by dollar votes. Consumers determine what will be produced. The *how* problem is solved by individual producers. Competition among producers will encourage them to combine resource inputs efficiently. The solution of the *for whom* problem is determined by who owns productive resources and by the relative prices of resources.

6. Specialization is responsible for productivity improvements. Specialization occurs because of the differences among people, land, and capital and because of the economies of large-scale production. The law of comparative advantage states that the factors of production will specialize in those activities in which their advantages are greatest or in which their disadvantages are smallest.

7. Transaction costs make profitable exchanges more difficult. Information costs encourage people to specialize in information.

Policy Focus: Policy makers must choose what goods and services are to be produced by private markets or by government decisions.

Key Terms

circular-flow diagram (p. 30)
economic problem (p. 30)
relative price (p. 33)
money price (p. 33)
principle of substitution (p. 34)
property rights (p. 34)
price system (p. 36)

equilibrium price (p. 36)
economies of scale (p. 39)
law of comparative advantage (p. 39)
money (p. 41)
transaction cost (p. 41)
information cost (p. 41)

Questions and Problems

1. In 1963, a typical car could be bought for about $2,000 and in 1994 a typical car sold for about $15,000. But on the average what cost $100 in 1963 costs about $500 in 1994. Did the relative price of a car increase or fall compared to most goods and services?

2. In the circular-flow diagram, how are the dollar costs of business firms related to the incomes of households?

3. If you own an automobile, what property rights do you

have? What restrictions are placed upon these property rights?

4. Explain why you can usually find the items you want at a grocery store without having ordered the goods in advance.

5. From the data in Table A, calculate the relative price of coffee. Explain your answer. (As an exercise in graphing, you may want to plot the various prices.)

TABLE A

	Price of Coffee (dollars per pound)	Price of Electricity (dollars per million BTUs)	Price of Tea (dollars per pound)
1970	0.535	5.83	0.390
1975	0.683	9.23	0.582
1980	1.70	14.09	0.858
1982	1.40	18.04	0.764

6. This chapter noted that not every product has a good substitute. Which of the following pairs of products are good substitutes? Which are poor substitutes? Explain the general principles you used to get your answers.
   a. Coffee and tea.
   b. Compact Chevrolets and compact Fords.
   c. Cars and city buses.
   d. Electricity and natural gas.
   e. Telephones and express mail.

7. Computer manufacturers want to sell more personal computers than customers want to buy at the going price. Explain why the equilibrium price could be higher or lower than the going price.

8. You own a 3-carat diamond ring which you no longer like. In fact, you would like to have a new color television set. How would you go about getting the television set in a barter economy? From this generalize about the efficiency of exchange in a barter economy versus a monetary economy.

9. "Specialization takes place only when people are different. If all people were identical, there would be no specialization." Evaluate this statement.

10. Assume that while shopping, you see long lines of people waiting to buy bread while fresh meat is spoiling in butcher shops. From these observations, what can you say about prevailing prices? What is your prediction about what will happen to the relative price of bread?

11. Bill can prepare 50 hamburgers per hour and wait on 25 tables per hours. Mike can prepare 20 hamburgers per hour and wait on 15 tables per hour. Hamburgers earn a profit of $0.60 each and tips are a dollar per table. If Bill and Mike were to open a hamburger stand, who should be the cook? Who the waiter? Would Bill do both?

12. In an hour's time, Jill can lay 100 tiles and can mortar 50 bricks. Tom can lay 10 tiles and 20 bricks in an hour's time. If every tile laid or every brick mortared pays $1, what would be the hourly earnings of Tom and Jill when they practice their comparative advantage?

13. Which of the following transactions would enter the circular flow and which would not?
   a. U.S. Steel sells steel to General Motors.
   b. General Motors sells a car to Jones.
   c. Jones takes a job from General Motors and receives $100 pay.
   d. Jones has his suit cleaned at the local dry cleaner and pays $5.
   e. Jones washes his dress shirt.

14. Why would an economy that used money be more efficient than the same economy that utilized only barter (where people exchanged their surplus goods for wanted goods)?

15. Unmarried males under 25 pay higher car insurance rates than married males. Yet, there are some unmarried males who are far safer drivers than the average married males. Why do these unmarried males still pay higher insurance rates?

Doing Economics

Interview two or more people who have been working for at least ten years. Inquire about how they chose their occupations. In particular, ask what alternative occupations they considered (or perhaps worked at for some time) and why they rejected these in favor of their current jobs. Find out what role (if any) the salary they expected to earn played in their decisions. What particular skills of each individual are utilized well in his or her current job? After completing the interviews, evaluate what role comparative advantage played in making the occupational decisions. How did the price system convey the information that the individuals needed to make the best occupational decision? Were any considerations other than comparative advantage important in occupational choice? How would these considerations affect the price system?

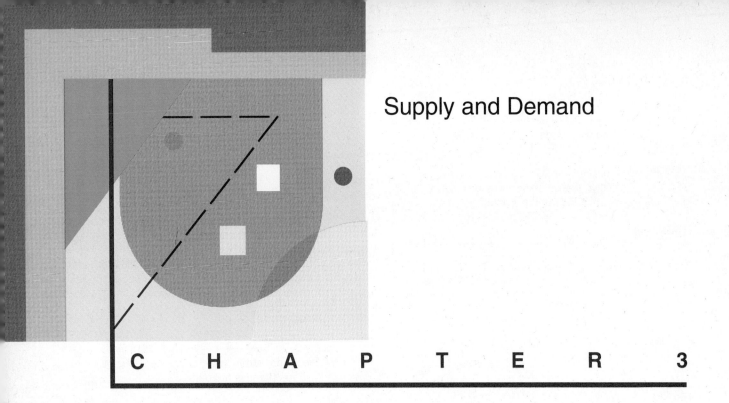

Supply and Demand

C H A P T E R 3

CHAPTER FOCUS   Just as some people think that all doctors prescribe "two aspirin and call me in the morning" for all ailments, people think that economists only use supply and demand to deal with all economic problems. Supply and demand are indeed powerful tools in the hands of the experienced economist. They explain how the forces of supply and demand determine prices. The previous chapter explained how economic decision-making is based on the price system; therefore, it is important to know where prices come from.

When supply and demand work smoothly, the resulting market prices attract little attention. However, when there are disruptions—such as cutoffs of the Mideast oil supply or panic purchases before and after massive hurricanes—there is a cry for intervention. Rather than letting supply and demand set prices, people then say, the government should intervene to hold prices down!

Sometimes it is easier to understand what supply and demand do during those very periods when prices are set by administrative means. This chapter shows that markets set equilibrium prices that strike balances between buyers and sellers. At any other prices, there will be imbalances. These imbalances, called shortages and surpluses, must be well understood by the public and policymakers alike to prevent poor public policy from being followed.

After studying this chapter you should be able to:

- Define perfect competition.
- State the law of demand.
- Understand the difference between changes in demand and changes in quantity demanded.
- See why the supply curve is usually upward sloping.
- Understand the difference between changes in supply and changes in quantity supplied.
- Appreciate the meaning of the equilibrium price.
- Understand the causes of shortages and surpluses.

MARKETS

People buy and sell goods through established channels and institutions. To understand the mechanics of supply and demand, we must narrow our vision to the study of the way a *single market* works. In each **market**, buyers and sellers are guided by price in their buying and selling decisions.

> A **market** is an established arrangement by which buyers and sellers come together to exchange particular goods or services.

Types of Markets

There are many types of markets. A retail store, a gas station, a farmer's market, real-estate markets, the New York Stock Exchange (where stocks are bought and sold), Chicago commodity markets (where livestock, grains, and metals are traded), auctions of works of art, gold markets in London, Frankfurt, and Zurich, labor exchanges, university placement offices, and hundreds of other specialized arrangements are all markets. A market brings together buyers and sellers of a particular good or service. The New York Stock Exchange brings together the buyers and sellers of corporate stock by means of modern telecommunications. Sotheby's auctions in London and New York bring together the sellers and buyers of rare works of art. The Rotterdam oil market brings together buyers and sellers of crude oil not under long-term contracts. The gas station brings together the buyers and sellers of gasoline.

In some markets, the buyers and sellers confront each other face-to-face (roadside farm markets). In other markets, the buyer never sees the seller (the Chicago commodity markets). Some markets are local (brining together local buyers and sellers); others are national (brining together buyers and sellers in all parts of the nation); others are international (bringing together buyers and sellers in all parts of the world). Real estate is traded in local markets; houses and buildings cannot be shipped from one place to another. College textbooks are usually exchanged in a national market. The New York Stock Exchange, the various gold exchanges, and the Chicago commodity exchanges bring together buyers and sellers from around the world.

Alfred Marshall (1842–1924)

Born in England in 1842, Alfred Marshall was to become Professor of Political Economy at Cambridge University. At the age of 75 he wrote:

> . . . the more I studied economic science, the smaller appeared the knowledge which I had of it, in proportion to the knowledge that I needed; and now, at the end of nearly half a century of almost exclusive study of it, I am conscious of more ignorance of it than I was at the beginning of the study.

Marshall developed many of his most important ideas while taking long walks in the high Alps. He would leave Cambridge in early June and return in October. According to Mary Marshall:

> He would walk with a knapsack on his back for two or three hours. He would then sit down, sometimes on a glacier, and have a long pull at some book. . . .

Marshall's masterpiece was his *Principles of Economics,* published in 1890. He combined simple graphical methods with wisdom and learning about the facts and circumstances of various industrious. Earlier economists emphasized the primacy of supply conditions in determining price. Marshall maintained that price was the outcome of both supply *and* demand forces, and used an analogy to make his point: "We might as reasonably dispute whether it is the upper or the under blade of a pair of scissors that cuts a piece of paper." Marshall was the first to use graphical methods in economics. The demand and supply curves in this book are drawn the way he drew them. We put price on the vertical axis and quantity on the horizontal axis because Marshall did it that way.

It is difficult to study economics without being Marshall's "student." His contributions grace microeconomics, macroecnomics, and the field of international trade.

Perfectly Competitive Markets

Markets exhibit different degrees of competition among the buyers and sellers. This chapter deals with a very special type of market called a **perfectly competitive market**.

A perfectly competitive market has the following characteristics:

1. The product's price is uniform throughout the market.
2. Buyers and sellers have perfect information about price and the product's quality.
3. There are a large number of buyers and sellers.
4. No single buyer or seller purchases or sells enough to change the price.

The principal characteristic of a perfectly competitive market is that buyers and sellers face so much competition that no person or group can control the price. The markets where most people buy and sell goods are not perfect. Buyers and sellers may not be perfectly informed about prices and qualities. Two homemakers pay different prices in nearby grocery stores for the same national brand of cookies. Chemically equivalent brand-name and generic drugs sell at different prices. AT&T, General Motors, and Saudi Arabia exercise some control over the prices they charge.

Many products, however, are exchanged in perfect markets. Stocks and bonds and commodities such as wheat, silver, copper, gold, foreign currencies, oats, pork bellies, soybeans, lumber, cotton, orange juice, cattle, cocoa, and platinum are bought and sold in perfectly competitive markets. Although markets like the local grocery store, the dry cleaner, the gas station, or the roadside stand are not perfectly competitive, they function in a way that *approximates* perfect competition. Perfectly competitive markets serve as a useful guide to the way many real-world markets function and are a valuable starting point for examining economic behavior.

DEMAND

As a consumer, you may want a good, but not buy it. You may want a Rolls-Royce, but it is unlikely that you can afford one. To *demand* a good or service a consumer must be willing and able to purchase it. The actual **quantity demanded** of a good depends on its price, holding all other factors constant.

> The **quantity demanded** is the amount of a good or service consumers are prepared to buy at a given price (during a specified time period), holding other factors constant.

The Law of Demand

People buy more of a good if its price falls; they buy less if the price rises, holding other factors constant. A fundamental law of economics is the **law of demand**.

> The **law of demand** states that as the price of a good falls the quantity demanded rises, holding other factors constant.

Chapter 2 studied the principle of substitution. As the price of any product goes up, people will tend to find substitutes for that product. If the price of gasoline rises, drivers will cut back on less essential driving, and more people will take the bus, or walk, or ride their bicycles to work. If the price of tea rises, more people will drink coffee, or cut back one or two cups a day, or buy a soft drink. If the price rises enough, some people will stop buying it entirely, and the number of users will fall. The universal and natural tendency is for people who consume or use the goods to *substitute other goods or services* when the price of a good goes up. Higher prices discourage consumption.

People also tend to buy less of a good as its price goes up because *they feel poorer*. If a person buys a new car every year for $5,000 (after trade-in), and the price rises to $9,000 (after trade-in), the person would need an extra $4,000 yearly income to maintain the old standard of living. The $4,000 increase in the price of the car is like a cut in income of $4,000. The rise in a price, especially of a good that is important in family budgets, reduces the amount of income left to purchase not only the good whose price has risen but also other goods. (See Example 1.)

The Demand Curve

The relationship between quantity demanded and price is called the **demand curve** or the **demand schedule**. The relationship is negative because of the law of

M&Ms and the Law of Demand

The law of demand states that the quantity demanded will increase as the price is lowered, as long as other factors that affect demand do not change. In the real world, factors that affect the demand for a particular product change frequently. Tastes change, income rises, and prices of substitutes and complements change. In 1984, the makers of M&M candy conducted an experiment that illustrates the law of demand. Over a 12-month test period, the price of M&Ms was held constant in 150 stores, and the content weight of the candy was increased. When the price is held constant and the weight increased, the price per ounce is lowered. In the stores where the price per ounce was dropped, sales rose by 20 to 30 percent almost overnight, according to the director of sales development for M&Ms. As predicted by the law of demand, a reduction in price causes the quantity demanded to rise, *ceteris paribus*.

SOURCE: "Why Do Hot Dogs Come in Packs of 10 and Buns in 8s and 12s?" *Wall Street Journal,*September 21, 1984.

demand; along a demand curve price and quantity go in opposite directions. To avoid confusion, we shall talk about the *demand schedule* when the relationship is in tabular form and about the *demand curve* when the relationship is in graphical form.

> The **demand curve** or **demand schedule** for a good shows the various quantities demanded at different prices over a specified time period, holding other factors constant.

Exhibit 1 shows a hypothetical demand curve for corn. Buyers in the marketplace will demand 20 million bushels of corn per month at the price of $5 per bushel (point *a*). It is important to state the units of the measurement for both the price and the quantity. In this example, price is in dollars per bushel, and quantity is in millions of bushels per month. Should the price of corn be lower—say, $4 per bushel—then the quantity demanded is higher. In this case, the quantity demanded at the lower price of $4 is 25 million bushels (point *b*). By continuing to decrease the price, it is possible to get buyers to purchase more and more corn. At the price of $1, quantity demanded will be 50 million bushels (point *e*).

The demand curve drawn through points *a* to *e* is labeled *D*. It has a negative slope. Since the relationship between price and quantity demanded is downward sloping, the law of demand is sometimes called the *law of downward sloping demand*.

Most of the demand curves used in this book are **market-demand curves**. A later chapter will discuss the demand curves of individuals and will show that market-demand curves are the sum of individual demand curves. The market-demand curve summarizes the actions of all the buyers in a particular market.

> The **market-demand curve** is the demand curve of all persons participating in the market for that particular product.

EXHIBIT 1   The Demand Curve for Corn

a. Graph of Demand Curve for Corn

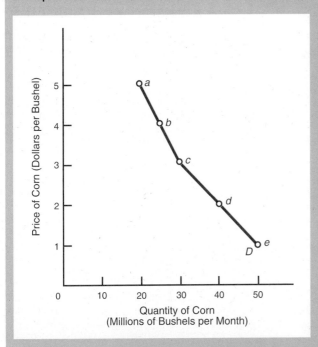

b. Demand Schedule for Corn

	Price (dollars per bushel)	Quantity Demanded (millions of bushels per month)
a	5	20
b	4	25
c	3	30
d	2	40
e	1	50

Panels (a) and (b) describe how the quantity of corn demanded responds to the prices of corn, holding all other factors constant. At *a*, when the price of corn is $5 per bushel, the quantity demanded is 20 million bushels per month. At *e*, when the price of corn is $1, the quantity demanded is 50 million bushels. The downward-sloping curve in panel (a) *(D)* is drawn through these points and is the demand curve for corn. Graphically, it shows the amounts of corn consumers would be willing to buy at different prices in the specified time period.

The demand curve shows the quantities people are prepared to buy at a different prices, *ceteris paribus*.

The *demand curve for corn* in Exhibit 1 refers to all buyers in the corn market. The corn market is an international market that brings together virtually all buyers of corn. The demand curve for Detroit real estate brings together all buyers of Detroit real estate. The demand curve for U.S. automobiles brings together the demand curves of all private, corporate, and governmental buyers of U.S. produced automobiles.

Factors That Cause the Demand Curve to Shift

The willingness of people to buy a good or service depends on a number of factors other than the price of the good or service itself. The demand curve for corn shows how corn purchases would change *if only the price of corn changed and all other factors remained the same.* Factors other than the price of corn can affect people's willingness to purchase corn. When those factors change, people may be willing to buy more (or less) corn at the same price as before. A change in one of the other factors would cause the demand curve to shift either to the right or to the left.

In the real world, other factors that affect demand are constantly changing; therefore, it is crucial to understand how changes in factors other than the good's own price affect the demand for a good. The main factors that can affect the demand for a good (in addition to its own price) are:

1. the prices of related goods,
2. consumer income,
3. consumer preferences,
4. the number of potential buyers, and
5. expectations.

The Prices of Related Goods.   Goods can be related to each other in two ways. Two goods are **substitutes** if the demand for one rises when the price of the other rises (or when the demand falls when the price of the other falls). Examples of substitutes are: coffee and tea, two brands of soft drinks, stocks and bonds, bacon and sausage, pork and beef, oats and corn, foreign and domestic cars, natural gas and electricity. Some goods are very close substitutes (two different brands of fluoride toothpaste), and others are very distant substitutes (Toyota cars and horsedrawn buggies).

> Two goods are **substitutes** if the demand for one rises when the price of the other rises (or if the demand for one falls when the price of the other falls).

Two goods are **complements** if increasing the price of one good lowers the demand for the other. Examples of complements are: automobiles and gasoline, food and drink, white dress shirts and neckties, skirts and blouses. When goods are complements there is a tendency for the two goods to be used jointly in order to achieve something more general (for example, automobiles plus gasoline equals transportation). An increase in the price of one of the goods effectively increases the price of the joint product of the two goods together. Thus, an increase in the price of one of the goods will reduce the demand for the other.

> Two goods are **complements** if the demand for one rises when the price of the other falls (or if the demand for one falls when the price of the other rises).

Income.   It is easy to understand how income influences demand. It is a fact of economic life that as incomes rise, people spend more on a great many **normal goods** and services. But as income increases, people also spend less on a few **inferior goods** and services.

> A **normal good** is one for which demand increases when income increases, holding all prices constant.

> An **inferior good** is one for which demand falls as income increases, holding all prices constant.

Lard, day-old bread, and second-hand clothing are examples of inferior goods for the market as a whole. For some people, inferior goods might be hamburgers, margarine, bus rides, or black-and-white TV sets. But most goods—from automobiles to water—are normal goods. All goods are normal at low enough levels of income.

Preferences.   To the economist, the word *preferences* means what people like and dislike without regard to budgetary considerations. One may *prefer* a 10-bedroom mansion but may only be able to afford a 3-bedroom bungalow. One may prefer a Mercedes-Benz but may drive a Volkswagen. One may prefer T-bone

EXAMPLE 1

Shifts in Demand: Wine, Health, and Recession

This chapter teaches that demand shifts as incomes and tastes change. Prices rise when demand increases and fall when demand falls.

The demand for wine, especially fine wines, is sensitive to income. When incomes are generally rising, the demand for wine rises, and there is upward pressure on wine prices. When incomes are generally falling the reverse happens. The prolonged U.S. business slump that began in 1990 caused the demand for wine to fall in the United States. Retail outlets had to discount the prices of their finer wines by 20 percent or more. The 1990s made wineries long for the booming 1980s—a period of rising incomes throughout the world.

All was not lost for wineries. The much-watched television show "60 Minutes" aired a segment in late 1991 which suggested that moderate wine consumption reduces the risk of heart attacks. After the original broadcast and its rebroadcast, sales of red wine shot up, reversing some of the decline caused by the slumping economy. People called the "60 Minutes" segment the 20 minutes that changed the industry.

When one winery ran an ad claiming that wine has therapeutic values as well as being recommended by the Bible, the government stepped in to ban this claim.

The public perception that wine is good for your health caused consumer preferences toward wine to improve, thereby increasing the demand for wine.

SOURCES: "Wineries and Government Clash Over Ads That Toast Health Benefits of Drinking," *Wall Street Journal,* October 19, 1992, p. B8. "Fine French Vintages Become a Hard Sell in Slumping Economy," *Wall Street Journal,* October 20, 1992, p. A1.

steaks but may eat hamburgers. Preferences plus budgetary considerations (price and income) determine demand. As preferences change, demand will change. If people learn that walking will increase their life span, the demand for walking shoes will increase. Business firms spend enormous sums trying to influence preferences by advertising on television, in newspapers, and in magazines. The goal of advertising is to shift the demand curve for the product to the right (See Example 2).

The Number of Potential Buyers. If more buyers enter a market, the demand will rise. The number of buyers in a market can increase for a number of reasons. Relaxed immigration barriers or a baby boom may lead to a larger population. The migration of people from one region to another changes the number of buyers in each region. The relaxation of trade barriers between two countries may increase the number of foreign buyers. If Japanese restrictions on imports of U.S. meat products were removed, the number of buyers of U.S. meat products would effectively increase. Lowering the legal age for alcoholic-beverage purchases will increase the number of buyers of beer.

Expectations. If people believe that the price of coffee over the next year will rise substantially (for whatever reason), they may decide to stock up on coffee. During inflationary times, when people find prices of goods rising rapidly, they often start buying durable goods, such as cars and refrigerators. The mere expectation of a good's price rising can induce people to buy more of it. Similarly, people can postpone the purchase of things that are expected to get cheaper. During the 1980s home computers grew cheaper and cheaper. Some buyers deliberately postponed purchasing home computers expecting that the good could

When the demand curve shifts to the left, *people want to buy smaller quantities of the good at each price.* A leftward shift of the demand curve indicates a *decrease in demand.* When the demand curve shifts to the right, *people want to buy larger quantities of the good at each price.* A rightward shift of the demand curve indicates an *increase in demand.*

EXHIBIT 2   Shifts in the Demand Curve: Changes in Demand

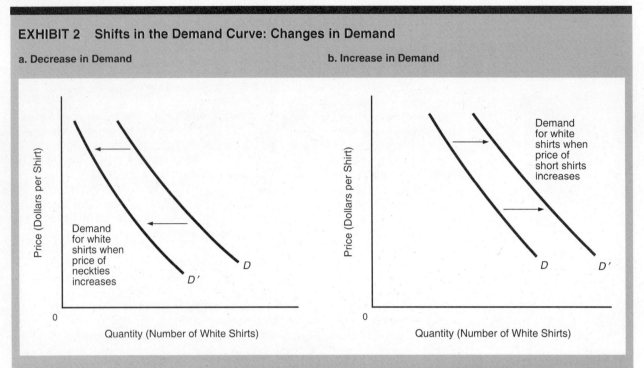

a. Decrease in Demand

b. Increase in Demand

Panel (a) shows a decrease in the demand for white dress shirts. Initially, the demand curve is *D*. If income decreases or if the price of some substitute falls or if tastes turn against white dress shirts, then at each price for white dress shirts the demand falls. The demand curve shifts to the left from *D* to *D′*. Panel (b) shows an increase in demand for white dress shirts. If income increases or if the price of some substitute increases or if tastes shift in favor of white dress shirts, then at each price demand increases. The demand curve will shift rightward from *D* to *D″*. A rightward shift reflects an increase in demand, and a leftward shift reflects a decrease in demand.

be purchased for less in the future. Finally, expecting income increases may dramatically affect consumer purchases in general.

Changes in any of the above five factors will *shift the entire demand curve* for the good. Exhibit 2 shows the demand curve for white dress shirts. This curve, *D*, holds constant such factors as the prices of complements and substitutes, income, preferences, and the number of buyers.

Demand curves shift to the right or left when factors other than the good's own price change. If consumer income increases, and if white dress shirts are a normal good, demand will increase (*D* will shift to the right). If preferences change and white dress shirts fall out of fashion, demand will decrease (*D* will shift to the left). If buyers expect prices of white dress shirts to rise substantially in the future, demand will increase.

> A change in a factor other than the good's own price that affects demand (such as prices of substitutes and complements, income, preferences, expectations, or the number of buyers) will cause the entire demand curve to shift.

SUPPLY

The **quantity supplied** of a particular good and service depends very much on the price of the product, holding other factors constant.

> The **quantity supplied** of a good or service is the amount of the good or service offered for sale at a given price, holding other factors constant.

The quantity supplied of a good should change when its price changes. As a general rule, the higher the price, the greater is the quantity supplied. A higher price for corn, for example, will induce farmers to cultivate fewer soybeans and plant more corn. A higher price for corn will cause farmers to ensure that corn is not wasted during harvesting or harmed by the weather or pests. A higher price for oil makes it more profitable for oil companies to take more risks when searching for new oil or when drilling for oil (for example, drilling deeper or through rock). In most cases, the higher the price of a good, the greater the quantity supplied.

The Supply Curve

The **supply curve** or **supply schedule** shows the different quantities supplied at different prices. Consider now the typical case of a positive relationship between price and quantity supplied. Panel (a) of Exhibit 3 shows a hypothetical curve for corn (drawn from the accompanying supply schedule panel (b)). When the price of corn is $5 per bushel, farmers are prepared to supply 40 million bushels per month (point *a*). As the price falls to $4, the quantity supplied falls to 35 million bushels (point *b*). Finally, when the price is $1 farmers are prepared to sell only 10 million bushels (point *e*).

EXHIBIT 3 The Supply Curve for Corn

a. Graph of Supply Curve for Corn

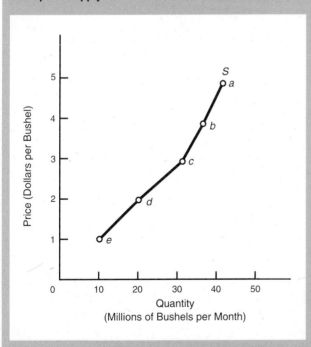

b. Supply Schedule for Corn

	Price (dollars per bushel)	Quantity Supplied (millions of bushels per month)
a	5	40
b	4	35
c	3	30
d	2	20
e	1	10

Panel (a) shows how the quantity of corn supplied responds to the price of corn. In situation *a*, when the price of corn is $5 per bushel, the quantity supplied by farmers is 40 million bushels per month. In the last situation, *e*, when the price is $1 per bushel, the quantity supplied is only 10 million bushels per month. The upward-sloping curve *(S)* drawn through these points is the supply curve of corn.

> The **supply curve** or **supply schedule** of a particular good or service shows the various quantities supplied at different prices, holding other factors constant, during a particular time period.

The curve drawn through points *a* through *e*, labeled *S*, is the supply curve. *It shows how much farmers are prepared to offer for sale at each price.* Along the supply curve, the price of corn and the supply of corn are positively related: in order to induce farmers to offer a large quantity of corn on the market, a higher price is required.

Factors That Cause the Supply Curve to Shift

Just as factors other than the good's own price can change the relationship between price and quantity demanded, other factors can change the relationship between price and quantity supplied, causing the supply curve to shift. The principal factors that can cause the supply curve to shift are:

1. the prices of other goods,
2. the prices of relevant resources,
3. technology,
4. the number of sellers, and
5. expectations.

The Prices of Other Goods. The resources that are used to produce any particular good can almost always be used elsewhere in the economy. Farmland can be used for corn or soybeans; engineers can work on cars or trucks; unskilled workers can pick strawberries or cotton; trains can be used to move coal or cars. As the price of a good rises, resources are naturally attracted away from other goods that use those resources. Hence, the supply of corn will fall if the price of soybeans rises; if the price of cotton rises the supply of strawberries may fall. If the price of trucks rises, the supply of cars may fall. If the price of fuel oil rises, less kerosene may be produced.

The Prices of Relevant Resources. The production and provision of goods and services requires certain resources that must be purchased in resource markets. As these resource prices change, the supply conditions for the goods being produced change. An increase in the price of coffee beans will increase the costs of producing coffee and decrease the amount of coffee that coffee companies are prepared to sell at each price; an increase in the price of corn land, tractors, harvesters, or irrigation will tend to reduce the supply of corn; an increase in the price of cotton will tend to decrease the supply of cotton dresses; an increase in the price of jet fuel will decrease the supply of commercial aviation at each price.

Technology. *Technology* is the knowledge that people have about how different things can be produced. If technology improves, more goods can be produced from the same resources. For example, if lobster farmers in Maine learn how to feed lobsters more cheaply with a new and cheaper combination of nutritious food, the quantity of lobsters supplied at each price will tend to increase. If a firm finds that the assembly line can be speeded up by merely rearranging the order of assembly, the supply of the good will tend to increase. If new oil-recovery procedures are discovered, the supply of oil will increase.

The Number of Sellers. If more sellers produce a particular good (perhaps because of high profits or in anticipation of high profits), the supply of the good

When the supply curve shifts to the left, *producers are prepared to sell smaller quantities at each price.* A leftward shift indicates a *decrease in supply.* When the supply curve shifts to the right, *producers are prepared to sell larger quantities at each price.* This rightward shift indicates an *increase in supply.*

will increase. The lowering of trade barriers (such as dropping cumbersome licensing requirements for foreign firms) may allow foreign sellers to enter the market, increasing the number of sellers.

Expectations. It takes a long time to produce many goods and services. When a farmer plants corn or wheat or soybeans, the prices that are expected to prevail at harvest time are actually more important than the current price. A college student who reads that there are likely to be too few engineers four years hence may decide to major in engineering in expectation of a high income. When a business firm decides to establish a plant that may take five years to build, expectations of future business conditions in that industry are crucial to that investment decision.

Changes in each of the above factors *will shift the entire supply curve.* Exhibit 4 shows the supply curve, *S,* for corn. The supply curve is based on a $10-per-bushel price of soybeans and a $2,000 yearly rental on an acre of corn land. If the price of soybeans rises to, say, $15 a bushel, then the supply curve for corn will shift leftward to *S'* in panel (a) because some land used for corn will be shifted to soybeans. If the rental price of an acre of corn land goes down from $2,000 a year per acre to $1,000 a year, the supply curve will shift to the right—to, say, *S″* in panel (b). The reduction in the land rental price lowers the costs of producing a bushel of corn and makes the corn producer willing to supply more corn at the same price as before.

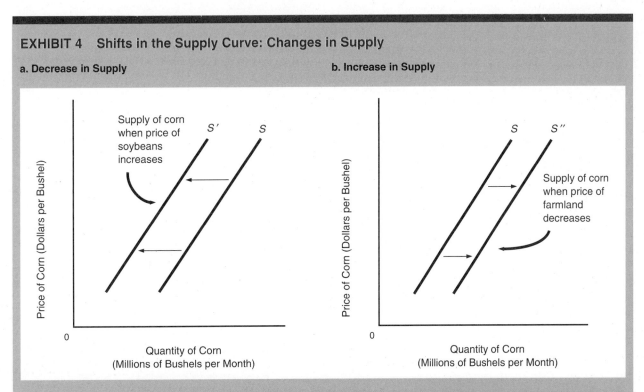

EXHIBIT 4   Shifts in the Supply Curve: Changes in Supply

a. Decrease in Supply

b. Increase in Supply

The supply curve of corn depends on the price of soybeans and on the price of farmland. When farmland is $2,000 an acre per year and soybeans are $10 per bushel, *S* might be the supply curve for corn. Panel (a) shows that if farmland stays at $2,000 per acre per year but soybeans fetch $15 instead of $10, profit-seeking farmers will switch farmland from corn to soybeans and cause the supply curve for corn to shift to the left fron *S* to *S'* (a decrease in supply). On the other hand, panel (b) shows that if soybeans remain at $10 per bushel and farmland falls from $2,000 to $1,000 per acre, the supply curve for corn will shift to the right from *S* to *S″* (an increase in supply).

EQUILIBRIUM OF SUPPLY AND DEMAND

Along a given demand curve, such as the one in Exhibit 1, there are many price/quantity combinations from which to choose. Along a given supply curve, there are similarly many different price/quantity combinations. Neither the demand curve nor the supply curve is sufficient by itself to determine the *market* price/quantity combination.

Exhibit 5 puts the demand curve of Exhibit 1 and the supply curve of Exhibit 3 together on the same diagram. Remember that the demand curve indicates what consumers are prepared to buy at different prices; the supply curve indicates what producers are prepared to sell at different prices. These groups of economic decision makers are (for the most part) entirely different. How much will be produced? How much will be consumed? How are the decisions of consumers and producers coordinated?

Suppose that the price of corn happened to be $2 per bushel. Exhibit 5 tells us the same thing that Exhibits 1 and 3 tell us separately: at a $2 price, consumers will want to buy 40 million bushels and producers will want to sell only 20 million bushels. This discrepancy means that at $2 there is a **shortage** of 20 million bushels.

> A shortage results if at the current price the quantity demanded exceeds the quantity supplied; the price is too low to equate the quantity demanded with the quantity supplied.

At a $2-per-bushel price, some people who are willing to buy corn cannot find a willing seller. The demand curve shows that a number of consumers are willing to pay more than $2 per bushel. Such buyers will try to outbid each other for the available supply. With free competition, the price of corn will be bid up if there is a shortage of corn.

The increase in the price of corn in response to the shortage will have two main effects. On the one hand, the higher price will discourage consumption. On the other hand, the higher price will encourage production. Thus, the increase in the price of corn, through the action of independent buyers and sellers, will lead both buyers and sellers in the marketplace to make decisions that will reduce the shortage of corn.

According to the demand and supply curves portrayed in Exhibit 5, when the price of corn reaches $3 per bushel, the shortage of corn disappears completely. At this **equilibrium** (or **market-clearing**) **price**, consumers want to buy 30 million bushels and producers want to sell 30 million bushels.

The equilibrium price equates the quantity demanded with the quantity supplied. If the price is not at equilibrium there will be a surplus or shortage.

> The **equilibrium (market-clearing) price** is the price at which the quantity demanded by consumers equals the quantity supplied by producers.

What would happen if the price rose above the equilibrium price of $3 per bushel? At the price of $4 per bushel, consumers want to buy 25 million bushels and producers want to sell 35 million bushels. Thus, at $4 there is a **surplus** of 10 million bushels on the market.

> A surplus results if at the current price the quantity supplied exceeds the quantity demanded; the price is too high to equate the quantity demanded with quantity supplied.

EXHIBIT 5   Market Equilibrium

This figure shows how market equilibrium is reached. On the same diagram are drawn both the demand curve for corn (from Exhibit 1) and the supply curve for corn (from Exhibit 3). When the price of corn is $2, the quantity demanded is 40 million bushels, but the quantity supplied is only 20 million bushels. The result is a shortage of 20 million bushels of corn. Unsatisfied buyers will bid the price up.

Raising the price will reduce the shortage. When the price of corn is raised to $4 per bushel, the quantity demanded is 25 million bushels while the quantity supplied is 35 million bushels. The result is a surplus of 10 million bushels of corn. This surplus will cause the price of corn to fall as unsatisfied sellers bid the price down to get rid of excess inventories of corn. As the price falls the surplus will diminish. The equilibrium price is $3 because the quantity demanded equals the quantity supplied at that price. The equilibrium quantity is 30 million bushels.

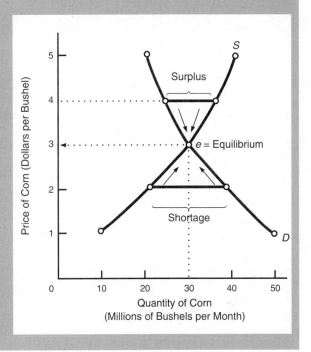

When there is a surplus some sellers will be disappointed as corn inventories pile up. Willing sellers of corn will not be able to find willing buyers. The competition among sellers will lead them to cut the price.

This fall in the price of corn will simultaneously encourage consumption and discourage production. Through the automatic fall in the price of corn, *the surplus of corn will therefore disappear.*

Again we find that the price will tend toward $3 and the quantity will tend toward 30 million bushels. This equilibrium point is where the demand and supply curves intersect. In Exhibit 5, there is no other price/quantity combination at which quantity demanded equals quantity supplied; any other price brings about a shortage of corn or a surplus of corn. The arrows in Exhibit 5 indicate the pressures on prices above or below $3 and how the amount of shortage or surplus—the size of the brackets—gets smaller as the price adjusts.

The equilibrium of supply and demand is stationary in the sense that once the equilibrium price is reached, it tends to remain the same. Movements away from the equilibrium price will be restored by the bidding of frustrated buyers or frustrated sellers in the marketplace. The equilibrium price is like a rocking chair in the rest position; give it a gentle push and the original position will be restored.

What the Market Accomplishes

The equilibrium price is discovered in the marketplace. The market coordinates the actions of a large number of independent suppliers and demanders. Their actions are brought together by the pricing of the good in a free market.

An equilibrium price accomplishes two basic goals. First, it *rations* the scarce supply of the commodity or service among all the people who would like to have it if it were given away free. Some people must be left out if the good is scarce. The price, by discouraging or restraining consumption, rations the good out to the various claimants of the good.

Second, the system of equilibrium prices *economizes on the information required* by individuals and firms. Buyers do not need to know how to produce the good, and sellers do not need to know why people use the good. Buyers and sellers need only be concerned with small bits of information, such as price, or small portions of the technological methods of production. The market can accomplish its actions without any one participant knowing all the details. Recall the pencil example discussed in Chapter 2: pencils are produced even though no single individual knows *all* the details for producing a pencil (from making the saw to felling the trees to making the rubber eraser).

The same is true of the corn-market example. Sellers of corn do not need to know anything about the buyers of corn, and vice versa. The price buyers pay tells sellers all they need to know, and the price sellers ask tells buyers all they need to know. When the price settles at equilibrium, the actions of buyers and sellers are harmonized.

CHANGES IN THE EQUILIBRIUM PRICE

Prices change. Sometimes prices go up, and sometimes they go down—and in relative-price terms, prices go down as often as they go up. Why do prices change? Equilibrium prices are determined by the intersection of the demand and supply curves. The only way for the price to change is for the demand or supply curves themselves to shift. The supply and demand curves can shift only if one or more of the factors *besides the good's own price* changes.

Change in Demand (or Supply) Versus Change in Quantity Demanded (or Supplied)

We make a careful distinction between movements along a demand curve and shifts in the entire curve. A change in the price of a good—as from p_2 to p_1 in panel (a) of Exhibit 6—causes a movement along the demand curve and is referred to as a **change in quantity demanded**. When a change in a factor other than the good's own price shifts the entire curve to the left or to the right, we call that a **change in demand**.

> A change (increase or decrease) in quantity demanded is a movement along the demand curve because of a change in the good's price. (See Exhibit 6).

> A change (increase or decrease) in demand is a shift in the entire demand curve because of a change in a factor other than the good's own price.

Similarly, panel (a) of Exhibit 7 shows that a rise in the price of a good (from p_1 to p_2) **changes the quantity supplied** but does not change the location of the supply curve. A **change in supply** occurs when a factor other than the good's own price changes, shifting the entire supply curve to the left or to the right.

> A change (increase or decrease) in quantity supplied is a movement along the supply curve because of a change in the good's price (see Exhibit 7).

EXHIBIT 6   Change in Demand Versus Change in Quantity Demanded

a. Change in Quantity Demanded

b. Change in Demand

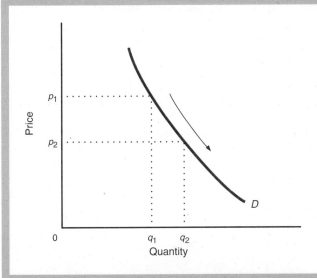 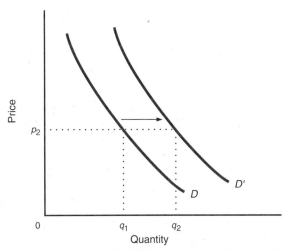

In panel (a), the increase in quantity demand (from q_1 to q_2) is due to the drop in price (from p_1 to p_2). The change in price causes the movement along the demand curve *(D)*. In panel (b), the increase in quantity (from q_1 to q_2) is due to a shift in the demand curve (an increase in demand) to *D'*, holding price constant. When demand increases, the whole demand curve shifts due to some change that leads consumers to buy more of the product at each price.

EXHIBIT 7   Change in Supply Versus Change in Quantity Supplied

a. Change in Quantity Supplied

b. Change in Supply

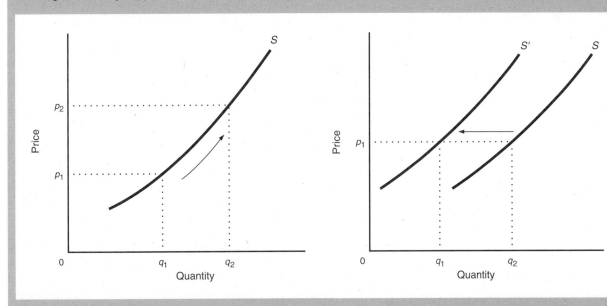

In panel (a), the increase in quantity supplied (from q_1 to q_2) is due to a rise in price (from p_1 to p_2). The change in price causes a movement along the supply curve S. In panel (b), the decrease in supply (from q_2 to q_1) is due to the shift in the supply curve (decrease in supply) from S to S', holding price constant. Firms wish to sell less at the same price.

> A **change** (increase or decrease) **in supply** is a shift in the entire supply curve because of a change in a factor other than the good's price.

The Effects of Change in Supply and Demand

Changes in supply or demand factors can change the equilibrium price and quantity in any given market. Consider first the effects of a change in supply.

Suppose a sudden and severe drought in America's breadbasket causes a substantial portion of the wheat crop to be lost. Exhibit 8 (a) illustrates the effect of the drought on the wheat market. The demand curve, *D*, and the supply curve, *S*, are based on conditions *before* the drought. The drought ruins about one half of the potential wheat crop. Now, at a price of $5 per bushel, instead of 50 million bushels being offered, only 25 million bushels are offered by farmers. Similarly, at all other prices smaller quantities of wheat are offered on the market. The supply curve for wheat has shifted to the left to *S'* (the supply of wheat has decreased). How will this supply reduction affect the demand curve?

When the supply curve for a single good, like wheat or corn, changes, the demand curve normally does not change. The factors influencing the supply of wheat *other than the price of wheat* have little or no influence on the demand for wheat. The severe drought will not shift the demand curve. In the analysis of a single market we can usually assume that the demand and supply curves are independent.

A decrease in supply causes the price to rise and the quantity demanded to fall. An increase in supply causes the price to fall and the quantity demanded to rise.

The supply curve has shifted to the left (supply has decreased); the demand curve remains unchanged. What will happen to the equilibrium price? Exhibit 8(a) shows that after the reduction in supply, the quantity supplied is less than the quantity demanded at the original equilibrium price. At the original price, there is a shortage of wheat. Therefore, the price of wheat will be bid up until a new higher equilibrium price is attained, at which quantity demanded and quantity supplied are equal. As the price rises, there is a movement up the new supply curve *(S')* as higher prices coax more wheat out of drought-ridden farmers.

A change in demand is illustrated in Exhibit 8(b). The initial situation is depicted by the demand curve for wheat, *D*, and the supply curve of wheat, *S*. The equilibrium price is $5 and the equilibrium quantity is 50 million bushels. Medical evidence is now uncovered showing that eating bread increases one's life span. This news would shift the demand curve for wheat to the right (from *D* to *D'*). People now want to buy more wheat than before at the same prices. The medical evidence, however, would not affect the supply of wheat. Because of the increase in demand, people want to buy more wheat at the original price of $5 than farmers are willing to supply. There is a shortage of wheat, and the price of wheat would rise until a higher price is established that equates quantity demanded and quantity supplied.

The rise in price causes a movement up the new demand curve, as higher prices cause people to cut back their purchases. *There has been no increase in supply, only an increase in quantity supplied* in response to the higher price.

An increase in demand causes the price to rise and the quantity supplied to rise. A decrease in demand causes the price to fall and the quantity supplied to fall.

Notice again that when the demand curve shifts due to some change in demand factors other than the good's price, there is no shift in the supply curve: the supply curve remains the same. The supply curve and the demand curve should be considered to be independent of one another at this level of analysis. In our example, the change in preferences should not affect the willingness of farmers to supply wheat at different prices during any given time period.

Exhibit 9 reviews the factors that cause shifts in supply and demand curves and shows how they affect equilibrium prices and quantities.

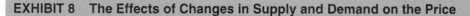

EXHIBIT 8   The Effects of Changes in Supply and Demand on the Price

a. Decrease in Supply

b. Increase in Demand

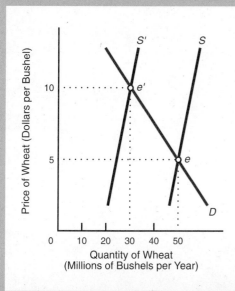

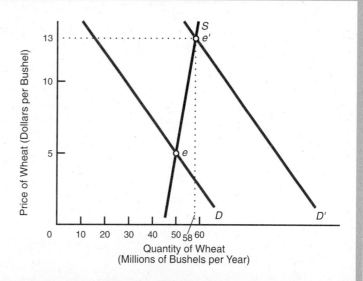

In panel (a), the natural disaster shifts the supply curve of wheat from S to S'. This decrease in supply raises the equilibrium price from $5 to $10. The movement from e to e' is a movement along the demand curve. Although the demand curve does not change, there is a decrease in quantity demanded from 50 million to 30 million bushels as the price rises from $5 to $10 per bushel. Panel (b) shows an increase in the demand for wheat because of, say, increased tastes for bread. The shift in the demand curve from D to D' depicts an increase in demand. This increase in demand drives up the equilibrium price from $5 per bushel to $13 per bushel. As price rises from $5 to $13, there is an increase in quantity supplied from 50 million to 58 million bushels that results from the movement along the supply curve, S.

Simultaneous Changes in Supply and Demand

In many instances, demand and supply can change at the same time. There can be nine combinations of supply and demand shifts (shown in Exhibit 10). Each combination yields different price/quantity outcomes. In some cases, the effects on price and quantity are known. In other cases, the effects are indeterminate. For example, as in Exhibit 10(e), a simultaneous increase in both supply and demand may raise or lower price. The price will rise if the demand shift exceeds the supply shift, as illustrated.

UNCONVENTIONAL USE OF SUPPLY AND DEMAND

The concepts of supply, demand, and the equilibrium price apply to a wide range of exchanges, even exchanges that appear to lie outside the traditional realm of economics. Anything that admits to being priced and exchanged freely can be analyzed by the tools of this chapter. In fact, the 1992 Nobel laureate in economics, Gary Becker, earned the award for his application of supply and demand to issues of marriage, crime, divorce, and discrimination. Economists now speak of "markets" for marriage and for crime. They note that in some traditional societies,

EXHIBIT 9   Shifts in Demand and Supply Curves: Effects on Prices and Quantities

Shifts in Demand Curves

Factor	Example	Result
Price of substitutes	Increase in price of coffee shifts demand curve for tea to right	Price of tea rises, quantity of tea rises
Price of complements	Increase in price of coffee shifts demand curve for cream to the left	Price of coffee falls, quantity of cream falls
Income	Increase in income shifts demand curve for automobiles to the right	Price of autos rises, quantity rises
Preference	Judgment that cigarettes are hazardous shifts demand curve for cigarettes to left	Price of cigarettes falls, quantity falls
Number of buyers	Trade agreement with Japan increases number of buyers of farm products and shifts demand curve to the right	Prices of farm products rise, quantity rises
Expectations of future prices	Expectation that PC prices will fall in future	Prices of PCs fall, quantity falls

Shifts in Supply Curves

Factor	Example	Result
Price of another good	Increase in price of corn shifts supply curve of wheat to left	Price of wheat rises, quantity falls
Price of resource	Decrease in wage rate of autoworkers shifts supply curve of autos to right	Price of autos falls, quantity rises
Technology	Higher corn yields due to genetic engineering shift supply curve of corn to right	Price of corn falls, quantity rises
Number of sellers	Trade agreement with USSR opens U.S. market to Soviet steel producers	Price of steel falls, quantity rises
Expectations	Expectation of higher ball bearing prices in the future causes more investment, shifting supply curve to right	Price of ball bearings rises, quantity rises

marriage proceeds as does any other market—the groom may pay a bride's price or the bride's family might provide a dowry. In modern societies there is less explicit use of prices, but marriages are formed and dissolved in a manner that resembles market transactions.

In the "market" for crime, the price of crime might be the amount that thieves can earn per day of mugging, robbing, or burglarizing. Even gambling appears to use prices to govern exchanges. The sports pages contain interesting market information every weekend during the National Football League season. Each game has a certain point spread, where one team is given an advantage over the other. The purpose of the point spread is to bring about equilibrium in the market for betting so that, for example, the number of people betting on favored team A equals the number of people betting on the underdog team B.

The extension of supply-and-demand analysis into non-economic areas such

Chapter 3   Supply and Demand

EXHIBIT 10   Summary of Effects of Supply-Curve and Demand-Curve Shifts

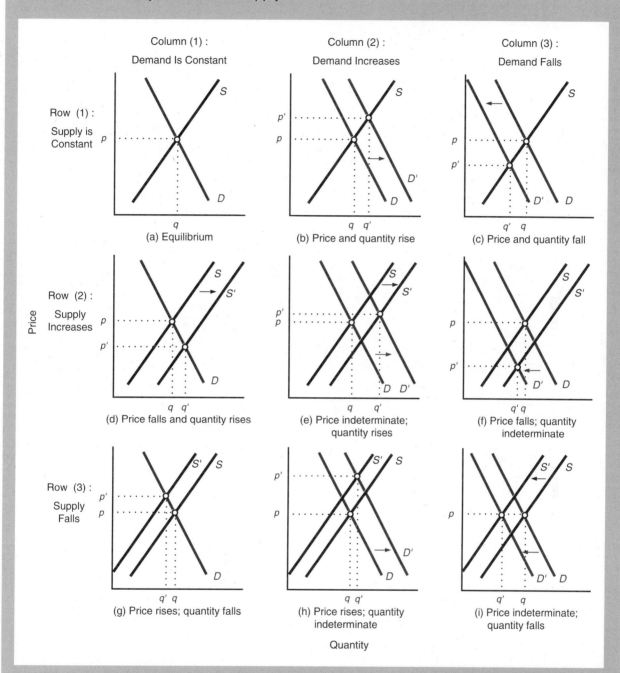

Column (1):

Demand Is Constant

Column (2):

Demand Increases

Column (3):

Demand Falls

Row (1):

Supply is Constant

Row (2):

Supply Increases

Row (3):

Supply Falls

Price

(a) Equilibrium

(b) Price and quantity rise

(c) Price and quantity fall

(d) Price falls and quantity rises

(e) Price indeterminate; quantity rises

(f) Price falls; quantity indeterminate

(g) Price rises; quantity falls

(h) Price rises; quantity indeterminate

(i) Price indeterminate; quantity falls

Quantity

This figure shows the effects of all possible combinations of shifts in supply curves and demand curves. As panels (e), (f), (h), and (i) demonstrate, the effects of simultaneous changes in supply and demand are sometimes indeterminate. If supply increases (shifts right) and demand decreases (shifts left), the price will fall. If supply decreases and demand increases, the price will rise. If, however, both the demand and supply curves move in the same direction (if both increase or if both decrease), the price effect depends on which movement dominates.

Interfering with Supply and Demand;
The 1974 Energy Crisis

Dramatic shifts in supply or demand can prompt a public outcry for the government to set prices in place of the market. After natural disasters, for example, the government penalizes merchants who raise prices (price gouging). When the Arab oil embargo threatened world gasoline supplies in 1974, the federal government was determined not to let gas prices rise through the roof. Prior to the embargo, gas was selling at 40 cents per gallon. With supplies cut off, the forces of supply and demand threatened to push the price toward $1—a price rise that was regarded as unacceptable at the time. To prevent such unconscionable price increases, the federal government began to allocate gas supplies to the various states and to set ceiling prices for gasoline.

The diagram shows the consequences of setting price ceilings during a period of dramatically reduced supply. With a price ceiling of 50 cents per gallon, the quantity demanded fell far short of the quantity supplied.

The American public will not soon forget the energy crisis of 1974. The government allocated ample supplies to some states. Other states received little gas, and gas shortages were severe. People had to get up early in the morning and wait in line for gas. A number of fatal shootings occurred at gas stations as impatient customers tried to cut in line. Gas station attendants were threatened at gunpoint by irate customers when they tried to shut the station in the evening.

The policy implication of the 1974 experience is that there are severe and unexpected costs when government allocation and price ceilings replace allocation by supply and demand. Although it is appealing to think of the government as holding prices to a reasonable level and preventing evil speculators from getting rich, the price of government intervention can be severe. The oil embargo is only one example. When rents threaten to rise in major cities, the public clamors for rent controls, which ultimately create housing shortages. When interest rates rise, there is

The Effect of Price Ceilings on the Market for Gasoline

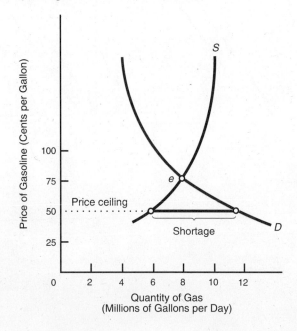

a public outcry for interest rate ceilings. Those least able to obtain credit (the poor), accordingly, are shut out of credit markets.

It is noteworthy that the European countries did not experience the lines and panics that characterized the U.S. gasoline market. Most of the European countries simply let the price of gas rise to its market level. People paid higher prices but lines and shootings were avoided.

as sociology, law, international relations, and anthropology has caused economics to be called the "imperialist" discipline of social science.

The first three chapters have focused on the way market economies use the price system to solve the economic problem. The next chapter looks at the way governments allocate resources.

Chapter Summary

The most important point to learn from this chapter is: In a perfectly competitive market, there is always an equilibrium price that coordinates the independent actions of firms that supply goods to the market and of consumers who demand goods from the market.

1. A perfectly competitive market consists of many buyers and sellers in which each buyer or seller accepts the market price as given.

2. The law of demand states that as price goes up the quantity demanded falls, and vice versa; the demand curve is a graphical representation of the relationship between price and quantity demanded—other things being equal. The demand curve is downward sloping.

3. As price goes up the quantity supplied usually rises; the supply curve is a graphical representation of the relationship between price and quantity supplied. The supply curve tends to be upward sloping because of the law of diminishing returns.

4. The equilibrium price/quantity combination occurs where the demand curve intersects the supply curve, or where quantity demanded equals quantity supplied at the market-clearing price. Competitive pricing rations scarce economic goods and economizes on the information necessary to coordinate supply/demand decisions. A shortage results if the price is too low for equilibrium; a surplus results if the price is too high for equilibrium.

5. A change in quantity demanded means a *movement along* a given demand curve; a change in demand means the entire demand curve shifts. A change in quantity supplied means a *movement along* a given supply curve; a change in supply means the entire supply curve shifts. Supply-and-demand analysis allows one to predict what will happen to prices and quantities when supply or demand schedules shift.

6. The concepts of supply, demand, and the equilibrium price can be applied to a wide range of exchanges.

Policy Focus: It may be appealing for the government to interfere with the forces of supply and demand by setting price ceilings. The public must recognize that such actions create shortages and require government rationing if chaos is to be prevented.

Key Terms

market (p. 47)
perfectly competitive market (p. 48)
law of demand (p. 49)
quantity demanded (p. 49)
demand curve or schedule (p. 49)
market-demand curve (p. 50)
substitutes (p. 52)
complements (p. 52)
normal goods (p. 52)
inferior goods (p. 52)

quantity supplied (p. 54)
supply curve or schedule (p. 55)
shortage (p. 58)
equilibrium (market-clearing) price (p. 58)
surplus (p. 58)
change in quantity demanded (p. 60)
change in demand (p. 60)
change in quantity supplied (p. 60)
change in supply (p. 60)

Questions and Problems

1. List the four characteristics of a perfectly competitive market. Explain why if any of the four conditions are not met, the principal characteristic of a perfectly competitive market (no person or group can control price) may not be met.

2. Suppose you live in a very cold climate and pay on the average 25 percent of your income for fuel. If the price of fuel rises by 15 percent, and there are no good substitutes for fuel, why would you cut back on fuel consumption?

3. Plot the supply and demand schedules for the hypothetical product in Table A as supply and demand curves.
   a. What equilibrium price would this market establish?
   b. If the state were to pass a law that the price could not be more than $2, how would you describe the market response?
   c. If the state were to pass a law that the price could not be less than $8 how would you describe the market response?
   d. If preferences changed and people wanted to buy twice as much as before at each price, what will the equilibrium price be?
   e. If, in addition to the above change in preferences, there is an improvement in technology that allows firms to produce this product at lower cost than before, what will happen to the equilibrium price?

TABLE A

Price (dollars)	Quantity Demanded (units)	Quantity Supplied (units)
10	5	25
8	10	20
6	15	15
2	20	10
0	25	5

4. American baseball bats do not sell well in Japan because they do not meet the specifications of Japanese baseball officials. If the Japanese change their specifications to accommodate American-made bats, what will happen to the price of American bats?

5. "The poor are the ones who suffer from high gas and electricity bills. We should pass a law that gas and electricity rates cannot increase by more than 1 percent annually." Evaluate this statement in terms of supply-and-demand analysis, assuming that equilibrium prices rise faster than 1 percent annually.

6. Much of the automobile-rental business in the United States is done at airports. What would be the predicted effect of a reduction in airfares on automobile-rental rates?

7. If both the supply and demand for coffee increase, what would happen to coffee prices? If the supply increased and the demand fell, what would happen to coffee prices?

8. Which of the following statements uses incorrect terminology? Explain.
   a. The recent fare war among the major airlines has increased the demand for air travel."
   b. "The recession of 90–91 has caused the demand for air travel to fall."

9. What are the factors held constant along the demand curve? Explain how each can shift the demand curve to the right. Explain how each can shift the demand curve to the left.

10. What are the factors held constant along the supply curve? Explain how each factor can shift the supply curve to the right. Explain how each factor can shift the supply curve to the left.

11. Why is the demand curve downward sloping?

12. Why is the supply curve normally upward sloping? Can you think of any exceptions?

13. What is the effect of each of the following events on the equilibrium price and quantity of hamburgers?

a. An increase in the price of steak (a substitute for hamburgers).
b. An increase in the price of french fries (a complement).
c. A given population becomes older.
d. The government requires that all the ingredients of hamburgers be absolutely fresh (that is, nothing can be frozen).
e. Beef becomes more expensive.
f. More firms enter the hamburger business.

Doing Economics

Think about the market for gasoline in the United States. Based on your experience, should the demand for gasoline vary over the seasons of the year? What about the supply? Now go to the Government Documents section of your school's library and find recent issues of *Monthly Energy Review,* a publication of the U.S. Department of Energy. In this publication, you should be able to find monthly data on retail gasoline prices and quantities sold. List the prices and quantities for unleaded gasoline month by month for a period of at least two years. Are there any major shifts in price? Thinking about the dates on which they occurred, what do you think caused them? Ignoring these major shifts, what pattern do you notice in the movements of prices over the seasons of the year? What is the pattern in quantity sold? Based on these observations, is this seasonal pattern likely to be explained by seasonal fluctuations in demand or supply? Does your evidence correspond to your intuitive prediction about seasonal movements in demand and supply?

14. "As a general rule, if *both* supply and demand increase or decrease, the change in price will be indeterminate." Is this statement true or false? Illustrate with a diagram.

15. "As a general rule, if demand increases and supply decreases, or vice versa, the change in quantity will be indeterminate." Is this statement true or false? Illustrate with a diagram.

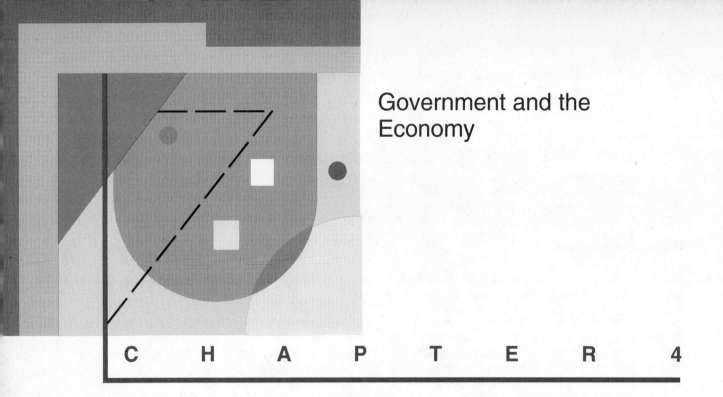

Government and the Economy

C H A P T E R 4

CHAPTER FOCUS This chapter addresses two fundamental policy issues: How should government raise the funds it needs to conduct its business in a fair and rational manner? What procedures and safeguards should democratic societies use to make sure that public funds are spent in the public interest?

The first question has been on the public mind since governments began taxing their citizens. Given that governments have to raise money to support government activities, what is the best and fairest way of sharing the burden? Social thinkers have given us two approaches. One is that those who benefit from the government service should pay for it. The other is that those who are better off should pay.

Economists can say a great deal about the consequences of different tax regimens; they cannot decide which type of tax system is the most fair. We shall return to the issue of fairness of the tax system in a later chapter.

How governments can ensure that public funds are spent efficiently and in the public interest is a question of more recent vintage. Early philosophers thought that democratically elected officials would automatically act in the interests of the majority. Centuries of logrolling and vote trading, however, have shown that majority rule can produce spending programs that favor special interests over the interests of the majority.

After studying this chapter, you will be able to:

- Explain why the relative size of government in the economy has grown.
- Define the ability-to-pay and benefit principles of taxation.
- Tell the difference between progressive and regressive taxes.
- Tell how the incidence of taxes can be changed by tax shifting.
- Define the types of government spending that actually use scarce resources.
- Understand how majority rule can result in inefficient government spending policies.
- Tell the reasons for government action.

GOVERNMENT SPENDING

Government operates businesses (for example, the government printing office, and weapons arsenals). Government provides for the national defense, education, police protection, streets and highways, public parks, and even garbage collection. The government pays for most of its spending by collecting taxes. People pay all kinds of taxes: income taxes, sales taxes, excise taxes, property taxes, and taxes on imported goods, called tariffs.

Types of Government Spending

Governments make two types of expenditures: **exhaustive expenditures** and **transfer payments.**

> Exhaustive expenditures are government purchases of goods and services that divert economic resources from the private sector, making them no longer available for private use.

> Transfer payments are simply transfers of income from one individual or organization to another by a combination of taxes and subsidies.

When the government buys a fleet of cars or hires a statistician, these are exhaustive payments because the fleet of cars and services of the statistician are no longer available to the private sector. Government transfer payments do not raise the amount of economic resources that the government consumes. Social Security transfers income from currently employed workers to retired or disabled workers. The federal government transfers funds to state and local governments through its various grants programs. Transfer payments affect the distribution of income among families but do not change the amount of goods and services exhausted (consumed) by government. Transfer payments may indirectly affect economic activity by affecting economic incentives: if Peter is taxed to pay Paul, both may work less.

Exhibit 1 shows that exhaustive government expenditures account for 19 percent of all goods and services produced by the economy. But exhaustive expenditures account for only 57 percent of government spending. Exhaustive government expenditures and transfer payments add up to 33 percent of the value of all goods and services produced by the economy.

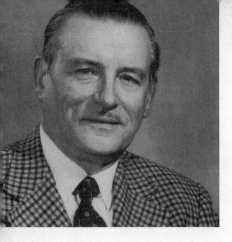

James Buchanan (1919–)

James Buchanan founded public-choice economics—the branch of economics that studies political economic decision-making. Buchanan started the Public Choice Society and promoted a new journal, *Public Choice*. He was born in 1919 in Tennessee, where his grandfather had been governor from 1891 to 1893. Buchanan received his Ph.D. in 1948 from the University of Chicago and taught at the University of Virginia and George Mason University. In 1986, he received the Nobel Prize in economics for his contributions to the study of government and the economy.

Prior to Buchanan, economists assumed that government functions were carried out efficiently. Monopoly, externalities, and macroeconomic instability were reasons given for government action. Yet few economists had considered *how well* government itself would perform its resource-allocation functions in place of private markets. It was simply assumed that government action would be better than private action. Buchanan raised the fundamental issue of how well democratic societies, operating under majority rule, allocate resources. Buchanan pointed out that when politicians seek to maximize their reelection chances they engage in logrolling and vote trading. Unwise public expenditures are the likely outcome. Buchanan predicted the difficulties of balancing federal budgets in majority-rule societies where government expenditures are popular and taxes unpopular. He also pointed out that majority-vote elections can reject public expenditures that are in the economic interests of the voters. Buchanan's main contribution has been to expand economics to include self-interested politicians and bureaucrats, who join Adam Smith's self-interested producers and consumers in pursuing their own self-interest.

Buchanan argues that constitutional constraints must be placed on democratic governments. Without such constraints he believes that attempts to, say, reduce the federal deficit must fail. He argues that the potential gains from reducing government expenditures and raising taxes would be dissipated by enormous lobbying efforts on behalf of special-interest groups.

Size of Government

Government revenues and expenditures have been increasing at a rapid pace. In 1929, receipts of local, state, and federal government were $11 billion and expenditures were $10 billion. In 1992, government receipts and expenditures were nearly $2 trillion each. Dollar figures such as these give an exaggerated view of the growth of government because of rising prices and growing output. The most relevant yardstick of the economic role of government is the share of total government spending of total economic output, or GDP. Exhibit 2 shows that government expenditures accounted for a small 6.5 percent of the value of all goods and services produced at the turn of the century. By 1950, government spending was 20 percent in the United States, and by 1992, this percentage had risen to 33 percent. Government economic activity has been increasing in the United States even after adjustment for growth distortion and inflation distortion.

Exhibit 2 shows the rise of government has been an international phenomenon. Government spending has risen as a percentage of economic activity in all the industrialized countries.

The rising share of government economic activity in the United States can be explained by a number of factors.

Government	Purchase of Goods and Services, Including Interest Payments (billions of dollars)	Purchase as Percent of Gross Domestic Product	Transfer Payments (billions of dollars)*	Total Expenditures for Goods and Services and Transfers (billions of dollars)	Total Expenditure as Percent of GDP
Federal	445	7.8	754	1,199	21.0
State and local	644	11.3	64	708	12.4
Total	1,089	19.1	818	1,907	33.4

*Federal transfers exclude grants to state and local governments.

SOURCE: *Economic Report of the President.*

EXHIBIT 2   Total Government Spending as a Percentage of GDP, U.S., and Other Countries, 1890–1991

The ratio of total government expenditures to total economic activity (or GDP) is a better measure of the changing role of government than measures of government spending alone. This exhibit shows the general increase in government spending as a percentage of total economic activity

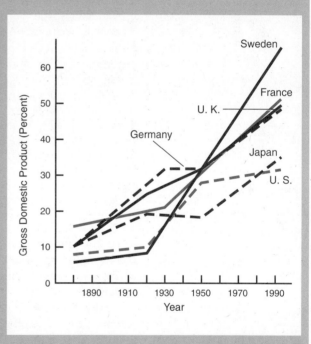

SOURCE: *World Development Report 1991* (Oxford: Oxford University Press, 1991), p. 139. Figures updated by authors.

1. Two world wars and the Cold War caused military spending to increase. The United States, as a military superpower, devoted an increasing share of its economic resources to national defense. On the eve of World War II, national defense accounted for 1.3 percent of total spending. At the peak of the Vietnam conflict, national defense accounted for almost 9 percent. The end of the Cold War should cause defense spending to drop as a percentage of total spending.

2. Government has increasingly taken responsibility for health, education, and income security. Prior to the Great Depression of the 1930s, it was primarily the responsibility of the individual to provide for family health, income security, and retirement needs. In 1929 government social-welfare programs cost a minute fraction of 1 percent of total economic activity, whereas today they account for more than 10 percent.

3. Modern urban societies require more government services—sanitation, traffic control, water supplies. Congested areas require more police protection than low-density farming communities. Modern industrial societies require a more complex legal system to carry out complex business contracts.

4. Democratic political processes increase government spending. Democratic politics can lead to logrolling, vote trading, and special interest legislation. Government spending decisions are determined by what benefits specific individuals and specific groups. Such actions cause the costs of government actions to be underestimated and government spending to rise.

The government's share of economic activity has been rising over the long run.

Shares of Federal, State, and Local Governments

Each society must determine at what level of government public services are to be provided. Should roads be built by federal, state, or local government? Should the municipalities, the states, or the federal government provide public education? There has been intense debate over these issues since the founding of this country. Some citizens fear a powerful federal government. Others consider the federal government to be more efficient and the best enforcer of national standards and legislation.

The federal government accounted for 61 percent of all government expenditures in 1991, while state and local governments accounted for 39 percent. Exhibit 3 shows that the larger share of federal spending dates from the post-World War II era.

TAXES

Most government spending is financed by taxes. In the early 1990s, personal income taxes amounted to 15 percent of personal income. The inclusion of sales, excise, and Social Security taxes raise the average tax burden to about 36 percent of personal income.

Exhibit 4 shows the relative importance of the various sources of government revenue to the federal government and to state and local governments. Note the importance of individual income taxes to the federal government. State and local governments depend on sales taxes, federal government revenue-sharing, and various fees and charges.

Efficiency, Fairness, and Social Goals

How governments tax is important for a number of reasons.

First, taxes affect economic behavior. People can typically alter their tax obligations by modifying their economic behavior. They pay lower sales taxes if they buy less; they pay lower income taxes if they earn less; they pay no property taxes if they own no property. Any tax that causes people to reduce their work effort, to be less innovative, or to take fewer business risks causes less output to be produced. With less output, there is less to go around for all.

Chapter 4   Government and the Economy

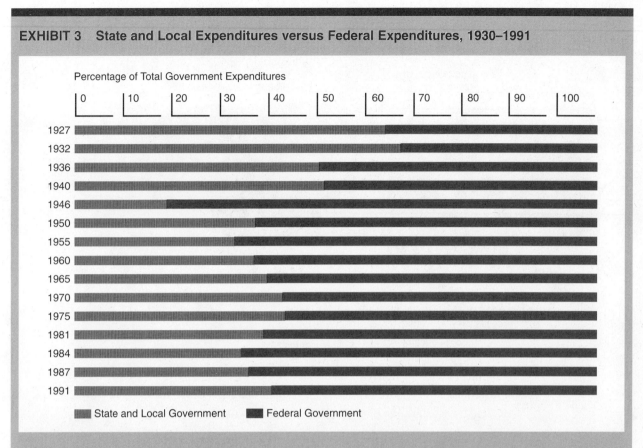

EXHIBIT 3   State and Local Expenditures versus Federal Expenditures, 1930–1991

Percentage of Total Government Expenditures

| | 0 | 10 | 20 | 30 | 40 | 50 | 60 | 70 | 80 | 90 | 100 |

1927
1932
1936
1940
1946
1950
1955
1960
1965
1970
1975
1981
1984
1987
1991

■ State and Local Government   ■ Federal Government

This graph shows that the dominance of federal over state and local spending is a fairly recent phenomenon. *Note:* Federal expenditures do not include grants in aid to state and local governments.
SOURCE: *Survey of Current Business; Historical Statistics of the United States*, vol. 2, pp. 1124–29.

Second, people should feel that taxes are fair. Poor people might think rich people are not paying their fair share. Rich people might think they are taxed too much. If people are convinced that the tax system is unfair, they try to evade taxes. Taxes are hard to collect when people consider the tax system unfair.

Third, taxes can be used to promote social goals. Taxpayers alter their economic behavior in response to taxes. The negative side is that people may reduce their work effort to reduce their taxes. The positive side is that the taxes can be used to encourage desirable activities or discourage undesirable activities. A high sales tax on cigarettes, for example, discourages smoking. Tax exemptions for military personnel encourages enlistment in the armed forces.

Principles of Fairness

The two principles of taxation are the benefit principle and the ability-to-pay principle.

Two principles of fairness underlie most taxes. The first is that the tax burden should be distributed according to benefits received. The second principle is that the tax burden should be distributed according to the ability to pay.

The Benefit Principle.   The *benefit principle* states that those who benefit from a public expenditure should pay the tax that finances it. The persons who benefit

Taxes

EXHIBIT 4 Sources of Government Revenue, 1992

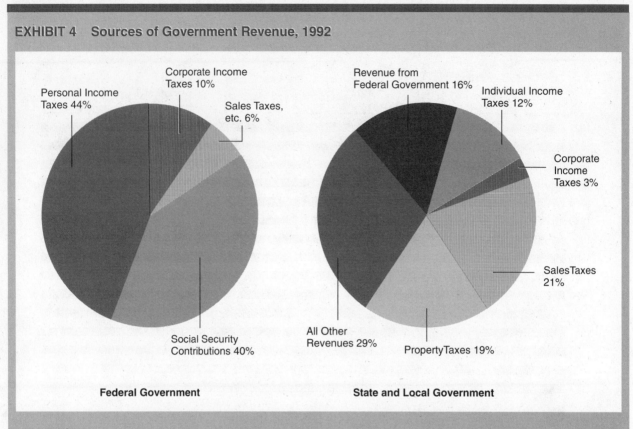

Personal Income Taxes 44%

Corporate Income Taxes 10%

Sales Taxes, etc. 6%

Social Security Contributions 40%

Federal Government

Revenue from Federal Government 16%

Individual Income Taxes 12%

Corporate Income Taxes 3%

Sales Taxes 21%

Property Taxes 19%

All Other Revenues 29%

State and Local Government

This exhibit shows that taxes are the major source of government revenues at all levels of government.

SOURCE: *Economic Report of the President*

from a new state highway, a new airport, or a flood-control project should pay. A prominent example of a benefit tax is the tax on gasoline that finances highway construction. In many communities, special taxes are assessed for road repairs, street lighting, and sidewalks. In these cases, the people who benefit pay for the government services from which they benefit.

If community members won't pay for a public project—if citizens vote against a flood-control project in their community—their votes show that they do not consider the project's benefits to outweigh its costs. If all taxes were levied on the principle that the beneficiaries bear the full burden of the tax (and if the beneficiaries were given the opportunity to vote on each public expenditure), taxpayers would only approve projects whose benefits equal or exceed their costs.

It is often difficult to determine exactly who benefits from different government expenditures. While it is obvious that automobile drivers benefit from public highways and that residents of New York City benefit from public expenditures on the New York subway system, other cases are less certain. Who benefits from national defense? Who benefits from police protection and from the legal system? Do the poor benefit more than the rich? In order to apply the benefit principle, one must first know who is the beneficiary.

Even if the beneficiaries could be identified, there is the question of whether they should pay. Many public expenditures are designed for the very purpose of benefiting the less able. It makes no sense to make the beneficiaries of welfare programs or job training programs pay because these programs' aim to raise the incomes of those least able to pay.

The Ability-to-Pay Principle. The second approach to fairness is the *ability-to-pay principle*. This principle maintains that those better able to pay should bear the greater burden of taxes, whether or not they benefit more. The rich benefit less from public education and from public hospitals because they use private hospitals and send their children to private schools, but because they are better able to pay, they should bear a heavier tax burden.

Like the benefit principle, the ability-to-pay principle has disadvantages. If those who benefit from a tax do not have to pay, public programs whose costs outweigh their benefits may be approved. If one group benefits from a flood-control project that is paid for by another group (and the first group has more votes), flood-control projects will be approved that yield only minimal benefits.

Incidence of Taxation: Who Actually Pays?

Surprisingly, the individual or company that is being taxed does not necessarily "pay" the tax. In many cases, the tax can be shifted to someone else. The **incidence of the tax** can fall on someone other than the designated payer of the tax.

> The **incidence of a tax** is the actual burden after considering the effect of the tax on actual prices paid or received.

A tax is shifted forward when the buyer of the product subject to a tax pays a portion of the tax by paying a higher price.

When a $1 tax is placed on each carton of cigarettes, cigarette manufacturers may reduce the supply of cigarettes. The previous chapter showed that a reduction in supply will raise price. When the price of cigarettes rises, the manufacturer has *shifted the tax forward* to the consumer. The consumer ends up paying at least part of the tax in the form of a higher price. If the $1 tax pushes up the price by $0.80, then 80 percent of the tax has been shifted to the consumer. Most of the tax burden is borne not by the manufacturer but by the consumer.

Virtually any tax—an income tax, a sales tax, an inheritance tax, or a tariff on foreign goods—can be shifted. Some taxes can be shifted almost entirely to others; other taxes must be completely paid by the individual or organization that nominally pays the tax.

Progressive and Regressive Taxes

With a progressive tax, the share of income paid as taxes rises with income. With a regressive tax system, the share falls as income rises.

Taxes can redistribute income. If Jones pays 50 percent of her income and Smith pays 10 percent of his income, the distribution of after-tax income has been altered in favor of Smith. Taxes can redistribute income in favor of poor people or rich people. If higher income people pay proportionately higher taxes, after-tax income will be redistributed in favor of poor people. A tax can be either **proportional, progressive, or regressive.**

> A **proportional tax** is one where taxpayers pay the same percentage of income as taxes irrespective of their income.

> A **progressive tax** is one where the higher the income, the larger is the percentage of income paid as taxes.

> A **regressive tax** is one where the higher the income, the smaller is the percentage of income paid as taxes.

The federal income tax is a progressive tax. For example, income tax rates in effect in the early 1990s started at 15 percent for moderate income families and rose to 34 percent for high income families. The higher the family income, the larger the percentage of income paid in taxes.

A sales tax varies proportionally with purchases with a 5 percent sales tax, a sales tax of $0.50 is paid for every $10 of purchases. Sales taxes are regressive because the wealthy spend a smaller portion of their income than the poor. Suppose the family with a $40,000 income spends $20,000 and saves the rest, while the family with $10,000 income spends every dime. Each pays a 5 percent sales tax; the higher income family pay sales tax of $1,000, or 1/40th of its income, while the poor family pays sales taxes of $500, or 1/20th of its income. Although the poor family spends fewer dollars on the sales tax, it spends a larger-percentage of its income.

What type of tax system is "best" is an issue of normative economics. Those who favor a progressive tax system believe that those with a greater ability to pay should bear a proportionally larger burden. They believe that those fortunate to be at the top of the income ladder should be willing to transfer income to those at the bottom. Those who favor proportional taxes (few favor regressive taxes) argue that progressive taxes depress initiative and risk-taking and divert efforts away from productive economic activities to tax avoidance.

The "best" tax is an issue of normative economics.

The U.S. tax system is a combination of progressive taxes (the personal income tax and corporate income tax) and regressive taxes (sales taxes). As Exhibit 5 shows, there is disagreement over how progressive the U.S. tax system is. (See Example 1 on the U.S. income tax.)

GOVERNMENT SURPLUSES AND DEFICITS

Government operates like a household or business firm. If its revenues (its income) exceed its outlays, it saves, or runs a **government surplus.** If, on the other hand, its outlays exceed its revenues, it is dissaving, or running a **government deficit.** The relationship between government revenue and outlays is shown by the government budget.

> A **government surplus** is an excess of government revenues over government outlays.

> A **government deficit** is an excess of government outlays over government revenues.

If households or firms spend more than they take in, they must finance the difference by borrowing. A government unit (be it a state, local, or federal government) that runs a deficit must borrow the difference as well. Governments borrow by selling IOUs (in the form of bonds and notes) both at home and abroad. Government borrowing accumulates as a **government debt.**

Government debt rises when government runs a deficit.

EXHIBIT 5   Two Views of the Tax Burden

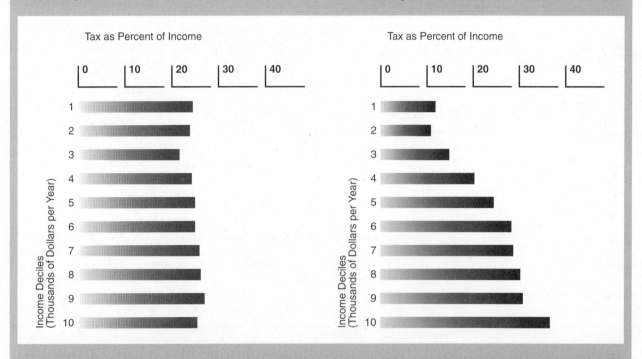

a. Pechman, 1980

b. Browning-Johnson, 1976

SOURCES: Joseph Pechman, *Who Paid the Taxes, 1966–85* (Washington, D.C.: The Brookings Institution, 1985). Edgar K. Browning and William R. Johnson, *The Distribution of the Tax Burden* (Washington, D.C.: American Enterprise Institute, 1979).

The U.S. tax system consists of different taxes at the local, state, and federal levels. When all taxes are combined, is the overall U.S. tax system regressive, proportional, or progressive?

The above chart shows that economists disagree on the answer. In a study conducted in 1985, Joseph Pechman concluded that the U.S. tax system is proportional over most income ranges. Only the very poor (those in the bottom 5 percent) and the very rich (those in the top 5 percent) pay a higher proportion of their income in taxes than other families.

A 1979 study by Edgar Browning and William Johnson found that the overall tax system was, as of 1976, highly progressive.

Why do economists come to different conclusions.[2] Taxes can be shifted forward to the consumer. It is difficult to determine whether taxes (such as sales taxes) are shifted forward to rich or to poor families. It is difficult to determine tax rates actually paid by the rich and the poor. The rich have been able to reduce their tax burden by investing in real estate and selling stocks and other assets at a profit. Poor families who received transfer payments have paid no income taxes and no social security taxes on this income.

> The **government debt** is the cumulated sum of outstanding IOUs that government owes its creditors.

A government debt can be reduced by running a surplus. If the government debt were $100 billion and government ran a $10 billion surplus, the government debt would be reduced by approximately $10 billion.

Exhibit 6 shows government budgets, surpluses, deficits, and debt in the United States. It shows that in total, government spent almost $2 trillion in 1991, or almost $200 billion more than it took in. The federal government ran a deficit, while state and local governments ran a surplus.

Government Surpluses and Deficits

EXAMPLE 1

The U.S. Income Tax: A Brief History

In 1913, the Sixteenth Amendment to the U.S. Constitution authorized the federal government to levy a personal income tax. Prior to World War II, the personal income tax was not a major source of federal government revenue. In the 1930s, it accounted for only about 14 percent of federal revenues. Tax rates were low. In the 1920s and 1930s, the tax rate on the lowest income bracket ranged from 1 to 4 percent and the tax rate on an income of $100,000 (the equivalent of more than $1 million in the early 1990s) was 55 percent in 1935. It was during World War II that the federal personal income tax became the federal government's most important revenue source. Tax rates on the bottom and top income brackets were raised (to over 20 percent for the bottom income bracket and to a high of 92 percent for the top income bracket). By the end of the war, the 1948 personal income tax accounted for 40 percent of all federal revenue.

The United States entered the postwar era with high personal tax rates. In 1951, for example, the tax rate on the top income bracket ($200,000 and above) was 91 percent. Tax rates of this magnitude were clearly unacceptable; therefore, various tax reforms altered the personal income tax system in three directions between 1951 and 1986. First, tax rates were reduced. By 1970, the tax rate on the lowest income bracket was 20 percent, and the tax rate on the top income bracket was 75 percent. The tax reform of 1981 lowered rates to a range of 11 to 50 percent and indexed tax rates to prevent them from being pushed up by inflation.

The second direction was to allow numerous deductions and exemptions from taxable income. Over the years, interest earned on bonds of state and local government (so-called *tax-exempt bonds*), contributions to retirement programs (such as Keogh accounts), taxes paid to state and local governments, medical expenditures, charitable contributions, fire and theft losses, and child-care costs for working mothers have been deductible. Capital gains were taxed at a lower rate than other forms of income.

The third direction of tax change was to use the personal income tax to promote economic or social goals. Tax credits for investments in equipment (the investment tax credit) were used to encourage capital formation. The deduction of certain forms of savings (such as in retirement accounts) from taxable income encouraged increased savings. Mortgage-interest deductions encouraged home ownership.

All these changes had made the federal income tax extremely complex. The system's critics felt it gave too many tax loopholes to the rich and that its high marginal tax rates discouraged hard work and risk takings.

In September 1986, Congress passed, and President Reagan signed, the Tax Reform Act of 1986. The number of tax rates was reduced from the previous fourteen (ranging from 11 percent to 50 percent) to three (15 percent, 28 percent, and 34 percent). The top rate on taxable income was lowered from 50 percent to 34 percent. Tax rates were adjusted for inflation by indexing tax-rate brackets, personal exemptions, and standard deductions to inflation. Many low-income families were removed from the tax rolls.

Deductions, exemptions, and exclusions from income were dramatically restricted to make up for the loss of tax revenue due to lower tax rates. Special tax treatment of certain industries such as oil drilling, cattle raising, and apartment construction was terminated. Capital gains income was no longer taxed at lower rates than ordinary income. Corporate income taxes were raised.

The 1992 presidential campaign focused on how to change the income tax system. The challenger, Bill Clinton, proposed to raise the top marginal tax rate to 36 percent, while President George Bush proposed to hold the line on tax rates. Both candidates proposed measures to encourage investment and saving.

EXHIBIT 6 Government Budgets and Debt, 1991

	Receipts (billions of dollars)	Expenditures (billions of dollars)	Surplus or Deficit (billions of dollars)	Total Debt (billions of dollars)	Total Debt as Percent of GDP
Total government	1,738	1,909	−171	3,860	68
Federal government	1,119	1,320	−201	3,618	64
State and local governments	771	741	30	242	4

SOURCES: *Statistical Abstract of the United States; Economic Report of the President*

People fear that expanding deficits depress saving, worsen trade balances, burden future generations, and raise interest rates. The validity of these fears will be explored in depth in later chapters.

REASONS FOR GOVERNMENT ACTION

If the private sector could deal with all resource-allocation decisions efficiently and fairly, there would be little need for government action. There are five economic problems that the market may not solve efficiently or fairly on its own.

Monopoly

Private markets may not work well when there is a single supplier of a commodity. If a monopoly firm controlled the nation's telephone system, steel production, or its airlines, that *monopolist* could restrict supply and drive up the price. The monopolist would earn monopoly profits, and consumers would pay in the form of higher prices. Income would be redistributed from the consumers to the owners of the monopoly. Monopoly cannot be avoided when for technological reasons the market has room for only one producer. When private markets are needlessly monopolized, laws against monopoly may be required. The threat of monopoly is one rationale for government action. Government action to control monopoly can take a variety of forms. A later chapter explains how governments can control monopoly.

Externalities

Private markets tend to work well when all participants bear the full costs and enjoy the full benefits of their actions. Private markets do not work well when private parties bear only a part of the costs and enjoy only a part of the benefits of their actions. **Externalities** cause private parties to make socially incorrect resource-allocation decisions.

> **Externalities** are present when private parties do not bear the full costs (or enjoy the full benefits) of their actions. A part of the costs (or benefits) is borne by third parties.

It is thought that private markets do not deal well with externalities. The firm that imposes costs on third parties will not automatically consider the *external* third-party costs in deciding how much output to produce. Instead, it bases its production decisions exclusively on its private costs.

Consider a chemicals firm that must dispose of 10 tons of waste by-products daily. Its cheapest method of waste disposal would be to burn them at a private cost of $1,000 per day. If the firm chooses to burn its waste by-products, however, it damages the health of residents living nearby, and it lowers the value of their property. The costs that the firm imposes on nearby residents amount to $100,000 per day. As long as the chemicals firm does not bear any of these third-party costs, private calculations would cause it to produce a large daily output of chemicals and to dispose of its waste products by burning. If, on the other hand, it had to pay the third-party costs along with its private costs, its costs of production would be raised, and it would produce less output. (In fact, the daily $100,000 cost may force it to close its doors.)

When external costs are present, the invisible hand of markets induces firms (who consider only their private costs) to produce "too much" output. The "correct" amount of output would be that output that the firm would voluntarily choose to produce if it bore both the private and the external costs of its activities. Later chapters will discuss remedies to the problem of externalities and the role of government in these remedies.

Public Goods

The private sector cannot supply **public goods**—goods that are publicly useful but not privately profitable. Public goods differ from private goods in two important respects:

> **Public goods** have two properties:
> 1. no one can be excluded from using the good once it is provided; and
> 2. the use of the good by one person does not detract from the use by another person

The best example of public goods is national defense. Consider the differences between national defense and private goods. In the case of private goods, consumers are rivals. If I buy the car, only I can benefit from it. If I buy a loaf of bread and eat it, you cannot. Public goods, such as national defense, do not involve this rivalry. My being protected by national defense does not detract from your being protected by national defense. In this case, consumers are not rivals.

Government intervention may be required because of monopoly, externalities, public goods, inequality, and macroeconomic instability.

In the case of private goods, it is quite easy to prevent nonpayers from enjoying the benefits. I can prevent you from using my car by locking the door. I can prevent you from enjoying my loaf of bread by eating it. Public goods are different. If I were to pay for national defense and you did not pay, there is no way I could prevent you from receiving the benefits of national-defense protection. Payers and nonpayers would have to be treated the same.

In private markets, if nonpayers enjoy the same benefits as payers, most people would not pay. Most people would want a *free ride*—letting someone else pay. If the number of free riders is substantial, private markets would not be able to provide the good. If few are willing to pay, why should a private firm produce the good?

Public goods are paid for by tax dollars and are provided by the government because of free riding and because consumers are not rivals. The price system, therefore, breaks down in failing to provide public goods. Yet society must have public goods to survive.

Inequality

There is no guarantee that private markets will solve the *for whom* problem to satisfy the ethical norms of society. If society, through its elected officials, decides that the income distribution generated by private markets is unfair, government can redistribute income. Governments redistribute income by taxing those who have "too much" more heavily than those who have "too little." Government can transfer income to those who have too little either by giving them transfer payments or by giving them goods and services (like free lunches, free medical care, and the like). The political process yields social judgments about the distribution of income in the form of income-tax legislation and antipoverty legislation.

Macroeconomic Instability

In solving the economic problem, the private sector may not provide a stable level of economic activity. It is a historical fact that market economies have been subject to fluctuations in output, employment, and prices—called *business cycles*. During booms, output grows rapidly, unemployment falls, and optimism prevails. Busts follow booms with declining output, rising unemployment, and falling stock markets.

The study of the instability of capitalism was pioneered by John Maynard Keynes during the Great Depression of the 1930s, and this theme remains a principal concern of macroeconomics. The major debate in modern macroeconomics is over the role of government in stabilizing the economy. Should the government attempt to stabilize the economy, or should the economy be left to recover from the business cycle on its own?

EVALUATING GOVERNMENT RESOURCE ALLOCATION

The Market Test

The private sector bases its decisions on the costs and benefits of alternative actions. Private economic decisions are affected by incentives (that is, the "carrots" and "sticks") that people face. The carrots are the benefits from engaging in an economic activity; the sticks are the costs of the activity. If a firm produces a product, its benefit is the revenue it earns from selling the product. Its cost is the opportunity cost of the resources used to make the product. If an individual buys a product, the benefit is the enjoyment from consuming the product; the cost is the opportunity cost of sacrificed alternatives.

In making decisions, the private sector weighs costs and benefits at the margin. Economists use **marginal analysis** to study private-sector decision-making.

> Marginal analysis examines the consequences of making relatively small changes from the current state of affairs.

The following chapters discuss marginal analysis as used in the private sector. In this chapter, it is important to understand only its basic principles. Marginal analysis teaches that private parties undertake an economic action *only if the marginal benefits of the action are greater than (or equal to) its marginal costs*. Consider the decision of Burger Bonanza about whether to expand its current hours of operation (11 A.M. to midnight) by opening for breakfast. Burger Bonanza would calculate how much extra revenue would be gained and the extra costs of opening earlier. If the extra (marginal) benefits exceed the extra (marginal) costs, Burger Bonanza would decide to open for breakfast. If the extra benefits fell short of the extra costs, Burger Bonanza would not change its hours of operation.

As long as private economic decisions follow the marginal rule that the marginal benefits must exceed or equal marginal costs, the private sector will produce goods and services that pass a **market test**.

> The **market test** ensures that goods and services in the private sector yield a benefit equal to or greater than their cost.

If only those activities are undertaken whose marginal benefits exceed their marginal cost, no activity will be selected that yields benefits less than costs. The market prevents costs from exceeding benefits. If private firms produce a product whose benefit to society is less than its cost, the firm will either go out of business or switch to producing other products. Goods and services produced by the private sector must pass the market test.

The Rationality of Public Choices

When the ballot-box is used instead of private economic decisions, majority-rule voting can result in public expenditures whose costs outweigh their benefits. Politicians, who are concerned about getting reelected, can have strong reasons for supporting programs whose costs exceed their benefits. Although voters can always vote out of office politicians who support unwise expenditures, voters typically do not vote on single issues. The senator who has supported a pork barrel spending program may have an excellent record on other issues. Voters must judge politicians on a wide range of issues.

Interest groups engage in vote trading and logrolling that cause public programs to be adopted that cost more than the benefits they bring in. Politicians representing one interest group trade votes with other politicians representing another interest group. They agree to pass spending programs that benefit both interest groups at considerable cost to the majority of taxpayers. Politician A tells politician B, "you vote for my project and I'll vote for yours," and both pay more attention to special interests than to the benefits of the majority. Politicians trade votes and logroll not out of greed or malice but because they want to be reelected. Special-interest groups that favor special-interest legislation contribute heavily to reelection campaigns. (See Example 2.)

Vote trading and logrolling typically do not cost politicians the votes of the majority who must bear the costs. Voters lack sufficient information on complex government programs to make well-informed choices. The benefits of special-interest legislation are concentrated on a few who well understand its implications. The costs of special-interest legislation are spread broadly, often among millions of voters, who stand to lose a few cents or a few dollars. The costs of each special-interest program are so small to the average voter that it would be irrational to gather information about the program.

Public choice economics explains why it is virtually impossible to balance the federal budget despite the best intentions. Politicians know it is in their interests to vote for public spending programs and against tax increases. Spending programs that benefit constituencies are popular. Tax increases are unpopular. As a consequence, insufficient revenue is raised to cover government spending. Balancing the budget would be easy if everybody knew what politicians were doing and what other people were receiving from government programs. (See Exhibit 7.)

EXAMPLE 2

Sugar: Special Interests and Logrolling

American sugar refiners, who refine imported sugar and then re-export it, can claim refunds for import duties paid on imported sugar. Current law allows them to claim refunds for duties paid up to five years from the date of the exports. In late 1987, a special-interest bill passed the Senate by a close vote to extend refunds for duties paid more than a decade ago.

Estimates of the costs of this program to taxpayers range from $65 to $200 million per year. The bulk of these payments would go to three large sugar refiners located in New York, Georgia, and Texas. One refiner alone would get at least $35 million per year. One opponent of the bill declared it "a government handout of the most outrageous kind."

The sugar bill illustrates the classic ingredient of special interest legislation. First, the legislation benefits a few people at lot. Major sugar refiners stand to gain millions of dollars per year in government payments. This prospect provides the incentive to contribute heavily to key elected political officials. Second, the sugar refiners and their political supporters can engage in vote trading and logrolling. In this case, sugar refiners received support from a diverse group of backers including the International Longshoremen's Association. They also arranged an agreement with the Sugarbeet Growers Association that senators from the sugarbeet growing states would not oppose the refund bill. Third, the costs of the sugar bill to the average taxpayer would be between $0.65 and $2.00 per year. Senators voting against the bill would save each of their taxpaying constituents only a little money. Voters, who stand to lose a little money, have less incentive to learn about the costs and benefits of the sugar bill. Most voters will remain "rationally ignorant"—they will not even know that such a bill has been enacted.

SOURCE: "Protecting Friends: Trade Bill is Full of Import Curbs Aiding Local Interests, and Major Fight Is Looming," *The Wall Street Journal,* November 12, 1987.

EXHIBIT 7 Majority Rule and Public Choice

Even without logrolling, vote trading, and imperfect information, majority-rule voting can lead to the approval of public-expenditure projects whose costs exceed their benefits. It can also cause projects to be rejected whose benefits exceed their costs. The accompanying table illustrates how this can happen.

Majority Rule and Public Goods

	Bridge A			Bridge B		
	Taxes	Benefit	Vote	Taxes	Benefit	Vote
Betty	$10	$2	Against	$10	$2	Against
Mary	10	11	For	10	8	Against
Harry	10	12	For	10	30	For
Totals	$30	$25	Wins	$30	$40	Loses

Suppose Betty, Mary, and Harry are the sole residents of a mini-community that is considering building a publicly financed bridge. The cost of bridge A is $30 and is to be divided equally among the three people. Each person will vote for the project only if their benefit exceeds their $10 tax share. If the project is worth $2 to Betty, $11 to Mary, and $12 to Harry, the bridge would be built because the majority (Mary and Harry) would vote for it. The total worth of the bridge to the community—$25 ($2 + $11 + $12)—is less than its $30 cost, and the bridge should not be built. But under majority-rule voting the bridge will be built.

On the other hand, majority rule may reject projects whose benefits exceed their cost. Suppose bridge B costs $30 as well, but Betty's benefits are $2, Mary's $8, and Harry's $30. The total benefit of the bridge is $40 (= $2 + $8 + $30), but since the taxes to finance the bridge are $10 each, only Harry would vote for the project. The bridge would not receive a majority of the votes, even though its benefits exceed its costs.

The Causes and Possible Cures of Special Interest Legislation

A key plank in independent presidential candidate Ross Perot's 1992 campaign was the urgent need to eliminate special-interest legislation. Perot presented himself as the only candidate unbeholden to special interests. He eloquently pointed out the dangers of continuing the present system of special-interest legislation, which he claimed was the prime cause of the burgeoning national debt.

Perot's comments are not new. The informed public is well aware of public harm caused by logrolling and vote trading. Examples abound: The U.S. dairy industry receives price support payments under a program passed by Congress and signed by the president which artificially raises milk costs to the consumer by $10 per year, while benefiting a few large dairy producers. The U.S. automobile industry receives protection from foreign imports that raises the average price of U.S.-produced automobiles by several hundred dollars per year. U.S. taxpayers pay up to $200 million per year to a few large sugar producers. (See Example 2.) These examples are routinely repeated at the state and local level.

In all cases, the ingredients are the same: A few people are helped a lot, while the majority must foot the bill. Votes are traded among special-interest groups. Spending bills are passed that clearly hurt the majority while helping a small minority. The general public, which loses in the form of higher prices, is only vaguely aware of what is happening. The pork barrel politician does not have to fear voter retaliation. Special-interest contributions supply an ample war chest and the voting public is confused by the vast array of issues on which to judge the incumbent.

Can a public policy be devised that will correct the abuses of special-interest legislation? A number of approaches have been suggested. First, strict limits should be placed on the campaign contributions of special-interest groups (typically called Political Action Committees, or PACs). If PACs cannot reward politicians for their votes, politicians will not support special-interest legislation. Second, term limits on politicians might be used to discourage "professional politicians." If elected officials knew in advance that their terms are limited, they would worry less about reelection war chests and more about the majority. Third, Congress may need to pass a balanced budget amendment. If the federal government is required to balance its budget on an annual basis, Congress would have to limit the amount of pork barrel legislation. Fourth, more political decisions should be made at the local level. The closer the link between the spending decision and the voting community, the less likely is the passage of special-interest legislation. If a local community votes on a local spending project for which it must pay, the wishes of the majority are more likely to be heard.

Special-interest legislation has been around for more than a century despite repeated efforts to correct obvious abuses. Its continuation suggests that it is not easy to devise public policy that deals effectively with this issue.

Chapter Summary

The most important point to learn from this chapter is: Politicians—like other economic actors—are motivated by self-interest. They want to be reelected or to increase their political power. As a consequence, public decisions to spend or tax may not be efficient even under majority rule.

1. Exhaustive government expenditures divert resources to the public sector. Transfer payments transfer resources from one group to another. Total government

expenditures are about one-third of total economic activity, and the government share of economic activity has been increasing over the years.

2. There are two competing principles of fairness in taxation. One is that taxes should be levied according to the benefits received; the other is that taxes should be allocated on the basis of ability to pay. Regressive taxes fall more heavily on poor people, progressive taxes fall more heavily on rich people, and proportional taxes are strictly proportional to income.

3. There is a government deficit if the government spends more than it takes in in taxes; the deficit is financed by selling government bonds. The government debt increases or decreases as the government runs a deficit or a surplus.

4. Cost/benefit analysis applied to government spending suggests that government activities should occur only when social benefits equal or exceed social costs. Cost/benefit analysis serves as a substitute for the market test that private goods must pass.

5. Government action may be justified to control private monopolies, correct externalities, provide public goods, achieve an equal distribution of income, and stabilize the private economy.

6. Majority rule may not select government projects where the benefits exceed the costs and may select projects where the benefits fall short of the costs. Vote trading and logrolling by politicians and the lack of information of voters explain such public-choice patterns.

> ***Policy Focus:*** **Society can devise policies, such as limitations on special-interest contributions, term limits, balanced-budget amendments, and more local spending decisions to limit the abuses of special-interest legislation.**

Key Terms

exhaustive expenditures (p. 71)
transfer payments (p. 71)
incidence of a tax (p. 77)
proportional tax (p. 77)
progressive tax (p. 77)
regressive tax (p. 77)
government surplus (p. 78)

government deficit (p. 78)
government debt (p. 78)
externalities (p. 81)
public goods (p. 81)
marginal analysis (p. 83)
market test (p. 84)

Questions and Problems

1. Explain how the market test for private spending balances costs and benefits and how cost/benefit analysis may substitute for the market test in the case of public spending.

2. Explain the different principles of fairness in taxation. Why can't the benefit principle simply be applied to all taxes?

3. Mr. Jones has a taxable income of $25,000. He pays a tax of $5,000. Ms. Smith has a taxable income of $50,000. How much tax would Smith have to pay for the tax system to be:
   a. proportional
   b. progressive
   c. regressive

4. A tax on shoe sales that requires the dealer to pay a $2 tax on every pair of shoes sold should not concern consumers because the dealer has to pay the tax. Evaluate this statement.

5. The state of Michigan hires an assistant professor to teach at one of its state universities. The state of Michigan pays an unemployed automobile worker $500 in unemployment compensation out of state funds. Which transaction is an exhaustive expenditure? How will the two transactions differ in their effect on resource allocation?

6. Explain how U.S. government expenditures as a proportion of GDP can be 35 percent while the government only uses 20 percent of U.S. resources.

7. Which of the following taxes satisfies the benefit principle? Which satisfies the ability-to-pay principle?
   a. A gasoline tax
   b. A progressive income tax
   c. A general sales tax
   d. A special levy on a community to build a dam

8. Professor Sailors grows roses; his neighbors benefit by his horticultural skills. Does the private market value Professor Sailors' roses appropriately?

Doing Economics

Obtain a copy of your local city's annual budget. (Check with local public libraries or with city officials if you have trouble locating a copy.) What are the major categories of revenues and expenditure for your local government? How do they differ from those of the federal government? How do you think they differ from those of other cities that are larger or smaller? For each of the major revenue categories, evaluate who is likely to end up paying the tax and whether the tax is proportional, progressive, or regressive. For each category of expenditure, consider whether it can be justified based on one or more of the reasons for government action discussed in the text.

9. A small town is bothered by mosquitoes. A private company will spray the town for $20,000. Is mosquito spraying a private or public good? Would the decision be a public or private one?

10. Explain why voters do not vigorously oppose tariffs on imported goods that raise prices to them while benefiting special interest groups?

11. Give at least three reasons for government intervention in private markets.

Microeconomics and the Product Markets

P A R T   T W O

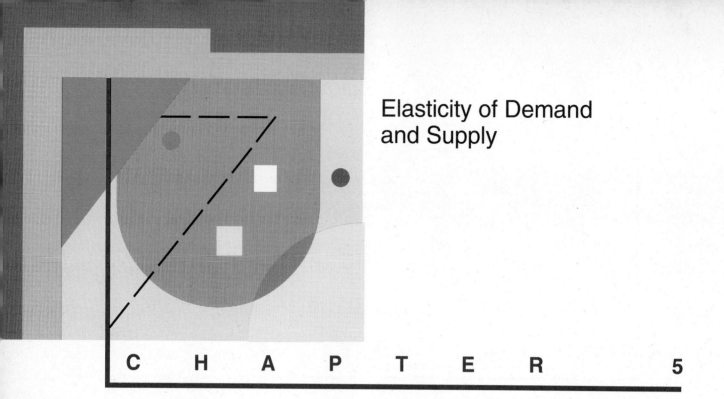

Elasticity of Demand and Supply

C H A P T E R 5

CHAPTER FOCUS   When prices rise, buyers look for substitutes. Higher prices encourage businesses to produce more of that product and less of others. In some cases, changes in prices evoke dramatic changes in consumer purchases and in businesses' willingness to sell products.

Elasticities describe responses to price changes. The sensitivity with which consumers and producers respond to prices depends on the product. Consumers are more sensitive to price changes when good substitute products are available. If no good substitutes are available, consumers won't cut back as much when the price rises.

Consumer price sensitivity affects pricing behavior in the marketplace. If firms know that an increase in price will cause a significant loss of markets, they will be hesitant to raise prices. If they know that people will continue to buy at higher prices, there will be less pressure on them to hold the line on prices.

Elasticity and policy are intertwined. The elasticity of consumer purchases has been used by the courts as a test of the degree of monopoly. The elasticity of consumer and producer responses to price changes has been used to determine the burden of proposed taxes. The degree to which markets are related can be judged by how much a price change in one market affects another market.

After studying this chapter, you will be able to:

- Measure the price elasticity of demand.

- Understand the relationship between price elasticity, price, and total revenue or expenditure.

- Predict how the price elasticity of supply changes between the immediate run, the short run, and the long run.

- Discuss how the burden of an excise tax is divided between consumers and producers.

- Understand how the income elasticity of demand is used to determine the dividing line between necessities and luxuries.

THE PRICE ELASTICITY OF DEMAND

The demand curve introduced in Chapter 3 shows how quantity demanded changes in response to changes in price, *ceteris paribus*. Economists use the **price elasticity of demand** to measure the *degree of responsiveness* of quantity demanded to a change in price. How does one measure how large or small the market response is to price changes? Absolute changes in price or quantity demanded are poor measures of responsiveness. If a $1 increase in the price of coal lowers quantity demanded by one ton, is this a large or small response? If the initial price is $2 per ton, a $1 change in price represents a 50 percent increase in price. If the initial price is $1,000, a $1 change in price represents a miniscule change in price. If the initial quantity were 1 million tons, the one ton change is very small, but if the original quantity were two tons, then the one ton change is large. To get a sense of whether a particular change in price is large or small, one must determine how large the change is relative to some initial position. In short, it is necessary to use *percentage* changes in quantity or price.

> The **price elasticity of demand** (E_d) is the percentage change in the quantity demanded divided by the percentage change in price.

The price elasticity of demand shows the percentage fall in quantity demanded per 1 percent rise in price. It also shows the percentage rise in quantity demanded per 1 percent fall in the price. For example, say the price of apples rises by about 10 percent (say, from $.50 a pound to $.55). If the quantity of apples demanded falls by 20 percent (say, from 1,000 bushels to about 800 bushels), the price elasticity would be 2 = 20 percent ÷ 10 percent. This means that every 1 percent increase in the price of apples will lower quantity demanded by 2 percent. Equivalently, a price elasticity of 2 means that a 1 percent reduction in the price will increase quantity demanded by 2 percent.

Calculating Price Elasticity of Demand

To compute the price elasticity of demand, one must calculate the percentage changes in quantity and in price. Imagine the price of pizza rises from $8 to $12. The percentage increase in the price appears to be 50 percent ($4 ÷ $8). But consider reducing the price of pizza from $12 to $8. Now the percentage fall in the

GALLERY OF ECONOMISTS

Paul A. Samuelson (1915–   )

Paul Samuelson was born in Gary, Indiana, in 1915. He spent his undergraduate days at the University of Chicago and went to Harvard for his Ph.D. Although an underachiever in high school, Samuelson became one of the greatest economists of the twentieth century. He went to MIT in 1940 and helped build one of the truly great departments of economics. His dissertation developed into *Foundations of Economic Analysis* (1947), setting the stage for the quantitative and mathematical economic reasoning now popular. Before Samuelson, economics reflected the verbal and diagrammatic approach popularized by Alfred Marshall. Samuelson showed economists more subtle kinds of mathematical reasoning. Samuelson's contributions to mathematical economic theory won him the Nobel Prize in economics in 1970. He was the first American to be so honored.

Samuelson has contributed to almost every branch of economics. In an autobiographical sketch, he said:

> My finger has been in every pie. I . . . [have written about] such diverse subjects as international trade and econometrics, economic theory and business cycles, demography and labor economics, finance and monopolistic competition, history of doctrines and locational economics.

Samuelson's carefully reasoned work on the effects of changes in the prices and income on quantities demanded is the scientific framework for the study of elasticities in this chapter.

price appears to be 33 percent ($4 ÷ $12). The price elasticity of demand between $8 and $12 should be the same for a movement from one price to another whether the price change is an increase or decrease. There should not be one elasticity for price decreases and another one for price increases. If percentage changes are calculated by dividing the change in price by the *average* price and the change in quantity by the *average* quantity, they will be the same for increases or decreases. In the above example, the percentage change in the price of pizza from $8 to $12 is 40 percent because the $4 price change is divided by $10—the average of $8 and $12. Because average prices and quantities represent the midpoints between the two prices and two quantities, this is called the **midpoints formula** for calculating price elasticity of demand.[1]

The **midpoints formula** for determining the elasticity of demand E_d for a given segment of the demand curve is:

$$E_d = \frac{\text{Percent Change in Quantity Demanded}}{\text{Percent Change in Price}}$$

$$= \frac{\dfrac{\text{Change in Quantity Demanded}}{\text{Average of Two Quantities}}}{\div \dfrac{\text{Change in Price}}{\text{Average of Two Prices}}}$$

---

[1]In symbols, if p_1 and p_2 are the two prices and q_1 and q_2 are the two quantities, the midpoints formula can be simplified as follows:

$$E_d = \frac{q_2 - q_1}{(q_1 + q_2)/2} \div \frac{p_2 - p_1}{(p_1 + p_2)/2} = \frac{q_2 - q_1}{p_1 - p_2} \times \frac{p_1 + p_2}{q_1 + q_2}.$$

EXHIBIT 1   Total Revenue and Elasticity

a. Elastic Demand

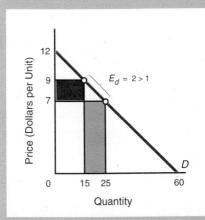

b. Unitary Elastic Demand

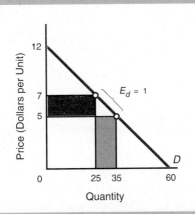

c. Inelastic Demand

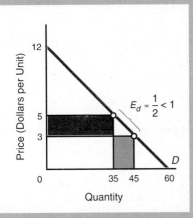

d. Demand Schedule

Price (dollars per unit), P (1)	Quantity (units), Q (2)	Total Revenue, TR = P × Q (3) = (1) × (2)	Direction of Change in Revenue (4)	Percentage Change in Quantity Demanded, $\frac{\Delta Q}{(q_1 + q_2)/2}$ (5)	Percentage Change in Price, $\frac{\Delta P}{(p_1 + p_2)/2}$ (6)	Coefficient of Price Elasticity, E_d (7) = (5) ÷ (6)	Conclusion (8)
(a) 9	15	135					
			Increase	$\frac{10}{20} = 50\%$	$\frac{2}{8} = 25\%$	$\frac{50}{25} = 2$	Elastic
(b) 7	25	175					
			No change	$\frac{10}{30} = 33.3\%$	$\frac{2}{6} = 33.3\%$	$\frac{33.3}{33.3} = 1$	Unitary Elastic
(c) 5	35	175					
			Decrease	$\frac{10}{40} = 25\%$	$\frac{2}{4} = 50\%$	$\frac{25}{50} = 0.5$	Inelastic
3	45	135					

The demand curve, D, is the same in panels (a), (b), and (c). Between the prices of $9 and $7, the elasticity of demand (E_d) is 2; demand is elastic. Panel (a) shows that a reduction in price raises revenue. The color shaded rectangle shows the revenue lost due to the lower price, and the black shaded rectangle shows the revenue gained due to the greater number of units sold. Because the black rectangle is greater in area than the colored rectangle, more revenues is gained than lost.

Between prices $7 and $5, E_d equals 1; panel (b) shows that the reduction in price has no impact on revenue. Finally, between the prices of $5 and $3, E_d is 1/2; demand is inelastic. Panel (c) shows that the reduction in price lowers revenue because more revenue is lost (color shading) than gained (black shading). Thus, the elasticity of demand varies along a linear demand curve with constant slope. Elasticity and slope are different.

The midpoints formula can be illustrated using the numbers in the demand schedule in Exhibit 1. Consider a change in price from $9 to $7. The change in price is $2, and the average price is ($7 + $9)/2 = $8. The percentage change in price is 25 percent ($2/$8 = 25 percent). When price falls from $9 to $7, quantity demanded rises from 15 to 25 units. The change in quantity is 10 units, and the average quantity is 20 units. The percentage change in quantity demanded is 50 percent (10/20 = 50 percent). Dividing the percent change in quantity demanded (50 percent) by the percent change in price (25 percent) yields a price elasticity of demand E_d of 2, as given in column 7 of Exhibit 1. The calculated elasticity is 2 whether the price rises from \$7 to \$9 or falls from \$9 to \$7.

Elastic and Inelastic Demand

Price elasticities of demand fall into three broad categories called elastic, inelastic, and unitary elastic:

1. When $E_d > 1$, demand is *elastic* (Q is strongly responsive to changes in P).
2. When $E_d < 1$, demand is *inelastic* (Q responds weakly to changes in P).
3. When $E_d = 1$, demand is *unitary elastic* (a borderline case).

Think of the dollar sales or revenue of the sellers of some product. The response of **total revenue** to price changes depends on elasticity.

> The **total revenue** of sellers *TR* is equal to the price of the commodity times the quantity sold:
>
> $$TR = P \times Q.$$

Along a demand curve, since price and quantity demanded always move in opposite directions, a change in price tugs total revenue in two directions. When the price falls, total revenue is tugged down because each unit sells at a lower price. However, the resulting increase in the quantity sold pulls revenue up. The net result depends on which effect dominates. What actually happens to total revenue when the price changes depends on the price elasticity of demand.

When $E_d > 1$, *TR* will move in the opposite direction of price because changing the price will change the quantity demanded by a greater percentage in the opposite direction.

If the price elasticity of demand is greater than 1 (demand is elastic), the percentage rise in quantity demanded is greater than the percentage fall in price. Revenue *increases* because the increase in quantity demanded more than offsets the *decrease* in price. This is illustrated in Exhibit 1. When the price changes from \$9 to \$7, a 25 percent change by the midpoints formula, quantity demanded changes by a larger percentage amount from 15 units to 25 units—a 50 percent change. As a consequence, total spending by consumers—which is the revenue received by sellers—rises from \$135 (= \$9 × 15) to \$175 (= \$7 × 25). In panel (a), the area shaded in color shows the loss in revenue from selling the first 15 units at \$7 rather than \$9; and the gray shaded area indicates the revenue gained from selling more units. Revenue rises because the gray shaded area exceeds the color shaded area when demand is elastic. Conversely, an increase in the price of the good from \$7 to \$9 will lower total revenue. Price and revenue move in opposite directions.

When $E_d < 1$, *TR* will move in the same direction as price because changing the price of the good will change quantity demanded by a smaller percentage in the opposite direction.

If the price elasticity is less than 1 (demand is inelastic), the percentage rise in quantity demanded is less than the percentage fall in price. Revenue *falls* because the *decline* in price is not offset by the relatively small rise in quantity. Demand is inelastic between the prices of \$5 and \$3 in Exhibit 1. When price falls by 50 percent from \$5 to \$3, the percentage increase in quantity demanded is 25 percent from 35 to 45. The relatively small percentage increase in quantity demanded is not enough to prevent revenue from falling. Revenue falls from \$175 (= \$5 × 35) to \$135 (= \$3 × 45). In panel (c), the color shaded area corresponding to the revenue loss exceeds the gray shaded area representing the revenue gain. Conversely, if the price rises from \$3 to \$5, total revenue rises. Price and revenue move in the same direction when demand is inelastic.

If the price elasticity of demand = 1 (unitary elastic), the percentage rise in quantity demanded equals the percentage fall in price. Revenue is unchanged because the decline in price is just offset by the rise in quantity. In Exhibit 1, demand is unit elastic between the prices of \$7 and \$5. When the price falls from

EXAMPLE 1

Vanity Plates and College Tuition: When Do Higher Prices Yield More Revenue?

The recession of the early 1990s forced states to seek out additional sources of state revenue. Insofar as raising the fees for various government services did not require voter approval, most states reexamined existing fees (tuition, licenses, and charges) to uncover additional sources of revenue.

All of the 50 states have public colleges and universities that charge tuition and fees, usually at highly subsidized rates. Most of the states offer vanity plates that permit users to have their own initials or a favorite slogan on their license plate.

Elasticity of demand explains why the states used increases in tuition and fees rather than increases in the price of vanity plates. Standard license plates are close substitutes for vanity plates. If the price of vanity plates rises, people cut back considerably on their purchases of vanity plates—so much so that the revenue from sales actually drops. The elasticity of demand for vanity plates is greater than unity. Students enrolled in state universities, however, will not drop out of school if tuition is raised. They may cut back somewhat on the number of courses, but enrollment tends to remain steady and revenues from tuition increase. The elasticity of demand for state college courses is less than unity. An increase in the price will raise revenue.

$7 to $5, 33 percent by the midpoints formula ($2 \div 6$), the quantity demanded increases from 25 to 35—again 33 percent ($10 \div 30$). The percentage changes are the same. Revenue stays constant at $175. In panel (b), the color shaded area is the same as the gray shaded area so that the loss in revenue due to lowering the price is just matched by the gain in revenue from selling more units. Alternatively, if price increases, the quantity demanded of the good will fall by exactly the same percentage so total revenue will still remain constant. Changes in the price of the good have no impact on total revenue when demand is unitary elastic (See Example 1.)

> When $E_d = 1$, TR will not change because price and quantity move by exactly offsetting amounts.

As the above example shows, one can determine whether demand for a particular product is elastic, inelastic, or unitary elastic by observing what happens to total revenue when price changes. This is called the **total-revenue test**.

> The **total-revenue test** is:
> 1. If price and total revenue move in different directions, $E_d > 1$ (demand is elastic).
> 2. If price and total revenue move in the same direction, $E_d < 1$ (demand is inelastic).
> 3. If total revenue does not change when price changes, $E_d = 1$ (demand is unitary elastic).

Elasticity and Slope

The elasticity and the slope of the demand curve are not the same. In Exhibit 1, the slope of the demand curve is constant between every pair of prices (the demand curve is a straight line). Yet, the price elasticity of demand falls as the price is reduced. For movements between $7 and $9, the price elasticity of demand was 2. For movements between $3 and $5, the price elasticity of demand was a lower $1/2$. Why is the price elasticity of demand higher at high prices than at low prices?

When the demand curve is a straight line, the quantity demanded increases by the same absolute amount for every $1 reduction in the price. But when price is high, and quantity is low, the percentage increase in price is small while the percentage increase in demand is large. Thus, elasticity will be high when the price is high. When the price is low, a $1 reduction in price means a higher percentage reduction in price for a smaller percentage increase in quantity demanded. Thus, elasticity will be low when the price is low. Along a straight-line demand curve, the price elasticity of demand falls as the price falls.

Perfectly Elastic or Perfectly Inelastic Demand Curves

The highest degree of elasticity possible—the greatest responsiveness of quantity demanded to price—is a perfectly horizontal demand curve. In Exhibit 2, any amount on demand curve D can be sold at the indicated price ($5). Such a horizontal demand curve demonstrates **perfectly elastic demand**. In other words, the market is willing to take any quantity of the good the sellers are prepared to supply at the going price.

Perfectly elastic demand curves are common in the real world. In perfectly competitive markets—defined in Chapter 3 as markets in which no single producer is large enough to influence the market price—each seller can sell all he or she wants at the market price. Single sellers do not have to lower their prices to sell more. Each corn or wheat farmer can sell all he wants at the prevailing market price and can't sell anything at a higher price.

> A horizontal demand curve illustrates **perfectly elastic demand**, in which case quantity demanded is most responsive to price.

The lowest degree of inelasticity possible—the least responsiveness of quantity demanded to price—occurs when the demand curve is perfectly vertical. In Exhibit 2, the vertical demand curve D' demonstrates **perfectly inelastic demand**. With demand curve D', 75 units of the good will be sold regardless of the price. The elasticity of demand is zero because if the price were to rise above $5, the percentage change in the quantity demanded would be zero.

A perfectly inelastic demand curve suggests that no matter how high the price rises, consumers will not cut back on the quantity demanded. The closest example would be insulin for the diabetic, but even in this case if the price rose higher and higher, eventually diabetics might reduce their dosages and accept some health loss rather than pay the higher price.

Demand curves can be perfectly inelastic *within a range of prices*. If insulin prices were to rise by 10 percent, the quantity demanded of insulin would probably not change. If the price of salt were to rise from $0.20 to $0.21 per pound, the quantity demanded would probably stay the same.

> A vertical demand curve illustrates **perfectly inelastic demand**, in which case quantity demanded is least responsive to price.

Determinants of Price Elasticity of Demand

The price elasticity of demand measures the degree to which consumers respond to changes in prices. The four determinants of the price elasticity of demand for a good are:

EXHIBIT 2   Perfectly Elastic and Perfectly Inelastic Demand Curves

The demand curve D is perfectly elastic; it is perfectly horizontal, or parallel to the quantity axis. The demand curve D' is perfectly inelastic; it is perfectly vertical, or parallel to the price axis. The elasticity-of-demand coefficient of D is infinitely large along the entire demand schedule. The elasticity-of-demand coefficient of D' is zero along the entire demand curve.

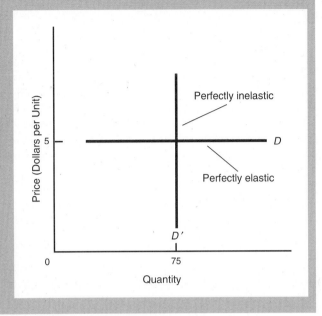

1. the availability of substitutes,
2. the relative importance of the good in the budget,
3. the amount of time available to adjust to the price change, and
4. whether the good is a necessity or luxury.

The Relative Importance of the Good in the Budget.   The more important a good is in the consumer's total spending, the more elastic should be the demand. When the price of salt changes, or toothpicks, or many other inexpensive items, a change in the price brings about a small change in quantity demanded. Why? A higher price of, say, salt does not cause the consumer to search out many new substitutes in order to save money. On the other hand, if the price of gasoline rises, an important item in the consumer's budget, it pays people to use less gasoline by driving smaller cars, riding bicycles, or taking the bus.

Time to Adjust to Price Changes.   Demand is more elastic the longer consumers have to adjust to price changes. Consider the response of consumers to higher electricity prices. Immediately after electric utility rates are increased, consumers can do little more than lower their heating thermostats in the winter and raise their air-conditioning thermostats in the summer. As time passes, additional substitutes for electricity become available. Extra insulation and more energy-efficient heating and air-conditioning equipment can be installed. If natural-gas prices have not risen as much, consumers can convert to natural-gas appliances when replacing the old system.

Many expenditures are conditioned by habit formation. Consumers are accustomed to buying certain products, and habits are hard to break. A family used to setting the thermostat at 72 degrees and to eating fresh vegetables will find it difficult to change when heating costs and vegetable prices rise.

Necessities Versus Luxuries.   As this chapter will discuss later in more detail, economists distinguish necessities from luxuries by defining *necessities* as products whose demand increases less rapidly than income.

Luxuries tend to have a higher price elasticity of demand than necessities. Chapter 3 noted that a reduction in price increases real income. Higher real incomes stimulate the demand for luxuries more than the demand for necessities, if everything else (the availability of substitutes, the importance of the good in the budget, the time allowed for adjustment) is equal.

THE INCOME ELASTICITY OF DEMAND

In Chapter 3 we saw that consumer demand depends not only on the product's own price, but also on consumer preferences, the prices of substitutes and complements, and consumer income. The elasticity concept is also applied to the other factors affecting demand.

A rise or fall in consumer income will affect the demands for different products. As consumer income rises, the demand for most products increases. The responsiveness of demand to consumer income is measured by the **income elasticity of demand (E_i)**.

> The **income elasticity of demand (E_i)** is the percentage change in the demand for a product divided by the percentage change in income *holding all prices fixed*.[2]

The income elasticity of demand is positive for most goods because the higher their incomes, the more consumers spend. If the income elasticity equals unity, a 1 percent increase in income will lead to a 1 percent increase in the demand for the good. Hence, consumers would continue to spend the same fraction of their income on the good as before income increased. If the income elasticity exceeds 1, people will spend a larger fraction of their incomes on the good as income rises. If the income elasticity is less than 1, people will spend a smaller fraction of their incomes on that good as income rises. The definitions of **necessities** and **luxuries** given earlier in this chapter can be refined using the income-elasticity-of-demand concept.

> **Necessities** are those products that have an income elasticity of demand less than 1.

> **Luxuries** are those products that have an income elasticity of demand greater than 1.

Using these definitions, goods such as food items would be necessities, while recreational vehicles would be luxuries. Notice, though, that the economist allows

---

[2]The midpoints formula for the income elasticity of demand is:

$$E_i = \frac{q_2 - q_1}{(q_1 + q_2)} \div \frac{i_2 - i_1}{(i_1 + i_2)},$$

where i denotes consumer income.

the terms *luxury* and *necessity* to be defined by the market choices people make rather than by individual perceptions about what is more "necessary" than something else.

THE CROSS-PRICE ELASTICITY OF DEMAND

A useful elasticity concept is the **cross-price elasticity of demand** that relates the responsiveness of the demand for one good to the price of some other good. The cross-price elasticity between coal and oil tells us the percentage increase in the demand for coal that results from a specified increase in the price of oil. For example, a cross-price elasticity of 0.5 tells us that a 10 percent increase in the price of oil increases the demand for coal by 5 percent. On the other hand, a cross-price elasticity of –0.25 between bacon and eggs tells us that a 10 percent increase in the price of eggs *reduces* the demand for bacon by 2.5 percent. Thus, the cross-price elasticity provides us with information about the extent to which the demand for one good falls or rises in response to a given percentage increase in the price of some other good.

> The **cross-price elasticity of demand** is the percentage change in the demand for the one good by the percentage change in the price of the other good.

THE PRICE ELASTICITY OF SUPPLY

The price elasticity of demand measures the responsiveness of *consumers* to price change. The **price elasticity of supply (E_s)** measures the responsiveness of *producers* to price changes. The elasticity of supply is calculated in the same way as the elasticity of demand, only now the Qs refer to quantities *supplied*, not quantities demanded. Indeed, the terms elastic, inelastic, and unit elastic have the same meanings on the supply side as on the demand side.

> The **price elasticity of supply (E_s)** is defined as the percentage change in the quantity supplied divided by the percentage change in price.

The price elasticity of supply is measured in the same way as the price elasticity of demand. The formula is the same as the midpoints formula above. The only difference is that the quantities refer to quantities supplied rather than quantities demanded.

Perfectly Elastic and Perfectly Inelastic Supply Curves

The highest degree of elasticity possible for a supply curve is a perfectly horizontal supply curve. In Exhibit 3, supply curve *S* illustrates the case of **perfectly elastic supply**. At the price of $10, producers of the good are willing to supply any amount of the good to the market at that price.

Most of the supply curves that the average consumer deals with are perfectly elastic. The grocery store is willing to sell any person all the milk, canned goods, and dairy products that person wants to buy at the prices set. Under normal

EXHIBIT 3   Perfectly Elastic and Perfectly Inelastic Supply Curves

The supply curve *S* is perfectly elastic because at a price of $10 any quantity of output can be offered on the market by sellers. The supply curve *S′* is perfectly inelastic because no matter how much the price rises, the quantity supplied remains the same.

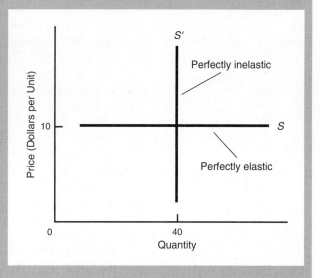

circumstances, however, all buyers together (the market) must offer higher prices to induce producers to increase the quantity supplied.

The lowest degree of elasticity occurs when the supply curve is perfectly vertical, as shown by supply curve *S′*. Such a supply curve demonstrates **perfectly inelastic supply**. The price elasticity of supply in this case equals zero. An increase in price has no effect on quantity supplied; therefore, the percentage change in quantity supplied is zero.

> A horizontal supply curve demonstrates **perfectly elastic supply;** quantity supplied is most responsive to price.

> A vertical supply curve demonstrates **perfectly inelastic supply;** quantity supplied is least responsive to price.

Elasticity of Supply in Three Time Periods

Just as the elasticity of demand depends on the amount of time the consumer has to respond to price changes, the elasticity of supply also depends on time. In general, the longer the period of time the producer has to adjust to changes in prices, the greater is the elasticity of supply.

Economists distinguish between three time periods during which producers adjust their supply to the new prices: the **immediate run**, the **short run**, and the **long run**.

> The **immediate run** is a period of time so short that the quantity supplied cannot be changed at all. In the immediate run—sometimes called the *momentary period* or *market period*—supply curves are perfectly inelastic.

Consider the case of a day's fish catch by fishermen selling to the Gulf Coast fresh fish market. In the immediate run, the fish catch is already in. If the price were to double unexpectedly at sundown, fishermen cannot return to their boats to bring in more fish. The immediate run supply curve is a vertical line (perfectly inelastic) as shown in Exhibit 4, panel (a).

In the short run, the fishermen have an opportunity to either increase or decrease their daily catch in response to price changes. If prices rise, they can work longer hours and hire additional helpers. The extra hours and extra help allow them to bring more fish to market in response to higher prices. Because of this flexibility, the short-run supply curve is not vertical but is upward-sloped. (See panel (b) of Exhibit 4.)

> The **short run** is a period of time long enough for existing firms to produce more goods but not long enough for existing firms to expand their capacity or for new firms to enter the market. Thus, output can be varied but only within the limits of existing plant capacity.

In the long run, the fishermen have even more opportunities to adjust their daily catch to changing prices. They have time to acquire new boats and equipment and to invest in new fish-finding technology. New fishermen can enter

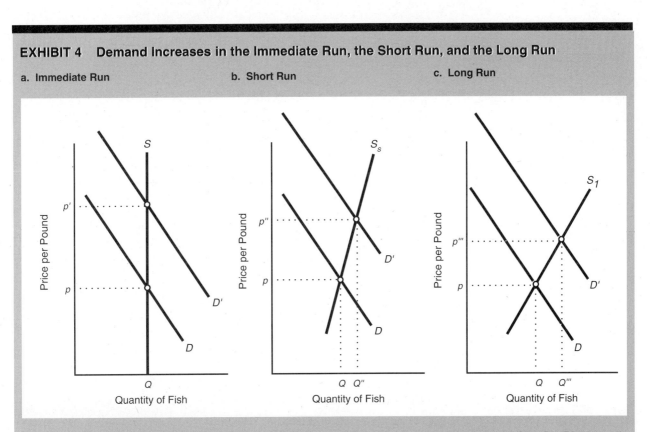

EXHIBIT 4   Demand Increases in the Immediate Run, the Short Run, and the Long Run

a. Immediate Run   b. Short Run   c. Long Run

In the immediate run, panel (a), the supply is fixed, and the supply curve is vertical. The increase in demand (from D to D') raises only the price (from p to p'), not the quantity. In the short run, producers can respond in a limited fashion to higher prices; hence the supply curve in panel (b) has a steep positive slope. As the market moves from the immediate run to the short run, the price drops from p' to p'' and the quantity increases from Q to Q''. In the long run, producers have the greatest flexibility to respond to higher prices. The long-run supply curve in panel (c) is even less steeply sloped. As the market moves from the short run to the long run, the price drops further (from p'' to p''') and the equilibrium quantity rises further from Q'' to Q'''.

EXAMPLE 2

Elasticities: Theory and Practice

Price Elasticities of Demand

	Short Run	Long Run
Tobacco products	0.46	1.89
Jewelry	0.41	0.67
Toilet articles	0.20	3.04
Owner-occupied housing	0.04	1.22
China and glassware	1.55	2.55
Electricity	0.13	1.89
Water	0.20	0.14
Medical care and hospitalization	0.31	0.92
Tires	0.86	1.19
Auto repairs	0.40	0.38
Durable recreation equipment	0.88	2.39
Motion pictures	0.88	3.69
Foreign travel	0.14	1.77
Gasoline	0.15	0.78

Source: Hendrick S. Houthakker and Lester D. Taylor, *Consumer Demand in the United States: Analyses and Projections* (Cambridge, Mass.: Harvard University Press, 1970), pp. 166–67; James L. Sweeney, "The Demand for Gasoline: A Vintage Capital Model," Department of Engineering Economics, Stanford University.

Price Elasticities of Supply

Wheat[a]	—	.93
Corn[a]	—	.18
U.S. oil[b]	—	.76
Natural gas[c]	—	.20
Urban housing[d]	—	5.30

Sources: [a]M. Nerlove, "Estimates of the Elasticities of Supply of Selected Agricultural Commodities," *Journal of Farm Economics* (May 1956); [b]E. W. Ericson, S. W. Millsaps, and R. M. Spann, "Oil Supply and Tax Incentives," *Brookings Papers on Economic Activity* (1974); [c]J. D. Khazzoom, "The FPC Staff's Econometric Model of Natural Gas Supply in the United States," *The Bell Journal of Economics* (Spring 1971); [d]B. A. Smith, "The Supply of Urban Housing," *Journal of Political Economy* (1976).

Income Elasticities

Motion-picture tickets[a]	3.4
Foreign travel[a]	3.1
Toys[a]	2.0
Automobiles and parts[b]	1.7
Clothing and shoes[b]	1.1
Furniture[b]	.9
Beef[c]	.5
Pork[c]	.3
Lard[c]	−.1

Sources: [a]H. S. Houthakker and L. D. Taylor, *Consumer Demand in the United States* (Cambridge, MA: Harvard University Press, 1970). [b]L. Philips, *Applied Consumption Analysis* (Amsterdam: North-Holland, 1974). [c]G. E. Brandow, "Interrelations among Demands for Farm Products and Implications for Control of Market Supply," Pennsylvania State University Agricultural Experiment Station Bulletin 680, 1961.

Calculated price elasticities of demand generally support theory. Long-run elasticities are larger than short-run elasticities. Elasticities appear to rise with the availability of substitutes. Medical care has fewer good substitutes than most of the other products listed, and it has lower short-run and long-run elasticities than products such as motion pictures, recreation equipment, gasoline, and foreign travel. In the short run, electricity has no good substitutes, and the short-run elasticity is low.

Income elasticities show that some items are highly elastic (movies, travel, and toys), while other goods (pork and lard) are inelastic.

the business. Accordingly, fish suppliers can respond more flexibly to changing prices. In the long run, the supply curve is more elastic than in the short run. (See panel (c) of Exhibit 4.)

> The **long run** is a period of time long enough for new firms to enter the market, for old firms to disappear, and for existing plants to be expanded. In the long run, firms have more flexibility in adjusting to price changes.

The elasticity of supply is larger in the long run than in either the short run or the immediate run. When the demand for a product increases, the immediate-run price will be higher than the short-run price, and the short-run price will be higher than the long-run price.

The effect on equilibrium prices and quantities of an increase in the demand for fish depends on the amount of adjustment time. Exhibit 4 shows that in the immediate run, an increase in demand raises price considerably, but does not affect quantity. In the short run, the increase in demand raises both price and quantity. Because fishermen are able to increase their catches by working longer hours and hiring more help, the increase in quantity supplied will hold down the price increase somewhat. In the long run, fishermen have even more flexibility in responding to higher prices, and there is an even larger increase in quantity supplied. This increase holds down prices even more.

The three time periods cannot be closely associated with calendar time. The amount of calendar time required to move from the short run to the long run varies with the type of industry. The electric-power industry may require a decade to expand existing power-generating facilities and to bring new plants on line. On the other hand, the fast-food industry can construct and open a new outlet in a few months.

Elasticity allows us to understand the extent to which changing prices and income affect supply and demand. The next chapter will look behind the demand curve to explain the law of demand. (See Example 2.)

Chapter Summary

The most important point to learn from this chapter is: The price elasticity of demand measures the degree to which Q responds to P for any good or service and indicates how total revenue changes along the demand curve.

1. The *price elasticity of demand* (E_d) is the percentage change in quantity demanded divided by the percentage change in price. Whether E_d exceeds, equals, or falls short of 1 determines how total revenue changes along the demand curve. E_d is typically calculated using the midpoints formula; the change in quantity is divided by the average quantity, and the change in price is divided by the average price.

Taxing Gasoline—Who Pays?

In the 1992 presidential election, third-party candidate Ross Perot proposed a $.50 per gallon tax on gasoline. The United States consumes about 110 billion gallons of gasoline per year at an average price of about $1.10 per gallon. How much would the price rise with a $.50 per gallon tax? Will consumers bear the entire burden and pay $1.60? How much revenue will be collected? In the newspapers it was often argued that $55 billion would be collected ($.50 × 110 billion). To illustrate the importance of the concepts of price elasticity of demand and supply, let us try to answer these questions.

To make the calculations simple we will suppose that the current price of gasoline is $1 and that 100 billion gallons are consumed per year. In the accompanying graph, this is shown as point *e* where the pretax demand and supply curves intersect.

The Burden of Tax

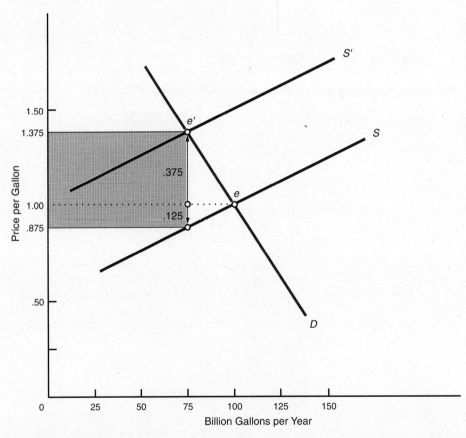

Curves *D* and *S* are the demand and supply curves for gasoline before the tax; the equilibrium price is $1. A tax of $.50 per gallon on sellers shifts the supply curve upward by exactly $.50 as sellers recoup their tax payments to the state. The new equilibrium price to buyers is found where the new supply curve, *S'*, intersects the old demand curve, *D*, at point *e'*; thus, the new price is 1.37^1/_2$ to buyers. Sellers must send $.50 (per gallon sold) to the tax collector; hence, sellers keep only $.87$^1/_2$ after paying tax. Notice that three-fourths of the burden of the $.50 tax ($0.37$^1/_2$) falls on buyers and one fourth of the burden (0.12^1/_2$) falls on sellers. This incidence reflects the fact that the elasticity of supply is approximately 4 times greater ($E_s = 2.4$) than the elasticity of demand ($E_d = 0.6$).

The tax of $.50 per gallon changes the supply curve. In order for sellers to earn $1 a gallon (after paying the tax), they must now charge $1.50; to earn $.87$1/2$ they must charge $1.37$1/2$. The tax will shift the supply curve up by exactly $.50—the amount of the tax. The tax does not change the demand curve. At each price (including taxes), consumers should continue to demand the same quantities as before. The new equilibrium must be less than $1.50 (the original price plus the tax) because at $1.50, the quantity demanded falls while the quantity supplied remains the same. Thus, at $1.50, there would be a surplus of gasoline on the market.

The new equilibrium point is *e′* at the price of $1.37$1/2$ and a quantity of 75 billion gallons per year. Sellers receive $.87$1/2$, with the tax collector picking up the $.50 difference. The government collects $37.5 billion in tax revenue ($.50 × 75 billion). This is much closer to what would happen to tax revenues than the estimates made in the newspapers.

The equilibrium price paid by consumers rises by $.37$1/2$ and the net price (price minus the tax) received by sellers falls by $.12$1/2$. Thus, consumers pay three-fourths of the tax and sellers pay one-fourth of the tax. Why is it that the consumer has the greater part of the burden than the seller in this particular example? The answer is found in the elasticities of demand and supply.

The demand curve in the accompanying exhibit is less elastic than the supply curve, as shown by the fact that curve *S* is flatter than curve *D*. Consumers, therefore, respond less to the price than do sellers. Since consumers are less sensitive to changes in the price of gasoline, they will pay more of the tax because they reveal less inclination to avoid the tax. We have assumed that the elasticity of demand along *D* between $1 and $1.37$1/2$ is approximately 0.6, and that the elasticity of supply along *S* is approximately 2.4.

In other cases, such as a tax on perfume, the elasticity of demand may exceed the elasticity of supply. In these cases, sellers will pay the greater burden of the tax because they are less sensitive to price changes than consumers. The consumer bears the greater burden of taxes when demand elasticities are less than supply elasticities, as is typical in the long run.

2. The cross-price elasticity is the percentage change in the demand for one good divided by the percentage change in the price of some other good. The income elasticity of demand is the percentage change in the demand divided by the percentage change in income. If this number is greater than 1, the good is a luxury; if it is less than 1, the good is a necessity.

3. The price elasticity of supply is the percentage change in quantity supplied divided by the percentage change in price. The price elasticity of supply depends on the time period of adjustment. Elasticity of supply is greater in the long run than in the short run and greater in the short run than in the immediate run.

4. The elasticites of demand and supply determine whether producers or consumers will bear the greater burden of a tax on a particular good. The group (producers or consumers) that bears the greater burden has the lowest price elasticity of demand or supply.

Policy Focus: **This chapter shows that it is elasticities that determine the incidence of a tax.**

Key Terms

price elasticity of demand (p. 91)
midpoints formula (p. 92)
total revenue (p. 94)

total-revenue test (p. 95)
perfectly elastic demand (p. 96)
perfectly inelastic demand (p. 96)

Questions and Problems

1. Using the demand schedule in Table A, calculate the price elasticities of demand for each successive pair of rows.

TABLE A

Price (dollars)	Quantity (units)
5	1
4	2
3	3
2	4
1	5

2. Suppose the long-run price elasticity of demand for tobacco is 2. A new tax increases the price of tobacco to consumers from $10 to $11 per carton. If Mr. Iron-lungs smokes 500 packages of cigarettes per year, what percentage decrease in quantity demanded would you predict? Approximately how many packages would be smoked at a price of $11 per carton (assuming 10 packages to a carton)?

3. Suppose the price of gasoline falls from $1.20 per gallon to $0.60 per gallon. Why would a driver's short-run adjustment to this price change be different from the long-run adjustment?

4. Assume that the basic monthly charge for a private telephone is $10.50 per month. If the rate were to rise to $11.00, would you expect a substantial reduction in the quantity demanded? Explain your answer. If, on the other hand, the basic monthly charge were $250.00 per month and the rate were to rise by the same percent as in the first case, what is your prediction about the change in quantity demanded?

5. When a professional football team raises its ticket prices by 10 percent, its sales revenues decline. From this information, what can you say about the price elasticity of demand for its tickets?

6. The University of Cowtown faces an inelastic demand for its dormitory rooms. What would you recommend that the university do in its annual budge meeting: raise the price, lower the price, or maintain the same price of dormitory rooms?

7. The income elasticity of demand for all services taken together is greater than one. As the economy grows, what would you expect to happen to the share of service industries in total output?

8. Used-car sales typically rise during economic recessions, while new-car sales decline during recessions. Explain why.

9. Assume that oranges have the following characteristics. The elasticity of demand is 0.2 and the elasticity of supply is 2. If government imposes a tax of $1 per crate of oranges, who would pay more of the tax (bear the larger burden of the tax): the consumer or the producer? Why? Draw a diagram illustrating your argument.

10. Evaluate the following statement: "The elasticity of demand for oranges is 0.2; therefore, California orange growers could raise their income by restricting their output."

11. Suppose the supply curve for the product X shifts to the right (supply increases). What happens to the total expenditure of consumers under each of the following conditions?
   a. The demand for X is price elastic.
   b. The demand for X is price inelastic.
   c. The demand for X is perfectly elastic.
   d. The demand for X is perfectly inelastic.

12. Suppose the supply curve for the product X shifts to the left (supply decreases). What happens to the total expenditure of consumers under each of the following conditions?
   a. The demand for X is price elastic.
   b. The demand for X is price inelastic.
   c. The demand for X is perfectly elastic.
   d. The demand for X is perfectly inelastic.

13. Suppose the demand for product X increases. What happens to the total revenue of sellers under each of the following conditions?
   a. The supply of X is elastic.
   b. The supply of X is inelastic.

14. Using the determinants of the price elasticity of demand, indicate for each of the following pairs of goods which one has the highest elasticity.
   a. Wheat and grains.
   b. Soft drinks and beverages.
   c. Cars and clothing.
   d. Toothpicks and beef.

15. Double the quantities demanded at each price in Table A above (for example, when the price is $5, assume 2 units are demanded; when the price is $4, assume 4 units

are demanded; and so on). What happens to the slope of the demand curve? What happens to the elasticity of demand between each successive pair of prices?

16. Who bears the burden of a tax on a good in each of the following circumstances?
   a. The supply curve is upward-sloping; demand is perfectly inelastic.
   b. The supply curve is upward-sloping; demand is perfectly elastic.
   c. The demand curve is downward-sloping; supply is perfectly inelastic.
   d. The demand curve is downward-sloping; supply is perfectly elastic.

17. The price elasticity of supply of perfume is 1. The price elasticity of demand for perfume is 2. How is the burden of the tax divided between producers and consumers?

Doing Economics

Has your campus cafeteria or bookstore changed the price of an item by a significant amount lately? If so, ask whether they would share information about the change in weekly or monthly sales that resulted from the price change. Based on the information that you receive from them, calculate the price elasticity of demand for the product. Does your estimate conform to your expectation based on the determinants of elasticity discussed in this chapter? Using this method for measuring elasticity assumes that the change in price moved quantity demanded along a fixed demand curve. This means that tastes, incomes, and the prices of related goods must be constant. Are these reasonable assumptions in this case? Explain.

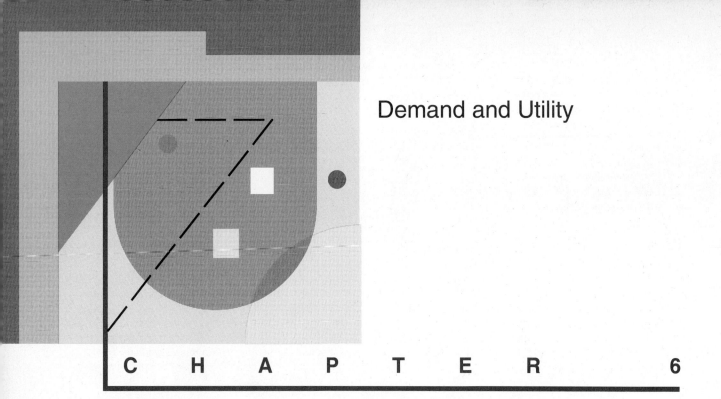

Demand and Utility

C H A P T E R 6

CHAPTER FOCUS   Why is there a law of demand? The answer that economists give is that
people buy more when the price of something is low because that makes
them better off. For example, in 1990s America, television entertainment is
very cheap: more channels are available, and high-quality color TV sets sell
for a fraction of what low-quality black-and-white TV sets cost two decades
earlier. Are consumers better off? *TV Guide* took a survey of its readers and
found that about half would refuse to give up television for less than a million
dollars! In other words, the value placed on watching television is
astronomical compared to the actual price.

    When people have only a limited amount to spend, they must spread their
expenditures over the available goods and services to get as much
satisfaction as possible. In doing so, they must weigh the costs of the good
compared to the extra satisfaction that it yields. Consumption is increased
until the price of the good just equals what one more unit of the good is worth
at the margin. As the TV example indicates, people may therefore get a lot of
satisfaction from something that has a very low price. This chapter focuses on
how the law of demand is the result of the rational calculation of costs and
benefits to consumers.

After studying this chapter, you will be able to:

- Understand how consumer preferences differ from demand.
- Know the law of diminishing marginal utility.
- Explain the principles under which the consumer's choices are in equilibrium.
- See how the law of demand is related to the law of diminishing marginal utility.
- Define the difference between income and substitution effects.
- Understand how to go from individual demand to market demand.

RATIONAL CONSUMER BEHAVIOR

The most important assumption of economics—the assumption upon which most economic ideas are based—is that individuals act to further their own self-interest. As buyers of goods and services, individuals spend their money to gain maximum satisfaction from their limited income. As owners of businesses, individuals operate their businesses to gain a maximum profit. As owners of factors of production, individuals use those factors to gain a maximum return. Economists assume that people act "rationally" in their own self-interest. Rational behavior does not mean that people are indifferent to family, friends, and society. People are entirely rational in helping others if they gain satisfaction from such benevolence.

Rational consumers spend their limited income buying goods and services. Consumers behave rationally when using their limited income to gain maximum satisfaction from the goods and services they consume.

CONSUMER PREFERENCES

Demand denotes the goods and services that households are prepared to buy given relative prices and consumers' income levels. If relative prices change or consumer income changes, the amounts people are prepared to buy change.

The amounts of goods and services that households are prepared to purchase depend not only on relative prices and income, but also on preferences or tastes. People have personal evaluations or **preferences** over the alternatives they face among the vast array of goods and services available.

> **Preferences** are a person's evaluations of goods and services independent of budget and price considerations.

People exhibit a wide variety of preferences. To satisfy the preference for entertainment, one person watches television, another goes to a movie, another learns how to pilot an airplane, yet another buys a book. Consumers' preferences determine how they would rank different combinations of goods and services in all conceivable situations. Smith prefers three apples and two oranges to one apple and five oranges, independently of apple and orange prices. Johnson prefers one apple and five oranges to three apples and two oranges, independently of apple and orange prices. Smith and Johnson have different preferences.

Nineteenth-century economists introduced a simple way of representing

preferences. They assumed people's preferences for goods or services are based on how goods or services add to their **utility**.

> **Utility** is the satisfaction that a person enjoys from consuming goods and services.

Marginal Utility

It is not possible to attach a meter to someone to measure satisfaction from consuming goods and services. (The appendix to this chapter explains why it is not even necessary to measure utility in specific units.) Suppose, however, that one could measure utility in terms of imaginary *utils,* or units of utility. From consuming 50 gallons of water per week, for example, a consumer enjoys 3,000 utils of satisfaction. From consuming 51 gallons, a consumer enjoys 3,010 utils.

The **marginal utility (*MU*)** of water is the extra utility enjoyed by increasing water consumption by one gallon. If 50 gallons yield 3,000 utils and 51 gallons yield 3,010 utils, the marginal utility of the 51st gallon of water is 10 utils.

> The **marginal utility (MU)** of any good or service is the increase in utility that a consumer experiences when consumption of that good or service increases by one unit, holding the consumption of all other goods and services constant. In general,
>
> $$MU = \frac{\Delta TU}{\Delta Q},$$
>
> where *TU* is total utility and *Q* is the quantity of the good.

The Law of Diminishing Marginal Utility

The **law of diminishing marginal utility** states that, as a general rule, as more of a good or service is consumed, its marginal utility declines. Thus, the first gallon of water per week has an enormous marginal utility because a consumer who has no water would have to use the first gallon to sustain life. The 20th gallon of water has a relatively small marginal utility because a person who already has 19 gallons would be able to use the 20th gallon for less important purposes. The marginal utility of water should decline rapidly as more water is consumed. Because the first gallon of water is essential to sustaining life, its marginal utility is astronomical. As more water becomes available, water can be applied to less urgent uses: to washing oneself, to washing clothes, to feeding pets, and eventually even to watering the lawn. By the time sufficient water is available for watering the lawn, the marginal utility of the last gallon is much smaller than the marginal utility of the first gallon. (See Example 1.)

> The law of diminishing marginal utility states that as more of a good or service is consumed during any given time period, its marginal utility declines, holding the consumption of everything else constant.

The **total utility** from all 20 gallons of water would be the sum of the marginal utilities of all units. Marginal utility is more important to explaining consumer demand than is total utility.

> Total utility is the amount of satisfaction (utility) obtained from consuming a particular quantity of a good or service. It is the sum of the marginal utilities of each successive unit of consumption.

MARGINAL UTILITY AND THE LAW OF DEMAND

The law of diminishing marginal utility explains the law of demand. Consumers will allocate their income among all the various goods in such a way that their total utility is maximized. When the price of any good falls, the consumer is motivated to buy more of the good.

Consider an individual consumer, Adam Smith. Adam Smith lives in a part of rural Scotland where only two goods can be bought—ale (A) and bread (B).

Adam Smith's preferences for both ale and bread are summarized in Exhibit 1. They do not change as time passes and as other things change. Columns 2 and 6 show the total utility of ale (TU_A) and bread (TU_B), respectively; columns 3 and 7 show the marginal utility of ale (MU_A) and bread (MU_B), respectively. These utility schedules apply to Adam Smith's consumption over a week's time period. In Smith's case, the utility of ale does not depend on how much bread he consumes, or vice versa.

Adam Smith's marginal utility schedule for ale is shown in Exhibit 2 and is graphed from the data in Exhibit 1. The first pint of ale (per week) yields a marginal utility of 40 utils; the second yields 30 utils; the third yields 20 utils; the fourth pint of ale yields a marginal utility of 10 utils. The total utility from consuming different quantities of ale is the sum of the bars up to the quantity of ale consumed. The total utility from consuming three pints of ale, for example, is 90 (= 40 + 30 + 20).

EXAMPLE 1

Why Diamonds Cost More Than Water

Adam Smith, in the *The Wealth of Nations* (1776), noted that "nothing is more useful than water; but it will purchase scarce anything; scarce anything can be had in exchange for it. A diamond, on the contrary, has scarce any value in use; but a very great quantity of other goods may frequently be had in exchange for it." The question at the root of this paradox is why prices often fail to reflect the usefulness of goods. Goods such as water and salt, without which human beings would perish, have low relative prices, whereas goods that have little practical value, such as diamonds, gold, and high fashion, have high relative prices.

Why is it that diamonds, whose total utility is much less than that of water, have a higher relative price than water? The law of diminishing marginal utility provides the answer to this paradox. On the one hand, the consumption of water takes place at a low marginal utility because the supply of water is large; on the other hand, the supply of diamonds is usually so limited that consumption takes place at a relatively high marginal utility. Although water's total utility is high, its marginal utility is low. Therefore, no one will sacrifice very much for an additional gallon.

The terms of the diamond/water paradox hold under normal supply conditions, but what happens when these conditions are disrupted? In the confusion at the end of World War II, food supplies were interrupted, and people gladly exchanged diamonds and precious metals for bread and potatoes in parts of Europe. The availability of food products was so limited that food products yielded a higher marginal utility (by preventing malnutrition) than did diamonds and precious metals. Similarly, when the American West was being settled in the nineteenth century, range wars were fought (and people were killed) over the control of water holes, and in arid parts of the world (Africa, the Middle East), armed conflicts still break out over water.

We know only Adam Smith's preferences for ale and bread. We cannot go from preferences to demand without knowing how much Smith has to spend on bread and ale per week and the prices of bread and ale. As noted in Chapter 3, demand depends not only on consumer preferences, but also on consumer income and prices. The combination of preferences, income, and prices explains the relationship between quantity demanded and price.

Adam Smith has $8 to spend on ale and bread per week. The price of ale (P_A) is $2 per pint, and the price of bread (P_B) is $0.50 per loaf. Smith could spend the entire $8 on ale, buying 4 pints of ale, or he could spend all $8 on bread, buying 16 loaves of bread. The most likely case, however, is that Smith will spend part of the money on ale and part on bread. For instance, he could purchase 3 pints of ale costing a total of $6 and 4 loaves of bread costing a total of $2 for a total weekly expenditure of $8. Smith is confronted with a choice: he can afford a number of combinations of ale and bread. Which combination will he actually select?

> To achieve maximum utility, consumers allocate their budget on goods in such a way that it is impossible to improve their total satisfaction by spending a bit more on one good or a bit less on the other.

As a rational consumer, Adam Smith will spend his limited income in such a manner as to obtain maximum satisfaction. Exhibit 1 shows that Adam Smith gets utility from consuming more of both ale and bread. How will he decide what affordable combination gives him the most satisfaction?

We will now demonstrate that Adam Smith maximizes his satisfaction when his budget is spent so that *the last dollar spent on each product (ale and bread) yields the same marginal utility.* This rule makes a lot of sense: If marginal utility per dollar of the last dollar spent is not the same for two products, the consumer can get more utility by switching the last dollar to the good with the greater marginal utility per dollar and still remain within budget.

Quantity of Ale (pints), Q_A (1)	Total Utility of Ale (utils), TU_A (2)	Marginal Utility of Ale (utils), MU_A (3)	Marginal Utility of Ale per Dollar (utils), MU_A/P_A (4)	Quantity of Bread (loaves), Q_B (5)	Total Utility of Bread (utils), TU_B (6)	Marginal Utility of Bread (utils), MU_B (7)	Marginal Utility of Bread per Dollar (utils), MU_B/P_B (8)
1	40	40	20	1	15	15	30
2	70	30	15	2	23	8	16
3	90	20	10	3	30	7	14
4	100	10	5	4	35	5	10
5	105	5	2.5	5	38	3	6
6	107	2	1	6	40	2	4

The table lists the quantities of ale and bread consumed per week by the consumer along with the utility the consumer attaches to each quantity. The marginal-utility-per-dollar figures are calculated by dividing marginal utility by price. The price of ale equals $2 per pint and the price of bread equals $0.50 per loaf.

EXHIBIT 2   Declining Marginal Utility

This figure graphs the data in columns 1 and 3 of Exhibit 1. The width of each bar represents one pint of ale. The vertical height or area of each bar represents marginal utility for that extra unit of ale. Total utility up to some quantity of ale is the sum of the areas of the bars to the left of that quantity of ale. For example, the total utility of 2 pints equals 70 (= 40 + 30); the total utility of 5 pints equals 105 (= 40 + 30 + 20 + 10 + 5).

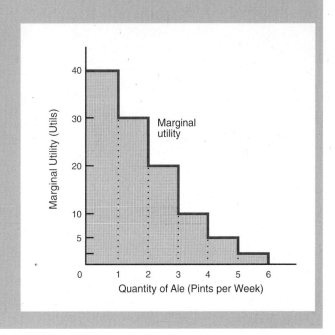

Maximum satisfaction requires that marginal utility per extra dollar spent on A be the same as the marginal utility per extra dollar spent on B.

Consumers select the affordable combination of goods that gives them maximum satisfaction by comparing marginal utility per dollar. In columns 4 and 8 of Exhibit 1, **marginal utilities per dollar** of ale and bread are calculated by dividing marginal utility by the price.

The **marginal utility per dollar** is the ratio MU/P and indicates the increase in utility from another dollar spent on the good.

EXHIBIT 3   The Steps to Consumer Equilibrium

	Available Choices	Decision	Income Remaining
1st Purchase ↓	1st pint of ale: $MU_A/P_A = 20$ 1st loaf of bread: $MU_B/P_B = 30$	Buy 1st loaf of bread for $0.50	$8.00 − $0.50 = $7.50
2nd Purchase ↓	1st pint of ale: $MU_A/P_A = 20$ 2nd loaf of bread: $MU_B/P_B = 16$	Buy 1st pint of ale for $2.00	$7.50 − $2.00 = $5.50
3rd Purchase ↓	2nd pint of ale: $MU_A/P_A = 15$ 2nd loaf of bread: $MU_B/P_B = 16$	Buy 2nd loaf of bread for $0.50	$5.50 − $0.50 = $5.00
4th Purchase ↓	2nd pint of ale: $MU_A/P_A = 15$ 3rd loaf of bread: $MU_B/P_B = 14$	Buy 2nd pint of ale for $2.00	$5.00 − $2.00 = $3.00
5th Purchase ↓	3rd pint of ale: $MU_A/P_A = 10$ 3rd loaf of bread: $MU_B/P_B = 14$	Buy 3rd loaf of bread for $0.50	$3.00 − $0.50 = $2.50
6th Purchase and 7th Purchase	3rd pint of ale: $MU_A/P_A = 10$ 4th loaf of bread: $MU_B/P_B = 10$	Buy 3rd pint of ale for $2.00 and 4th loaf of bread for $0.50	$2.50 − $2.00 = $0.50 $0.50 − $0.50 = $0 } Equilibrium

This table shows the step-by-step process by which a consumer makes purchasing decisions that will maximize satisfaction. In choosing at each step between a unit of ale and a unit of bread, the consumer determines which commodity has the highest marginal utility per dollar and buys that commodity. The data are taken from Exhibit 1. The consumer has $8 to spend. The consumer ends up buying 3 pints of ale and 4 loaves of bread, which is the equilibrium combination because marginal utility per dollar is equal for the two goods and all income is spent.

Note that the concept of marginal utility per dollar is a rate measure like miles per hour. Just as one can drive 50 miles per hour without driving for a full hour, marginal utility per dollar does not require the spending of a full dollar.

Exhibit 3 shows a step-by-step process by which Adam Smith could allocate his income between bread and ale. The first loaf of bread costs $0.50 and yields a marginal utility of 15; the marginal utility *per dollar* is 30 (= 15/$0.50) for the first loaf. The first pint of ale costs $2 and yields a marginal utility of 40, but the marginal utility *per dollar* is only 20 (= 40/$2) for the first pint. Because the first loaf of bread has a higher marginal utility per dollar, Smith would first buy one loaf of bread at a cost of $0.50, leaving $7.50 to spend. Smith now finds that the marginal utility per dollar is higher for the first pint of ale (20) than for the second loaf of bread (16), so he purchases a first pint of ale for $2, leaving $5.50 to spend. Marginal utility per dollar is higher for the second loaf of bread (16) than for the second pint of ale (15), so Smith's third purchase is the second loaf of bread. Smith continues to select the product with the higher marginal utility per dollar until his

$8 budget is exhausted. Smith is in **consumer equilibrium** when he buys 3 pints of ale and 4 loaves of bread—where he has spent his entire income of $8 (3 pints at $2 each and 4 loaves at $0.50 each) and where the marginal utility per dollar is 10 utils for both ale and bread.

> **Consumer equilibrium** occurs when the consumer has spent all of the budget and marginal utilities per dollar are equal on each good purchased ($MU_A/P_A = MU_B/P_B$).

The consumer is not inclined to change purchases from an equilibrium position where marginal utilities per dollar are equal unless some other factor changes. How other factors—such as income or changes in preferences—affect consumer equilibrium will be discussed below.

The Law of Demand

The law of demand follows from the analysis of consumer behavior. When the price of ale is $2, Adam Smith purchases (demands) 3 pints of ale, given that his income is $8 and the price of bread is $0.50. The price/quantity combination of $2/3 pints of ale is one point (*r* in Exhibit 4) on Smith's demand curve.

Other points on the demand curve can be calculated by repeating the whole process at a different price of ale, keeping income at $8 per week and the bread price at $0.50 per loaf.

If the price of ale falls from $2 to $1 per pint, the marginal utility per dollar for ale is now higher than the marginal utility per dollar for bread at the old equilibrium of 3 pints of ale and 4 loaves of bread. Ale purchases will be increased because it now yields more satisfaction for each additional dollar spent. Expenditures will be reallocated between the two goods until the $8 is spent and marginal utilities per dollar are again equal—this time at 5 pints of ale and 6 loaves of bread purchased. Thus, when the price of ale is $1, the quantity demanded of ale is 5 pints. This price/quantity combination of $1/5 pints is a second point (*t*) on the demand curve

---

EXHIBIT 4   From Marginal Utility to the Demand Curve

This curve shows Adam Smith's demand curve for ale calculated from Exhibit 1. If the price of bread is $0.50 per loaf and weekly income is $8, consumer equilibrium can be calculated at the price of ale equal to $2 per pint. The equilibrium quantity of 3 pints of ale is the quantity of ale demanded when the price of ale equals $2 (point *r*). The equilibrium quantity can also be calculated for a price of ale equal to $1 per pint. The resulting equilibrium quantity of ale (5 pints) is the quantity of ale demanded when the price of ale equals $1 (point *t*).

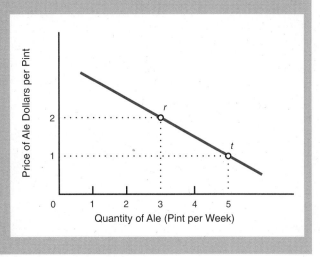

EXAMPLE 2

Marginal Utility, "All You Can Eat for $10," and the Daily Newspaper

Many restaurants offer buffets where customers can eat all they want for a specified price. Such offers are possible because the marginal utility of food diminishes rapidly. Depending on the individual's appetite, extra helpings yield smaller and smaller marginal utilities. In fact, they rather quickly yield negative marginal utility— the consumer's utility was higher before the extra helping. Although more food costs the consumer nothing, people will limit the amount of food they consume.

Rapidly diminishing marginal utility explains why the daily newspaper is dispensed from coin-operated boxes that permit people to take as many copies as they want. Newspaper companies know that the marginal utility of a second newspaper is zero for most people and they don't worry about people taking more than one. Owner's of coin-operated dispensers of other products (soft drinks, candies, etc.) know that they cannot give the customer the opportunity to take more than one.

in Exhibit 4. The law of demand holds because, holding all other facts constant, a decrease in the price causes an increase in the quantity demanded. (See Example 2.)

Every point on a given consumer's demand curve satisfies the conditions that MU/P is the same for all goods the consumer is buying and that all income is spent—that is, the consumer is maximizing utility at that price/quantity combination.

Income and Substitution Effects

When the price of a good falls, two things happen. First, consumers can buy the goods and services they used to buy *plus* what can be bought with their new savings. A decrease in price is like an increase in income in the sense that it enables consumers to purchase more goods of any type, including more of the good whose price has fallen. The part of the increase in quantity demanded caused by such an increase in income is called the **income effect**. Second, the cheaper good now yields a higher marginal utility per dollar. Consumers bent on maximizing satisfaction will substitute this now cheaper good for other products. This part of the increase in the quantity demanded of the cheaper good is called the **substitution effect**.

> When the price of a good falls people buy more of it because of the **income effect**—a price reduction is like an increase in income that in itself normally leads to larger demands for all goods and services, including the one whose price has fallen.

> When the price of a good falls, people buy more because consumers tend to substitute the good whose price has fallen for other relatively more expensive goods. This is called the **substitution affect**.

In Exhibit 4, before the drop in the price of ale from $2 to $1, the consumer purchased 3 pints of ale and 4 loaves of bread for a total of $8 worth of ale and bread. At the lower price of $1 per pint of ale, the consumer can purchase the same 3 pints of ale and 4 loaves of bread for $5. The consumer now has $3 left over that can be spent on either ale or bread. This $3 is like an increase in income. The effect of this increase in real income on purchases of ale is the income effect.

In addition to having the extra $3, the relative price of ale has dropped (the ratio of ale price to bread price has fallen from 4 to 2). Because of the lower relative price of ale, the consumer is now getting more marginal utility *per dollar* out of ale than bread, and therefore switches to buying more ale. This switch from bread to ale is the substitution effect.

The size of the income effect from a price change depends on how much of the good is being consumed. If the price of a Rolls-Royce goes up or down, there is no income effect for the vast majority of people. But if the price of gasoline rises, every driver would be affected—and those who used the most gasoline would be affected the most. Thus, the income effects for changes in the prices of food, clothing, and housing can be quite substantial. The income effects of changes in the prices of goods that are relatively unimportant in the consumer's budget are small or trivial.

The size of the substitution effect depends on the ease with which other goods can be substituted for a good. There are more substitutes for a movie than for a pair of eye-glasses, and the substitution effect would be correspondingly larger.

The theory of rational consumer behavior predicts that the law of demand holds true. The theory of rational consumer behavior explains why people consume a variety of goods and services.

MARKET DEMAND

We have used the law of diminishing marginal utility to demonstrate that a rational consumer will purchase less of a product, *ceteris paribus*, if its price rises. In other words, the demand curves of individual consumers have negative slopes.

But prices are established in markets, and the individual consumer is usually only a small part of the market. The **market-demand curve** for a particular good combines the demand curves of all participants in that market.

> The **market-demand curve** shows the total quantities demanded by all consumers in the market at each price. It is the summation of all individual demand curves in that market.

Exhibit 5 shows the demand curves for ale for two consumers, Jones and White, who constitute all the buyers in the market for ale. (In reality, there would be many buyers of ale, but two buyers allow us to make the point as simply as possible.) At a price of $3 per pint, Jones demands 0 pints and White demands 1 pint. The market quantity demanded at the $3 price can be obtained by adding the two quantities demanded together (0 + 1 = 1 pint). At a price of $2 per pint, Jones demands 2 pints and White demands 3 pints. The market quantity demanded at the $2 price is 2 + 3 = 5 pints.

The market-demand curve is downward-sloping for the same reasons that the individual demand curves are downward-sloping. In addition, as price decreases more consumers might be enticed to buy a product. For example, when the price of ale is above $3 Jones is not in the market; at a price of $0.50, even more buyers may enter the market.

EXHIBIT 5   From the Individual Demand Curve to the Market Demand Curve

a. Jones' Demand   **b. White's Demand**   **c. Market Demand**

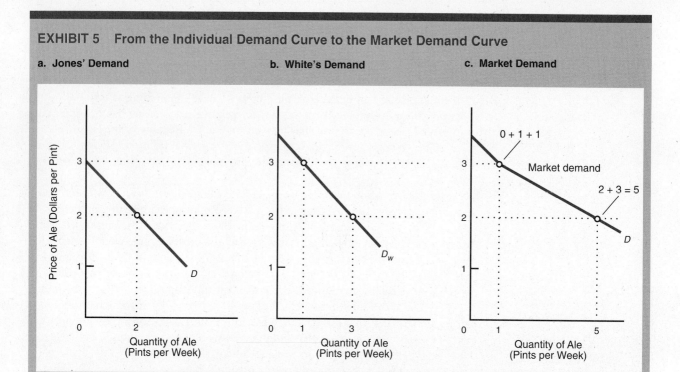

The market-demand curve is the horizontal summation of all individual demand curves; it is calculated by summing all individual quantities demanded at each price. Here, the market has only two consumers, but the principle applies to markets with any number of consumers.

This chapter examined the relationship between consumer behavior and the demand curve for goods and services. The next chapter shifts to the supply side of the market and examines how businesses are organized and the markets in which they operate.

Chapter Summary

The most important point to learn from this chapter is: When the consumer is in equilibrium the ratio of marginal utility to price is the same for each good purchased. The law of demand follows from this equilibrium condition.

1. Preferences are people's evaluations of goods and services independent of budget and price considerations. *Demand* denotes the goods and services that consumers are prepared to buy given income and relative prices.

2. The satisfaction that is obtained from consuming goods and services is called utility. Marginal utility is the increase in total utility obtained when consumption of a good is increased by one unit. The law of diminishing marginal utility states that the marginal utility declines as more of a good or service is consumed.

3. The law of diminishing marginal utility explains the law of demand. When the price of a commodity drops, two effects will be set in motion: The income effect occurs when

Should We Allow Price Gouging?

Natural disasters raise prices. After massive hurricanes such as Hurricane Andrew, which destroyed much of the Florida coast in the summer of 1992, the prices of building-repair materials tend to shoot up. With the many destroyed homes, gaping roofs, and open store windows, the marginal utility of building materials such as plywood increases, and the market demand increases.

Many states have ordinances that protect consumers from "price gouging" in the wake of natural disasters. These ordinances require that shop owners and speculators not benefit from the hardship of others. Even though people are prepared to pay a higher price of plywood after hurricanes, merchants cannot raise prices. If they do, they can be fined or even jailed!

Are anti-price-gouging laws really in society's best interest? Let us take a simplified example. The accompanying diagram shows a price of $5 per unit of plywood before the hurricane. Assume each "customer" buys 1 unit of plywood. At this price, two customers buy plywood. The hurricane increases demand. Without price controls, the price would rise to $11 with three customers buying at this price. If the law requires that the original $5 price be held, six people now wish to buy plywood, but only two customers can be satisfied.

The demand curve shows what people would have been willing to spend at different prices. After the hurricane, one customer would have been willing to pay $15, another $13, another $11. The first three customers would have been willing to pay $11 or more; the next three customers would have been willing to pay from $5 to $9.

This chapter teaches that the price people are willing to pay reflects that good's marginal utility to that person. The person willing to pay $15 places a higher value on plywood (perhaps to replace a missing roof) than the person willing to pay $5 (to

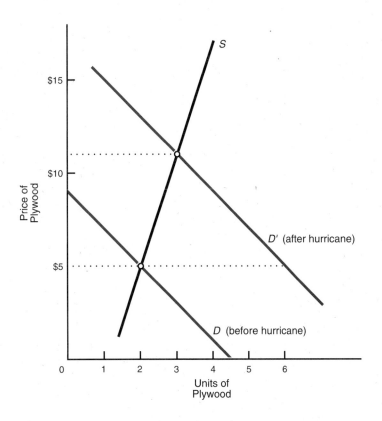

replace part of the front porch). If the price is held at $5, plywood will be distributed to two lucky customers according to the luck of the draw. If the person willing to pay only $5 is standing in line before the person willing to pay $15, plywood goes to a buyer who places a low value on the good. Let's assume that the luck of the draw results in customers 5 and 6 getting the plywood. For them, the plywood has a combined value of $12 ($5 + $7). For the excluded customers 1 and 2, the plywood would have a combined value of $28 ($15 + $13).

Goods allocated by price will always go to those buyers who place the highest value on the good. If goods are allocated by standing in line or by the luck of the draw, buyers who place a high value on the good may lose out to those who place a much lower value on the good. There is a loss to society if the person who desperately needs plywood to replace a roof cannot buy plywood, while the person who needs plywood for a minor front-porch repair can buy plywood.

the price decrease raises the real income of the consumer and when this increase in income is used to purchase additional goods and services. The substitution effect occurs because the fall in the relative price of the good motivates the consumer to substitute the good for other goods.

4. The marked-demand schedule summarizes the demand schedules of all individuals participating in the market. The market-demand curve will have a negative slope because individual demand curves have negative slopes.

Policy Focus: **Anti-price-gouging laws may not be in society's interest because they may result in goods going to buyers who place a relatively low value on them.**

Key Terms

preferences (p. 109)
utility (p. 110)
marginal utility (*MU*) (p. 110)
law of diminishing marginal utility (p. 111)
total utility (p. 111)

marginal utility per dollar (p. 113)
consumer equilibrium (p. 115)
income effect (p. 116)
substitution effect (p. 116)
market-demand curve (p. 117)

Questions and Problems

1. People spend a much larger fraction of their income on transportation in the 1980s than they did in the 1880s, when the horse and buggy was popular. Does this mean that consumer preferences for transportation services are basically unstable?

2. One of the most basic changes in consumer buying patterns in the late 1970s and early 1980s was the switch from "gas guzzlers" to fuel-efficient cars. Does this switch indicate that consumer preferences changed between the late 1970s and early 1980s?

3. For which good do you think marginal utility will decline more rapidly: hot dogs or best-seller paperbacks?

4. Use the marginal-utility information in Exhibit 1 to calculate the quantity demanded of ale at a price of $4 per

pint. What do you do when marginal utility per dollar cannot be exactly equated on the last units sold?

5. Again using Exhibit 1, calculate the quantity demanded of ale at the price of $2 but at a weekly income of $11. Compare this result with the answer at $8. Which is larger? Why?

6. There are 1,000 identical consumers in the market with the same income and the same preferences. When the price of *X* is $50 per unit, the typical consumer is prepared to purchase 20 units of *X*. When the price is $40 per unit, the typical consumer is prepared to purchase 25 units of *X*. Construct the market-demand curve for *X* (assume the demand curve is a straight line).

7. A consumer spends total weekly income on goods *A*

and *B*. The last penny spent on *A* yields a marginal utility of 10; the last penny spent on *B* yields a marginal utility of 20. Is it possible for the consumer to be in equilibrium? If so, what are the exact conditions?

8.   Ms. White consumes only goods *X* and *Y*. Column 1 of the table below shows the marginal utility she derives from various units of *X*; column 2 shows the marginal utility she derives from various units of *Y*. Her income is $20, the price of *X* is $2 per unit, and the price of *Y* is $4 per unit. Use Table A to answer the following questions:
   a. How much of *X* and *Y* will Ms. White demand?
   b. Check your answer by using the consumer-equilibrium conditions. (Is all income spent? Does $MU_x/P_x = MU_y/P_y$?)

TABLE A

Units of X	MU_x	Units of Y	Mu_x
1	20	1	2,000
2	16	2	200
3	12	3	20
4	10	4	10
5	6	5	4

9.   Can the equilibrium conditions be applied to more than two goods? How?

10.   The price of ale is $10, the price of bread is $5, and the marginal utility of bread is 50 utils when the consumer is in equilibrium. Can you deduce how much is spent on ale? Can you deduce the marginal utility of ale?

11.   The price of oranges is $0.25 each, and the price of grapefruit is $0.50 each. Assuming that all income is spent in each case, determine whether or not the consumer is in equilibrium in each of the following circumstances. If consumer equilibrium does not occur, determine the good of which the consumer will purchase more and explain why.
   a. The marginal utility of oranges, MU_O, equals 10, and the marginal utility of grapefruit, MU_G, equals 15;
   b. $MU_O = 50$ and $MU_G = 100$;
   c. MU_O is twice that of MU_G;
   d. MU_G is twice that of MU_O.

12.   Ms. Jones buys 100 cokes per year at $0.50 per coke and 20 pizzas at $5 each. Does doubling the price of cokes to $1 per coke have a larger or smaller income effect than raising the price of pizzas to $6? Explain your answer.

Doing Economics

One difficulty in applying supply-and-demand analysis is dealing with goods or services that are similar but not quite identical. For example, an apartment close to the center of a city (or close to campus) offers similar services to one far away, but is more desirable to some consumers because it reduces the amount of time spent commuting. Consumers choose between close-apartment/short-commute and distant-apartment/long-commute alternatives. From the analysis in this chapter, you know that a consumer (in equilibrium) balances the *MU/P* of each consumption alternative. Assuming that consumers are in equilibrium, you may be able to infer something from the differential in price about how much people dislike long commutes. From newspaper ads or personal inquiry, collect information on rents asked for otherwise comparable apartments in several areas at varying distances from the center of your city (or from your campus, if most of the apartments you consider are rented to students). Estimate the length of the commute from each area. What can you infer about the marginal disutility of commuting a particular length of time? What potential problems exist in this analysis?

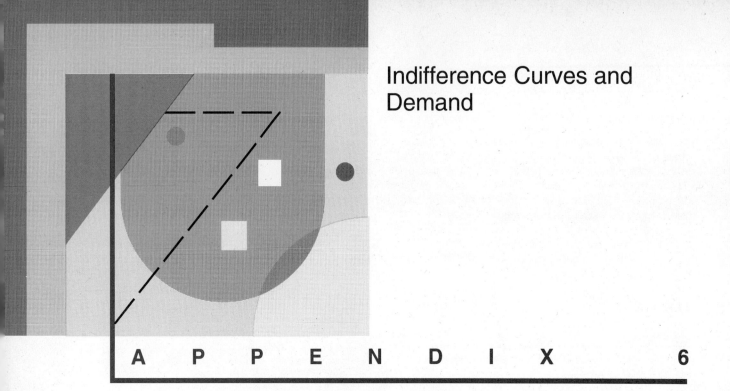

Indifference Curves and Demand

APPENDIX FOCUS   The preceding chapter on demand and utility showed how the law of diminishing marginal utility can be used to explain the law of demand. In equilibrium, consumers will equate marginal utilities per dollar on the last unit of items consumed. If the price of good *A* rises, the marginal utility per dollar of *A* will be *less* than that of other goods. The law of diminishing marginal utility states that the marginal utility of *A* will increase if less of *A* is consumed. Therefore, consumer equilibrium is reattained by consuming less of *A*. Because of diminishing marginal utility, there will be a negative relationship between price and quantity demanded.

   The law of diminishing marginal utility does explain the law of demand, but it requires that people be able to measure the *utility* they obtain by consuming various quantities of goods and services.

   Because of skepticism about the measurement of utility, economists were forced to find an alternative approach to understanding consumer behavior. The search culminated in *indifference-curve theory*.

CONSUMER PREFERENCES

Indifference-curve theory does not require that consumers be able to measure utility in any specific units of measurement but does assume that consumers are able to rank their preferences for combinations of goods. The consumer should be able to choose between 4 pints of ale and 5 loaves of bread on the one hand and 8 pints of ale and 1 loaf of bread on the other. If the consumer does not prefer one combination to the other, the consumer is said to be *indifferent*.

Exhibit 1 diagrams the preferences of a particular consumer. The horizontal axis measures the quantity of ale consumed by the individual per week. The vertical axis measures the quantity of bread consumed by the individual per week. At point *a*, 6 loaves of bread and 1 pint of ale are consumed. At *a*, the consumer is willing to give up 3 loaves of bread for 1 more pint of ale. This trade-off would move the consumer to point *b* where 3 loaves of bread and 2 pints of ale are consumed. At point *b*, the consumer is no longer willing to give up 3 loaves of bread to acquire 1 more pint of ale. The consumer is now willing to give up only 1 loaf of bread to acquire 1 more pint of ale. This trade-off would put the consumer at point *c*, consuming 2 loaves of bread and 3 pints of ale per week. Finally, to acquire 1 more pint of ale, the consumer is willing now to give up only half a loaf of bread, moving the consumer to point *d*. The consumer is indifferent between points *a, b, c,* and *d* and feels equally well off at any of these points.

A curve can be drawn, through points *a, b, c,* and *d,* which represents all the possible consumption patterns that keep the consumer at the same level of satisfaction. This curve is called an **indifference curve** because every point on the curve yields the same satisfaction even though the consumption pattern is different at each point. The indifference curve shows that a person can be flexible, and is willing to substitute one good for another.

> An **indifference curve** shows all the alternative consumption patterns that yield the same total satisfaction to a particular consumer and among which the consumer is indifferent.

An indifference curve is downward-sloping because as long as both goods yield satisfaction, more is better than less. The only way for the consumer's satisfaction to stay the same when more of one good is consumed is to consume less of the other good.

The Law of the Diminishing Marginal Rate of Substitution

The shape of an indifference curve provides useful information about preferences. Indifference-curve analysis substitutes the concept of the **marginal rate of substitution (MRS)** for the concept of marginal utility.

> The **marginal rate of substitution (MRS)** is how much of one good a person is just willing to give up to acquire one unit of another.

Thus, the marginal rate of substitution is just a fancy name for an acceptable trade-off between two goods or for the person's *valuation* of an additional unit of one good in terms of the other. For example, consider how many hot dogs you would be willing to sacrifice for an additional pizza. If you would give up 3 hot dogs

EXHIBIT 1　An Indifference Curve

When given the choice among the commodity bundles along an indifference curve, the consumer is indifferent. Consumption pattern *a* yields the same satisfaction to the consumer as *b, c,* or *d*. The absolute value of the slope of an indifference curve is the marginal rate of substitution and shows—in this case—how much bread the consumer is just willing to sacrifice for one more pint of ale.

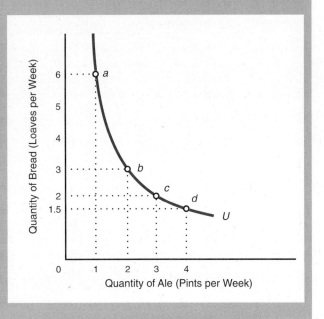

for 1 pizza, your marginal rate of substitution of hot dogs for pizza is 3. That quantity of hot dogs is your personal valuation of pizza in terms of hot dogs.

In Exhibit 1 the marginal rate of substitution of bread for ale from point *c* to point *d* is 0.5 (one-half of a loaf of bread for 1 pint of ale). Geometrically, the absolute slope of the tangent at any point on the indifference curve measures the marginal rate of substitution of good *B* for good *A*. The flatter is the slope of the indifference curve, the lower is the relative valuation the consumer places on *A* (compared to *B*).

An indifference curve is always convex when viewed from below (bulges toward the origin). The convex curvature of the indifference curve is explained by the **law of diminishing marginal rate of substitution**: as more ale is consumed relative to bread, the consumer is willing to give up less and less bread to acquire additional units of ale because bread is getting more valuable and ale is getting less valuable. When one moves from point *a* down to point *d* and beyond, the indifference curve gets flatter and flatter because the relative valuation placed on ale is decreasing compared to bread.

> The law of diminishing marginal rate of substitution is that as more of one good (*A*) is consumed along a given indifference curve, the amount of the other good (*B*) that the consumer is willing to sacrifice for one more unit of good *A* declines.

Indifference curves can be drawn to represent any level of satisfaction. Exhibit 2 shows the same consumer at three different levels of satisfaction. Higher indifference curves for any one consumer represent higher levels of satisfaction. Each consumer has an entire map of indifference curves, one for every level of satisfaction. Exhibit 2 shows only three indifference curves. Whether a person is poor or well off is determined by the person's income and the relative prices of goods.

EXHIBIT 2 The Map of Indifference Curves

There is an infinite number of indifference curves for each consumer; three indifference curves for a particular consumer are shown here. The higher the indifference curve, the greater is the well-being of the consumer. The indifference map shows that commodity bundle *e* is preferred to bundle *d* because the former is on a higher indifference curve. Indifference curve U_3 represents a higher level of satisfaction than U_2 and U_2 represents a higher level than U_1. The level of satisfaction along each indifference curve is constant.

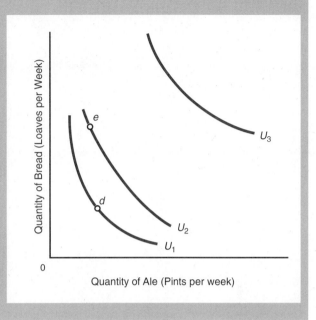

Indifference curves are subjective and unique to each person. Nevertheless, they have in common the following five properties:

1. Indifference curves that show preferences between two goods from which consumers derive benefits are downward-sloping.
2. They are bowed toward the *origin* (the point where the axes meet), which reflects the law of diminishing marginal rate of substitution.
3. Consumers are better off when they move to a higher indifference curve.
4. Indifference curves cannot intersect each other, because an intersection would indicate that the consumer is simultaneously worse off and better off. (Even though indifference curves do not intersect, they need not be parallel.)
5. The set of indifference curves does not move as a result of market circumstances (changes in income or prices).

A consumer's equilibrium position on an indifference curve is determined by the consumer's budget. What the consumer can buy depends on income and prices. The consumer can buy more when income rises for given prices; the consumer can buy more when prices fall for a given income.

The Budget Line

Suppose the price of ale is $2 per pint and the price of bread is $0.50 per loaf. Assume the consumer has $8 to spend per week on ale and bread. If the entire $8 is spent on ale, the consumer can buy 4 pints of ale. This combination corresponds to point *m* in Exhibit 3. If the entire $8 is spent on bread, 16 loaves of bread can be purchased. This combination corresponds to point *n*. The **budget line** connecting points *m* and *n* represents all the other combinations of ale and bread the consumer is able to buy by spending the entire $8 income on the two goods.

EXHIBIT 3   The Budget Line

With a budget of $8, the consumer can buy 16 loaves of bread at a price of $0.50 per loaf or 4 pints of ale at a price of $2 per pint. Spending $4 on each good would buy 8 loaves of bread and 2 pints of ale (point p). The budget line shows the choices open to the consumer. The consumer can afford to buy any combination of goods on the budget line. Points above the budget line, such as k, cannot be purchased with the consumer's income. The slope of the budget line is the ratio of the price of ale to the price of bread; in this case, the slope is 4.

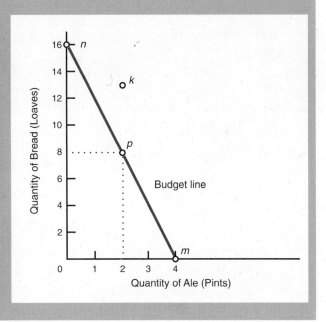

The **budget line** is all the combinations of goods the consumer is able to buy given a certain income and set prices. The budget line shows the consumption possibilities available to the consumer.

The budget line in Exhibit 3 has a negative slope with an absolute value of 16/4 = 4. This negative slope is the price of ale in terms of bread: $P_A/P_B = \$2/\$0.50 = 4$. The slope indicates that if the consumer wants to buy one more pint of ale, the consumer must give up 4 loaves of bread. In other words, 4 loaves of bread represent the opportunity cost of consuming one more pint of ale.

Algebraically, point m in Exhibit 3 is income divided by the price of ale because point m shows the maximum possible consumption of ale. Point n is income divided by the price of bread. The absolute value of the slope of the line nm is then determined as follows:

$$\text{Slope} = \frac{\text{Income}}{P_B} \div \frac{\text{Income}}{P_A} = \frac{P_A}{P_B}.$$

Indifference curves show how the consumer ranks *different* market baskets; the budget line shows what the consumer *is able* to buy. Combining the information represented by the indifference curve and the budget line shows what combination of goods the consumer *will* buy.

CONSUMER EQUILIBRIUM

The consumer achieves equilibrium by choosing a consumption pattern that maximizes the consumer's satisfaction on the budget line. Exhibit 4 shows

EXHIBIT 4 Consumer Equilibrium

The consumer's optimal consumption pattern is at point *e*. A point like *d* is attainable (on the budget line) but is not as good as *e* because it places the consumer on a lower indifference curve (U_0). Point *f* is better than *e* (the consumer is on a higher indifference curve, U_2) but is not attainable with the given set of income and prices. At *e*, the indifference curve U_1 is tangent to the budget line. Thus, the slope of the indifference curve equals the slope of the budget line. This tangency is equivalent to the marginal-utility rule for maximizing utility ($MU_A/P_A = MU_B/P_B$) discussed in the chapter.

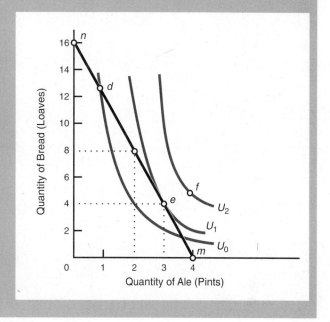

The consumer is in equilibrium when the budget line is just tangent to the highest attainable indifference curve. Two conditions are then satisfied: (1) The consumer is on the budget line. (2) The consumer's marginal rate of substitution of bread for ale equals the price ratio of ale to bread (P_A/P_B).

The marginal rate of substitution of bread for ale (*MRS*) equals the ratio of the ale's marginal utility (MU_A) to the bread's marginal utility (MU_B):

$$MRS = \frac{MU_A}{MU_B}.$$

the optimal consumption pattern. The consumer is *able* to locate anywhere on the budget line, but *the rational consumer will select that consumption combination that falls on the highest attainable indifference curve*. This combination is point *e*: by consuming 4 loaves of bread and 3 pints of ale the consumer can reach indifference curve U_1. Any other point on the budget line will fall on a *lower* indifference curve. At the optimal consumption pattern, represented by point *e*, the budget line is tangent to (touches the curve only at one point and has the same slope as) the indifference curve.

Equivalently, consumer equilibrium occurs at that point on the highest attainable indifference curve where the marginal rate of substitution equals the price ratio. At point *e*, the consumer's marginal rate of substitution is 4 because the consumer is willing to trade off 4 units of bread for one unit of ale. The price ratio, as we have shown, is also 4.

There is a link between indifference-curve analysis and marginal-utility theory. The marginal rate of substitution of bread for ale can also be indicated by the marginal utilities of ale and bread. For example, if the marginal utility of ale (MU_A) is 20 and the marginal utility of bread (MU_B) is 5, it takes 4 extra loaves of bread to compensate the consumer for the loss of only 1 pint of ale. But if $MU_A = 10$ and $MU_B = 5$, the marginal rate of substitution of bread for ale is only 2.

The condition for equilibrium can now be translated into the equal-marginal-utility-per-dollar rule for consumer equilibrium described in this chapter. At point *e*, the slope of the indifference curve is MU_A/MU_B. The slope of the budget line is P_A/P_B. The indifference-curve equilibrium rule is equivalent to $MU_A/MU_B = P_A/P_B$. A little algebraic manipulation shows that this equation is equivalent to the marginal-utility-per-dollar rule for equilibrium: $MU_A/P_A = MU_B/P_B$.

EXHIBIT 5   The Effect of an Income Change

When the price of ale is $2 per pint and the price of bread is $0.50 per loaf, a fall in income from $8 to $4 causes a parallel shift in the budget line from nm to hj. The equilibrium changes from e_1 to e_0, which is on a lower indifference curve.

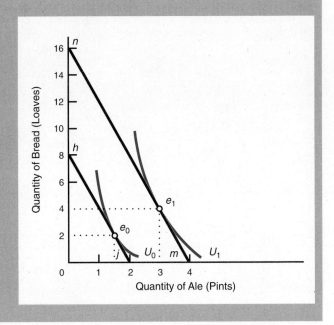

THE EFFECT OF AN INCOME CHANGE

The consumer's equilibrium position will be affected if income changes, if the price of ale changes, or if the price of bread changes. Exhibit 5 shows how a reduction in the consumer's income from $8 to $4 leads to a reduction in the demand for both ale and bread. We assume the price of ale stays at $2 per pint and the price of bread remains at $0.50 per loaf. The budget line shifts down from nm to hj, because now the consumer can purchase a maximum of only 2 pints of ale or 8 loaves of bread. Instead of 4 loaves of bread and 3 pints of ale being consumed, now only 2 loaves of bread and 1.5 pints of ale are consumed at the new equilibrium (point e_0).

Notice that when income changes, holding prices constant, the budget line shifts in a parallel fashion. This shift occurs because the slope of the budget line is P_A/P_B, which has been assumed constant. The budget line shifts down when income falls and up when income rises. Clearly, utility falls as income falls and rises as income rises.

THE EFFECT OF A PRICE CHANGE

Now consider the effects of a change in one of the prices, holding income and the other price constant. Exhibit 6 shows how a fall in the price of ale from $2 to $1 per pint leads to an increase in the quantity of ale demanded. The initial equilibrium situation is represented by the combination e_1, where the price of ale is $2 and the price of bread is $0.50. Reducing the price of ale to $1 will allow the consumer the option of purchasing as many as 8 pints of ale, because the income remains $8. The budget line will now swing outward from nm to nr.

EXHIBIT 6 The Effect of a Price Change on Consumer Equilibrium: The Law of Demand

Assuming that income is $8 and the price of bread is $0.50, when the price of ale falls from $2 to $1 per pint, the budget line swings outward from nm to nr because the consumer is able to buy as many as 8 pints of ale. The consumer seeks out a new equilibrium combination, e_2, where the indifference curve U_2 is tangent to the new budget line nr. A fall in the price of ale from $2 to $1 thus increases the quantity of ale demanded from 3 pints at point e_1 to 5 pints at point e_2.

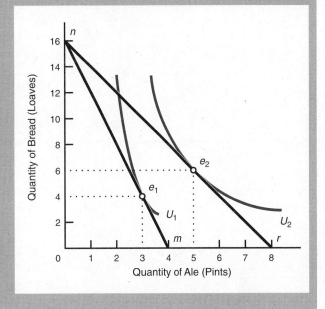

When the price of one good falls, an increase in real income occurs, as shown by an outward swing of the budget line.

The new equilibrium position occurs at e_2. At this point, the consumer buys 5 pints of ale and 6 loaves of bread. Before the price change, the consumer bought 3 pints of ale and 4 loaves of bread. The law of demand is confirmed: lowering the price of ale increases the quantity of ale demanded.

The consumer is clearly made better off (moves to a higher indifference curve) by the fall in the price of ale. Clearly, the consumer gets a bonus from low prices; the lower is the price of a good bought by a consumer, holding income and other prices constant, the greater is the consumer's welfare.

Why are demand curves downward-sloping? The chapter pointed out that there are two reasons for the law of demand: the substitution effect and the income effect. When the price of a good falls, people will tend to substitute the good for other goods because its relative price has fallen. Thus, the substitution effect tends to increase the quantity of a good demanded when the price falls. In addition, when the price of a good falls, people have more money to spend on all goods. If you are accustomed to buying one $10,000 car per year, a price reduction to $8,000 is like a $2,000 increase in income! If a good is normal, increases in income increase demand for the good. Thus, the income effect of a price reduction will also increase the quantity demanded of the good. Indifference-curve analysis can be used to illustrate the income effect and the substitution effect.

Exhibit 7 shows a consumer with the initial budget line vw and the initial equilibrium at point e. The consumer is purchasing q units of ale. When the price of ale falls, the budget line shifts to vz. The quantity of ale demanded is now q'' at the new equilibrium point, e''. The consumer is better off after the drop in the ale price because curve U'' is higher than curve U.

The change in equilibrium from e to e'' can be broken down into a two-step process to isolate the roles of the *income effect* and the *substitution effect* on the change in the equilibrium position.

When the price of ale falls, the ratio of the price of ale to the price of bread changes. *If the consumer were interested only in maintaining the current level of welfare*

The Effect of a Price Change   **129**

EXHIBIT 7   Substitution and Income Effects

When income is $8 per week, bread costs $0.50 per loaf, and ale costs $2 per pint, the initial equilibrium is point *e*. When the price of ale falls from $2 to $1 per pint, the budget line swings outward from *vw* to *vz*. The new equilibrium is point *e″*. The substitution effect is obtained by drawing the budget line *st* parallel to *vz* but tangent to the original indifference curve, *U*. Thus, the substitution effect is the distance *qq′* and the income effect is the distance *q′q″*. In the case of a normal good, the income effect reinforces the substitution effect.

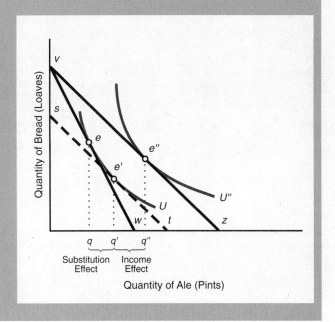

achieved on curve U, the consumer would increase the quantity demanded of ale until he or she reached the point on curve *U* where line *st* is tangent to *U* (*st* is a budget line with a slope that reflects the *new* ratio of ale price to bread price that results when the price of ale falls). The point on curve *U* where *st* is tangent to *U* is point *e′*. At *e′*, the consumer buys more ale and less bread without changing the level of satisfaction. This change in the quantity demanded of ale from *q* to *q′* is the **substitution effect** of the change in the price of ale.

> The **substitution effect** is the change in quantity of *X* demanded that occurs when the price of *X* changes and the consumer is compensated to keep utility constant.

At point *e′*, however, the consumer is not spending all the income available to him or her. Because of the drop in the price of ale, the consumer has more income available to spend on *both* bread and ale. The consumer's new budget line resulting from the lower ale price is *vz*, which has the same ale-price-to-bread-price ratio as *st* but which makes possible for the consumer a position on a higher indifference curve. The consumer who wished to maximize satisfaction would not stay at *e′* but would shift to *e″*, a point on the highest indifference curve attainable given budget line *vz*. The consumer making this shift would increase the quantity demanded of ale still further from *q′* at *e′* to *q″* at *e″*. This new equilibrium, unlike *e′*, *does* satisfy all the conditions of consumer equilibrium. The increase in quantity demanded from *q′* to *q″* as a result of the additional income made available is the **income effect** of the change in the ale price.

> The **income effect** is the change in the quantity of *X* demanded that is attributable to the welfare change that accompanies the price change.

The importance of the distinction between the substitution and income effects is that we can see that for normal goods the demand curve must be downward-sloping. In Exhibit 7, the price of ale falls and the substitution effect increases quantity demanded from q to q' along the convex indifference curve U. The move from e' to e'' is like any income increase. If ale is a *normal* good, for which demand increases with income, more ale will be consumed. In effect, a reduced price of ale gives the consumer more income to spend on both ale and bread. Thus, for a normal good, the income effect also indicates more ale will be consumed. It follows from the above analysis that if a good is normal, the demand curve for the good must be downward-sloping.

Appendix Summary

1. Indifference-curve analysis requires only that consumers be able to state whether they prefer one combination of goods to another combination or whether they are indifferent. An indifference curve plots those combinations of goods that yield the same level of satisfaction to the consumer. In indifference-curve analysis, the law of the diminishing marginal rate of substitution replaces the law of diminishing marginal utility. It states that the greater is the quantity of good X that the individual consumes relative to good Y, the smaller will be the quantity of good Y that the consumer is willing to sacrifice to obtain one more unit of good X. The budget line shows the choices of goods open to the consumer.

2. Maximizing satisfaction requires that the consumer seek out the highest indifference curve while remaining on the budget line. This point occurs at the tangency of the indifference curve and the budget line.

3. A change in income causes a parallel shift in the budget line. The budget line shifts down if income decreases and up if income increases. The new equilibrium is simply the new tangency of the new budget line with an indifference curve.

4. A reduction in the price of one commodity swings the budget line outward. The new equilibrium takes place at the point of tangency between a higher indifference curve and the new budget line. The consumer is made better off by the price reduction because the consumer is able to locate on a higher indifference curve. The effects of a price change on quantity demanded can be broken down into a substitution effect, which maintains the existing utility level, and an income effect, which results from the change in the consumer's level of utility.

Key Terms

indifference curve (p. 123)
marginal rate of substitution (*MRS*) (p. 123)
law of diminishing marginal rate of substitution (p. 124)

budget line (p. 125)
substitution effect (p. 130)
income effect (p. 130)

Questions and Problems

1. Assume that the consumer's income is $100, the price of ale is $5 per pint, and the price of bread is $4 per loaf
   a. Draw the consumer's budget line.
   b. How does the budget line shift if the price of bread rises to $10, holding the price of ale at $5.
   c. How does the budget line shift if the price of ale rises to $10 holding the price of bread at $10?
   d. How does the budget line shift if income doubles at $200, holding the prices of ale and bread at $5 and $10, respectively?

2. Why are indifference curves downward-sloping? Why are they bowed toward the origin?

3. Why must the equilibrium position be a point of tangency between the budget line and an indifference curve?

4. Illustrate a situation in which income increases and the demand for one of the goods falls.

5. Deduce the law of demand for a normal good using the distinction between substitution and income effects when the price of the good rises.

6. Assume that the marginal rate of substitution of good X for good Y is $MRS = 6$, that the price of good X is $1 per unit, and that the price of good Y is $3 per unit.
   a. Illustrate the consumer's current position on the budget line relative to an indifference curve.
   b. Explain why the consumer would buy more of good Y.

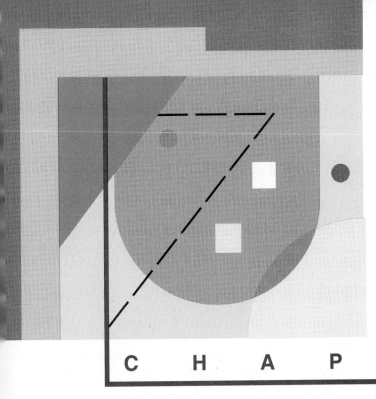

Business Firms, Information, and Contracts

C H A P T E R 7

CHAPTER FOCUS   In olden times, businesses were run simply. One or several individuals would own the business, take the risks, and make the decisions. Most modern businesses cannot be run in such a direct way. Millions or even billions of dollars of capital are required—much more than one or two owners could manage. The failure of a such a large venture would destroy the personal wealth of the owners if they were held personally liable. Modern businesses employ thousands of persons spread among various divisions both at home and abroad.

The complexity of modern business fostered new forms of business organization. The corporation now accounts for most production. Modern corporations are run by professional managers whose goals and interests may differ from those of the owners (the shareholders). Relations among businesses are coordinated by contracts that may prove to be unfavorable if not constructed properly.

The modern corporation raises a fundamental question: How to run a company in which there is a separation of ownership from management. There is general agreement that companies should serve the interests of the owners. When professional managers run the show, contracts are complex, and information is scarce, devising an organization that actually serves the interests of the owners is not easy.

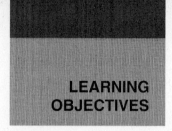

After studying this chapter, you will be able to:

- Define the goals of business firms.
- Understand the advantages and disadvantages of corporations, partnerships, and individual proprietorships.
- Know how information costs affect the contracts between parties to a business contract.
- Understand how opportunistic behavior affects business contracts.
- Understand the role of intermediaries as information specialists.

BUSINESS FIRMS AND THEIR GOALS

Business firms can take on a variety of legal forms, and they operate in different competitive conditions when selling their outputs and buying their inputs. Business firms have an owner or owners, who stand to receive the firm's profits. They are run by managers, who can be either the firm's owners or a hired management staff. The firm's managers direct the factors of production controlled by the firm to carry out tasks. The fourth factor of production (after labor, land, and capital), the **entrepreneur**, motivates the firm to discover profit-making opportunities.

> An **entrepreneur** organizes business firms to take advantage of profit opportunities. The entrepreneur evaluates risks, introduces innovations, and foresees new markets. The entrepreneur benefits from the firm's success and suffers the consequences of the firm's failure.

The business firm has external and internal dealings. On the outside, it deals with other firms in markets. It buys materials and services from other businesses and it sells its products to other businesses. Its transactions with other firms are coordinated by markets. General Motors buys its steel and plastics from other manufacturing firms, and it sells its automobiles to GM dealers. Resources are also allocated *within* the business firm by managerial coordination. Business firms own some factors of production (like plant and equipment). They also have contractual relationships with factors of production. The firm has labor contracts with its employees. It has contractual leases with the owners of buildings and land. The firm's manager has the authority to direct such factors of production to carry out specified tasks. The managers of GM can assign tasks to GM workers. The management of GM can use the plant and equipment owned by GM as it sees fit. Such managerial coordination of factors of production takes place without the use of markets.

Production is carried out by business firms whose goal is profit maximization.

The chapter on demand and utility emphasized that consumers want to spend their limited income to obtain maximum utility. Business firms have a primary goal: **profit maximization**.

> **Profit maximization** is the search by firms for the product quality, output, and price that give the firm the highest possible profits.

The search for profits is a dominating force in business life. The owners of the business firm are compensated with the profits that the firm earns. The value of the

GALLERY OF ECONOMISTS

Adolf A. Berle (1895–1971)

Adolf A. Berle conducted pioneering studies of the separation of ownership and management in modern corporations. Prior to Berle's studies, economists thought of business firms as being managed by independent entrepreneurs who served both as the firm's owners and managers. Conflicting objectives between the owners and the managers would be impossible because they were one and the same. Berle's contribution was to show that management was separated from ownership in modern corporations. This being so, professional managers were in a position to manage the corporation in their own interests and not in the interest of stockholders.

Berle graduated from Harvard College, served in Army Intelligence during World War I, and was a member of the American delegation to the Paris Peace Conference. After joining the Columbia faculty, Berle became a member of Franklin Roosevelt's famous Brain Trust and was a close advisor to the President. Berle's most famous work (written with Gardner Means) was *The Corporation and Private Property*, published in 1932.

In recent years, Berle's contributions have gained new attention. Modern economics has become more interested in potential conflicts between principals (the shareholders of a corporation) and agents (the management of a corporation). Many of Berle's predictions concerning the behavior of corporation management have been borne out by modern theory and experience.

firm ultimately depends on its profits. The firm that earns no profits will have no value in the long run. Firms that do not maximize profits may be forced out of business by competitors who offer higher quality products produced at lower cost. They can be taken over by someone else who knows how to earn a higher profit.

FORMS OF BUSINESS ORGANIZATION

Businesses are organized as sole proprietorships or as corporations. Each form has its advantages and disadvantages.

Business enterprises are organized as *sole proprietorships, partnerships,* and *corporations.* Which form a business enterprise takes determines who makes business decisions, how capital is raised, who bears the risk of business failures, and how profits are taxed. (See Exhibit 1 for a profile of American business.)

Sole Proprietorships

The **sole proprietorship** is the least complex form of business enterprise.

> The **sole proprietorship** is owned by one individual who makes all the business decisions, receives the profits that the business earns, and bears the financial responsibility for losses.

The individual who has accumulated or borrowed funds can set up a sole proprietorship. No legal work is required, although the individual proprietor will often seek legal and accounting advice. Once in business, the proprietor is responsible for all business decisions—how many employees to hire, what products to produce, how to market these products. Other than being required to

EXHIBIT 1   A Profile of American Business

a. Proprietorships, Partnerships, and Corporations, 1991

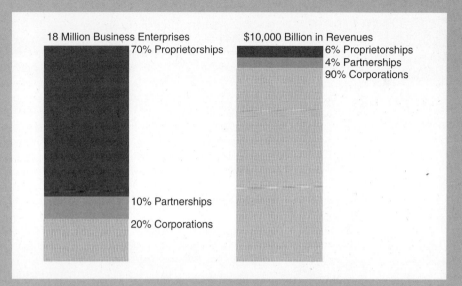

18 Million Business Enterprises
70% Proprietorships
10% Partnerships
20% Corporations

$10,000 Billion in Revenues
6% Proprietorships
4% Partnerships
90% Corporations

SOURCE: *Statistical Abstract of the United States.* Updated by authors.

**b. Proprietorships, Partnerships, and Corporations,
by Industry, 1991**

Industry	Number of Firms (thousands)			Business Revenues (billions of dollars)		
	Nonfarm Proprietorships	Partnerships	Corporations	Nonfarm Proprietorships	Partnerships	Corporations
Mining	168	65	45	19	29	315
Construction	1,467	77	339	80	30	446
Manufacturing	304	27	312	17	24	3,873
Transportation, public utilities	551	21	138	37	11	995
Wholesale and retail trade Wholesale Retail	3,032	238	1,010	322	114	3,239
Finance, insurance, real estate	1,172	843	556	40	88	1,559
Services	5,211	324	986	177	108	582

SOURCE: *Statistical Abstract of the United States.* Updated by authors.

observe the law and honor legal contracts, the owner is free to make wise or foolish decisions.

For the sole proprietorships, decision-making authority is clear-cut: it resides with the owner. The individual proprietor receives profits that the business earns, and this income will be taxed only once. (As we shall show, this is not true of the corporation, whose income is often taxed twice.)

The main disadvantage of the sole proprietorship is that the owner has *unlimited liability* (responsibility) for the debts of the company. The owner enjoys

EXHIBIT 1 A Profile of American Business *(Continued)*

c. Business Failures in the United States, 1970–1991

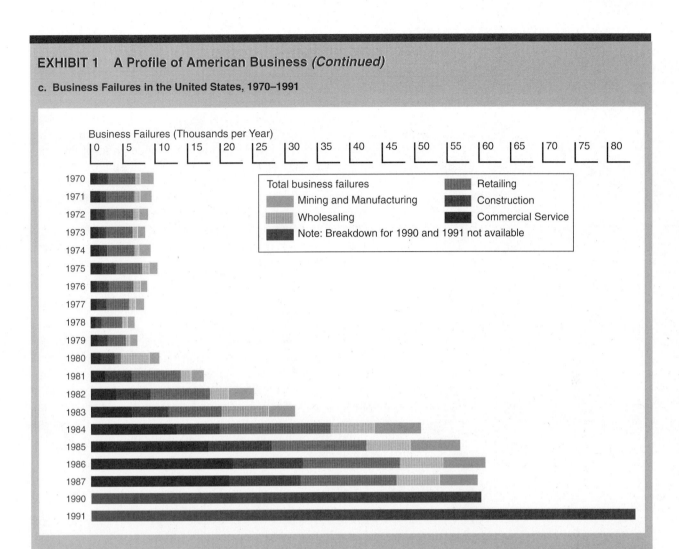

SOURCE: *Survey of Current Business;* Dun and Bradstreet Corp., Monthly Failure Report.

Panel (a) shows that although the proprietorship dominates in terms of numbers, the corporation produces 90 percent of output. Panel (b) shows that partnerships and proprietorships are important in services and construction. Panel (c) shows the rising rate of business failures in the United States.

the profit of the business if it is successful, but if the business suffers a loss, the owner is personally liable. If the company borrows money, purchases materials, and runs up other bills that it cannot cover, the owner must personally cover the losses. Sole proprietorships have a *limited ability to raise financial capital.* The owner can raise financial capital by reinvesting profits or borrowing. Lending money to a sole proprietorship can be risky, because so much depends upon the owner. As a consequence, sole proprietorships cannot raise as much financial capital as other business forms.

Partnerships

A **partnership** is much like an individual proprietorship but with more than one owner.

> A **partnership** is owned by two or more people (called partners) who make all the business decisions, share the profits of the business, and bear the financial responsibility for any losses.

Like the individual proprietorship, partnerships are easy to establish. Most partnerships are based on an agreement that spells out the ownership shares and duties of each partner. The partners may contribute different amounts of financial capital to the partnership; there may be an agreement on the division of responsibility for running the business; partners may own different shares of the business. One partner may make all the business decisions, while the other partner (a "silent partner") may only provide financial capital. A partnership can be a corner gas station or a nationally known law firm or brokerage house.

Partnerships are also easy to set up. The company profits go to the partners and are taxed only once. Partnerships offer a greater opportunity to specialize and divide managerial responsibility: the better salesperson will be in charge of the sales department, the talented mechanical engineer will be in charge of production. Partnerships can raise more financial capital than a sole proprietorship because the partners can pool their borrowing power.

The main disadvantage of partnerships is the unlimited liability of the partners. A business debt incurred by one is the responsibility of all partners. Each partner stands to lose money if the company is a commercial failure. "Two heads are better than one" *if* the two heads agree. But if partners disagree, decision-making can become quite complicated. There is no longer one single person who is in charge. Partnerships can be immobilized when partners disagree on fundamental policy. Partnerships become more complicated as the number of partners grows.

Corporations

The **corporation** was created to overcome the disadvantages of proprietorships and partnerships.

> A **corporation** is a business enterprise that is owned by its stockholders. The corporation has the legal status to act as a single person. The stockholders elect a board of directors that appoints the management of the corporation. Management is charged with the actual operation of the corporation.

A *corporate charter* is required to set up a corporation. The laws of each state are different, but, typically, for a fee, corporations can be established (incorporated) and can become legal "persons" subject to the laws of that state. Officers of the corporation can act in the name of the corporation without being personally liable for its debts. If corporate officers commit criminal acts, however, they can be prosecuted as individuals.

The corporation is owned by individuals (stockholders) who have purchased shares of *stock* in the corporation. A stockholder's share of ownership of the corporation equals the number of shares owned by that individual divided by the total number of shares outstanding. Owners of shares of stock have the right to vote on corporate matters (like electing the board of directors). The management of the corporation is required by law to issue periodic reports to its shareholders describing the corporation's financial and business activities. The profits of the corporation can either be reinvested or distributed to shareholders as dividends.

Corporations often have thousands or millions of shares outstanding, and these shares are typically owned by a large number of stockholders. Billionaire H. Ross Perot's 11 million shares of General Motors stock made him GM's largest shareholder (with 2 percent of GM stock) before he sold his shares in early 1987. There are usually too many shareholders to involve them in decision-making. For this reason, there is usually a *separation of ownership and management*. The board of directors appoints a management team that makes decisions for the corporation. The board of directors can fire the management team if it sees fit.

The main advantage of the corporation is *limited liability*. The owners of the corporation (the stockholders) are not personally liable for the debts of the corporation. The corporation's creditors can lay claim to the assets of the corporation (its bank accounts, equipment, supplies, and real-estate holdings), but they cannot file claims against the stockholders. The worst thing that can happen to stockholders is that the value of their stock will decline (in extreme circumstances, it can become worthless).

Corporations have more options than other business forms to raise financial capital. Proprietorships and partnerships can only raise financial capital outside the firm by borrowing from lending institutions. Corporations, on the other hand, can sell bonds and sell new shares of stock. Limited liability makes it easier to sell new shares (called issuing stock) because buyers of the new stock are not personally liable for the debts of the corporation. Lenders (such as buyers of corporate bonds) are more willing to make long-term loans to corporations because corporations can remain in business for a long time. (How corporations raise capital is described in more detail in the appendix to this chapter.) Many major U.S. corporations are more than a century old. Few corporations have the same owners and officers that they had when the corporation was founded.

Separating ownership and management allows the corporation to recruit a professional management team and to bring in new management. The owners of businesses (individuals with money to invest) do not always make the best managers.

The profits (earnings) of the corporation can either be distributed to shareholders as dividends or reinvested (plowed back) into the corporation. The profits of the corporation are subject to a federal income tax. In many states, corporations must also pay a state income tax. If the corporation chooses to plow back all profits into the company, corporate profits will be taxed only once, but if it distributes some of its profits to shareholders in the form of dividends, shareholders must pay income taxes on these dividends. Corporate profits can, therefore, be taxed twice, first by the corporate income tax and second by the personal income tax on dividends.

Corporations can have thousands or even millions of different owners (stockholders). It is difficult to get the owners to agree (or even assemble), even when important issues are at stake. Power struggles among shareholder factions can paralyze decision making. It is difficult to mobilize widely dispersed stockholders to get rid of incompetent management. Shareholders want the best return from their shares of stock; however, the professional management team may be more interested in preserving their jobs or in maximizing their personal income or perquisites than in profit maximization. (See Example 1.)

Limited liability and an ability to raise large sums of capital have made the corporation the dominant form of business organization. Corporations can be huge, employing hundreds of thousands of people both at home and in foreign branches. The largest U.S. corporations are profiled in Exhibit 2.

The three different forms of business organizations have their advantages and disadvantages. The fact that the major portion of the U.S. economy's output is produced by corporations attests to the advantages of the corporation (See Exhibit 3 for a summary of advantages and disadvantages of the different business forms.)

The corporation offers limited liability to its owners. Corporations have more options in raising financial capital.

EXAMPLE 1

Unlimited Liability and Lloyds of London

Lloyds of London, the centuries-old insurance syndicate headquartered in London, England, made its reputation for its willingness to insure virtually anything. Lloyds insured actresses's legs, renowned jewels, and hazardous shipments. Lloyds is one of the last great businesses that operates on the basis of unlimited liability. Various insurance packages are underwritten by "Names"—individual investors who must make good on claims, even if they must draw on all their personal assets to do so.

The years 1991 and 1992 were disastrous for the insurance industry. The Gulf War, numerous national disasters and airline crashes, and product liability claims caused billions of dollars of losses for Lloyds of London insurance syndicates. Lloyds of London Names therefore had to sell virtually all their personal assets to cover these losses. One Name—a former heavyweight boxing champion—had to sell his championship belts. Other Names had to sell their noble titles and their estates.

As a consequence of these losses, Lloyds of London is no longer willing to insure many high risk activities. Policies that were previously sold by Lloyds of London are no longer available. Hence, Lloyds of London has decided to restructure its way of doing business so that its investors may underwrite insurance with limited liability. The world's last major example of unlimited liability is in the process of disappearing.

PRINCIPALS AND AGENTS

Most economic dealings are governed by contracts. In some cases, these contracts are not written but parties to the contract implicitly understand its terms. Examples of contracts are employment contracts negotiated by unions, contracts for the delivery of natural gas at specified prices, or leasing contracts for office buildings.

Sole proprietorships, partnerships, and corporations enter into business contracts in which they act either as a **principal** or as an **agent**.

> A **principal** engages an agent to act subject to the principal's control and instruction.

> An **agent** is a party that acts for, on behalf of, or as a representative of a principal.

Firm A is a principal when it signs a contract with an employee (the agent) that calls for the employee to perform specific services at a specified wage for Firm A. The Boeing Corporation acts as a principal when it contracts with Rolls Royce (the agent) to supply jet engines for its aircraft. Chrysler Corporation acted as a principal when it hired Lee Iacocca (the agent) to serve as its chief executive officer.

Contracts and Information Costs

Business firms use contracts to specify the relationship between the principal and the agent. A typical contract requires the agent to perform services for the principal (to deliver goods, to build a house, to perform a certain type of work). Some

EXHIBIT 2 The Fifty Largest U.S. Industrial Corporations, Ranked by Sales

Rank 1987	Rank 1986	Company	Sales (millions of dollars)
1	1	GENERAL MOTORS Detroit	101,781.9
2	2	EXXON New York	76,416.0*
3	3	FORD MOTOR Dearborn, Mich.	71,643.4
4	4	INTERNATIONAL BUSINESS MACHINES Armonk, N.Y.	54,217.0
5	5	MOBIL New York	51,223.0*
6	6	GENERAL ELECTRIC Fairfield, Conn.	39,315.0*
7	8	TEXACO White Plains, N.Y.	34,372.0*
8	7	AMERICAN TEL. & TEL. New York	33,598.0
9	9	E.I. DU PONT DE NEMOURS Wilmington, Del.	30,468.0
10	11	CHRYSLER Highland Park, Mich.[1]	26,257.7
11	10	CHEVRON San Francisco	26,015.0*
12	12	PHILIP MORRIS New York	22,279.0*
13	15	SHELL OIL Houston[2]	20,852.0*
14	13	AMOCO Chicago	20,174.0*
15	17	UNITED TECHNOLOGIES Hartford	17,170.2
16	19	OCCIDENTAL PETROLEUM Los Angeles	17,096.0
17	18	PROCTER & GAMBLE Cincinnati[3]	17,000.0
18	20	ATLANTIC RICHFIELD Los Angeles	16,281.4
19	14	RJR NABISCO Atlanta	15,868.0
20	16	BOEING Seattle	15,355.0
21	21	TENNECO Houston	15,075.0
22	35	BP AMERICA Cleveland[4]	14,611.0*
23	22	USX Pittsburgh	13,898.0*
24	27	DOW CHEMICAL Midland, Mich.	13,377.0
25	26	EASTMAN KODAK Rochester, N.Y.	13,305.0
26	23	MCDONNELL DOUGLAS St. Louis	13,146.1
27	24	ROCKWELL INTERNATIONAL Pittsburgh[5]	12,123.4
28	25	ALLIED-SIGNAL Morristown, N.J.	11,597.0
29	34	PEPSICO Purchase, N.Y.	11,500.2
30	30	LOCKHEED Calabasas, Calif.	11,370.0
31	37	KRAFT Glenview, Ill.	11,010.5*
32	31	PHILLIPS PETROLEUM Bartlesville, Okla.	10,721.0
33	28	WESTINGHOUSE ELECTRIC Pittsburgh	10,679.0
34	32	XEROX Stamford, Conn.[6]	10,320.0
35	29	GOODYEAR TIRE & RUBBER Akron, Ohio	10,123.2
36	46	UNISYS Blue Bell, Pa.	9,712.9
37	39	MINNESOTA MINING & MANUFACTURING St. Paul	9,429.0
38	44	DIGITAL EQUIPMENT Maynard, Mass.[3]	9,389.4
39	36	GENERAL DYNAMICS St. Louis	9,344.0
40	40	SARA LEE Chicago[3]	9,154.6
41	59	CONAGRA Omaha[7,8]	9,001.6
42	•	BEATRICE Chicago[2]	8,926.0[10]
43	33	SUN Radnor, Pa.	8,691.0
44	50	GEORGIA-PACIFIC Atlanta	8,603.0
45	41	ITT New York[6]	8,551.0
46	45	UNOCAL Los Angeles	8,466.0*
47	43	ANHEUSER-BUSCH St. Louis	8,258.4*
48	47	CATERPILLAR Peoria, Ill.	8,180.0
49	51	HEWLETT-PACKARD Palo Alto, Calif.[11]	8,090.0
50	53	JOHNSON & JOHNSON New Brunswick, N.J.	8,012.0

Listed are the 50 largest U.S. industrial corporations ranked by business sales. The annual sales of certain large U.S. industrial corporations—like General Motors and Exxon—exceed the annual output of many industrial economies. The annual sales of General Motors, for example, equal the annual production of Belgium. The annual sales of the six largest U.S. industrial corporations exceed the annual production of the United Kingdom—a fact that underscores the importance of big business in the U.S. economy.

SOURCE: *Fortune*, April 28, 1988; Updated from *Fortune*, April 1993.

EXHIBIT 3   Advantages and Disadvantages of Different Forms of Business Organization

Type of Firm	Advantages	Disadvantages
Individual Proprietorships	1. Business is simple to set up. 2. Decision making is clear-cut; the owner makes the decisions. 3. Earnings are taxed only once as personal income.	1. The owner has unlimited liability; the owner's personal wealth is at risk. 2. The company has a limited ability to raise financial capital. 3. Business dies with owner.
Partnership	1. Business is relatively easy to set up. 2. More management skills are available; two heads are better than one. 3. Earnings are taxed only once as the personal income of the partners.	1. There is unlimited liability for the partners. 2. Decision-making can be complicated. 3. The company has a limited ability to raise capital. 4. Partnerships can be unstable.
Corporation	1. There is limited liability for owners. 2. Company is able to raise large sums of capital through issuing bonds and stock. 3. Company has an unlimited life span. 4. Company is able to recruit professional management and to change bad management.	1. Corporate income is taxed twice; once as corporate profits, then as personal income (dividends). 2. There are greater possibilities for management disagreements. 3. There is the possibility of conflicting goals between the owners of the corporation (the *principals*) and management (the *agents*).

contracts set the rules for principal/agent relationships within the firm. An employment contract, for example, spells out the duties and responsibilities of the employee (the agent). Other contracts set rules for principal/agent relationships among firms. A delivery contract, for example, calls upon the supplier of a good (the agent) to provide the principal with specified goods at specified prices.

Information is costly because resources are required to gather and process information.

Business firms operate with imperfect information. They are unable to specify contracts with agents containing every last detail, and they are unable to monitor perfectly the agent's performance. Business firms operate with imperfect information *because information is costly*.

Opportunistic Behavior

Just as firms must economize on the use of land, labor, and capital inputs used to produce output, so must they economize on the resources devoted to gathering and processing information. As a consequence of imperfect information, firms enter into contracts that permit agents to engage in **opportunistic behavior**.

> **Opportunistic behavior** occurs when the agent is able to formally fulfill a contract while engaging in behavior that is not in the interests of the principal.

Costly information requires that principals write contracts with agents that specify only the agent's general obligations. Employment contracts, for example, specify that the employee work a specified number of hours. The contract does

EXAMPLE 2

Carl Icahn, Texaco, and the Principal/Agent Problem

As we have seen in this chapter, corporate management's goals may differ from shareholders' goals. At times, management may act in its own interest rather than in the interest of the shareholders. This conflict is called the principal/agent problem.

Two giant oil concerns—Texaco and Pennzoil—became involved in a massive legal battle over Texaco's acquisition of Getty Oil. Texas courts ruled that Texaco had illegally acquired Getty Oil at the expense of Pennzoil and ordered Texaco to pay $10 billion in damages to Pennzoil. The possibility that Texaco would have to pay such a huge settlement pushed down Texaco's share prices, but the uncertainty about whether Pennzoil would ever collect failed to raise Pennzoil's share price. Here was a situation in which shareholders of both Texaco and Pennzoil would benefit from a settlement.

The noted corporate raider, Carl Icahn, owned significant shares of both Pennzoil and Texaco at the time. (Icahn was Texaco's largest single shareholder). As a major shareholder, Icahn stood to gain from a settlement, and he pressured Texaco's officers to settle with Pennzoil for $3 billion in cash. In an interview, Icahn told of a conversation with Texaco's president, Jim Kinnear, concerning the need to settle the suit and get on with Texaco's business.

> Icahn asked Kinnear, "What happens if you can't make a deal?" And he said, "Well I can just go fishing." And I said, "What happens if there's no company when you get back?" And he said, "Well I'll still have my fishing pole." That's sort of amazing, because Kinnear might have his fishing pole, but what would all the shareholders have? The other shareholders wouldn't even have a fish.

SOURCE: "Icahn: 'We're Fed Up': The Raider Talks About His Stake in Texaco," *Newsweek*, January 4, 1988, p. 36.

not specify the quality of work that must be performed. Contracts for the delivery of spare parts cannot specify to the last detail the exact qualities and specifications of the spare parts. Even if such employment or delivery contracts specified the obligations of the agent to the last detail, the principal would find it too costly to monitor every last detail of contract fulfillment. (See Example 2.)

Costly information gives agents the opportunity to fulfill the general terms of the contract, while engaging in opportunistic behavior. Workers can work the specified number of hours but work carelessly and do low-quality work. Spare-parts suppliers can substitute cheaper materials.

By devoting more resources to monitoring and by devising incentive systems, business firms can limit opportunistic behavior. To prevent sales personnel from slacking off, business firms can offer employees bonuses that depend on increased sales. Corporations can offer executives incentives to act in the best interests of the shareholders. Business firms can deny repeat business to suppliers who have behaved opportunistically. The real world supplies many examples of incentive schemes that successfully limit opportunistic behavior.

Because information is costly, agents can engage in opportunistic behavior.

In some cases, it is not possible to set up monitoring systems or to devise incentive schemes that effectively control opportunistic behavior. Military contracting appears to be one example. Assembly-line production appears to be another example. It is especially hard to control opportunistic behavior when agents are able to alter their behavior after entering into a contract. (See Example 3.)

EXAMPLE 3

Moral Hazard and Contracts

Business firms find it particularly difficult to devise contracts when agents have an opportunity to change their behavior after the contract is signed. This difficulty is called the *moral-hazard problem.*

The basic consequence of the moral-hazard problem is that firms can offer only those contracts that will not be flagrantly abused by their agents. The kinds of contracts offered must be limited to those that will minimize the moral-hazard problem. In some instances, the moral-hazard problem is so severe that certain contracts cannot be written at all, at least not by private profit-maximizing companies.

A moral-hazard problem would be present if a manufacturing firm agrees to buy highly specialized machine tools to produce specialized component parts for a diesel engine manufacturer. It would be difficult to devise a contract that would protect the component-parts manufacturer against abuse by the diesel manufacturer, who would be the firm's only potential customer. The diesel manufacturer could give every assurance that it would deal fairly with the component-parts manufacturer, but there is no guarantee that the diesel manufacturer would not alter its behavior after the contract was signed. A moral-hazard problem would also be present if a pump manufacturer were to enter into contracts with industrial users to replace without charge any pump that fails within a five-year period. The industrial user might fail to service the pump properly or even sabotage the pump to obtain a new one free of charge.

Contracting parties who stand to suffer will adopt measures to prevent opportunistic behavior. The pump manufacturer's guarantee may put the burden of proof on the pump user to demonstrate that the pump broke under normal usage and with proper maintenance. Or the manufacturer may insist on a stiff installation fee for replacement pumps. The component-part manufacturer would insist upon a long-term contract that guaranteed a certain level of purchases by the diesel manufacturer at specified prices before acquiring the specialized tools.

INTERMEDIARIES AND THE INFORMATION BUSINESS

Any business transaction or contract requires two parties. In business contracts, there must be a principal and an agent. In business transactions there must be a buyer and a seller. In order for transactions to take place and for contracts to be signed, the parties must be aware of each other's existence. They must have information concerning the fact that the other party is a potential participant in a business deal. The fact that information is costly applies not only to the monitoring of agents by principals but also to the information required to consummate business deals.

The Role of Intermediaries

Most business firms specialize in producing goods or services. Business firms must find buyers for their goods, and they must find factors of production and materials. Business firms require information in order to survive.

While most firms produce and sell goods and services, some produce "information" that enables other firms to conduct their transactions. Such firms

How Can Boards Reclaim the Company for Its Owners?

The 1980s and early 1990s were characterized as the "era of greed." Prominent Wall Street bankers and brokers were sent to jail. The terms "greenmail" and "poison pills" were originated to describe the selfish behavior of corporation presidents who placed their own interests above the company. (See Example 2.) The chief executive officer of the corporation was often the chairman of the board of directors, a situation akin to students grading their own papers. A much-publicized trip to U.S. executives to Japan in 1992 succeeded in focusing attention on their astronomical salaries despite poor operating performance.

Public policy can be used to prevent corporate abuse of the interests of shareholders, and in the early 1990s, changes were made in the governance of corporations. The basic approach has been to create legal conditions that encourage and even force the board of directors to act in the interests of the shareholders. Insofar as many boards of directors are dominated by professional management, public policy has aimed at making the outside directors of the board more active and responsive.

In 1989, in the wake of the savings-and-loan scandals, federal regulators were given the power to require boards of directors to pick up more of the costs of federal bailouts. In June 1992, the Securities and Exchange Commission enacted reforms that gave shareholders greater power to force change in poorly performing companies. Specifically, corporations had to provide shareholders with details of executive pay and how it related to the company's stock performance.

The most highly publicized consequence of these reforms was the forced resignation of General Motors' chairman and chief executive officer in October 1992. General Motors, over the years, had acquired a reputation of management waste, complacency, and lack of innovation. GM's share of the automobile market had fallen, and management had made a number of disastrous errors in the design and implementation of new models. Said one specialist: "GM's been the type of . . . nonperforming company whose board should have stepped in long before this."

GM had 11 outside directors drawn either from high-level positions in other industries or from academe. These outside directors hired their own counsel, appointed an outside director to head its executive committee, and finally forced the resignation of GM's chief executive officer. As a consequence of this action, declared one specialist, "CEOs are starting to learn that it's not their company, it's not their board, and directors are starting to say their accountability is to the shareholders."

SOURCE: "The High Energy Board Room," *New York Times*, October 28, 1992, C1.

Firms run by intermediaries specialize in information concerning exchange opportunities.

are run by **intermediaries**, or "middlemen," who specialize in information concerning exchange opportunities between buyers and sellers.

> **Intermediaries** specialize in information either to bring together two parties to a transaction or to buy in order to sell again.

Real-estate brokers, grocery stories, department stores, used-car dealers, auctioneers, stockbrokers, and travel agents are all intermediaries. All these professions "mediate" or stand between ultimate buyers and sellers in return for a fee.

Why are firms willing to pay for information from information specialists? Suppose that a company is willing to sell its multimillion-dollar corporate jet for no less than $20 million and that somewhere a potential buyer is willing to pay at most $25 million for such an airplane. Someone with information about this exchange opportunity could act as an intermediary and bring the two together. It would be possible for the seller to get $20 million, for the buyer to pay $25 million, and for the intermediary to charge as much as $5 million for the service of bringing the two together. The intermediary could collect the difference either in the form of a fee or buy the jet for $20 million and then resell it for $25 million. In both cases, the intermediary is receiving a fee for information.

The Value of Intermediaries

Transactions arranged by intermediaries take place all the time. Home buyers and sellers are brought together by realtors who charge a fee. Stock-market brokers bring together buyers and sellers of a particular stock. Auction houses bring together sellers of rare works of art and potential buyers and charge a fee for this service.

Do intermediaries "earn" their fees? Parties to transactions can in most situations avoid paying the intermediary fee. Homemakers could drive to farmers' markets and to wholesale distributors of meats and dairy products. The seller of the corporate jet could try to find a buyer without using an intermediary. The intermediary, by specializing in bringing together buyers and sellers, is able to provide the service at a lower cost than if the individuals involved performed the service themselves. As long as people voluntarily pay for the services of intermediaries, the intermediary is supplying information at a lower cost than could the user of information services.

We have seen that business organization is the first step in the supply side of product markets. The next chapter examines the role of production costs in determining product supply. The appendix to this chapter discusses financial markets for corporate stocks and bonds and how corporations raise financial capital by selling bonds and issuing stock.

Chapter Summary

The most important points to learn from this chapter are: Corporations are the dominant form of business organization because of limited liability. The owners of corporations are not personally liable for the corporation's debts. Limited liability allows the corporation to raise more financial capital and to deal better with uncertainty.

1. Business firms allocate the land, labor, and capital resources they control by managerial coordination. Business firms work both through market allocation in their dealings with other firms and consumers and through managerial allocation.

2. The goal of business firms is the maximization of profits.

3. The three forms of business organization are the *sole proprietorship* (a business owned by one individual), the *partnership* (a business owned by two or more partners who share in making business decisions), and the *corporation* (a business enterprise owned by stockholders).

4. Business enterprises operate in a world of imperfect information. They enter into contractual relationships with the factors of production and with other business firms.

A principal/agent problem exists when agents are able to act opportunistically contrary to the interests of the principal. Principals must devise monitoring and incentives schemes to limit opportunistic behavior.

5. Information is costly. Some firms therefore specialize in information. Whenever individuals and firms voluntarily purchase information from intermediaries, the intermediary is supplying the information at lower cost than they themselves would have incurred.

Policy Focus: **The separation of ownership and management in the corporation requires policy measures to ensure that corporations are run in the interests of their owners, the shareholders.**

Key Terms

entrepreneur (p. 134)
profit maximization (p. 134)
sole proprietorship (p. 135)
partnership (p. 137)
corporation (p. 138)

principal (p. 140)
agent (p. 140)
opportunistic behavior (p. 142)
intermediaries (p. 145)

Questions and Problems

1. What are some of the reasons business firms maximize profits?

2. What are some disadvantages of the sole proprietorship?

3. Sole proprietorships are, on average, smaller than partnerships and partnerships are smaller, on average, than corporations. Use the legal features of business organizations to explain why.

4. In the real world, limited partnerships exist in which the liability of each partner for the debts of the company is limited. Explain why such partnerships may be more attractive than the traditional form of partnership.

5. Explain why corporations can issue bonds that mature in the next century while partnerships and proprietorships can borrow for only short periods of time.

6. Indicate which of the following is an advantage of the corporate form of business:

   a. conflicts of interest between stockholders and management.
   b. continuity of management.
   c. double taxation of corporation income.
   d. limited liability.

7. Explain what is meant by limited liability.

8. What prevents principals and agents from always being in complete agreement?

9. For the following transactions, explain which party is the principal and which is the agent and why:

   a. Smith hires a remodeling company to add a room to her house.
   b. A university buys a computer from IBM.
   c. An engineer signs a contract with Aramco to work for a year in Saudi Arabia.

10. What is the information in which intermediaries specialize?

Doing Economics

The association between a college or university and its students has a rich pattern of principal-agent relationships and information problems. Potential students have imperfect information about the quality of the education that they can obtain from alternative schools. How did you go about gathering quality information on colleges you considered? What measurable pieces of information did you use to signal quality? Do intermediaries play an important role in this market? How do you monitor quality as you progress through your studies? Is there a moral-hazard problem?

Another information problem in schools relates to grading. Faculty must ensure that each student has achieved a sufficient level of understanding to be certified as passing the course. Explain why this problem is one of moral hazard. How do faculty resolve this problem? Why is the problem different in, say, a math class versus a literature class? How do the means used by instructors reflect these differences?

Yet another problem relates to how the school monitors the behavior of its faculty. How does the school get information on faculty performance? (Ask one of your instructors if you do not know.) How is this information used to provide incentives for good performance? How does the tenure system affect these incentives?

Corporate Finance and Financial Markets

A P P E N D I X 7

A P P E N D I X   F O C U S   The corporation has a number of advantages over proprietorships and partnerships. One advantage is its greater ability to raise capital in financial markets. This appendix explains how corporations raise funds by selling bonds and by issuing stock. Interest rates and bond prices are determined in bond markets. The appendix discusses bond prices and the inverse relationship between interest rates and bond prices. Stock prices are determined in stock markets. The appendix shows that stock prices depend on the present and future earnings of the company. It discusses the efficient stock market hypothesis and explains how stock markets influence the allocation of resources.

After studying this appendix, you will be able to:

■ Calculate the present value of an asset.

■ Explain how the prices of bonds are established and the relationship between interest rates and bond prices.

■ Understand why the stock price reflects the present value of future earnings and why the price/earnings ratio is a barometer of future earnings.

■ Know the meaning of a stock price index.

■ Comprehend the rational stock market hypothesis.

■ Discuss how stock markets serve as guides to resource allocation.

HOW CORPORATIONS RAISE CAPITAL

Limited liability and continuity give corporations an edge in raising financial capital. Corporations have options for raising capital that are not available to sole proprietorships or to partnerships. Corporations, like proprietorships and partnerships, can borrow money from banks and from other lending institutions, and they can plow profits back into the business. In addition to these traditional forms of raising capital, corporations can:

1. sell bonds, or
2. issue (sell) new shares of stock.

Corporations raise capital by selling bonds and issuing new shares of stock.

Corporations sell **bonds** through intermediaries to individuals and businesses that have accumulated savings.

> Corporate **bonds** are IOUs that obligate the corporation to pay a fixed sum of money (the principal) at maturity and a fixed sum of money annually (the *interest* or *coupon*) until the maturity date.

Like other things, bonds have a price. The price of a bond is the sum people pay to acquire the bond. Bond prices and interest rates are intimately linked because the interest payments are paid over a period of time. To understand the linkage between bond prices and interest rates, one must first understand present value.

Present Value

Bonds are obligations to make payments at specific dates over a specified period of time. The payments of interest and principal are spread out over time. Some money will be received in the near future; other money may be received in the distant future. When dealing with money payments that are spread out over time, one must keep in mind a fundamental principle: A dollar today is worth more than a dollar tomorrow because it can earn interest.

A dollar today is worth more than a dollar tomorrow because it can earn interest.

Consider the following example in which 10 percent is the prevailing annual rate of interest paid throughout the economy. When $100 is deposited in a savings account, $10 interest will be earned at the end of one year. At 10 percent interest,

$100 today will be equal to $110 a year from now. If the interest rate had been 20 percent, $100 today would be equal to $120 a year from now.

Look at the process in reverse. If a bank were to offer to pay $110 one year from now, what would people be willing to pay today for this offer? At 10 percent interest, the most people would be willing to pay now in order to receive $110 in one year is $100. Thus, the **present value (PV)** of a future payment of $110 is $100 at 10 percent interest.

> The **present value (PV)** of money to be received in the future is the most anyone would pay today in order to receive the money in the future; alternatively, the present value of a future sum of money is the amount that must be invested today to generate that future sum of money.

The price of an IOU such as a bond that promises to make specified payments at specified future dates is the present value of those payments. We just showed that no one would pay more than the present value, and no one could buy for less than the present value. At 10 percent interest, $110 a year from now is worth $100. If I offer $105, no one would sell.

Formulas explain how to calculate present values. The longer the time period over which payments are made, the more complicated the formula. The present value (PV) of each dollar to be paid in one year at the interest rate i (i stands for the rate of interest in decimals) is:

$$PV = \frac{\$1}{1 + i}.$$

If the interest rate is 10 percent, then $i = 0.10$ and $1 + i = 1.10$. The PV of each dollar equals $0.9091. If $10,000 is the sum to be paid in one year, the PV equals $9,091 ($10,000 times 0.9091). The price of an IOU of $10,000 to be paid in one year's time is $9,091 at a 10 percent interest rate.

The present-value formula becomes more complicated when the time span is greater than one year. At an annual interest rate of 10 percent, how much would someone be willing to pay now for an IOU that paid $121 two years from now? The answer follows the same reasoning as before. Consider how much money would have to be deposited today at a 10 percent interest rate to have $121 in two years? If the sum PV were deposited at interest rate i, it would be worth $PV \times (1 + i)$ one year from now. That sum would then earn a second year's interest and by the end of the second year would be worth $PV \times (1 + i) \times (1 + i)$, or $PV (1 + i)^2$. Setting the sum, $PV(1 + i)^2$, equal to $121 and dividing by $[(1 + i)^2]$ yields:

$$PV = \frac{\$121}{(1 + i)^2}.$$

At a rate of interest of 10 percent, the present value of $121 to be received two years from now is $100 (= $121/1.1^2). At 10 percent interest, the price of a $121 IOU to be paid in two years would be $100.

This result can be generalized. The present value of a sum to be received in three years is that sum divided by $(1 + i)^3$; the present value of a sum to be received in four years is that sum divided by $(1 + i)^4$; and so on. The present value (PV) of a dollar to be received in n years is

$$PV = \frac{1}{(1 + i)^n}.$$

The present value (PV) of a dollar to be received in n years is

$$PV = \frac{1}{(1 + i)^n}.$$

At a 10 percent interest rate, $100 received one year from now has a present value of $90.91; $100 to be received five years from now has a present value of only $62.27. The further out in the future the money is to be received, the lower is its present value.

Present-value formulas show that the present value of money to be received in the future falls as the interest rate rises. In the above example, the present value of $121 to be received two years from now is $100 at an interest rate of 10 percent ($121 ÷ $1.1^2 = 100). At an interest rate of 20 percent, the *PV* of $121 to be received two years from now falls to $84 ($121 ÷ $1.2^2 = 84). There is an inverse relation between present value and interest rates.

This principle is illustrated by an IOU that pays interest forever. Suppose someone has a bond that pays $100 per year *in perpetuity* (forever). What is this IOU worth (its market price) today? If the interest rate were 10 percent, a $1,000 deposit would earn $100 per year in interest. This $1,000 is the present value of the $100 perpetual interest stream. If the interest rate doubled to 20 percent, a $500 deposit would earn $100 a year in perpetuity. Hence, $500 would be the present value of the $100 perpetual income stream at a 20 percent rate of interest.

The formula for the present value (*PV*) of an asset that yields a perpetual income stream is:

$$PV = \frac{R}{i}$$

where R = the annual income and i = the rate of interest expressed in decimal form. At an interest rate of 10 percent, the present value of $100 a year in perpetuity is $100 ÷ 0.10$, or $1,000. (This formula is important in understanding stock prices, as explained later in this appendix.)

Bond Prices

Corporations acquire funds to finance business expansion by selling bonds. Once the bond is sold, the buyer can resell it, but such sales of second-hand bonds do not add directly to the corporation's financial capital. The interest and principal payments on corporate bonds represent a legal obligation for the corporation, just like any other debt it has. The purchaser of the bond has loaned the corporation money, and in return the corporation has promised the lender fixed interest payments until maturity and payment of the principal at the date of maturity. Interest and principal payments on corporate bonds have a claim on company earnings prior to dividends. The company has no choice but to make interest payments unless it is declared **bankrupt**.

A corporation can be declared **bankrupt** if it cannot pay its bills or its interest obligations.

Because purchasers of corporate bonds have prior claims on company earnings, bonds offer a relatively secure return. As long as the corporation does not become bankrupt, the bondholder will receive the promised annual interest payment (as well as the principal payment at the date of maturity).

Nevertheless, corporate bonds are not a riskless investment because bond prices fluctuate in the second-hand market. If the bond owner wishes to sell the bond before the date of maturity, the price received for the bond may well be less than the price paid for the bond.

As interest rates fall, bond prices rise and vice versa.

Bond prices, like the price of any IOU, are the present discounted value (PV) of the fixed interest payments and principal. But as demonstrated above, there is an inverse relationship between interest rates and present values. As interest rates rise, investors pay *less* for the bond's stream of interest payments. As interest rates fall, investors will pay *more* for the bond's stream of interest payments.

Stock Issues

Corporations can sell additional shares of **stock** as a second means of raising financial capital.

> A share of **stock** represents the ownership of 1/*n* percent of the corporation, where *n* is the number of shares outstanding. Owners of shares can vote on corporate matters and receive dividends proportional to their share holdings.

Suppose ZYX corporation has 100,000 shares of stock that are already owned by stockholders. These outstanding shares of stock can be bought and sold in markets for second-hand stock, called stock exchanges. Each share of stock currently sells for $10 on the second-hand market for stocks.

The corporation decides that it needs to raise $500,000 to build a new plant and arranges with an intermediary to sell 50,000 new shares of stock to potential buyers. The company will prepare a statement called a *prospectus* that describes the financial condition of the company and the proposed uses to which the raised funds will be put.

The amount of money potential buyers will be willing to pay for the 50,000 new shares depends upon their assessment of the impact of the proposed investment on ZYX corporation earnings. If investors expect the new plant to raise company earnings substantially, they will offer a higher price than if they expect the investment to have a small effect.

Experts believe that corporations will issue new stock only if they can avoid a decline in the price of the stock in the second-hand market. Let us suppose this is the case with ZYX corporation. The 50,000 new shares sell for a $10-per-share price, and ZYX corporation raises $500,000 through the stock issue.

The corporation now has 150,000 shares owned by stockholders rather than the previous 100,000. The owners of the new 50,000 shares are entitled to vote on corporate matters and to receive dividends. Unlike corporate bonds that legally obligate the corporation to pay fixed interest payments, the corporation is not obligated to pay dividends. The corporation pays dividends only if sufficient profits are left over after meeting interest and other obligations. When corporations experience hard times, dividends are frequently cut or even omitted.

Stock Markets

Stock prices (the prices of shares of stock of corporations) are determined by supply and demand in second-hand markets, called **stock exchanges**.

> A **stock exchange** is a market in which shares of stock of corporations are bought and sold and prices of shares of stock are determined.

There are many organized stock exchanges in the United States and in other countries, located in New York City, London, Denver, Frankfurt, Tokyo, Zurich, and Paris. In each stock exchange the shares of particular corporations are traded. The shares of French companies are traded in Paris, the shares of Japanese companies are traded in Tokyo, and so on. The world's largest stock exchanges are located on New York City's Wall Street: the New York Stock Exchange (NYSE) and the American Stock Exchange (ASE). The New York Stock Exchange lists about 50 billion shares of stock, and most days millions of shares worth hundreds of billions of dollars change hands. The shares of the largest American and multinational corporations are traded on the New York Stock Exchange, which provides a good example of how stock exchanges works.

Stock prices are determined by supply and demand in stock exchanges.

Stock Prices. Like any organized market, the NYSE brings together all buyers and sellers of a particular commodity. In this case, it brings together all buyers and sellers of shares of corporations like General Motors, Kodak, or IBM. The number of shares of IBM stock outstanding is fixed (unless IBM decides to issue new shares of stock), and the owners of these shares will be prepared to sell their shares at different prices. The supply curve of IBM shares on September 3, 1993, is shown as curve S in Exhibit 1. The higher is the price, the greater is the number of IBM shares current owners will be prepared to sell; the supply curve is positively sloped. On the demand side of the market are potential buyers of IBM stock. Their demand curve for IBM shares on September 3, 1993, is shown as curve D. The lower is the share price, the greater is the number of IBM shares people will be prepared to buy, and the demand curve is negatively sloped. The equilibrium price of IBM shares (on September 3, 1993) is that price ($46.75) at which the number of shares demanded equals the number of shares supplied. The equilibrium number of shares traded (8.2 million) is referred to as the *volume* of IBM transactions.

Stock prices, like other market prices, are determined by supply and demand. When the supply or demand curves shift, stock prices change. For example, on

EXHIBIT 1   Determination of IBM Stock Prices

This figure diagrams the supply (S) and demand (D) curves for shares of IBM stock on September 3, 1993. The supply curve is positively sloped because owners of IBM stock will offer more shares for sale at high prices than at low prices. The demand curve is negatively sloped because buyers of IBM shares will be prepared to buy more at low prices than at high prices. The equilibrium price is that price at which the quantity demanded equals the quantity supplied. Share prices fluctuate daily because of shifts in supply and demand. This equilibrium price reflects the consensus present value of the future earnings per share of IBM.

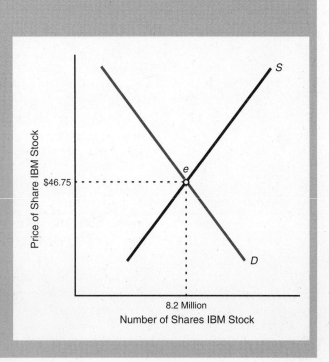

September 3, 1993, the price of IBM shares reached a low of 44^1/_2$ and a high of 46^3/_8$. The change in the price of IBM shares would be caused either by an increase in demand, a reduction in supply, or a combination of the two.

Exhibit 1 explains in a mechanical way how stock prices are determined, but it does not explain what lies behind the supply and demand curves: the different assessments of the future profits of the corporation. The owner of a share of stock benefits from the profits that the corporation earns now and in the future. The share owner of a corporation receives dividends that the corporation pays out of profits (if any) and benefits from reinvested profits that increase future profits. Share prices, therefore, depend on the present and future earnings of the corporation. Present earnings may be known, but future earnings are uncertain. They depend on factors such as the general state of the economy, the quality of management, and shifts in consumer demand. Because the future is unknown, different people will have different views of what the future holds. Some will see a bright future of rising profits and dividends. Others will foresee a bleak future of declining economic fortunes.

Stock prices depend on the present and future earnings of the corporation.

Stock Prices as Present Values.   The price of a share of stock is determined by the present and future profits of the corporation. The price depends upon the anticipated future profits per share of outstanding stock, or **earnings per share**.

> Earnings per share (*EPS*) is the annual profit of the corporation divided by the number of shares outstanding.

No one knows for sure what future profits will be. Suppose Jones, an optimist, expects earnings per share of ZYX Corporation to be $10 from now to eternity (in perpetuity). Smith, a pessimist, on the other hand, expects earnings per share of ZYX Corporation to be $5 from now to eternity. As the earlier discussion of present value showed, money to be earned in the future is worth less than money now. The anticipated future profits of ZYX Corporation need to be converted by both Jones and Smith into a present value. Applying the perpetuity formula (at a 10 percent interest rate), the present value of the anticipated profit stream of one share of stock is $100 ($10/0.10) for Jones and $50 ($5/0.10) for Smith. Jones would be a willing seller of ZYX stock at a price greater than $100 and a willing buyer at a price less than $100. Smith would be a willing seller at a price above $50 and a willing buyer at a price below $50. At a $75 price, Smith would sell and Jones would buy.

The price of a share of stock is the perceived present value of the future earnings per share of the stock.

The demand and supply curves of stock show that potential buyers and sellers assess differently the future earnings of corporations. The share price settles at that price at which the quantity of shares demanded equals the quantity supplied. This equilibrium price is the consensus of participants in the market concerning the present value of the future earnings of the corporation.

Price/Earnings Ratios.   Stock prices fluctuate because the future is unknown. No one knows for sure what the future earnings of any company might be. There will be disagreement among those who currently own the stock and those who are considering buying the stock. No one can predict for sure the future behavior of the economy. No one can predict for sure whether a particular company's fortunes will improve, deteriorate, or remain the same. When a company announces the development of a new product, the investment community may be convinced that this development will raise future earnings. This event will change investors' assessments of the present value of the company, and the stock price will rise.

The **price/earnings (*PE*) ratio** signals whether investors believe that the

A high *PE* ratio indicates that investors believe that current profits understate the future profits of the corporation.

profits of the company, or earnings per share, will rise or fall from their current profit levels.

> The **price/earnings** (*PE*) ratio is the stock price divided by the earnings per share.

If the average company has a *PE* ratio of 6, companies with a *PE* ratio greater than 6 are expected to have profits rising at above-average rates. Companies with a *PE* ratio less than 6 are expected to have profits rising at below-average rates.

Stock Indexes. The share prices of corporations reflect the present discounted value of future profits. At times, share prices tend to rise generally in stock exchanges. At other times, they tend to fall generally. **Stock-price indexes** measure the ups and downs of average stock prices.

> A **stock-price index** (such as the Dow Jones Industrial Average, the Standard & Poor Index, or the New York Stock Exchange Index) measures the general movements of stock prices.

The different stock-price indexes measure movements in general stock prices differently. The Dow Jones Industrials Index measures the movement of 30 industrial stocks (such as Exxon, AT&T, and Du Pont). The New York Stock Exchange Index measures the average price of all stocks exchanged on the New York Stock Exchange. Although the different stock-price indexes do not yield identical results, they typically agree that stock prices are generally rising or falling but disagree on the magnitude of the rise or fall.

If buyers and sellers of stocks generally expect corporate profits to rise more rapidly, average stock prices should rise. The present value of future corporate earnings would rise, and buyers would be willing to pay more for stocks. Rising optimism about future corporate profits should cause stock-price indexes to register increases. When interest rates rise, the present values of future corporate earnings fall (because of the inverse relationship between present value and interest rates). The falling present values of corporate earnings should generally depress stock prices.

Anticipated corporate profits and interest rates are only two factors that explain general movements in stock prices. There are literally millions of participants in modern stock markets. Rumors of war, deaths of political leaders, drought, pronouncements of Wall Street gurus, and even trivial events can cause fluctuations in stock prices. It is often said that anyone who really understands the stock market is so rich that they do not have to bother dispensing advice to others on how to get rich.

The Efficient Stock Market Hypothesis

The efficient stock market hypothesis says that stock prices change because information about the company changes.

There are two opposing views of why stock prices change. One view is that the stock market is *irrational*. Potential buyers and sellers of stock are subject to changes in moods and whims. They turn overnight from being optimists to being pessimists for no apparent reason. They try to guess what other potential buyers and sellers are thinking. The opposing view—the **efficient stock market hypothesis**—is that the stock market reacts rationally to changes in information.

> The **efficient stock market hypothesis** states that stock prices are determined by the information currently available on the present and future earnings of corporations. Changes in stock prices are due to changes in the information available on present and future earnings of corporations.

As noted above, the price of IBM shares on September 3, 1993, varied from a low of $44^1/8$ to a high of $46^3/8$. The efficient stock market hypothesis says that these price fluctuations would have been due to changes in the information available concerning IBM's current and expected profits. Proponents of the irrationality of stock market theory would argue that such changes occurred for no rational reason.

The efficient stock market hypothesis appeared to suffer a setback on "Black Monday," October 19, 1987, when in one day stock prices plummeted by almost one quarter. Analysts were hard pressed to explain how stock prices could fall in value so much in one day, when there was no apparent change in information concerning expected corporate profits.

Stock Prices and Resource Allocation

Corporations can issue new stock to raise financial capital. Once the stock is issued, it is traded on the various stock exchanges, and the buying and selling of stock do not have a *direct* effect on the corporation's financial capital. The gains from rising stock prices accrue to the individual holders of the issued stock.

The price of stocks does have an important effect on the allocation of capital resources. Consider what would happen if ZYX corporation's research-and-development team develops a promising anticancer drug and obtains Food and Drug Administration approval to market this drug. The investor community will realize (probably well before government approval is even granted) that ZYX corporation's earnings will rise substantially, so the price of the stock will rise rapidly. In our earlier example, the price of ZYX stock was $10, and the company was able to raise $500,000 by selling 50,000 new shares of stock. If, on the other hand, the prospect of the new drug raises the price of the stock to $50 (the new plant would be built to manufacture the new drug), the issue of 50,000 new shares would raise $2,500,000 instead of $500,000.

Rising stock prices make it easier for corporations to raise financial capital.

As stock prices rise, corporations find it easier to raise financial capital for expansion. Corporations with falling stock prices cannot raise large sums of money for expansion. In this sense, the second-hand markets for corporate stocks serve as barometers that signal the direction of the allocation of financial capital. Stockholders can express their dissatisfaction by "voting with their feet." By selling their shares, they drive down the price of the stock. If dissatisfaction is widespread, the stock price can fall considerably, preventing the firm from raising much capital by selling new shares.

Appendix Summary

1. A dollar today is worth more than a dollar tomorrow. The present-value formula allows one to compute what a stream of dollars to be received in the future is worth today.

2. The price of a bond reflects the present value of the interest payments and principal. If interest rates rise, this present value falls. Hence the relationship between bond prices and interest rates is inverse.

3. Corporations raise capital by issuing new shares of stock. Once issued, stock is bought and sold in stock exchanges. The price of a share of stock is the present value of the future earnings per share of stock. The price/earnings ratio signals whether stock markets believe that profits will be rising or falling.

4. Stock indexes measure general movements in the prices of shares.

5. The efficient stock market hypothesis maintains that stock prices depend upon the information that is currently available concerning the present and future profits of the corporation. Changes in stock prices are due to changes in this information.

6. Rising share prices allow a corporation to raise more financial capital by issuing new shares of stock. Hence rising stock prices tend to affect the allocation of resources.

Key Terms

bonds (p. 150)
present value (p. 151)
bankrupt (p. 152)
stock (p. 153)
stock exchange (p. 153)

earnings per share (p. 155)
price/earnings ratio (p. 155)
stock-price index (p. 156)
efficient stock market hypothesis (p. 156)

Questions and Problems

1. Without any change in information concerning a corporation's earnings prospects, the price of the corporation's stock falls by 25 percent. Would this fall support the efficient stock market hypothesis? Explain your answer.

2. Using the present-value formula, explain why a rise in the interest rate would tend to drive down stock prices.

3. The earnings per share of ABC corporation was 10, then dropped to 5. What does this change tell us about people's evaluation of the future earnings of ABC corporation?

4. What is $150,000 to be paid two years from today's date worth now? Do you have enough information to answer the question?

5. Answer the previous question at an interest rate of 10 percent and an interest rate of 5 percent. Compare the answers and explain what fundamental present-value principle is illustrated.

6. What is $100,000 put in a 5 percent saving account going to be worth in three years?

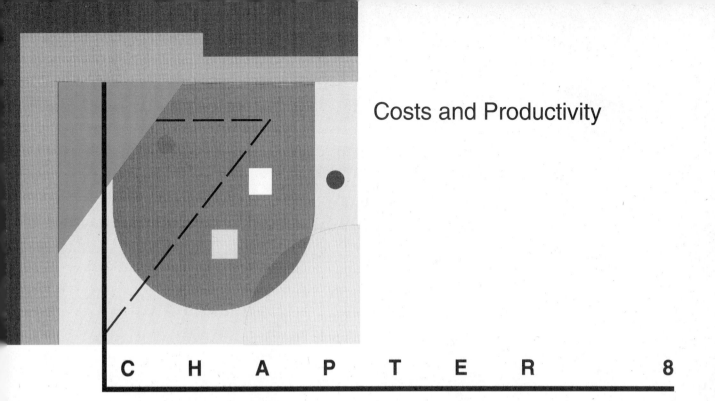

Costs and Productivity

C H A P T E R   8

CHAPTER FOCUS This chapter shows that the costs that affect economic decision-making are opportunity costs. If a firm takes a particular action, like producing more output or purchasing new equipment, the costs of that action are what must be given up or sacrificed.

Instinct suggests incorrectly that the costs that really matter to businesses are their dollar costs. If an automobile dealer buys 20 cars for $12,000 and another 20 at $16,000 after the price has risen, the opportunity cost to the dealer of selling a car is $16,000, not $12,000 or $14,000. If the dealer sells one of the $12,000 cars, it will cost $16,000 to replace.

This principle of costs applies generally. If a shopping center, which cost $200,000 to build, is destroyed by a hurricane, the cost of this disaster is not $200,000 but how much it would cost to replace the shopping center (which could be more or less than the original cost).

Opportunity costs measure the resources that have to be sacrificed in order to take an action. Resources must be paid their opportunity costs. If they are offered a return less than their opportunity costs, they will go into an alternate activity.

After studying this chapter, you will be able to:

- See why opportunity costs include explicit and implicit costs.
- Explain the difference between economic profits and accounting profits.
- Understand the average/marginal rule.
- Define marginal physical product and use it to explain the law of diminishing returns.
- Distinguish between fixed and variable costs.
- Discuss the relationships between average variable, average total, and marginal costs.
- Explain the difference between the short-run and the long-run cost curves (and the shape of the long-run curve).

OPPORTUNITY COSTS

Business decisions are based upon opportunity costs. The notion of opportunity cost was introduced in Chapter 1: the opportunity cost of any action is the next best alternative that has to be sacrificed. In this chapter, we look more closely at opportunity costs in the context of the business firm.

Explicit and Implicit Costs

Economists look at costs in a way that differs from the common perception of costs as something that must be paid out of one's pocket. Consider the following case. Suppose your rich aunt gives you a brand new sports car, which has a market value of $15,000. She tells you: "This car is yours to keep or to sell. If you sell it, the $15,000 is yours. If you keep it, I'll pay for all gas, oil, maintenance, repairs, and insurance." This car is a generous gift. But is the car truly free? In fact, the car is not free. There is a cost to *using* the car.

The opportunity cost of using the car under these conditions may actually be higher than the annual cost of a small car. Consider selling the car today as opposed to keeping the car for one year. If the car were sold today for $15,000 and the money invested at 6 percent interest, the money would grow to $15,900 ($900 is the interest on $15,000 at 6 per cent per year). On the other hand, if the car were sold in one year, its resale value would decline due to depreciation. Suppose the resale value falls to $11,000. Selling the car today brings $15,900 in one year; selling in one year brings $11,000 in one year. Hence, the decision to sell the car today means that in one year you will have $4,900 more money than if the car is sold in one year. Using the car for one year will cost you exactly $4,900. The "free" car is far from free if the car is used! The lesson is that *costs are not necessarily what has been paid but what has been given up by taking one action rather than another.* **Opportunity cost** is the measure of what has been given up.

> The **opportunity cost** of an action is the value of the next best forgone alternative.

As the car example shows, an opportunity cost may be an **implicit cost** or an **explicit cost**.

Economists use opportunity costs that include both explicit and implicit costs.

Johann Heinrich von Thunen (1783–1850)

J. H. von Thunen was born in Germany in 1783. With the help of a small inheritance he bought a run-down 1,200-acre estate named Tellow that became a model farm and attracted visitors from all over Europe. The farm was his economic model. Thunen kept incredibly accurate records on the relationship between inputs and outputs. Years ahead of his time, he even offered his employees a profit-sharing plan. His major study, *The Isolated State with Respect to Agricultural and Political Economy,* was published in 1826 after more than twenty years of work and established him as an international authority on agriculture. Thunen was so excited about his discoveries in economics that he had one of his laws engraved on this tombstone.

Thunen put marginal productivity and costs on a secure foundation. His meticulous records revealed the law of diminishing marginal productivity. He conceived the experiment of recording the consequences of changing the input of capital, holding labor constant, or changing the input of labor, holding capital constant. Not only did he discover the law of diminishing marginal product, he stated the rules that would minimize a firm's costs of production and discovered many of the principles that govern the economics of how the city and farm interact.

An **explicit cost** (also called an *accounting cost*) is incurred when an actual payment is made.

An **implicit cost** is incurred when an alternative is sacrificed but no actual payment appears to be made.

Consider a business firm that produces stereos. Resources are required to produce stereos. Skilled workers must be hired, component parts must be purchased, and precision machinery must be available. The business firm could not acquire these resources without paying their owners. Skilled workers have alternative employment opportunities. The component parts are used by other manufacturers. How much would the business firm have to offer? The firm must offer each factor of production its opportunity cost. If skilled workers could earn $25 per hour in their next best employment alternative, the stereo manufacturer must offer at least $25 per hour. If the owners of the precision machines could rent them for $5,000 per month in their next best alternative, the stereo firm must offer at least that. (See Example 1.)

> Business firms must pay the factors of production their opportunity costs to attract resources. If firms make offers below opportunity costs, resources will seek out alternate employment.

Opportunity Costs as the Sum of Explicit and Implicit Costs

Some of the business firm's factor payments are explicit (as money changes hands), and some may be implicit. The manager of the firm must consider the opportunity costs (the value of those resources if used in their next best alternative) of the resources owned by the firm. The hired resources (labor, land, equipment) have explicit costs that must be paid to acquire them.

For example, pharmacist Smith owns and operates Smith's Drugstore. Smith has put $60,000 of her own money into the business. As a pharmacist, Smith could earn $2,000 per month from a chain drugstore. Smith's capital investment in the

EXAMPLE 1

Air Force Pilots, Commercial Pilots, and Opportunity Costs

The 1980s were a boom period for the nation's commercial airlines. While Air Force pilots with the rank of colonel earned $60,000 per year, not including benefits, commercial pilots with the same experience earned in excess of $100,000. In the 1980s, the dropout rate of Air Force pilots reached 50%. These high dropout rates suggest that military pay and compensation had fallen below civilian compensation. The military was not paying pilots their opportunity cost.

The 1990s presented a completely different picture. With the rising number of airline bankruptcies and declining commercial airline traffic, the pay of commercial pilots stagnated and even fell. The pay of Air Force pilots rose with inflation during the 1990s and exceeded compensation in the private sector. Instead of being worried by a high dropout rate, the Air Force now had to worry about a surplus of Air Force pilots. Air Force pilots were being paid in excess of their opportunity costs.

---

drugstore may earn $500 per month invested elsewhere. This $2,500 (= $2,000 + $500) is an *implicit* cost of doing business. (Although this $2,500 is a true opportunity cost, no money changes hands.) The explicit (accounting) costs are Smith's rent payments on the building, inventory costs, business taxes, and wage payments to clerks and other pharmacists. These explicit monthly payments add up to $37,000 per month. Smith's total opportunity cost (per month) is the sum of explicit costs ($37,000) and implicit costs ($2,500), or $39,500.

Economic Profits

Economists measure profits using opportunity costs. Conventional accounting measures of profits often leave out implicit costs. Thus, **economic profits** are not always the same as profits reported by the usual accounting standards. Accounting profits can give a misleading picture of the firm's well-being, because they can sometimes ignore important implicit costs. Economic profits—which consider both explicit and implicit costs—signal whether or not resources are being directed to their best use.

Economic profits consider both explicit and implicit costs.

> **Economic profits** are the excess of revenues over total opportunity costs.

If Smith's Drugstore has monthly sales of $40,000, it has accounting profits of $3,000 per month because accounting costs = $37,000. Smith's economic profit, however, is only $500 because accounting costs ignore the implicit costs that must be paid to Smith for using Smith's entrepreneurial talents and funds. She is earning $500 more than the sum of money necessary to persuade the entrepreneur/owner to commit her talent and financial resources to the business. If accounting profit were below $2,500, the entrepreneur would not enter the business because Smith would be better off working for a chain pharmacy and drawing interest on her savings.

What would happen if revenues exactly equaled total opportunity cost (which would occur at an accounting profit of $2,500)? In this case, Smith would just be enticed to enter the business because she is earning the opportunity costs on the personal resources she devotes to the business. When revenues and total opportunity costs are equal, economic profit is zero.

Average/Marginal Rules

In economics, the relationship between *average* values or quantities and *marginal* values or quantities comes up again and again. This chapter examines the relationship between average costs and marginal costs. Later chapters will discuss the relationship between average revenues and marginal revenues. There is a common arithmetical background to all average/marginal relationships that can be illustrated with a familiar example.

Suppose that you are taking a course in chemistry and that there are eight (equally weighted) examinations. Your performance for the course is determined by your average score on all exams. Exhibit 1 shows how the average score is computed and graphs both marginal and average scores. On test number 1, you score 80 points; your average is 80. On test number 2, you score only 50; your *total* score is now 130 (= 80 + 50), and your average falls to 65 (= 130/2). Your average is the total accumulated points scored divided by the number of exams taken.

The marginal score is the increase in the total accumulated points obtained by taking one more exam. The marginal score is simply your score on the last examination taken. On the first exam your average and marginal scores are the

> Whenever the marginal value exceeds the previous average value, the new average value will rise. Whenever the marginal value is below the previous average value, the new average value will fall.

same: 80. The second exam score is 50, which is below the previous average of 80. What will happen to the new average? *Whenever the marginal value is below the previous average value, the new average will fall.* In this case, the average falls from 80 to 65 because it is *pulled down* by the low marginal test score. The third exam score is 100, well above the 65 average to that point. What will happen to the new average? *When the marginal score is above the previous average test score, the new average will rise.* The average will be *pulled up* by the high marginal score.

A second rule is illustrated by the final marginal test score. The average test score of the first seven exams is 70. The eighth exam score is 70. Because the marginal score, thus, *equals* the previous average score, the new average will remain the same because the marginal value will pull the average neither up nor down.

> If the marginal value equals the previous average value, the new average will not be changed.

Baseball fans are also familiar with these average/marginal rules. If a batter enters a game with a batting average of 0.250 (25 hits every 100 times at bat) and goes two for four on that day, the average will rise because the marginal score (0.500) is higher than the previous average score (0.250). If the player had gone one for four on that day, the average score would not have changed because the marginal score equals the previous average. If the player had zero hits, the average would have fallen because the marginal score was below the previous average.

COST CURVES IN THE SHORT RUN

A business firm expands the volume of its output by hiring or using additional resources. Every good or service is produced by a combination of resources (land, labor, capital, raw materials, entrepreneurial or managerial talent). The package of resources used depends on the prices and productivity of resources and on the time available to the firm for altering output. Prices and productivity are important because profit-minded businesses will use resources depending on their prices and productivity. Time is important because time is required to change the level of resource use. Some resources can be adjusted immediately. Other resources require considerable time to change.

EXHIBIT 1 Average and Marginal Relationships

a. Test Scores

Test	Test Score = Marginal Score	Average Test Score	Explanation
0		0	
1	80	80	Average and marginal values are the same.
2	50	65	When the marginal score is below the previous average, the new average falls.
3	100	76.67	When the marginal score is above the previous average, the new average rises.
4	70	75	When the marginal score is below the previous average, the new average falls.
5	60	72	When the marginal score is below the previous average, the new average falls.
6	50	68.22	When the marginal score is below the previous average, the new average falls.
7	80	70	When the marginal score is above the previous average, the new average rises.
8	70	70	When the marginal score equals the previous average, the new average is unchanged.

b. Graph of Test Scores

Panel (b) graphs the data from panel (a). Whenever the marginal score is less than the previous average score, the average score declines. Whenever the marginal score is greater than the previous average score, the average score rises. If the marginal score equals the previous average score, the average score will not change.

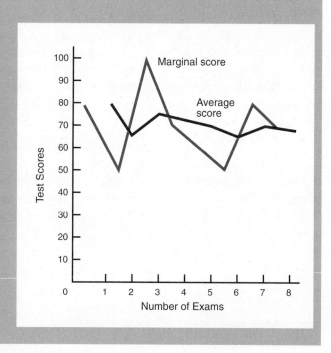

Short Run and Long Run

Suppose economic conditions are such that a business firm wishes to expand its volume of output. To expand output, it must expand resources. Some resources can be expanded quickly. The firm could ask its employees to work overtime. It may be able to recruit new employees on a moment's notice. Additional raw materials may be only a telephone call away. The firm's other inputs cannot be

In the short run, some factors of production are fixed. In the long run, all factors are variable.

expanded quickly. The installation of a new piece of capital equipment or the construction of a new plant may require significant time. The firm may have to wait for a lease to expire before moving into larger quarters. The business firm must wait for some resources to be expanded. In the meantime, the firm has to expand output by increasing those inputs that can be readily increased.

Economists distinguish between the **short run** and the **long run** when considering the time necessary to change input levels.

> The **short run** is a period of time so short that the existing plant and equipment cannot be varied; such inputs are fixed in supply. Additional output can be produced only by expanding the variable inputs of labor and raw materials.

> The **long run** is a period of time long enough to vary all inputs.

The long run is not a specified amount of calendar time. The long run may be as short as a few months for a fast-food restaurant, a couple of years for a new automobile plant, or a decade or more for an electrical power plant. Generally speaking, engineering complexity determines whether the long run is a matter of weeks or years in actual calendar time.

Fixed and Variable Costs

In the short run, there are both fixed and variable costs. In the short run, some factors (such as plant and equipment) are fixed in supply; even if the firm wanted to increase or reduce them, it would not be possible in the short run. The costs of these fixed factors are **fixed costs (FC)**. The firm pays these costs even if it produces no output. In the short run, greater output is obtained by using more of the *variable inputs* (such as labor and raw materials); the costs of these variable factors are **variable costs (VC)**. The sum of variable and fixed costs is **total costs (TC)**.

> **Fixed costs (FC)** are those costs that do not vary with output.

> **Variable costs (VC)** are those costs that do vary with output.

> **Total costs (TC)** are fixed costs plus variable costs:
> $$TC = VC + FC.$$

In the short run some costs are fixed. As the time horizon expands, more and more inputs can be varied. *In the long run, all costs are variable.* In other words, in the long run fixed costs are zero.

In the long run, all costs are variable. Thus, in the long run, fixed costs are *zero*. In the short run, some costs are fixed, and total costs consist of fixed plus variable costs.

We have seen that the costs of an action are measured in terms of the next best alternative sacrificed. In the short run there is no way to change fixed costs; they remain the same no matter what the firm decides. If the firm is considering expanding its output, this action has no effect on resources that are fixed. In the short run, fixed resources have no alternate use. The decision to increase output in the short run means an increase in variable inputs and, therefore, in variable costs. Variable inputs do have alternative uses, and they must be paid their opportunity costs.

The Law of Diminishing Returns

Production costs depend on input prices and technology. Production costs rise as input prices rise, *ceteris paribus,* and they fall as productivity improves, *ceteris paribus.* In this section, we are interested in what happens to the costs of production as firms expand the level of output in the short run.

The prices of the land, labor, and capital used in the enterprise are determined by conditions outside the firm (in the markets for those resources). Except in unusual circumstances, input prices would not be affected by the decision of a firm to expand its output. The firm's technology is determined by the ability of the management team to absorb the engineering and technical knowledge relevant to the firm's business. For all practical purposes, the firm's technology is fixed in the short run. The firm's technology dictates the relationship between increases in inputs and increases in outputs in the short run. In fact, the relationship between increases in input and increases in output follows a distinctive pattern in the short run, called the **law of diminishing returns**.

> The law of diminishing returns states that as ever larger amounts of a variable input are combined with fixed inputs, eventually the extra product attributable to each additional amount of the variable input must decline.

The extra product that is attributed to an additional unit of an input, holding other inputs fixed, is called the **marginal physical product (*MPP*)** of the input. It is calculated by taking the ratio of the change in output to the change in the variable input. The law of diminishing returns asserts that as more of a variable input is used, diminishing or declining marginal physical product must eventually be encountered by any firm. Alternatively, the law means that additional units of output become harder to produce when the point of diminishing returns is reached.

> The **marginal physical product (*MPP*)** of a factor of production is the change in output divided by the change in the quantity of the input, holding all other inputs constant.

To understand the law of diminishing returns, think about the average daily output of a shrimp boat along the Texas Gulf Coast. The fixed inputs would be the boat, along with its engine and nets (and other fishing equipment), as well as the ocean. The variable inputs would be the number of workers (shrimpers) used. Exhibit 2 shows the daily output (in terms of bushels) as a function of the number of shrimpers. Panel (b) shows the total output curve, panel (c) shows the marginal product curve, and panel (a) shows the underlying data.

If the boat is operated by only one shrimper, his or her time must be divided between piloting the boat, setting the nets, pulling in the nets full of shrimp, and unloading the nets. A lone shrimper catches 2 bushels per day. A second shrimper brings the total output to 12 bushels per day. An additional shrimper will allow the two persons to specialize somewhat and to save time switching from job to job. A third shrimper proves even more valuable, raising daily output to 32 bushels. The fourth shrimper raises output to 62 bushels, the fifth to 82, the sixth to 92 and so on.

Panel (c) and column 3 of panel (a) show the marginal physical product (*MPP*) of each additional shrimper. By definition, the *MPP* is the change in output per unit change in the input. Raising the input of shrimpers from 0 to 1 raises

EXHIBIT 2   The Law of Diminishing Returns, Shrimp Fishing

a. Total Product and Marginal Physical Product Schedules

Number of Shrimpers	Daily Output	Marginal Physical Product
0	0	
		2
1	2	
		6
		10
2	12	15
		20
3	32	25
		30
4	62	25
		20
5	82	15
		10
6	92	7.5
		5
7	97	4
		3
8	100	2.5
		2
9	102	1.5
		1
10	103	

This exhibit shows the relationship between the variable inputs and output. Panel (b) shows the total daily output; panel (c) shows the marginal physical product. Both graphs are based on the data in panel (a). When the total daily output is increasing rapidly, the marginal physical product curve (*MPP*) is increasing. When the total daily output is increasing but at a slower and slower rate, the *MPP* curve is declining.

b. Total Product

c. Marginal Physical Product

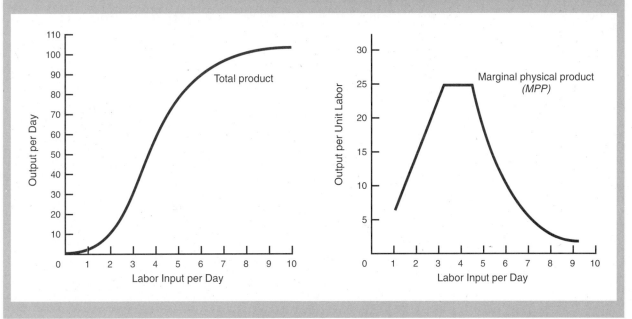

output by 2 bushels. Adding the 6th shrimper raises output from 82 to 92 bushels for an *MPP* of 10 bushels. Adding the 10th shrimper raises output from 102 to 103 bushels for an *MPP* of 1 bushel.

Marginal physical product can be calculated for one-unit increases in the input (as done above) or for increases of more than one unit. Consider the calculation of *MPP* when the number of shrimpers is increased by two. Raising the input of shrimpers from 0 to 2 increases output from 0 to 12 bushels. *MPP* is the change in output (12 bushels) divided by the change in inputs (two units)—or 6 bushels. The *MPP* of moving from 8 to 10 shrimpers is 1.5 units (3 bushels/2 shrimpers).

In panel (a) the *MPP* of increasing the number of shrimpers by one unit is given *in between* the relevant rows. When the *MPP* is calculated by increasing the labor input by 2 units, the results are given in boldface. For example, when the input increases from 4 to 6, output increases by 30 units from 62 to 92; thus, the *MPP* for the input level 5 (in between 4 and 6) is 15 (= 30/2) in boldface.

As the graph in panel (c) shows, diminishing returns set in after the fourth shrimper. Prior to the fourth shrimper, each additional shrimper had a higher *MPP*. Starting with the fourth shrimper, each additional shrimper has a lower *MPP* than the previous shrimper. What is the explanation? As more shrimpers are added to the fixed inputs of a boat and fishing equipment, the benefits from each shrimper being able to specialize in a particular activity are soon exhausted. By the time the fifth shrimper is added, the variable inputs may start to get in each other's way. The tenth shrimper adds only 1 bushel of shrimp to the daily output.

The law of diminishing returns—illustrated with the shrimp-boat example—applies to the production of any good or service. When some inputs are fixed, adding more variable inputs means that each variable input has less of the fixed input with which to work. When the fixed input becomes "crowded" with variable inputs, the law of diminishing returns sets in.

The law of diminishing returns explains why MPP eventually declines in the short run.

Marginal and Average Costs

The behavior of costs depends on the law of diminishing returns. Indeed, productivity and costs are inversely related. The higher the productivity, the lower are the costs; the lower the productivity, the higher are the costs.

Marginal Costs.   Recall that total cost equals variable costs plus fixed costs. Notice that as output increases, both total cost and variable cost increase by the same amount. Suppose, for example, that when the output of shrimp increases by 2 bushels, total (and variable) costs rise by $10. The change in costs divided by the change in output is called the **marginal cost (*MC*)** of production. In this example, $MC = \$5 = (\$10 \div 2)$. In other words, *MC* is the increase in cost per unit increase in output. If the increase in output is only one unit, the *MC* is simply the increase in costs associated with increasing output by one unit. Marginal cost can be determined for any increase in output—one unit, two units, or any number.

> Marginal cost (*MC*) is the change in total cost (or equivalently in variable cost) divided by the increase in output or, alternatively, the increase in costs per unit increase in output.
>
> $$MC = \frac{\Delta TC}{\Delta Q} = \frac{\Delta VC}{\Delta Q}.$$

Business decisions are based on marginal costs (See Example 2.)

Average Costs.   While marginal costs look at the change in costs per unit change in output, average costs spread total, variable, or fixed costs over the entire quantity of output.

To determine whether the firm should operate in the short run or temporarily close down, the firm must consult its **average variable cost (*AVC*)**. By definition, *AVC* is obtained by dividing variable costs by output. Fixed cost per

Why Economic Decisions Are Based on Marginal Costs

Economic decisions are based on the marginal (opportunity) cost. Suppose you are in a supermarket and the manager announces that in the next five minutes you can buy two bottles of your favorite soft drink for the price of one. You hurry over and buy two bottles for $1 (the normal price of one bottle). When you arrive back at your home, your neighbor, who has unexpected company, asks to buy from you one bottle. What price would you charge? You have purchased two bottles for $1, for an average price of $0.50. There are three options: (1) Assume the bottle you are selling your neighbor is the "free" bottle and charge nothing. (2) Charge the average price of $0.50. (3) Charge $1. As a profit-maximizer, you should choose option 3. Why? It would cost you $1 to buy another. The two-for-one offer has expired, and you must now pay the regular price. The marginal cost of the action (parting with the bottle of soft drink) is $1. If you part with the bottle for the average cost ($0.50), your wealth would be reduced by $0.50 when you replace the bottle at a $1 price. The moral of this story is that profit-maximizing people and businesses make economic decisions on the basis of opportunity costs, not dollar costs.

SOURCE: Thomas Wyrick, "Marginal-Cost Policy Making and the Guy Next Door," *Wall Street Journal*, April 12, 1984.

---

unit produced is called **average fixed cost (*AFC*)** and is calculated by dividing fixed costs by output. To determine whether the firm is making economic profit on each unit produced, the firm must calculate its **average total cost (*ATC*)**; it is calculated by dividing total cost by output. Alternatively, *ATC* is just the sum of *AFC* and *AVC*.

> Average variable cost (*AVC*) is variable cost divided by output:
>
> $$AVC = VC \div Q.$$

> Average fixed cost (*AFC*) is fixed cost divided by output:
>
> $$AFC = FC \div Q.$$

> Average total cost (*ATC*) is total cost divided by output, or the sum of average variable cost and average fixed cost:
>
> $$ATC = TC \div Q = AVC + AFC.$$

The Cost Curves

Exhibits 3 and 4 assemble cost and output information for a hypothetical firm that produces a single product. The costs shown include all opportunity costs (explicit and implicit). The firm is operating in the short run because fixed costs are present. The enterprise has fixed costs of $48 per day. It consists primarily of the interest on the firm's capital, lease payments, and depreciation. As more output is produced, variable costs must rise because more inputs, such as labor and raw materials, must be hired or purchased. Exhibit 4a graphs total costs, variable costs,

EXHIBIT 3 The Short-Run Costs of a Hypothetical Enterprise

Cost Schedules in the Short Run for a Hypothetical Enterprise

Quantity of Output (units), Q (1)	Variable Cost (dollars), VC (2)	Fixed Cost (dollars), FC (3)	Total Cost (dollars), TC (4) = (2) + (3)	Marginal Cost (dollars), MC (5)	Average Variable Cost (dollars), AVC (6) = (2) ÷ (1)	Average Fixed Cost (dollars), AFC (7) = (3) ÷ (1)	Average Total Cost (dollars), ATC (8) = (4) ÷ (1) = (6) + (7)
0	0	48	48			∞	∞
				20			
1	20	48	68	15	20	48	68
				10			
2	30	48	78	8	15	24	39
				6			
3	36	48	84	5	12	16	28
				4			
4	40	48	88	6	10	12	22
				8			
5	48	48	96	10	9.6	9.6	19.2
				12			
6	60	48	108	16	10	8	18
				20			
7	80	48	128	26	11.4	6.9	18.3
				32			
8	112	48	160	38	14	6	20
				44			
9	156	24	180				

This exhibit shows the family of cost schedules for a hypothetical business enterprise operating in the short run with total fixed cost of $48. The table shows the basic data. *Variable cost* (column 2) rises with the level of output. *Total cost* (column 4) is the sum of total fixed cost and total variable cost. *Marginal cost* is shown in column 5; and *average variable, average fixed,* and *average total cost* are shown in the remaining columns.

The family of short-run cost curves consists of *MC, AVC, ATC,* and *AFC.*

and fixed costs; panel (b) graphs average variable costs, average total costs, and marginal costs. Exhibit 3 gives the basic underlying data for the firm.

In Exhibit 3, variable and total costs are shown in columns 2 and 4. Exhibit 4a shows the same data graphically. The marginal-cost figures in column 5 are shown *in between* the various output levels, because they are in this case the extra cost of going from one output level to another. The boldface figures are the marginal costs of increasing output by 2 units and are shown in between the respective output levels. For example, the *MC* of going from 0 units of output to 2 units of output is $15. This $15 *MC* figure between the output levels of 0 units and 2 units is displayed at the output level of 1. Similarly, the marginal cost in going from output level 5 to output level 7 is $16, because the increase in variable cost is $32 (from $48 to $80) and the increase in output is, again, 2. Thus, the *MC* figure for $Q = 6$ is $16 (= $32/2).

In the example, *MC* at first falls and then rises. Marginal costs first fall because as the first few units of output are produced, the variable inputs experience higher and higher marginal physical products as they specialize in different aspects of production. But eventually the law of diminishing returns sets in. At this point, it takes a larger increase in the variable inputs to produce a given increase in output. The law of diminishing returns dictates that marginal costs must eventually rise as output increases. As diminishing returns set in, marginal costs rise.

In Exhibit 3, column 6 divides variable costs by output to arrive at *AVC.*

EXHIBIT 4   The Short-Run Costs of a Hypothetical Enterprise

a. Total, Variable, and Fixed Costs

b. The Cost Curve

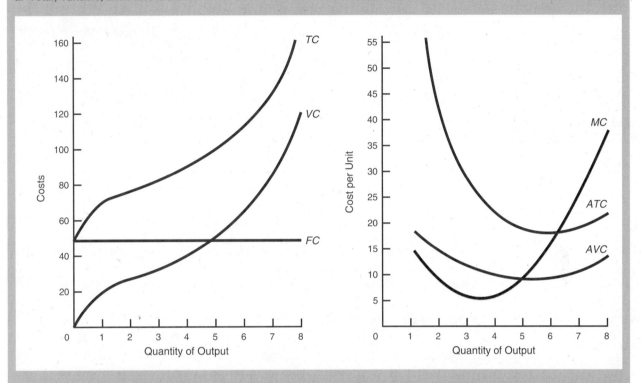

In Exhibit 4, the marginal and averages figures (except for average fixed costs) are graphed. Average total cost is the sum of average variable cost and average fixed cost. Note that *ATC* approaches *AVC* as output grows and that *MC* intersects both curves at their minimum points.

Column 7 divides fixed costs by output to arrive at *AFC*. Notice that *AFC* declines throughout because the same fixed cost is being spread out over more and more units of output. Finally, column 8 divides total cost—column 4—by output to obtain *ATC*.

Exhibit 4b shows the graphical relationship between marginal cost and average variable cost or between marginal cost and average total cost. Recall the average/marginal relationship, explained earlier. When *MC* is below *AVC* (or *ATC*), the margin is pulling down the average. Thus, in increasing output from 3 units to 4 units, *AVC* falls from $12 to $10, and *ATC* falls from $28 to $22. (Also see the data in Exhibit 3, columns 6 and 8.) The marginal cost of $4 is below *AVC* and *ATC* and pulls them both down. When output is 5 units, *MC* is slightly above *AVC*, and so just begins to pull *AVC* upward. When output is larger than 5 units, *MC* exceeds *AVC* and is pulling average variable costs up. When output is smaller than 5 units, *MC* falls short of *AVC* and is pushing average variable costs down.

Cost curves show what happens to costs of production as the level of output changes. Exhibit 4b illustrates an important principle: the *MC* curve intersects the *AVC* and *ATC* curves at their minimum points because of the average/marginal rule. At the minimum point, the average value is neither rising nor falling; therefore, the marginal and average values must be equal.

Notice that minimum *ATC* occurs after the minimum *AVC*. This must occur because when AVC reaches its minimum point, by definition, MC is equal to AVC but is still below ATC. Thus, when AVC is minimized, the ATC curve must still be falling by the average-marginal rule. When the ATC curve reaches its minimum point, the plant is being operated at its most efficient level. We shall see in the next chapter that competition forces the firm to produce at such a level.

Because $ATC = AVC + AFC$, the distance between the AVC and ATC curves represents AFC. As a given fixed cost is spread over a larger and larger output, AFC gets smaller and smaller. Thus, the AVC and ATC curves get closer together as output rises.

MC equals *ATC* and *AVC* at their respective minimum values.

LONG-RUN COSTS

The basic characteristic of the long run is that enterprises do not have any fixed costs; all costs are variable. In the long run, the business enterprise is free to choose any combination of inputs to produce output. Once long-run decisions are executed (the company completes a new plant, the commercial-farming enterprise signs a 10-year lease for additional acreage), the enterprise again has fixed factors of production and fixed costs. In the long run, enterprises are free to select the cost-minimizing level of capital, labor, and land inputs. Long-run cost-minimizing decisions are based on the prices the firm must pay for land, labor, and capital.

Shifts in Cost Curves

Take the case of Acme Steel Company, which produces steel tubes. Acme Steel can determine the average total cost curves it would face with different-size plants. With a small plant and highly unspecialized machinery, Acme Steel would face the average total cost curve ATC_1 in Exhibit 5. Notice that with this cost curve, ATC reaches its lowest point at output level q_1. With a slightly larger plant and somewhat more specialized equipment, Acme Steel's average total cost would be lower for sufficiently larger levels of output, such as at q_2. The average total cost curve associated with the larger plant and more specialized equipment is ATC_2. The remaining ATC curves show the average costs for even larger plants. The curve ATC_3 yields the most efficient plant size for producing the output level q_3.

The Long-Run Cost Curve

Exhibit 5 demonstrates that there is a different ATC curve for each level of fixed input. For every plant size, there is a different average total cost curve. If there is an infinite number of fixed input levels from which to choose, there would be an infinite number of associated ATC curves. Recall that in the long run all costs are variable; therefore, there is no distinction between long-run variable costs and long-run total costs—there is only **long-run average cost (*LRAC*)**.

> Long-run average cost (*LRAC*) consists of the minimum average cost for each level of output when all factor inputs are variable (and when factor prices and the state of technology are fixed).

In the long run, the enterprise is free to select the most effective combination of factor inputs because none of the inputs is fixed. The long-run cost curve "envelopes" the short-run cost curves, forming a long-run curve that touches each

EXHIBIT 5 Shifts in Cost Curves with Changing Plant Size

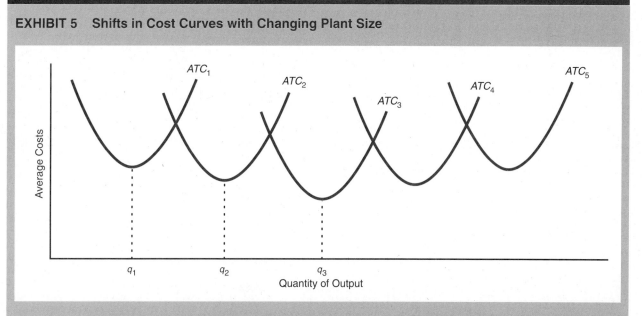

In this exhibit, economies of scale are achieved with larger plant sizes up to the plant size ATC_3. When diseconomies of scale are encountered, larger plant sizes entail larger unit costs, as with ATC_4 and ATC_5.

short-run curve ($SRATC$) at only one point, as shown in Exhibit 6. In the short run, the fact that some factors of production are fixed causes the average-total-cost curve to be U-shaped. The law of diminishing returns need not apply to the long run because, in the long run, all inputs are variable.

Economies and Diseconomies of Scale

The long-run average-cost curve will also be U-shaped, as shown in Exhibit 6. Why would long-run average costs ($LRAC$) first decline as output expands and then later increase as output expands even further? The reason is that firms experience first economies of scale, then constant returns to scale, and finally diseconomies of scale as output expands.

Economies of Scale. The declining portion of the $LRAC$ curve is due to economies of scale that arise out of the indivisibility of the inputs of labor and physical capital goods or equipment. In a large firm, the division of labor will be much more specialized than in a small firm. Workers are able to specialize in various activities, increase their productivity or dexterity through experience, and save time in moving from one task to another. People are simply indivisible: it is difficult for one person to be one part mechanic, two parts supervisor, and three parts electrician and still remain as efficient as one who specializes in just one of these tasks. The classic example of worker specialization is the assembly line of an automobile plant. The same principles apply to machines. A small firm might have to use general-purpose machine tools whereas a large firm might be able to build special equipment or machines that will substantially lower costs when large quantities are produced. Small-scale versions of certain specialized machines simply cannot be made available.

Economies of scale can occur because of the greater productivity of specializa-

EXHIBIT 6   The Long-Run Average-Cost Curve as the Envelope of the Short-Run Average-Total-Cost Curves

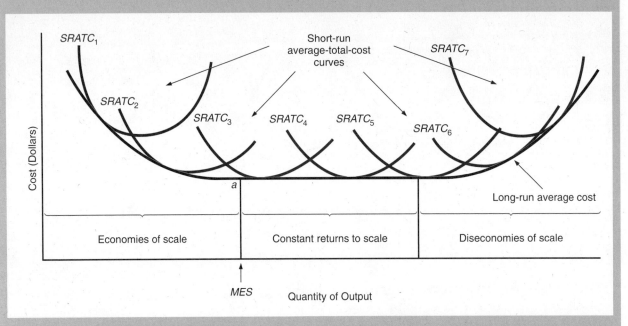

For each level of fixed input, there is a corresponding short-run average-total-cost curve. The long-run average-cost curve is the envelope of the short-run average-total-cost curves. The long-run average-cost curve is *U*-shaped. The declining portion shows economies of scale. The rising portion shows diseconomies of scale. The horizontal portion shows constant returns to scale.

tion in any of a variety of areas, including technological equipment, marketing, research and development, and management. The optimal rate of utilization for some types of machinery may occur at high rates of output. Some workers may not be able to perfect specialized skills until a high rate of output allows them to concentrate on specific tasks. As the output of an enterprise increases with all inputs variable, average costs will decline because of the **economies of scale** associated with increased specialization of labor, management, plant, and equipment. (See Example 3.)

Long-run costs decline because of economies of scale.

> Economies of scale are present when an increase in output causes average costs to fall.

Constant Returns to Scale.   Economies of scale will become exhausted at some point when expanding output no longer increases productivity. The evidence suggests that for a large range of outputs there will be **constant returns to scale**, where the average costs or production remain constant.

> Constant returns of scale are present when an increase in output does not change average costs of production.

Diseconomies of Scale.   As the enterprise continues to expand its output, eventually all the economies of large-scale production will be exploited, and

The Do-It-Yourself Car: Economies of Scale

Classic Motor Carriages, a company located in Florida, sells to do-it-yourself hobbyists a kit of automobile parts that can be assembled in one's own garage. Not included is the automobile drive train (which contains the engine and transmission), which the hobbyist can obtain already assembled. Even with the advantage of starting with an assembled drive train, Classic Motor Carriages estimates that it would take a person 200 hours to assemble the car. To get some idea of the advantages of specialization and large-scale production, consider General Motors' assembly plant in Tarrytown, New York. The plant employs 2,000 workers per 8-hour shift and turns out approximately one car per minute (about 500 cars per day). Dividing 500 cars by the 2,000 workers yields one car for every four workers—or, equivalently, one-fourth of a car per worker per day. Under conditions of specialization, large capital use, and mass production, the average worker produces one complete car every four days. The difference between four days (or 32 hours) per worker and 200 hours per worker illustrates in dramatic fashion the concept of economies of large-scale production.

SOURCES: Roger W. Shmenner, *Production/Operations Management: Concepts and Situations* (Chicago: SRA, Inc., 1981), chap. 5, and the authors.

long-run average costs will begin to rise. The rise in long-run average costs as the capital stock of the enterprise expands is the result of **diseconomies of scale**.

> **Diseconomies of scale** are present when an increase in output causes average costs to increase.

Diseconomies of scale can be caused by a series of factors. As the firm continues to expand, management skills must be spread over a larger and larger firm. Managers must assume additional responsibility, and managerial talents may eventually be spread so thin that the efficiency of management declines. The problem of maintaining communications within a large firm grows, and red tape and cumbersome bureaucracy become commonplace. Large firms may find it difficult to correct their mistakes. Employees of large firms may lose their identity and feel that their contributions to the firm are not recognized. As the output of an enterprise continues to increase, average cost will eventually rise because of the diseconomies of scale associated with the growing problems of managerial coordination.

Because of economies and diseconomies of scale, the long-run average cost curve is U-shaped.

This chapter examined how production costs behave in the short run and in the long run. The next chapter will study how perfectly competitive firms use these costs to determine their output level.

Chapter Summary

**The most important point to learn from this chapter is:
Marginal costs increase because of the law of diminishing returns.**

Two Prices for Natural Gas?

In the United States, the price of natural gas has been regulated since 1938. The latest act, the Natural Gas Policy Act of 1978, deregulated must of the natural-gas industry, allowing the prices of "new" gas to be set by the marketplace. "Old" gas remains a significant exception to market pricing. Natural gas previously committed to pipelines remains subject to price regulations that have kept the price of "old" gas significantly below the price of "new" gas.

Legislators argue that because "old" gas was discovered at a time when costs were low, it would be inappropriate for the producers of "old" gas to receive as much as "new" gas producers, who produce at a higher cost. Allowing the price of natural gas from all sources to be set by supply and demand would give windfall profits to producers of "old" gas.

This chapter teaches that opportunity cost appropriately measures the costs of an activity. With the price of "old" gas held below market rates, the natural-gas price paid by users is an average of the cost of producing "old" and "new" gas. Assume, for example, that "old" gas costs $1 per million btu and "new" gas costs $3 per million btu, and that half the gas is "old" gas and half is "new" gas. The price the consumer pays is therefore approximately $2. The opportunity cost of "old" gas is, however, $3. Once this gas is used, the producer must incur a cost of $3 to replace that gas.

In effect, the consumer is buying natural gas (at $2) at less than its opportunity cost ($3). The consumer will therefore be encouraged to use natural gas in uses that are worth only $2 to that consumer, below the opportunity cost of $3.

Economists have noted another defect of controlling the price of "old" gas. Modern technology (water flooding, fracturing, chemical treatment) allows producers of "old" gas to increase their production. It may be cheaper to increase the production of gas from old fields than to discover and develop new fields. Yet with the price of "old" gas controlled, producers of "old" gas have no incentive to use these new methods. They are better off developing new fields at higher costs than improving old fields.

This analysis suggests a full deregulation of natural gas to allow the prices of both old and new gas to be determined by supply and demand.

SOURCE: Ronald Braeutigam and R. Glenn Hubbard, "Natural Gas: The Regulatory Transition," in Leonard Weiss and Michael Klass (eds), *Regulatory Reform: What Actually Happened* (Boston: Little, Brown & Co., 1986), pp. 137–168.

1. The opportunity cost of an action is the value of the next best forgone alternative. Economic profit is defined as total revenue minus opportunity costs. When economic profits are zero, the firm is still earning an accounting profit. The average of a series of values falls when the marginal value is below the previous average value; the average stays constant when the marginal value equals the previous average; the average rises when the marginal value exceeds the previous average.

2. In the short run, the time period is so short that existing plant and equipment cannot be varied; in the long run, all inputs are variable. Variable costs are those costs that vary with output; fixed costs do not vary with output. In the long run, all costs are variable.

3. Marginal physical product is the increase in output divided by the change in the quantity of an input, holding all other inputs constant. The law of diminishing returns states that as one input is increased (holding other inputs constant), the marginal physical product of the variable input will eventually decline.

4. Marginal cost is the increase in cost divided by the increase in output. Average variable cost (*AVC*) is variable cost divided by output; average total cost (*ATC*) is total (fixed plus variable) cost divided by output. The average-variable-cost and average-total-cost curves tend to be *U*-shaped, with the *MC* intersecting *AVC* and *ATC* at their minimum values.

5. In the long run, there are different-sized plants. Associated with each size of plant is a particular short-run average-total-cost curve. The envelope of all such short-run average-total-cost curves is the *long-run average-cost curve.* The long-run average-cost curve gives the minimum unit cost of producing any given volume of output. Along the long-run average-cost curve, the firm is choosing the least-cost combination of inputs. Economies of scale prevail when increasing output lowers average costs of production. Constant returns to scale prevail when increasing output does not change average costs of production—in which case, the long-run average-cost curve in constant or horizontal. Diseconomies of scale prevail when increasing output lowers the average unit costs of production.

Policy Focus: **Charging prices below opportunity costs for "old" gas creates a gap between what people pay for natural gas and its opportunity cost.**

Key Terms

opportunity cost (p. 160)
explicit cost (p. 160)
implicit cost (p. 160)
economic profits (p. 162)
short run (p. 165)
long run (p. 165)
fixed costs (*FC*) (p. 165)
variable costs (*VC*) (p. 165)
total costs (*TC*) (p. 165)
law of diminishing returns (p. 166)

marginal physical product (*MPP*) (p. 166)
marginal cost (*MC*) (p. 168)
average variable cost (*AVC*) (p. 168)
average fixed cost (*AFC*) (p. 169)
average total cost (*ATC*) (p. 169)
long-run average cost (*LRAC*) (p. 172)
economies of scale (p. 174)
constant returns to scale (p. 174)
diseconomies of scale (p. 175)

Questions and Problems

1. In Lower Slobovia, the army is recruited by a draft and each recruit is paid $50 a month. In Upper Slobovia, the army is voluntary and each recruit must be paid $500 a month. Is the cost of the military cheaper in Lower Slobovia?

2. Why do economists measure profit differently than accountants?

3. A firm's accounting costs are $15,000 per month. In addition, the firm's implicit opportunity costs are $5,000. What are the firm's total opportunity costs? If revenue were $22,000, how much economic profit would the firm earn?

4. Your uncle gives you a "free" car and pays for the insurance, gas, oil, and repairs. You are told you may sell the car any time. Assume the car is now worth $20,000 and will have an estimated value of $12,000 after one year. If the interest rate is 10 percent, how much does it cost you to use the car for one year?

5. Contrast the average-total-cost (*ATC*) curve of a firm that has very large fixed costs relative to variable costs with the *ATC* curve of a firm that has very small fixed costs relative to variable costs.

6. Explain why fixed costs should not affect business decisions in the short run.

7. Answer the following questions using the production-function information in Table A.
   a. What is the *MPP* between 3 and 5 units of output?
   b. Derive the *MPP* schedule. Does it obey the law of diminishing returns?

TABLE A

Labor (units)	Output (units)
0	0
1	5
2	15
3	20
4	23
5	24

8. At the current output level, the average total cost (*ATC*) is $25, and marginal cost (*MC*) is $15. If output were increased by one unit, what would happen to the new average total cost? To the new average variable cost? If *ATC* were to stay at $25 and *MC* were to increase to $25, what would happen to the next *ATC*?

9. Suppose *FC* = $25, *VC* = Q^2, and *MC* = $2Q$. Draw the *AFC, AVC, MC,* and *ATC* curves. At what output level does the minimum *ATC* occur?

10. What is the role of the law of diminishing returns in explaining the shape of the marginal cost curve?

11. If *MC* rises, what conclusion can be drawn about whether *ATC* or *AVC* is rising or falling?

12. What is the opportunity cost of a worker to a firm that mistakenly pays the worker $40 an hour instead of the worker's wage of $25 an hour?

13. A firm increases its output by 50 units and finds that its costs, in the short run, increase by $200. What is its marginal cost of production over this range?

14. Suppose 30 units of labor produce 100 widgets and 40 units of labor produce 200 widgets. If each unit of labor is paid $10, what is the marginal cost of producing widgets between those two output levels?

15. Using Table B, plot all the short-run total-cost and average-cost curves discussed in this chapter. Do the cost curves have the expected shapes? Explain your answer.

TABLE B

Output (units)	Fixed Costs (dollars)	Variable Costs (dollars)
1	10	5
2	10	8
3	10	12
4	10	20
5	10	40

Doing Economics

If there is an empty seat next to you in economics class, it appears that the marginal cost (from the point of view of the college) of adding a student is zero. Is this true? Explain. It is profitable to fill the seat if the increased revenue the college receives exceeds its marginal cost. What implications does this have for the pricing and supply behavior of your college?

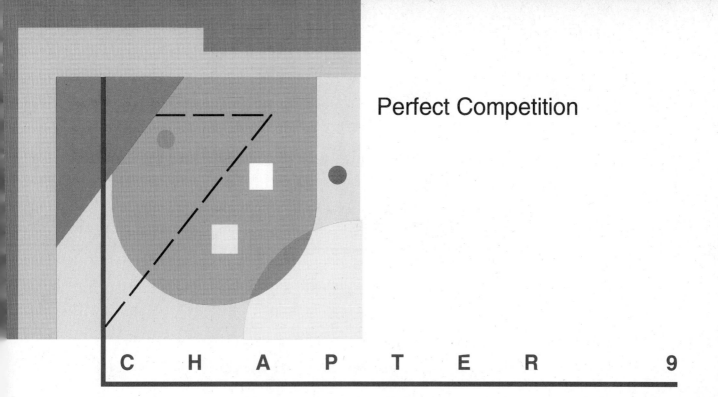

Perfect Competition

C H A P T E R   9

CHAPTER FOCUS   Most people have seen competition and the lack of competition. If they work for a manufacturing or service company, they know that rival firms are competing with them for customers. They know the importance of holding their market share. In their jobs, people understand that other people are willing to take their place or that another company may want to hire them away. Accordingly, they encounter competition in the job market, just as their employer encounters competition in the market for products. If they work for the electric light company or for the only cable television company in town, they see that they have to hustle less to sell their product and have to worry less about the actions of rival firms.

   Adam Smith in his *Wealth of Nations* emphasized the benefits of competition. It is competition that makes the self-centered baker or shoemaker produce the products desired by consumers. It is competition that causes firms to seek out new ways of doing things and to develop new products.

   This chapter describes how businesses operate in the most competitive of all markets—the perfectly competitive market.

After studying this chapter, you will be able to:

- See why perfectly competitive firms are price takers, and why price equals marginal revenue.
- Understand the profit maximization conditions for the firm under perfect competition.
- Discuss how the supply curve of the market is related to the marginal cost curves of each firm.
- Determine the shape of the long-run supply curve for both constant-cost and increasing-cost industries.
- Explain why perfect competition is efficient.

THE FOUR MARKET MODELS

An industry is a collection of firms producing a similar product (such as steel, aluminum, milk, wheat, or automobiles). Each industry is characterized by how much competition is present. Economists distinguish among four basic market models: *perfect competition, monopolistic competition, oligopoly,* and *monopoly.*

These markets will be discussed in detail later on. Briefly, *perfect competition* exists in an industry where individual firms have no control over the market price, and new firms are perfectly free to enter the industry. Perfect competition is most likely in an industry where there are many small producers of a homogeneous product, such as farming. *Monopolistic competition* prevails when there are many small producers of a differentiated product and new firms can enter freely. Local supermarkets and service stations are examples of monopolistic competitors. When firms are large relative to the market (such as General Motors or Ford), and there are impediments to the entry of new firms, the industry is *oligopolistic.* Automobile companies, steel companies, soap manufacturers, and cereal producers are examples of oligopolies. Finally, a *pure monopoly* exists when an industry's product is supplied by only one firm. Examples of pure monopolies are the local telephone service or cable-TV service.

The remainder of this chapter deals with firms that operate in perfectly competitive markets. The three other markets are discussed in the following chapters.

CHARACTERISTICS OF PERFECT COMPETITION

Almost every seller exercises some influence over price, but the more competition the seller faces the less control the individual seller can exercise over the prices charged. In the limiting case, the seller has absolutely no control over price. When the price is given to the individual seller by the market, the seller is said to be a **price taker**. In a perfectly competitive industry, each individual seller faces so much competition from other sellers that the market price is taken as a given. The price is something to which the perfectly competitive firm reacts. It cannot influence the market price through its actions.

> A **price taker** is a seller that does not have the ability to control the price of the good it sells.

The characteristics of perfectly competitive markets account for the inability of a single firm to influence the market price. In perfect competition, all firms in the industry sell a homogeneous or identical product. No firm exercises an advantage over other firms in terms of quality, location, or other product features. If Firm A charges a higher price than Firm B for the identical product, no rational buyer will buy from A. In a perfectly competitive market, buyers have perfect information about the prices charged by different sellers. Every buyer would know if Firm B's price is lower than Firm A's price. Moreover, there are so many firms that no single firm can affect market supply by increasing or decreasing its output.

In an industry characterized by **perfect competition**:
1. There is a large number of buyers and sellers in the market.
2. Each buyer and seller has perfect information about prices and product quality.
3. The product being sold is homogeneous; it is not possible (or even worthwhile) to distinguish the product of one firm from that of other firms.
4. There are no barriers to entry into or exit from the market; there is freedom of entry and exit.
5. All firms are price takers: No single seller is large enough to exert any control over the product price, so each seller accepts the market price as given.

The Conditions for Perfect Competition

Most industries are not perfectly competitive, but the model of perfect competition is much more useful than the strict conditions would indicate. In real-world markets, there are many industries that closely *approximate* the conditions of perfect competition. In such markets, the number of producers may not be large

Competition and World Trade

Economics teaches that a market consists of all potential buyers and sellers of a good or service. Both domestic and foreign firms serve as sellers in markets, and the presence of foreign sellers increases the amount of competition in a market. Competition in a market is determined by the number of foreign and domestic competitors.

The last thirty years have seen a dramatic expansion in world trade. From 1970 to 1988, world trade increased more than 6 percent per year, which is about twice the growth of economic activity in general. The high growth of international trade was made possible by the dismantling of barriers to international competition any by the development of modern telecommunications. Business enterprises no longer operate in isolated national markets. They must compete not only with domestic rivals, but also with rival producers located thousands of miles away. Around the globe, more and more businesses find that their chief competitors in markets are located in other countries.

The growth of international trade and competition means that it is no longer valid to measure competition according to the number of domestic producers in a market. Although there are only three major U.S. automobile manufacturers, they face stiff competition from rivals located in Germany, Italy, France, Japan, Brazil, and South Korea. Restaurants in Paris, Frankfurt, and Tokyo must compete for customers with McDonalds and Burger King. Buyers of precision machinery receive competitive bids from manufacturers in Switzerland, Hong Kong, Canada, and New Zealand.

The growth of international competition has made the theory of competition more relevant. International trade has increased the amount of competition in world markets.

enough to make each firm a perfect price taker, but the amount of control over price may be negligible. Information on prices and product quality may not be perfect, but consumers may have a significant amount of information at their disposal. The product may not be perfectly homogeneous, but the distinctions among products may be inconsequential. The number of firms actually in the industry may not be exceptionally large, but a large number of firms may be waiting in the wings to enter on short notice if economic profits are earned. (See Example 1.)

This chapter shows that perfect competition yields important insights into the functioning of markets. It describes the competitive forces that attract resources from one industry to another. It describes how businesses that have little control over price select the level of output that is best for them. It shows that firms operating in competitive markets produce output at minimum average cost in the long run. The model of perfect competition also shows why profits to be driven down to normal returns in competitive markets.

The Firm and the Industry

The difference between the perfectly competitive firm and the market (or the industry as a whole) is illustrated in Exhibit 1. Panel (b) shows the market demand curve, D, for the product. When the market price is $7, the quantity demanded in the market is 10,000 units. The individual firm, shown in panel (a), can sell all it wants (from a practical standpoint) at the going market price of $7. Whether the firms sells 3 units or 10 units, the price is still the $7 market price.

EXHIBIT 1 **Market Demand Versus Firm Demand**

a. The Firm b. The Market

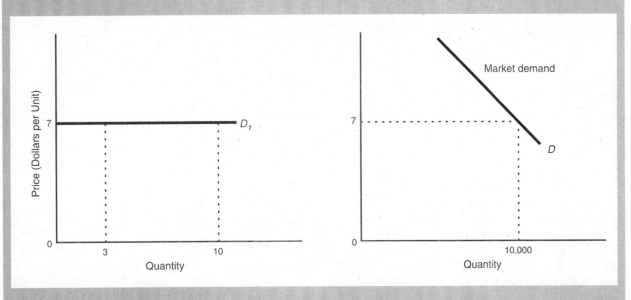

The market demand curve, *D*, in panel (b) shows the total market demand for a homogeneous product being produced by many relatively small firms. The demand curve, *D₁*, in panel (a) shows how the demand is perceived by the individual firm. Because the individual firm is so small relative to the market, it cannot significantly influence the market price. The firm is, thus, a price taker and can sell all it wants at the going price.

The demand curve facing the perfectly competitive firm is *horizontal* or *perfectly elastic* at the going market price.

The perfectly competitive firm can sell all it wants at the prevailing market price. This means that the demand curve *that the individual firm faces is perfectly elastic*.

The individual firm in a perfectly competitive market produces very small amounts relative to the market as a whole. An individual firm cannot change the market price by altering the quantity of the good it offers in the marketplace. Because the individual firm faces a perfectly elastic demand schedule, the firm is a price taker. If the firm tried to sell at a price higher than the market price, it would sell nothing.

THE SHORT-RUN SUPPLY CURVE

Perfectly competitive firms have no control over price; they are price takers. They do not have to decide what price to charge. The market does that. Therefore, the major decision they must make is how much output to produce. In the short run, a perfectly competitive firm makes its output decisions by varying the quantity of its variable inputs (such as labor, raw material, or energy) that are used with its fixed plant and equipment.

Selecting Output to Maximize Profit

Business firms use marginal analysis to decide *how much* to produce. The firm determines whether it is producing the "right" amount of output by considering what would happen if it either increased or reduced the level of output. If producing another unit of output raises the *profit of the firm (or reduces its losses),* more output should be produced. If reducing output by one unit raised profit, output should be reduced. Adjustments in the level of output will continue to be made as long as each change adds more profit or reduces losses.

Marginal costs play a key role in the firm's search for the right level of output. The preceding chapter showed that marginal cost (*MC*) is the increase in costs that results from increasing output by one unit. Marginal costs tell the firm what is happening to costs as it considers marginal changes in output. In considering marginal changes in output, the firm must compare marginal costs with changes in revenues.

The **profit-maximization rule** is that output should be produced up to the point where the extra cost of an additional unit of output (marginal cost) is just equal to the extra revenue derived from the additional unit of output, or the **marginal revenue (*MR*)**.

> Marginal revenue (*MR*) is the increase in total revenue (*TR*) that results from each one-unit increase in the amount of output:
>
> $$MR = \frac{\Delta TR}{\Delta Q}.$$

> The **profit-maximization rule** is that a firm will maximize profits by producing that level of output at which marginal revenue (*MR*) equals marginal cost (*MC*).

As long as an extra unit of output adds more to revenues than to costs, the profits of the firm are increasing (or its losses are being reduced). If the marginal cost of an additional unit of output exceeds its marginal revenue, the profits of the firm would be reduced (or its losses increased) if output is expanded. The profit-maximizing rule is a general rule that applies to all firms—be they perfectly competitive, oligopolistic, or monopolistic. Each firm will produce that level of output at which marginal revenue and marginal cost are equal.

The relationship between marginal revenue and price is different for perfectly competitive firms than for other types of firms (the importance of this distinction will be clear after studying the next chapter). For example, a monopolist can determine the price. By setting a high price, the monopolist loses sales; by setting a low price, the monopolist gains sales. Briefly, for a monopolist, marginal revenue will generally be less than the price because increasing the number of units sold lowers the price. But the competitive firm can sell all it wants at the going market price. To a competitive firm, the price (*P*) measures the extra revenue of an additional unit of output, or the marginal revenue (*MR*), because the extra unit sold is sold without depressing the market price. The increase in revenue brought about by increasing output by one unit, therefore, equals *P*.

Consider the hypothetical competitive firm described in Exhibit 2. The costs are the same as the firm studied in Exhibit 3 of the previous chapter. Both the table and the graph can be used to show how much the firm decides to produce. Panel (b) shows the basic data. The firm's average variable costs (*AVC*) for different levels of output are shown in column 2. The firm's average total costs (*ATC*) are shown in column 3. Total costs are shown in column 4, and the firm's marginal costs (*MC*) are shown in column 5. Panel (a) shows the same information in

EXHIBIT 2   The Profit-Maximizing Firm

a. Short-Run Profits

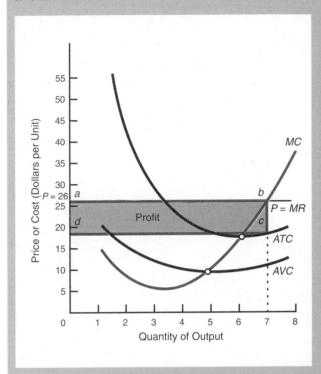

The market price is $26. The firm maximizes profits at an output level of 7 units (where $P = MC$). At $P = \$26$, price exceeds ATC by the distance bc. Total profit is the rectangle $abcd$ in panel (a) and is $54, as shown by column 8 of panel (b).

b. Cost and Revenue Schedule

Output (1)	Average Variable Cost (2)	Average Total Cost (3)	TC (4)	Marginal Cost (5)	P = Marginal Revenue (6)	Revenue (7)	Profit (8)
0	—	∞	$48		$26	$0	−$48
				$20			
1	$20	$68	68	15	26	$26	−32
				10			
2	15	39	78	8	26	52	−26
				6			
3	12	28	84	5	26	78	−6
				4			
4	10	22	88	6	26	104	16
				8			
5	9.6	19.2	96	10	26	130	34
				12			
6	10	18	108	16	26	156	48
				20			
7	11.4	18.3	128	26	26	182	54
				32			
8	14	20	160	38	26	208	48
				44			
9	17.3	22.7	204				

graphical form. The graphs of the various cost curves show again that the difference between the *ATC* and *AVC* curves measures average fixed cost (*AFC*) and that the *MC* curve intersects both the *AVC* and *ATC* curves at their minimum points.

The minimum points on the *AVC* and *ATC* curves are important to keep in mind. In Exhibit 2b, column 2 shows that the minimum average variable cost is $9.60—which occurs when output equals 5 units. Column 3 shows that the minimum average total cost is $18 and occurs when output equals 6 units.

Whether the firm can make a profit or not depends upon the price.

Three Cases

In the short run, the firm's objective would be either to maximize profits or, if necessary, to minimize losses. Once the market price is set, the firm can find itself in one of three positions:

1. the price may be high enough that the firm can make economic profits;
2. the price may be low enough that the firm stays in business but produces at a loss; or
3. the price may be so low that the firm's best option is to temporarily shut down and hope for the price to rise.

As the above three outcomes illustrate, prices affect output decisions. At very low prices, the firm may have to shut down. At higher prices, it produces a positive amount of output. The firm's supply curve shows how much it is prepared to sell at each price. We shall demonstrate that the quantity supplied at each price is simply the firm's profit-maximizing output (or its loss-minimizing output).

The Profitable Firm.   Let us start with the price of $26. Because the firm is perfectly competitive, $P = MR = \$26$. Columns 4, 7, and 8 in Exhibit 2b show the total cost, total revenue, and the profit (positive or negative) of the firm. If the firm produces 5 units, where the average total cost (*ATC*) is $19.20, it can make a profit of $34. However, the firm can do better. When output is 5 units, *MC* equals $10. Since $MR = \$26$, the firm can increase its profits by producing more units. The increase in revenue exceeds the increase in costs. If output is increased to 6 units, profit increases to $48. Profit increases from $34 to $48 because the increase in revenue ($26) exceeds the increase in costs ($12) by $14. As long as $MR > MC$, the firm can do better by producing more output. Profit will be maximized when $MR = MC$. This occurs when output equals 7 units and profit is $54.

The graph in Exhibit 2a tells the same story. The line labeled $P = MR$ shows the marginal revenue (which is the same as price) of the firm. At any point along this line, the firm's total revenue equals the price times the quantity at that point. When $P = \$26$, profit is maximized where the $P = MR$ line intersects the *MC* curve—which occurs at an output level of 7 units. The vertical difference between the $P = MR$ line and the *ATC* curve at that point—the distance *bc*—shows profit per unit of output. Total profit is determined by multiplying this difference by the output of 7 units. Total profit is measured by the rectangle *abcd*.

The Loss-Minimizing Firm.   Let us turn to the second case where the market price is not high enough for the firm to make a profit. Since the minimum *ATC* is $18, any lower market price must bring about losses. Consider a price of $16. The firm cannot make a profit. Instead, it must worry about minimizing its losses. Exhibit 3a and 3b uses the same cost figures, but columns 6, 7, and 8 of the table now reflect the lower $16 price. If the firm produced an output of zero, column 4

EXHIBIT 3   The Loss-Minimizing Firm

a. Short-Run Losses

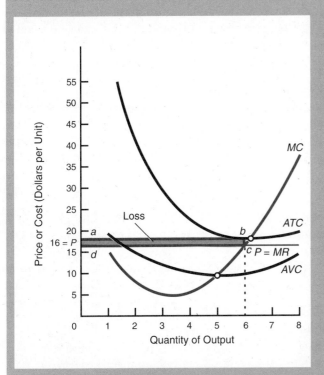

In this case, minimum *ATC* is $18, but *P* = $16. The firm loses money. But the firm minimizes its losses by adjusting output to 6 units, where *P* = *MC*. By shutting down, the firm would lose its fixed costs of $48. By producing where *P* = *MC*, the firm's losses are only $16 because the firm can cover not only its variable costs but also some portion of its fixed costs.

b. Cost and Revenue Schedules

Output (1)	Average Variable Cost (2)	Average Total Cost (3)	TC (4)	Marginal Cost (5)	P = Marginal Revenue (6)	Revenue (7)	Profit (8)
0	—	∞	$48		$16	0	−$48
				$20			
1	$20	$68	68	15	16	$16	−52
				10			
2	15	39	78	8	16	32	−46
				6			
3	12	28	84	5	16	48	−36
				4			
4	10	22	88	6	16	64	−24
				8			
5	9.6	19.2	96	10	16	80	−16
				12			
6	10	18	108	16	16	96	−12
				20			
7	11.4	18.3	128	26	16	112	−16
				32			
8	14	20	160	38	16	128	−32
				44			
9	17.3	22.7	204				

shows that total costs would still be $48—the firm's fixed costs do not go away if it shuts down. The firm's revenue would be zero, as shown in column 7, and its loss (its negative profit) would be −$48.

If the firm shuts down, it loses its entire fixed costs of $48. Can the firm do better? If the firm's revenue exceeds its variable costs, something will be left over to cover some portion of its fixed cost. If the firm can pay even a small portion of its fixed costs by staying in business, it is better off. The minimum AVC ($9.60) occurs when output is 5 units. By producing 5 units, the firm's price exceeds AVC by $6.40. The difference between the price and AVC generates revenues that can be used to cover some of the fixed costs. If the firm produced 5 units of output, its loss is −$16, as shown in column 8. At an output of 5 units, the firm is still not minimizing its losses. The price of $16 still exceeds the marginal costs of $10. An additional unit of output would add $16 to revenue and only $10 to costs. According to the profit-maximizing rule, the firm should produce more. The firm's losses are minimized when the output is 6 units, where $P = MC$. In panel (a), this occurs at point c, where the $P = MR$ line intersects the MC curve. The firm's losses *per unit of output* are measured by the distance bc, or $P - ATC = \$16 - \$18 = -\$2$. When it produces 6 units, the firm loses $2 per unit. The firm's total losses of −$12 (the 6 units times the $2 loss per unit) are shown by the rectangle abcd.

The Shutdown Case.   In both cases so far, the price of the product exceeded the minimum AVC of $9.60. If the price falls short of the minimum AVC, what should the firm do? The firm should temporarily shut down. After all, if the price falls short of average variable cost, the firm's revenues must fall short of variable costs. In this case, it loses not only its fixed cost, but also that portion of its variable cost that is not covered by dollar sales. Thus, the firm's **shutdown rule** holds that output should be zero when the price is less than minimum average variable cost.

> The **shutdown rule** is: If the firm's price at all levels of output is less than average variable costs, it minimizes its losses by shutting down.

Exhibit 4 shows the competitive firm when the price is only $8. Column 8 in panel (b)'s table shows that its losses are minimized when output is zero. When the firm produces nothing, its losses are limited to its fixed cost of $48. Any additional output, since the price does not cover AVC, must increase the firm's losses. By producing the first unit, for example, the firm's AVC is $20. Since the price is only $8, the firm loses −$12 on the first unit. Thus, its losses increase from −$48 to −$60 as output rises from 0 to 1 unit. The $P = MR$ line is less than AVC for any output. The firm's losses are minimized when output equals zero. In column 8, its losses are −$48 for output equal to 0. For any positive level of output, the firm loses more money than by shutting down. In panel (a)'s graph, the price line $P = MR$ lies everywhere below the AVC curve.

The three cases explain the competitive firm's supply curve. The supply curve shows the output levels that competitive firms are prepared to supply at each price. In each case, the profit-maximizing level of output increased as the price increases.

The Industry Supply Curve

The behavior of the profit-maximizing firm explains the short-run behavior of the perfectly competitive industry of which it is a part. Recall that the short run is a period so short that old firms cannot build new plants and equipment; new firms cannot enter; old firms cannot leave. There are a fixed number of competitive

Perfectly competitive firms choose that level of output where $P = MC$—or, in graphical terms, where the P (=MR) line intersects the MC curve—provided price is greater than the minimum level of AVC. This holds whether the firm is maximizing its profit or minimizing its losses.

The competitive firm's supply curve (how much it is willing to sell at different prices) is that portion of the firm's MC curve above the AVC curve. It shows the profit-maximizing level of output for the firm at different price levels. Because the marginal cost curve is positively sloped, the competitive firm's supply curve is also positively sloped.

EXHIBIT 4 The Shutdown Case

a. Zero Output

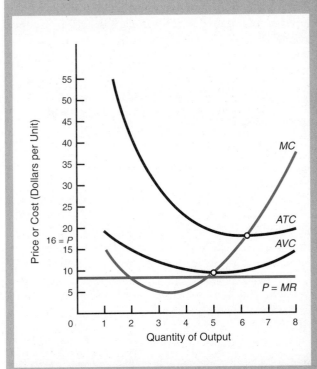

The firm minimizes its losses by shutting down if the price is less than *AVC*. In this case, *P* = $8 and the minimum *AVC* is $9.60.

b. Cost and Revenue Schedules

Output (1)	Average Variable Cost (2)	Average Total Cost (3)	*TC* (4)	Marginal Cost (5)	*P* = Marginal Revenue (6)	Revenue (7)	Profit (8)
0	—	∞	$48		$8	0	−$48
				$20			
1	$20	$68	68	15	8	$8	−60
				10			
2	15	39	78	8	8	16	−62
				6			
3	12	28	84	5	8	24	−60
				4			
4	10	22	88	6	8	32	−56
				8			
5	9.6	19.2	96	10	8	40	−56
				12			
6	10	18	108	16	8	48	−60
				20			
7	11.4	18.3	128	26	8	56	−72
				32			
8	14	20	160	38	8	64	−96
				44			
9	17.3	22.7	204				

firms of given sizes. Each firm's supply curve is its MC curve above its AVC curve.

In the short run, the **market** or **industry supply curve** is the sum of the profit-maximizing or loss-minimizing outputs of every firm at each price. Exhibit 5 shows how the market supply curve is derived in the simple case of four identical firms, but the principles are the same for any number of firms. To simplify, we have considered an even simpler marginal cost curve than in the previous example.

> In the short run, the **market supply curve** is the horizontal summation of the supply curves of each firm, which in turn are their MC curves above minimum AVC.

The marginal cost curve (above AVC) for a single firm is shown as $S_1 = MC$. The firm wishes to sell 0 units at a price of $15, 2 units at a price of $20, 3 units at a price of $25, 4 units at $35, and 5 units at $50. The curve S_4 shows the market supply curve for all four firms. Graphically, the market supply curve is the *horizontal* summation of each firm's supply curve. With four identical firms, no industry output is supplied at a price of $15. At a price of $20, 8 units are supplied (the four firms times 2 units each). At a price of $50, the industry is prepared to supply 20 (four firms times 5 units each). The supply curves S_2 and S_3 show what the market supply curves would be with only two and three firms in the industry. Additional firms simply shift the market supply curve to the right.

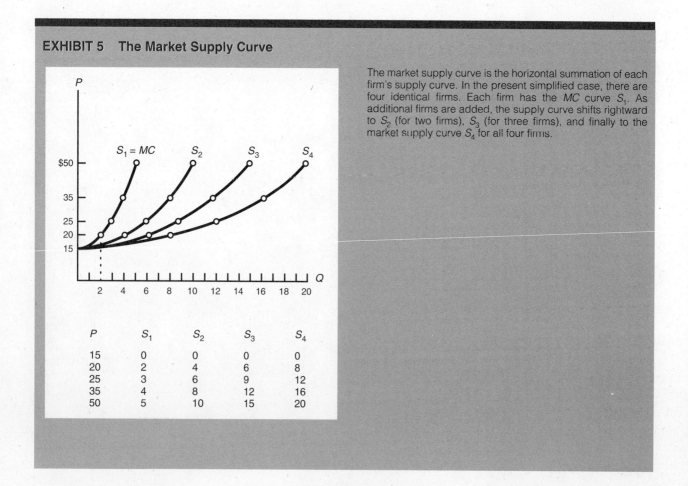

EXHIBIT 5   The Market Supply Curve

The market supply curve is the horizontal summation of each firm's supply curve. In the present simplified case, there are four identical firms. Each firm has the MC curve S_1. As additional firms are added, the supply curve shifts rightward to S_2 (for two firms), S_3 (for three firms), and finally to the market supply curve S_4 for all four firms.

P	S_1	S_2	S_3	S_4
15	0	0	0	0
20	2	4	6	8
25	3	6	9	12
35	4	8	12	16
50	5	10	15	20

Short-Run Equilibrium

The market or industry equilibrium is determined when the market price equilibrates the market supply with the market demand for the good. Exhibit 6 shows how the short-run equilibrium price is determined, using the hypothetical firm of Exhibits 2 through 4. Panel (a) shows the individual firm, and panel (b) an industry consisting of 1,000 such firms. The supply curve S in panel (b) is the horizontal summation of each firm's MC curve above AVC. For example, at the price $26 each firm sells 7 units and the industry sells 7,000 units. The market demand curve, D, intersects the market supply curve at the price of $26. At $26, the quantity demanded equals the quantity supplied (7,000). The $26 price becomes the firm's horizontal demand curve. In response to this price, the firm produces 7 units of the output, where the MC curve intersects its demand curve. The profit-maximizing behavior of the individual firm is consistent with the profit-maximizing behavior of all the firms in the market.

Panel (a) shows a representative firm that is *making an economic profit: ATC* at the profit-maximizing output level of 7 units is $18.30; therefore, the firm is making a per-unit profit of $7.70 (= $26 – $18.30) on each of the 7 units for a total of $54 economic profit. The representative firm could just as easily have made losses, because in the short run the firm will not shut down as long as it can pay part of its fixed costs.

EXHIBIT 6   Short-Run Equilibrium: The Firm and the Market

a. The Firm   **b. The Market**

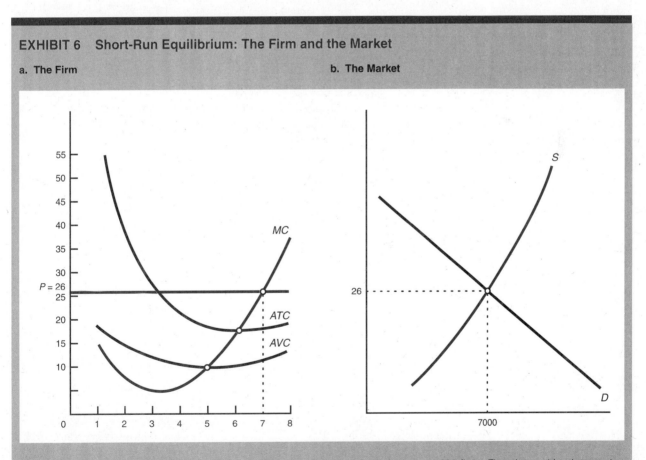

Panel (a) shows the representative firm; panel (b) shows the market, in which there are 1,000 firms. Firm demand is when market demand and supply are in equilibrium at the point of a $26 price and an equilibrium market output of 7,000 units. The individual firm produces 7 units of output and makes a profit of $54 ($7.70 × 7 units) from the per-unit profit of approximately $7.70.

The effect of economic profits on perfectly competitive industries is felt primarily in the long run when new firms can enter the industry and established firms can exit. As competitive firms respond to economic profits or losses, the industry short-run supply schedule shifts, and prices change.

Economic Profit Attracts Resources

Profit equals revenue minus costs. As noted in the preceding chapter, *economic profits* equal revenues minus opportunity costs, not just revenue minus accounting costs. *Opportunity costs* are the best alternatives sacrificed by the business firm when it engages in some particular production plan. *Included in these alternatives is the return that could be earned by the owner/entrepreneur if the owner's money capital, labor, and managerial time had been used elsewhere.* Economic losses are incurred when the return to the resources used in the business firm is less than the normal return those resources could earn in the next best alternative. When economic profits are zero, the business firm is earning a **normal profit**.

> A **normal profit** requires zero economic profit or accounting profit equal to a normal competitive return on the resources used in the firm.

The persistence of economic profits ($P > ATC$) or economic losses ($P < ATC$) is not a stable or equilibrium situation in the long run for a competitive industry. If economic profits continue, there will be an incentive in the long run for new firms to enter the industry. New firms will cause the price of the good to fall and economic profits to disappear. On the other hand, if there are economic losses, some firms will choose to exit from the industry. When long-term leases expire or an unprofitable plant can be sold, the firm no longer has these fixed costs and is free to leave the industry. The disappearance of firms will raise the price of the good and eliminate the losses. Thus, economic profits and losses tend to the normal level. Only when a normal profit is being earned will the industry be at rest—in long-run equilibrium. Long-run equilibrium occurs when firms no longer wish to either enter or leave the industry.

Entry and Exit

Perfectly competitive industries move toward normal profit by the entry and exit of firms. For the economy as a whole, entry and exit are opposite sides of the same coin. If it is profitable to enter one industry, resources must be exiting another industry. In other words, if revenue exceeds opportunity costs in some industries, revenue falls short of opportunity costs in other industries.

Entry. Consider the perfectly competitive industry consisting of 100 firms shown in panel (b) of Exhibit 7. Panel (a) shows the ATC and MC curves of a typical firm in this industry; ATC is the short-run average-total-cost curve in an efficient scale of plant. Panel (b) shows the market supply curve derived by summing the supply curves of 100 such firms. When the market demand curve is *D,* the equilibrium price is \$10. At this price, the representative firm is making zero profits (a normal profit). The demand curve facing the representative firm is D_1; each of the 100 firms produces 7 units of the product, making for a market output

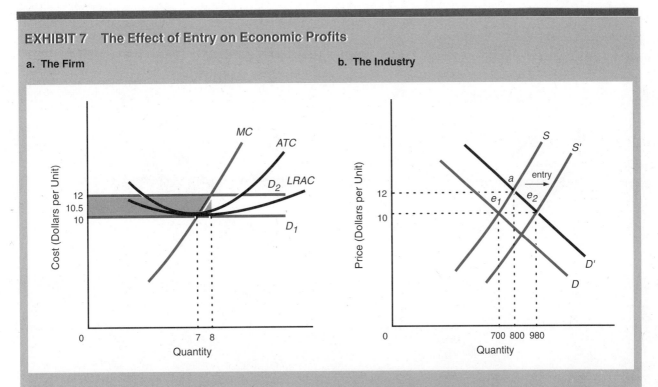

EXHIBIT 7   The Effect of Entry on Economic Profits

a. The Firm

b. The Industry

The initial long-run equilibrium is e_1, at the intersection of D and S in panel (b). When demand shifts to D', the short-run equilibrium price rises to $12 (point a), creating economic profits for the individual firm facing the new demand curve D_2 in panel (a). In the long run, new firms enter until the supply curve shifts to S'. The long-run equilibrium is established at point e_2, where price again equals $10. Each firm returns to producing 7 units of output, but the number of firms rises from 100 (700 ÷ 7) to 140 (980 ÷ 7).

of 700 units. The industry is in long-run equilibrium. With a normal profit, there is no inducement either to enter or exit.

Suppose that consumers increase their demand for the product, and the market demand curves shifts from D to D'. The short-run equilibrium price rises to $12, and the short-run equilibrium output of the industry rises to 800 units. At this higher price, the firm's short-run equilibrium is now at 8 units of output, where price and marginal cost are equal. The typical firm now makes economic profits. In the short run, which may be a few months or many years, the individual firm will enjoy above-normal returns. This is not a long-run equilibrium because economic problems act as an inducement for new firms to enter the industry.

In the long run, above-normal profits will attract more firms. *As these new firms enter the market, the supply curve shifts to the right,* because the market supply is the sum of individual supply curves. The entry of new firms will continue as long as economic profits are positive. But as the supply curve shifts to the right (to S'), the market price falls, putting a squeeze on profits. Eventually, in the new long-run equilibrium, economic profits must again be zero. The new long-run (and short-run) equilibrium is e_2, which is at the old equilibrium price of $10. In the new long-run equilibrium, the individual firm again produces 7 units, but there are now 140 such firms producing 7 units each (or 980 total units for the market as a whole).

Exit.   The reverse of entry is exit. Like entry, the exit of firms leads to a long-run equilibrium with the representative firm earning a normal profit. In part (b) of Exhibit 8, the initial demand and supply curves are D and S in panel (b). The

EXHIBIT 8   The Effect of Exit on Economic Losses

a. The Firm

b. The Industry

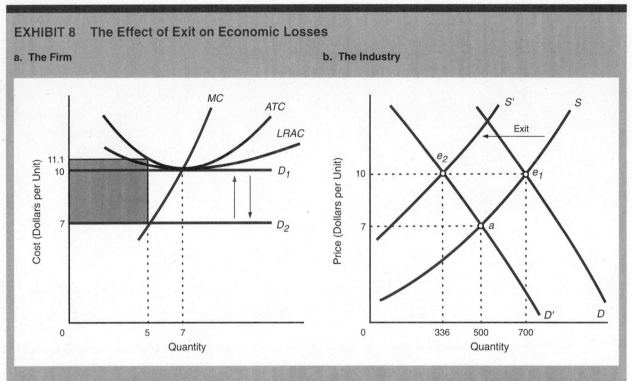

The initial long-run equilibrium is e_1, the intersection of D and S in panel (b). Demand drops to D', causing the short-run equilibrium price to fall to $7 (point a). The representative firm in panel (a) makes losses as D_1 shifts downward to D_2. The exit of firms in the long run shifts the supply curve to S', which lifts the price back to $10 and eliminates losses. Each firm returns to producing 7 units of output, but the number of firms falls from 100 (700 ÷ 7) to 48 (336 ÷ 7).

equilibrium is at e_1, which is both a short-run and a long-run equilibrium. There are 100 firms. Point e_1 is a short-run equilibrium point because, in Exhibit 8b, the market quantity supplied equals the market quantity demanded and because, in Exhibit 8a, $P = MC$ for the representative firm. The market is in long-run equilibrium because when price is $10 (the firm demand curve is D_1), the representative firm makes a normal profit.

Suppose now that consumers reduce their demand for the product, and the market demand curve shifts from D to D' in Exhibit 8b. When the demand curve shifts from D to D', the short-run equilibrium shifts from e_1 to a. The short-run price falls to $7, and the short-run quantity falls to 500 units, with the representative firm producing 5 units. Because $7 is less than ATC, the representative firm has economic losses. In the long run, firms will begin to exit (the weaker ones first). The exit of firms shifts the industry supply curve to the left until economic losses are eliminated (at S'), and price is driven back up to the original $10. The new equilibrium is at e_2, where total output is 336 units, and there are now only 48 firms, which again produce an average of 7 units each.

Characteristics of Long-Run Equilibrium

Exhibits 7 and 8 show a perfectly competitive market in long-run equilibrium. The industry is brought to a long-run equilibrium by entry in response to economic profits and exit due to losses. Consider the characteristics of this long-run equilibrium.

Perfectly competitive firms will operate at maximum efficiency (produce at minimum *LRAC*) in the long run. Long-run equilibrium occurs for the competitive industry when economic profits are zero and long-run average costs are minimized.

In the long run, the firm operates at an efficient scale of operation. The *ATC* curve for the optimal plant will have a minimum average cost equal to the minimum average cost on the long-run average-cost curve. The long-run equilibrium for the representative firm occurs at q_0, where $P = ATC = LRAC$.

When $P = MC$ and $P = ATC = LRAC$ at the long-run equilibrium output, and when *MC* intersects *ATC* at its *minimum point,* the perfectly competitive firm is producing at the lowest average cost in the long run.

Both forces together bring about *efficient* production, or production in which the good is being produced at the minimum cost to society. The firm in a competitive industry cannot be inefficient in the long run; the firm cannot select an inappropriate plant size. The plant size in Exhibit 7 must be the best possible size for producing 7 units, or the firm would not be around in the long run.

The Long-Run Industry Supply Curve

In Exhibits 7 and 8, increases or decreases in demand serve to raise or lower price in the short run. But in the long run, prices remain the same! In the case of Exhibit 7, the increase in demand is answered by an increase in supply that drives the price back down to the original level. Similarly, in Exhibit 8, the decrease in demand is answered by a decrease in supply that drives the price back up to the original level. The **long-run industry supply curve** determines what happens to price when demand changes.

> The **long-run industry supply curve** shows the quantities that the industry is prepared to supply at different prices *after* the entry or exit of firms is completed.

Constant-Cost Industries.   The long-run industry supply curve corresponding to Exhibits 7 and 8 is perfectly elastic (horizontal) at the price of $10, which equals the minimum unit cost of production (minimum *LRAC*). The case of a perfectly elastic industry supply curve is illustrated in Exhibit 9, where S_L is the long-run industry supply curve. Shifts in demand, such as the shift from *D* to *D'*, simply change the equilibrium quantity in the long run; there is no change in prices or costs. When shifts in demand do not change prices or cost in the long run, the industry is a **constant-cost industry**.

If the individual firms' cost curves remain the same when the industry expands (or contracts), the industry will be a constant-cost industry. Firms in constant-cost industries purchase labor, raw materials, lands, and the like at the same prices whether the industry is expanding or contracting. The constant-cost industry's demand for resources is a relatively small part of the total demand, and the industry's factor inputs usually are not highly specialized. (See Example 2)

> A **constant-cost industry** is relatively small and, hence, can expand or contract without significantly affecting the terms at which factors of production used in the industry are purchased. The long-run industry supply curve for a constant-cost industry is horizontal.

Increasing-Cost Industries.   As the number of firms in an **increasing-cost industry** expands, the prices of the factors of production used by that industry are bid up. Industries whose factor purchases make up a large percentage of the market and industries that use factors of production specialized to that industry are

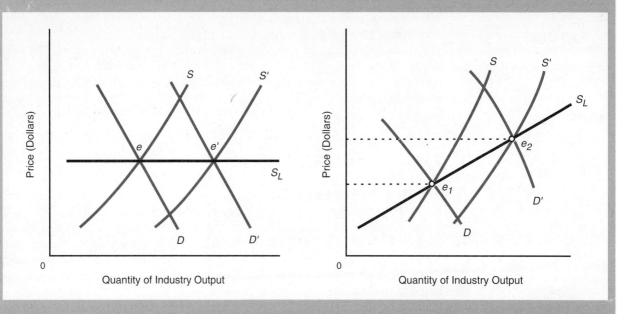

EXHIBIT 9 Long-Run Supply Curves

a. Constant-Cost Industry

b. Increasing-Cost Industry

Costs are constant for a constant-cost industry. In Panel (a), when demand increases, as from D to D', in a long run the price stays the same and only quantity increases as supply increases by a corresponding amount from S to S'. Price must stay the same to keep economic profits at zero. Thus, the long-run supply curve, S_L, is perfectly elastic. For an increasing-cost industry, costs increase when demand expands. In Panel (b), initially D and S are the demand and supply curves. When demand shifts to D', the long-run equilibrium price increases from p_1 to p_2. The entry of new firms and the rise in costs cause the short supply curve to shift only to S'. The long-run supply curve, S_L, is upwardly sloping but is still more elastic than the short-run supply curves, such as S or S'.

usually increasing-cost industries. Thus, when the industry is expanding, the individual firms must pay higher prices for their resources—so their costs of production will rise.

> As an **increasing-cost industry** expands, the factor prices of resources used in the industry are bid up. As the industry contracts, the prices of these factors fall. Hence, the long-run industry supply curve for an increasing-cost industry is upwardly sloping.

The long-run adjustment in an increasing-cost industry is illustrated in Exhibit 9. The equilibrium is initially at e_1, with the demand curve at D. The demand curve shifts to D', raising the price in the short run to the level indicated at point a. The typical firm now earns economic profits. New firms enter, the industry expands, and the price of the good itself falls, squeezing profits toward zero, as in a constant-cost industry. But factor prices are also bid up as the industry expands, and this increase in factor costs and the increase in the number of firms cause the supply curve to shift from S to S'. In the final equilibrium, indicated at e_2, profits have been squeezed to zero by the entry of new firms *and* rising costs. The long-run supply curve is shown as S_L.

Two of the most important characteristics of perfectly competitive industries are: (1) that perfectly competitive firms will operate at minimum average cost in

Competition, Freedom of Entry, and One-Hour Photo Processing

As recently as 10 years ago, people had to wait overnight for film to be developed. In the early 1980s, French and Japanese manufacturers revolutionized the photo-processing industry by developing low-cost minilabs that could fit into a corner space in a pharmacy or any other small retail establishment. When introduced, these minilabs required an investment of $33,000. As technology was perfected, the price of the minilabs dropped substantially.

The one-hour photo-processing business is characterized by minimal barriers to entry. Anyone who wants to enter the business can do so by buying the necessary equipment. The first entrepreneurs to offer one-hour processing made considerable, but transitory, profits. Later investors, attracted by these profits, entered the business and competed for customers without restriction.

Economic theory states that entry into competitive businesses will cease when all participants earn normal profits. The one-hour photo-processing industry reached this level of saturation in the early 1990s, when one-hour processing was available in virtually every pharmacy, in addition to specialized outlets.

the long run and (2) that perfectly competitive firms will produce that quantity of output at which price equals marginal cost in both the short run and the long run. These characteristics will be important to keep in mind when evaluating the other types of markets—monopoly, oligopoly, and monopolistic competition—that will be studied in the chapters that follow.

The next chapter will examine the behavior of firms that are able to exercise some control over price. Monopolists exercise considerable control over their prices; monopolistically competitive firms have only limited control over their prices.

Chapter Summary

The most important point to learn from this chapter is: In a perfectly competitive market, price equals marginal cost and, in the long run, competition forces firms to produce at the minimum point on their long-run average-cost curves.

1. A perfectly competitive market exists when there is a large number of sellers and buyers, when buyers and sellers have perfect information, when the product is homogeneous, and when there is freedom of entry and exit. These conditions ensure that each seller will be a price taker.

2. In the short run, the number of firms in the industry is fixed, and the firm has fixed costs. In the long run, the number of firms can change through entry and exit, and fixed costs become variable costs. If the market price covers average variable cost, the competitive firm will produce that quantity of output at which price and marginal cost are equal. The firm's supply curve is its marginal cost curve above average variable cost. The industry supply schedule is the horizontal summation of all the

Does the U.S. Need an Industrial Policy?

Critics of U.S economic policy argue that the United States has lost its competitive edge because it does not have an industrial policy. "Industrial policy" can mean a number of things, but in this context it means that the U.S. government should be actively involved in assisting companies or entire branches of the economy in their development. This assistance could be in the form of guaranteed loans, research-and-training grants, or tariff protection. Basically, the government would identify potential "winners" in the international marketplace and then give these winners the assistance they need to establish themselves in the world marketplace.

There are good reasons to oppose active industrial policy. Experience has shown that competitive markets do a good job in weeding out winners from losers. If a business has a good business plan, it will be able to convince private capital markets to fund it. It does not need government funding or subsidized funding if the idea is good. Private entrepreneurs are better at identifying and seeking out profit opportunities than are government bureaucrats sitting in Washington. A government agency in charge of picking winners would be more likely to pick losers than winners.

The most important business ideas and innovations have come from private entrepreneurs. The personal computer market, for example, was pioneered by lone individuals working out of their garages or basements. Larger computer companies passed up the opportunity to develop the personal computer and had to force their own bureaucracies to get involved in personal computers. Major innovations in automobile marketing and manufacturing were the results of Henry Ford's ideas at the turn of the century. The common feature of these innovations was that they were the result of the entrepreneurial drive of a small number of individuals working under competitive conditions. It is unlikely that this drive could be unleashed by an entrenched government bureaucracy, which would naturally favor the larger established firms, lacking in necessary entrepreneurial drive.

Advocates of U.S. industrial policy point to Japan, where the powerful Ministry for Industry and Trade (MITI) has purportedly provided the assistance and guidance that promoted the emergence of Japanese electronics and automotive manufacturers as world leaders.

Japan's industrial policy has not only been a small part of the economy, but the agency in charge, MITI, has been consistently wrong. For example, MITI first wanted only one automobile company. Market forces led them to continually revise their targets until MITI eventually recognized the need for seven automobile companies. The Japanese consumer products that have been so important on world markets (TVs, stereos, automobiles, and VCRs) are not the industries fostered by industrial policy in Japan in the last two decades. They targeted steel and semiconductors, but both industries have generated lower rates of return than other nontargeted industries. No one knows whether these industries created enough positive spillover effects on the rest of the Japanese economy to justify the subsidies.

supply schedules of individual firms in the industry. The price at which the quantity supplied equals the quantity demanded is the market price.

3. In the long run, firms enter competitive industries where economic profits are being made. They exit from industries where a below-normal profit is being earned. Economic profits must be zero for the competitive industry to be in equilibrium. In the long run, goods are produced at minimum average cost with price equal to marginal cost for the average competitive firm.

4. Constant-cost industries have horizontal long-run supply curves, increasing-cost industries have upwardly sloping long-run supply curves.

Key Terms

price taker (p. 180)
perfect competition (p. 181)
marginal revenue (*MR*) (p. 184)
profit-maximization rule (p. 184)
shutdown rule (p. 188)

market or industry supply curve (p. 190)
normal profit (p. 192)
long-run industry supply curve (p. 195)
constant-cost industry (p. 195)
increasing-cost industry (p. 195)

Questions and Problems

1. A firm can sell all it wants at the price of $49.73. What is the firm's marginal revenue?

2. A firm is contemplating whether to produce its 10th unit of output and finds its marginal costs for the 10th unit are $50 and its marginal revenue for the 10th unit equals $30. What advice would you give this firm?

3. A firm has fixed costs of $100,000. It receives a price of $25 for each unit of output. Average variable costs are lowest (equal to $20) at 1,000 units of output. What advice would you give this firm? Would this advice be the same in the short run as in the long run?

4. How is the firm's supply curve related to its marginal cost curve?

5. The representative firm in the widget industry, which is perfectly competitive, is making a large economic profit. What predictions can you make about what will happen in this industry in the long run?

6. What is the difference between a constant-cost industry and constant returns to scale (where the long-run average-cost curve is horizontal)?

7. In the short run, explain what would happen to an industry's price and output if the demand for the product suddenly fell because of bad publicity.

8. In Exhibit 1, the table shows fixed costs are $48. If fixed costs were raised to $60, how would the supply schedule be affected in the short run? How would the supply schedule be affected in the long run?

9. Imagine that a firm faces the cost schedule given in Table A.
    a. Calculate the firm's profit or loss for each level of output when the price is $5.99, when the price is $6.01, and when the price is $10.01.
    b. How many units of output will the profit-

maximizing or loss-minimizing firm produce at those three prices?
    c. What is the firm's supply schedule?

TABLE A

Quantity, Q	Variable Cost, VC	Fixed Cost, FC	Total Cost, TC
0	$0	$5	$5
1	6	5	11
2	14	5	19
3	24	5	29
4	36	5	41

10. You observe the (competitive) airline industry making economic losses. What do you expect to happen to ticket prices, to the quantity of airline passengers, and to the number of airline companies as time passes?

11. You observe a highly profitable new industry producing a product of advanced technology (such as computers). What do you expect to happen to the price of the product, to profits, to the industry's output, and to the number of firms as time passes?

12. Explain why, in the long run, the industry supply curve is perfectly horizontal in the case of a constant-cost industry.

13. What is the key difference between a constant-cost industry and an increasing-cost industry?

14. The long-run elasticity of supply for cucumbers is estimated to be 2.20. Is the cucumber industry a constant-cost industry? Explain.

15. If dry cleaning is a constant-cost industry, what would you expect to happen to the price of dry cleaning in a particular town in both the short run and the long run as the size of the town increases?

Doing Economics

Consider the retail market for gasoline in your city. How closely does it approximate the textbook conditions for perfect competition? Now go out and observe the price of regular unleaded gasoline at ten or more stations. As you record your price data, you may wish to note the location and chain name of each station, as well as any other particular distinguishing characteristics. In a perfectly competitive market, each seller charges the same price. Do your data support the hypothesis that the local gasoline market is perfectly competitive? How would you explain any price variation that you may have observed? Do you think that sellers in this market face perfectly elastic demand curves? Do you think that they make economic profits?

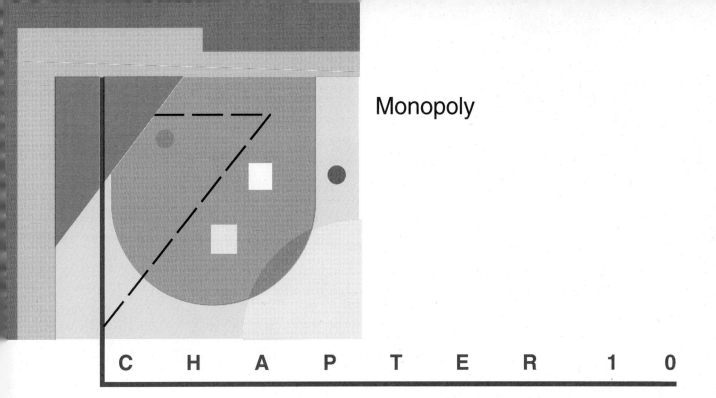

Monopoly

C H A P T E R 1 0

CHAPTER FOCUS

The word "monopoly" evokes the image of evil capitalists oppressing downtrodden consumers with high prices. Monopoly brings to mind oil-rich countries forcing high prices on consumers in both rich and poor countries, of greedy pharmaceutical firms treading on the poor and the sick with outrageous drug prices, and of cable-TV companies with ever-increasing monthly charges.

Economists, heeding the early warnings of Adam Smith in 1776, emphasize the dangers of monopoly. A monopoly raises prices, restricts output, and reduces economic efficiency. The invisible hand works best when competition is present. It does not work effectively when markets are monopolized.

Monopolies can arise for a number of reasons. They can be dictated by technology: One firm produces output much more efficiently than two or more firms. Surprisingly, a major source of monopoly is government. Governments, through licenses, franchises, and other means, can create monopoly markets. In fact, much of the activity of lobbyists at the local, state, and federal levels devoted to receiving monopoly rights to produce and sell some output.

After studying this chapter, you will be able to:

- Discuss the conditions giving rise to monopoly.
- Calculate marginal revenue for a monopolist
- See how the monopolist maximizes profit.
- Understand that a profit-maximizing monopoly cannot be efficient from a social standpoint.

CHARACTERISTICS OF MONOPOLY

Literally, *monopoly* means "single seller." The definition of monopoly focuses on the conditions necessary for there to be only one producer in the market and on the control over price which that one producer has.

Definition of Monopoly

A **pure monopoly** has the following characteristics.

> A **pure monopoly** exists
> 1. when there is one seller in the market for some good or service that has no close substitutes,
> 2. when the seller has considerable control over price, and
> 3. when barriers to entry protect the seller from competition.

Like perfect competition, examples of monopoly in this pure form are rare, but the theory of pure monopoly does shed light on the behavior of firms that approximate the conditions of pure monopoly. Many firms possess at least a little bit of monopoly power. For example, a corner at a particularly busy intersection may be the best spot in town for a service station, and only one firm can occupy that spot. For purposes of clarity our discussion will focus on firms with a great deal of monopoly power.

Limitations on Monopoly Power

"Pure" monopoly is hard to find in the real world for several reasons. First, substitutes of some kind exist for almost all products. National magazines and TV news substitute for local newspapers; stainless steel and copper substitute for aluminum; aluminum foil substitutes for cellophane; foreign imports substitute for domestically produced goods. A pure monopoly requires that there be no good substitutes, but where does one draw the line between good and poor substitutes? Modern technology is good at creating new products to substitute for a monopoly product.

Second, a sole supplier in a particular market may not act like a pure monopolist if it fears that rival firms may enter the market. If the monopolist's economic profits become too high, rivals may find ways to overcome existing barriers to entry. In other words, there is the competition from *potential* substitutes.

Joan Robinson (1903–1983)

Joan Robinson, born in England in 1903, was the daughter of Major General Sir Frederick Maurice and Helen Marsh. She married the economist E. A. G. Robinson in 1926 and began a long teaching career at Cambridge University in the same decade. Her most important work, *The Economics of Imperfect Competition,* was published in 1933. In that masterpiece she completed the Marshallian tradition by examining the detailed consequences of monopoly and monopolistic competition for the pricing of both goods and factors. She was one of the first economists to point to the advantages of price discrimination. She argued: "It may happen, for instance, that a railway would not be built, or a country doctor would not set up in practice, if discrimination were forbidden."

While in her seventies, she traveled for one month in central Africa. The economist Luigi Pasinetti remarked that it was amazing how she endured ". . . living in most primitive conditions with raw food, lack of facilities and exposure to harsh tropical weather, day and night."

Joan Robinson contributed to many areas of economics—international trade, macroeconomics, Marxian economics, the theory of wages, and economic growth. She was perhaps the greatest economist to deserve—but not receive—the Nobel Prize before she died.

Barriers to Entry

If new firms could freely enter the market, there would be no monopoly. In cases where a single firm is earning an economic profit, additional firms would enter, thereby destroying the monopoly. To exist as a monopoly, the existing monopoly must be protected in some manner from the entry of new firms into the market.

The basic source of any monopoly power is the presence of *barriers to entry*. A barrier to entry is anything that gives the existing firm an advantage over new firms that might seek to enter the market. Five factors tend to give existing firms advantages over new entrants. They are:

1. economies of scale,
2. patents,
3. exclusive ownership of raw materials,
4. public franchises, and
5. licensing.

Economies of Scale.   New firms enter markets at smaller levels of output than established firms. If the industry is characterized by economies of scale, the average costs of the new firm will be higher than the average costs of an established firm. The lower average costs of large established firms (the result of economies of scale) protects them from the entry of new firms. The established firm can offer goods to the market at a lower price due to its lower production costs. A *natural monopoly* illustrates the case when the cost advantages of established firms are extreme. A natural monopoly occurs when economies of scale are so large that there is room for only one firm in the industry. Competition is either unworkable or highly inefficient. Examples of possible natural monopolies are the local public utilities that deliver telephone services, gas services, water services, and electricity.

Patents. American *patent* laws allow an inventor the exclusive right to use the invention for a period of seventeen years. During that period, the patent prohibits others from using the invention; the patent holder is protected from competition. The IBM Corporation's patents on tabulating equipment, the Xerox Corporation's patents on copying equipment, the United Shoe Machinery Company's patents on shoemaking machinery, and Smith Kline's patent on the drug Tagamet are examples of this type of entry barrier. The Bell System (now AT&T) achieved a monopoly in the nineteenth century when Alexander Graham Bell was granted a patent just hours before a rival inventor. Even if rival firms wish to enter the market, they are not legally allowed to do so. The patent-holding firm has a legal monopoly to the product as long as the patent remains in effect.

Exclusive Ownership of Raw Materials. Established companies may be protected from the entry of new firms by their control of critical inputs or raw materials. The International Nickel Company of Canada used to own virtually all the world's nickel reserves; virtually all the sales of the world's diamond mines are under the control of the DeBeers Company of South Africa.

Public Franchises. State, local and federal governments grant to individuals or organizations exclusive *franchises* to be the sole operator in a particular business. Competitors are legally prohibited from entering the market. The U. S. Postal Service is a classic example of a public franchise. According to its franchise, only the U. S. Postal Service has the right to deliver and pick up postage from patrons' postal boxes. Along tollways, the state grants exclusive franchises to operate restaurants and service stations; duty-free shops in airports and at international borders are also franchise operations. Most public utilities operate under state or local franchises.

Licensing. Entry into an industry or profession may be regulated by government agencies and by autonomous professional organizations. The Federal Communications Commission licenses radio and television stations and controls entry into the lucrative broadcasting industry. Most countries license airlines and, thus, limit entry into the industry. Every state regulates attorneys, nurses, teachers, physicians, and real-estate agents.

HOW MONOPOLISTS MAXIMIZE PROFITS

The most fundamental difference between monopoly and perfect competition is that the competitive firm must accept whatever price the market dictates. The perfectly competitive firm is literally a *price taker*, while the monopolist is a **price maker**. The monopolist has its own market demand curve. Thus, the monopolist has the problem of searching the demand curve for the profit-maximizing price. Such price-making behavior is not restricted to just *pure* monopolies. Even the local grocery store has some control over price and must determine the right price.

> A **price maker** is a firm with the ability to control to some degree the price of the good or service it sells.

Exhibit 1 illustrates the difference between price takers and price makers. The demand curve facing the price taker, panel (a), is perfectly elastic because the price is dictated by the market and because more units can be sold without lowering the

EXHIBIT 1   Price making Versus Price Taking

a. The Price Taker

b. The Price Maker

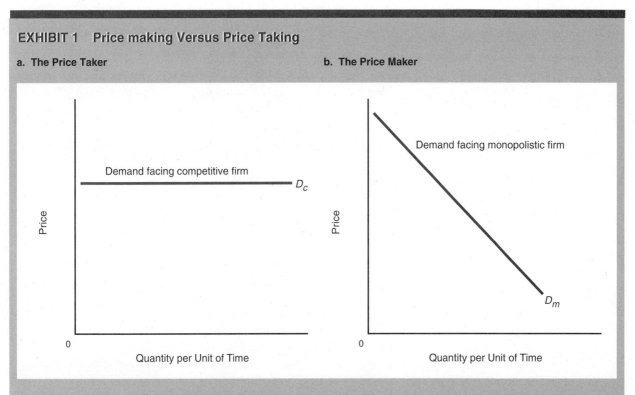

In panel (a), the demand curve D_c facing the competitive firm is perfectly horizontal, meaning that the firm can sell additional units without lowering its price. The price taker can sell all it wants at the going market price. In panel (b), the demand curve D_m facing the monopolistic firm is downward-sloping.

price. In contrast, the price-making firm, shown in panel (b), must lower its price on all units sold in order to sell more.

Price and Marginal Revenue

In the previous chapter we defined **marginal revenue** as the extra revenue generated by a unit increase in output. To a perfectly competitive, price-taking firm, the price of the good in the market measures the marginal revenue to the firm. To the monopolist, or price maker, price no longer measures marginal revenue. Let's consider why this is so.

> Marginal revenue *(MR)* is the increase in revenue divided by the increase in output caused by the change in price; in other words, it is the additional revenue raised per unit increase in quantity sold.

The monopolist, unlike the price taker, faces a negatively sloped demand curve. This means that the monopolist *must lower price in order to sell more output.* The perfectly competitive firm can sell all it wants at the market price. It need not have a lower price to sell more. Take the case of the monopolist who wishes to produce more output. To sell that extra output, the monopolist must lower price on all units sold. The effect on the monopolist's revenue from producing more output is uncertain. By selling more units of output, the monopolist's revenue expands, but having to sell at a lower price contracts revenue. Marginal revenue tells which effect dominates.

Marginal revenue tells what happens to revenue when output is changed by a small amount. Equivalently, marginal revenue tells what happens to revenue when price is changed by a small amount. Marginal revenue is the ratio of the change in revenue divided by the change in output brought about by the change in price.

The fact that price makers must lower the price to sell additional units of output means that marginal revenue must be less than price. When a price maker sells one more unit, the extra revenue generated equals the (new) price of the extra unit minus the loss in revenue from having to reduce the price on output that was previously sold at a higher price. In other words, price exceeds marginal revenue because a new but larger output "spoils the market" for the old output level that was previously sold at a higher price.

For a price maker, price is greater than marginal revenue: $P > MR$.

For example, suppose a price maker faces a demand schedule in which one unit per week can be sold if the price is $19; two units can be sold if the price is $17. The total revenue is the number of units multiplied by the price per unit for that quantity. When the number of units sold is 1, revenue is $19 (= $19 × 1); when the number of units sold is 2, revenue is $34(= $17 × 2). Marginal revenue is the extra revenue raised by increasing output by one unit. Therefore, the change in revenue can be calculated by comparing revenues at each output level. The marginal revenue of a change from one to two units is $34 − $19 = $15.

This example illustrates why price is greater than marginal revenue for the price maker. The price of the second unit ($17) is greater than the marginal revenue for the second unit ($15). To sell the second unit, the firm must lower price on both the first and second units from $19 to $17. The firm gains $17 in revenue on the sale of the second unit but loses $2 on the sale of the first unit. Hence, the marginal revenue of the second unit is $17 − $2 = $15. In effect, selling one more unit spoiled the market on the first unit because the price falls.

Marginal revenue per additional unit sold is measured by taking the ratio of the change in revenue to the change in total units sold brought about by the change in price. It is not necessary to change the number of units sold by only one unit, as in the above example. To illustrate, imagine that a producer of chocolates can sell 500 boxes at $10 per box and 600 boxes at $9 per box. At a price of $10, the firm's revenue would be $5,000; at a price of $9, the firm's revenue is $5,400. The change in revenue is $400 and the change in quantity sold is 100. Thus, the marginal revenue is $MR = \$400/100 = \$4$. Again, notice that the marginal revenue of $4 is less than the new $9 price.

Monopoly Equilibrium in the Short Run

Consider now the profit-maximizing strategy of a pure monopolist. We will study the case of the short run, where the monopolist has fixed plant and equipment. The key to monopoly is that each firm has its own demand curve and that to sell more of its product the price must be lowered. To the monopolist, the law of demand means that it cannot have both higher prices *and* a higher output. The monopolist faces a tradeoff between higher prices or higher output. (See Example 1.)

The previous chapter gave a general rule for the profit-maximizing firm—be it a price taker or a price maker. This rule gives the optimal strategy for any firm:

The price-making firm should lower price as long as the marginal revenue of the extra output sold exceeds the marginal cost of production.

Any firm should undertake those actions that raise revenues more than costs. If producing an extra unit adds more to revenues than to costs, the firm's profits are raised (or losses reduced).

Exhibit 2 shows the profit-maximizing strategy of a monopolist. The cost figures are the same as those studied in Exhibit 3 in the chapter on "Costs and

What Price for a Cancer Cure?

Ever since studies by the National Cancer Institute concluded that taxol, a substance that comes from the Pacific yew tree, provides an effective treatment for ovarian and lung cancer, cancer patients have waited for its appearance on the market. Up until November 1992, taxol was available only on an experimental basis from the National Cancer Institute.

In November 1992, taxol was approved for release on the open market. The drug company with the monopoly right to market taxol decided to sell taxol at a monthly cost of $300 to users. Although there was a public outcry about the high price of taxol, many desperate patients, who saw in it a chance for cure, would have been willing to pay much more for treatment.

How did the drug company settle on the $300 per month price? Just as in the case of other products, the company had to consider the tradeoff between higher prices and a smaller number of units sold. A $1,000-per-month price would have discouraged too many users, who understand its experimental nature. Monopolists price their product so as to achieve a maximum profit. In the case of taxol, the marginal cost of producing more taxol is very high because of the limited supply of Pacific yews. The profit-maximizing monopolist will restrict sales to that level at which the marginal revenue from more sales just equals the marginal costs of producing more output.

Even a monopolist producing an essential product does not charge the highest possible price. If the price is too high, too few units are sold and profits will not be maximized.

Productivity." The new information is the demand curve, shown as the downward-sloping D curve in panel (b) and in columns 1 and 2 of panel (a) in Exhibit 2. Nothing is demanded at a price of $46. When the price is $41, one unit is demanded. To sell two units, the price must be lowered to $36, and so forth. Column 3 shows the revenue produced at each level of output ($P \times Q$), and column 4 shows marginal revenue at each output level. In panel (b), MR is the **marginal revenue curve**. It shows that for any output level price P exceeds MR.

> The **marginal revenue curve** shows how much marginal revenue is at each level of output.

The marginal revenue values in column 4 of Exhibit 2a are positioned vertically between the rows corresponding to the relevant output levels. Each number that appears in color in column 4 is the marginal revenue when output increases by 2 units. For example, the MR for the output level 3 is determined by raising output from 2 units to 4 units. Increasing the output from 2 units to 4 units raises revenue from $72 to $104. The increase in revenue is $32. Since marginal revenue is the increase in revenue divided by the increase in output, MR is $16 (= $32/2).

Exhibit 2's cost figures are just the ATC and MC studied in previous chapters. Like the marginal-revenue values in Exhibit 2a's column 4, the marginal-cost values in column 7 are shown in between the relevant output levels. Again, each number in color represents the marginal cost of increasing output by 2 units (one above and one below the given output level).

EXHIBIT 2   Monopoly Equilibrium

a. Cost and Revenue Schedules

Output (units), Profit = Q (1)	Price or Average Revenue, P = AR (2)	Total Revenue, TR = P × Q (3) = (1) × (2)	Marginal Revenue, MR (4)	Average Total Cost, ATC (5)	Total Cost, TC (6)	Marginal Cost, MC (7)	Profit = TR − TC, (8) = (3) − (6)
0	$46	$ 0		∞	$ 48		−$48
			41			20	
1	41	41	36	$68	68	15	−27
			31			10	
2	36	72	26	39	78	8	−6
			21			6	
3	31	93	16	28	84	5	9
			11			4	
4	26	104	6	22	88	6	16
			1			8	
5	21	105	−4	19.2	96	10	9
			−9			12	
6	16	96	−14	18	108	16	−12
			−19			20	
7	11	77	−24	18.3	128	26	−41
			−29			32	
8	6	48		20	160		−112

b. Monopoly Profit

The table in panel (a) shows the demand and marginal-revenue schedules of a price maker. The demand schedule is given in the first two columns. Because all customers are charged in the same price, price and average revenue are the same. Revenue—in column 3—equals P × Q. Marginal revenue is the increase in total revenue brought about by increasing output by 1 unit. Panel (b) shows the same data in graphical form. The downward-sloping demand curve is D and the marginal revenue curve is MR. The monopolist's profit is maximized by producing 4 units of output, where profit equals $16, and the monopolist charges a price equal to $26. A lower or higher price brings smaller profits.

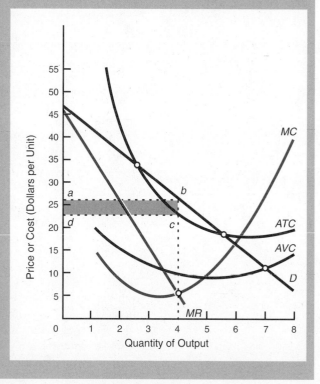

The monopolist has an incentive to lower price and expand output when marginal revenue exceeds marginal cost. Suppose our monopolist is charging $41—the highest price possible without losing all customers. At $P = \$41$, the firm is losing money because $P < ATC$. The firm's losses are $-\$27$. If the firm lowers its price to $36, its revenue increases by $31, and its cost increases by only $10. By lowering the price, the firm cuts its losses to $-\$6$. A price of $36 is better for the monopolist than a price of $41.

The $36 price is still not the "best" price for the monopolist. It pays the firm to continue to lower the price. When it lowers the price to sell 3 units, the firm's MR exceeds MC. The firm finally maximizes its profit by lowering the price to $P = \$26$ and producing exactly 4 units of output. At this point, $MC = MR = \$6$. To expand output any further lowers profit because costs rise by more than revenue. The firm's maximum profit is $16, which is achieved by charging a price of $26 and selling 4 units of output.

To maximize profit, the monopolist selects that output at which marginal revenue and marginal cost are equal. In Exhibit 2b, the MR and MC curves intersect at a point below the demand curve (because for a monopolist MR is less than P). To determine the price that maximizes profit, simply draw a vertical line through the intersection of MR and MC until it meets the demand curve. The vertical line drawn at 4 units of output meets the demand curve at $P = \$26$—the profit-maximizing price. Profit per unit of output is measured by the distance bc between the price and average total cost. Total profit is shown by the shaded rectangle $abcd$, which is the amount of output multiplied by the profit per unit.

The Loss-Minimizing Monopolist

In the short run, the monopolist need not make a profit. Exhibit 3 shows a case in which at the price where $MC = MR$ the monopolist is making a loss. With the given demand and marginal revenue curves, the firm's loss-minimizing price and output are $P = \$23$ and $Q = 3$ units, respectively. The firm's $ATC = \$28$ at that output, and thus is losing $5 per unit produced. It pays the firm to produce 3 units instead of 0 units because it is more than covering its variable costs (AVC is less than P at that point).

Being a monopoly does not guarantee automatic economic profits. Every patent issued by the U.S. patent office is a monopoly, but only a handful of those patents issued are actually used because price is less than average cost for most patentholders. Monopolies can incur losses just like competitive firms. The major distinction is that monopoly profits have a tendency to persist over time, while the above-normal profits of competitive firms are squeezed out by the entry of new firms.

Monopoly Profits in the Long Run

When there is competition in an industry, the distinction between the short run and the long run is critical. In the short run, the number of firms in the industry is fixed; in the long run, new firms can enter the industry or old firms can exit in response to economic profits or losses. The long-run entry and exit of firms ensures that economic profits will be squeezed out of perfectly competitive industries.

In the case of the monopolist, the long-run/short-run distinction is not as important because barriers to entry prevent new firms from entering the industry and squeezing out monopoly profits. There is no automatic tendency for monopoly profits to be eliminated by the *entry of new firms*.

Monopolies maximize short-run profits, or they minimize short-run losses, by producing where $MC = MR$. The monopoly price is not the highest price possible, but it exceeds the marginal cost of production.

EXHIBIT 3 A Loss-Minimizing Monopolist

The monopolist is minimizing losses by producing where *MC* = *MR* at *Q* = 3 units because at that point *P* > *AVC*. Its losses are equal to the rectangle *abcd*.

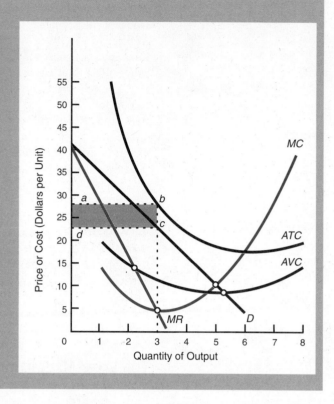

Unlike competitive profits, monopoly profits can persist for long periods of time.

In the real world, it is difficult to find pure monopolies because of actual or potential substitutes and because absolute barriers to entry are rarely present. Exceptional monopoly profits have historically promoted the development of closer substitutes for the monopolist's product. The railroads' monopoly over freight transportation was eventually broken by the development of trucking and air freight; AT&T's monopoly over long-distance telephone service was broken by the advent of microwave transmission.

Although monopoly profits will not automatically be driven down to the normal return, there is a tendency for high monopoly profits to promote the development of substitutes in the very long run. (See Example 2.)

Price Discrimination

Thus far this chapter has dealt with price makers who charge the same price to all buyers. This is not necessarily the case. Customers often pay different prices for the same product. Movie prices are often lower for senior citizens; doctors and lawyers often charge wealthy clients more than poor clients; airlines charge business travelers higher fares by requiring advance ticket purchases and minimum stays for discounts. All of these situations are examples of **price discrimination**.

Price discrimination exists when the same product or service is sold at different prices to different buyers.

EXAMPLE 2

Intel's Microprocessor Monopoly

Intel Corporation's 80386 microprocessor is the chip of choice for IBM and IBM-compatible computers. Microprocessors are fingernail-sized wafers of silicon containing circuitry that functions as a personal computer's brain. Intel's virtual monopoly of the microprocessing industry stems from its Microcode patent, the strength of its brand-name identification (the 80386 name), and its reputation for technological innovation. Advances in processing speed and reductions in the cost of Intel's microprocessors have resulted in a steep drop in personal computer prices over the past decade.

Intel's monopoly is facing challenges on several fronts. First, Advanced Micro Devices has used reverse engineering to develop an 80386 clone with different circuitry that mimics the 80386. Second, Advanced Micro has received permission to call its reverse-engineered microprocessor the 80386. Third, Intel has been charged with antitrust violations by companies seeking to develop their own microprocessors. Intel has responded to these challenges with an attempt to maintain its monopoly by producing better chips. Its new microprocessor will run 51 percent faster and cost 34 percent less than previous versions.

This example illustrates the constant challenges faced by firms in monopoly positions. The most effective way to preserve a monopoly is to continually innovate and produce better products than potential competitors.

Not all monopolists can engage in price discrimination. They can do so only if a number of conditions are met. These conditions are:

1. The seller must exercise some control over the price (price discrimination is possible only for price makers).
2. The seller must be able to distinguish easily among different types of customers.
3. It must be impossible for one buyer to resell the product to other buyers.

If the firm is not a price maker, it cannot control its price. The seller who cannot distinguish between customers will not know which buyers should be charged the lower price. The electric company meters electricity usage and can readily distinguish high-volume from low-volume users; doctors and lawyers can often identify wealthy clients on the basis of appearance, home address, and stated profession. By placing advance-purchase and minimum-stay requirements on tickets, airlines can create conditions that many business travelers cannot meet. If one buyer can sell to another, low-price buyers can sell to high-price buyers, and no one will be willing to pay the high price. For example, poor clients cannot resell legal and medical services to the wealthy; industrial users of electricity cannot sell their electricity to households; airline tickets with a one-week-minimum-stay requirement cannot be sold to someone departing on a two-day business trip. (See Example 3.)

If the above conditions are met, the seller can divide the market into distinct groups. A profit-maximizing seller will then charge prices according to the price elasticity of demand of each group. A low price elasticity means the buyer is less sensitive to price than a buyer with a relatively high price elasticity. If residential users of electricity have a more elastic demand for electricity than industrial users, it pays the electric company to charge a higher price to the less price-sensitive industrial users. If business travelers have a lower price elasticity of demand, the airlines will charge them higher prices.

EXAMPLE 3

Price Discrimination: Manufacturer's Coupons

Grocery shoppers are familiar with manufacturer's coupons that arrive through the mail or can be clipped out of the daily newspaper. Economic theory explains why some manufacturers offer coupons and others do not. In effect, the holder of the coupon is entitled to buy the product at a lower price than others. If Nabisco places a coupon offering 50 cents off one of their cereals in the daily newspaper, this means that you can buy the cereal at a lower price than other shoppers. Manufacturer's coupons are a form of price discrimination. The coupon issuer reasons as follows: Anyone taking the trouble to cut out the coupon has a higher elasticity of demand than other shoppers. Without the 50 cents off, many shoppers would not buy the cereal. The 50-cent price reduction, therefore, brings about a substantial increase in quantity purchased from careful shoppers. Shoppers not taking the trouble to clip out the coupon have a lower price elasticity of demand. Their purchases are not strongly affected by the 50-cent reduction. We have seen that price discrimination is possible only when the manufacturer has price-making power, when high-price-elasticity customers can be identified, and when low-price buyers cannot resell the product. Manufacturer's coupons follow this pattern. Typically, manufacturers in highly concentrated markets (with only a few sellers), such as cereal or soap manufacturers, offer coupons. Such manufacturers exercise significant market power. Requiring coupons to obtain the lower price allows manufacturers to differentiate high-elasticity from low-elasticity customers. Although low-price buyers could theoretically sell to high-price buyers, the price difference usually is not big enough to cause this to happen.

When price discrimination is possible, the higher is the price elasticity of demand, the lower will be the price charged.

To see how price discrimination raises profits and why the price varies with demand elasticity, take the case of an electric utility that charges the same price in both residential and industrial markets. Assume the demand of residential users is more price elastic than is the demand of industrial users. Why is this monopolist not gaining the maximum profit possible?

Recall that marginal revenue is less than price because it is necessary to cut the price on all units to sell additional output. The more elastic is demand, the smaller the cut in price necessary to stimulate a unit increase in quantity demanded. Thus, at the same price, the electric company's marginal revenue from selling another unit to residential customers would exceed its marginal revenue from selling another unit to industrial customers. Accordingly, it would pay the firm to shift output from industrial users to residential users by raising the industrial price and lowering the residential price. The process of raising the price to the users with a low price elasticity of demand and lowering price to users with a high price elasticity of demand would continue until the marginal revenue the firm earns in each market is the same.

MONOPOLY AND EFFICIENCY

Most economists believe that competition is more efficient than monopoly. Let us first see why competition is efficient.

The Case of Perfect Competition

The chapter on perfect competition demonstrated that perfectly competitive markets produce output at minimum average cost in the long run. It did not point out another property of perfect competition that leads to an efficient outcome: Market equilibrium in perfectly competitive markets brings about the right balance between consumer utility and the costs of production.

Perfect competition forces firms to produce where price equals marginal cost. The price consumers pay measures the *marginal benefit* they receive from consuming another unit. Marginal cost measures the *opportunity cost society pays to produce another unit of the good*. When price equals marginal cost, there is **economic efficiency** because consumers are buying what they want at the minimum cost to society. When the economy is efficient, the resources of society are being used in such a way that the total economic pie is as large as possible. When efficiency prevails, to give one person a larger slice of the economic pie means someone else must get a smaller slice. When the economy is inefficient, a larger pie can be produced and everyone gets a larger piece.

> **Economic efficiency** is present when society's resources are so organized that it is impossible to make everyone better off by *any* reallocation of resources; in other words, making one person better off must be at the expense of someone else.

Monopoly and Contrived Scarcity

The basic argument against monopoly is that monopolies maximize profit by restricting output to the scale where price exceeds marginal cost. Remember that monopolies maximize profit where $MR = MC$, but $P > MR$. Therefore, price will exceed marginal cost at that output which maximizes monopoly profit. Perfectly competitive industries, on the other hand, produce that quantity of output at which $P = MC$. This means that if everything else is equal, perfectly competitive industries tend to produce more output and sell at a lower price than monopolists. Monopoly restricts output to obtain a profit-maximizing price. By restricting output —or *contriving scarcity*—monopolists produce less output than is socially optimal.

We compare the monopoly outcome with the perfect competition outcome in Exhibit 4. We consider an industry in which a single monopoly producer can produce output at exactly the same average cost as a large number of perfectly competitive firms (there are no economies of scale; average costs are the same for all levels of output). Average cost and marginal cost are the same: $AC = MC$. Marginal cost ($= AC$) is a constant $4 per unit.

If the industry were organized as a monopoly, it would produce 300 units of output because at that output level MR equals MC. Both equal $4. The monopoly would sell the 300 units at the monopoly price of $7. Monopoly profits are represented by the color shaded area, which equals $900.

If the industry were perfectly competitive, free entry would squeeze out any economic profits. Free entry would cause output to expand to 600 units, at which point price ($4) would equal marginal cost ($4) and economic profits would disappear (the price of $4 equals average cost).

Monopolies are *inefficient* because they restrict output so as to be able to sell at a price greater than marginal cost. Why is $P > MC$ an inefficient outcome? We consider only the case where there are no externalities (Chapter 4), so that private and social values or costs coincide. Price measures marginal benefit to consumers, and marginal cost measures marginal cost to society; therefore, when $P > MC$, society gains by producing more of the monopolized good. A monopolized good is characterized by **contrived scarcity** because too little is produced. The economy

The direct comparison of monopoly and perfect competition demonstrates that, under identical cost conditions, a monopoly produces less output and charges a higher price than a perfectly competitive industry. The monopoly restricts output and sells at a price that is greater than marginal cost. The perfectly competitive industry does not restrict output and sells at a price equal to marginal cost.

EXHIBIT 4   Monopoly and Competition Compared

This industry has constant returns to scale where $AC = MC = 4 for all levels of output. If the industry were perfectly competitive, price would be $4 and output would be 600 units. If this industry were a single-firm monopoly, price would be $7 and output would be 300 units, with a monopoly profit of $900 (= $3 × 300). Monopoly profit is the grey area. The monopolist creates profits by the contrived scarcity of 300 units (the monopolist produces 300 units less than the competitive industry). The loss from contrived scarcity is the white area.

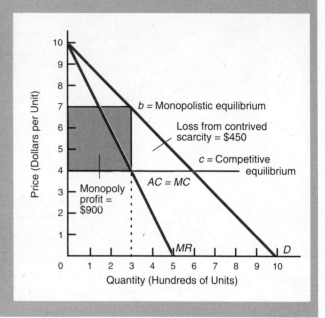

would be better off—more efficient in the sense of making it possible to give more to everyone—if more of the monopolized good were produced. This can be demonstrated in Exhibit 4 where the monopoly firm sells its 300 units of output at a price of $7—the $7 price is $3 greater than the marginal cost of $4. Society values an extra unit of output at $7, while it costs only $4 to produce an extra unit of output. Price greater than marginal cost signals a social opportunity. If $P > MC$, there is a social payoff to producing more of the good. Remember that marginal cost is the opportunity cost at the margin—what is being given up elsewhere. To say that price exceeds marginal cost is to say that the resources used in the production of this particular good have a higher marginal benefit to society than those resources have elsewhere because marginal costs measure opportunity costs.

> **Contrived scarcity** is the production of less than the economically efficient quantity of a good by a monopoly.

When $P > MC$, one more unit of output adds more to social welfare than to social costs, and it is possible make everyone better off by producing more of the monopolized good (and less of other goods). Exhibit 4 even shows how to measure the net gains to removing the inefficiency of contrived scarcity. When contrived scarcity is removed (by converting the industry to perfect competition), the social gain exceeds the monopolist's loss of profit. Since consumers gain more than the monopolist loses, it is possible to make everyone better off by taxing consumers and redistributing the proceeds to the monopolist.

Monopoly-Profit-Seeking Behavior

Monopoly is inefficient because output is restricted. The costs of monopoly can be far more severe, however. Monopolies are not costlessly granted to certain individuals or companies. *People seek monopoly power.* Let us reconsider Exhibit 4. Instead of considering a move from the monopoly output to the competitive output, think about the reverse. If the industry were perfectly competitive, the price/quantity combination would be $4/600 units, or point *c*. If someone could turn this industry into a monopoly, that person could gain the potential monopoly profit of $900 (grey color area). People would be willing to spend real resources—or engage in **monopoly-profit-seeking behavior**—to turn the industry into a monopoly and acquire the monopoly profit.

> **Monopoly-profit-seeking behavior** is the activity of anyone trying to achieve or maintain a monopoly in order to gain the monopoly profits.

A prime example of monopoly-profit-seeking behavior would be lobbying. Monopolies can be achieved and maintained through government charters, franchises, and regulation. There are more than 10,000 registered lobbyists in Washington, D.C. The offices they occupy, the secretarial services they employ, and their own labor could be used elsewhere in a world of scarcity. A prominent case is the lobbying in Congress by American automobile manufacturers for protection from foreign imports.

Monopoly-profit-seeking behavior can lead to substantial social losses. To limit such behavior, it would be necessary to lessen substantially the possibility of "buying" monopoly through the manipulation of government. This is easier said than done.

Monopoly and Innovation

The discussion of monopoly so far has emphasized its negative features. Monopolies contrive scarcity. They cause resources to be wasted as people attempt to gain monopoly power. In terms of the production-possibilities frontier discussed in Chapter 1, monopolies cause the economy to operate inside the frontier. Chapter 1 also emphasized that technological progress causes the production-possibilities frontier to shift outward. If monopolies do a better job of creating technological advances, this advantage may compensate for monopoly's disadvantages.

Economists have long debated whether monopoly (or big business) or competition is better suited to creating new technology. *Monopoly* and *big business* are not the same; but more often than not, monopolies (or companies that possess considerable monopoly power) are giant concerns. Giant corporations like AT&T, Du Pont, and IBM maintain enormous, privately financed laboratories and employ thousands of scientists. Indeed, Nobel Prizes for the discovery of the laser, superconductors, and the transistor were awarded to scientists employed by giant corporations.

The ability of large companies to finance research and product development has convinced economists such as Joseph Schumpeter and John Kenneth Galbraith that big businesses are more likely to come up with significant scientific inventions than competitive businesses. Big corporations with profits protected by barriers to entry can devote more of their resources to research and development (R&D). Both Schumpeter and Galbraith argue that the most significant innovations of the industrial era can be traced to giant concerns, not to small competitive firms.

Studies of major innovations fail to answer conclusively the question of monopoly and innovation. The evidence shows that both small, competitive firms and giant concerns with considerable market power have produced major innovations. A study of the case histories of 61 important twentieth-century inventions found that less than one-third were discovered in large industrial laboratories. A

Should Cable TV Be a Monopoly?

At first glance, it appears that cable TV must be a monopoly. To have more than one cable-TV company in a community would require building separate underground cables to homes. If each company had to have its own underground cables, the costs of delivering cable service likely would be raised so much that consumers would pay lower prices if there were only one cable-TV company in town.

Studies by a number of economists show that communities served by more than one cable-TV company pay lower rates. The competition for customers between rival companies gives lower rates to customers, who have a choice, despite the higher cost of parallel underground cables. Why is it that competition yields lower cable-TV rates? First, competition forces cable-TV companies to hold their costs down so that they can offer their service at competitive rates. Second, when local communities grant cable-TV companies a local monopoly, they often require that the cable-TV company offer 100 channels, public-access channels, and talk-back systems, all of which raise costs above what a competitive system would have required. Third, cable-TV companies have to spend considerable sums on lobbying state and local government to receive the monopoly right to operate. This money spent on monopoly rent-seeking raises the cost to the consumer.

It is a matter of public policy to decide what is the better market structure for cable TV. The local government can decide to franchise only one cable-TV company for the entire community. Alternatively, local government can operate on an open-access basis, whereby more than one company is allowed to compete for cable customers. Experience to date suggests that customers are better off with competition.

Despite the obvious benefits of competition, most local cable-TV service is provided by monopoly suppliers. The result has been that cable-TV rates have risen much more rapidly than other prices, causing a backlash of consumer resentment. The U.S. Congress in 1992 passed legislation giving regulatory agencies at the state and local level the power to set the rates for cable-TV services, just as they set electricity rates and rates for local telephone service.

It is doubtful that government regulation will result in lower prices and better service for consumers. Public policy has passed up an opportunity for competition, which would have benefited consumers.

---

little more than one-half were the product of academic investigators or of individuals working independently of any research organization.[1] F. M. Scherer summarizes the evidence and its bearing on public policy:

> *No single firm size is uniquely conducive to technological progress. There is room for firms of all sizes. What we want, therefore, may be a diversity of sizes, each with its own special advantages and disadvantages.*[2]

Diversity can be important to technological innovation. A small firm might discover a new product or process, but a large firm may be needed to put the invention on the shelf for the consumer. Basic ideas may come from small firms or even individuals, but a large laboratory may be needed to develop the idea so it can be put to practical use.

---

[1] John Jewkes, David Sawers, and Richard Stillerman, *The Sources of Invention* (New York: St. Martin's Press, 1959), pp. 71–85.

[2] F.M. Scherer, *Industrial Market Structure and Economic Performance,* 2nd ed. (Boston: Houghton Mifflin, 1980), p. 418.

The most important point to learn from this chapter is: Compared to perfect competition, monopolists restrict output and raise product prices above marginal costs of production.

1. A pure monopoly exists when there is one seller producing a product that has no close substitutes. Barriers to entry keep out competitors. The monopolist is a price maker and has considerable control over price. Pure monopoly is rare in the real world because of substitutes and because of the absence of absolute barriers to entry, especially in the long run. Sources of monopoly are: economies of scale, patents, ownership of critical raw materials, public franchises, and collusion.

2. Price makers face downward-sloping demand curves; they must lower their price in order to sell more. For price makers, price will exceed marginal revenue. When marginal revenue is positive, demand is elastic; when marginal revenue is negative, demand is inelastic.

3. Monopolists maximize profits by producing that output quantity at which marginal revenue and marginal cost are equal or by charging that price at which $MR = MC$. Once the monopolist has chosen the optimal output, the market will dictate the price, and vice versa.

4. Price makers can raise their profits through price discrimination. Buyers with inelastic demand will pay higher prices than those with elastic demand.

5. In perfect competition, economic efficiency is present because society's resources are so organized that it is impossible to make at least one person better off by any reallocation of resources without harming someone else. Efficiency prevails where price equals marginal cost. Monopoly is inefficient because price exceeds marginal cost and monopoly-profit-seeking behavior absorbs resources.

6. Schumpeter and Galbraith argue that large business firms or large concentrations of monopoly power are conducive to technological progress. Studies of major innovations show that diversity of industrial organization is required for innovation.

Key Terms

pure monopoly (p. 202)
price maker (p. 204)
marginal revenue (p. 205)
marginal revenue curve (p. 207)

price discrimination (p. 210)
economic efficiency (p. 213)
contrived scarcity (p. 213)
monopoly-profit-seeking behavior (p. 215)

Questions and Problems

1. The ABC corporation can sell 5 widgets at a price of $20 each and 10 widgets at a price of $12. What is its marginal revenue per additional unit sold?

2. The XYZ corporation can sell 100 plastic oranges at a price of $2 and 300 at a price of $1 What is its marginal revenue per additional unit sold?

3. Explain why a price maker can choose either its profit-maximizing output level or its profit-maximizing price. Why is it that when one choice is made, the firm has no choice about the other?

4. A monopolist produces 100 units of output, and the price elasticity of demand at this point on the demand curve is 0.5. What advice would you give the monopolist? From this information, what can you say about marginal revenue?

5. A price maker produces output at a constant marginal cost of $5 and has no fixed costs. The demand curve facing the price maker is indicated in Table A.
    a. Determine the price maker's profit-maximizing output, price, and profit.

b. Show that by producing more or less output, the firm would decrease its profit.

c. Explain what happens to marginal revenue when output is raised from 15 to 20 units.

TABLE A

Price (dollars)	Quantity Demanded (units)
12	0
10	5
8	10
6	15
4	20

6. A food concession in a sports stadium makes an economic profit of $100,000 in the first year of operation. Explain what will happen to profits in subsequent years

a. if the concessionaire is granted an exclusive franchise to stadium concessions, and

b. if potential competitors have the freedom to set up concession stands in the stadium.

In the latter case, can the concessionaire do anything to protect long-run profits?

7. Prices of movie tickets and tickets to sports events and concerts are typically lower for children than for adults. Explain why, using the theory of price discrimination.

8. Assume a monopoly is making an economic profit. The monopoly is sold to the highest bidder. Would the new owner make an economic profit? Why or why not?

9. Explain why marginal revenue is less than price for a price maker.

10. A natural water fountain is discovered in the middle of a city. The demand schedule for the drinking water is shown in Table B. There is no cost of production.

TABLE B

Price (cents per drink)	Quantity Demanded (drinks per day)
6	0
5	10
4	20
3	30
2	40
1	50
0	60

a. Draw the demand curve.

b. Calculate marginal revenue for each level of output.

c. How would the city maximize its revenues from the water fountain?

11. Restate the reason why $P = MC$ is the condition for economic efficiency.

12. Why do economists say that monopolists contrive scarcity?

13. Explain why monopolists produce too little output from the standpoint of economic efficiency.

14. What does the evidence indicate about the relationship between the size of business firms and technological progress? Is technological innovation a "monopoly" of large business enterprises?

15. What is the difference between monopoly-profit-seeking losses and the losses that result when the monopolist produces at marginal revenue = marginal cost?

16. Why is production at an output level where marginal cost = marginal revenue socially inefficient for monopolies but socially efficient under perfect competition?

17. The marginal cost of production for a hypothetical drug is $2 per dozen. The demand schedule for the drug is shown in Table C

a. Calculate the marginal revenue by centering a 2-unit increase in output at each output level (for example, at the output level 2, consider the marginal revenue going from one unit of output to 3 units of output).

b. What is the monopoly price for the drug?

c. Calculate monopoly profit.

d. How does the monopoly output compare to the perfectly competitive output?

TABLE C

Price (dollars per dozen)	Quantity (dozens)
10	0
9	1
8	2
7	3
6	4
5	5
4	6
3	7

Doing Economics

A monopoly is a situation in which consumers have no good alternative to consuming a particular product or service. Is this situation faced by students at your college in selecting courses, owing to restrictive graduation requirements? Are there particular departments or individual professors who have monopoly power with respect to student choices? What are the incentives for faculty in such courses? How do these incentives differ from those in courses for which many substitutes exist? Are these differences in incentives reflected in the style and popularity of the "monopoly" courses?

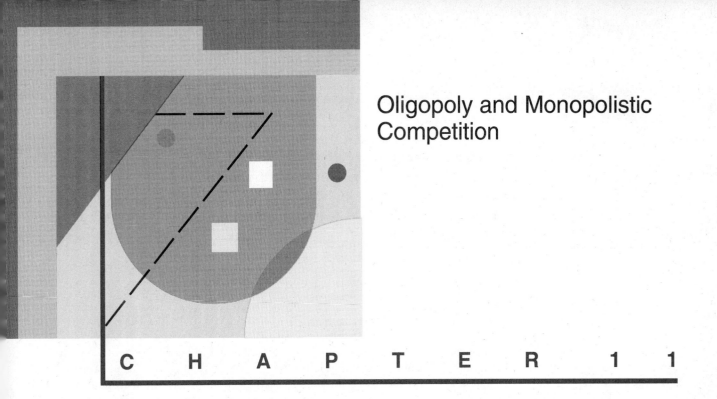

Oligopoly and Monopolistic Competition

C H A P T E R   1 1

CHAPTER FOCUS Most of the output of the U.S. economy is produced by firms that are somewhere between perfect competition and monopoly. These firms range from household names like Exxon, Ford Motors, Proctor and Gamble, Burger King, and Alcoa to the corner grocery store or the neighborhood dry cleaners. All of these firms can select their own prices, but they all have to worry about competition. In markets where competitive pressures are intense, a small increase in price may cause a precipitous decline in market share. Even when immediate competitive pressures are not intense, firms must worry about the long-term effects of price increases on their market position.

This chapter is about how firms that are neither perfectly competitive nor monopolistic deal with these competitive pressures. There is no single approach. Some producers band together to behave as a monopoly; others work out through custom and practice procedures for coexistence; yet others get involved in competitive pricing wars. Some firms adopt complex pricing strategies to see how their competitors will react.

When the number of producers is small, the conduct of business becomes like a game of strategy. To survive in the marketplace, managers must be sure that they play the competitive game as well as or better than their competitors.

After studying this chapter, you will be able to:

■ Understand how monopolistic competition differs from monopoly and perfect competition in the short run and the long run.

■ See the difference between nonprice and price competition.

■ Learn how concentration is measured for different industries.

■ Understand how the prisoners' dilemma game explains oligopoly behavior.

■ Explain the kinked-demand curve model of oligopoly.

■ Describe the different ways oligopolists can collude.

■ Name the economic obstacles to collusion.

MONOPOLISTIC COMPETITION

Recall from the monopoly chapter that the monopolist's price depends on the monopolist's output. Firms that can affect prices by changing output are *price makers*. Price-making firms are not necessarily monopolists. In fact, few price makers are monopolies. Price makers can be anything from a pure monopoly to a firm closely resembling a perfect competitor. The characteristic common to all price makers is the downward-sloping demand schedule they face. To sell more of their product, they must lower their price.

Characteristics of Monopolistic Competition

Usually some basis exists for distinguishing between the goods and services produced by different sellers. These distinctions may be based on the physical attributes of the product (hamburgers at one restaurant are different in some respects from hamburgers at other restaurants), on location (one gas station may be more conveniently located than another), on the type of service offered (one dry cleaner offers two-hour service, another offers one-day service), and even on imagined differences (one type of aspirin is perceived as "better" than another). The point is that there are usually differences—real or imagined—among products. Sellers of these different products have some monopoly power over the customers who prefer their product. How much monopoly power they have depends on the strength of this preference.

In **monopolistic competition**, the degree of control over price is quite limited because of the large number of firms and the existence of close substitutes.

> **Monopolistic competition** is an industry in which:
> 1. the number of sellers is large enough so that each seller acts independently of the other;
> 2. the product is differentiated from seller to seller;
> 3. there is free entry into and exit from the industry;
> 4. sellers are price makers (although to a very limited degree).

With a large number of sellers, each seller presumes that its decisions have no discernible effect on the rest of the market. The many other sellers would not be expected to react to the actions of any single seller. Monopolistic competitors hence make their decisions independently—without expecting to affect the decisions of others. Monopolistic competitors are price makers because of product

Edward Hastings Chamberlin (1899–1967)

Edward Chamberlin, the father of modern industrial organization, was born in La Conner, Washington. He received his Ph.D. from Harvard University in 1927 and a full professorship from that institution ten years later.

Throughout his career, Chamberlin viewed the real world as a mixture of monopoly and perfect competition. His Ph.D. thesis, published in 1933 as *Theory of Monopolistic Competition,* continued through eight editions. In it Chamberlin attempted to convince readers that the polar concepts of monopoly and perfect competition were inadequate to describe the real world. He stimulated economists' interests in oligopoly, advertising, product differentiation, and economies of scale. Along with Joan Robinson, he is credited with discovering the theory of monopolistic competition. In the 1960s, his theory of monopolistic competition came under heavy attack from economists such as George Stigler. Not only has Chamberlin's theory survived the attack, it has been given new life by modern economists.

differentiation. Differences in products (by physical traits, location, type of service, or imagined differences) give the seller some limited control over price. The seller who raises price will not lose all customers (as would the perfect competitor); some loyal customers will have a strong enough preference to accept the higher price.

Profit Maximization in the Short Run

The chapters on perfect competition and monopoly explained how firms maximize profits in competitive and monopolistic markets. The key difference between monopolistic competition and perfect competition is that the product is differentiated from firm to firm. Firms find it advantageous to differentiate their product because it allows them some measure of control over the price. Take the hypothetical firm of Jolley's Turkey Farm. In the beginning, Jolley's Turkey Farm is just like any of the thousands of other turkey farms. It is a small fraction of the total turkey market, and its turkeys are undifferentiated—buyers cannot distinguish Jolley Farm turkeys from any other turkey. In other words, we begin with Jolley operating in a perfectly competitive market. Exhibit 1a begins with Jolley Farm selling turkeys for 18 cents per pound and producing at the minimum point on its *ATC* curve. Jolley Farm's demand curve is perfectly elastic (horizontal) at the 18 cents market price. Jolley Farm is in long-run equilibrium, earning a zero economic profit. This outcome is identical to the long-run equilibrium of perfect competition described in the chapter on perfect competition.

After careful consideration, Jolley Farms management decides to differentiate their turkeys from other turkeys by spending a few cents per turkey to add a plastic thermometer that pops out when the turkey is done. With this unique feature, Jolley Farm starts advertising a "great tasting Jolley Farm turkey that you can't cook wrong." The advertising campaign is successful: people start looking for Jolley Farm turkeys in their supermarkets. Because of the thermometer, they are prepared to pay slightly more.

Exhibit 1b shows the consequences of product differentiation for the demand for Jolley Farm turkeys. As a monopolistically competitive firm selling a differentiated product, Jolley Farm now faces a downward-sloping demand curve. The firm's marginal-revenue curve lies below its demand curve, just as a monopolist's

Product differentiation is the key difference between monopolistic competition and perfect competition.

EXHIBIT 1   Monopolistic Competition in the Short Run and Long Run (Jolley's Turkey Farm)

a. Before Product Differentiation

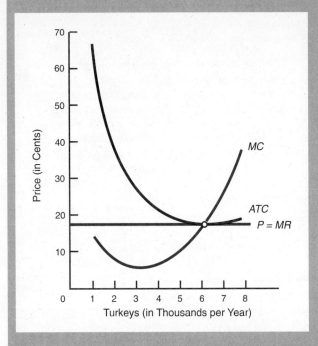

b. After Product Differentiation

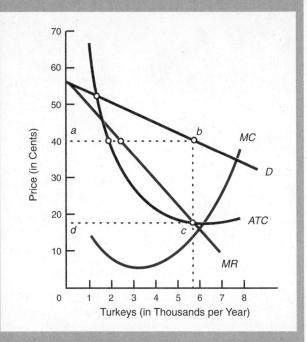

c. Demand Curve After Long-Run Adjustments

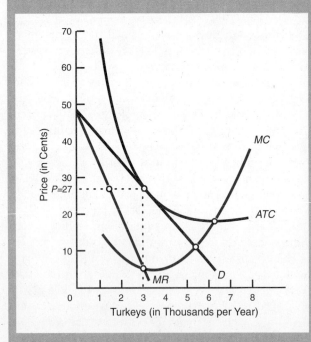

Panel (a) shows Jolley's Turkey Farm in long-run competitive equilibrium earning zero profits. Through product differentiation, Jolley's Turkey Farm succeeds in shifting its demand curve to D in panel (b). Jolley's Turkey Farm now can make an economic profit by setting the price at 40 cents, where marginal revenue equals marginal costs. This economic profit will encourage new firms to enter and rivals to differentiate their products. Panel (c) shows Jolley's demand curve after long-run adjustments have taken place. Rival firms introduce their own product-differentiating devices, and Jolley's demand curve shifts to the right and becomes more elastic. In long-run equilibrium, Jolley's demand curve must be tangent to the ATC curve. The firm charges a price that just equals average total cost, yet marginal revenue equals marginal cost, and output falls short of the most efficient level.

does. Profits are maximized where *MC* equals *MR*. Jolley Farm maximizes its profit at the price of 40 cents per pound and makes a substantial economic profit of *abcd*. Product differentiation has raised Jolley Farm's profit, but Jolley will have trouble keeping this profit in the long run.

Monopolistic Competition in the Long Run

In the long run, monopoly and monopolistic competition are strikingly different. Barriers to entry protect the monopolist from new competitors. If a monopoly earns substantial profits, new firms will not automatically enter to squeeze out those profits. Monopolistic competition, however, shares with perfect competition the characteristic of *freedom of entry*. Free entry means that if a monopolistic competitor earns economic profits in the short run, new firms can (and will) enter the market, eventually driving these profits down to zero.

Return 'to the example of Jolley Farm. Other turkey farmers have noticed Jolley's success. Now they begin to differentiate their products. Some copy Jolley Farm's pop-up thermometer, others add new features: One firm adds a self-basting feature, another stresses that it produces turkeys without artificial chemicals, and others use other product-differentiating devices. Jolley Farm's demand curve now shifts to the left (demand drops) because some of Jolley's customers are attracted to some other brand. Jolley Farm's demand curve also becomes more elastic as the number of very close substitutes (brand-name turkeys) on the market increases.

In the long run, new firms can enter monopolistically competitive markets. Each new entrant will reduce the demand facing Jolley Farm. As in the case of perfect competition, the entry of rival brands ends when economic profits have been driven down to zero.

The long run equilibrium of a monopolistically competitive firm is shown in Exhibit 1c. In the long run, new firms will enter until economic profits are driven down to zero. At zero profits, Jolley Farm's demand curve *D* must be tangent to its *ATC* curve. In the long run, Jolley Farm's profits will equal zero where the price is approximately 27 cents per pound and output is 3,000 turkeys per year. Since profits are maximized at the price of 27 cents, it must be that at the output of 3,000 units marginal revenue equals marginal cost (the condition required for profit maximization).

The level of output at which Jolley Farm's average total cost is minimized is 6,000 units (at that output level, *MC* = *ATC*). Jolley Farm's optimal production capacity is 6,000 units. Yet Jolley Farm produces only 3,000 units—only one-half of optimal capacity. Jolley Farm produces below optimal capacity because of product differentiation. As long as the monopolistic competitive firm faces a downward-sloping demand curve, its long-run equilibrium output falls below optimal capacity. There is *excess capacity,* making monopolistic competition appear less efficient than perfect competition. Excess capacity is the price we must pay for the variety introduced by product differentiation.

> Product differentiation yields only short-run profits. Entry of new firms and product differentiation of established firms eliminate economic profits in the long run.

> Monopolistic competition is characterized by excess capacity in the long run.

Advertising, Brand Names, and Product Differentiation

The entry of new firms and the loss of economic profits are facts of life for monopolistic competitors. Monopolistic competitors, by definition, produce goods and services that are different. If they can use **nonprice competition** to make their product different from their competitors, customer loyalty will be stronger. The stronger is this customer loyalty, the smaller will be the loss of customers as new firms enter and the less elastic will be the demand for their product.

Monopolistically competitive firms use advertising and brand names as sources of nonprice competition. They clearly identify their product with a brand name (such as "Jolley Turkey Farm"), and they use advertising to convince customers that their brand is better than competitive brands. In fact, nonprice competition—successfully applied—yields short-run profits for the firm and can delay profit loss. Once loyal customers are convinced that Jolley Farm turkeys are easier to prepare (are more nutritious, more lean, and so on), they will continue to be willing to purchase Jolley Farm turkeys at the same price despite the existence of close substitutes. When advertising creates strong brand loyalty, the entry of new firms does not increase the price elasticity of demand as much.

Nonprice competition yields both long-run and transitory profits. Profits on some brand-name products, like Bayer aspirin or Borden's condensed milk, have persisted for a long time. Advertising and brand names have successfully differentiated these products from substitutes, despite relative freedom of entry. Even though all aspirin and condensed milk are basically the same, many consumers are convinced that these particular brands are better. In other cases, nonprice competition yields only transitory profits. Advertising cannot always convince consumers that one particular product is indeed better (that California oranges are better than other oranges, for example). Also, in many cases competitors can duplicate the means of product differentiation. If the gas-station owner differentiates the product by staying open all night or by offering a free car wash, then competitors can do the same. Any gains from product differentiation are then temporary.

Advertising brand names are sources of nonprice competition.

OLIGOPOLY

The industries that make headlines fall somewhere between monopoly and monopolistic competition. The Fords, the IBMs, and the General Foods compete with a relatively small number of rivals. They are aware of their rivals' actions, and they must consider their rivals' responses before making their pricing and output decisions. These industries share certain characteristics.

An **oligopoly** is an industry that is dominated by a few relatively large firms.

An **oligopoly** is an industry characterized by:
1. moderate to high barriers to entry,
2. a relatively small number of firms in the industry,
3. recognized mutual interdependence, and
4. price making (firms are able to exercise varying degrees of control over price).

There is diversity among oligopolies. Some have high barriers to entry; others have more moderate barriers. The degree of control over price varies. Some oligopolies produce a homogeneous product (aluminum); others produce a heterogeneous product (automobiles). The common denominator is mutual interdependence. How oligopolies deal with mutual interdependence is the subject of most of this chapter.

Mutual interdependence is the common denominator of oligopoly.

DETERMINANTS OF CONCENTRATION

An oligopoly is an industry in which there are a relatively small number of firms. In some oligopolistic industries, there are only two or three firms that completely dominate industry sales. In other oligopolistic industries, there are ten to fifteen firms that share the market fairly evenly. Within oligopoly, there is great diversity as to the number of firms and the dominance by key firms.

Barriers to Entry Revisited

Whenever there are a relatively few firms in a profitable industry, there probably are barriers to entry. With free entry (as perfect competition and monopolistic competition show), profits entice new entrants, and the number of firms increases. The last chapter discussed *barriers to entry* in the context of monopoly. For a monopoly, the entry barriers could be such factors as economies of scale, patents, the exclusive ownership of raw materials, public franchises, and licenses. The same factors are at work in oligopoly, except that the entry barriers must be low enough to allow at least two firms to remain in the industry. In the case of monopoly, entry barriers are stronger because there is only one firm in the industry. In oligopoly, there is an additional barrier to entry—product differentiation. Monopolists, as sole producers, do not need to worry about differentiating their product. Oligopolists, however, face rival firms. For them, product differentiation can be an important source of profits.

Barriers to entry explain the relatively few firms in oligopoly industry.

Experts on industrial organization have attempted to classify industries according to the strength of barriers to entry. They have concluded that industries such as distilled liquors, newspapers, drugs, automobiles, and heavy electrical equipment have high barriers to entry. Clothing, printing, cement, and footwear have low barriers to entry. Industries with high barriers are likely to be populated by a relatively small number of oligopolistic producers. Industries with low entry barriers are likely to be populated by a relatively larger number of producers. As the following discussion shows, the relative number of firms influences the way firms react to mutual interdependence.

Measuring Concentration

There is no magic formula for measuring the extent of oligopoly. A statistical tool economists use to gauge oligopoly is the **concentration ratio**.

> An *x*-firm **concentration ratio** is the percentage of industry sales (or output, or labor force, or assets) accounted for by the *x* largest firms.

The 4-firm sales concentration ratio, for example, is the percentage of industry sales accounted for by the four largest firms in the industry. Exhibit 2 shows concentration ratios for U.S. industrial concerns. Concentration ratios are an imperfect guide to the extent of oligopoly for four reasons.

First, concentration ratios do not reflect competition from foreign producers or from substitute products at home. The 4-firm concentration ratio of the U.S. automobile industry is 90 percent—a figure that fails to measure the competition of foreign imports. The 4-firm concentration ratio in metal cans (54 percent) does not reflect the competition from stainless steel and plastic.

EXHIBIT 2 Concentration Ratios

Industry	4-Firm Concentration Ratio (percent)	Number of Firms
Motor vehicles and car bodies	90	352
Cereal and breakfast foods	87	33
Photographic equipment	72	717
Tires and inner tubes	69	114
Aircraft	72	137
Metal cans	54	161
Soaps and other detergents	65	683
Cookies and crackers	58	316
Semiconductors	40	755
Farm machinery	45	1,516
Blast furnaces and steel mills	44	271
Toilet preparations	32	648
Hardware	32	1,127
Gray iron foundries	30	692
Men's footwear	26	110
Petroleum refining	32	200
Women's footwear	50	123
Periodicals	18	3,759
Motor homes	56	144
Paper mills	33	122
Pharmaceutical preparations	22	640
Canned fruits and vegetables	29	462
Nonwoven fabrics	9	91
Men's and boy's suits	34	285
Radio and TV equipment	37	572
Corrugated and solid fiber boxes	26	952
Sawmills	15	5,252
Wood household furniture	20	2,771
Nuts and bolts	16	834
Valves and pipe fittings	20	372
Women's dresses	6	5,398
Ready-mix concrete	8	3,749

SOURCE: U.S. Department of Commerce, "Concentration Ratios In Manufacturing", *1987 Census of Manufacturers,* MC87-S-6.

Second, concentration ratios may not measure concentration in the relevant market. The 4-firm concentration ratio in the concrete business is only 8 percent, but it is nearly 100 percent in some local markets.

Third, many markets, such as newspapers, cement, and real estate, are local or regional. Concentration ratios for percentages of national sales are misleading in such markets. A local or regional firm may dominate its relevant market, but the national concentration ratio may not reflect this fact.

Fourth, concentration ratios do not measure *potential* competition. They do not indicate those industries in which new firms can overcome existing barriers to entry. One airline may account for 90 percent of the flights between two cities, but the number of *potential* entrants into this market may be large.

Although concentration ratios can be misleading, they can—if used with care—provide insights into how concentrated an industry is. Combined with additional information, such as the amount of foreign competition, and applied to meaningful market definitions, concentration ratios indicate which industries are indeed populated by a relatively small number of firms. Oligopoly theory explains why this makes a difference. It shows that oligopolies with two to three dominant producers behave differently from those with eight to ten producers.

Concentration ratios are a statistical tool for measuring the extent of oligopoly.

OLIGOPOLY THEORY

When oligopoly firms are interdependent, the marginal revenue resulting from a price change depends on how rival firms respond to the price change.

Oligopoly theory is more complicated than perfect competition, pure monopoly, or monopolistic competition because there is no one theory of oligopoly. In either perfect competition or monopoly, the firm need only equate marginal cost and marginal revenue. In the case of oligopoly, things are not that simple. Because of mutual interdependence, the marginal revenue an oligopolist gains from changing price depends on the actions and reactions of rival firms. If these reactions cannot be predicted, the oligopolist will not know the marginal revenue of a pricing action.

Mutual Interdependence

An oligopolistic industry was defined as one with a "relatively small" number of firms. What is meant by "relatively small"? There are a relatively small number of firms in an industry when each firm must consider the reactions of rival firms. One firm must consider how a rival firm will respond to its actions and vice versa. When firms in an industry must consider the responses of rival firms, the industry is characterized by **mutual interdependence**.

> **Mutual interdependence** is characteristic of an industry in which the actions of one affect other firms in the industry and in which these interrelationships are recognized.

Mutual interdependence is the most important feature of oligopoly. In making decisions concerning prices, quantities, and qualities of output, mutually interdependent firms must consider the reactions of rival firms. In some oligopolistic industries, the pattern of reaction may be easy to anticipate by all participants; it may be dictated by custom or agreement. In other industries, the reactions of rival firms may be unpredictable, and participants use strategy to outguess and outmaneuver their rivals.

The Prisoners' Dilemma

Oligopolists must use strategic behavior to outguess their rivals if they are to earn large profits. One way to understand oligopolistic industries is to study the strategies that people use in strategic games. Oligopoly is like a game where there are two or more players, each trying to figure out what the other players will do. *Game theory* is the study of the strategies people follow when players receive different rewards or payoffs depending on the strategies or "plays" of all the players.

The **prisoners' dilemma game** analyzes a situation much like that often faced by oligopolistic producers. It explains why some oligopolists cooperate with rivals while others try to outmaneuver them. In the game, two bank robbers have been apprehended by the police; they are being interrogated in separate rooms. If both talk, both go to prison for five years. If one talks and the other remains quiet, the one who talks is set free while the silent bank robber receives a 20-year jail sentence. If neither talks, both get only a year for carrying a concealed weapon. Each prisoner is in a dilemma. Each knows that by keeping quiet both can get off with a light one-year sentence. But each suspect has an incentive to talk—each can get off free if he or she confesses while the other keeps quiet. Game theory

Tit-for-Tat and the Prisoners' Dilemma

Robert Axelrod has studied how best to play the prisoners' dilemma game, particularly when it is repeated over and over so that players can learn from experience. Axelrod invited 14 authorities on the game to compete in a prisoners' dilemma tournament. Each contestant was required to submit a strategy for the following game: For each of the 200 rounds of the game, each player's strategy should give either a C (cooperate) or D (don't cooperate—defect) response. If both players produced a C, then each received 3 points. If both produced a D, then each received 1 point. If one offered a D while the other offered a C, the defecting player got 5 points and the cooperating player 0 points. The winning program was the shortest program of all—called Tit-for-Tat by its author, Anatol Rapoport. The Tit-for-Tat strategy is very simple: Offer a C on the first move, and then do whatever your opponent did on the previous move. As long as your opponent cooperates, you cooperate too. If your opponent defects, you punish by defecting on the next move. The Tit-for-Tat program amassed the highest number of points in the first tournament and beat out 62 entrants from six countries in Axelrod's second tournament. The simplest winning strategy achieved its victory by being cooperative. Game theorists are studying whether or not people naturally employ cooperative behavior in real-life business "games" that are played frequently.

SOURCE: William F. Allman, "Nice Guys Finish First," *Science* 84 (October 1984): pp. 25–32.

concludes that both will confess even though they would both be better off if both kept silent. (See Example 1.)

> A **prisoners' dilemma game** is a game with two players in which both players benefit from cooperating, but in which each player has an incentive to cheat on the agreement.

The Oligopolist's Dilemma

The prisoners' dilemma is much like the oligopolist's dilemma: cooperate with rivals or act independently. In both cases, the consequence of one "player's" decision depends on the decision of another "player". Suppose Firm A and Firm B each sell a differentiated product. Suppose also that when the two products have equal prices, both firms enjoy exactly the same profit. If one charges a slightly lower price than the other, however, that firm will make larger profits.

Exhibit 3 shows a set of outcomes. Each firm has the option of choosing a price of either $20 or $19. Firm A's price choices are shown down the left side; Firm B's price choice are shown along the top. The *profits* earned by Firm A and Firm B are determined by the prices the two firms choose. Firm A's profit payoffs are shown in the lower-left corner of each box (in grey); Firm B's profit payoffs are shown in the upper-right corner of each box (in color). When both charge $20, both earn $2,500; when both charge $19, both earn $1,500. When one charges $20 and the other charges $19, the lower-priced firm earns $3,000 while the higher-priced firm earns only $1,000.

The two oligopolists are like the two prisoners. One stands to gain a high profit (at the expense of the other) by selecting the lower price while the rival selects the

EXHIBIT 3   Profit Payoffs to a Two-Firm Oliogopoly

Each square (cell) shows the profits that each firm would earn when various combinations of prices are charged by the two firms. Firm A's profits are shown in grey in the lower left-hand corner of each cell, and Firm B' s profits are shown in color in the upper right-hand corner of each cell. For example, if A charges $19 and B charges $20, A would earn a profit of $3,000 and B would earn $1,000. This exhibit illustrates the oliogopolist's dilemma: If both charge low prices ($19), they both earn an intermediate-level profit ($1,500). If both agree to charge a high price ($20), they both earn a high profit ($2,500). However, if one cheats on the agreement and charges a lower price ($19 versus $20), the cheater earns a very high profit ($3,000) while the noncheater earns a low profit ($1,000)

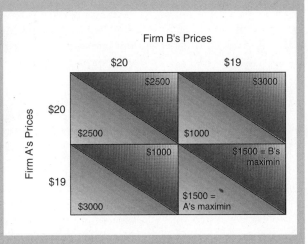

higher price. Both stand to earn a decent profit if both select the lower price. If both select the higher price, they each earn a substantial profit. Yet, like the prisoners in isolated cells, each oligopolist must make a pricing decision not knowing what the other firm will do.

What would each firm consider as it makes its pricing decision? Each might reason: "My rival probably won't risk charging the higher $20 price for fear that I would select the lower $19 price. Therefore, my rival will select the lower $19 price. If I select the higher $20 price, my rival will get the larger share of profit ($3,000 versus my $1,000). I therefore decide to select the lower $19 price." If each firm reasons the same and decides to select the lower price, the two firms are in equilibrium. They have correctly anticipated each other's actions and they have chosen the appropriate strategy. If each believes the other will charge $19, each should charge $19. When both actually charge $19, each has guessed correctly, and each is able to employ the best strategy for the situation in which the *other* charges $19.

In this situation, A and B would both decide to select prices of $19 and pocket a profit of $1,500 each. They are, however, aware that if both charged $20, they could each carn a profit of $2,500. If A and B played this game repeatedly over a fairly long period of time, it is likely that A and B would realize that they are both better off charging higher prices. They might learn to cooperate and choose the strategy (a $20 price) that maximizes joint profits. There is another way they could settle immediately on a $20 price: They could simply agree that both would charge the higher price.

Kinked Demand

The prisoner's dilemma shows that oligopolists must try to anticipate the actions of rival firms. If they anticipate properly, they will have adopted their best strategy. If they anticipate incorrectly, they will have to revise their strategy. The behavior of an oligopoly can take many forms. One of the simplest ways oligopolistic firms might anticipate the behavior of their rivals is illustrated by the **kinked-demand curve**. Subsequent sections show other ways.

In an oligopolistic industry characterized by kinked demand, firms match

Oligopolist firms must make decisions not knowing what other firms will do. They will select the correct strategy if they correctly anticipate the strategy of their rivals.

price reductions but ignore their rivals' price increases. Suppose Ford's rivals tend to match Ford's price *cuts* but hold their prices when Ford raises its price. Ford would face a more elastic demand for price increases than it would for price reductions. Price hikes would cost Ford substantial business; price cuts would be matched by General Motors, Chrysler, and Toyota so that Ford's demand would not increase at their expense. The demand curve would have a "kink" in it at the current price as shown in Exhibit 4.

> A **kinked-demand curve** results when rival firms match a firm's price decreases but don't match the firm's price increases.

Exhibit 4 shows an oligopoly firm facing a kinked-demand curve. The current price charged by this firm is $12. Because rival firms do not follow price increases but do match price cuts, the firm's demand curve, *D,* is more elastic above the $12 price than below the $12 price. Thus, the firm's demand curve has a kink at the current price. Because of the kink, the *MR* curve drops sharply at the price of $12. Marginal revenue is $7 at a price just above $12 and only $2 at a price just below $12. Because the marginal-revenue curve has a vertical segment (*feg*) just below the demand kink, there is a *range* of *MR* values associated with the $12 price. The oligopolist maximizes profits at the price of $12 if the *MC* curve intersects the *MR* curve anywhere in the vertical segment *feg.*

The kink in the demand curve means that if the firm's *MC* curve shifted up or down within the range *f* to *g*, *MR* would still equal *MC* at the current price! The firm would not change its output and price. Moreover, there could even be slight changes in demand without altering the profit-maximizing price.

The kinked-demand model says that in industries in which rivals match price reductions but ignore price increases, prices should remain relatively stable. They should not change with every change in market demand and in marginal cost as in perfectly competitive industries.

A kinked-demand curve results when rivals ignore price increases but match price reductions. When the demand curve is kinked, prices should be relatively stable.

EXHIBIT 4   The Kinked-Demand Curve

This firm's rivals follow price reductions but not price increases. For prices below the current $12 price, the demand curve, *D,* is less elastic than it is for prices above $12. The marginal-revenue curve, *MR,* drops sharply from *f* to *g.* The *MC* curve can shift up or down (as long as it remains within this vertical portion of the *MR* curve) without changing the firm's price or output decisions.

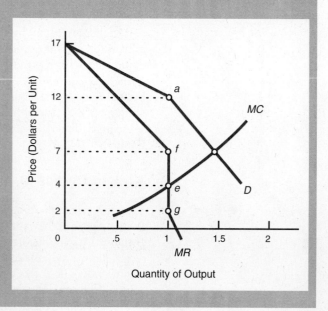

Oligopoly Coordination

The kinked-demand model of oligopoly assumes there is no overt coordination among firms. Each firm knows that price increases will not be followed but that price reductions will be, and firms make their pricing decisions on this basis. The prisoners' dilemma, however, showed that there are substantial gains through coordination. If the two prisoners could agree beforehand not to confess, they would both get off lightly. If both oligopolists in Exhibit 3 agree to charge the higher price, they can both earn higher profits. These examples show that oligopolists can benefit from coordination.

Oligopoly coordination takes a variety of forms. Oligopolists can *collude* on pricing and output decisions. They can enter into formal agreements either in secret (if such agreements are against the law) or in the open (in cases where such agreements are legal and even sanctioned by government). Coordination can take on looser forms when it is based upon custom, habit, or informal agreement. The effectiveness of coordination varies from oligopoly to oligopoly. In some cases, coordination is rigidly enforced; in other cases, it is loosely enforced and tends to break down.

Cartel Agreements.   The most direct way for an oligopoly to coordinate pricing and output policy is to enter a **cartel** agreement, binding on all parties, to set the prices or market shares of each producer. If successful, such agreements allow the oligopolistic firms to earn monopoly profits for the industry as a whole.

> A **cartel** is an arrangement that allows the participating firms to coordinate their output and pricing decisions to earn monopoly profits.

Exhibit 5 shows an oligopolistic industry consisting of three identical firms (with the same costs and producing the same product). Barriers to entry are so high that the three firms need not worry about attracting new entrants should profits be high. The three identical firms agree to each share one-third of the market and to charge the same monopoly price. The industry demand curve is D. Firm A's demand and marginal-revenue curves (which are the same as those of Firms B and C) are shown as D_A and MR_A. Because all three firms are part of a cartel agreement to share the market equally, Firm A's demand curve is D_A, $(= \frac{1}{3} \times D)$. The monopoly price is determined by drawing the MR_A curve corresponding to D_A and locating its intersection with the MC curve. Firm A would maximize its profit by producing 100 units at a price of $50 per unit (point a). The other two firms also charge $50 and produce 100 units each. Industry output is 300 $(= 3 \times 100)$.

Firm A is strongly tempted to cheat. The two rival firms are selling 200 units at the price of $50. Firm A could charge $49.50 and sell slightly more than its third. As long as its secret sales remain small and don't drive down the cartel price, $49.50 is now essentially the cheating firm's marginal revenue. The marginal revenue of $49.50 clearly exceeds marginal cost ($20) to each firm. Hence, substantial gains accrue to the firm that breaks the cartel agreement. Firms B and C are subject to the same temptation. Cheating on the agreement has its long-run costs. When the other firms detect cheating, they will break the agreement. Price warfare could erupt, and economic profit would be driven down. (See Example 2.)

Greed both creates and destroys cartels. Cartels offer their members a share of monopoly profits as long as every member adheres to the cartel agreement. Each cartel member, however, can gain by cheating on the agreement if the others do not cheat. Cartel members are like the two prisoners of the prisoners' dilemma. If one cheats and the other does not, the cheater wins. If both cheat, they both lose.

EXHIBIT 5   Collusive Oligopoly

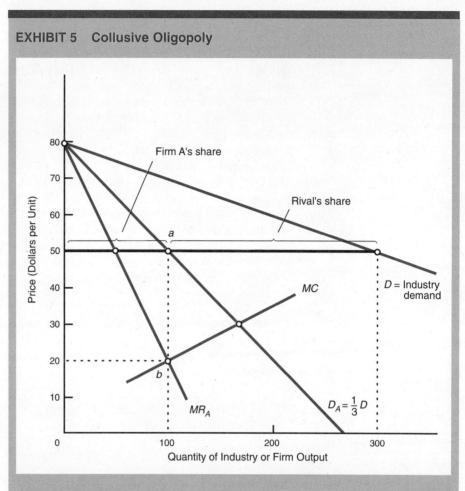

Curve *D* represents the industry demand curve. The industry consists of three oliogopolistic firms who agree to share the market equally and charge the same price. D_A is the demand schedule of Firm A; it is one-third of the industry demand schedule. MR_A is the marginal-revenue curve of Firm A. Firm A maximizes profits by producing that output at which *MC* equals *MR*, or 100 units at $50 per units (point *a*). Firm A is tempted to cheat on the agreement because if it lowers price a little, it gains sales from its two rivals. As long as A's lower price exceeds A's marginal cost, Firm A's profits will increase. If all three firms cheat, however, a competitive bidding war should break out, and they could end up earning virtually no economic profits.

The desire to earn monopoly profits causes interdependent firms to form cartels. Interdependent firms can get an even larger share by cheating on the cartel agreement. This explains why cartels are unstable.

If both do not cheat, they are better off than if both cheat, but each one constantly is tempted to cheat.

Cartels are unstable because it is difficult to enforce cartel agreements. Very few cartels succeed over the long run. Most, like the ill-fated sugar, cocoa, tin, and coffee cartels, either disappear quickly or have no noticeable effect on prices.

There are numerous examples of cartel agreements on pricing. The Organization of Petroleum Exporting Countries (OPEC) meets regularly, with full coverage by the world's press, to attempt to set the price of crude oil. The International Air Transport Association (IATA) also meets openly with the blessing of the member country governments to set air fares for travel between countries.

With some minor exceptions, formal price-setting agreements violate U. S. law, but a number of price-conspiracy cases have come to light. While formal secret agreements continue, there are other less risky ways to coordinate prices. These methods are discussed in the next sections.

EXAMPLE 2

Yakutia Diamonds Threaten the DeBeers Cartel

The DeBeers Company, founded by Cecil Rhodes in 1871 in the diamond fields of South Africa, has proven to be the world's most lasting and effective cartel. DeBeers has controlled world diamond prices since the 1930s through its Central Selling Organization (CSO). The CSO is DeBeers' marketing arm, through which virtually all the world's diamonds are sold. Although only 15 percent of today's world diamond production originates in South Africa, the CSO has purchasing pacts with the world's major diamond producers (such as the former Soviet Union, Zaire and other African nations, and Australia). DeBeers prevents its *buyers* from cheating by inviting only a select group to its London sales every five weeks. Buyers must accept the cartel price or risk not being invited to subsequent sales. DeBeers also prevents cheating by diamond *producers* by offering faithful members stable contracts, stable prices, and financial security. Third, DeBeers has ways to punish disloyal members. When Zaire attempted to leave the cartel in 1981, DeBeers flooded diamond markets with low-quality diamonds similar to those from Zaire to drive their price down.

The collapse of the former Soviet Union poses the most serious threat to the DeBeers cartel in recent history. Under the Soviet regime, a top-secret government agency cooperated with DeBeers to market Russian raw diamonds produced almost exclusively in remote Yakutia—the population-poor but resource-rich Russian republic located in the polar north.

In the confusion that accompanied Moscow's central power collapse and Yakutia's growing control over its diamond resources, Yakutia mine operators began to sell their diamonds, which could potentially account for more than 20 percent of the world market, to buyers other than DeBeers. In high-level negotiations with Russian and Yakutian officials, DeBeers sought to convince the new Russian and Yakutian authorities that all Yakutia diamonds should be marketed through DeBeers. If DeBeers fails to achieve agreement, its long-time monopoly over world diamond sales would end.

Informal Agreements.   Informal agreements can also be used to coordinate pricing and output decisions. The most notable case of informal agreement was that of the so-called Gary Dinners of the early twentieth century. Mr. Gary, president of U. S. Steel Corporation, would invite steel-company executives representing more than 90 percent of the industry to dinner and urge them to cooperate in holding prices. Gary dinners and their like confirm Adam Smith's perception that "people of the same trade seldom meet together, even for merriment and diversion, but the conversation ends in a conspiracy against the public, or in some contrivance to raise prices."

Price Leadership.   A more subtle method of collusion occurs when a recognized **price leader** sets industry prices. When a price leader sets prices, there is no kinked-demand curve because rival firms follow the price leader's price decreases and price increases. The price leader keeps a sharp eye on market demand and costs that are common to all firms.

> A **price leader** is a firm whose price changes are consistently imitated by other firms in the industry.

Examples of price leadership are plentiful. In the ready-to-eat breakfast-cereal industry, whose "big three" corporations are Kellogg's, Post, and General Mills,

Kellogg's is the price leader for most product lines while General Mills and Post lead for their own best product lines.

Conscious Parallelism. The most subtle form of collusion is **conscious parallelism**. Conscious parallelism occurs when oligopoly firms behave in the same way even though they have not agreed to act in a parallel manner. Examples would be the submitting of identical bids or switching to high season rates at the same time of year without any formal agreement to do so.

> Conscious parallelism is the coordination of actions of producers without formal or even informal agreements. All firms use their understanding of the industry to make their own decisions and anticipate the behavior of rival firms.

Conscious parallelism is explained by the use of *focal points* to set prices. A focal point is an obvious benchmark by which prices or output could be coordinated without an explicit agreement. Oligopolist firms are intimately acquainted with the way things work in their own industries. Business practices followed in the industry are well-known. The focal points may be certain standardized business practices—such as common percentage markups, the use of round numbers, the charging of prices like $4.95, and policies like "splitting the difference" or charging high season rates at the same time each year. As long as each oligopolist understands these standard practices, it can anticipate how rival firms will behave. If all firms in the oligopolistic industry use standard focal points, they will behave in a parallel fashion, even without formal agreements.

Obstacles to Collusion

Despite the considerable gains from cooperation, oligopolists often do not cooperate. They cheat on cartels. They suddenly abandon focal points. The price leader raises prices and other firms don't follow. Some industries are characterized by cooperative behavior. Others are characterized by cheating and breaking of formal or informal agreements. The chances for effective and lasting collusion decrease when there are:

1. many sellers,
2. low entry barriers,
3. product heterogeneity,
4. high rates of innovation,
5. high fixed costs, and
6. difficulty of detecting cheating.

Many Sellers. The more firms there are in the industry, the more difficult it is to agree on common prices. When there are two sellers, there is only one communication link: when there are three sellers, there are three different information links: A must agree with B, B must agree with C, and C and A must agree. When there are 10 sellers, there are 45 ways information must flow! The number of information channels increases at a faster rate than the number of sellers increases. It becomes far more difficult to coordinate collusive actions as the number of colluders grows.

Low Entry Barriers. If it is easy for new firms to enter an industry, existing firms may not find it worthwhile to enter into cumbersome agreements to raise

Oligopolies can coordinate their actions without formal agreements through price leadership and conscious parallelism.

prices. Effective collusion would only bring in new firms. High prices create profitable opportunities for new firms. There would be no lasting benefits to the original firms that worked out the pricing agreement. Higher prices would simply encourage new firms—who are not parties to the agreement—to enter, and this entry would continue until prices were driven back down to where a normal return was earned.

Product Heterogeneity. The more differentiated the product is from firm to firm, the more difficult it is for the industry to achieve coordination or collusion. Reaching an agreement creates both costs and benefits. It is costlier to reach an agreement if the product is not homogeneous. Because steel is homogeneous, an agreement on prices and market shares between large steel producers may be fairly easy to conclude. But an agreement between McDonnell Douglas and Boeing over the relative prices of MD-11s and Boeing 747's may be quite difficult because of product differences and complexity. An agreement between the producers of high-quality goods and low-quality goods may break down because of disagreement over quality differences. It would be difficult for a fast-food chain like McDonald's to enter into a pricing agreement with a full-service restaurant chain like Red Lobster because of the difficulty of agreeing on the proper relative price.

High Rates of Innovation. If there is a high rate of innovation in an industry, collusive agreements will be more difficult to reach. The costs of reaching an agreement are higher when the industry is constantly turning out new products and developing new techniques. For example, it would be difficult for Eastman Kodak and Polaroid to reach an agreement because of rapid technological change in the camera and instant-development industry. The same would be true of the personal-computer market—characterized by virtually monthly advances in technology.

High Fixed Costs. The higher fixed costs are relative to total costs, the more likely is cheating on the pricing agreements. As long as the price covers average variable costs, there is something left over to pay fixed costs. By granting a secret price concession, a firm may gain much in the short run if marginal costs are very low. Thus, the benefits to secret price reductions are increased by high fixed costs.

Detecting Cheating. If it is easy to cheat without being detected, firms will tend to break a collusive agreement. It is easier to cheat on price agreements when actual prices charged by one party cannot be known with certainty by the other parties to the agreement. For example, barbers often agree to charge uniform prices within a city because the prices of haircuts must be posted. Rival barbers can easily detect barbers who undercut the agreed-upon price. When the terms of price negotiations are not revealed (as in the cases of long-term oil-delivery contracts or purchases of commercial aircraft by the airlines), it is easier to cheat on pricing agreements. When the cartel lacks an effective punishment for cheaters, enforcing discipline is difficult.

OLIGOPOLY AND EFFICIENCY

The previous chapter described positive features of perfect competition and negative features of monopoly. In their extreme form—the cartel—oligopolies are basically monopolies, and they share the inefficiencies of monopolies. In its other extreme—an oligopoly with ten or so firms engaging in a bitter price war—it resembles perfect competition.

Economists have debated whether oligopolies that are dominated by one or

Predatory Pricing

The antitrust laws of the United States prohibit predatory pricing. Predatory pricing occurs when one firm deliberately lowers its prices for the purpose of driving rival firms out of business. These laws will be studied in the next chapter. Predatory pricing was allegedly used by John D. Rockefeller to create Standard Oil at the turn of the century.

Is predatory pricing a problem? A company that wishes to drive its rivals, who have the same costs, out of business must charge prices that the competitors cannot match. This would require pricing below average variable costs. Any price above average variable cost would leave the rival firm above its shutdown point, and the firm would continue to operate. Accordingly, the predator would have to incur extra losses to drive a rival firm out of the market. For predatory pricing to pay off, the increase in profits due to the rival's departure would have to more than offset the losses from predatory pricing. Unless barriers to entry are very high, the rival firm could either return after the price has been raised or a new firm (that may have bought the assets of the failed firm cheap) may enter the market with low average costs.

If the market is comprised of a low-cost producer and high-cost producers, government policy should not force the efficient producer to keep prices high enough to cover the higher average variable costs of rivals, even if it means their demise. If the management of one firm has done a better job at containing costs, it should be able to reap the rewards.

The most highly publicized case of possible predatory pricing was the decision by American Airlines in the spring of 1992 to cut its full-fare tickets by one-half. American Airlines, the financially strongest U.S. airline, was accused in formal complaints by Continental, TWA, and Northwest of using "predatory" prices that they could not match and survive.

An examination of American Airline's "predatory pricing" reveals that American Airlines continued to price above its average variable cost and that American's low fares were a consequence of the weak demand for air travel resulting from the 1990–91 recession.

If the weaker airlines cannot survive in a low-fare climate, it is because they made serious mistakes in the 1980s. Specifically, they all borrowed too much money for an expansion that never came and ended up with excessive interest costs.

In the fall of 1993, the courts ruled that American Airlines had not engaged in predatory pricing.

The rules against predatory pricing should not be used to protect companies that have raised their average costs due to poor business decisions.

Even if American Airlines were pursuing a policy of predatory pricing, it is doubtful that it would achieve the desired result. As the weaker airlines go into bankruptcy, new investors can buy their assets at bargain-basement prices and keep the airline operating at much lower average costs. These new low-cost airlines might even pose a serious threat to American Airlines.

SOURCE: "The Airline Mess," *Business Week,* July 6, 1992, pp. 50–55.

two giant firms are necessarily inefficient. Some believe there is little difference between such oligopolies and monopoly. Others believe that if superior performance gained this domination, the outcome is efficient.

The noted Austrian economist Joseph Schumpeter argued that technological progress—the moving force behind economic progress—often establishes some firms as dominant in their industry. This dominance, however, does not last. Through the process of "creative destruction," Schumpeter believed that new ideas and new technologies eventually replace the old. The dominant concerns of yesteryear—the Western Unions and the U.S. Steels—are inevitably replaced by new dominant concerns—the IBMs and the Microsofts. These new dominant firms will eventually be replaced. Creative destruction means that the monopoly power created by technological innovation will not last forever.

If one or two firms dominate an industry because they have played the game better than others (Schumpeter's "creative destruction"), are not high profits their just reward? This important issue will be discussed in the following chapter on antitrust policy.

Chapter Summary

The most important point to learn from this chapter is:
Most markets fall between the extremes of monopoly and perfect competition. There is no single model or explanation of oligopoly because of strategic behavior. For every possible strategy—price leadership, collusion, focal points—there is a different explanation for how the industry behaves.

1. Monopolistic competition prevails when there are many small firms producing a differentiated product and there is free entry. The number of firms is so large that the actions of one firm have no impact on other firms.

2. An oligopoly is an industry characterized by a small number of firms, barriers to entry, mutual interdependence, and price making. The number of firms is so small that the actions of one firm will not have a significant effect on other firms in the industry.

3. An industry's concentration ratio is the percentage of domestic sales accounted for by the top (four or eight) firms. It is an imperfect measure of oligopoly power.

4. The prisoners' dilemma game explains the dilemma of oligopolists. It is a game situation in which it pays both players to cooperate, but it also pays each to cheat provided the other cooperates. Oligopolists are often in the same situation. There are benefits to cooperation, but it pays to cheat if other oligopolists do not cheat.

5. Oligopolies can exercise varying degrees of control over price. Because of mutual interdependence, the oligopolist's demand curve cannot be defined until the reaction of rival firms is known. The demand curve can vary from the kinked-demand curve to the market sharing of a cartel. Methods of oligopoly coordination range from formal agreements (cartels) to informal arrangements, such as price leadership or conscious parallelism. Collusive agreements, if successful, allow the participating firms to earn monopoly profits. Because there are incentives to cheat on the cartel agreement, however, collusive agreements tend to be unstable.

6. Collusion is difficult when there are many sellers, low barriers to entry, heterogeneous products, high rates of innovation, high fixed costs, and easy price cheating.

Policy Focus: **Predatory pricing is best controlled by the incentives of firms to make a profit in a competitive environment.**

Key Terms

monopolistic competition (p. 220)
nonprice competition (p. 223)
oligopoly (p.224)

concentration ratio (p. 225)
mutual interdependence (p. 227)
prisoners' dilemma game (p. 227)

kinked-demand curve (p. 229)
cartel (p. 231)

price leader (p. 233)
conscious parallelism (p. 234)

Questions and Problems

1. Consider the four-firm concentration ratio for motor vehicles shown in Exhibit 2. Is this figure an accurate measure of the extent of oligopoly? Explain.

2. What is the relationship between the small number of firms and mutual interdependence in oligopoly theory? Why was mutual interdependence not considered in the chapter on monopoly and monopolistic competition?

3. Firm ZYX is one of three equal-sized firms in the widget market. It currently charges $20 per widget and sells 1 million widgets per year. It is considering raising its price to $22 and needs some estimate of what will happen to its widget sales. Why would it be difficult to make such an estimate?

4. Firm ZYX and the two other widget manufacturers meet in secret and agree to charge a uniform price of $50 and share the market equally (each gets one-third of sales). At the price of $50, each firm's marginal cost is $10. What are the rewards to cheating on the agreement if ZYX does not get caught? What is likely to happen if all three try to cheat?

5. Try to apply the prisoners' dilemma game to advertising in highly concentrated oligopolies.

6. Why is nonprice competition encountered frequently in oligopolistic industries?

7. In which situation would oligopoly prices be more stable: when rival firms match both price increases and price reductions; or when rival firms match price reductions but not price increases?

8. How does oligopoly theory explain why there are so many different types of oligopoly behavior—collusion, nonprice competition, conscious parallelism, price leadership?

9. Mel and Alice own the only two diners in a small town. If they agree to serve small portions, they can make larger joint profits. Is this cartel agreement stable?

10. How is the prisoners' dilemma game similar to a cartel?

11. Consider an industry that consists of three equal-sized firms. Their marginal cost of production is $2.99 at each level of output. The industry demand schedule is given in Table A. Assume that the three firms divide the market equally.
   a. What is the demand schedule facing each firm?
   b. What will be the cartel price and quantity?
   c. What is the incentive for each firm to cheat on the agreement?

TABLE A

Price (dollars per unit)	Quantity Demanded (units)
15	3
12	6
9	9
6	12
3	15

Doing Economics

Airlines are often characterized as an oligopoly in the United States. Are there barriers to entry in the airline industry? Is the product homogeneous or differentiated? Do you think that airlines are mutually interdependent? What evidence can you use to support this? Look in the financial press or in a major financial publication to find a report of airline quarterly or annual profit or loss. Are airlines making economic profits? Pick a pair of cities (one near you) between which at least three airlines fly. Call the airlines' local or toll-free reservations numbers and inquire about coach-class fares, both unrestricted and with advance-purchase and overnight-stay restrictions. Do all the airlines quote the same price? Does it seem that there is significant price competition between airlines? (Be careful answering this.) What about nonprice competition? If you have seen airline commercials on television, do they advertise price or nonprice aspects of their service?

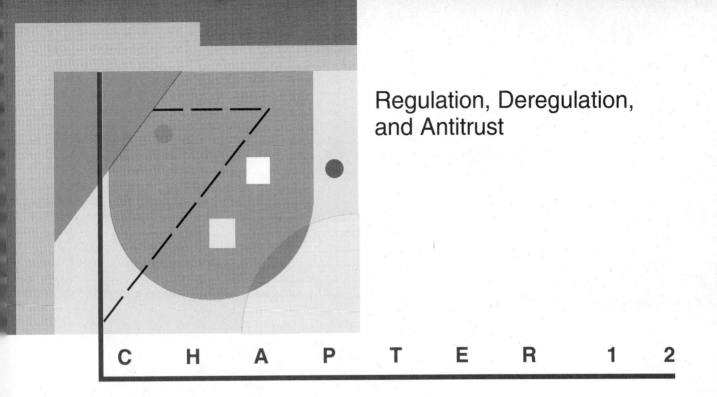

Regulation, Deregulation, and Antitrust

C H A P T E R   1   2

CHAPTER FOCUS

Government can protect citizens from monopoly. If a powerful monopoly is uncontrolled, it can charge its customers high, monopoly prices. Historical and contemporary examples of monopoly abuse of consumers abound: One need only think of the robber barons of the 19th century, charging farmers monopoly prices for rail transport and families high prices for kerosene and fuel oil, or of drug manufacturers charging sick people monopoly prices for medications produced under monopoly patents.

Public policy can provide protection against monopoly in a variety of ways: Government regulatory bodies can actually set the prices that monopolists are permitted to charge. Legislators can pass laws that prohibit certain types of market behavior or even prohibit monopoly outright. Oversight commissions can monitor potential abuses by monopolists.

The choice of appropriate public policy toward monopoly is sometimes difficult. Patents that grant pharmaceutical manufacturers monopolies may be necessary to promote research and development. If businesses are prohibited from aggressive competition, they may behave less forcefully in the marketplace. What should public policy do about monopolies that are won in a fair competitive struggle?

After studying this chapter, you will be able to:

- Describe the pricing formula of regulators and its problems.
- Explain how regulatory lag might raise the efficiency of regulated enterprises.
- Discuss the deregulation movement.
- List the legislation that makes up U.S. antitrust laws.
- Discuss the rule of reason.
- Explain why superior innovation creates problems in interpreting the Sherman Act.

REGULATION

One way to control monopoly power is to regulate monopoly prices and services. Such regulation is carried out by regulatory agencies of federal, state, and local government. Municipal and state governmental agencies regulate the rates of the local gas, electric, and phone company. Federal regulatory agencies regulate companies that serve national markets. Regulation at the state and local level is primarily directed at monopolies—the electric, gas, water, and telephone companies. However, state and local regulators also regulate businesses, such as taxicabs and barber services, that are potentially competitive. At the national level, federal regulatory commissions regulate a number of industries, some of which are potentially competitive. (See Exhibit 1.)

Some businesses are regulated for reasons that have nothing to do with monopoly power. Manufacturers of prescription drugs are regulated to ensure the safety and purity of their products. Manufacturers of automobiles are regulated to ensure that their cars meet emission and safety standards. Restaurants are regulated to ensure that they meet cleanliness standards. This chapter is not about such regulation. It is about regulation designed to control monopoly power.

The Scope of Regulation

It is difficult to estimate what proportion of the U.S. economy is regulated because most businesses are regulated in some way. On the one hand, regulated industries could include only those industries (such as communications, utilities, and insurance) in which rates and prices are controlled by government agencies. According to this criterion, as much as 10 percent of national output may be produced by regulated firms. If businesses that are government-supervised (such as the drug or meatpacking industries) are added, the regulated sector may be as high as one-fifth of national output.

Regulation of Prices

Monopolies abuse power by charging monopoly prices to earn monopoly profits. To protect the public from monopoly power, therefore, regulators must lower prices below the monopoly price. In addition to controlling prices, regulators issue licenses and franchises, and establish rules for product quality and safety. Their most important business, however, is to regulate monopoly prices.

Government uses **rate regulation** to control monopoly power.

George J. Stigler (1911–1992)

George Stigler was awarded the Nobel Prize in Economic Science in 1982 for his notable contributions to microeconomics and to industrial organization. Stigler grew up in Seattle, attended the University of Washington, and received his Ph.D. from the University of Chicago. At Chicago, Stigler studied under three prominent economists, Frank Knight, Henry Simons, and Jacob Viner, who taught him that "great reputation and high office deserve little respect in scientific work." Instead, Stigler learned to listen to the argument, look at the evidence, and ignore the position, degrees, and age of the speaker. After teaching at Iowa State University, the University of Minnesota, Columbia University, and a stint at the National Bureau of Economic Research, Stigler returned to the University of Chicago.

Stigler made scientific contributions in a number of areas of economics, ranging from the history of economic thought to microeconomics and to industrial organization. Stigler is best known for his pioneering contributions to the theory of the economics of information. He proposed that costly information explains why prices for seemingly identical products differ in the marketplace. Stigler's use of information costs to explain price dispersion is important to this chapter because economists had largely viewed price differences as the result of market power. In addition to theoretical work, Stigler pioneered empirical testing of theoretical propositions. Stigler's work on information economics was supported by his empirical observation that price dispersion is less for products that make up a significant portion of family expenditures.

Stigler's work on the economics of regulation is particularly relevant to this chapter. In his first paper on this subject, Stigler found that early state regulation of electrical utilities in the United States had a surprisingly weak effect on electricity prices. Stigler later sought to explain the weak effects of regulation by pointing out that regulators typically serve the interests of the regulated, shielding them from market forces.

Rate regulation is government control of the prices (rates) that regulated enterprises are allowed to charge.

Regulators must decide what prices regulated firms can charge. They must use a reasonable pricing formula that is "fair" to both the regulated firm and to its customers.

The Regulatory Pricing Formula. Consider how a government regulatory commission would go about setting the price (rate) for a regulated monopoly. If the firm were unregulated, it would charge the (monopoly) price that maximizes its profit. The regulatory commission's job to protect customers from monopoly pricing would require it to set the price below the monopoly price.

The regulatory commission must set "reasonable" prices. It cannot set a rate below operating costs plus a "fair" rate of return on invested capital. If regulators fail to allow regulated monopolies to earn a fair rate of return, the monopoly could appeal to the courts. In addition, regulators must allow a fair return on invested capital to attract further investment. If returns are too low, no new power plants or

Regulators set prices to cover operating costs plus a rate of return on capital.

underground gas pipelines would be built. The requirement that rates must be reasonable has caused regulators to use a simple pricing formula: Price equals average operating cost plus a fair rate of return on invested capital.

EXHIBIT 1   Federal Regulatory Commissions

Commission	Established	Purpose
Interstate Commerce Commission	1887	Regulates railroads, interstate oil pipelines, and interstate motor and water carriers.
Federal Power Commission	1920	Regulates power projects and the interstate transmission of electricity and natural gas.
Federal Communications Commission	1934	Regulates interstate telephone and telegraph service and broadcasting.
Securities and Exchange Commission	1934	Regulates securities markets.
The Civil Aeronautics Board	1938	Supervised domestic and international aviation until its dissolution at the end of 1984.

This pricing formula creates two problems. First, regulated monopolies may lose their interest in combining resources efficiently to minimize costs. Second, the formula may encourage regulated monopolists to overinvest in capital. Let us consider each problem.

Inflated Costs.   The pricing formula automatically passes increases in operating costs (whether justified or not) on to the consumer in the form of higher prices. If operating costs increase, so does the regulated price. The regulated firm need not be overly concerned with minimizing its production costs. Regulators typically do not have the information to determine whether reported costs are padded or legitimate. Regulators are reluctant to substitute their judgments on what costs are reasonable for those of management. (See Example 1.)

Overinvestment.   The pricing formula calls for a fair rate of return on invested capital. If regulators determine that 10 percent is a fair rate of return, the regulated firm's profit cannot exceed 10 percent of its invested capital. If the company has $10 million worth of invested capital and the profit-rate ceiling is 10 percent, this company can earn a maximum profit of $1 million per year.

An unregulated company will add to its invested capital only if the resulting increase in profits justifies the investment cost. The regulated monopoly, however, can increase its profits merely by acquiring more capital. By investing an additional $5 million, the regulated company can now earn $1.5 million profit per year. Regulated firms have an incentive to acquire more capital than unregulated firms. This incentive leads to inefficiencies because regulated firms invest at the margin in projects with lower rates of return than those acceptable to unregulated firms.

Price regulation causes inflated costs and overinvestment in capital.

Regulatory Lag

Rate regulation appears to eliminate rewards to efficiency and innovation *if regulators raise rates immediately when operating costs rise*. In reality, rate increases are typically not granted on a timely basis. Regulated utilities must appeal to regulatory officials to raise rates, and red tape and foot dragging can create substantial delays. If rate increases are delayed while operating costs rise, the regulated firm will not earn its fair rate of return.

Regulatory lag pressures regulated monopolies to economize on costs. If

EXAMPLE 1

Who Should Pay the Cost of Nuclear Power?

When capital capacity expands, short-run cost curves shift out. Once the investment has been undertaken, the industry operates on a new cost curve and cannot return to its original cost curve even if demand does not expand. In the case of electrical power, there is a substantial lag between the decision to build generating plants and their completion. Electrical utilities must make decisions based on the projected demand for electrical power ten years hence. Most nuclear power plants were planned during the late 1960s and early 1970s, when the demand for electricity was expanding rapidly. Electrical utilities started constructing nuclear power plants while anticipating steady increases in demand. With growing demand, the shifting out of the cost curve would mean that the industry could operate a lower average cost. In fact, the first nuclear power plants that came on stream did so in a period of expanding demand, and they proved quite profitable.

The energy crisis of the mid- and late 1970s had a profound impact on electricity demand. With rising energy prices, consumers cut back on energy usage, and the demand for electricity stopped growing. As new power plants came on stream, they could not be operated efficiently at the lower-than-anticipated demand levels of the late 1970s and early 1980s. The plants ordered more than a decade earlier were being finished at a time when no one wanted them.

The accompanying figure illustrates the economic problem of nuclear power. The figure shows an electrical utility that expected to be generating 600 megawatts of electricity in 1992. It therefore built a nuclear power plant to expand its capacity. The completion of the nuclear power plant shifts its cost curve from ATC to ATC'. ATC' yields a much lower cost for generating 600 megawatts than ATC. However, the 1992 demand for electricity is much less than expected. Only 400 megawatts are generated. The electrical utility (now located on ATC') generates this lower-than-expected output at high cost.

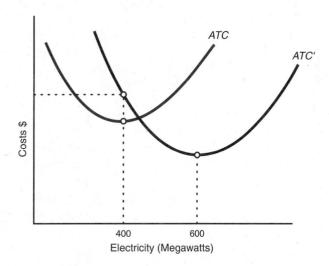

As a regulated industry, the rates of electrical utilities have traditionally been set to cover ATC. The fact that the electrical utilities that chose nuclear power were operating at higher costs than other electrical utilities raised a difficult issue for regulators: Should customers of the utility pay for the failure to choose the right ATC curve or should the company itself pay?

Regulators in California and in New England decided to make the utilities that chose nuclear power pay by not allowing them to charge customers prices high enough to recover their investment in nuclear power. The companies argued that this was unfair. If they had made a similar wrong decision that had not involved unpopular nuclear power, they would have been allowed to recover their investment. They were simply being penalized for the unpopularity of nuclear power.

operating costs rise and if years are required for the approval of higher rates, company earnings fall. By the time higher rates are granted, they are already outdated, and the incentive to hold down costs is still present. Regulatory lag is especially harmful to profits during inflationary periods when costs increase faster than rates.

> **Regulatory lag** occurs when government regulators adjust rates some time after operating costs and invested capital have increased.

Regulatory lag reintroduces some incentives for regulated firms to use their resources efficiently, but it is only a partial (and very imperfect) solution to the fundamental problem: How can regulators encourage efficient operation when they are basically guaranteeing a fair rate of return?

The Effects of Regulation

To evaluate the effects of regulation, the rates, services, and costs that would have existed in the absence of regulation have to be compared to regulated rates. To compare actual regulated rates with unregulated rates, researchers have examined the history of U.S. utilities. Surprisingly, these studies show that the regulation of prices has made very little difference.

Why has regulation not had more of an impact on prices? First, the staffs of regulatory agencies are small and underpaid and cannot compete with the large and well-paid staffs of the regulated firms. Only the regulated firms know the details of the company's operation, and they can sidestep orders from the regulatory commission. Profits in excess of the fair rate of return can be concealed by creative accounting.

Second, the monopoly power of regulated monopolies may be exaggerated. If there arc indeed effective substitutes (natural gas for electricity) or if industrial or commercial customers are prepared to move to another utility region if rates become excessive, then rate regulation does not make much difference.

Third, regulators tend to be loyal to the industry they regulate. Regulators often are closer to the companies they regulate than to the public they represent. Regulators are often recruited from the ranks of the regulated companies and often join the regulated companies upon leaving the regulatory agency. (See Example 2.)

DEREGULATION

Regulation is not limited to monopolies. There are numerous examples of regulation of potentially competitive industries. Examples of potentially competitive industries that are (or have been) regulated by federal agencies are radio and

EXAMPLE 2

Does Regulation Protect the Consumer or the Regulated Company?

City councils typically determine what taxicab companies will be allowed to operate in the city. State regulatory commissions determine what trucking companies can transport goods within the state and according to what rules. The rationale for government regulation in both cases is that someone must protect the public from dangerous unlicensed operators who operate according to their own rules. If taxi and trucking companies were free to make up their own rules and operate where they wished, the public interest might be harmed. During the 1992 election campaign, one candidate for a transportation regulatory commission spoke of the dread of sighting an unlicensed truck in one's rear-view mirror.

The consumer ultimately pays for regulation. In the case of taxicabs, the city will typically limit the number of taxicab operators. Licensed companies are usually those that have contributed to the campaigns of local public officials. New operators will not be allowed into the market on the grounds that they are unsafe. Only one taxicab company may be allowed to pick up passengers at the municipal airport. By limiting access to the market, the city council raises the price of the service.

State regulatory agencies limit the number of trucking companies allowed to operate within the state. Not only is the number limited, they are also required to follow complex and often arbitrary rules. For these reasons, it has proved cheaper for customers to ship materials across a state border to take advantage of cheaper interstate rates (such as from Houston to Dallas via Baton Rouge, Louisiana, rather than directly from Houston to Dallas).

Although the argument that regulation is required to protect public safety is persuasive, in reality, regulation often serves the economic interests of the companies being regulated.

television broadcasting, trucking, telecommunications, stock brokerage, passenger and freight airlines, railroads, and banking. In addition, state and local governments regulate numerous businesses that are potentially competitive, such as barbers, veterinarians, insurance, and taxicabs.

Economists tend to favor deregulation of potentially competitive businesses.

Most economists favor deregulation of industries that are potentially competitive. Deregulation advocates argue that it is better to let firms make decisions themselves—rather than bureaucrats—when the market is competitive. The public will likely get better service at lower cost.

Whenever regulation raises costs and prices, it creates social costs. Regulation cost between an estimated 0.7 percent and 1.8 percent of total national output in the late 1970s. If such percentages applied today, the costs of regulation would be $42 to $108 billion per year.[1]

Deregulation Legislation

In October 1978, President Jimmy Carter signed the Airline Deregulation Act, the first of the major deregulation acts. The Airline Deregulation Act allowed the airlines, rather than the Civil Aeronautics Board, to set fares and to select routes. Service to smaller communities was to continue for 10 years, financed by

---

[1]Robert E. Litan and William D. Nordhaus, *Reforming Federal Regulation* (New Haven: Yale University Press, 1983), p. 23.

government subsidy if necessary. The act phased out the Civil Aeronautics Board by the end of 1984. Other federal deregulation legislation followed. The Motor Carrier Act of 1980 curbed the Interstate Commerce Commission's control over interstate trucking. The Staggers Rail Act of October 1980 gave the railroads more flexibility in setting their own rates and allowed railroads to drop unprofitable routes. The Depository Institutions Deregulation and Monetary Control Act of 1980 eliminated interest-rate ceilings and allowed savings-and-loan associations to offer checking accounts. The Thrift Institutions Restructuring Act enabled savings-and-loan institutions to operate on a more equal footing with commercial banks. The 1982 Bus Deregulatory Reform Act allowed intercity bus lines to operate without applying for federal licenses in many circumstances.

Since 1972, the Federal Communications Commission has been gradually deregulating the television-broadcast industry by increasing the number of channels, removing barriers to direct satellite broadcasting, licensing new low-power television stations, and removing restrictions on cable television.

In 1975, the Securities and Exchange Commission made the brokerage fees charged by stockbrokers on the New York Stock Exchange freely negotiable. Prior to this, U.S. brokers were required to charge fixed commissions for stock transactions and were not allowed to compete on price. In the 1960s, the Federal Communications Commission began authorizing competitive long-distance telephone companies to build microwave networks. In a settlement with the Justice Department in 1982, rival long-distance companies gained access to the same connection to local telephone networks as did AT&T.

The Results of Deregulation

The early years of deregulation were anything but tranquil. Airline deregulation occurred during two costly recessions and a period of escalating fuel bills. Deregulation of trucking was fought by unions and by major trucking firms. Banking deregulation occurred during a period of soaring interest rates, bank failures, and an international debt crisis. Rival long-distance telephone companies did not gain equal access to local telephone exchanges until the mid-1980s.

Deregulation should be judged by its effects on prices, costs, and quality of service. Experience has shown that deregulation leads to lower prices for most but not all consumers. Air fares remained below what they would have been had regulation continued. Trucking rates fell. Stockbroker commissions on large trades fell. Bank customers enjoy more competitive rates on their savings. Long-distance phone rates are lower than under regulation. Firms previously protected by regulation lowered their costs, and these lower costs were passed on to their customers.

Deregulation has increased diversity of services, and has given consumers more choices. Customers have more trucking firms from which to choose. Airline customers can choose among a larger number of fares, destinations, and types of service. Banking customers can write checks on savings accounts. Television viewers have many more viewing channels. Long-distance customers can select among a number of long-distance companies offering different prices and services.

Deregulation has had both winners and losers. Customers in high-cost markets have had to pay more. Firms that could not meet competitive pressures have gone out of business or have been acquired by more successful firms. Employees have seen their earnings fall as firms have sought ways to lower their costs. Airline pilots, flight attendants, and baggage handlers would be earning more if there had been no deregulation. Bank profits would probably be higher if regulation had continued.

Deregulation has meant lower prices to most, but not all, consumers.

ANTITRUST LAW

Rather than regulating monopolies directly, the government can set the legal rules of the game through **antitrust legislation**.

> Antitrust legislation is legislation that controls market structure and conduct.

Antitrust law is made up of different pieces of legislation passed over the years and of court interpretations of these laws.

The Sherman Act of 1890

The Sherman Act of 1890 is the main piece of antitrust legislation.

The cornerstone of antitrust legislation is the Sherman Antitrust Act of 1890. The Sherman Act was enacted as a reaction to the public outrage against the monopoly abuses of the late nineteenth century in the railroad, steel, tobacco, and oil industries. People were convinced that too much monopoly power was bad, and Congress responded by passing the Sherman Act.

The Sherman Act contains two sections. Section 1 provides that

every contract, combination in the form of a trust or otherwise, or conspiracy, in restraint of trade or commerce among the several States, or with foreign nations, is hereby declared to be illegal.

Section 2 provides that

every person who shall monopolize, or attempt to monopolize, or combine or conspire with any other person or persons to monopolize any part of the trade or commerce among the several states, or with foreign nations, shall be guilty of a misdemeanor. . . .

Section 1 prohibits a particular type of market *conduct* (conspiring to restrain trade), while section 2 outlaws a particular market *structure* (monopoly). The vague language of section 2 has led to varying court interpretations over the years. Section 2 prohibits *monopolization*, not *monopolies*. Although the act of creating a monopoly is clearly prohibited, the legality of existing monopolies is unclear.

The Clayton Act and the Federal Trade Commission Act, 1914

The Sherman Act prohibited "acts in restraint of trade" but did not specify actual restrictive or monopolistic practices that were illegal. Moreover, the Sherman Act did not establish any agency (other than the existing Department of Justice) to enforce the provisions of the Sherman Act.

The Clayton Act of 1914 declared illegal the following four specific monopolistic practices if their "effect was to substantially lessen competition or tend to create a monopoly":

1. price discrimination (charging different prices to different customers for the same product),
2. exclusive dealing and tying contracts (requiring a buyer to agree not to purchase goods from competitors),
3. acquisition of competing companies, and
4. *interlocking directorates* (in which the directors of one company sit on the board of directors of another company in the same industry).

The Clayton Act gave private parties the right to sue for damages for injury to business or property as a result of violations of the antitrust laws, along with other penalties.

The Federal Trade Commission Act established the Federal Trade Commission (FTC). The FTC's role was to secure compliance with the ban on "unfair methods of competition" stated in the FTC Act. It was empowered to prosecute unfair competition and also to issue cease-and-desist orders to violators.

Other Antitrust Legislation

The Robinson-Patman Act of 1936 amended the anti–price-discrimination section of the Clayton Act. The basic purpose of the Robinson-Patman Act—which was passed during Depression times, when the rate of failure for small businesses was high—was to protect small businesses from the competition of the growing chain stores who were passing along discounts for large purchases to customers in the form of lower prices. Because the act sought to protect small businesses from the lower prices of large competitors, many authorities regard the Robinson-Patman Act as anticompetitive.

The Wheeler-Lea Act of 1938 extended the general ban on "unfair methods of competition" to include "unfair or deceptive" acts or practices. The FTC was empowered to deal with false and deceptive advertising and the sale of harmful products.

The Celler-Kefauver Act of 1950 broadened the Clayton Act's ban on corporate mergers by limiting mergers that occurred through the acquisition of one company's assets by another company. This antimerger provision applied if the acquisition served to lessen competition substantially or to create a monopoly.

Exhibit 2 provides a brief summary of antitrust legislation.

Interpretation of the Sherman Act

American antitrust policy is decided in the courts as well as in Congress. The Sherman Antitrust Act, the mainstay of antitrust legislation, left unresolved a basic issue: Do antitrust laws prohibit only market *conduct* that leads to monopoly, or is monopoly by the fact of its existence a violation of antitrust law?

The "Rule of Reason." In early court rulings, the courts interpreted the Sherman Act as outlawing specific market *practices* in restraint of trade (mergers, price fixing, price slashing to drive out competition), not the existence of monopoly in and of itself. This interpretation became known as the **rule of reason**.

> The **rule of reason** stated that monopolies were in violation of the Sherman Act only if they engaged in unfair or illegal business practices. Being a monopoly in and of itself was not considered a violation of the Sherman Act.

The early landmark tests of the Sherman Act were the Standard Oil and American Tobacco Company cases, both tried in 1911. In both cases, the court ruled that these companies should be broken up into smaller companies (many of the major oil companies of today are spinoffs of Standard Oil). Both Standard Oil and American Tobacco accounted for more than 90 percent of output in their respective industries. The court's ruling, however, was not based on their 90 percent market share. The court ruled that Standard Oil and American Tobacco

EXHIBIT 2   Antitrust Laws of the United States

Acts	Enacted	Purpose
Sherman Act	1890	Prohibits business behavior that limits competition and attempts to monopolize.
Clayton Act	1914	Specifies illegal business practices that restrict competition.
Federal Trade Commission Act	1914	Established Federal Trade Commission to prosecute unfair competition and issue cease-and-desist orders.
Robinson-Patman Act	1936	Protected small businesses from growing competition of chain stores.
Wheeler-Lea Act	1938	Banned unfair or deceptive methods of competition.
Celler-Kefauver Act	1950	Broadened ban on corporate mergers.

The rule of reason declared that monopolies that did not use unfair business practices were not in violation of the Sherman Act.

violated the Sherman Act because they had both engaged in unreasonable business practices, not because they were in fact monopolies.

The implication of the Standard Oil and American Tobacco rulings was that if a monopoly does not engage in unfair business practices, it is not in violation of the Sherman Act.

Alcoa.   The rule of reason prevailed until the Aluminum Company of America (Alcoa) case of 1945. The courts ruled that Alcoa was in violation of the Sherman Act because it controlled more than 90 percent of the aluminum-ingot market in the United States. Although Alcoa was also accused of using unfair pricing (setting ingot prices too high relative to aluminum sheet prices), the courts ruled that Alcoa was in violation of the Sherman Act because of its 90-percent market share.

The rule of reason said that companies that used unfair business practices that would ultimately lead to monopoly were in violation of the Sherman Act, while companies that were already monopolies, if they were well behaved, did not violate the Sherman Act. The Alcoa case appeared to reject this interpretation. In its place a *structure test* was applied in which size was the determining factor. Actual monopolization, not the attempt to monopolize, was Alcoa's offense.

Definition of Market.   The Alcoa decision raised a fundamental issue: If the existence of monopoly is itself a violation of the Sherman Act, how is the market to be defined? Alcoa controlled 90 percent of the virgin aluminum-ingot market in 1945, but it had to compete in the scrap ingot market and to face competition from stainless steel, lead, nickel, tin, zinc, copper, and imported aluminum. In the 1945 Alcoa decision, aluminum substitutes were not included in Alcoa's market.

Subsequent court cases established a broader interpretation of what constitutes a market. The Du Pont cellophane case of 1956 established that the market should be defined to include products that are "reasonably interchangeable" with cellophane (such as aluminum foil, waxed paper, or vegetable parchment). The IBM case (which was dismissed in 1982) again used a broad interpretation of the market. Although IBM dominated the mainframe computer market in the early 1980s, its shares of other computer markets were relatively small: 20 percent of the minicomputer market, 18 percent of the word-processor market, and less than 5 percent of the telecommunications and computer-services markets.

Superior Innovation   The Alcoa case raised concern that the Sherman Act would be used to punish businesses that had gained a dominant position through superior innovation and risk-taking. What about businesses that had gained a dominant position by fairly outcompeting rivals? Subsequent court cases have established the principle that firms that have fairly gained dominant positions in their markets have not violated the Sherman Act. In 1972, a smaller competitor charged that Eastman Kodak's method of introducing its pocket-sized instamatic camera gave Kodak an unfair advantage over other film processors. The court ruled in favor of Eastman Kodak, concluding that Kodak had earned certain advantages as a result of "reaping the competitive rewards attributable to efficient size." The principle that superior firms should not be punished for success was upheld in subsequent court rulings.

The Alcoa ruling required the courts to define the market and how to deal superior innovation.

MERGERS

One business firm can gain monopoly power by merging with another. If one company acquires another company, the new and larger company will likely have more market power than the two single firms. Antitrust legislation—directed against the creation of monopoly power—must therefore determine what types of mergers are to be permitted.

The Clayton Act of 1914 and the Celler-Kefauver Act of 1950 prohibit the acquisition of one company by another if this action reduces competition. The test for whether a merger is to be allowed is therefore whether the merger creates "monopoly power." There is no simple way to determine by how much a merger lessens competition. Federal agencies that deal with mergers have had to make this judgment.

There are three types of mergers. Mergers may be a **horizontal merger**, a **vertical merger**, or a **conglomerate merger**.

The three types of mergers are horizontal, vertical, or conglomerate mergers.

> A horizontal merger is a merger of two firms in the same line of business (such as an insurance company merging with another insurance company or a shoe manufacturer merging with another shoe manufacturer).

> A vertical merger is a merger of two firms that are part of the same materials, production, or distribution network (such as a personal-computer manufacturer merging with a retail computer-distribution chain or a machinery manufacturer merging with a machinery-parts supplier).

> A conglomerate merger occurs when one company takes over another company in a different line of business.

The courts (especially since 1950) have adopted a virtual prohibition of horizontal mergers between two companies if both have substantial market shares. Exceptions are allowed when one firm takes over another firm that is on the verge of bankruptcy. For example, Jones & Laughlin Industries and Youngstown Steel were allowed to merge in 1978 to form the third largest steel producer. The approval of a multitude of airline mergers in the 1980's was motivated by the desire to keep these insolvent airlines in business.

Vertical mergers violate the Clayton Act if a buyer merges with a supplier, thereby restricting supplies to rivals, or if the merger results in a transfer of significant market power. On these grounds, Du Pont (a major supplier of automotive fabrics and finishes) was required to sell its 23 percent of General

EXAMPLE 3

Coke, Pepsi, Dr. Pepper, and Seven-Up

In early 1986, Coca-Cola announced its intention to acquire Dr. Pepper and Pepsi announced its intention to purchase Seven-Up. At the time, Coke and Pepsi accounted for two-thirds of the carbonated-drink market, while Dr. Pepper and Seven-Up accounted for another 11 percent.

In July 1986, a federal district court ruled against the two mergers. The purchases by Coke and Pepsi of their smaller rivals would not be allowed. The court ruling hinged on the following economic arguments. First, the courts ruled that the carbonated-drink market is distinct from the beverage market (fruit juices, coffee, tea, and other beverages). Coke and Pepsi accounted for a much smaller percentage of the beverage market, but combined they accounted for $2 out of every $3 of sales of carbonated drinks. Second, the courts ruled that Coke and Pepsi possessed significant market power. They were able to raise prices in specific sales regions without the loss of a significant number of customers. Third, the courts ruled that there were significant barriers to entry into the carbonated drink market. If the mergers were allowed, it was unlikely that new companies could and would enter the market. Although smaller companies could economically manufacture carbonated-drink concentrate, the advertising cost of launching a new product was in the range of $50 million. Another barrier to entry for a new drink is that vending machines have only a limited number of buttons—only four to six different brands can be accommodated. A final barrier to entry is that bottlers must operate at an economical scale of operations. The concentrate can be produced economically by small manufacturers, but bottling requires at least a 10 percent market share before profits can be achieved.

SOURCE: Lawrence J. White, "Application of the Merger Guidelines: The Proposed Merger of Coca-Cola and Dr Pepper," John Kwoka and Lawrence White (eds.), *The Antitrust Revolution* (Glenview, Ill.: Scott, Foresman and Company, 1989, pp. 46-79.

Motors stock in 1957 because Du Pont's influence over GM gave it a competitive advantage over other automotive suppliers. For similar reasons, Brown Shoe Company was not allowed in 1962 to acquire Kinney (a large shoe-retailing chain). The ban on vertical mergers between moviemakers and movie theaters was eased in 1986 in response to technological change in the entertainment industry. (See Example 3 for another example.)

The major exception to the prohibition of mergers among large companies is the conglomerate merger because it does not involve merger of competing companies. U.S. Steel was permitted to acquire Marathon Oil and Du Pont was allowed to acquire Conoco because the merging companies operated in different markets.

Conglomerate mergers have led to a substantial increase in the share of corporate assets controlled by the largest U.S. corporations over the past 30 years. The 451 largest corporations controlled 50 percent of corporate assets in 1960; by 1990, they controlled approximately 75 percent of corporate assets.

The pace of mergers in the United States has been uneven over the years (see Exhibit 3). In part, this pattern reflects the fact that antimerger legislation has changed over the years, as has the rigorous enforcement of antimerger legislation. It has been especially difficult to stop conglomerate mergers because the government has to prove that the proposed merger will actually reduce competition. When two companies in different lines of business merge, it is extremely difficult to prove that the merger will lessen competition.

EXHIBIT 3   Mergers in the United States, 1890–1992

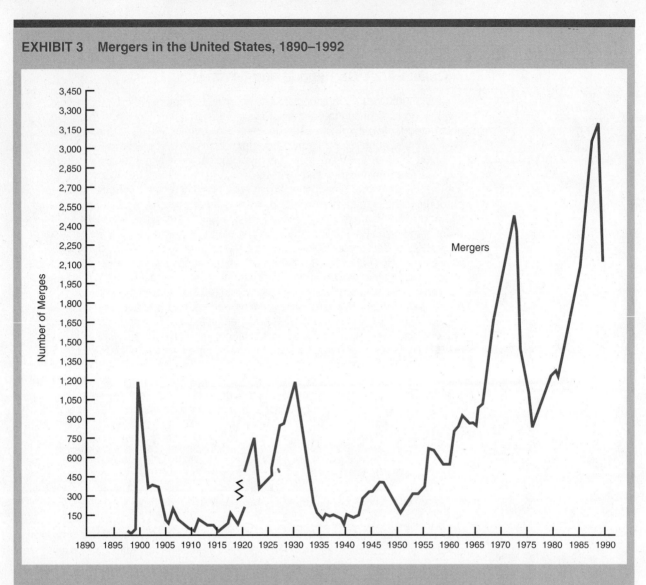

SOURCE: The National Bureau of Economic Research and the Federal Trade Commission, *Mergers and Acquisitions* updated data courtesy of W. T. Grimm and Company.

DO WE NEED ANTITRUST LAWS?

A number of economists argue that the costs of antitrust laws outweigh the benefits to consumers. Antitrust battles force corporations to spend billions of dollars on legal expenses, and litigation can stretch over decades. The IBM case, for example, lasted 13 years before its dismissal, cost the government more than $12 million, and cost IBM even more.

Some experts argue that the growth in international trade has largely antiquated antitrust laws, which were passed in the early part of this century. Major U.S. corporations that account for substantial shares of U.S. production must now compete with foreign companies. Modern technology is able to develop substitutes for the products that monopolists sell, and substitutes threaten all monopolies with

Should We Reregulate Airlines and Banking?

Deregulation began in earnest in the United States in 1978 and was hailed as the major achievement of the Carter and Reagan presidencies. The deregulation laws of the late 1970s and 1980s are discussed in this chapter.

Has deregulation been a success or failure? Critics of deregulation point to two industries, airlines and banking, as proof that deregulation has failed and should be reversed.

We maintain that regulation has been healthy for the U.S. economy, should not be reversed, and should be expanded into new areas such as intrastate trucking.

The Airline Deregulation Act of 1978 gave the airlines the freedom to set their own fares and pick their own routes. Prior to this act, the Civil Aeronautics Board awarded routes and set rates. The consequence was that consumers paid high prices and pilots and flight attendants received high salaries. In the years that followed, the number of airlines expanded to include new airlines such as Air California, People Express, Midway, and many others. A number of commuter airlines were established to serve smaller communities.

The 1980s and early 1990s were difficult for the airlines. The deep recession of 1980–81 and the rise in fuel prices associated with the Iran-Iraq war cut deeply into airline profits. Terrorism reduced the revenues of U.S. carriers with international routes, and the recession of 1990–91 again destroyed airline profits. In this newly competitive environment, weak airlines either failed or were taken over by stronger airlines. By the early 1990s, the U.S. airline industry had been reduced to three strong carriers with a number of weak airlines fighting for survival.

How can we argue that deregulation was good for the airline industry in light of this history? Deregulation has been good for airline customers. Prior to deregulation, flying was reserved for the wealthy and for business travelers on expense accounts. Since deregulation, flying has become accessible to virtually all. Airlines fares today are about 40 percent what they would have been without deregulation. Today the airlines offer more variety in terms of types of fares, connections, and services than before deregulation. The airlines have had to improve their productivity in the new competitive environment. Labor productivity in commercial aviation has risen more rapidly than productivity in other branches.

Many people blame the Depository Institutions Deregulation and Monetary Control Act of 1980 for the banking crises and failures that occurred subsequent to deregulation. This act reduced the legal distinction between banks and savings-and-loans institutions and allowed financial institutions to select their own investment activities and interest rates. Prior to this reform, savings-and-loans institutions were restricted primarily to making real-estate loans and could not issue checking accounts.

The root causes of the banking crises of the 1980s and 1990s were not deregulation but other factors. First, savings-and-loans associations, which were forced to make primarily real-estate loans under strict banking regulation, were caught with unprofitable loans in the 1970s as interest rates rose and real-estate values fell. Second, government bank-insurance programs encouraged banks to make risky loans knowing that their customers were insured by government bank-insurance programs. Third, the government felt that it could not afford to let big banks fail, no matter how badly managed, for fear that such failures would threaten the stability of the banking system.

What would happen if the airlines and banks were to be reregulated? First, customers would be denied the benefits of competition. Airlines could again pass cost increases along to consumers and airline ticket prices would rise. Banks again would have to follow strict rules concerning loans and investments. Second, government agencies would either directly or indirectly manage the nation's airlines and banking system. Some government agency would determine what airlines could fly where and at what prices. Another agency would tell banks what activities they could engage in and what interest rates they could charge.

Reregulation would raise prices to consumers, deprive them of diversity and quality, and lower productivity. There is no evidence that government regulators can do a better job running airlines or banks than can private management. In fact, many of the current problems of the airlines and banks can be traced to improper government policies (such as requiring savings-and-loan institutions to invest in real estate and poorly devised deposit insurance programs).

potential competition if their monopoly profits are too high. Finally, monopolies may indeed be the result of superior innovation and better management. To break up efficient companies may reduce rather than increase efficiency. Punishing successful companies could signal that aggressive innovation will be punished rather than rewarded.

The next chapter deals with agriculture, an industry that illustrates many of the principles of supply, demand, and competitive markets.

Chapter Summary

The most important point to learn from this chapter is:
There is no simple way for government to control monopoly power in the public interest. Price regulation leads to inefficiencies and antitrust legislation can punish superior competition.

1. Regulation of monopolies aims at preventing monopoly profits while allowing the monopoly to operate profitably and efficiently. Regulated monopolies are normally allowed to charge a price that covers operating costs plus a "fair" rate of return on invested capital. This pricing formula encourages inefficiency because higher costs can be passed on to the consumer and higher investment will automatically yield higher profits. Regulatory lag provides some incentive to minimize costs.

2. Deregulation frees competitive industries from government supervision. There has been a substantial move to deregulation since 1978.

3. Antitrust legislation seeks to control market structure and market conduct by setting legal rules for business. The Sherman Act outlaws actions that restrain trade and outlaws the act of monopolization. The Clayton Act specifies particular business practices that illegally restrain trade. The Federal Trade Commission Act established the Federal Trade Commission and banned unfair methods of competition. The Celler-Kefauver Act toughened the antimerger provisions of the Clayton Act. The "rule of reason" that only unreasonable restraint of trade violates the Sherman Act was applied by the courts until 1945. The rule of reason apparently was overturned in 1945 with the Alcoa decision when the courts ruled that size alone is a violation of the Sherman Act. In subsequent cases, the courts have ruled that monopolies created by superior technological achievement do not violate the Sherman Act.

4. The law prohibits mergers between firms in the same industry if both have substantial market shares. Exceptions are allowed when one firm takes over another that is on the verge of bankruptcy. Conglomerate mergers are usually not opposed because they do not involve mergers of competing companies.

Policy Focus: **A return to regulation of airlines and of banking would raise prices to consumers and lower efficiency.**

Key Terms

rate regulation (p. 240)
regulatory lag (p. 242)
antitrust legislation(p. 247)
rule of reason (p. 248)

horizontal merger (p. 250)
vertical merger (p. 250)
conglomerate merger (p. 250)

Questions and Problems

1. Explain why regulation of potentially competitive industries is not consistent with the objectives of regulation.

2. Explain why the Alcoa case of 1945 caused the definition of what constitutes the relevant market to become critical to antitrust cases.

3. You are the president of a regulated monopoly. You know that the regulators will allow you to set rates to cover operating costs plus a "fair" rate of return on invested capital. How would you behave? Would you behave differently if you were not regulated?

4. One explanation why regulating utilities has not made much difference in utility rates is that utilities face competition. How can a monopoly like an electrical power utility face competition and still be a monopoly?

5. You operate a regulated monopoly that sells in both a competitive and a monopolistic market. How would your company's price and output decisions differ in the two markets? What steps might you take to improve your position in the competitive market?

6. Deregulation of the television-broadcasting industry has been opposed by the three major networks. How would deregulation affect their profits?

7. Explain the contradiction raised by the rule of reason.

8. Why would innovative and risk-taking firms such as Boeing and Eastman Kodak oppose the Alcoa decision?

9. Explain why the government is more likely to approve a conglomerate merger, even of two giant firms, than a horizontal merger.

10. "Several ill-informed people have suggested doing away with our antitrust laws. To do so would return us to the robber barons of the nineteenth century." Evaluate this statement.

11. Would regulatory lag tend to raise or lower economic efficiency? Why?

12. Identify the following according to the type of merger:
    a. A merger of General Motors and Chrysler.
    b. A merger of Prudential Insurance with McDonalds.
    c. A merger of Hyatt Hotels and American Airlines.
    d. A merger of U.S. Foods with Safeway Stores.
    e. A merger of U.S. Steel with Ford Motor Company.
    f. A merger of B. F. Goodrich with General Motors.

Doing Economics

Consider the dormitory food service for your campus. How well does it satisfy the conditions listed in the text for a monopoly? What kinds of barriers to entry protect its position? Do you think it earns economic profits? Why or why not? Describe the demand situation faced by the food-service provider once it has won your school's contract and once the number of students subscribing to the board plan is determined. How are the provider's costs related to the quality of the food it serves? What incentives does it have in terms of food quality? If possible, examine a copy of the contract between the school and the food service or interview the college official in charge of food service. In what ways do the terms of the contract constitute "regulation?"

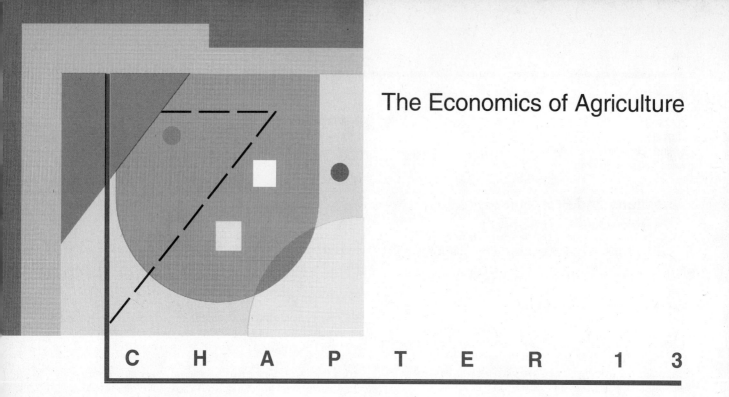

The Economics of Agriculture

C H A P T E R 1 3

CHAPTER FOCUS
The Great Depression of the 1930s focused attention on farming. In just three years (1929 to 1932), farm income fell to one-third of its previous level. The collapse of farm income was due to the collapse of farm prices. In 1932, farmers received less than half of what they had received in 1929 for their products.

The U.S. Congress and President Franklin Roosevelt responded to collapsing farm incomes by introducing programs aimed at stabilizing farm prices and farm incomes. In the early 1930s, it was widely accepted that farming exemplified the American life-style. Most nonfarming families still had friends and relatives in farming, and they could easily sympathize with the plight of farmers. Low prices were viewed as the culprit. So farm programs to raise farm prices were put in place in the 1930s. The Agricultural Adjustment Act of 1933 established the principle that farmers were entitled to higher prices (because agricultural prices had fallen more than other prices) and that it was the government's responsibility to support agricultural prices if they threatened to fall too low in private markets.

The American "farm problem" really consists of two problems. The first is the variability of farm prices, which causes farm incomes to fluctuate. The second is the long-run decline in farm prices relative to nonfarm prices. The second problem means that market forces hold the increase in farm incomes below the increase in incomes in nonfarm occupations.

This second problem has reduced the attractiveness of farming as a business and as a source of employment. The numbers of farms and the amount of farm employment have been shrinking for more than a half-century.

Public policy has tried to come to grips with the farm problem in an effort to halt the perceived decline of the farm sector of the U.S. economy.

After studying this chapter, you will be able to:

- Explain why farm prices are more variable than other prices and why they have declined relative to nonfarm prices.

- Know the consequences of price fluctuations and falling relative prices for American farmers.

- Discuss the ways farm prices and farm incomes can be raised by government policy.

- Understand the role of futures markets in allowing farmers to cope with uncertainty.

THE BUSINESS OF FARMING

Facts and Figures

Farming is a $100 billion business that accounts for about 2 percent of total output produced by the U.S. economy. In 1992, 3 million people worked on the 2 million American farms. The median farm family income was about $30,000. Eighty-seven percent of American farms were owned by individuals or families, 10 percent were owned by partnerships, and only 3 percent were owned by corporations. Although the rise of corporate farming has been widely publicized, American farming is still primarily a family business. Even though corporate farms account for only 3 percent of all farms, they account for 24 percent of the value of farm products. Corporate farms are much larger than family farms.

Farming and Competition

The American farm industry comprises about 2 million firms producing products such as wheat, corn, turkeys, chicken, livestock, and soybeans. Although corporate farms are much larger on average than family farms, they are still too small to dictate the prices of farm products. In other words, farms are price takers in product markets.

The individual farm faces a perfectly elastic demand curve. It is a price taker in product markets.

In perfectly competitive markets, the market demand curve is downward sloping, while the demand curve facing the individual firm is horizontal. As a price taker, the farm controls only one decision: How much output to produce? Based on market prices, the farmer must decide how much corn, cotton, or wheat to plant, or how many pounds of chickens, pigs, turkeys, and hogs to raise.

In the chapter on perfect competition we saw how a perfectly competitive firm would make these decisions. The farmer, as a perfectly competitive producer, produces that quantity at which price and marginal cost are equal. By equating price and marginal cost, the farmer maximizes profit. If prices do not cover variable costs, the farmer should temporarily shut down operations. If prices continue to not cover average variable costs in the long run, the farmer would have to leave farming.

Each farm follows the price equals marginal cost rule; therefore, the market supply curve for a particular farm product is the sum of the marginal cost curves of the thousands of farms that make up this particular market. The market supply curve is positively sloped. The market demand curve for a particular farm product is negatively sloped, and the equilibrium price is that price that equates quantity supplied and quantity demanded.

GALLERY OF ECONOMISTS

Ernst Engel (1821–1896)

Ernst Engel, a German statistician known for the discovery of the Engel curve and Engel's law, was born in Dresden. Engel's work with a French sociologist interested him in household budget surveys—a subject that would play an important role in his later work. Engel served as the director of the Prussian statistical bureau in Berlin, a post he resigned in opposition to Bismarck's protectionist policies. In 1885, he was among the founders of the International Statistical Institute.

Engel's study of the family budgets that he collected in various European countries convinced him that there was a strong negative association between the share of household expenditures on food and family income. This relationship is one of the first functional relationships ever established in economics, and it is this empirical proposition that has come to be known as Engel's law.

Engel's law is relevant to farming because it says that the income inelasticity of the demand for food products is less than unity. Demand is income inelastic when the demand for the product rises at a slower rate than income. If demand rises slower than income, the share of the product in total expenditures will fall. Engel's law explains why the share of resources devoted to agriculture falls with economic development and why farm prices have not kept pace with nonfarm prices.

TRENDS IN FARM PRICES AND FARM INCOMES

The incomes of owners of firms in the industry are affected by the prices their products receive. Farm products have inelastic price elasticities of demand. If the price falls by 10 percent, the quantity demanded of farm products will rise by far less than 10 percent. Demand for farm products is inelastic, for several reasons. First, food is a necessity. Second, in an aggregate sense, there are no substitutes for food. Third, any particular food item makes up a small portion of a family's total expenditures, and this reduces one's incentive to be price conscious. With inelastic demand, agricultural prices are positively related to total revenue or gross income. Thus, earnings in agriculture are positively related to agricultural prices. When prices rise, earnings from farming rise. When prices fall, earnings from farming fall. (See Example 1.)

The demand for farm products is inelastic. Agricultural income and farm prices are positively related.

Agricultural prices behave differently from manufacturing or service prices. It is these differences in price patterns that contribute to the farm problem. Most agricultural prices fluctuate more than nonfarm prices and agricultural prices have declined relative to other prices in the long run.

Farm Prices Fluctuate More Than Other Prices

Exhibit 1a plots the prices of some major farm products along with the prices of selected manufactured products. The difference between the two series is the much greater variability of farm product prices.

The variability of farm prices reflects itself in the variability of farm income. Farm income and farm prices are plotted in Exhibit 1b, which shows that the ups-and-downs of farm income follow the ups-and-downs of farm prices, as one would expect with inelastic demand. The lesser variability of manufacturing prices is a consequence of more elastic demand and the more stable supply conditions in manufacturing.

EXAMPLE 1

Price Elasticities of Demand in Agriculture

This chapter emphasizes the relatively low price elasticities of demand for agricultural products. The following chart gives estimates of the price elasticities of demand for various farm products along with some price elasticities for nonfarm products. Notice that the price elasticities of demand for farm products tend to be less than unity (although there are some exceptions). The price elasticities of demand for manufactured goods or services tend to be greater than for farm products.

Price Elasticities of Demand

Agricultural Products		Nonagricultural Products	
Milk	0.14	Automobiles	1.35
Eggs	0.23	Beer	1.13
Potatoes	0.30	Housing	1.00
Chicken	1.20	Alcohol	0.92
Lettuce	0.30	Tires	0.86
		Recreation equipment	0.88
		Tobacco products	0.46
		China and glassware	1.55

SOURCES: Hendrick S. Houthakker and Lester D. Taylor, *Consumer Demand in the United States: Analyses and Projections* (Cambridge, Mass.: Harvard University Press, pp. 166–67); Heinz Kohler, *Intermediate Microeconomics,* 2nd ed. (Glenview, Ill.: Scott, Foresman, 1983); George E. Brandow, "Interrelations Among Demands For Farm Products and Implications of Control of Market Supply," *Pennsylvania Agricultural Experimental Station Bulletin 680*, 1961, Table 1; Ralph T. Byrnes and Gerald W. Stone, *Microeconomics,* 3rd ed. (Glenview, Ill.: Scott, Foresman, 1987), pp. 105, 108.

The data on farm prices and farm income underscore the risks associated with farming. Farmers are unable to control farm prices because they act as price takers in competitive markets. Many of their costs are for nonfarm products such as machinery and chemical fertilizers which are more stable than farm prices, resulting in a cost-price squeeze. Farm profits are squeezed by falling output prices and rising input prices. When farm prices decline, farm profits and income tend to fall. If farm prices fall substantially, farmers find that their revenues do not cover their variable costs, and they must shut down.

Exhibit 2 uses supply, demand, and price elasticity to explain the greater variability of farm prices. The greater variability is deeply rooted in the nature of the supply and demand for farm products. The market demand curves for agricultural products tend to be relatively price inelastic, for the reasons noted above. On the supply side, agriculture is also different from manufacturing or services. Unlike manufacturing, the supply of agricultural products is subject to weather conditions. When temperatures are right and the amount of rainfall is right, harvests are abundant—the supply curve shifts to the right. When it is either too hot or too cold or too dry or too damp, the supply curve shifts to the left.

Exhibit 2 explains the effects on agricultural prices of the combination of an inelastic demand curve and a shifting supply curve. With an inelastic demand curve, relatively small increases in supply cause substantial drops in price. Relatively small decreases in supply cause substantial increases in price.

Shifting supply curves along inelastic demand curves are an important reason for volatile farm prices. There are even more reasons why farm prices are so

The shifting supply curve of agricultural products due to weather conditions causes movements up and down the inelastic demand curve for agricultural products, resulting in considerable variability in price.

EXHIBIT 1 Farm Prices and Farm Income

a. The Greater Variability of Farm Prices

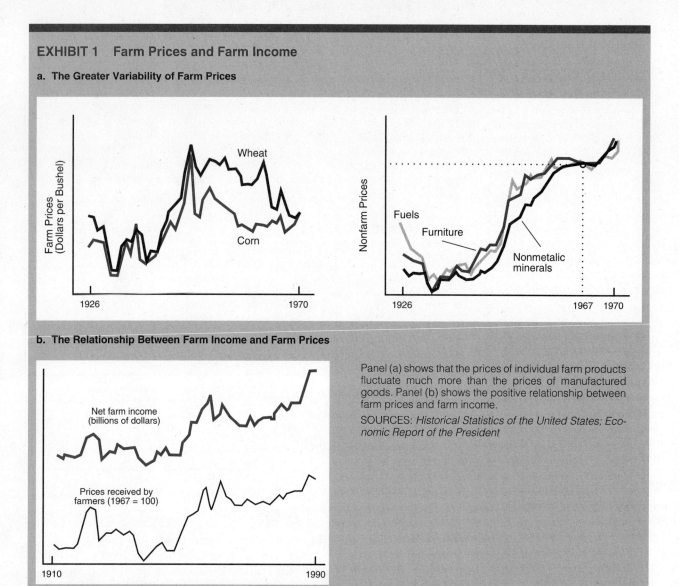

b. The Relationship Between Farm Income and Farm Prices

Panel (a) shows that the prices of individual farm products fluctuate much more than the prices of manufactured goods. Panel (b) shows the positive relationship between farm prices and farm income.

SOURCES: *Historical Statistics of the United States; Economic Report of the President*

volatile. Because of the time lag between planting and selling, farmers do not know what prices their crops will bring at market time. Farmers can mistakenly expect a high price and plant too much of one crop. Many farm products, like fruits and vegetables, are highly perishable. They must be sold before they spoil, even if prices are temporarily low.

Declining Relative Prices

Exhibit 3 plots long-term trends in farm and nonfarm prices. This exhibit shows that the *relative price* of farm products has declined over the long term. The relative price of farm products is measured as the ratio of prices which farmers receive to the prices which farmers pay. Exhibit 3 shows that not only is farming subject to greater price variability, it is also subject to a long-term decline in relative farm prices.

Supply, demand, and income elasticity explain the long-term decline in

EXHIBIT 2   Why Farm Prices Fluctuate

The demand curve for farm products is inelastic. We begin with the supply curve for "normal" weather conditions, S, which yields an equilibrium price of P. The supply curve under bad weather conditions, S', yields a much higher price, P', as the supply curve moves up the inelastic demand curve. The supply curve for good weather conditions, S", yields a much lower price, P", as the supply curve moves down the inelastic demand curve.

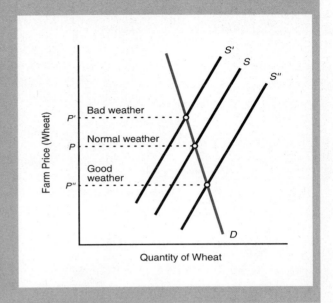

EXHIBIT 3   Trends in Agricultural and Nonagricultural Prices, 1910–1991

These data show that agricultural prices have risen less rapidly than nonagricultural prices over the long run.

SOURCES: *Historical Statistics of the United States; Economic Report of the President*

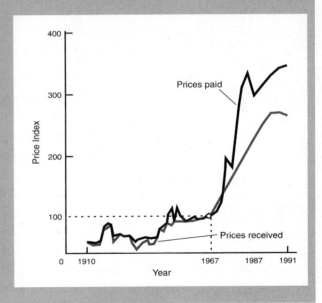

relative farm prices. In order to explain changes in prices over time, one must examine the factors that cause supply and demand curves to shift systematically over time.

Shifts in Supply.   Weather factors cause only short-run changes in supply. Technological improvements do, however, cause long-run increases in supply.

Technological improvements reduce the marginal costs of producing a given level of output and hence shift the supply curve to the right. If agricultural and nonagricultural firms experience equal rates of technological progress, then technological improvements would not explain the decline in the relative price of agricultural products (because both supply curves shift at the same rate). If, however, technological progress in agriculture is more rapid, then more rapid technological advances in agriculture explain at least part of the decline in relative agricultural prices. In fact, farm productivity has risen about 25 percent faster than nonfarm productivity since 1929, and the more rapid rise of productivity would depress farm prices relative to nonfarm prices.

The U.S. government has made substantial investments in agricultural technology through the Agricultural Experimental Stations located at land grant universities and through the U.S. Department of Agriculture. The government's Cooperative Extension Service has worked to disseminate technology information to farmers and to rural residents. No similar federal program exists for manufacturing. One need only think of the advances in hybrid seeds, biotechnology, and growth hormones to understand the rapid technological advances in agriculture.

The frequent complaints about farm crises shift attention from the fact the American agriculture is (along with Canada) the most productive in the world. (See Example 2.)

Shifts in Demand. The decline in relative agricultural prices is also explained by shifts in demand. A long record of statistical research has confirmed that the demand for agricultural products is income inelastic. (See discussion of Engel's law in Gallery of Economists.) Income inelasticity means that when incomes rise by 1 percent, the demand for the income-inelastic product rises by less than 1 percent. Services and manufactured goods tend to be either unitary elastic or elastic, meaning that the demands for these goods rise at the same rate or faster than income.

The inelastic income elasticity of farm products means that as incomes grow over time, the demand curve for farm products will shift out relatively little because we do not eat much more. Farm-product demand curves shift out less than the demand curves for nonfarm products. The largest part of the increase in demand for farm products results from increases in population rather than from increases in income.

Shifts in Supply and Demand Together. The supply curve of agricultural products has shifted out more to the right than the supply curve of nonagricultural products, owing to the more rapid technological progress of agriculture. The demand curve for agricultural products shifts less to the right than the demand curve for nonagricultural products as income rises. Exhibit 4 shows the effect of the shifts on agricultural and nonagricultural prices. Over the long run, the prices of agricultural products rise less rapidly than the prices of nonagricultural products, resulting in real price declines for agricultural products.

Agricultural prices have fallen relative to other prices because of rapid increases in farm productivity and income inelasticity of farm products.

THE DECLINING SHARE OF AGRICULTURE

The relative shift of labor resources out of agriculture over the past century has been substantial. In 1880, three out of four U.S. residents lived in rural areas. A century later, only one in five lived in rural areas. The shift of labor force was even more dramatic. In 1880 one in five American workers was employed in agriculture. A century later only one in one hundred was employed in agriculture.

How Productive Are American Farms?

The focus on the problems of American farming have diverted attention from its enormous success. American farms are the most productive in the world, along with Canadian farms. American farmers produce the surpluses that have been used to feed not only American families but families the world over. The success of American agriculture is explained by its rapid technological progress. American farmers now apply biotechnology and genetic engineering to raise the output of dairy and meat products, use the most sophisticated forms of chemical fertilizers, and use the research of the massive American farm research establishments located in land grant universities.

The accompanying table shows that the average American farm worker produces more than double the most productive European farmer, 15 times the Russian farmer, and 80 times the Chinese farmer.

Total Grain Production per Agricultural Worker, 1990

Country	Grain Production (millions of metric tons)
United States	84
France	41
Germany	25
Italy	9
Russia	7
Poland	5
Japan	3
China	1

Source: Handbook of Economic Statistics, 1990, Tables 23 and 99. Grains includes the major grains plus rice.

Economics teaches that factors must be paid their opportunity costs. As agricultural prices fall relative to nonagricultural prices, more and more people discover that agricultural employment does not pay them their opportunity costs. Accordingly, families move from farms to cities. They leave family farms or their jobs as hired hands on farms and find employment in nonagricultural occupations.

With declining real prices, only innovative farmers using technological advances and the most efficient production practices can lower costs faster than real prices fall. These farmers continue to earn profits and stay in farming without assistance. It is because of these highly efficient farms that only a small percentage of the labor force is required to feed the population and export farm goods to the rest of the world.

THE AGRICULTURAL CRISIS OF THE 1980s

The focus of this chapter has been the long-run economic forces that have shaped American agriculture. The 1980s was a period of "crisis" for American agriculture that concentrated even more attention on the farm problem.

The transformation of American agriculture actually began at the beginning of the 1970s, when the world turned to the U.S. to sell its large stocks of grains and

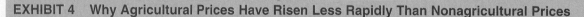

EXHIBIT 4   Why Agricultural Prices Have Risen Less Rapidly Than Nonagricultural Prices

a. Agricultural Prices

b. Nonagricultural Prices

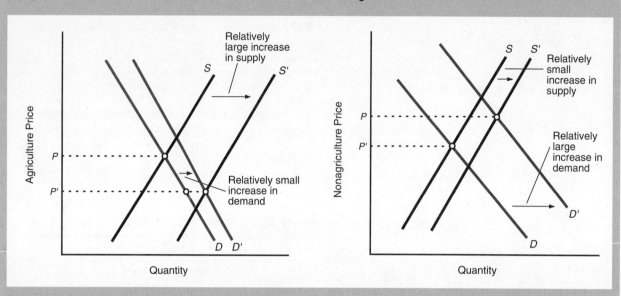

In both panels (a) and (b), the demand curve shifts to the right (demand increases) as income rises. But the demand curve for agricultural products shifts less than the demand curve for nonagricultural products. Because of more rapid technological progress in agriculture, the supply curve of agriculture shifts more to the right than the supply curve of nonagricultural products. The result is that nonagricultural prices rise more rapidly than agricultural prices over the long run.

oilseeds. In 1970, weather for raising crops had been poor worldwide, and only the U.S. had sufficient stocks of agricultural products to prevent hunger and political unrest. New customers for American farm products included the Soviet Union, which concluded large grain purchase agreements with the United States. Corn exports more than doubled from 1970 to 1972, driving the price of corn up from $1.08 per bushel in 1971 to $3.02 in 1974. As these figures show, the explosion of world purchases of American farm products caused farm prices to soar.

These events made farming a profitable business. This new situation caused two developments that continued to affect agriculture throughout the 1980s. First, U.S. farmers and the U.S. government became convinced that the expanding world market would continue to raise the demand for U.S. farm products. President Gerald Ford encouraged farmers to plant "fencerow to fencerow," and American farmers responded by borrowing to buy or rent more land and equipment. Second, the rise in market prices made it easy for the federal government to raise support prices because the high market prices made these moves initially costless.

The 1980s saw American farming expecting a further growth in world demand. This would raise farm prices even more and cause the immense investments in equipment and land made in the 1970s to pay off. Instead of rising farm prices, the 1980s was a period of generally falling farm prices. The decline in farm prices had a number of causes. First, the 1980s saw resumption of the downward course of farm prices. Second, the 1980s saw the rapid growth of agricultural output in other parts of the globe. Soviet grain harvests improved, and countries like India and even Saudi Arabia became relatively self-sufficient in certain agricultural commodities.

As farm prices fell, farm profits fell. Farmers who had borrowed heavily could no longer pay their costs of production and meet their interest and principal payments. Farm loans that had been secured by farm land were no longer covered because of a sharp drop in farm land prices. The net income of farmers fell, and a substantial percentage of American farmers operated at a loss and went out of business.

Major suppliers of agricultural inputs, such as International Harvester, went out of business after sustaining large losses, and a large number of rural banks folded. Price supports were lowered in an effort to reduce the need to purchase surplus agricultural products. Excess supply became so great that in 1983 the government paid farmers for not planting grain and cotton. Despite these efforts, harvests continued to be plentiful, and farm surpluses continued to build up. The cost of farm programs escalated as the federal government attempted to correct the problems in its programs while sustaining the income level of the agricultural sector.

The drought in the summer of 1988 was yet another disaster to befall farmers. It added to the growing number of farm bankruptcies and to the already declining number of farms. The number of farms shrank from almost 4 million in 1960 to 2 million by the end of the 1980s.

SPECULATION AND FUTURES MARKETS

Government farm programs (discussed below) aim to reduce the instability of farm incomes associated with fluctuating farm prices. It should be noted that private market forces also deal with the problem of variability of farm prices. Special private markets in which agricultural products are bought and sold now for delivery at a future date allow farmers to reduce the risks of price fluctuations.

Speculators affect the prices of commodities like wheat, corn, and pork bellies.

> **Speculators** buy and sell for the purpose of profiting from price fluctuations.

The business of speculation in commodities like wheat, corn, and pork bellies is so highly specialized that markets have developed that separate the business of storing commodities from the business of speculation. The grain speculator need not worry about what the purchased grain looks like, where it is stored, and how much to take out of storage.

Speculators can buy and sell commodities in a **futures market**.

> A **futures market** is one where a buyer and seller agree now on the price of a commodity to be delivered at some specified date in the future.

In the type of market most people know best there is an actual outlay of cash (or the arrangement of credit) for the immediate delivery of a good. The market in which a good is purchased today for immediate delivery is called a **spot (cash) market**.

Most of the goods consumers buy and sell are transacted in spot markets. In the grocery store, consumers pay now for goods that are delivered now. Stocks, foreign exchange, gold, and commodities like wheat, pork bellies, lumber, and copper are traded in organized exchanges. The organized markets in which commodities are traded are called *commodities markets*. In commodities markets, contracts can be made now for payment and delivery now.

Futures markets work quite differently from spot markets. *Futures contacts* are bought and sold in futures markets. In a futures contract, the terms (the price and the quantity) of a future transaction are set today. The buyer of a futures contract contracts today to purchase a specified quantity of a good (say, wheat) at a specified price at some specified date in the future. Both delivery and payment are to be made in *in the future*. The seller of a futures contract is obliged to deliver the specified quantity of the good at the specified price at the specified future date. The seller of a futures contract does not even have to own the commodity at the time of the sale.

For example, on January 1, the spot price of wheat is $3 per bushel. This means that buyers can buy wheat for immediate delivery at $3 per bushel. On the same day, the futures price of July wheat is $3.40. This means that buyers and sellers can enter into a contract on January 1 to buy wheat to be delivered in July at $3.40. The fact that wheat to be delivered seven months hence sells for more than wheat now means that speculators believe that wheat prices will rise over the next seven months.

Consider the farmer and the futures market. One substantial risk to the farmer is that prices will fall unexpectedly between the time the farmer plants and the time the farmer markets output. The farmer must decide what crops to plant without knowing what farm prices will be at harvest time. The existence of a futures market reduces uncertainty. If the farmer's crop will be harvested and sold six months hence, the farmer can contract to sell that output for delivery six months hence in the futures market.

Take the example of a farmer who plants a crop in April to be harvested in October. The spot price of the crop is $8 per bushel in April, but the futures price for October delivery is $9. The farmer can sell the crop for October delivery at $9 per bushel. If the spot price in October is $10 per bushel, the farmer has lost because the farmer has already sold at $9 per bushel. If the spot price in October is $7 per bushel, the farmer has gained. In either case, the farmer has been able to reduce the risks of price fluctuations by being able to sell in futures markets. Without futures markets, the farmer would have to bet on getting a favorable spot price at the time of actual delivery.

> In futures markets, prices are set now for products to be delivered in the future. In spot markets, prices are set for goods that are delivered at the time of the transaction.

> Farmers can use futures markets to reduce the risks of price fluctuations.

GOVERNMENT FARM PROGRAMS

Price Supports

Government farm programs use price supports to raise agricultural prices above the prices that would prevail in competitive markets. Exhibit 5 shows how price support programs work. The government sets a *support price* of wheat, for example. The price is called a support price because the government stands ready

EXHIBIT 5   How Government Farm Price Supports Work

The price *P* is the price that would be in effect in the absence of a government price support program. It is the equilibrium price. If, however, the government is willing to purchase any wheat not purchased by private buyers at a support price *P'*, and if this support price is above the equilibrium price, then the government must buy the surplus (the difference between the quantity supplied and the quantity demanded at the support price). By being willing to buy at the support price, the government ensures that the price will not fall below the support price.

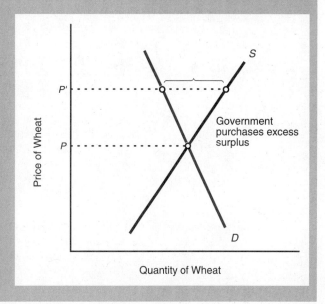

to purchase any wheat that is not purchased by private wheat buyers at this price. If the support price is above the private market price, then the government must buy the *excess supply, or surplus* of wheat. The government can accumulate this wheat to be sold when the support price is below the market price or to give wheat to needy countries through its foreign-aid program.

Who benefits and who loses from price supports? The farmer able to sell at higher prices benefits. The business that sells inputs to farmers also benefits as the demand for their goods and services increases. The consumer of farm products loses because the support program raises farm prices and hence food prices. The loss to consumers is a hidden loss. The consumer is not necessarily aware of what food prices would have been without the support program. Tax-payers pay for the program directly through higher taxes.

Direct Payments to Farmers

An alternative to price supports, incorporated in farm programs in 1973, is direct government payments to farmers. The magnitude of the direct payments, called *deficiency payments*, depends on the difference between the market price and a *target price* established by the government. For example, if the target price is $5 per bushel but the agricultural product is selling for $4 per bushel, the farmer receives $1 per bushel as a direct payment from the government. This is a simplified, but reasonably accurate portrayal of how a deficiency payment works. (See Exhibit 6.)

Direct deficiency payments do not increase the price paid by consumers. It puts the entire burden of the higher price on taxpayers. Some of the benefits are passed through to the suppliers of agricultural inputs, who are able to sell larger quantities of farm machinery, chemical fertilizers, and land to farmers at higher prices.

EXHIBIT 6 Direct Payments to Farmers With Target Prices

The government sets the target price, and farmers supply output *a* on the supply curve. With a supply of *ca* units, private markets will set a price of *cb* to clear the market. Farmers receive a direct payment of *ba* for each unit of output, for a total direct payment equal to *ab* × *Oc*.

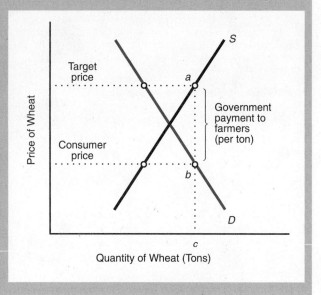

Supply Control Programs

A third approach to raising farm prices is to reduce the supply of agricultural products. Because farmers operate in a competitive industry, it is not possible for them to form cartels to regulate output. If, however, government programs were to cause farmers generally to limit output, then agricultural prices would rise. Remember, with inelastic demand, a reduction in supply pushes up prices considerably.

American farm policy includes programs that provide economic incentives to farmers to restrict their sown acreage. Crop farmers are required to *set aside* a certain portion of land to qualify for the government program. Payments are made to farmers who put part of their land into soil conservation uses rather than planting them in crops.

The number of farms has continued to shrink despite government programs to prop up the American farmer. American farming remains the most productive in the world. (See Example 2.) The major policy issue is whether government intervention should continue or whether farm prices and farm incomes should be set by the marketplace, as are other prices and incomes.

A number of sectors of the economy have experienced declining relative prices, such as personal computers, natural gas, and long-distance telephone service, but they have not been protected from market forces by the government. In fact, most economists would argue that market forces have made them more healthy while making the consumer better off. The most innovative firms survive, and technological advances are passed on to the public in the form of higher quality products and lower prices. American farming, like personal computers and long-distance telephone service, has experienced rapid technological growth. The elimination of government supports would mean that marginal farms would not survive, just as marginal computer manufacturers do not survive when

Is It Up to Government to Solve the Farm Problem?

Although American farming is the most productive in the world, the government has intervened heavily in the business of farming since the 1930s. The perception has been that the government must act decisively to prevent the collapse of the American farm. The decline in the number of farms, the failure of farm prices to keep pace with other prices, and the massive failure of farms in the 1980s are cited to justify government farm programs.

The government has created a complex system of price supports, direct payments, and supply controls to aid the farmer. The goal of these policies has been to keep agricultural prices from falling too much relative to other prices. In this way, it was felt, the family farm would be preserved and American farming would remain healthy.

computer prices drop. The public policy question is whether the loss of marginal farms justifies expensive farm programs that cost both taxpayers and consumers dearly.

Chapter Summary

**The most important point to learn from this chapter is:
Agriculture is a perfectly competitive industry that has inelastic demand curves, unstable supply curves, and low income elasticities. These factors cause agricultural prices to be unstable and to fall relative to other prices over the long run.**

1. Farming is a competitive business dominated by the small firm—the family farm. The farm acts as a price taker in product markets.

2. The farm problem is caused by fluctuations in farm prices as a result of shifting supply and inelastic demand, and by the long-term decline in farm prices relative to other prices. The long-term relative price decline has been caused by rapid technological progress, a price-inelastic demand, and an income-inelastic demand.

3. Futures markets allow farmers to reduce their risks by being able to enter into contracts now for future delivery of crops.

4. The 1970s was a period of rising world demand for American farm products. Farm prices rose, and farming was profitable. Increased world production drove prices down in the 1980s, causing farm profits to fall, and the number of farms to decline.

Policy Focus: **We must decide whether American farming, unlike other branches, requires special protection from market forces.**

Key Terms

speculators (p. 265)
futures markets (p. 265)

spot (cash) market (p. 265)

Questions and Problems

1. The demand curve facing a particular farm is perfectly elastic. This means that that farm can sell all it wants at the market price. Why do not farms supply an infinite amount if they can sell all they want at the prevailing price?

2. The government sets a price support for butter at $1.00 per pound. Explain what will happen to government purchases if the price established without government purchases is $1.00. If it is $1.20?

3. Explain the role of the income elasticity and the price elasticity of demand in accounting for the farm problem.

4. Why do farmers not form their organization of wheat-growing producers to control the amount of wheat produced?

5. Why does the text call price supports a hidden payment to farmers?

6. If productivity is rising rapidly in agriculture, what will be the effect of acreage restrictions? Would acreage restrictions be more likely to raise prices if there were no technological progress?

7. Using supply and demand curves, explain what would happen to wheat prices if Japanese laws protecting Japanese wheat farmers were abolished.

8. The chapter asserts that futures markets help farmers cope with risks. Explain why this is so.

9. Explain who pays for supply control programs, price support programs, and direct payments to farmers.

10. What are the differences between spot and futures markets?

Doing Economics

Most agricultural products have strong seasonal production cycles. For example, look at the monthly data on production and consumption of a major agricultural product such as cotton (listed under Textile Products) or rice (listed under Food and Kindred Products) in the blue-colored pages of a recent issue of the *Survey of Current Business,* a publication of the U.S. Department of Commerce that is available either in the government documents or general periodicals section of most libraries.

What is the seasonal pattern in production? Do you think the demand for these products moves very much over the seasons of the year? What do the data on consumption (or shipments of processed product) and exports say about the seasonal pattern of consumption? What seasonal pattern of price change would you predict? What is the actual seasonal pattern of prices? How do you explain this difference? Does the behavior of "stocks" (inventories) give you a clue?

Factor Markets

P A R T   T H R E E

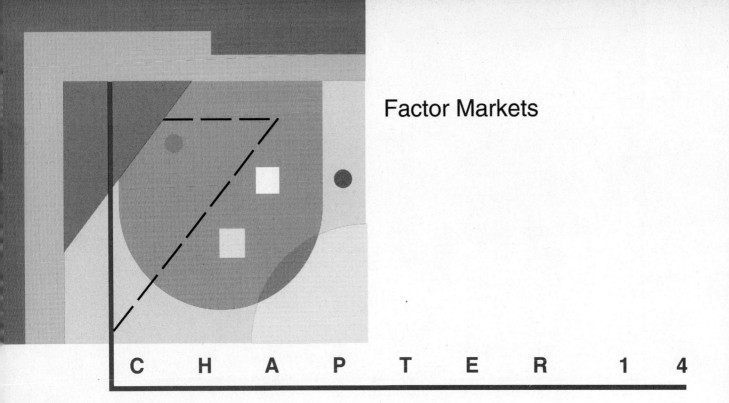

Factor Markets

C H A P T E R 1 4

CHAPTER FOCUS   Although few of us own and operate businesses, most of us supply factors to businesses. If we have a job, we provide our physical and intellectual skills to our employers. If we own stocks, bonds, or certificates of deposits, we provide businesses with capital (credit) that they can use to expand and modernize their businesses. We may even own a tractor, truck, or Roto-Rooter that we lease out directly to businesses to use as capital. If we own farmland that has been leased to a farmer or a corner lot on which a gas station is located, we have supplied the land necessary to operate these businesses.

Almost everyone works at a job at some time in life. We therefore have a lot of practical experience with labor markets. In fact, about 75 percent of all income is earned as labor income. Earnings from capital are less significant, while earnings from the ownership of land are, at an economywide scale, relatively small.

This chapter focuses on factor markets in general. The following chapters will describe specific factor markets such as those for labor, capital, and land.

<table>
<tr><td>**LEARNING OBJECTIVES**</td><td>After studying this chapter, you will be able to:</td></tr>
</table>

- Calculate the marginal contribution of a factor to a firm's revenue.
- See the difference between price makers and price takers in the factor markets.
- Explain the profit-maximizing rule in the factor market.
- Understand the least-cost rule for hiring inputs.
- Describe how the functional distribution of income is determined.

THE CIRCULAR FLOW DIAGRAM

The circular flow diagram introduced in Chapter 2 shows the connecting link between product markets and factor markets. Exhibit 1 shows that firms produce goods and demand factors, but that households demand goods and supply factors. Households and firms meet in two distinct markets: the market for goods and the market for factors.

This is a highly simplified picture. In the real world, firms also demand factors from other firms. The Ford Motor Company buys tires from B. F. Goodrich and computer services from International Business Machines. General Mills buys wheat from farmers or grain elevators. However, the principles that govern the firm's purchases of labor or capital from households are identical to those that determine its purchases of inputs that are produced by other firms.

Firms hire inputs for the same reason they produce outputs: it is profitable. Similarly, households demand the output of firms for the same reason they supply factors: it adds to their utility. The circular flow diagram shows that everything takes place simultaneously.

THE TWO FACES OF THE FIRM

The firm shows two faces to the outside world. One face is that of a *seller of the goods and services it produces* in product markets. As a seller, the firm can be either a price taker or a price maker (as described in an earlier chapter). The other face is that of a *buyer of inputs* in factor markets. A firm can produce no output without factor inputs. In a factor market, the firm can again be either a price taker or a price maker.

Price Making and Price Taking in the Factor Market

The definitions of a **price taker** and **price maker** in factor markets are analogous to the definitions of price takers and price makers in product markets.

> A **price taker** in a factor market is a buyer of an input whose purchases are not large enough to affect the price of the input. The price-taking firm must accept the market price as given.

John Bates Clark (1847–1938)

John Bates Clark was born in Providence, Rhode Island, in 1847. His discovery of the marginal productivity theory of factor payments made him the first world-famous American economist. His book, *The Distribution of Wealth* (1899), argued that each factor of production—land, labor, and capital—is paid the value of its marginal product. Clark argued that unions had no effect on marginal productivity and, therefore, no impact on wages. He believed in compulsory arbitration of labor disputes, and that wages should be set at the level prevailing in comparable employments.

Clark taught at Carleton, Smith, and Amherst colleges and finished his career at Columbia University. His superb command of language once prompted one of his critics to complain that his literary skills gave him an unfair advantage. The American Economics Association honors him every year by bestowing the John Bates Clark medal to the best economist under the age of forty.

EXHIBIT 1   The Circular Flow of Economic Activity

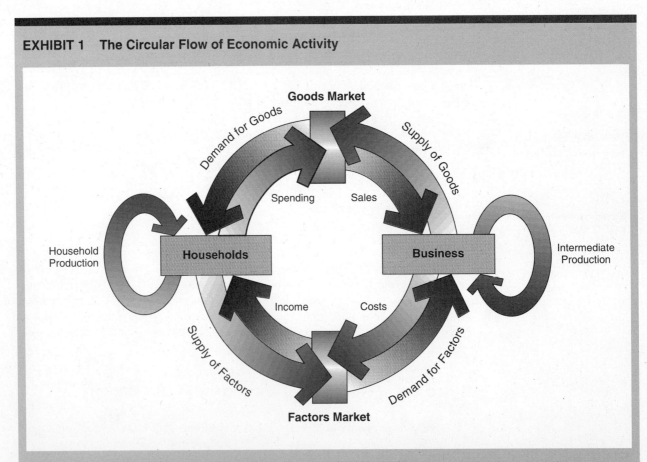

The circular flow diagram shows that firms operate simultaneously in the product market and in the factor market. The upper half of the circular flow shows the flows of products and purchases between the business and household sectors. The bottom half shows the flows of factors from households to business firms and the payment of factor income from business firms to households for the factors of production.

> A **price maker** in a factor market is a buyer of inputs whose purchases are large enough to affect the price of the input.

Exhibit 2 shows the four possible market conditions the firm may face in its role as either a seller of products or a buyer of factor inputs and in its role as either a price taker or a price maker:

1. The firm may be a price taker in both the product and factor markets—panels (a) and (b).
2. The firm may be a price maker in both the product and factor markets—panels (c) and (d).
3. The firm may be a price taker in the product market and a price maker in the factor market—panels (a) and (d).
4. The firm may be a price maker in the product market and a price taker in the factor market—panels (b) and (c).

There is no necessary link between the amount of competition a firm faces on one side of the market and the amount it faces on the other side. A monopolist may purchase its land, labor, and capital inputs as a price taker. A perfectly competitive firm may be a price maker in the factor market. Although there are numerous exceptions, in the most likely scenario the firm will face more competition on the input (factor) side than on the output (product) side. In selling its products, the firm faces competition from other firms that produce either the same product or a product that serves as a substitute for the goods it produces. As demonstrated in previous chapters, such competition may be limited. The picture is different in factor markets. Factors, unless highly specialized, can typically be used by different firms and by different industries. Essentially all firms compete with one another for skilled and unskilled labor; they all compete with one another for capital and for land. The firm, therefore, faces competition for inputs not only from those firms with which it competes in the product market but also from firms in entirely different industries. Oil companies, universities, law offices, and retailers all compete for skilled secretaries. Restaurants, motels, gas stations, retailers, and home builders all compete for land in major cities.

A firm will usually face more competition from other firms when hiring inputs than when selling outputs.

As with most generalizations, there are exceptions to the rule that firms face more competition on the input side than the output side. A textile mill located in a small, isolated town may face little competition from other employers when hiring local labor, while its sales on the output side may be in a perfectly (or near perfectly) competitive product market. Certain skilled people—professional athletes, for example—are so specialized that they are suited for employment in only one industry. The employer is, therefore, likely to be a price maker in this factor market. Certain types of capital—such as oil-drilling rigs—are suited to only one use, unlike trucks, lathes, and computers. Firms purchasing such specialized equipment are more likely to be price makers.

When the firm has the power to influence the price at which it purchases inputs, the firm has **monopsony** power.

> A **monopsony** is a firm that faces an upward-sloping supply curve for one or more factors of production. A *pure monopsony* is a firm that is the only buyer of some input.

Like pure monopoly, pure monopsony is rare. Few firms are the sole buyer of a factor of production. Even if the isolated textile mill—which appears to have a

EXHIBIT 2   The Two Faces of the Firm: Product Market and Factor Market

a. Product Demand—Firm Faces Many Competitors for Output

b. Factor Supply—Firm Faces Many Competitors for Inputs

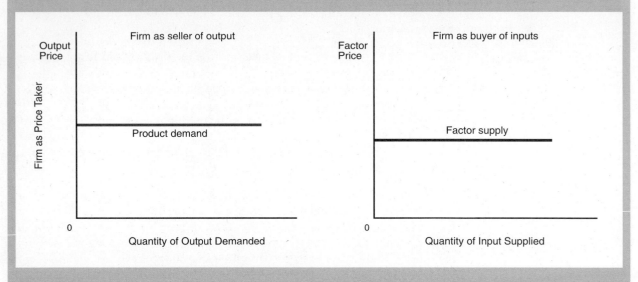

c. Product Demand—Firm Faces Many Competitors for Output

d. Factor Supply—Firm Faces Many Competitors for Inputs

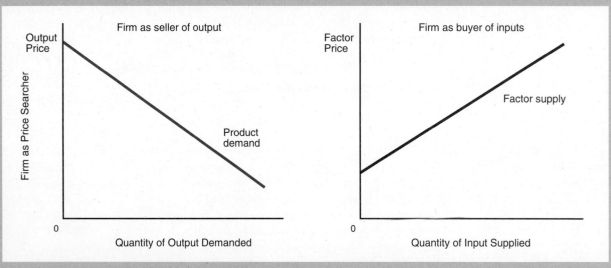

Panels (a) and (b) show a price-taking firm in the product and factor markets, respectively. Price taking on the product side means that the firm can sell all it wants at the existing market price (demand is perfectly elastic). Price taking in the factor market means that the firm can hire all the factors it wants at the prevailing factor price (factor supply is perfectly elastic). Panels (c) and (d) show price making in the product and factor markets, respectively. Price making on the product side means that the firm faces a downward-sloping product demand curve. To sell more, it must lower its price. Price making on the factor side means that the firm faces an upward-sloping factor supply curve. To hire more factor inputs, the firm must pay a higher factor price.

monopsony over the local labor market as the sole major employer in town—offers wages that are too low, people may move to other cities, or outside firms might be attracted into the market by the prospect of cheap labor. This textile mill faces competition from factories located in other cities (in the case where people move) and also from new firms entering the local labor market.

Marginal Factor Cost

The concepts of marginal revenue and marginal cost play a decisive role in the theory of product markets described in the preceding chapters. Profit-maximizing firms produce that level of output at which marginal revenue and marginal costs are equal. If they follow the $MC = MR$ rule, they will maximize profits or minimize losses. In the theory of factor markets, there are concepts analogous to marginal cost and marginal benefit that are applicable to the input side of the firm. Inputs have costs and benefits to the firm, just as production has costs and benefits to the firm. In making its input decisions, the most important cost the firm must consider is the additional cost of hiring one more unit of an input, or **marginal factor cost (MFC)**. As with other marginal measures, it is calculated by dividing the increase in costs by the increase in the amount of the factor in question.

> Marginal factor cost *(MFC)* is the extra cost to the firm per unit increase in the amount of the factor; it is the increase in costs divided by the increase in the amount of the factor.

The price of a factor of production is the wage (in the case of labor) or the rental (in the case of capital or land) that the firm must pay to hire or use the factor. Recall that, in the product market, price exceeds marginal revenue if the firm is a price maker but that price equals marginal revenue when the firm is a price taker. Being a price taker means that the buyer is too small a part of the market to affect the factor's price.

In the factor market, if the firm is a price taker, marginal factor cost is simply the factor's market price. The firm can hire one more unit of the factor (or more than one unit) at the going market price. The firm's actions have no effect on the input's price.

If the firm is a price maker in the factor market, the firm's marginal factor cost will exceed the market price of the factor. As a price maker, the firm is a large enough portion of the particular factor market so that it cannot buy more of the factor without driving up its market price. To use one more unit of the input per period, the firm must pay the same higher price for all units that it would need to pay for the last unit hired. In other words, the extra unit of the factor will cost the firm not only its market price but also the higher price paid on units hired at a cheaper price.

For example, Exhibit 3 shows that because Firm A is a price taker, it can rent as much farmland as it wants at the market price of $500 per acre. It currently rents 100 acres. For this firm, the price of the input and the marginal factor cost are equal. Firm B is a price maker that currently rents 1,000 acres at $500 per acre, but B would have to pay $500.10 to rent 1,001 acres. The marginal factor cost of Firm A is the market price of $500. The marginal factor cost of Firm B is the price of the 1,001st acre ($500.10) plus the $100 extra ($0.10 $\times$ 1,000) it must pay for the original 1,000 acres. Thus, the marginal factor cost of Firm B at an input level of 1,000 acres is $600.10, which is higher than the factor price ($500). Thus, B's MFC curve lies everywhere above the factor's supply curve. Monopsony is important because the additional cost of hiring a factor exceeds its price.

As noted earlier, price taking is more likely in factor markets than is price making (monopsony). The remainder of this chapter will examine the behavior of firms that are price takers in factor markets—firms in which marginal factor cost and factor price are the same. The next chapter will study the role of monopsony in the labor market.

For price makers in factor markets, marginal factor cost is greater than the factor prices; for price takers in factor markets, marginal factor cost equals factor price.

EXHIBIT 3   Competition Versus Monopsony in the Market for Inputs

a. Firm A

b. Firm B

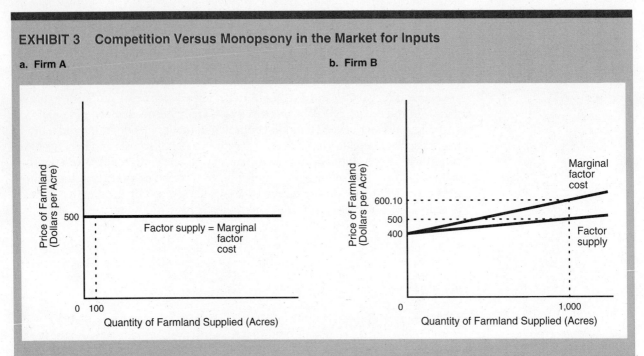

Panel (a) shows a price-taking firm that can hire all the inputs it wants at the going market price. The horizontal supply curve facing the firm is its marginal-factor cost curve. Panel (b) shows a price-making firm on the factor side that must pay higher input prices to get larger quantities of the input. To use more input per period requires a higher price for all quantities of the input; therefore, the extra cost of hiring one more unit of input is the price plus the increase in the cost of using the old input quantity. Thus, the *MFC* curve lies above the factor's supply curve.

THE FIRM'S DEMAND FOR FACTORS OF PRODUCTION

The firm's demand for a factor input depends on the input's physical productivity and on the demand for the good the factor is being used to produce.

The chapter on "Costs and Productivity" defined the production function as showing the relationship between output and inputs. Recall that we define a factor's *marginal physical product (MPP)* as the increase in output divided by the increase in the amount of the factor, holding all other factors constant.

All production functions exhibit the *law of diminishing returns*. As explained earlier, the law states that as ever larger quantities of a variable factor are combined with fixed amounts of the firm's other factors, the marginal physical product of the variable factor will eventually decline.

Derived Demand

Consumers buy products because they yield consumer satisfaction. The firm buys factors of production for a different reason. Inputs are purchased because they produce goods and services that create revenue for the firm. No matter how productive the input is in producing output, that input will not be demanded unless it produces an output that commands a positive price in the marketplace. The garment industry buys sewing machines because they help to produce suits, shirts, and dresses that consumers will buy. Automobile workers are hired because they help produce automobiles that people will buy. Wheat land is rented because it

Derived Demand: Air Travel, and Aircraft Leases

This chapter teaches that the demand for factors of production is a derived demand. The demand for the factor depends on the demand for the product that the factor assists in producing. A clear case in point has been the worldwide slowdown in passenger air travel that characterized the early and mid-1990s. The U.S. recession and its spread to Europe caused a sharp cutback in the volume of air travel and exerted downward pressure on ticket prices.

Air travel is produced by combining labor (pilots, flight attendants, mechanics) and capital (aircraft). If the demand for the product (air travel) falls, there should be a comparable decline in the demand for these two factors of production. Accordingly, the decline in pilot, flight attendant, and mechanics wages and in aircraft prices and lease rates should mirror declines in passenger air travel.

True to form, wages and salaries in commercial aviation have fallen dramatically behind wages in other industries in the early 1990s. Even more hard-hit have been the prices of new and used aircraft. A Boeing 737 that would have leased for $100,000 per month in 1990 leased for $40,000 per month in late 1992.

---

yields wheat that people will consume. If the most productive tailor in the world made only three-armed shirts, the demand for the tailor's services would be zero because the demand for three-armed shirts is zero. The demand for workers, the demand for wheat land, and the demand for tailors are all examples of **derived demand**. (See Example 1.)

> The demand for a factor of production is a **derived demand** because it results (is derived) from the demand for the goods and services the factor of production helps produce.

The principle of derived demand is essential to understanding the workings of factor markets. If consumers reduce their demand for lettuce, the demand for workers employed in lettuce growing, the demand for farmland used for lettuce, and even the demand for water used in farm irrigation would also fall. When demand for automobiles falls, there is unemployment in Detroit. When world demand for Boeing commercial aircraft grows, there is rising employment in Seattle and Wichita (the cities where Boeing is located). In short, the nature of the market for the good itself will be reflected in the derived demand for the factors used to produce it.

Joint Determination of Factor Demand

Another elementary but important fact about the demand for factors of production is that the production of a good generally requires the cooperation of different factors of production. Farm workers can produce no corn without land; corn land without farm labor is useless. Both corn land and farm workers require farm implements (ranging from hand tools to sophisticated farm machinery) to produce corn.

The farm worker's marginal physical product will be less if the cooperating factor is one square yard of farmland rather than one acre. The farm worker's

In general, the marginal physical product of any factor of production depends on the quantity and quality of the cooperating factors of production.

EXHIBIT 4 Marginal Revenue Product

Labor (workers), L (1)	Units of Output, Q (2)	Price P (3)	Total Revenue, TR (4) = (2) × (3)	Marginal Revenue Product, MRP (5) = (6) × (7) = Δ(4) ÷ Δ(1)	Marginal Revenue, MR (6) = Δ(4) ÷ Δ(2)	Units of Marginal Physical Product, MPP (7) = Δ(2)
0	0	$24	$ 0			
				$95	$19	5
1	5	19	95			
				40	10	4
2	9	15	135			
				9	3	3
3	12	12	144			

Columns 1 and 2 give the production function (the amount of output produced by 0, 1, 2, and 3 units of labor input). Columns 2 and 3 give the demand schedule facing the firm. Marginal revenue product *(MRP)* is calculated by taking the increase in total revenue associated with one-unit increases in the labor input. It can also be calculated by multiplying *MR* times *MPP*. Marginal revenue in column 6 is calculated by dividing the increase in revenue in column 5 by the difference between rows in column 2. Marginal physical product in column 7 is the increase in output for every unit increase in the factor, or the difference between rows in column 2.

marginal physical product will be higher on one acre of fertile Iowa land than on one acre of rocky New England land. The marginal physical product of the farm worker will be higher when working with modern heavy farm machinery than with hand implements. The interdependence of the marginal physical products of land, labor, and capital makes the problem of factor pricing in a market setting difficult to analyze.

Marginal Revenue Product

The demand for a factor of production—land, labor, or capital—is a derived demand. The factor is valuable because the firm sells the output on the product market. Thus, the dollar value of an extra worker, an extra unit of land, or an extra machine is that factor's **marginal revenue product *(MRP)***—or the revenue from selling the marginal physical product (*MPP*) that the factor produces.

> The **marginal revenue product** *(MRP)* of any factor of production is the extra revenue generated per unit increase in the amount of the factor.

There are two ways to calculate a factor's marginal revenue product. Both methods yield the same value.

Method 1. Calculate marginal revenue product by simply changing the quantity of the factor and observing the change in revenue. According to this direct method, marginal revenue product is the change in total revenue (*TR*) divided by the change (increase or decrease) in the factor.

$$MRP = \frac{\Delta TR}{\Delta \text{Factor}}$$

Exhibit 4 demonstrates this method. The different quantities of labor the firm employs are given in column 1, and the resulting output is given in column 2.

Columns 1 and 2, therefore, represent the production function. Column 3 shows the market prices that clear the market for the various output levels produced. This firm is a price maker in the product market because the price falls with higher output levels. The firm's total revenue (price times quantity of output) is given in column 4. Because marginal revenue product, in column 5, is the difference between the revenues generated at consecutive levels of labor input, it is recorded between the rows corresponding to the input levels. The revenue generated when one worker is employed is $95; the revenue when two workers are employed is $135. The marginal revenue product is, therefore, $135 – $95 = $40. In other words, the firm's total revenue would increase by $40 if the firm hired a second worker.

Method 2. The marginal physical product (*MPP*) is the increase in output associated with a one-unit increase in the factor but does not indicate the dollar value of this extra output. Marginal revenue (*MR*) indicates the increase in revenue associated with an increase in output of one unit. By multiplying *MR* and *MPP* we indirectly obtain the marginal revenue product. Therefore:

$$MRP = MR \times MPP.$$

The marginal revenue product of a factor can be calculated directly by determining the increase in revenue at different input levels or indirectly by multiplying marginal physical product times marginal revenue.

That this formula works for the price maker is shown in Exhibit 4. Because the firm increases its output from 5 to 9 units as a consequence of adding a second unit of labor, marginal physical product equals 4 units. The 4 extra units of output add $40 to revenue, or $10 per extra unit ($40/4); therefore, the marginal revenue is $10. Using the formula, *MRP* = *MR* × *MPP*, one can calculate that marginal revenue product equals $10 × 4, or $40. Thus, the indirect method of calculating marginal revenue product yields the same answer as the direct method. The marginal revenue product in column 5 is just the product of *MR* in column 6 and *MPP* in column 7.

PROFIT MAXIMIZATION

In the product market, the firm maximizes profit by producing that output at which marginal revenue and marginal cost are equal. The firm also is guided by profit maximization in the factor market. Profit-maximizing decisions in the product market are also profit-maximizing decisions in the factor market because deciding on the quantity of inputs determines the level of output.

The *MRP* = *MFC* Rule

To understand how firms choose the profit-maximizing level of factor inputs, consider the case of a firm deciding how much unskilled labor to hire. *The firm will hire one more unit of unskilled labor if the extra revenue (the extra benefit) the firm derives from the sale of the output produced by the extra unit exceeds the marginal factor cost of the extra unit of unskilled labor.* As long as the extra benefit of a decision is larger than the extra cost, the firm's profits must increase. Recall that if the firm is a price taker, marginal factor cost will be the market wage. As in any other economic activity, a firm will hire inputs to the point where marginal benefits equal marginal costs.

The firm will continue to hire inputs as long as their marginal revenue product (*MRP*) exceeds their marginal factor cost (*MFC*). Since in this chapter we are

EXHIBIT 5   Firm Equilibrium: The Hiring of Factor Inputs

The firm's derived demand for Factor A is the marginal-revenue-product curve. The supply schedule of Factor A as seen by the firm is perfectly horizontal at the market price of $14. Equilibrium (e) will be reached at a price of $14 and a quantity of 110 units of Factor A. At this point, marginal revenue product equals marginal factor costs.

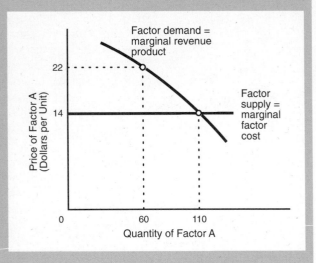

assuming that the firm is a price taker in the factor market, the market prices of the inputs the firm uses (wage rates, rental rates, interest rates) are the marginal factor costs of these inputs. The marginal benefit of an additional unit of factor input is its marginal revenue product. As long as the marginal revenue product exceeds the price of the input, it pays the firm to hire the factor. If the marginal revenue product of Factor A is $40 and its price is $30, it pays the firm to hire the factor. By hiring an additional unit of the factor, the firm increases its profit by $10 (= $MRP - MFC$).

The Demand Curve for a Factor

Exhibit 5 shows the marginal-revenue-product curve of Factor A. The MRP curve is downward sloping because the greater the amount of Factor A used, the lower will be its marginal physical product (because of the law of diminishing returns). Also, if the firm is a price maker in the product market, higher levels of output mcan a lower marginal revenue. Thus, as the quantity of Factor A increases, both marginal physical product and marginal revenue tend to decline, so that MRP (which is $MR \times MPP$) declines. The firm will hire Factor A until its price equals marginal revenue product.

The *MRP* curve is the firm's demand curve for a factor because the firm hires that factor quantity at which the price of the factor equals the marginal revenue product of the factor.

In Exhibit 5, the supply curve of Factor A to the firm is horizontal at the market price of $14. The price-taking firm in the factor market can hire all it wants at $14. If the firm hired only 60 units of Factor A (point *a*), it would not maximize its profit: at 60 units, A's MRP equals $22 and A's MFC equals $14. The firm's incentive to hire additional factors continues as long as MRP exceeds $14. Thus, the firm will continue to hire to the point where MRP and MFC are equal, which occurs at 110 units of Factor A (point *e*). The firm will be in equilibrium (earning a maximum profit or minimizing its losses) when each factor is employed up to the point where marginal factor cost (which equals the price of the factor when the input market is competitive) equals the marginal revenue product of the factor. Since the firm adjusts its factor use to the point where the price of the factor equals the marginal revenue product, the firm's demand curve for a factor is the MRP curve or schedule.

In the product market, the rule of profit maximization is $MC = MR$. In the factor market, the rule becomes $MRP = MFC$ for each factor. These rules are logically the same. They are just different sides of the same coin. If the firm is maximizing profit, then it must be that marginal cost equals marginal revenue and marginal revenue product equals marginal factor cost. The rules are different ways of looking at the same process.

COST MINIMIZATION

The rules of profit maximization explain the behavior of firms in the factor market. These rules predict that firms will employ that level and combination of inputs that maximizes their profit. In the product market, firms produce that level of output (and charge the associated price) that maximizes their profit.

Because profit is revenue minus costs, to maximize profit it is necessary to minimize the cost of producing a given quantity of output. We have explained how a firm selects the optimal level of *one* factor input. But firms produce output with cooperating factors. How will they know when they are combining *all* their inputs in a least-cost fashion?

Most important to the firm is the effectiveness of labor and capital compared to their costs. Assume a worker can pick 20 pounds of pecans per hour. If the worker is paid $4 an hour, this means that each additional dollar spent on labor yields 5 pounds of pecans (= 20/$4). A pecan-picking machine may have an (*MPP*) of 100 pounds of pecans per hour and cost $10 an hour. A dollar spent on the machine yields 10 pounds of pecans (= 100/$10) per dollar. Thus, the machine would be more cost-effective than the worker. The firm could produce pecans more cheaply by substituting pecan-picking machines for workers. To determine the cheapest method to produce pecans, or any good or service, the firm will look at the marginal physical product *per dollar of cost*. The rational firm will minimize costs when the effectiveness of each factor is the same per dollar of cost. As the firm substitutes machines for labor, the law of diminishing returns will lower the *MPP* of machines and raise the *MPP* of workers until, at the margin, the effectiveness per dollar is equalized. (See Example 2.)

The marginal physical product *per dollar* of a factor is its marginal physical product divided by its price. The price-taking firm takes both the wage rate for labor (W) and the rental rate on capital (R) as given. As the above example shows, if the marginal physical product per dollar of labor is smaller than the marginal physical product per dollar of capital, the firm is not combining inputs in a least-cost fashion. It can produce the same output at lower cost by substituting capital for labor until:

According to the least-cost rule, the firm is producing at minimum cost only if the marginal physical products per dollar of the various factors are equal.

$$\frac{MPP_L}{W} = \frac{MPP_K}{R},$$

where MPP_K is the marginal physical product of capital.

THE MARGINAL-PRODUCTIVITY THEORY OF INCOME DISTRIBUTION

Economists distinguish between the **functional distribution of income** and the **personal distribution of income**. Both are determined in the factor markets.

Paying for Merchandise

The sensitivity of factor demand to factor prices is nowhere more evident than in comparisons between countries. Compare a department store in the United States, where clerical wages are $1,000 to $1,500 per month, to one in the Philippines, where clerical wages are $50 per month. In an upscale U.S. department store the clerk that helps you find the merchandise is often the one that takes your money or credit card. An upscale department store in the Phillipines, on the other hand, will have an army of clerks just to check you out. There may be five or six clerks at each of many check-out stands. One clerk will enter your purchase on the cash register, another might verify your credit card, a third will verify the correctness of your bill, and perhaps another will wrap your merchandise!

> The **functional distribution of income** is the distribution of income among the four broad classes of productive factors—land, labor, capital, and entrepreneurship.

> The **personal distribution of income** is the distribution of income among households, or how much income one family earns from the factors of production it owns relative to other families.

The profit-maximizing and least-cost rules resolve the *how* problem in economics. They show how firms go about combining inputs to produce output. These same rules also resolve the *for whom* problem.

Factors of production, unless they are highly specialized (such as 7-foot-tall basketball players), are demanded by many firms and by many industries. For example, the market demand for truck drivers will come from a wide cross section of American industry: the steel industry, retailers, the moving industry, and the local florist will all have a derived demand for truck drivers. The demand for urban land will also come from a broad cross section of American industry: heavy industry requires land for plant sites; motel chains require land for motels; home builders require land for subdivisions. Similarly, the demand for capital goods will come from a cross section of American industry.

How the price (wage) of truck drivers is determined is shown in Exhibit 6. The truck drivers' wage rate reflects two forces: the derived demand for truck drivers as represented by their marginal revenue product and the supply of truck drivers. At equilibrium, the market wage will equate quantity supplied and quantity demanded, and the wage will equal the marginal revenue product. In other words, truck drivers will be paid their marginal revenue product. The same is true of the other factors of production. According to the **marginal-productivity theory of income distribution**, skilled labor and unskilled labor will each be paid its marginal revenue product. Capital will be paid its marginal revenue product. Land will be paid its marginal revenue product.

> According to the **marginal-productivity theory of income distribution**, the functional distribution of income between land, labor, and capital is determined by the relative marginal revenue products of the different factors of production. The price of each factor will equal the marginal revenue product of that factor.

The market supply curve of truck drivers is upward-sloping, which indicates that individuals are prepared to work more hours as truck drivers at high wages than at low wages. The market demand curve is derived from the marginal-revenue-product curve of truck drivers across several industries. Equilibrium is achieved at point e, where the quantity supplied of truck drivers equals the quantity demanded. At the equilibrium wage of $15, there are 10,000 labor hours used in the various industries using truck drivers.

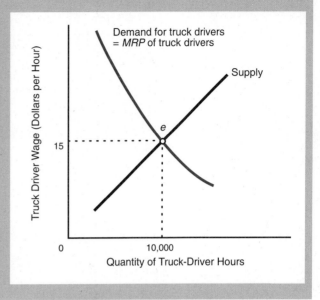

Marginal Productivity and Factor Incomes

The marginal-productivity theory of income distribution suggests that a productive factor is usually paid its marginal revenue product. The marginal revenue product of one factor depends on the quantity and quality of cooperating factors. Two textile workers, one in the United States and the other in India, may be equally skilled and diligent, but one works with a $50 sewing machine while the other works with a $100,000 advanced knitting machine. The New England farmer may be just as skilled as the Kansas farmer but may have a low *MRP* because of the low quality of the land. Marginal revenue product also depends on the supplies of factors. The supply of residential land is limited in Hawaii but abundant in Iowa. The equilibrium *MRP* of land is, therefore, higher in Hawaii. If women are limited to employment in only a few professions, they will *overcrowd* these professions and drive down the *MRP* and, thus, wages. Finally, marginal revenue product, as stated earlier, depends on the demand for the product being produced. If product demand falls, so will the factor's *MRP*.

> The marginal-productivity theory of income distribution states that a competitively determined factor price reflects the factor's marginal revenue product. Marginal revenue product is the result of (1) the relative supplies of the different factors, (2) the quantity and quality of cooperating factors, and (3) the market demands for the goods the factors produce.

The marginal-productivity theory states that each factor of production will be paid its marginal revenue product. If the world is sufficiently competitive, the theory suggests that each factor of production will be paid its marginal physical product in value terms. When the firm is a price taker in the product market, $MR = P$ and, therefore, $MRP = P \times MPP$. Thus, for example, the wage rate $W = P \times MPP$. Each factor is then paid the dollar equivalent of its marginal physical product.

This chapter discussed how factor markets work, but each factor market—the labor market, the capital market, and the market for land—has its unique features. In the labor market, the supply of labor is determined by how individuals choose among market work, work in the home, and leisure. These are choices not faced by the owners of capital and land. Moreover, the labor market is affected by the organization of workers into unions and by the effect of education and training on labor's marginal physical product. In the capital market, intertemporal choices are

Should Factors Be Paid Their Market Value or Their "Comparable Worth?"

This chapter explains the general principles of price determination in factor markets. The following three chapters look at price determination in labor, land, and capital markets. Over time, social critics have argued that prices determined in factor markets can be "unfair" or that they may not reflect the "true value" of the factor. Why should professional baseball players earn more than college professors or even the president of the United States? Why should credit-card companies receive 18 percent interest from credit-card holders? Why should high-fashion models, who are fortunate to have perfect complexions and figures, earn $5,000 per hour, while a hard-working office manager earns $10 per hour?

In most cases, the market determines the price paid the factor of production, be it judged as reflecting the true worth of the factor or not. Public policy has correctly been wary about interfering in the market process and dictating a different price.

Public policy has played a role in making sure that employees have a right to "equal pay for equal work." This principle has been applied to cases in which women earn less than men even though they perform exactly the same work as men. The principle of equal pay for equal work is well established in law and in practice.

A more difficult policy issue is whether people should be guaranteed equal pay for "comparable" work. Compare the pay of female guards in women's prisons with that of male guards in men's prisons. Typically, male guards have received more than female guards, yet the work is "comparable." Should some government agency step in and dictate that male and female guards earn the same pay?

Courts in Oregon and Washington have dictated that employers must pay workers with comparable jobs the same pay. In Washington, a committee assigns points to each job on the basis of knowledge and skills, mental demands, accountability, and working conditions. The committee awarded nurses the highest evaluation, well above computer systems analysts. Clerical supervisors were rated above chemists, and electricians were rated below beginning secretarial workers. In all of the above cases, the labor market had assigned different relative wages than the comparable worth commission.

Which verdict should be followed—the verdict of the market or that of a comparable-worth rating commission? We would argue that the market is a more reliable guide. First, there is doubt that experts will be able to find and agree on rational formulas for determining comparable worth. Second, if people are paid the "comparable worth wage," surpluses will develop in professions that have been assigned comparable worths above the market wage. Too many people will wish to work in secretarial positions and too few as electricians. Third, if wages are based on comparable worth rather than on market conditions, the "law of unintended" consequences will cause some employers to replace women with men in occupations such as coaching.

We would argue that the costs of using a comparable wage system outweigh its benefits.

---

involved: buyers of capital can receive the benefits of capital over a long period of time; suppliers of capital must choose between consumption today and more consumption tomorrow. The market for land is characterized by the relative fixity of the supply of land.

The next three chapters will examine each factor market in detail, but these discussions will build upon the general theoretical framework established in this chapter.

Chapter Summary

**The most important point to learn from this chapter is:
In a market economy the problem of distributing the national output among cooperating factors is solved by profit-maximizing firms paying each factor its marginal revenue product.**

1. Firms operate in two markets: the product (output) market and the factor (input) market. Firms sell their output in the product market, and they buy inputs to produce output in the factor market. The *what* problem is solved in the product market. The *how* and *for whom* problems are solved in the factor market. Marginal factor cost (*MFC*) is the extra cost of hiring one more unit of the factor of production. A price-making firm in the factor market will have a marginal factor cost that is greater than price. A price taker in the input market will have a marginal factor cost equal to the price of the input.

2. The firm's demand for a factor of production will depend upon the demand for the product being produced and upon the factor's productivity. The marginal physical product (*MPP*) of a factor of production is the increase in output that results from increasing the factor by one unit, other things equal. The demand for a factor of production is a derived demand because it depends on the demand for the goods and services the factor helps produce. Production requires the cooperation of the factors of production. The marginal physical product of one factor will depend on the quantity and quality of cooperating factors. Marginal revenue product (*MRP*) is the increase in revenue brought about by hiring one more unit of the factor of production.

3. Profit-maximizing firms will observe the following rule in factor markets: factors of production will be hired to the point where *MFC* = *MRP*. The *MFC* = *MRP* rule in the factor market is equivalent to the *MR* = *MC* rule in the product market. If firms are perfectly competitive in the factor market, they will hire the various factors of production to the point where the *MRP* of each factor equals its price.

4. The least-cost rule for firms is to hire factors of production so that *MPP* per dollar of one factor equals the *MPP* per dollar of any other factor.

5. The marginal-productivity theory of income distribution explains the functional distribution of income (among the four classes of production factors) and the personal distribution of income (among households).

Policy Focus: **The costs of replacing market wages by comparable worth formulas exceed the benefits.**

Key Terms

price taker (p. 273)
price maker (p. 273)
monopsony (p. 275)
marginal factor cost (*MFC*) (p. 277)
derived demand (p. 279)

marginal revenue product (*MRP*) (p. 280)
functional distribution of income (p. 283)
personal distribution of income (p. 283)
marginal-productivity theory of income distribution (p. 284)

Questions and Problems

1. The *MPP* of a 100th worker is 33 units of output. The marginal revenue of the firm for the corresponding level of output is $2, the price of the product is $3, and the wage rate is $99.

287

a. Is the firm maximizing its profit?

b. What would the wage rate have to be for 100 workers to maximize profit?

2. Explain how workers in Country X could earn $10 per hour while workers in the same industry in Country Y earn only $0.50 per hour. Do the higher wages in Country X mean that workers in this country work harder than those in Country Y?

3. The last unit of land rented by a farmer costs $100 and increases output by 1,000 bushels. The last unit of capital costs $1,000 to rent and increases output by 20,000 bushels. Is this farmer minimizing costs? If not, what should he or she do?

4. In Soviet industry, capital grew about 10 times as fast as labor. What would you expect to happen to the marginal physical product of capital?

5. Workers are paid $20 per hour; the price of the output is $2. What is the best estimate of the marginal physical product of labor? (Hint: use the profit-maximizing rule.)

6. A manufacturing plant in a small town accounts for 85 percent of employment in the town. The plant receives a large contract and decides to expand its work force by 40 percent. What will be the relationship between marginal factor cost and the wage rate in this case? Construct a graph to illustrate your answer.

7. One type of equipment—such as specialized oil-drilling equipment—can be used only in one particular industry. Another type—such as general-purpose lathes—can be used in a wide variety of industries. How would the

amount of competition differ for these two types of equipment?

8. Complete Table A by filling in columns 4 and 5.
a. Is the firm maker or a price taker in the product market?
b. If the wage rate is $55, how many units of labor should the firm hire?

TABLE A

Labor (number of workers, L (1)	Units of Output, Q (2)	Price, P (3)	Units of Marginal Physical Product, MPP (4)	Marginal Revenue Product, MRP (5)
0	0	$8		
1	10	8		
2	17	8		
3	23	8		
4	28	8		

9. Assume that the marginal physical product (MPP) of a first worker is 20 units of output, that the MPP of a second worker is 30 units, that the MPP of a third worker is 20 units, and that the MPP of a fourth worker is 15 units. If four workers are hired, how many units of output are produced?

10. An additional engineer costs a firm $50,000 per year; an additional lathe operator costs $20,000 per year. Do you have enough information to determine which worker the firm should hire? If not, what information do you need?

Doing Economics

On most campuses, student labor is used for many tasks, from filing in offices to food-service assistance to helping in academic laboratories. Much of this labor is provided under federal work-study programs as part of students' financial-aid package. Under the work-study program, educational institutions pay only a small part (currently 20 percent) of the cost of student employees, with federal funds making up the rest. How would this affect the demand by campus employers for work-study vs. regular student employees? What sort of equilibrium do you predict if students eligible for work-study are as productive

as those who are not? (Remember that the college's hourly cost of work-study labor is below the minimum wage.) How are the results different if work-study students on average have lower productivity than other students? Now try to find out from your college's administration or from a personal survey of campus workers what fraction of student workers are supported on work-study and what kinds of jobs are typically staffed with work-study students and what jobs are performed by other student employees. Do your results accord with your predictions?

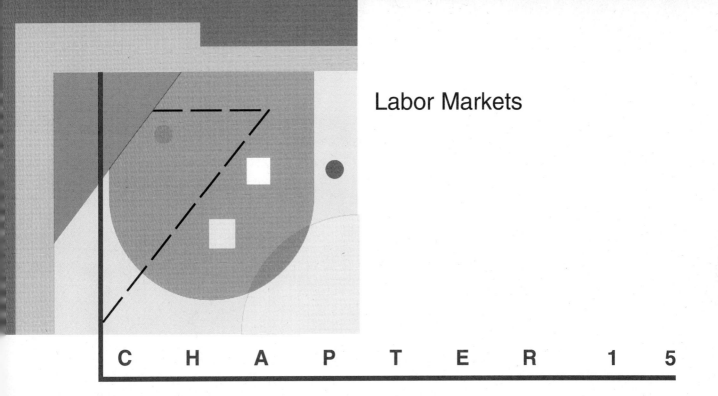

Labor Markets

C H A P T E R   1 5

CHAPTER FOCUS   Some 75 cents out of each dollar is earned as wages and salaries. The remaining 25 cents is for dividends, profits, rents, etc. Except for the relatively few who live on dividends, profits, and rents, our economic livelihoods depend on what we earn in the labor market. Individuals who work hard at high-paying jobs do well, in contrast to those who lack marketable skills and who must work at minimum wages.

More than 110 million people work in the American labor force. They earn an average hourly wage of over $10. A skilled surgeon earns $5,000 per hour, a corporate lawyer earns $200, a management consultant $125, an automotive worker $25, and a fast-food employee $4.25. Why do some people command high wages while others command low wages? What determines the overall level of wages in the economy?

- Understand how labor differs from other factors of production.
- Explain why wages would differ even if people were all identical.
- Explain why wages would differ even if all jobs were the same.
- Describe the principal/agent problem and how it fosters incentive payments.
- Use the backward-bending supply curve to explain why the average workweek is shorter.
- Understand why more women have entered the work force.

HOW LABOR DIFFERS FROM OTHER FACTORS

The preceding chapter explained how factor markets work and gave general rules that apply to land, labor, and capital inputs. The labor market differs from other factor markets because of the human element. Four features of labor make it different from the other factors of production:

1. A person cannot be bought like an acre of land or a piece of equipment; slavery is against the law. Land and capital assets can be bought and sold. Employers cannot "buy" labor. Employers and workers enter into contracts that specify the time period of employment and the conditions of employment.
2. If land and machines are not put to productive use, they stand idle, and the owners do not normally benefit. When people do not work in the labor market, they can spend time in work in the home or in leisure.
3. Unlike land and capital, people have preferences regarding the type of work and the location of the work. A drilling rig doesn't care whether it is placed in permafrost or in a tropical climate. Farm land does not care whether it is planted in wheat or cotton. People do care where they work and under what conditions they work.
4. People live in families in which there is often specialization. One family member may have a strong attachment to the labor market (as the major breadwinner), another may specialize in work in the home. Some family members may cross over regularly between work in the home and work in the labor force.

WAGES AND INCENTIVE PAYMENTS

Wages are the payments people receive for working. Wages may be paid on an hourly, daily, or monthly basis. Payment on a monthly basis of a specified amount (that does not vary with the number of hours worked) is typically called a salary. Some wages are based on how many units of output are produced per unit of time (hour, month, year)—called piece rates. In addition to their wages and salaries, workers can also receive incentive payments in the form of bonuses and premiums.

Nominal wages differ from *real* wages. The dollar wages received by workers

Gary Becker (1930–   )

Economists have been accused of being imperialists because they apply economics to other disciplines, like education, sociology, law, home economics, and demography. The most prominent "economic imperialist" is Gary Becker, professor of economics at the University of Chicago.

Becker made his mark by applying the cost/benefit logic of economics to education, discrimination, social behavior, fertility, and marriage. In his doctoral dissertation, Becker wrote that pay differentials between white and black workers could be explained by a taste for discrimination by both employers and employees. Becker's demonstration that people invest in education just as businesses invest in capital served as a starting point for the field of human capital in economics. Becker suggested in an article published in 1968 that crime can be analyzed just like other occupations, and that people become criminals depending upon the expected benefits of crime and its costs in terms of the likelihood of arrest and punishment. Becker's writings demonstrate that people respond to price effects and income effects in their social interactions as well as in their economic interactions. Economic considerations enter into the selection of marital partners, the decision on how many children to have, and even into questions of religion and suicide. By applying economic logic to family decision making, Becker has been able to provide clearer explanations for the increase in the percentage of working women and for declining fertility. Becker's writings have been controversial among economists and other social scientists because they have expanded economics into new areas that had previously been regarded as outside the realm of economics. Becker's work was honored with the 1992 Nobel prize in economics.

are their nominal wages. However, the purchasing power of dollar wages differs from region to region, and it changes as the general price level changes. Real wages are nominal wages adjusted for differences in the prices of the things people buy. For example, in 1969, the average manufacturing worker's nominal wage was $3.19 an hour. In 1992, the average manufacturing worker's nominal wage was almost four times higher at about $12 per hour. But over the same period, consumer prices also increased by nearly three times. Real wages scarcely changed over this period, although nominal wages rose by a factor of almost four. To understand trends in real wages it is also important to include fringe benefits, such as pensions and medical insurance. From 1973 to 1992 real manufacturing wages appeared to fall. But when fringe benefits are included, total real wages paid in manufacturing actually rose.

Workers normally base their labor force decisions on real wages, not on nominal wages. What counts is what the nominal wage will buy. If nominal wages are two times higher in Alaska but prices are three times higher, people would not move to Alaska for the higher nominal wages. If prices and nominal wages change at the same rate, there has been no change in real wages, and we would expect no changes in the number of hours people wish to work.

Why are some workers paid incentive wages in the form of bonuses, prizes, and premiums? Employees often have personal objectives that are different from the firm's objectives. One employee's objective may be to maximize the amount of income earned on a particular job. Another employee may wish to minimize job stress and exertion without being fired. As long as the employer and employee have different objectives, a **principal/agent problem** exists.

People base their labor force decisions on real wages.

EXAMPLE 1

First-Class Fares for Coach: The Principal/Agent Problem

Business travel costs corporations billions of dollars per year, and it is in the company's interest to hold down travel expenditures. If corporation employees shared this goal, they would seek out the most economical airline tickets on their own, and the corporation need not worry. The airlines, however, realize that a principal/agent problem exists with regard to airline travel. They therefore offer first-class seats to business travelers who purchase full-fare coach tickets (often at twice the expense of economy tickets). They offer free travel to business travelers who accumulate miles on that airline's frequent-flier program. Employees book more expensive flights just to take advantage of the frequent-flier program.

The travel departments of major corporations claim that this principal/agent problem costs corporations millions of dollars per year. Corporations, however, are not in a position to eliminate these abuses because it costs too much to monitor employee travel.

> A **principal/agent problem** exists between the firm and any of its employees when the firm (as the principal) and the employee (as the agent) have different goals and objectives for the employee's behavior.

Incentive pay systems seek to deal with principal/agent problems between employee and employer.

The employer cannot constantly monitor each employee's performance under normal conditions. Employers must motivate workers to act spontaneously in the firm's interests. To prevent assembly-line workers from shirking responsibility, the firm may pay them bonuses for exceeding production norms or goals. Professional athletes may receive performance-based incentive contracts. A baseball player may receive a bonus for every extra-base hit over 50 in a season. A company may give its employees an annual bonus if the company exceeds a profit goal it set for itself. All these bonus and incentive schemes are designed to improve the work performance of the agent (the worker) without raising the monitoring costs of the principal (the employer).

It is not easy to design incentive-pay systems that eliminate the principal/agent problem entirely. Assembly-line workers may achieve their bonuses by increasing the quantity of output while reducing the quality of their work. Professional baseball players may lose games by attempting to get extra-base hits when a sacrifice fly is required. The more specific is the incentive target, the more likely the employee is to achieve the target by sacrificing some other worthwhile outcome (such as sacrificing quality for quantity). The more general the incentive target— such as a bonus based on company profits—the less likely the employee is to believe that his or her actions affect the outcome. (See Example 1.)

THE DEMAND FOR LABOR

Wage rates are determined in labor markets by supply and demand. Labor exists in all sorts and sizes. People are different. They have different skills, training, and temperaments. Jobs are different. To learn about product prices, we must begin by studying a single product, such as oranges. The same is true of wages. We must begin by studying the wage determination of a specific type of worker. In the next sections, we look at how computer programmer wage rates are determined by the forces of supply and demand.

The Firm's Demand for Labor

How does a firm decide how much labor of a single type to hire at different wage rates? According to the preceding chapter, profit-maximizing firms hire factors up to the point where the marginal factor cost (MFC) equals its marginal revenue product (MRP).

Exhibit 1 applies the rule to the labor market for computer programmers. Together, the graph and data show a firm that is perfectly competitive in the computer-programmer market (it must take the market wage rate as given), and therefore its marginal factor cost is equal to the market wage rate. This firm can hire all the labor it wants at the prevailing market wage rate. Its labor-supply schedule is a horizontal line (perfectly elastic) at the market wage.

The firm shown in Exhibit 1 happens to be a price taker in the product market as well as in the factor market. Its marginal revenue product equals its product price, P, times labor's marginal physical product (MPP). The profit-maximizing firm will demand the quantity of labor at which $W = MRP$. The MRP of the

---

EXHIBIT 1   The Firm's Demand for Computer Programmers

a. Graph of Demand for Computer Programmers

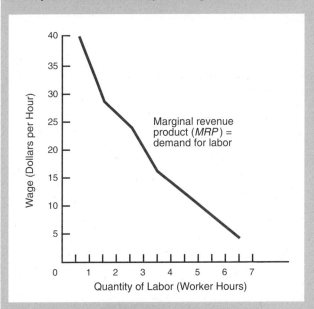

b. Table of Demand for Computer Programmers

Labor Input (hours) (1)	Quantity of Output (lines programmed) (2)	Marginal Physical Product (lines), MPP (3)	Marginal Revenue Product, MRP = P × MPP (4)
0	0		
		20	$40
1	20		
		14	28
2	34		
		12	24
3	46		
		8	16
4	54		
		6	12
5	60		
		4	8
6	64		
		2	4
7	65		

The graph uses the data in panel (b). The labor demand curve shows the marginal revenue product of different quantities of labor hours. This firm is competitive in both the labor market and the product market. The price of the output is $2 per unit. The firm uses 4 programmer hours when the wage rate is $16 per hour (where the marginal revenue product is equal to the market wage). If the market wage rate rises to $28 per hour, the firm would employ only 2 programmer hours because the marginal revenue product of the second hour equals $28. Columns 1 and 2 of panel (b) show the amounts of output that are associated with various amounts of labor input for this firm. Columns 3 and 4 give the marginal physical product and marginal revenue product for each level of input. Since the price of the output is $2 per program line, MRP = $2 × MRP. Both columns 2 and 3 show that under these circumstances, the law of diminishing returns applies to the labor input. Panel (a) graphs the data from columns 1 and 4.

second programmer hour is $28; therefore, the firm will demand 2 programmer hours. If the market wage falls to $16 per hour, the firm would react by hiring more programmer hours. As the firm increases employment, *MRP* will fall because of the law of diminishing returns. The firm will continue to increase labor until the last hour's *MRP* just equals the market wage of $16. At a $16 wage, the firm would use 4 programmer hours because the *MRP* of the fourth hour is $16.

The individual firm's demand curve for labor is its marginal-revenue-product curve. Because the marginal-revenue-product curve is negatively sloped, the firm demands more labor at a low wage rate.

The quantity of labor demanded varies inversely with the wage rate, which can be seen by comparing columns 1 and 4 in Exhibit 1b or by observing the downward-sloping shape of the demand curve. The demand curve is nothing more than the marginal-revenue-product curve. At each wage, that quantity of labor is demanded at which $W = MRP$. More labor will be hired at lower wages than at higher wages, *ceteris paribus*.

The Market Demand for Labor

Earlier chapters explained that the market demand curve is constructed from individual demand curves. Exhibit 1 showed the demand curve for computer programmers of a single firm. The market demand curve for computer programmers is the summation of all the demand curves of firms that hire computer programmers. If there are 400 firms demanding computer programmers, the market demand for computer programmers is the summation of the demands of all 400 firms that purchase labor of that type. The market demand curve shows how the total quantity of labor demanded varies as the wage changes.

The market demand curve for labor of a particular type—computer programmers—is given in Exhibit 2. This market demand curve shows the quantities of computer programmer hours that are demanded by all 400 employers of that type of labor at different wage rates. Because the labor-demand curves of individual firms are negatively sloped, the market demand curve will be negatively sloped as well.

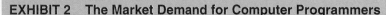

EXHIBIT 2 The Market Demand for Computer Programmers

The market labor demand curve for programmers shows the number of programmer hours that would be demanded by all firms that hire programmers at different wage rates. Because the demand curves of each firm are negatively sloped, the market labor demand curve is also negatively sloped.

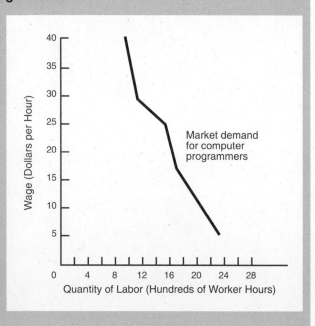

THE LABOR SUPPLY CURVE

Employers must pay workers a wage that is at least equal to the opportunity cost of the next best alternative that the worker sacrifices in accepting that employment.

The market demand curve for labor of a single type explains only one side of the labor market. The market labor supply curve explains the other side of the market. The wage rate for labor of that type is determined by both supply and demand.

The amount of labor supplied depends on the wage rate, *ceteris paribus*. Workers, in choosing where to work, compare the wage they can earn in one occupation with their opportunity cost (the wage they could receive from employment in the next best occupation). The higher is the wage offered for labor of that type, the greater will be the number of workers who offer their services.

The employer who fails to pay workers their opportunity costs will have no workers because they would all take the next best alternative, which then becomes their best alternative.

Exhibit 3 is a market supply curve that shows the number of hours computer programmers are willing to work at different wage rates. The supply curve is positively sloped because at higher wages, computer-programming employment becomes more attractive relative to employment in other occupations. Computer programmers will, therefore, shift hours from other occupations for which they are qualified (engineering, accounting, math) into programming work. The market labor-supply curve is the summation of the individual labor-supply curves of computer programmers.

LABOR-MARKET EQUILIBRIUM

Wage rates are determined in labor markets by the interaction of supply and demand. The market demand curve for labor of a single type is negatively sloped;

EXHIBIT 3   The Market Supply of Computer Programmers

This market labor supply curve shows the number of hours programmers are willing to work at different wage rates, all other things remaining the same. The labor supply curve is positively sloped because at higher wages, programmer employment is more attractive relative to other types of employment.

EXHIBIT 4   Equilibrium in the Market for Computer Programmers

The market supply of programmers (from Exhibit 3) and the market demand for programmers (from Exhibit 2) are brought together in this figure. The equilibrium wage rate is $16 per hour. At the $16 wage, the quantity demanded (1,600 hours) equals the quantity supplied. At wage rates above $16, there is a surplus (quantity supplied exceeds quantity demanded); at wage rates below $16, there is a shortage of labor (quantity demanded exceeds quantity supplied)

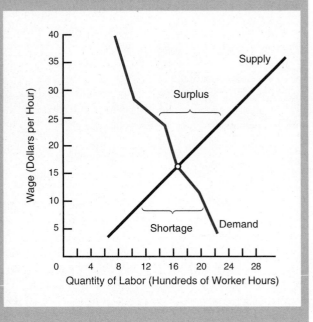

the market supply curve of labor of a single type is positively sloped. The labor market coordinates the activities of firms and workers by setting an equilibrium wage rate.

The market supply and demand curves for computer programmers given in Exhibits 2 and 3 are brought together in Exhibit 4. The wage rate of $16 equates the quantity of programmer hours supplied with the quantity of programmer hours demanded, or 1,600 hours. At any other wage, the quantity demanded will not equal the quantity supplied.

In a competitive labor market, wage rates adjust until they equal the equilibrium wage rate. If there is a **labor surplus**, some workers willing to work at the prevailing wage will be without jobs. At the wage rate of $25 there are more workers willing to work than the quantity demanded by firms, and the market wage would fall. If there is a **labor shortage**, some firms wishing to hire workers at the prevailing wage rate will go away empty-handed. In Exhibit 4, at the wage rate of $10 the quantity of labor demanded exceeds the quantity of labor supplied, and the wage rate would rise.

> A **labor surplus** occurs when the number of workers willing to work at the prevailing wage rate exceeds the number firms wish to employ at that wage rate.

> A **labor shortage** occurs when the number of workers firms wish to hire at the prevailing wage rate exceeds the number willing to work at that wage rate.

Not all wages are permitted to adjust to surpluses or shortages due to regulations, trade groups, and certification. In Exhibit 4, if a law were passed making it illegal for the employers of computer programmers to pay less than $25 per hour, there would be a surplus of computer programmers. A number of

At any wage other than the equilibrium wage, there will be a labor surplus or shortage.

computer programmers, who are prepared to work at $25 per hour, would be without work. A number of states and the federal government have minimum-wage laws that require that qualifying employees not be paid less than a specified minimum wage.

Shifts in Labor Supply and Demand

Unless something happens to prevent it, the market wage is that wage which equates the quantity of labor demanded with the quantity of labor supplied. In this regard, labor markets are just like product markets. The price of labor will settle at that wage that equates quantity demanded with quantity supplied. The price of labor—the wage—will remain fixed at this rate until the labor demand curve shifts or the labor supply curve shifts. Changes in labor supply and demand change wage rates. If any of the factors capable of shifting a demand or supply curve were to change, the equilibrium would be disrupted and a new wage rate would be established. The factors that cause labor demand and supply curves to shift are discussed below, along with their effects on the wage rate.

Factors Causing Shifts in Labor Demand and Supply Curves

Shifts in the Demand. Factors other than wages affect the demand for a particular type of labor. If one of these factors changes, the demand curve for labor will shift. The demand for labor of a particular type increases (the demand curve shifts to the right), *ceteris paribus*, when:

1. the demand for the final product produced using that type of labor increases. If the demand for the final product increases, there will be an increase in that product's price. This price increase will raise the marginal revenue product of labor, shifting the demand curve to the right.
2. the price of a substitute factor of production increases. Substitute factors are those that can be substituted for the type of labor in question in the process of production. Automated equipment may be substituted for bank tellers; sophisticated word-processing equipment may be substituted for secretaries; skilled labor may be substituted for unskilled labor. If the prices of substitute factors increase, firms will increase their demand for labor of that type.
3. the price of a complementary factor of production decreases. Complementary factors are those that are used in combination with the factor in question. Materials, such as steel, aluminum, and plastics, are used in combination with labor to make automobiles, for example. If the prices of these materials fall the demand for labor will rise.
4. the productivity (marginal physical product) of labor increases. When the marginal physical product of labor rises (when labor productivity increases), the marginal revenue product of (and, therefore, the demand for) labor rises.

The demand for labor changes when the prices of substitute or complementary factors change, when product prices change, and when labor productivity changes.

Exhibit 5, panels (a) and (b), shows the effects of increases and decreases in the demand for labor. If demand increases, *ceteris paribus*, the wage rate rises. If demand falls *ceteris paribus*, the wage rate falls.

Shifts in Supply. The supply of labor to a particular occupation increases when:

1. the wages that can be earned in related occupations fall. The wages paid in other occupations affect the supply of labor to a particular occupation. If

EXHIBIT 5   Effects of Changes in Labor Supply and Demand on Wages

a. Effects of Changes in Labor Demand

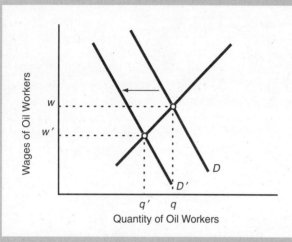

b. Effect of Changes in Labor Productivity

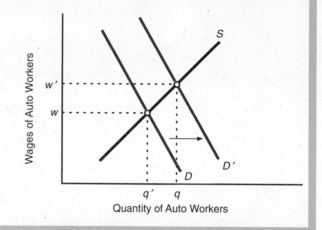

c. Effect of Change in Price of Substitute Factor

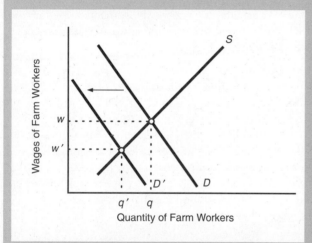

Panel (a) shows that a fall in the price of oil reduces the demand for oil workers—their wages drop. Panel (b) shows that an increase in the labor productivity of auto workers raises the demand for automobile workers—their wages rise. Panel (c) shows that a fall in the price of farm machinery reduces the demand for farm workers—their wages fall. Panel (d) shows that the wage rate of truck drivers falls from S to S' as wages of taxi drivers increase. Panel (e) shows that new bullet-proof vests and headgear make police work less dangerous, increasing the supply of police officers—the wage rates of police officers fall.

d. Effects of Changes in Labor Supply

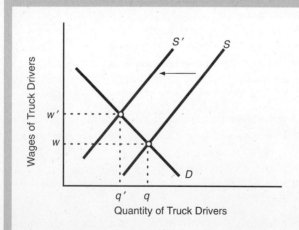

e. Effect of Change in Job Conditions

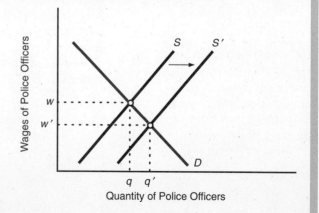

the wages of mathematicians fall, the supply curve of computer programmers should shift to the right. More people will find computer programming as the occupation that pays them their opportunity cost.

2. the conditions of work in that occupation improve. Other things remaining the same, people prefer to avoid heavy, unpleasant, or dangerous work in harsh climates. A decrease in the unpleasantness or danger associated with a particular job will increase the supply of labor to that industry. If, for example, new filters are discovered that make working in an asbestos plant perfectly safe, the supply of labor to the asbestos industry would increase.

The supply of labor to a particular occupation is affected by wages in other occupations and by the conditions of work in that occupation.

Exhibit 5, panels (c) and (d), gives examples of shifts in the labor supply curve and the resulting impact on wages. Increases in labor supply reduce the wage rate, and decreases in supply raise the wage rate.

WAGE STRUCTURE

The preceding explanation of wage rates for labor of a specific type did not explain why some people earn more than others or why some occupations command a higher wage than others. These wage differences occur, very simply, because *people are different* and because *jobs are different*. If all people were the same and if all jobs were the same, then everyone would earn the same wage in competitive labor markets. People don't earn the same wage. Some earn $2 million per year; others earn $5 per hour. The following discussion explains the structure of wages.

Compensating Wage Differentials

Underground coal miners are paid more than workers in manufacturing industries. For example, in the United States underground coal miners are paid more than 50 percent more than the average wage in nonagricultural industries.

Why are coal miners paid more than most other production workers? Coal mining does not require highly specialized skills or training; the skills that most manufacturing workers possess could readily be used in underground coal mining. The reason for the wage difference is the difference in the nature of the job.

The general desirability of a job can shift the labor supply curve. People prefer to avoid dirty, monotonous, and dangerous jobs, other things equal. Coal mining is a dangerous profession with a high fatality and disability rate.

Exhibit 6 shows the effect of differences in the danger of the occupation on relative wages. For simplicity, the demand curve for coal miners is assumed to be identical to the demand curve for textile workers. The labor supply curves are quite different. The position of the coal miners' supply curve (higher than the textile workers' supply curve) reflects the fact that workers prefer, *ceteris paribus*, less dangerous employment. To get an equivalent supply of coal miners, coal-mine employers must offer higher wages than textile employers. The higher wages paid to attract workers to dangerous and unpleasant occupations are called **compensating wage differentials**.

> **Compensating wage differentials** are the higher rewards that are required to induce people to enter occupations that have undesirable job characteristics.

Compensating wage differentials explain why welders on the Alaskan pipeline have to be paid so much (to compensate for the harsh climate and higher living

EXHIBIT 6   Wages in Coal Mining and Textiles

The demand curve for coal miners is drawn to be identical to the demand curve for textile workers. Wages are higher for coal miners because the quantity supplied of coal miners is less than the quantity supplied of textile workers.

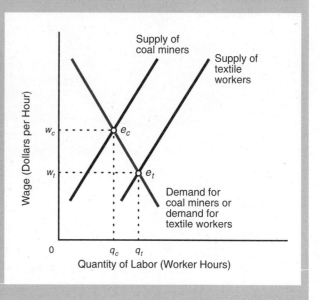

Compensating wage differentials are needed to induce people to enter unpleasant or dangerous occupations.

costs) or why sanitation workers are usually better paid than clerical workers (to compensate for the unpleasantness and social stigma). They also explain, in part, the decline in U.S. real wages since 1973. When fringe benefits are counted, total real wages have increased.

Numerous studies confirm that compensating wage differentials are indeed paid to offset undesirable job characteristics. Although individuals do differ a great deal (some enjoy heavy outdoor work and would detest office work; others enjoy work in the office but hate being outdoors), almost everyone wishes to avoid injury and disease. Wages are positively associated with the risk of being killed or seriously injured on the job. (See Example 2.)

Noncompeting Groups

Differences among people are a second source of differences in wages. Both jobs *and* people are different. Some individuals are qualified by mental and physical skills and training for a wide variety of occupations. Others are qualified for only a few occupations. Only a limited number of people have the peculiar abilities to become brain surgeons, trial lawyers, or theoretical physicists. Surgeons must have extremely sensitive and sure hands; trial lawyers must be articulate and be able to think quickly; theoretical physicists must have an enormous analytical aptitude. The number of individuals qualified to be professional athletes is limited to those possessing the necessary physical attributes. On the other hand, the number of individuals who are qualified to be stock clerks, management trainees, factory workers, and so on is much greater.

People are different for two basic reasons: first, people are born with different mental and physical abilities; second, people acquire different skills and talents through experience and training. Because of these differences, only certain groups of people qualify to fill certain jobs. Only women with slim figures and perfect complexions can become high-fashion models. Only people with good analytical

EXAMPLE 2

Compensating Wage Differentials: Land Mine Disposal in Kuwait

After the end of the Gulf War, a costly cleanup campaign was begun in Kuwait. Literally hundreds of thousands of land mines had been laid by the Iraqi forces to slow the advance of the Allied forces. These land mines had to be cleared.

The Kuwaiti government awarded contracts to American, British, and French firms to bring in specialists to remove the land mines. These firms had to pay technicians $80,000 to $100,000 per year, tax free, and all transportation and living expenses, to work at mine removal. Supervisors were paid even more. Mine disposal requires little advanced training for the technicians, who would have earned only a small fraction of this pay if they had worked in their next best alternative. The extra pay was a compensating wage differential paid to compensate workers for the danger of the job. In the course of the mine disposal work, more than a dozen technicians were killed.

skills can become mathematicians and physicists. Only individuals with superior athletic ability can become professional athletes. Because of these differences, people divide into **noncompeting groups** in the labor market.

> **Noncompeting groups** are groups of people who are differentiated by natural ability and abilities acquired through education, training, and experience to the extent that one group does not compete with another for jobs.

Because people are different, the labor force is divided into noncompeting groups.

Differences among people restrict movement among occupations. If the earnings of professional athletes or physicians were to double overnight, people lacking the necessary physical attributes and training would not be able to enter these two professions to compete for jobs.

LEISURE AND HOUSEHOLD PRODUCTION

Individuals do have options other than work in the labor force. These other options affect the total supply of labor to the economy. Individuals must choose among work in the labor force, **household production**, and **leisure**.

> **Household production** is work in the home and includes child care, meal preparation, and cleaning.

> **Leisure** is time spent in any activity other than work in the labor force or work in the home.

What determines how an individual allocates his or her time among these three activities? Opportunity costs explain how individuals decide how much time to devote to labor-force work, to leisure, and to work in the household.

Backward-Bending Labor Supply

The opportunity cost of leisure is the income (or household production) that must be given up to enjoy leisure. The opportunity cost of leisure, therefore, rises when the price of market work rises. As real wages rise over time, we would expect the quantity of market work that each person performs to increase. This has not happened. Real wages at the end of the 1980s were five times real wages 75 years earlier, but average hours worked have fallen. Why have people responded to rising real wages by working fewer hours? The backward-bending labor supply curve explains this phenomenon.

Exhibit 7 shows a labor supply curve relating wages and hours worked per person. It is drawn to be *backward-bending*—it has a section with a negative slope. The chapter on "Demand and Utility" identified two effects of a price change on the consumption of goods: the *income effect* (the impact of the change in real income that results from a price change) and the *substitution effect* (the substitution of cheaper goods for more expensive goods that results from a price change).

The increase in wages also results in income and substitution effects. In effect, the wage is the "price" of leisure. The increase in wages raises the relative price of leisure and motivates individuals to substitute other things—in this case, market work—for leisure, thereby discouraging leisure. Also, the increase in wages increases income (an income effect), making more income available to purchase leisure. Typically, as income rises, more consumption of a good occurs—if the good is a *normal good* (a good the demand for which increases as income rises). If the substitution effect of a wage increase discourages leisure, and the income effect of a wage increase encourages leisure, what then will be the overall effect on leisure of the wage increase? The overall effect depends on which effect is stronger, the substitution effect or the income effect.

In Exhibit 7, the labor supply curve is upward-sloping until a wage of $10 per

If the income effect of higher wages dominates the substitution effect, the labor supply curve will be backward bending.

EXHIBIT 7   The Backward-Bending Labor-Supply Curve

When the wage is only $2 per hour and hours worked are only 15 hours per week, a dollar increase in wages adds up to only an additional $15 per week; the income effect is weak. When wages are $4 per hour and hours worked are 25 per week, a dollar increase in wages is like an extra $25 per week; the income effect is stronger. When wages are $10 per hour and 45 hours are worked per week, the income effect is even stronger. The income effect begins to dominate the substitution effect after wages reach $10 per hour. Further increases in wages cause hours worked per person to actually decline, as shown by the backward-bending section of the labor supply curve.

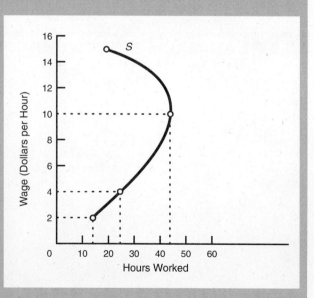

Technology, Employment, and Wages

Workers have an ambivalent attitude toward technology. They fear that advances in technology will deprive them of their jobs and livelihoods. The Communist philosopher Karl Marx warned that new technologies would displace workers by machines, creating a vast army of unemployed workers. A famous English movie of the 1950s showed English textile workers trying to foil the introduction of a more durable synthetic textile. Does new technology cost jobs? Is it a mistake for governments to promote research and development?

Public policy in the United States has been geared toward the production and creation of new technology. Government agricultural research has helped make American farming the most productive in the world. The National Science Foundation and other government agencies use government funds to promote new technologies, such as the supercomputer and supercollider. The private sector spends even more on research and development. Do these public and private investments in technology mean fewer jobs and lower wages?

This chapter teaches that the demand for labor depends on its productivity. If a new technology in computer technology makes the computer assembler twice as productive as before, the demand for computer assemblers will increase. Labor-saving techniques raise labor productivity; employers are now prepared to hire more workers at the same wage as before. As the demand for computer assemblers increases, more will be hired at a higher equilibrium wage.

If technology advances drive down wages, we would see a negative relationship between labor productivity and real wages. The accompanying table shows a clear positive relationship between labor productivity and real hourly wages. During periods of rapid advances in labor productivity, real wages also rise rapidly. During periods of slow labor productivity growth, wage growth is also slow.

What is the net outcome of higher technology? Real wages are higher; the national income of the country is higher. What about employment? High technology does not create unemployment, but it does have a side effect on employment. As real wages rise, people choose to take more of their time in leisure. The average workweek falls with rising affluence. This is the backward-bending labor supply curve discussed in this chapter.

	Average Annual Growth Rates Output per hour	Real Wages per hour
1960–69	2.7	2.7
1970–79	1.3	1.1
1980–86	1.3	.7
1987–90	0	−.3

Source: *Economic Report of the President.*

hour is reached. Below $10 the substitution effect of higher wages dominates the income effect of higher wages. At wage rates above $10, the quantity of labor supplied falls as the wage rate increases because the income effect dominates the substitution effect. Above $10, the labor supply curve bends backward.

Over the long run, mechanization has raised labor productivity, which translates into higher real wages. Higher real earnings enable people to opt for more leisure and fewer hours worked. Mechanization has enabled people to have more leisure while still earning high incomes.

Opportunity Costs and Household Production

One of the most striking changes in the U. S. labor force has been the substantial increase in the number of women working in it. At the turn of the century, only one in five women worked in the labor force. By the early 1990s, more than 50 percent of women worked in the labor force. A number of reasons account for the dramatic rise in women's numbers in the labor force: changing social roles, high divorce rates and one-parent families, more part-time jobs, and antidiscrimination legislation.

Opportunity costs provide another plausible explanation. Whether people work in the labor force or in household production depends in part on the value of their household production relative to the wage they could earn in market employment. If work in the home (child care, cleaning, food preparation) is worth, say, $10 per hour, and the market wage a woman could earn in the labor market is $8 per hour, she would not enter the labor force. The opportunity cost of labor-force work—household production—exceeds the market wage. If, however, the market wages of women rise more rapidly than the value of household production, then one would expect women to enter the labor force. For more women, market wages exceed the value of home production.

The real wages of women have risen substantially since the 1940s. With rising real wages, more and more women have found that market work yields returns greater than the value of home production, and they have entered the labor force.

This chapter examined how labor markets work. The next chapter will look at the effect of labor unions on the labor market.

Chapter Summary

The most important point to learn from this chapter is:
Wage rates are determined by supply and demand like any other price. People earn different wages because jobs are different and people are different.

1. Labor markets operate like other factor markets, but labor is different because workers desire leisure and because workers have preferences concerning different jobs. Labor cannot be bought and sold like the other factors of production. A labor market brings buyers and sellers of labor services together. Employers use incentive-pay schemes to deal with the principal/agent problem.

2. If firms are price takers, they hire labor to the point where $W = MRP$. The firm's MRP schedule is its labor demand schedule. The labor demand curve will be negatively sloped both for firms and for the market. The labor demand curve will shift if the demand for the firm's final product changes, if the price of either substitute factors or complementary factors changes, or if the productivity of labor changes.

3. The labor supply curve for a particular occupation will be positively sloped because workers must be paid their opportunity costs. The labor supply curve will shift if job conditions or wages in other industries change.

4. The equilibrium wage rate is that wage at which the quantity demanded of labor of a single type equals the quantity supplied. A shortage exists when the quantity demanded exceeds the quantity supplied at that wage. A surplus exists when the quantity supplied exceeds the quantity demanded at that wage. A new equilibrium wage/quantity combination will result when either the market supply or market demand curve shifts.

5. People are paid more who work in jobs that have undesirable characteristics. Noncompeting groups are workers with different abilities who do not compete for the same jobs. Wage differences are explained by job differences and differences among people.

6. When wage rates in general rise, the opportunity cost of leisure increases, as does income. Whether or not the aggregate labor supply curve will be backward-bending depends on the relative strengths of the income and substitution effects. Whether people work in household production or in the market labor force depends on the value of time in the home compared to the market wage.

Policy Focus: **Improvements in technology raise labor productivity, increase the demand for labor, and raise wages.**

Key Terms

principal/agent problem (p. 291)
labor surplus (p. 296)
labor shortage (p. 296)
compensating wage differentials (p. 299)

noncompeting groups (p. 301)
household production (p. 301)
leisure (p. 301)

Questions and Problems

1. Suppose between 1990 and the year 2000 wages increase from $10 an hour to $20 an hour. If the prices of the goods workers buy more than double, what would happen to real wages?

2. Explain why labor's special features cause the labor market to work differently from the other factor markets.

3. A price-taking firm in both its product and factor markets is currently employing 25 workers. The 25th worker's marginal revenue product is $300 per week, and the worker's wage is $200 per week. Is this firm maximizing its profits? If not, what would you advise the company to do?

4. There is a close positive association between labor productivity and wages. Using the theory presented in this chapter, explain this relationship.

5. State law in New Jersey requires that employees in licensed gambling casinos be residents of New Jersey for a specified period of time. What effect does this legislation have on the demand for casino employees in New Jersey?

6. During recessions and periods of falling wages, the number of volunteers for the all-volunteer army rises. Explain why this supply of labor rises.

7. Explain why a worker in India earns much less than a worker in West Germany.

8. "If all jobs were the same, everyone would earn the same wage." Evaluate this statement.

9. "If all people were the same, everyone would earn the same wage." Evaluate this statement.

10. You are a surgeon earning $200,000 per year. When the demand for your services increases, the charge for each operation increases by 25 percent. What effect will this increase have on the number of operations you perform?

11. Rank each of the following jobs according to the difficulty of devising an incentive-pay system that is compatible with the firm's overall objectives. Explain your ranking.
   a. Janitorial work performed at night in an office building.
   b. Assembly-line work in a washing-machine factory.
   c. Traveling sales work.
   d. The creation of hand-carved figures for a crafts company.
   e. Professional basketball playing.

12. Referring to Exhibit 1b, explain what would happen to the wage of computer programmers if the number of program lines produced per hour were to double for each level of labor input. Explain what would happen if the price of the product fell to $1.

13. Draw hypothetical labor supply and labor demand curves for truck drivers. Shift the curves to show what happens when:
   a. truck driving becomes more safe.
   b. truck drivers become more efficient.
   c. truck drivers must be licensed by a state agency.
   d. the earnings of surgeons increase.
   e. the earnings of moving-equipment operators fall.

14. What is a simple economic explanation for the shorter average U.S. workweek?

Doing Economics

This project explores wage differentials among student employees on your campus. Take a survey of student employees. Find students who work for at least ten different campus employers and ask them about their wage, how long they have worked at that job, what kind of work they do, the conditions in which they work, and the training or educational background required for the job. Can you explain the wage differentials you observe based on the factors discussed in this chapter? How important do specific skills or training seem to be? How important is experience? Are working conditions important at all?

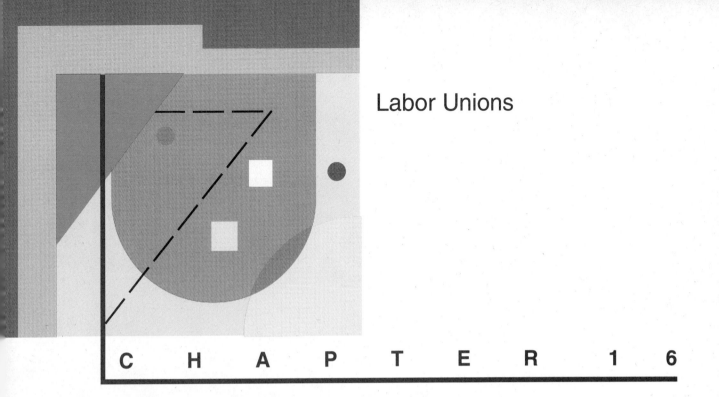

Labor Unions

C H A P T E R   1 6

CHAPTER FOCUS   People have strong views about unions. To some, unions protect helpless workers from cruel employers. Without union protection, workers would be forced to work for low wages under miserable working conditions. Without collective action, workers stand little chance against well-organized and powerful employers. To others, unions are symbols of corruption and inefficiency. Union leaders are associated with organized crime and with under-the-table contributions to shady political figures. Unions require that employers follow work rules, called featherbedding, that raise costs and reduce competitiveness. Unions can call strikes that disrupt the national economy, such as strikes of transportation workers or of sanitation workers.

    This chapter examines the role of the union in the economy. Is the union a positive force, as some believe, or a negative force?

After studying this chapter, you will be able to:

- Understand why the union's share of the labor force has been declining.
- See how unions deal with the trade-off between higher wages and lower employment.
- Explain how collective bargaining with the threat of strike raises union wages.
- Discuss why it is clear that unions raise wages in unionized industries but not clear whether they raise or lower wages in nonunionized industries.
- Describe the two views of efficiency and labor unions.

WHAT IS A UNION?

People join together in clubs, political parties, and other groups for gain and pleasure. As workers, they join together in **labor unions**.

> A **labor union** is a collective organization of workers whose objective is to improve conditions of pay and work.

The labor union's primary objective is to improve employment conditions for its members. These improvements concern higher pay, greater job security, or safer working conditions.

Labor unions fall into three categories that depend on the type of work and industry and on skill requirements. The three types of unions are **craft unions**, **industrial unions**, and **employee associations**.

> A **craft union** is a collective organization that represents workers of a single occupation.

> An **industrial union** is a union that represents employees of an industry or a firm, regardless of their specific occupation.

> An **employee association** is an organization that represents professional employees within a particular profession for the purpose of maintaining professional standards and affecting conditions of work and pay.

Examples of craft unions are barbers unions, plumbers unions, and electricians unions. Examples of industrial unions are the United Automobile Workers (a union representing automobile workers of all types) and the United Mine Workers (a union representing all types of workers engaged in mining). Examples of employee associations are the National Education Association, the American Association of University Professors, the American Bar Association, the American Medical Association, and state employee associations. The employee associations were founded to maintain professional standards, but in recent years they have become increasingly involved in the primary union function to improve employment conditions for their members.

The three types of unions are craft unions, industrial unions, and employee associations.

Unions perform a variety of functions. Their most visible function is to engage in *collective bargaining* with the employers of their members. Instead of each

H. Gregg Lewis (1914–1992)

Economists have been interested in unions since they became a part of the industrial scene centuries ago. It was widely suspected that unions affected wages and productivity, but no one knew by how much. H. Gregg Lewis did the pioneering empirical work on the effect of unions on the economy. Invited to comment on a paper on labor unions in the 1950s, Lewis noticed that virtually everyone had an opinion on the effects of unions on wages, although no one had analyzed the necessary data. Returning to the University of Chicago, where he taught labor economics, Lewis and his graduate students began collecting and analyzing data on union and nonunion wages. The result of this research was Lewis' *Unionism and Relative Wages in the United States*, published in 1963. In this pioneering work, Lewis estimated the extent to which unions raised wages in different industries, and his estimates have served as the foundation for subsequent studies on the effects of unions on wages. Lewis' neighbor in Chicago was the president of the meat packers' union, with whom Lewis had an amiable difference of opinion concerning the effects of unions on wages and employment.

Lewis received his Ph.D. in economics from the University of Chicago, where he taught from 1939 to 1975. Lewis taught at Duke University from 1975 to his retirement in 1985. He served as vice president of the American Economic Association and was named a distinguished fellow of the association. Lewis began his academic studies as an engineer, and his interest in mechanical drawing generated an interest in modern design. As an amateur artist, Lewis exhibited contemporary art mobiles. Were it not for the Great Depression, Lewis declared, he might have ended up as a furniture designer and not as a pioneering researcher in labor economics.

employee negotiating individually with the employer concerning wages, fringe benefits, and work conditions, the union represents all members in negotiations or discussions with employers. Unions may bargain collectively about a number of issues, ranging from wage rates, vacation pay, and group health insurance to job-security provisions, lay-off rules, and safety conditions.

DECLINE OF UNIONISM

In the United States, there are fewer than 18 million union members; fewer than one in five people in the labor force belong to unions (see Exhibit 1). In the 1930s, union members accounted for between 6 and 7 percent of the labor force. This percentage rose in the late 1930s and 1940s and peaked at 25 percent in the mid-1950s. Since then, the share of union members has fallen steadily to under 17 percent in 1992.

Union membership as a percentage of employment has declined in recent years, for several reasons. In 1990, 22 percent of male workers and 15 percent of female workers belonged to unions. The percentage of women in the labor force has been rapidly increasing, and women have tended historically not to join unions. The share of white-collar workers in total employment has been rising as well; white-collar employees also tend not to join unions. Exhibit 2 shows that higher percentages of blue-collar workers than white-collar workers belong to unions. The shift in employment to services (which is only 7 percent unionized) has also reduced unionization. Moreover, there has been a well-publicized shift in popula-

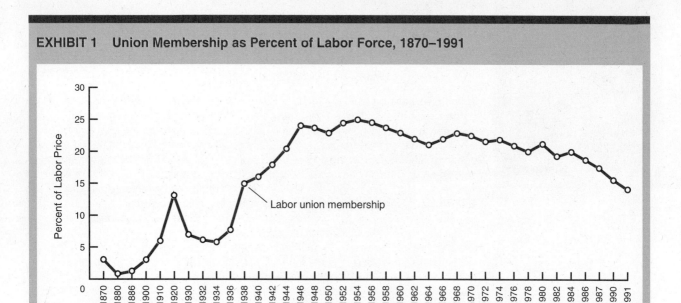

EXHIBIT 1   Union Membership as Percent of Labor Force, 1870–1991

Labor union membership

Fewer than one in five people in the labor force in the United States belong to a union. Union membership rose from 6.7 percent in the 1930s to a peak of 25 percent in the 1950s before declining to recent levels.

SOURCES: *Statistical Abstract of the United States; Handbook of Labor Statistics; Historical Statistics of the United States, Colonial Times to 1970,* 1976, part I

The share of union members of the labor force has been falling because of the rising labor force shares of women and of white-collar employment.

tion from the northeastern and midwestern states to the southern and southwestern states, which are the states where union membership has been weakest.

The rapid unionization of public employees after 1964 has kept the percentage of union members from falling even more. In 1964, only 8 percent of state- and local-government employees belonged to unions. By 1992, the proportion had risen to 43 percent. The rise in public-sector unionism, while significant, has not been sufficient to stem the fall in the share of union members in total employment. Unionism in the United States is less well developed than in other industrialized economies. (See Example 1.)

HISTORY OF UNIONISM

Unions were not a powerful force in American life until the late 1930s, although the first national conventions of labor unions met as early as 1869 to lobby for restrictions on Chinese immigration. Union membership expanded rapidly after 1886 when the traditional craft unions banded together in the American Federation of Labor (AFL) under the leadership of Samuel Gompers, the "father of the American labor movement." Gompers made a lasting imprint on the American labor-union movement through his espousal of a nonpolitical, nonsocialist approach to unionism. Gompers believed that unions should be organized by craft and should not include unskilled workers.

Unskilled and semiskilled workers joined the Knights of Labor (organized in 1869), which experienced phenomenal growth in the early 1880s. Unlike the AFL, the Knights of Labor was committed as much or more to political goals as to wage increases. When violence in Chicago's Haymarket Square in May of 1886

EXHIBIT 2   Characteristics of Union Members: U.S. Labor Force

Category	Percent in Union	Median Weekly Earnings	
		Union Workers (dollars)	Nonunion Workers (dollars)
Total Work Force	18.6	494	372
16–24 years	7.4	335	252
25–34 years	16.5	473	378
35–44 years	23.6	518	438
45–54 years	25.5	523	431
55–64 years	24.4	504	401
65 years and over	10.7	470	306
Men	21.8	524	430
Women	14.9	416	312
White	17.7	503	384
Men	21.2	537	452
Women	13.7	423	317
Black	25.4	423	290
Men	28.0	470	305
Women	22.9	390	276
Hispanic	16.8	417	276
Men	18.5	451	291
Women	14.5	368	255
Full-time workers	20.9	494	372
Managerial and professional specialty	15.2	581	584
Technical, sales, and administrative support	12.1	431	346
Service occupations	15.1	406	226
Precision production, craft, and repair	28.2	568	405
Operators, fabricators, and laborers	29.0	448	287
Farming, forestry, and fishing	4.6	379	239
Private nonagricultural wage and salary workers	13.7	485	368
Mining	19.7	572	561
Construction	22.6	634	393
Manufacturing	23.1	458	400
Transportation and public utilities	34.1	561	458
Wholesale and retail trade, total	7.0	402	298
Finance, insurance, and real estate	3.1	399	407
Services	7.0	402	352
Government	43.6	506	419

Source: U.S. Bureau of Labor Statistics, *Employment and Earnings,* annual. The above data are for 1990.

stiffened employer resistance to the Knights of Labor and turned public opinion against organized labor, the Knights of Labor suffered a fatal collapse.

One reason for the difficulty in organizing the American labor force into unions is the unfavorable political climate that prevailed until the 1930s. Antitrust laws (the Sherman Antitrust Act of 1890) were applied against "monopolistic" labor unions; companies used private police forces, threats, and intimidation to prevent labor unions from forming. It was not until 1932 that the government adopted a conscious policy favoring the free organization of unions. Prior to 1932, management was often able to obtain court orders that prohibited union activity, and employers were allowed to require new employees to sign "yellow dog" contracts, in which the employee had to agree not to join a union as a condition of employment.

Industrial unionism (which suffered a severe setback with the collapse of the Knights of Labor) made a comeback in the 1930s under the leadership of John L. Lewis. The failure of the AFL to organize unskilled and semiskilled workers in

EXAMPLE 1

Labor Unions in International Perspective

There are significant differences between the labor union movements in the United States and in Europe. Although associations of journeymen existed in the form of medieval guilds, labor unions were not organized in Europe until the nineteenth century. The United Kingdom reversed earlier antiunion acts when it passed the Trade Union Act of 1871, which guaranteed legal recognition for labor unions. On the Continent, unions were organized on industrial rather than craft lines, and they engaged in more partisan political activity. In Germany, for example, unions were responsible for much social legislation prior to World War I.

In Europe today, labor organizations tend to be either constituted as or affiliated with political parties, usually from the left wing. In England, the labor unions joined forces with the socialists to form the Labour Party in 1893. In Sweden, there is a close alliance between the two major labor unions and the Social Democratic Party. In Italy, Belgium, and the Netherlands, rival Christian and socialist trade union movements are present. Unlike its European counterparts, the American labor movement has avoided forming a political party, remaining instead within the framework of the two-party system.

The United States is one of the least unionized industrial economies. Between 65 percent and 90 percent of workers in Scandinavian countries are unionized. The proportions for Germany, Japan, and the United Kingdom hover around one-third. The United States resembles France, Switzerland, Hong Kong, and Taiwan, where unionization rates are 20 percent or less.

The industrialized countries have developed many types of labor unions. In Germany, unions are organized on an industry basis and are grouped into federations. Collective bargaining usually takes place at industrywide levels, and compulsory arbitration is often used to settle disputes. German enterprise laws require that union representatives sit on management boards in large companies. The German labor movement plays a prominent role in the German Social Democratic Party.

Sweden is dominated by a highly disciplined and comprehensive labor movement. Virtually all blue-collar workers belong to the Confederation of Trade Unions, and white-collar workers belong to one of two other unions. As close allies of the Social Democratic Party, Swedish unions have developed profit-sharing plans and have pushed for social welfare policies to equalize the distribution of income.

The Japanese economy is characterized by company unionism. Each company has its own union that cuts across all craft and class boundaries. Japanese union presidents are key workers who are often promoted to the ranks of management. Japanese unions typically foster cooperation between management and workers and commonly adopt a management perspective. The founding slogan of the Nissan Company labor union is "Those who truly love their union, love their company."

UNION MEMBERS AS A PERCENTAGE OF THE LABOR FORCE

Country	Percentage	Country	Percentage
Israel	90%	Canada	31%
Sweden	90	Netherlands	29
Finland	80	Japan	29
Belgium	70	France	20
Norway	66	Switzerland	20
Denmark	65	Taiwan	18
Austria	62	Singapore	17
Italy	42	Hong Kong	15
United Kingdom	37	United States	14
Ireland	36	South Korea	10
Germany	34		

Source: *The World Factbook 1990.*

assembly-line production caused conflicts within the AFL organization. As a consequence, the Congress of Industrial Organizations (CIO) was formed in 1936 to organize workers on an industrial rather than a craft basis.

In 1955, the AFL and CIO merged to form the combined AFL–CIO. The AFL–CIO continues to try to bring major non-AFL–CIO unions back into the AFL–CIO. In 1985, the United Automobile Workers rejoined the AFL–CIO. In late 1987, the AFL–CIO scored a major victory when the nation's largest independent union—the Teamsters—joined the AFL–CIO.

UNION LEGISLATION

Until the passage of federal legislation in the 1930s, the courts ruled on union activities using common-law principles. Common law, however, presented the courts with difficult choices. On the one hand, it is a common-law principle that intentional harm to private property is illegal. Yet strikes, picketing, and boycotts are designed to place economic hardship on the private property of employers. On the other hand, the right of people to combine for mutual assistance was also accepted by common law. In the early nineteenth century, the courts typically held that union efforts to raise wages through strikes, picketing, and boycotts constituted criminal conspiracies. Under such rulings, union leaders were criminally prosecuted and sued for damages. The basic legality of trade unionism was not settled until 1842 when the Supreme Court of Massachusetts ruled that union legality depended on union objectives. Unions in themselves were not illegal. Following the 1842 ruling, peaceful strikes for improved wages, hours, or working conditions were generally accepted as legal, while violent strikes or sympathy strikes to aid workers in other industries were not accepted by the courts.

In the 1880s, employers began using court *injunctions* to prevent strikes, pickets, and boycotts. The injunction was originally designed to prevent threatened damage to property under conditions when regular court processes would be too slow. Employers could go to sympathetic judges when threatened with strikes to obtain a restraining order which could close down a picket line or head off a strike within a matter of hours. The use of injunctions was eventually broadened to safeguarding businesses' "justifiable expectation of profit." The liberal use of injunctions in the late nineteenth and early twentieth centuries made it very difficult for unions to strike a company without being restrained by an injunction. The company only needed to claim that the strike threatened damage to the employer's property. In the early twentieth century, court rulings further weakened unions by upholding "yellow dog" contracts. In effect, the courts ruled that employers could legally require a nonunion pledge as a legitimate condition for employment. A further problem for unions was the uncertainty about whether the restraint-of-trade provisions of the 1890 Sherman Act were meant to apply to union activities.

Two pro-union laws passed during the Great Depression paved the way for the growth of the organized labor movement in the 1930s and 1940s. The Norris-LaGuardia Act of 1932 declared that a worker "has full freedom of association, self-organization, and designation of representatives of his own choosing, to negotiate the terms and conditions of his employment . . . " and that workers should be "free from the interference, restraint, or coercion of employers" in the choice of union representatives. The Norris-LaGuardia Act restricted the use of court orders and injunctions to combat union organizing drives and strikes and prohibited "yellow dog" contracts. The National Labor Relations Act (the

Wagner Act) of 1935 defined specific unfair labor practices. Employers were required to bargain in good faith with unions representing a majority of employees, and it became illegal to interfere with employees' rights to organize into unions. The National Labor Relations Board (NLRB) was established and given the authority to investigate unfair labor practices. The NLRB was also authorized to conduct elections to determine which union the employees wanted, if any, to represent them.

The Norris-LaGuardia Act of 1932 and the Wagner Act of 1935 encouraged union growth in the 1930s and 1940s. Exhibit 1 makes it clear that until these laws were passed, labor unions were relatively insignificant in size. After World War II, unions lost some of their popular support. The Taft-Hartley and Landrum-Griffin acts were the result of anti-union sentiment. The Taft-Hartley Act of 1947 gave states the right to pass *right-to-work laws* that prohibited the requirement that union membership be a condition for employment. *Closed-shop agreements* that required firms to hire only union members were outlawed for firms engaged in interstate commerce. Major strikes that could disrupt the economy could be delayed by an 80-day cooling-off period if ordered by the president.

The Landrum-Griffin Act of 1959 was designed to protect the rights of union members and to increase union democracy. It included provisions for periodic reporting of union finances and for regulating union elections.

> The Norris-LaGuardia Act of 1932 and the Wagner Act of 1935 were pro-union laws that spurred the growth of labor unions.

UNION OBJECTIVES

What are the objectives of labor unions? Surprisingly, the answer to this question is not as obvious as it appears. Unions would like to obtain higher wages, better fringe benefits, and safer working conditions for their members. They would also like to prevent the unemployment of their members. Are the two objectives of higher wages and lower unemployment compatible—given the fact (demonstrated in the previous chapter) that the firm will hire more labor at low wages than at high wages, *ceteris paribus*?

Assume that two different unions—A and B—collectively bargain about wages with management. For simplicity, we assume that workers in each union are earning the same wage (w_c) and that employment is the same in both cases (at l_c). The demand curve for each union's labor force is shown in Exhibit 3. Demand curves for labor, just like demand curves for goods and services, can be either elastic or inelastic. The demand curve in the case of Union A is inelastic: moving from point c to point a in panel (a) means a large percentage increase in the wage (to w_a) compared to the percentage reduction in the quantity of labor demanded (from l_c to l_a). The demand is elastic in the case of Union B: moving from c to b in panel (b) means a small percentage increase in the wage compared to the percentage reduction in the quantity of labor demanded (from l_c to l_b).

The leadership of Union B is faced with a dilemma. If it pushes for wages higher than w_c—such as w_b—the number of jobs available to union members will decline from l_c to l_b. Jobs will be traded off for higher wages, and the rank and file of the union will likely be dissatisfied with the union leadership. This **wage/employment tradeoff** is less acute in the case of Union A because the same increase in wages loses fewer jobs (because of the difference in elasticity between A and B).

> Unions are faced with a wage/employment tradeoff when bargaining for higher wages.

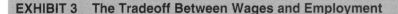

EXHIBIT 3   The Tradeoff Between Wages and Employment

a. Inelastic Demand: Union A   **b. Elastic Demand: Union B**

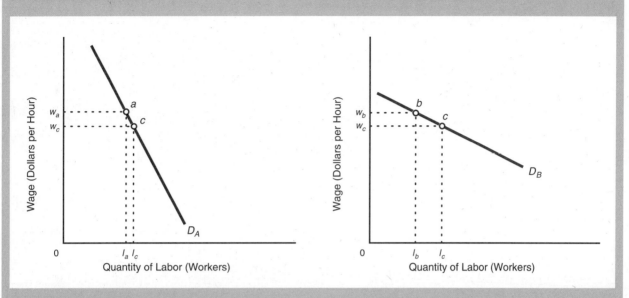

The demand curve for the members of Union A is relatively inelastic, while the demand curve for the members of Union B is relatively elastic. If both unions, in the collective-bargaining process, push for the same wage increases, more jobs will be lost by workers in Union B (where demand is elastic) than by workers in Union A.

> The **wage/employment tradeoff** confronts any labor union that faces a downward-sloping demand curve: higher wages means sacrificing the number of jobs; lower unemployment means sacrificing higher wages.

Example 2 provides an example of the tradeoff.

How Unions Deal with the Tradeoff

The wage/employment tradeoff explains why unions try to increase the demand for labor and to reduce the elasticity of demand for labor. If they succeed in increasing demand for labor, labor unions can obtain both higher wages and higher employment. By reducing the elasticity of demand for labor, unions can raise wages with a smaller cost in lost employment.

Unions attempt to increase the demand for union labor and lower its elasticity of demand in a variety of ways. Unions lobby for tariffs and quotas on competing foreign-produced products to increase the demand for the products produced by union workers. Unions conduct advertising campaigns telling the public to "look for the union label" or to "buy American." Unions have opposed relaxing immigration laws. Unions have traditionally supported raising the minimum wage—an act that makes unskilled labor more expensive relative to the more skilled workers that tend to belong to unions.

Unions have lobbied for minimum staffing requirements. The unions unsuccessfully lobbied for the MD-80 aircraft to be staffed by three cockpit personnel

EXAMPLE 2

The Wage/Employment Tradeoff: A Union Strikes for Lower Wages!

One of the most unusual strikes in union history was called in September 1984 by the New Jersey Building and Construction Trades Council of the AFL–CIO on behalf of unionized insulation installers. The goal of the strike, which lasted two days, was to force employers to agree to pay union workers $1.60 an hour less than the employers had offered! Why would a union go on strike to gain lower wages? The union leadership interpreted management's offer as a subtle attempt to price union members out of the market. The higher wage would have provided firms with an excuse to hire more non-union labor, causing a decline in union membership. In this case, the union members clearly understood the wage/employment tradeoff. They were willing to accept lower wages for more jobs.

SOURCE: "Union Asks for Lower Wages to Save Jobs," *Christian Science Monitor*, September 24, 1984.

(two pilots and a flight engineer) rather than the two pilots that airline management wanted. Staffing requirements that call for the use of additional labor for jobs that have become redundant (such as fire stokers on diesel-powered locomotives) are called *featherbedding*. Unions may also bargain for rules that make it difficult or impossible to substitute other grades of labor for union labor. In construction, unions specify which jobs can be performed only by electricians and by no one else, and there are sanctions against builders who hire nonunion employees. Work rules are often a subject of negotiation along with wage rates when unions bargain with management.

Limitations of Labor Supply

Some unions seek to drive up the wage by limiting the supply of union labor. In these cases, the union controls who will be allowed to work in a particular occupation by means of certification and qualification requirements. In craft unions, the number of union members can be limited by long apprenticeships, by rules limiting entry into the union, by difficult qualifying exams, and by state licensing. In the process of limiting labor supply, the union screens out unqualified workers but may also exclude some qualified people who are prepared to work in that occupation.

Unions can raise wages by limiting the supply of labor.

Exhibit 4 shows the effect of limiting labor supply on wages. The decrease in supply (from S to S') moves the equilibrium wage/employment combination from e to e'; at e' wages are higher, but fewer jobs are available. When unions seek to control wages through limitations on the supply of union labor, it is especially important to prevent employers from substituting nonunion labor. For this reason, craft unions favor rigid certification requirements and rules prohibiting nonunion workers from performing certain tasks.

Collective Bargaining

Industrial unions that represent all the workers in a particular industry have a more difficult time limiting the supply of labor. Such unions can indeed affect overall

EXHIBIT 4   The Effect on Wages of Limiting Supply

By limiting entry into the profession, a craft union shifts the labor supply curve to the left (from S to S'), and the wage rate of union members is raised above what it would have been without the union.

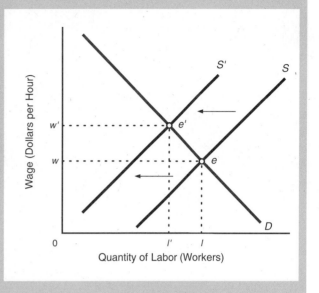

labor supply conditions by favoring restrictions on immigration, mandatory retirement, shorter workweeks, and laws against teenage employment. But they, unlike plumbers, electricians, and physicians, find it difficult to control the number of union members. Industrial unions, therefore, use **collective bargaining**, sometimes coupled with the threat of **strike**, to raise the wages of union members.

> **Collective bargaining** is the bargaining of unions as representatives of all union employees with management.

> A **strike** occurs when all union workers cease working until the employer agrees to specific union demands.

Industrial unions raise wages through collective bargaining with the threat of strike.

Collective bargaining gives workers a stronger voice than they would have if each worker bargained separately with management. The threat of strike is the union's strongest weapon in collective bargaining.

The effect of the collective-bargaining process (with threat of strike) is represented in Exhibit 5. The supply curve, S, represents the supply of labor to the industry *if each individual were to bargain separately with management*. When the union threatens to strike, the union is, in effect, telling management that: at wages less than w_c, no labor will be supplied; at the wage of w_c, management can hire as much labor as it wants up to l_c; as wages increase above w_c, management can hire ever-increasing amounts of labor beyond l_c. Thus, the new labor supply curve with the threat of a strike is shown by the heavy line that connects w_c, on the vertical axis with point c and then continues up the original supply curve above point c. Without the threat of strike, the supply curve would be the original curve S, and point e would be the equilibrium wage/employment combination. With the threat of a strike, the demand curve would meet the new supply curve at point a, and the firm would hire l_a workers at a wage of w_c.

EXHIBIT 5   Collective Bargaining with the Threat of Strike

The supply curve, S, represents the labor supply if there were no union. The heavy blue supply curve that is S' to the left of point c and S above c is the supply curve with collective bargaining because no union labor will be supplied at a wage below w_c. Point e is the equilibrium wage/employment combination without collective bargaining or threat of a strike; point a is the equilibrium wage/employment combination with collective bargaining. The benefit to union members is that a higher wage is achieved (w_c is higher than w_e). The cost is that the number of jobs is reduced. Some union members who are willing to work at w_c are without jobs in the industry (the number represented by the difference between l_c and l_a is the number left without jobs).

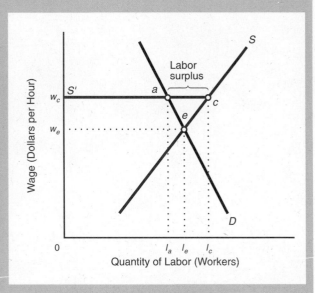

From the standpoint of union members, collective bargaining has its costs and benefits. The benefits are the higher wages that collective bargaining brings (w_c is higher than w_e). The costs are that some union members who are willing to work at the negotiated wage will not be employed. Although l_c workers are willing to work at w_c, only l_a workers will be hired. The unemployment effects of collective bargaining are softened by numerous rules within the union governing which members will be laid off first. Typically, union members who have *seniority* (have been in the union the longest time) are laid off last.

Collective Bargaining with Monopsony

If employers have monopsony power over their labor market, the tradeoff between higher wages and union employment does not hold. An employer has monopsony power if the employer accounts for a large enough portion of total hiring in that labor market to affect the market wage. The labor supply curve to a monopsonistic firm is not horizontal at the prevailing market wage because the employer cannot hire all the labor it wants at the market wage. Instead, to hire more labor, the monopsonistic firm will have to offer higher wages to all its employees.

Consider a monopsonist faced with the upward-sloping labor supply schedule given in Exhibit 6. The wage rate is not the marginal factor cost (*MFC*) in the case of the monopsonist. To hire one more unit of labor, the monopsonist must pay a higher wage not only to the new worker but also to workers previously hired. To hire the second worker, the monopsonist must pay a higher wage ($7 rather than the previous $5) to the first worker. The *MFC* of the second worker is, therefore, the wage paid the second worker ($7) plus the increase in the wage of the first worker ($2) for a total of $9. The *MFC* exceeds the wage in the case of the monopsonist.

The figure in Exhibit 6 shows the employment and wage rate offered by a monopsonist with and without collective bargaining. *Without collective bargaining,*

The marginal factor cost of the monopsonist is greater than the wage rate paid by the monopsonist because the monopsonist must raise the wage of all workers to increase employment.

EXHIBIT 6   Monopsony and Collective Bargaining

a. The Monopsonist's Marginal Factor Cost

Labor (workers), *L* (1)	Wage (dollars per hours), *W* (2)	Labor Cost (dollars) (3) = (1) × (2)	Marginal Factor Cost (dollars), *MFC* (4)
1	5	5	
			9
2	7	14	
			13
3	9	27	
			21
4	12	48	

b. Collective Bargaining: When *MFC* Exceeds the Wage

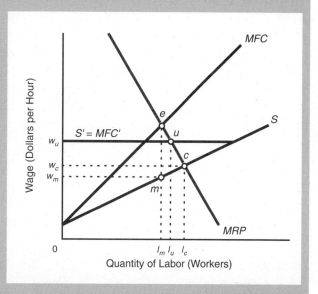

Because this industry is monopsonistic, *MFC* is greater than the wage at each quantity of labor. The monopsonist will hire that quantity at which *MFC* = *MRP* and pay the wage that corresponds to that labor quantity on the supply curve, or w_m. Without unions, *MFC* = *MRP* at point *e*; the monopsonist will hire l_m workers and pay the wage of w_m. If a union collectively bargains for a wage of w_u, the monopsonist's *MFC* curve shifts to *MFC'* because of the change in labor supply and becomes a horizontal line at w_u; *MFC'* will now equal *MRP* at point *u*. In this case, collective bargaining actually increased both wages (from w_m to w_u) and union employment (from l_m to l_u).

the monopsonist hires that quantity of labor at which *MFC* and *MRP* are equal (but will pay the wage corresponding to that quantity on the labor supply curve). The monopsonist hires l_m workers and pays a wage of w_m.

Since *MFC* exceeds the wage rate, the monopsonist will hire less labor than would be the case if the industry were competitive in the labor market and each firm treated the wage rate as its *MFC*. The competitive industry would operate at point *c*, where *S* (which equals the competitive firm's *MFC*) equals *MRP*. *Monopsony results in lower wages and fewer people being employed as compared to the case of the competitive employer.*

When facing a monopsonistic employer, collective bargaining can raise both employment and wages. If a union collectively bargains for a wage of w_u, the monopsonist's *MFC* curve becomes a horizontal line at w_u. Collective bargaining makes the supply of union labor perfectly elastic (horizontal) at the union wage. By demanding w_u the union makes this wage the *MFC* of the monopsonist. In this case, *MRP* = *MFC'* at point *u*, where the monopsonist hires l_u of labor.

> Collective bargaining can raise both wages and union employment when the firm is a monopsonist.

There are no measures of the degree of monopsony in labor markets. Monopsony in factor markets is less likely than monopoly in product markets because virtually all employers compete among themselves for the factors of production. Although cases of monopsony can be found, the observed behavior of labor unions—the obvious efforts of unions to soften the wage/employment tradeoff—suggests that monopsony is not prevalent and that in most cases unions must trade off jobs for higher wages.

THE EFFECT OF UNIONS ON WAGES

Unions can affect the wages of their members by limiting the supply of union labor, by increasing the demand for union labor through staffing requirements and programs to increase the demand for the product, and through collective bargaining. Considerable effort on the part of many labor economists has gone into estimating the extent to which unions have been able to raise the wages of their members relative to comparable nonunion workers.

Effect on Union Wages

Studies of the effect of unions on wages find that unions have indeed succeeded in raising the wages of their members above what those wages would have been without unions. In the mid-1990s, union members earned about one-third more per week than nonunion members. The effects of unions have varied among industries, over time and by gender and race as shown in Exhibit 7. From 1967 to 1975, the wage advantage of union members increased from around 12 percent to a near 17 percent advantage. Studies show that, historically, craft unions in construction and transportation have achieved the largest relative wage effects (20–25 percent). Industrial unions have had a smaller relative wage effect (10–15 percent). In competitive industries such as textiles and apparel, unions have had the smallest impact on relative wages. Whatever the case, union members earn more on average than nonunion workers.

> Unions have succeeded in raising the wages of their members above nonunion wages.

Effect on Nonunion Wages

It is more difficult to establish the effect of unions on the general level of wages or on the wages of nonunion workers. Theory suggests that unions could either depress or increase the wage rates of nonunion workers.

Exhibit 1 showed that less than one U.S. worker in five is a union member. The economy's labor force is made up of both unionized and nonunionized sectors, with the nonunionized sector numerically dominant. If unions bargain for substantial increases in the union wage and trade off jobs for large wage increases, unemployed union members can "spill over" into the nonunion sector. The young union members with low seniority are the ones most likely laid off in the unionized

EXHIBIT 7   Union Wage Advantages

	Percentage Union Wage Effect			Percentage Unionized		
	1967	1973	1975	1967	1973	1975
All workers	11.6	14.8	16.8	23	26	25
White males	9.6	15.5	16.3	31	33	31
Black males	21.5	22.5	22.5	32	37	37
White females	14.4	12.7	16.6	12	14	14
Black females	5.6	13.2	17.1	13	22	22

SOURCE: Orley Ashenfelter, "Union Relative Wage Effects: New Evidence and a Survey of Their Implications for Wage Inflation," in *Econometric Contributions to Public Policy,* eds. R. Stone and W. Peterson (New York: St. Martin's, 1979), Tables 2.1 and 2.2.

Are Unions "Good" or "Bad" for Efficiency?

Public policy plays a major role in determining the overall level of health of unionism. Until the passage of pro-union federal legislation in the 1930s, unions played a relatively small role. President Ronald Reagan's decision to fire striking air-traffic controllers in August 1981 dealt a severe blow to the American labor movement.

To determine what stance public policy should take toward unions, it is important to determine the effect of unions on economic efficiency.

Do Unions Decrease Efficiency?

The traditional view is that unions have a negative effect on productivity. The reasons for this view include the following:

1. Unions bargain for staffing requirements *(featherbedding)* that prevent employers from using labor and capital in the most efficient manner. If union rules prevent carpenters from turning a screw on any electrical fixture, for example, the economy will operate below its potential.
2. Union strikes disrupt output and cause the economy to produce below its production potential. Strikes in major industries, like steel and rail transportation, can disrupt other sectors of the economy and cause losses of real output.
3. If workers of comparable quality are paid different wages because one belongs to a union and the other is in nonunion employment, the economy loses potential output. In both the unionized and nonunionized sectors, workers will be employed to the point where their wage equals their *MRP*, but the *MRP*s of union workers will be higher than those of comparable nonunion workers. The economy could have increased its output by reallocating workers from the nonunionized sector (where *MRP* is lower) into the union sector (where *MRP* is higher).

Do Unions Increase Efficiency?

A new breed of economists maintain that unions actually improve productivity. Unions improve productivity by acting as a *collective voice* for union members. Without unions, if workers are dissatisfied with their employer, their only recourse is to quit and seek another job. When workers "vote with their feet" to punish bad employers, the resulting job turnover costs the economy lost output. With high turnover, employees must learn new jobs and spend time in often lengthy job searches.

Unions can have a positive effect on productivity in three ways. First, when worker grievances are handled by the union, workers need not leave the firm in order to bring about an improvement in their work conditions. If fewer workers quit—because the union gives them a voice for their protests or complaints—the firm can reduce its hiring and training costs, and the work groups will function more smoothly. Workers with a voice are more willing to train in skills that are useful in only that industry. Second, senior workers (who are most important politically in the union organization) are more likely to provide informal training and assistance in enterprises where unions give them a voice. When the union provides a channel of communication between workers and management, the improved flow of information can increase the efficiency of the enterprise. Third, a well-established seniority system tends to reduce friction between junior and senior workers.

The empirical evidence suggest the following effects of unions on productivity. First, there is strong evidence that the presence of unions causes a dramatic reduction in employee turnover (see Exhibit 8). Although the quit rates of young workers (who happen to be the first laid off in unions) are only slightly reduced by unionization, other workers' quit rates are reduced by the presence of unions from 34

EXHIBIT 8 Unions, Turnover, and Productivity

a. Effect of Unions on Quit Rates

Sample	Percentage by which Quits Are Reduced by Unionism
All workers, 1968–78	45
All workers, 1973–75	86
Men 48–62 in 1969	107
Men 17–27 in 1969	11
Manufacturing workers	34–48

Source: Richard Freeman and James Medoff, "The Two Faces of Unionism," *The Public Interest* 57 (Fall 1979): p. 79.

b. Effect of Unions on Productivity in U.S. Industries

Industry	Percentage Increase in Output per Worker Due to Unions
Manufacturing, 1972	20–25
Wooden furniture, 1972	15
Cement, 1953–76	6–8
Underground coal, 1965	25–30
Underground coal, 1975	(−20)–(−25)
Construction, 1972	29–38
Construction, office buildings, 1973–74	30
Construction, retail stores and shopping centers, 1976–78	51

Sources: Richard Freeman and James Medoff, "The Two Faces of Unionism," *The Public Interest* 57 (Fall 1979): p. 80; Kim Clark, "The Impact of Unionization on Productivity: A Case Study," *Industrial and Labor Relations Review* (July 1980): pp. 451–69; and Ronald Ehrenberg and Robert Smith, *Modern Labor Economics*, 4th ed. (New York: HarperCollins, 1991), p. 483.

to 107 percent. Second, empirical studies find that productivity is generally higher in industries with higher rates of unionization.

The final chapter remains to be written on this issue. If unions do indeed promote efficiency, a more supportive public policy towards unions could be called for.

Higher wages in the unionized sector can depress the wages of nonunion workers by causing unemployed union members to spill over into nonunion employment.

sector when there is a tradeoff between higher wages and fewer jobs. When they seek employment in the nonunionized sector, the labor supply curve in the nonunionized sector shifts to the right (increases), and wages in the nonunionized sector are bid down.

On the other hand, unions could possibly raise wages in the nonunionized sector in two ways. First, employers of nonunion workers may fear that if they do not match union wage increases, pressure will build among their workers to form a union. Second, when a unionized worker is laid off, there is a possibility that that worker will not spill over into the nonunionized sector but will wait until he or she is recalled to a job in the union sector. The unemployed union member is least likely to "spill over" when there is a substantial wage differential between the nonunion and union job, when the likelihood of recall is high, and when unemployment benefits are generous. If unemployed union workers do not spill over into nonunionized jobs, the downward pressure on nonunion wages would be removed.

The empirical evidence on the question of union effects on nonunion wages is not decisive, but it does suggest that unions depress wages in nonunionized jobs. In cities where the percent of unionized workers is high the wages of nonunion workers are lower than in other cities where there is less unionization.

This chapter continued the discussion of labor markets begun in the preceding chapter by examining how unions affect wages and economic efficiency. The next chapter will turn to the nonlabor factors of production: land, capital, and entrepreneurship.

The most important point to learn from this chapter is:
Unionized workers face a tradeoff between higher wages and fewer jobs. In collective bargaining, unions must balance this tradeoff in their bargaining strategy.

1. A union is a collective organization of workers and employees whose objective is to improve the work conditions of its members. A craft union represents workers of a particular occupation. An industrial union represents workers of a particular industry. Currently less than 20 percent of the labor force belongs to unions—a decline from the high of 25 percent in the 1950s. The declining percentage is due to the rise of white-collar employment, the rising share of women in the work force, and the shift of industry to the South and Southwest. The most substantial gains in union membership have been in public employment.

2. During the nineteenth century, the courts used common-law rulings and injunctions to limit union activity. The formation of unions was aided by pro-labor legislation beginning with the Norris-LaGuardia Act of 1932, which facilitated union-organizing drives. The National Labor Relations Act of 1935 made it illegal for employers to interfere with the rights of employees to organize. The Taft-Hartley Act of 1947 reacted against the pro-union legislation of the 1930s.

3. Unions must weigh the advantages of higher wages against the disadvantages of less union employment. Unions respond to the tradeoff between jobs and employment by increasing the demand for union labor and by promoting measures to reduce the elasticity of demand for union labor. In collective bargaining, the union's most potent weapon is the strike threat. If the employer is a monopsonist, the wage/employment tradeoff does not exist.

4. Unions are able to raise the wages of union members relative to comparable nonunion members. The amount wages are raised varies by industry and by union. Unions can have both a positive and a negative effect on nonunion wages. When unions raise wages in the union sector, the workers who are laid off spill over into the nonunion sector, and the increase in labor supply lowers nonunion wages. However, when unions raise wages in the union sector, nonunion employers may raise wages because they fear the formation of a union if they do not raise wages.

Policy Focus: **Public policy can either promote or retard the development of unions. It is therefore important to understand the effect of unions on productivity. There are two views on the effect of unions on productivity. The traditional view maintains that unions adversely affect labor productivity. The new view argues that unions give workers a voice in the workplace and that this raises the labor productivity of union workers.**

Key Terms

labor union (p. 308)
craft union (p. 308)
industrial union (p. 308)
employee association (p. 308)

wage/employment tradeoff (p. 314)
collective bargaining (p. 317)
strike (p. 317)

Questions and Problems

1. The elasticity of demand for labor (the percentage change in quantity of labor demanded divided by the percentage change in the wage) is 1.5 in the widget industry and is 0.5 in the ratchet industry. Which industry would be easier to unionize? In which industry is the tradeoff between employment and higher wages more costly?

2. If you were the president of a major industrial union, what would your attitude be toward unlimited immigration? What would your attitude be toward the minimum-wage law? Explain.

3. Why do industrial unions not use the craft-union technique of restricting labor supply to raise union wages?

4. Explain why both the automobile unions and the management of the automobile industry favor import restrictions on imported cars.

5. Assume that you belong to a union of bank tellers. What would your attitude be toward automated bank tellers? Explain.

6. Explain why the impact of higher union wages on nonunion wages might depend on whether laid-off union members waited to be rehired as opposed to searching for jobs in nonunionized industries.

7. Which of the following policies would unions tend to favor? Explain your answer.
   a. Liberal immigration laws.
   b. Free trade.
   c. Reductions of quotas on foreign goods.
   d. A higher minimum wage.

8. If unions do succeed in raising productivity, what effect would this productivity increase have on the costs of production of unionized companies versus nonunionized companies?

9. Explain why common-law principles made it difficult for judges in the eighteenth and nineteenth centuries to rule on the legality of strikes.

10. Strikes have been called the strongest weapon available to industrial unions in collective bargaining. Explain how strikes can be used to change the labor-supply curve. What shape does the labor-supply curve have with and without the threat of strike?

11. If unions lower quit rates, why would productivity be expected to increase?

12. How is "featherbedding" used to raise union wages? What does "featherbedding" mean?

Doing Economics

Try to obtain an interview with a local union leader. Ask her what the objectives of her union are. How relatively important are high wages, improved benefits, expanded employment, dealing with grievances and working conditions, improved productivity, political action, and other union objectives? Does she view the union and the employer(s) as fundamentally in partnership or in conflict?

What examples can she give of how the presence of the union enhances productivity through a more orderly operation of the workplace? Does she believe that pushing for higher wages or benefits necessarily reduces the amount of employment? Which of the arguments against unions presented in the text does she agree with and which ones does she dispute?

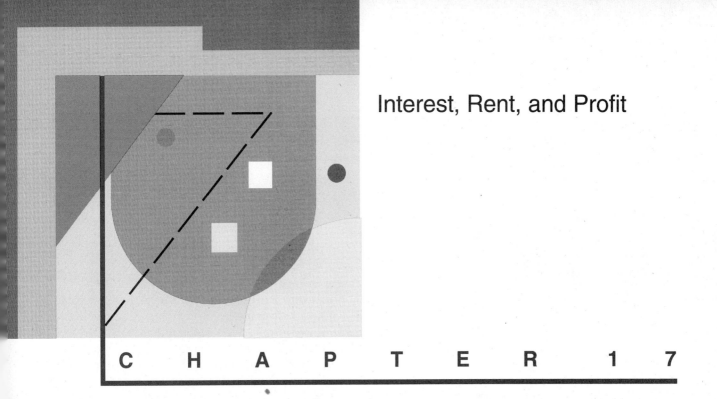

Interest, Rent, and Profit

C H A P T E R   1 7

CHAPTER FOCUS   This chapter is about the factors of production other than labor. They account for about 25 cents of every dollar earned by participants in the economy. These other factors—capital, land, and entrepreneurship—are less visible and less well understood, but they make essential contributions to economic well-being.

   The average American manufacturing worker works with over $100,000 worth of manufacturing equipment. Through the process of past investment, American workers find themselves in a favorable position relative to workers in less-developed economies. The combination of labor with vast amounts of capital makes workers highly productive and makes it possible for them to earn relatively high wages. An American manufacturing worker working with primitive equipment would earn much less. What if this capital had not been accumulated?

   What if no entrepreneur had been around to detect business opportunities? If farsighted persons, willing to take risks, had not foreseen the profit opportunities in automobile manufacturing, personal computers, fast-food chains, or commercial jet manufacturing, there would be little capital, little employment, and low wages.

   Some people possess or own unique resources. Some women have perfect complexions and become supermodels earning astronomical salaries; others have unique athletic skills; yet others are fortunate to own valuable real estate located in the center of prosperous cities. How and why should people be rewarded for possessing these unique resources?

After studying this chapter, you will be able to:

■ Understand how interest rates are related to productivity and thrift.

■ Discuss why interest rates differ between different people and different assets.

■ Explain the function of economic rent.

■ Identify the sources of economic profit.

CAPITAL AND INTEREST

Ultimately, the function of production is to provide for consumption. Capital goods such as trucks, conveyors, lathes, cranes, and computers are ultimately useful only because they enable us to consume more goods and services. Cars and shirts and milk are produced indirectly by first producing capital goods. Indirect or roundabout production is typically more productive than direct production. Capital goods enlist the mechanical, electrical, and chemical powers of nature to expand the production possibilities of society far beyond what otherwise could be accomplished by unaided human hands or minds. Productivity is raised when a net is used instead of bare hands to catch fish. Productivity is raised when workers use an automated assembly line rather than hand tools to assemble cars.

Capital and Saving

Saving is necessary for a society to invest in capital goods. Resources must be diverted from producing consumption goods to producing capital goods. When people save, they buy stocks and bonds or deposit their funds in bank accounts. While some of these funds are used to finance consumption expenditures, the rest are channeled into investments in new buildings, plants, and machinery.

Interest is the price paid for borrowed funds or credit. Because capital is productive, a dollar invested today in capital goods yields more than a dollar tomorrow. But people are impatient. To be convinced to save a dollar today, they must be rewarded with more than a dollar tomorrow. Business firms that wish to invest are willing to pay interest and savers demand that interest be paid. Interest coordinates the number of dollars that businesses want to invest with the number that people want to save.

> **Interest** is the price of credit. Interest is set where the amount businesses wish to invest is balanced with the amount people are prepared to save.

Credit Markets

Interest plays its coordinating role in credit markets. **Credit markets** bring suppliers of credit (savers) together with demanders of credit (businesses that wish to invest). Credit markets, also called *capital markets,* make possible the production of capital goods.

> **Credit markets** are markets for borrowing and lending funds.

GALLERY OF ECONOMISTS

Frank Knight (1885–1972)

Frank Knight was born on a farm in Illinois, the first of eleven children, two others of whom became economists. Knight attended a series of small colleges and then spent two years at the University of Tennessee before going to Cornell to study philosophy. He switched to economics a year later and wrote a dissertation that appeared in 1921 as his classic work, *Risk, Uncertainty, and Profit.* Knight taught at Cornell, Iowa, and the University of Chicago, where he spent the rest of his teaching career. He served as president of the American Economic Association in 1950. In addition to contributing to the theory of profits, Knight explained how the efficiency of markets depends on property rights to resources being clearly defined.

In *Risk, Uncertainty, and Profit,* Knight sought to explain why profits exist even in competitive markets. Knight argued that profits are a reward for risk and uncertainty. Although some risks can be calculated, Knight thought that certain risks cannot be reduced to objective measures. In a changing business environment with technological advances, certain business risks will be unknown because they are unprecedented. Entrepreneurs who take unprecedented risks are rewarded by positive profits even in competitive industries. Knight's major contribution to economics was to provide a satisfactory explanation of profits in a competitive environment.

Robinson Crusoe, living alone on a deserted island, had no need for credit markets. Crusoe would simply *save* (give up some present consumption) so he could *invest* (produce capital goods). When Crusoe took three days off from fishing to weave a net (a capital good), he was both saving and investing. Similarly, farmers both save and invest by taking time off from current production to drain a swamp or build a dam (that is, to produce capital goods).

In a modern economy, however, credit markets are required to bring savers and investors together. Unlike Crusoe or the farmer draining land, the saver and the investor are typically not the same. Financial assets—stocks, bonds, bank credit, and trade credit—are used to finance capital goods. Credit markets make possible the separation of the act of saving from the act of investing.

Credit markets allow specialization. Business firms specialize in knowing profitable investment opportunities. They know when to build a new plant, buy new equipment, or to set up an advanced research and development lab. Households specialize in saving. They usually do not have the information to use their saving to act on profitable investment opportunities. There is, therefore, a natural trade that can be set up between households and businesses. In credit markets, firms wishing to invest in capital goods borrow from households (and other businesses).

The Rate of Interest

The **interest rate** measures the cost of borrowing to acquire capital goods. It is usually expressed as an annual percentage rate. If $1,000 is borrowed on January 1 and $1,100 (the $1,000 borrowed plus $100 interest) is repaid on December 31 of that same year, the $100 interest represents a 10 percent rate of interest on an annual percentage basis. If the loan were for only six months, and $1,050 were repaid on June 30, the $50 interest still represents a 10 percent annual rate.

EXAMPLE 1

Interest Rates, Present Value, and Insulation

Home owners are bombarded by press advertising and solicitations exhorting them to insulate their homes. The main argument for such sales pitches is that the reduction in heating bills will more than compensate for the cost of the insulation.

Present value calculations provide a means of assessing whether a home owner should insulate or not. Take the simple case where the homeowner determines that insulation will save an extra $200 per year on heating costs. At an interest rate of 10%, the homeowner could earn $200 per year from a deposit of $2,000 in a savings account. At a 10% interest rate, if the insulation cost less than $2,000, its installation could be justified. If the insulation cost more than $2,000, the homeowner would be better off putting the money in a deposit account and using the interest to pay the higher heating bill.

In this example, the present value of the heating-bill savings of $200 per year equals $2,000. If the interest rate had been a lower 5%, the present value of savings would have been a higher $4,000. If insulation had cost less than $4,000, its use could be justified.

> The **interest rate** measures the yearly cost of borrowing as a percent of the amount loaned.

As a price of credit or borrowing, the interest rate shows the terms of trade between things today and things tomorrow. For example, consider a $12,600 car today and the same $12,600 car in one year (ignore inflation). An interest rate of 5 percent means that the car next year can be bought with only $12,000 of today's purchasing power. Put $12,000 in the bank, and it will grow to $12,600 in one year at an interest rate of 5 percent ($12,000 + $600 interest). Consider now a 10 percent interest rate. To buy the same $12,600 car in one year requires that a person put only $11,455 in the bank. The higher interest rate makes the future car cheaper relative to the present car. Similarly, a lower interest rate makes a future car more expensive relative to the present car. This is why analysts suppose that higher interest rates discourage present-day car sales. (See Example 1.)

Interest-Rate Determination

The interest rate is determined in credit markets by the supply and demand for credit. The total amount of credit (also called *loanable funds*) supplied to credit markets consists of the total amount of lending from all households, businesses, and governments or bank credit made available to borrowers in credit markets.

The Supply of Credit. For credit markets as a whole, the supply of funds made available to credit markets comes primarily from the net savings of businesses and households during that period. The supply curve in Exhibit 1 shows the quantity of funds savers are prepared to make available to lenders at each interest rate. This supply curve of credit is positively sloped because a larger quantity will be saved (made available to lenders) at high interest rates than at low interest rates, *ceteris paribus*.

EXHIBIT 1 Interest-Rate Determination in Credit Markets

The supply curve shows the quantity of credit offered by lenders at different interest rates; lenders will offer more at high interest rates. The demand curve shows the quantity of credit demanded by borrowers at different interest rates; less will be demanded at high interest rates. The credit market is in equilibrium at an interest rate of 9 percent, where the quantity demanded equals the quantity supplied.

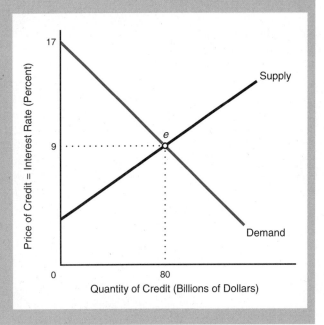

The Demand for Credit.

The demand for credit is made up principally of the demand for new investments in capital goods of businesses. Households also demand credit for automobile loans, consumer loans, and home mortgages, but this chapter will concentrate primarily on business investment.

What determines business demand for capital goods? New capital raises the output (and, therefore, the revenue) of the firm for a number of years because capital goods are in use for more than a single year. A machine will be used for 8 years on average, and a plant will be used for 35 years on average.

Business firms will want to invest in capital goods when the return on their investment exceeds the interest they could earn by placing those funds in the bank. Investment in new capital goods will be carried out until the **rate of return on capital** equals the rate of interest.

> The **rate of return on capital** measures the annual return of the capital investment as a percentage of the investment cost.

To see how interest rates affect the demand for credit by business firms, consider the hypothetical Ajax Sheet Metal Company. When the interest rate is exceptionally high, say 20 percent per year, Ajax may only be willing to borrow funds to replace essential but worn-out capital equipment (such as a machine for flattening the metal). At an interest rate of 15 percent, Ajax may consider adding robots to the manufacturing process. As interest rates fall further, to say 10 percent, Ajax might purchase more modern versions of its rolling machines. At an extremely low interest rate, such as 5 percent, Ajax might even double the size of its factory.

The law of diminishing returns applies to capital just as it applies to labor. Additional capital-investment projects will yield successively lower rates of return. In making their investment plans, businesses will consider a variety of investment projects. Successive projects bring lower and lower rates of return due to the law

The demand curve for credit is
negatively sloped because at
high interest rates there are
fewer investment projects that
have a rate of return equal to
or greater than the interest
rate.

The equilibrium interest rate
equates the quantity of credit
demanded with the quantity
supplied.

of diminishing returns. As interest rates fall, the firm can carry out investment projects with lower rates of return.

The demand curve for credit in Exhibit 1 is downward-sloping. The demand curve reflects the rate of return on capital investment projects because business firms will be willing to add to their capital stock as long as the rate of return of investment projects exceeds the rate of interest. The demand curve shows the quantity of credit funds businesses are prepared to borrow for capital investments at each interest rate.

The Equilibrium Interest Rate.   Like any other price, the equilibrium (market) rate of interest established by the credit market is that rate at which the quantity of credit supplied equals the quantity demanded.

In Exhibit 1, when the interest rate is 9 percent, there are $80 billion worth of investment projects that yield a rate of return of 9 percent or above. Since the quantity of credit supplied equals the quantity demanded at that rate, the equilibrium rate of interest is 9 percent.

Productivity of Capital and Thrift.   The demand for credit reflects the basic productivity of capital. Firms demand funds for investment as long as rates of return are greater than or equal to the rate of interest. Anything that makes capital more productive will shift the demand curve to the right and cause the interest rate to rise. The supply curve of funds supplied to credit markets reflects the basic thriftiness of the population. Anything that causes the population to be more thrifty (that is, to save more at each interest rate) will shift the supply curve to the right and cause the interest rate to fall.

The impacts of productivity improvements and changes in thrift on interest rates are shown in Exhibit 2. If an important technological breakthrough raises the productivity of capital, the demand curve for credit would shift to the right and would drive up the interest rate, *ceteris paribus,* as in Exhibit 2, panel (a). If there were a change in tax laws to reward those families that save, the supply curve would shift right and lower the market rate of interest, *ceteris paribus,* as in Exhibit 2, panel (b).

The Structure of Interest Rates

Although the interest rate is the price of credit, this price is not the same for all borrowers. Some borrowers pay higher interest rates than others. Savings-and-loan associations may pay as little as 2 percent when they borrow from their depositors. Individuals who borrow from the savings-and-loan association may be charged interest rates of 8 percent for automobile and home-mortgage loans. The U.S. treasury may pay 3 percent to purchasers of its six-month treasury bill and 4 percent on a three-year treasury bond, while a near-bankrupt company must pay 21 percent on a six-month bank loan. *Different interest rates are paid on different financial assets.* Interest rates differ because of differences in the conditions of *risk, liquidity,* and *maturity* associated with a loan.

Risk.   Borrowers with high credit ratings pay lower interest rates than borrowers with low credit ratings. Lenders must be compensated for the extra risk associated with lending to borrowers with low credit ratings if they are to be competitive and earn a normal profit. If certain types of borrowers are known to be more likely not to repay a loan, that type of borrower will be charged a higher interest rate. The extra interest higher-risk borrowers are required to pay is called a *risk premium.*

Liquidity.   A financial asset that can be turned into cash quickly or with a small penalty is said to be *liquid.* People may be willing to hold savings accounts paying 5 percent interest when six-month certificates of deposits pay 10 percent simply

EXHIBIT 2   Interest Rates, Productivity, and Thrift

a. Increase in Productivity

b. Increase in Thriftiness

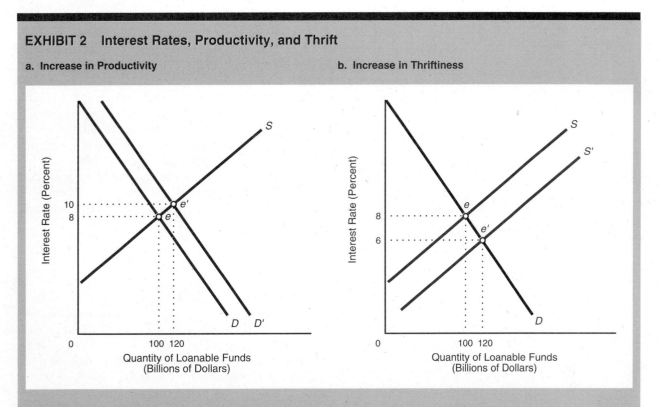

Panel (a) shows that an increase in the productivity of capital raises interest rates and panel (b) shows that an increase in thriftiness of the population lowers interest rates.

because the savings account can be turned into cash quickly and without penalty. The general rule is that interest rates will vary inversely with liquidity, *ceteris paribus*.

Maturity.   Interest rates will also vary with the term of maturity. A corporation borrowing $1,000 for one year may pay a lower rate of interest than if it borrows the same $1,000 for two years. If the credit market expects the interest rate on one-year loans to be 6 percent during the first year and 12 percent during the second year of a two-year loan, the interest rate on a two-year loan will be 9 percent. If $1,000 were invested for one year at 6 percent, it would yield $1,060 in one year; if the $1,060 were then reinvested at 12 percent it would yield $1,180. On the other hand, if $1,000 were invested at 9 percent for two years, it would also yield $1,180 at the end of the second year. Thus, $1,000 invested at 6 percent for one year with the proceeds invested for one more year at 12 percent is the same thing as investing $1,000 for two years at 9 percent. Roughly speaking, the two-year interest rate (expressed as an annual rate) will be an average of the one-year interest rates the credit market anticipates over the two years.

RENT

The differentiating feature of land and other natural resources is their relative inelasticity of supply. Land and natural resources are nature's bounty, and the quantity supplied is not affected by the price received as a factor payment.

The rent on land is a relatively small proportion—about 2 or 3 percent—of the total of all payments to factors of production. Even though land rents account for such a small portion of factor payments, relative inelasticity of supply can characterize productive factors other than land and natural resources. Because other types of factor payments resemble land rents, the study of rents for land and natural resources is much more important than the small percentages of factor payments to land suggests.

"Rents" paid for apartments, cars, tools, or moving trucks should not be confused with *economic rents*. "Rental payments" for the temporary use of a particular piece of property owned by someone else can be returns to land, labor, or capital. Apartment rent is a payment both to land (for the land on which the apartment building sits) and to capital (for the structure itself). Thus, the common term *rent* is simply a price or rental rate rather than a payment to a specific factor of production.

Pure Economic Rent

Exhibit 3 shows the determination of the competitive price—called rent in the case of land—for a fixed amount of land. The supply curve is completely inelastic: more land is not forthcoming at higher prices. The demand curve is like any other demand curve. It is determined by the marginal revenue product of land (*MRP*). The competitive rent paid to land is that price which equates the fixed quantity supplied with the quantity demanded. As such, the equilibrium price rations the fixed supply of land among the various claimants for the land. Exhibit 3 shows the case of **pure economic rent**.

> A **pure economic rent** is the price paid to a productive factor that is completely inelastic in supply. Land is the classic example of such a factor.

The main economic role of pure economic rent is to assure that the factors of production that are fixed in supply are used in the highest and best use. Pure economic rent in a competitive market serves as a guide to efficient resource use by rationing the available supply to the most efficient use. In Exhibit 3, the same quantity of land would be supplied, no matter what the price per acre ($0, $900, $1,400), as shown by the vertical supply curve. The quantity demanded, however, does depend on the price. At a zero price, the quantity demanded would be very large. At that zero price, prime agricultural land might be demanded for use as a garbage dump or as a junkyard for old cars. A higher price of land will cut off the various demands for the land that have a low *MRP*.

If the price is too high, the land will not be fully used, and there will be an excess supply. If the price is too low, the land may not be put to its best use. Land rents that are below equilibrium can allow land to be put to uses that yield relatively low *MRP*s. Efficiency requires that the price be set where the quantity supplied equals the quantity demanded of land. Although pure economic rent does not affect the amount of the fixed factor supplied to the market, it does ensure that the fixed factor is put to its best use.

When something is perfectly inelastic in supply, the price does not affect the quantity supplied. Taxing a good, service, or factor of production often reduces supply. Such is not the case for land. Land can be taxed without affecting its supply. This feature has made land a favorite object to tax.

Notice that changes in pure economic rent are completely demand-determined. Supply and demand analysis teaches that movement from the equilibrium price must be caused either by a shift in the demand curve or a shift in the supply curve. In the case of land, the supply curve is fixed. Shifts in supply are not possible. The price of

The pure economic rent that is paid to a productive factor does not affect the quantity supplied because the supply is perfectly inelastic.

EXHIBIT 3　Pure Economic Rent

Because the supply of land is fixed at 1,000 acres, the supply curve, *S* is perfectly inelastic. The equilibrium rent of $900 per acre at *e* gives rise to pure economic rents, since the land has no alternative uses. The entire rental payment is a surplus over opportunity costs. In this case, opportunity costs are zero. If the demand curve for land increases from *D* to *D'*, due to an increase in the demand for the product the land is used to produce, the economic rent will rise from $900 to $1,400 per acre at *e'*. Changes in economic rents are demand determined because supply is fixed.

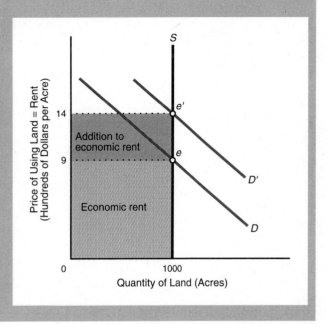

anything that is perfectly inelastic in supply must, therefore, be demand-determined. If the demand curve in Exhibit 3 shifts from *D* to *D'* due to technological advances in the use of the land or increases in the final demands for goods that the land is used to produce, competitive economic rents will be bid up.

Economic Rent and Other Factors of Production

Pure economic rents represent an extreme case of factor payment. At the other extreme is a payment to a factor that just equals its opportunity cost. A factor of production that is perfectly elastic in supply earns no economic rents because the factor is paid its *opportunity cost* (its earnings in its next best alternative use). For example, a small farmer must compete with other farmers and potential users of the land. If the farmer does not pay what the land could earn in its next best use, the land will be used elsewhere.

In between factors of production that are perfectly elastic in supply and those that are perfectly inelastic are numerous cases where factors of production earn some surplus return over their opportunity costs, or **economic rent**.

> **Economic rent** is the excess of the payment to the factor over its opportunity cost.

The major distinction between *economic rent* and *pure economic rent* is that a factor that earns pure economic rent has an opportunity cost of zero. A factor that earns economic rent has an opportunity cost that is positive but smaller than the payment to the factor.

The amount of economic rent earned by a factor depends on the perspective from which the factor is viewed. The corn land rented by an Iowa farmer does not earn economic rent—because the *individual* farmer is paying the land's opportu-

EXAMPLE 2

Babe Ruth and Economic Rents

The legendary baseball player, Babe Ruth, who played for the New York Yankees during the 1920s and early 1930s, was the highest-paid professional athlete of his day. Babe Ruth's remarkable batting skills helped him set batting records, many of which have yet to be surpassed. Babe Ruth's salary as a baseball player illustrates the concept of economic rent. Although Ruth earned more than the president of the United States, he would have been able to earn very little in his next best alternative. Ruth grew up in an orphanage and had little formal education. If he had not become a baseball player, he would have worked as a manual laborer. The difference between his actual salary and what Ruth would have earned outside baseball is the economic rent that Ruth earned. Babe Ruth often declared that he would play baseball for no salary; yet he was the highest-paid athlete of his day.

If Babe Ruth was willing to work for only a fraction of his baseball salary, would it not have been better to pay him, say, what he would have earned as a day laborer? The economic rent received by Babe Ruth ensured that he would be engaged in that activity that created the highest marginal product. If Babe Ruth had worked as a day laborer, millions of people would have been denied the entertainment and enjoyment gained from watching him play.

nity cost—but Iowa corn land *in general* does earn economic rent. In other words, *rents accrue to factor owners, not factor users.* The economic rent of John Smith as an engineer differs from the economic rent of John Smith as an engineer *for General Motors Corp.* Smith can earn $30,000 per year working for GM, $29,000 working for Ford, and $20,000 working in his best nonengineering job. Smith's economic rent as a GM engineer is $1,000 (the excess of his earnings over his opportunity cost); his economic rent as an engineer is $10,000 (the excess of his earnings as an engineer over his next best nonengineering alternative).

The prices paid to an attractive movie star, a late-night talk-show host, the winningest pitcher in major-league baseball, Iowa farm land, and offices in New York City surprisingly have much in common: a large fraction of the factor's income is economic rent. These factors receive payments in excess of their opportunity cost (their earnings in their next best alternative use). The factor payment assures that the factor is employed efficiently in its highest and best use. Paying one of the world's most talented tenors $50,000 per performance assures that he devotes himself to opera and not to working as a plumber. (See Example 2.)

Although people often resent individuals with inherited talents, rare skills, or good looks who earn substantial salaries, other factors as oil-drilling rigs, Iowa corn land, and high-speed computers earn similar rewards; namely, payments in excess of their opportunity costs. Although land rents account for only a small portion of total factor earnings, economic rents are paid to a wide variety of economic factors. Actors, professional athletes, musicians, surgeons, professors, television-repair persons, and even nobility can earn economic rents.

PROFITS

Economic profit is revenue above the firm's opportunity costs. Hence, it is the firm's economic rent.

Sources of Economic Profits

Firms have three basic sources of economic profits. The first source is the existence of barriers to entry in an industry or business. Such economic profits, called *monopoly profits,* are the basis of popular misgivings about profits. The second source of profits is provided by the dynamic and ever-changing nature of the economy. Such profits arise from the uncertain or risky nature of economic activity. The third source of economic profits is innovation. The individual (or group of individuals) who engages in risk taking and innovation is called an *entrepreneur.* For this reason, economic profits that are not the result of monopoly restrictions are often considered the reward to entrepreneurship.

Entry Restrictions.   As we have shown, monopolies can earn a profit rate in excess of normal profits. Moreover, unlike competitive profits, which are transitory in nature, monopoly profits can persist over a long period of time. In other words, under conditions of monopoly, businesses can earn revenues that exceed the opportunity costs of the factors they employ. In this sense, monopoly profits are like economic rents; for this reason, economists often refer to monopoly profits as *monopoly rents.* Monopoly profits can also be earned in a potentially competitive industry where entry is restricted by government licensing or franchising. If monopoly profits cannot be competed away by the entry of new firms, existing firms can enjoy monopoly rents.

Examples of monopoly profits due to entry restrictions are not hard to find. Cable-television franchises are granted by municipal authorities and by local governments. Once the franchise is granted, the cable-television company is protected by law from the entry of competitors. In many cities, taxicab drivers must be licensed, and entry into the business is controlled by the high cost of the license. Monopoly profits in the prescription-drug industry are protected by patents. Economies of scale also limit the entry of competitors into power generation, telecommunication services, and parcel deliveries.

Risk Taking.   If there were no entry restrictions, if people could predict the future perfectly, and if there were no costs for obtaining information about current market opportunities, there would be no economic profit. All businesses would earn normal profits. If an opportunity arose to earn economic profits, it would be anticipated and the free entry of new firms would serve to keep profits down to a normal return.

Unfortunately, no one can predict the future. Industry is unprepared for wars, changes in fashions and preferences, weather, and new inventions. Even with free entry, at any given time, some industries will earn economic profits and others will suffer negative economic profits. Unanticipated shifts in demand or costs cause economic profits to rise and fall. The majority of people wish to limit their exposure to the ups and downs of the economy; they want a steady income. Therefore, there must be rewards to those who are willing to risk the ups and downs of economic fortunes. Just as those who lend money to poor credit risks require risk premiums, so those who want to earn economic profits must be willing to bear risks.

Uncertainty turns the quest for profits into something resembling a game of chance in which there will be winners and losers even in the long run. All is not fair in love, war—and business. As in a game of chance, profits will average out to a normal return over all firms, but there will be a wide range of profit outcomes with a few big winners, a few big losers, and a larger number of intermediate winners and losers.

Economists have studied the relationship between the rate of profit and risk (as

Why Usury Laws Don't Necessarily Help the Poor

Earlier chapters discussed what happens when prices are not allowed to adjust to equilibrium. If wage rates are held above equilibrium, there will be unemployment of labor of that type. The same thing can happen in the case of interest rates. If interest rates are not allowed to adjust to their equilibrium rate, credit shortages or surpluses develop.

Usury laws place ceilings on interest rates charged by lenders. A particular state, for example, might pass a law stating that credit-card companies cannot charge more than 18 percent per annum or a law stating that no one can charge more than 15 percent interest. Such usury laws are in effect in many states and countries. Usury laws have considerable popular support because they claim to protect the poor from excessive interest rates charged by the rich. Insofar as the rich are the large lenders and the poor are the ones who borrow, usury laws are thought to redistribute wealth from the rich to the poor.

An interest-rate ceiling is said to be *effective* if the legislated rate is below the market interest rate that would have prevailed without the usury law. If the usury law sets the maximum interest rate at 20 percent, and the prevailing interest rate is 10 percent, then the ceiling is not effective (except in rare cases). If the ceiling is set at 15 percent and the market interest rate would have been 17 percent, the ceiling rate is effective.

If an interest-rate ceiling is effective, there will be an excess demand for loans. In the accompanying figure, an interest-rate ceiling of 7 percent creates a $50 billion shortage of loanable funds. Some people who wish to borrow at the ceiling rate cannot obtain loans. Lenders will be made worse off by the ceiling (at least those lenders that abide by the law) because they are able to lend fewer funds at lower interest rates. The borrowers who actually obtain financing at lower rates are made better off because they borrow at interest rates below market rates. Those shut out of the loan market lose the returns they could have gained if they had had funds for investment.

Interest-rate ceilings redistribute wealth from the unlucky (those who are unable to obtain financing at the ceiling rate) to the lucky (those who are able to get financing at the ceiling rate). Are the poor—whom the usury law is supposed to help—likely to be among the lucky few who obtain loans? When there is excess demand in credit

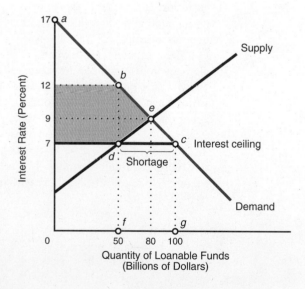

markets, lenders will engage in *credit rationing*. They approve loans to their best customers and to those who have the best credit ratings. The lucky few who obtain loans will be the rich. In fact, interest-rate ceilings typically force the poor to seek loans from disreputable lenders who are willing to disobey the usury law and lend at rates above the ceiling.

The policy conclusion: Usury laws or interest ceilings that are designed to help the poor often achieve the opposite result. It is better to let the market allocate scarce loanable funds. This is yet another example of the law of unintended consequences in economics.

---

measured by the variability of profits) and find (although there is some dispute on this matter) that profit rates are indeed higher in risky industries. Firms and industries that are subject to greater risk earn *risk premiums*. Entrepreneurs and stockholders earn higher average profits for bearing more risk than others.

Innovation. Blind luck cannot explain all economic profits. The economy is in a constant state of flux. New technologies are developing; consumer tastes are changing; new markets are being discovered. Resource availabilities are changing. To be an innovator requires ability, foresight, luck, and the willingness to bear risk.

Business history is replete with success stories of business geniuses—Henry Ford and the Model-T, Edwin Land and the Polaroid camera, Richard Sears and Alvah Roebuck and mass retailing, and Louis Marx and his children's toy empire. Ability and entrepreneurial genius explain the success of each of these companies. More was involved than a game of chance with an uncertain outcome. Yet even ability does not guarantee success. Many able people are trying to become the next Henry Ford or the next Sears or Roebuck, but few succeed.

The last three chapters surveyed how the economy determines wages, rents, interest, and profit—the payments to the productive factors of labor, land, capital, and entrepreneurship. The next chapter will turn from the functional distribution of income to the personal distribution of income and will address questions like: How equally or unequally is income distributed among persons? What has happened to the personal distribution of income? How does America's income distribution compare to that of other countries? What can be done about poverty?

Chapter Summary

**The most important points to learn from this chapter are:
Interest rates ration the scarce supply of loanable funds among all those who might demand credit. All factors may earn economic rent, if they earn more than their opportunity cost. Profit is a return to risk and uncertainty.**

1. Interest is payment for the use of capital. The supply of capital is the result of past saving and investment decisions. Interest rates are determined in credit markets, which make possible the specialization of savings and investment decisions. The structure of interest rates depends on risk, liquidity, and maturity. Interest rates are determined in the market for loanable funds by the demand and supply of credit.

2. Rent is payment for the use of land or natural resources. Pure economic rent is the payment to a factor of production that is completely inelastic in supply and is demand determined. Economic rent is the excess of the payment to a factor over its opportunity cost.

3. The sources of economic profits are: restrictions to entry into an industry, uncertainty, and entrepreneurship.

Policy Focus: **Usury laws (interest-rate ceilings) designed to help the poor achieve the opposite result. They make it difficult if not impossible for the poor to obtain credit.**

Key Terms

interest (p. 326)
credit markets (p. 326)
interest rate (p. 328)

rate of return on capital (p. 329)
pure economic rent (p. 332)
economic rent (p. 333)

Questions and Problems

1. Explain what would happen to interest rates if the productivity of capital goods increased.

2. This chapter emphasized that the credit market is another example of specialization in economics. Explain how this specialization works and its effect on economic efficiency.

3. If you borrow $10,000 from the bank and repay the bank $12,000 in one year, what is the annual rate of interest?

4. A new business owner remarked: "The bank ripped me off, they charged me 15 percent interest while they charged my biggest competitor only 12 percent." What would you tell the business owner?

5. Explain what would happen to interest rates if the thriftiness of the population decreased.

6. A company has four investment projects that yield returns of 20 percent, 15 percent, 10 percent, and 5 percent. Explain how the company will decide which of these projects to carry out.

7. Distinguish between *pure economic rents* and *economic rents*.

8. "Pure economic rents play no useful role in the economy because the supply of the factor in question is fixed. The factor will be supplied no matter what rent is paid." Evaluate this statement.

9. Why should the profit rate be higher in businesses that are risky? How do we measure risk?

10. What would be the logic of taxing pure economic rents as opposed to taxing other kinds of factor incomes?

11. Identify the sources of economic profits earned:
   a. by steel companies after the government imposed restrictions on competitive steel imports from foreign countries.
   b. in the coal industry after the Organization of Petroleum Exporting Countries quadrupled the price of oil in 1974.
   c. by a firm that developed a surefire method of increasing gas mileage.

12. The demand schedule for a particular acre of land is given in Table A. How much is the economic rent in equilibrium?

Table A

Rent	Quantity
$1,000	1/4
900	1/2
800	3/4
700	1
600	1 1/2

Doing Economics

There are many different kinds of "loans" in our economy. Student loans, car loans, and home mortgages are common loans from financial institutions to consumers. Savings deposits and certificates of deposit are the reverse. Corporate bonds (long-term) and "commercial paper" (short-term) are loans from investors to corporations. Government securities reflect borrowing by the government from whoever buys them. Using both direct surveys of nearby financial institutions and published data on financial markets from a newspaper, collect information about the interest rates and characteristics of a wide variety of kinds of loans on a particular day. How much of the variation can you explain by differences in risk, liquidity, and maturity? (Be sure to consider whether each loan is guaranteed or insured by the government.) For homogeneous loans such as those to the government, are long-term interest rates higher or lower than short-term rates today? What does that imply about the market expectation of future short-term rates on these loans?

Income Distribution and Poverty

C H A P T E R 1 8

CHAPTER FOCUS   Philosophers have argued for centuries: What is a fair distribution of income? Should society allow extremes of wealth and poverty? Is it society's role to ensure that no poverty exists? Although there is agreement that extremes in wealth and poverty should be avoided, there is less agreement about what constitutes the "right" distribution of income.

In every organized society, the government has a role in determining the distribution of income. Through its power to tax and to redistribute goods like education, public medicine, and welfare payments, the government affects how income is distributed. What families earn in factor markets determines the distribution of income before government action. If the government taxes the rich much more than the poor and distributes goods primarily to the poor, the actual distribution of income can differ significantly from the factor-market distribution.

Although there is general agreement that poverty is bad and that societies should avoid extremes of wealth and poverty, there is a lack of agreement on the appropriate balance. If the government were to take too much away from the rich to give to the poor, there would be little incentive to become rich. There would be less risk taking, less sacrifice for training and education, and less hard work.

After studying this chapter, you will be able to:

- Understand the Lorenz curve and how it measures the distribution of income.
- Explain the natural law, utilitarian, and Rawls views of distributive justice.
- Know the sources of inequality of income distribution.
- Discuss how to measure poverty and trends in poverty.
- Describe the negative income tax.

MEASURING INCOME INEQUALITY

Some people earn high incomes; others earn low incomes. If one person earned all the income, this would clearly be the most unequal distribution of income possible. If everyone earned exactly the same income, this would be the most equal distribution of income possible. The Lorenz curve measures where the actual income distribution falls between these two extremes.

The **Lorenz curve** measures the degree of inequality in the distribution of income.

> The **Lorenz curve** shows the percentage of all income earned by households at successive income levels. The cumulative share of households (ranked from lowest to highest incomes) is plotted on the horizontal axis and the cumulative share of income earned by the cumulative percent of households is plotted on the vertical axis.

The Lorenz curve measures the distribution of income.

Lorenz curves are normally plotted in *quintiles,* or fifths. A household in the top fifth of the income distribution earns more than at least 80 percent of all households. A household in the bottom fifth earns less than at least 80 percent of all households.

Exhibit 1 gives the U.S. distribution of income in 1929, 1970, and 1991. The table in panel (a) shows the cumulative percentage of households and their cumulative share of income. In 1991, the bottom fifth of households accounted for 4.6 percent of all income. The cumulative share of income of the first two quintiles (the lowest fifth and the second fifth) was 15.4 percent—the bottom 40 percent of U.S. households accounted for 15.4 percent of all income. The top 20 percent earned 44.3 percent of all income. The Lorenz curve is plotted in panel (b) of the exhibit and shows exactly the same information as the table.

If all households earned exactly the same income, there would be perfect equality in the distribution of income. Perfect equality is shown by a 45-degree line drawn through the Lorenz curve. If income were equal, the bottom 20 percent of households would receive 20 percent of all income, the bottom 40 percent of households would receive 40 percent of all income, and so on.

If the 45-degree line shows a perfectly equal distribution of income, then the more bowed the Lorenz curve is from the 45-degree line, the more unequal is the distribution of income. Changes in the income distribution between two points in time can be seen in movements of the Lorenz curve. The less bowed the Lorenz curve becomes, the more equal the income distribution becomes. Lorenz curves for different countries show which countries have a more equal distribution of income. (See Example 1.)

GALLERY OF ECONOMISTS

John Stuart Mill (1806–1873)

John Stuart Mill was one of the most influential social philosophers of the nineteenth century. He was educated by his father, James Mill, the famous British philosopher, economist, and historian. He rose to a high position in the East India Company and during his years there contributed to various periodicals and discussion groups. Mill's first important book, *A System of Logic*, was published when he was thirty-seven. His most important work, *Principles of Political Economy*, appeared in 1848. Mill married Harriet Taylor, a widow, with whom he had been in love for twenty years. He worked with his wife, and through her influence became interested in women's rights, socialism, social reform, and humanitarianism. Mill served as a member of parliament in the 1860s, after which he retired to France. Mill's famous *Autobiography* appeared one year after his death.

In his *Principles of Political Economy*, Mill wrote that society could distribute income according to whatever rules it thinks best. Mill recognized that various schemes could be used to distribute income, and that it was up to society to select that system that it felt was best. If society chose a system of private property, Mill felt that society should first eliminate "initial inequities and injustice." Resources should be divided fairly among people, so that "all might start . . . on equal terms." Individuals should be compensated by society for "injuries of nature" and less robust members should be given compensation that would place them on par with others. Once this initial "fair" distribution of resources was made, however, it should not be interfered with. "Individuals would be left to their own exertions and to the ordinary chances, for making advantageous use of what has been assigned to them." By not interfering, society would be insured that people would have the incentives to use their resources to best advantage.

The U.S. distribution of income has become more equal over the past half-century.

The Lorenz curves for the United States in 1929, 1970, and 1991 tell us that the U.S. distribution of income is far from equal—a not surprising result. More important, they tell us that, over the past half-century, there has been a distinct trend toward more equality. The 1991 Lorenz curve lies *inside* the 1929 curve. Households in the top fifth accounted for 54.5 percent of all income in 1929 but for a smaller 44.3 percent in 1991. The top 5 percent accounted for 30 percent of all income in 1929 but for a much smaller 17.4 percent in 1991. The *middle class* (households in the third and fourth quintiles) increased its relative standing most over the past half-century: its share of income rose from 33.1 percent to 40.4 percent.

SOURCES OF INEQUALITY

Households earn different incomes for a variety of reasons. Household income consists of two basic types—income earned from labor and from **wealth**.

> **Wealth** is the value of assets that represent claims to land and capital resources. Such assets yield returns in the form of dividends, interest, rent, or capital gains.

Examples of income earned from wealth are land rents, dividends, and interest payments. Three out of every four dollars earned in the economy are earned from

EXHIBIT 1

a. The U.S. Distribution of Income, 1929, 1970, and 1991

Quintile of Households	1929		1970		1991	
	Share of Income (percent)	Cumulative Share of Income (percent)	Share of Income (percent)	Cumulative Share of Income (percent)	Share of Income (percent)	Cumulative Share of Income (percent)
Lowest fifth	3.9	3.9	5.5	5.5	4.6	4.6
Second fifth	8.6	12.5	12.2	17.7	10.8	15.4
Third fifth	13.8	26.3	17.6	35.3	16.6	32.0
Fourth fifth	19.3	45.6	23.8	59.1	23.8	55.8
Highest fifth	54.5	100.0	40.9	100.0	44.3	100.0
Top 5 percent	30.0		15.6		17.4	

b. Lorenz Curves of the U.S. Income Distribution, 1929, 1970, and 1991

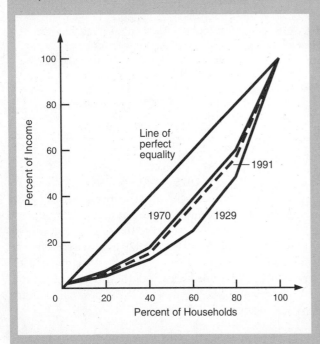

These Lorenz curves are drawn using the data in panel (a). The Lorenz curve measures the cumulative percentage of households (ranked from lowest to highest incomes) on the horizontal axis and the cumulative percentage of income earned by these households on the vertical axis. If all households earned the same income (perfect equality), the Lorenz curve would be a 45-degree line. The more the Lorenz curve is bowed away from the line of perfect equality, the greater is the inequality in the distribution of income. The 1929 and 1991 Lorenz curves show that for more than 50 years there has been a trend toward more equality in the U.S. distribution of income.

SOURCE: *Historical Statistics of the United States; Statistical Abstract of the United States*

Income is earned from labor and from wealth.

labor; therefore, the main income differences among households are due to different earnings from labor. However, earnings from wealth are more concentrated among a few households, and they contribute to the more extreme disparities between the rich and everyone else.

Differences in People and in Jobs

The chapter on labor markets emphasized that people earn different wages and salaries because jobs are different and people are different.

EXAMPLE 1

International Comparisons of Income Distribution

The accompanying figure shows the income distribution in four countries—Sweden, the United States, Hungary and Brazil. The figure illustrates two important facts about the distribution of income. First, income tends to be more unequally distributed in low-income countries than in rich countries. Brazil is representative of low-income countries, and it has an income distribution that is much more unequal than other countries. Second, demographic characteristics and government policy affect the distribution of income. Sweden has about the same average income as the United States, but Sweden's income distribution is more equal. Sweden's greater equality is explained by the greater homogeneity of the Swedish population and by the greater role of the Swedish state in redistributing income. Third, planned socialism equalizes income distribution. Although Hungary is relatively poor, its income is more equal.

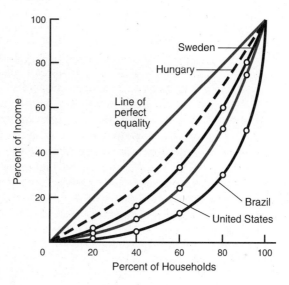

SOURCE: *The World Bank*

Compensating Differentials and Risk.   To encourage people to take unpleasant and dangerous jobs, *compensating wage differentials* must be paid. Sanitation workers earn more than bank clerks and often schoolteachers because of compensating wage differentials. Compensating wage differentials mean that some inequality is a consequence of occupational choice.

Uncertainty affects inequality. Different occupations involve different degrees of income risk. The wheat farmer, whose crops may be destroyed by blights and droughts, has a more uncertain income than the union employee with seniority. Individuals have differing attitudes towards risk. *Risk seekers* are more willing to incur risks than others, while *risk avoiders* are reluctant to take on risks. If society has only a small number of risk seekers, the distribution of income will be unequal. Some of those willing to incur risks will strike it rich and rise to the top income level. Other risk seekers will be less fortunate and fall to the bottom level. The vast majority—the risk avoiders—will be in the middle.

Ability and Human Capital. The chapter on labor markets emphasized that people divide into *noncompeting groups* in the labor market. Those who have the ability, talents, and skill to become doctors, lawyers, and physicists compete among themselves for such jobs. Those who have the athletic ability and determination compete among themselves for jobs as professional athletes. Those who have few skills compete among themselves for manual labor jobs. Even though one group earns substantially more than other groups, there is little crossing over from lower- to higher-paying groups.

Although natural ability accounts for some large earnings (such as for professional athletes and entertainers), they are not the most important source of income inequality. Mental and physical abilities are distributed much more evenly among the population than is income.

The skills, ability, and training we acquire through **human-capital investment** are much more important in explaining income unequality.

> **Human-capital investment** is the expenditure of resources on schooling, health, and training.

When individuals make human-capital investments, they acquire new skills and abilities that raise their productivity. They also enter into noncompeting groups. Only those persons who have invested in medical training and certification can compete for jobs as physicians.

Human-capital investments require the sacrifice of economic resources. Tuition must be paid; earnings must be sacrificed until a college degree is obtained; people must bear the personal and financial costs of moving to an area where jobs are more abundant. Human-capital investments also offer rewards. They qualify people for higher-paying and more satisfying jobs. Human-capital investment has its costs and benefits.

Income inequality due to human capital is partly the result of deliberate choice. Individuals choose between more money now (going to work after high school) and more money later (going to college and not earning money now). Individuals who place a high value on having money now are less likely to acquire human capital.

Income inequality due to human capital can be reduced by social policy. Some individuals are in a better position to pay for human-capital investment. If society bears the main cost of human-capital investment (in the form of subsidized public education), there will be less income inequality. Over the years (especially in the 1960s), various government programs have been used to increase the human capital of the poor and the young. These government programs (such as the Job Corps, Manpower Training and Development, and Neighborhood Youth Programs) all have been aimed at training disadvantaged persons to learn marketable skills.

Differences in human capital are more important for explaining income inequality than are differences in natural ability.

Chance and Inheritance

Chance. Accidents and poor health can unexpectedly destroy one's earning capacity. Choosing to train for a profession (such as teaching English or modern languages) in which there is an unexpected decline in demand can lead to low earnings. Likewise, having the good fortune to train for a profession (such as petroleum engineering in the 1970s) in which there is an unexpected increase in demand can have a significant positive and unplanned effect on earnings. Luck determines whether individuals earn the economic rents discussed in the preceding

Chance, Luck, and Earnings: The Vietnam Draft Lottery

No one has been drafted into the armed forces since 1972. Congressional authority to conscript expired in July 1973, largely as a consequence of the unpopular drafts of the Vietnam War. There were five draft lotteries during the Vietnam War period. Birth dates were drawn by lottery, and men with birth dates drawn early were the first to be drafted.

Sufficient time has passed to allow economists to determine the effect of being drafted for Vietnam upon earnings after return to civilian life. Earnings information from the Social Security Administration show that white male veterans in the 1980s earned 15 percent less than comparable nonveterans. Vietnam veterans were earning about $4,000 less per year than nonveterans in the early 1990s.

Why did service in Vietnam reduce lifetime earnings? One explanation is that people who served in Vietnam lost about two years of experience in the civilian labor market. In addition, some employers may have systematically avoided hiring Vietnam veterans.

Although earnings statistics clearly show that Vietnam veterans earn less, they are less clear on the effects of service in World War II on earnings. In fact, many studies show the effect of World War II service to be positive or at least neutral on lifetime earnings.

SOURCE: Joshua Angrist, "Lifetime Earnings and the Vietnam Era Draft Lottery," *American Economic Review*, 80 (June 1990): pp. 313–36.

chapter. Having the good fortune to be in the right place at the right time can have a marked impact on relative income. (See Example 2.)

Chance and luck have short-term effects on income distribution. Spells of unemployment pass; the entrepreneur who has good luck in one period has bad luck in the next. The other factors (ability, human capital, and occupational differences) have longer-run effects.

Inheritance and Wealth. Income from wealth is distributed more unequally than income from labor. **Personal wealth** is held in the form of assets (stocks, bonds, real estate, precious metals) that represent ownership of capital and land resources.

> **Personal wealth** (or net worth) is the value of one's total assets minus one's liabilities.

Stocks pay dividends and capital gains. Interest is earned on bonds. Rental income is earned from real estate. In the late 1980s, the top 1 percent of wealth holders in the United States accounted for 37 percent of all wealth. The top 10 percent accounted for about 68 percent of all wealth. Wealth is distributed more unequally than income. The top 10 percent of families accounted for 68 percent of all wealth, while the top 10 percent of families earned 34 percent of all income (Exhibit 2).

Wealth is distributed more unevenly than is income.

Wealth can be created either by its current owner or by previous generations. One important cause of the unequal distribution of wealth is *inheritance*, or the passing of wealth from one generation to the next. Wealth passes from one

EXHIBIT 2　Distribution of Wealth in the United States

Population Segment	Share of Total Wealth (percent)	
	1963	1989
Top 0.5 percent	25	29
Top 1 percent	32	37
Top 10 percent	64	68

Sources: *Statistical Abstract of the United States*, 1981, 453; *Federal Reserve Bulletin, Survey of Consumer Finances*, 1992.

generation to the next because of several factors. First, the children of the wealthy, in addition to inheriting assets, typically receive better educations and training and develop important social contacts. Second, the children of the wealthy tend to marry wealthy spouses.

Discrimination

Discrimination occurs when qualified individuals are blocked from entering higher-paying jobs and occupations or when workers with equal skills and qualifications performing the same tasks are treated differently on the grounds of race, sex, or creed. Individuals who are denied equal access to education, training, and union membership will be limited in their career opportunities.

During the postwar period, the median income of nonwhite households has averaged about 60 percent that of white households. The postwar trend in the ratio of nonwhite to white incomes has been upward, beginning at 51 percent in 1947 and rising to an average of 61 percent in the mid-1970s. The economic downturns of the late 1970s and early 1980s caused a slight reversal of the upward movement, so that in 1991, the ratio of median nonwhite to white income was 56 percent.

Substantial differences also exist in the average incomes of males and females. Women who work full time have had an average income equal to slightly more than 60 percent of male incomes since the late 1950s. Although the ratio has improved since 1947, the female/male income difference remained almost constant until 1980, after which it jumped from 60 percent to 70 percent of men's earnings.

Studies of discrimination conclude that about one-half of observed differences in earnings can be attributed to objective factors like schooling, training, or years of experience. In fact, women have on average about as much education as men.

The fact that not all of the difference in earnings can be explained by factors such as schooling or labor market experience suggests the presence of discrimination in labor markets. Labor market discrimination does not normally assume the form of discriminating between two workers (of different race or sex) performing the same job. In fact, there are federal laws guaranteeing equal pay for equal work. More often discrimination occurs when nonwhites or women are channeled into occupations regarded as "suitable" for them. This channeling may be the result of the employee's own preferences (a woman may want to be a schoolteacher and nothing else) or employer discrimination (an employer may be unwilling to hire women for assembly-line work). As a consequence, these "suitable" professions—say, nursing and teaching for women or bus driving for black males—become *crowded,* and the relative earnings of these professions are driven down. (See Exhibit 3.)

EXHIBIT 3   Why Women Earn Less

Empirical studies of male/female earnings differences seek to determine how much of the 30 percent to 35 percent female earning gap is explained by "objective" factors such as less education or less experience. Empirical studies find that the gap is not satisfactorily explained by objective differences among men and women. Researchers agree that a major cause of the female earning gap is the concentration of women into low-paying professions.

One study of the personnel practices of 373 firms found that in 60 percent of them, men and women were perfectly segregated by job title. In other words, there was not a single job type in those establishments to which the employer assigned both sexes. Another study, based on wage surveys, found extensive segregation in white-collar job titles within firms, despite the availability of women for each job title. If a firm hired men for a particular job title, it hired no women for that title. Since salary is usually set by job title, such segregation allows employers to create different pay scales for men and women. Sometimes, however, the disparity is not so subtle. Research has demonstrated that even within narrowly defined occupations, for which it is relatively certain that the jobs have similar duties, men earn more than women (see table below).

Average Weekly Wages for Women and Men in Selected Narrowly Defined Occupations, 1985

Occupation	Women	Men
Secretaries	$278	$365
Stock and inventory clerks	265	326
Bookkeepers, accounting and auditing clerks	263	341
Expediters	257	413
Machinists	257	408
Bus drivers	257	404
General office clerks	255	323
Cost and rate clerks	254	483
Sales workers, furniture and home furnishings	252	307
Grinding, abrading, buffing machine operators	251	330
Production inspectors, checkers, examiners	249	406
Traffic, shipping and receiving clerks	247	305
Electrical and electronic equipment assemblers	243	284
Packaging and filling machine operators	234	286
Printing machine operators	225	363
Molding and casting machine operators	222	347
Painting and paint-spraying machine operators	218	313
Solderers and brazers	216	287
Photographic process machine operators	208	297
Butchers and meat cutters	204	326
Bakers	202	301
Truck drivers, light	200	281
Slicing and cutting machine operators	192	303
Hotel clerks	191	279
Sales workers, apparel	168	281

Note: These figures are estimates of medians of usual weekly earnings of employed wage and salary workers who usually work full-time. They are based on data collected by the Bureau of Labor Statistics, but the medians have been computed on a basis that differs slightly from the method used to produce the official BLS estimates. Moreover, BLS does not officially issue figures on wages for groups of less than 50,000, while some of the wages quoted in the table are for groups of size 19,000–50,000. Wage estimates included in the table have a standard error of estimate less than 10 percent.

SOURCE: Barbara Bergmann, "Does the Market for Women's Labor Need Fixing?" *Journal of Economic Perspectives* 3 (Winter 1989): pp. 43–60.

DISTRIBUTIVE JUSTICE

Philosophers have debated **distributive justice** for centuries.

> Distributive justice is present when society's resources are distributed fairly among the members of society.

The first chapter explained the difference between normative economics (what ought to be) and positive economics (what is). Questions of distributive justice—is it fair to have extremes of wealth and poverty? What is a just distribution of income?—are matters of normative economics. Over the years, different philosophies have been formulated.

Natural Law

According to the natural-law philosophers of the seventeenth century, each individual has the right to the fruits of his or her labors. In terms of modern economic theory, this philosophy supports income distribution according to marginal productivity. When owners of the factors of production are paid their marginal-revenue product, factors that are more productive receive higher rewards. Their factors have contributed more to output; therefore, they deserve more income. Inequality is justified by the fact that some factors contribute more to output than others.

When income is distributed according to marginal productivities, the owners of factors of production are encouraged to raise the marginal productivity of their factors. Individuals are encouraged to invest in human capital; owners of capital are encouraged to save to acquire more capital; entrepreneurs are encouraged to assume risks. If factors of production were not paid in accordance with marginal productivity, there would be a tendency to reduce effort, to acquire less capital, and to take fewer risks. The end result would be that the economy would earn less income in total. (See Example 3.)

The natural law view of distributive justice is consistent with income distribution according to marginal productivity.

Most economists agree that there is a tradeoff between more equality and more income. If income were redistributed from those who possess high-priced factors of production to those less fortunate (by means of a high tax on the fortunate, for example), the efficiency of the economy would decline, and less income would be available for society as a whole. Redistributing income from the fortunate to the unfortunate is like transferring water from one barrel to another with a leaky bucket. In the process of making the transfer, water (income) is lost forever. If the leak is a slow one, then the costs to society of the redistribution are small. If the leak is large, then the losses of total income will be substantial. Society must decide whether the costs of greater equality are worth the price.

Critics of the natural-law philosophy point out that distribution according to productivity can be quite unfair. Some individuals will inherit factors with high productivities; others will be fortunate to be born with superb natural abilities; those who are lucky will receive high rewards.

Utilitarianism

Natural-law philosophy argues that inequality allows individuals to reap the fruits of their efforts and raises economic efficiency. The *utilitarian theory* argues, to the contrary, that an equal income distribution is better for society.

The law of diminishing marginal utility (studied in an earlier chapter) supplies the basic rationale for the utilitarian view of distributive justice. If people are basically alike, then the total utility of society will be greatest when income is distributed equally because everyone is subject to the law of diminishing marginal utility. If Jones were rich and Smith were poor, Jones would be getting much less utility from his last dollar than Smith. If income were shifted from Jones to Smith, Smith's utility would increase more than Jones' would decrease. Therefore, the

Christy Turlington: Fashion Model at $1.75 Million per Year

In 1991, 23-year-old high-fashion model Christy Turlington earned $1.75 million. Her 1992 earnings were twice this figure. Turlington is the face of Calvin Klein fragrances in the United States, and she represents Guerlaine in France. She represents on the side other cosmetic firms at $25,000 per day.

Asked by a major business magazine whether she wasn't embarrassed to earn so much, Turlington answered: "There's a tremendous amount of money made in fashion and cosmetics. When you think of my earnings as commission, it's not that ridiculous." Turlington went on to explain that no one would pay her $25,000 per day if she did not pull in enough business to more than cover the $25,000.

Rightly or wrongly, market economies pay the factors of production according to their contributions to revenues. The high earnings that anger many people are explained by the fact that that particular person adds a considerable amount to revenues.

SOURCE: James W. Michaels, "Should Anyone Earn $25,000 Per Day?" *Forbes,* May 25, 1992, p. 10.

In the utilitarian view, society's welfare is maximized when income is distributed equally.

decrease in inequality would increase the total utility of society. If indeed everyone is alike, then the total utility of society would be greatest when income is distributed perfectly equally among individuals.

The criticism of utilitarian theory is that people are indeed different. Some care little for money and worldly goods; others care a great deal. Therefore, it is not at all certain that the rich person gets less marginal utility from his or her last dollar than does the poor person. Critics also point out that it would be difficult to encourage effort and to persuade people to accumulate capital and take risks when income is evenly divided.

Rawlsian Equality

A different argument for equality has been proposed by philosopher John Rawls. Rawls maintains that a "fair" distribution of income is the distribution that people would want if they knew nothing in advance of their chances of being rich or poor. In reality, people start out in life with a pretty good idea of whether they will be rich or poor. If people did not know in advance whether they would be rich or poor, what type of income distribution would they prefer? According to Rawls, rational, self-interested individuals would act as risk avoiders. They would favor an equal distribution of income because they themselves might end up at the bottom of the ladder.

Because distributive justice is a matter of normative economics, there will be disagreement on what constitutes a fair distribution of income.

The policy implication of Rawls' notion of distributive justice is that government should step in to equalize the distribution of income. The government should push society toward that income distribution that people would favor if they did not know in advance who would be privileged and who would not be privileged. Without government action, an unequal distribution of income would prevail because the rich would not favor a change in the prevailing distribution of income. A change toward more equality could not take place voluntarily. It could only be accomplished by government.

GOVERNMENT POLICY AND INCOME DISTRIBUTION

People earn wages, rent, interest, and profit in factor markets. These earnings do not constitute the *final* distribution of income because government can redistribute income among households. If Jones earns $50,000 and Smith earns $10,000, and the government takes $20,000 from Jones and gives it to Smith, both end up with $30,000. Government alters the distribution of income through taxes and money transfers and through the distribution of valuable public services.

Exhibit 4 shows the effect of taxes and public services on the distribution of income. The Lorenz curve *before income and payroll taxes* is shown as curve *B*, and curve *A* shows the Lorenz curve *after taxes*. Income and payroll taxes equalize the distribution of income only slightly.

Household income consists of money income and **in-kind income**.

> **In-kind income** consists primarily of benefits—such as free public education, school-lunch programs, public housing, or food stamps—for which the recipient is not required to pay.

The Lorenz curve *C* shows the distribution of income *after taxes* and *after the distribution of in-kind income*. Comparison of Lorenz curves *A* and *C* indicates that the distribution of income becomes much more equal when all sources of income and in-kind benefits are included as income because the poor receive a larger share of public services than the rich.

Calculations of the effect of in-kind service are inexact. It is difficult to place an appropriate price tag on in-kind benefits. The recipient of a public service that costs $20 to produce (say, a vaccination in a public health clinic) may value that service at less than $20 or may even place a zero value on the service. Nevertheless,

---

EXHIBIT 4   The Effect of Income Taxes and Payroll Taxes and Benefits on the U.S. Distribution of Income

Income and payroll taxes have only a minor equalizing effect on the U.S. distribution of income, as shown by the difference between curve *A* (the distribution before taxes) and curve *B* (the distribution after taxes). The Lorenz curve *C* shows the distribution after both taxes and in-kind benefits are included. Comparing it with *A* shows that the inclusion of in-kind benefits makes the distribution of income more equal. The figures are for 1972.

SOURCE: Based on Edgar K. Browning, "The Trend Toward Equality in the Distribution of Net Income," *Southern Economic Journal* 43, 1 (July 1976): p. 914.

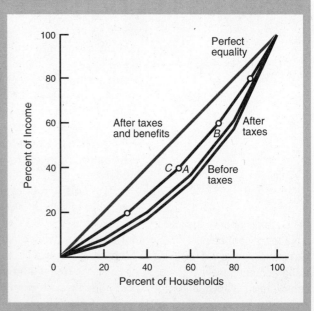

Public policy alters the distribution of income through the tax system and the distribution of in-kind income.

it is clear that the distribution of in-kind benefits to the poor has a more substantial impact on the distribution of income than taxes.

Each society must determine by how much government should alter the distribution of income.

POVERTY

The causes of poverty are the same as the causes of income inequality. The poor are poor because of their limited endowments of ability and skills, their limited amount of human capital, bad luck, discrimination, and (some might even argue) conscious choice. The poor are poor because their capacity to earn a "sufficient" income is, for some reason, impaired.

Defining poverty is not an easy task. Analysts will always disagree over what constitutes a poverty income. Some define poverty in terms of the amount of income necessary to provide a family of a certain size with the minimum essentials of food, clothing shelter, and education. This approach provides an **absolute poverty standard**.

An **absolute poverty standard** establishes a specific income level for a household of a given size, below which the household is judged to be living in a state of poverty.

Poverty can be measured either according to an absolute poverty standard or a relative poverty standard.

But is an absolute measure of poverty appropriate? Poverty can, after all, be relative. A person's sense of poverty depends on the incomes of others in the community. Thus, a person whose income is 10 percent of everyone else's may feel poor even if that income is above the level required to purchase the minimum essentials. Similarly, the American conception of poverty does not necessarily match that of other countries. The American poor would he considered wealthy in many Asian and African nations. Yet, they are still categorized as poor because they measure themselves against other Americans, not against the poor in other countries. A second approach to poverty, therefore, is a measurement in relative terms. A **relative poverty standard** might classify a household as poor if the household's income is, say, less than 25 percent of an average household's income.

A **relative poverty standard** defines the poor in terms of the income of others in some defined group.

If an absolute standard is used, increasing real living standards will push more and more families above the poverty line. According to a relative standard, poverty can be eliminated only by equalizing the distribution of income. If both the rich and the poor experience equal percentage increases in income, the poor will not have improved their relative position.

Trends in Poverty

Exhibit 5 shows the official statistics on the number of persons below poverty levels in the United States for the period 1959–1991. According to the absolute poverty standards of the U.S. government, the number of persons in households below the poverty level declined from 39.5 million to 34.1 million between 1959 and 1991.

EXHIBIT 5 Poverty in the United States

a. Persons Living in Households with Money Incomes Below Poverty Levels, 1959–1991

Year	Number of Persons Below Poverty Level (millions)	Percentage of Population	Poverty Income for Household of Four (dollars)
1959	39.5	22.4	2,973
1960	39.9	22.2	3,022
1965	33.2	17.3	3,223
1966	28.5	14.7	3,317
1968	25.4	12.8	3,553
1970	25.4	12.6	3,968
1972	24.5	11.9	4,275
1974	24.3	11.6	5,038
1976	25.0	11.8	5,815
1978	24.5	11.4	6,662
1979	25.3	11.6	7,412
1980	29.3	13.0	8,414
1981	31.8	14.0	9,287
1982	34.4	15.0	9,862
1983	35.3	15.2	10,178
1984	33.7	14.4	10,609
1985	33.1	14.0	10,989
1986	32.4	13.6	11,285
1987	32.2	13.4	11,611
1988	31.7	13.0	12,092
1989	31.5	12.8	12,675
1990	33.6	13.5	13,207
1991	34.1	14.1	13,682

Sources: *Economic Report of the President;* U.S. Bureau of the Census.

b. Characteristics of Poverty

Category	Percentage of Families Below Poverty Levels
Race	
White	17.8
Black	27.8
Hispanic	23.4
Size of family	
2 persons	8.2
3 persons	9.8
4 persons	10.1
5 persons	13.5
7 or more persons	32.3
Education of family head	
Less than 8 years	25.5
8 years	15.9
1–3 years high school	19.2
4 years high school	8.9
1 or more years college	3.6
Families headed by single mothers	45.0
Age of family head	
15–21 years	30.4
25–31 years	14.9
35–41 years	9.4
45–51 years	6.3
55–61 years	7.4
65 or more years	6.6
Did not work	23.4

Source: *Statistical Abstract of the United States.* These figures are for 1989.

Assistance According to Demonstrated Need or Negative Income Tax?

The Current Welfare System

The current welfare system is founded on the principle that public assistance should be granted primarily on the basis of need. For this purpose, the government has established a number of programs—such as Aid to Families with Dependent Children (AFDC), the food stamp program, public housing, and Medicaid—in which the amount of public assistance is based on family income. Welfare authorities determine what resources the family has (totaling the earnings of the family head, contributions from relatives, and so on) and grant public assistance on the basis of the perceived need. The greater the resources of the family, the less public assistance it receives. The welfare family is, therefore, discouraged from working because additional earnings—if detected by welfare authorities—will cause a reduction in public assistance. Proposals have been made to build better incentives into the existing system. In particular, it has been suggested that welfare recipients be permitted to keep a specified percentage of extra earnings without a reduction in existing public assistance.

Documenting needs and resources is costly, requiring an army of welfare workers to staff the program. Dollars that could have been devoted to public assistance are diverted into the bureaucratic costs of operating the system.

Exhibit 6 shows the effects of current government welfare programs. It shows that welfare programs more than halve the number of poverty households, although they are less successful in reducing poverty among black and hispanic families.

The Negative Income Tax

Economists have proposed that the current system be replaced by a **negative income tax**.

> A **negative income tax (NIT)** would supplement incomes by giving recipients who earn less than the *break-even income* an amount equal to a minimum acceptable income and subtracting a given percentage of each extra dollar the family earns on its own.

A negative income tax would work as outlined in Exhibit 7. First, the government would set a floor below which family incomes would not be allowed to fall. For purposes of illustration, Exhibit 7 sets this floor at $6,000 for a family of four. Second,

EXHIBIT 6 The Percentage of Persons Below Poverty Before and After Government Antipoverty Programs

Classification	All Households (percent)	White Households (percent)	Black Households (percent)	Hispanic Households (percent)
Income before taxes and cash payments	19.4	16.7	37.3	29.9
Income after cash payments	12.8	10.0	30.7	26.2
Income after cash and in-kind payments	8.9	6.9	21.2	19.4

Source: U.S. Bureau of the Census, *Current Population Reports*. The above data are for 1986.

EXHIBIT 7 The Negative Income Tax

a. Graph of Negative Income tax

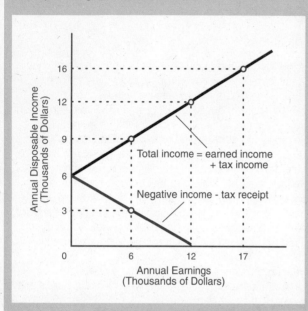

b. Table of a Negative Income Tax

Earnings (dollars)	Amount of Negative Income Tax Received (dollars)	Total Disposal Income = Earned Income + Tax Receipt (dollars)
0	6,000	6,000
3,000	4,500	7,500
6,000	3,000	9,000
9,000	1,500	10,500
12,000	0	12,000

Panel (a) is based on the data in panel (b). It illustrates a hypothetical negative income tax with a negative tax rate of 50 percent and a $6,000 floor income. A family with $0 income would receive $6,000 in benefits. Any family that earned more than $0 would have their $6,000 benefits reduced by $0.50 for every dollar earned. A family earning $3,000 would receive $4,500 in addition to the $3,000 they earned. Up to an income of $12,000, families would still receive some benefits in addition to their income (benefits equal to $6,000 minus $0.50 times the amount of income earned). At an income of $12,000, families would receive no benefits in addition to their income.

the government would set a negative tax rate. In our example, this negative tax rate is 50 percent.

As Exhibit 7 shows, a family earning $0 would be guaranteed $6,000. If the family earned income, it would be allowed to keep 50% of its earnings until it reached a break-even level of earnings.

The negative income tax offers two advantages over the existing system. First, it preserves work incentives up to the break-even income level by allowing low-income families to keep a prescribed portion of earnings. Second, it promises to do away with the costly bureaucracy of the existing welfare system. Administration of the negative income tax would be carried out by the same authority—the Internal Revenue Service—that administers the current personal-income-tax system.

As a percent of the U.S. population, the figure declined from 22.4 percent to 14.1 percent. Progress has been uneven, however. Large percentage declines were experienced in the 1960s; subsequently, the number of people below the poverty level remained roughly the same through the 1970s, rose with the severe recessions of the early 1980s, declined with the recovery of the mid-1980s, and rose with the recession at the outset of the 1990s.

A long-run decline in poverty rates is to be expected in a world of rising living standards. Rising real output pulls up the poor along with the rich. Similarly, as the figures show, the incidence of poverty remains quite sensitive to general economic downturns.

Who Are the Poor?

Exhibit 5, panel (b), provides a statistical profile of poor families in the United States. The poor tend to be disproportionately black and of Hispanic origin. They tend to live in large families; the family head seems to have little education, to be young, and to be female. Over 40 percent of the American poor are children under the age of 18. The poor tend to concentrate in central cities and in rural areas. Contrary to popular myth, a majority are working poor. Similarly, only 64 percent of the poor receive some form of cash assistance from government antipoverty programs.

These figures suggest that for the majority of families, poverty results from a limited earning capacity. Employment *per se* does not pull them out of poverty. Only in poor families headed by females do a majority of household heads not hold jobs.

The official poverty income standard does not provide for an attractive standard of living. The 1991 poverty income standard of about $13,500 for a family of four allowed for $3.00 per person each day in food expenditures. A Gallup poll asking Americans what poverty income would be required to make ends meet yielded a figure 50 percent larger than the official poverty standard.

Even the most avid supporters of the existing welfare system recognize its deficiencies. It destroys work incentives, it breaks up homes, it fosters one-parent families, and it has created a massive bureaucracy that the poor have come to regard as their enemy.

The negative income tax promises to do away with the bureaucracy and restore, at least partially, work incentives. It is for these reasons that most economists favor the negative income tax over the current system.

Income-maintenance programs offer only a short-run solution to the poverty problem. The long-run solution of poverty requires an attack on the fundamental sources of poverty—limited human capital and discrimination—that are responsive to government action.

To provide a long-run solution to the problem of poverty, government policy should aim at eliminating job-market discrimination and race and sex discrimination in education. Moreover, government policy should encourage the children of the poor to invest in human-capital resources. The problem is how to devise a policy that does not defeat itself by reverse discrimination or by making the tradeoff between equity and efficiency too costly. The intended effects of legislation can often differ dramatically from the actual effects.

In the 1960s and 1970s, the government embarked on a series of training programs (called the "Great Society" programs in the 1960s) aimed at providing education and training for the children of the poor. Many of these programs have been abandoned in recent years, but they represented an important social effort to eliminate the root sources of poverty.

This chapter examined the causes of inequality in the distribution of income and directed attention to the role of government in the redistribution of income to the poor. The next chapter will focus on externalities.

Chapter Summary

The most important point to learn from this chapter is:
The challenge to a society that wishes to have a more equal

distribution of income is to redistribute income without substantially reducing the total amount of income.

1. The distribution of income among households is determined first in factor markets. Household income is the sum of the payments to the factors of production that the household owns. The government may change this distribution of income through taxes and the distribution of public services. The Lorenz curve measures inequality in the distribution of income. It shows the cumulative percent of all income earned by households at successive income levels. If the Lorenz curve is a straight 45-degree line, income is distributed perfectly equally. The more the Lorenz curve bows away from the 45-degree line, the more unequal is the distribution of income. The U.S. distribution of income has become more equal since 1929.

2. The sources of inequality are: different abilities, discrimination, occupational differences, different amounts of human-capital investment, chance and luck, and property inheritance.

3. The distribution of income is made more equal by taxes and especially by the distribution of in-kind services.

4. There are different views on what constitutes distributive justice. Natural-law theory calls for a distribution of income according to the marginal productivity of the resources owned by households. The utilitarian school believes an equal distribution of income maximizes total utility. John Rawls calls for a distribution of income that maximizes the utility of the least-fortunate members of society.

5. Poverty can be measured either in absolute or relative terms. The absolute measure is based on an estimate of the minimum income necessary to allow a household to buy the minimum essentials. The relative standard measures poverty in terms of the household's location in the income distribution. According to government absolute measures of poverty, the number of those living below the poverty line has declined substantially since the 1950s. If in-kind payments are included in income, slightly more than 8 percent of Americans are living below the poverty line. Poor Americans tend to be nonwhite, poorly educated, members of households headed by females, and either very young or very old.

Policy Focus: **The current welfare system requires a large bureaucracy and discourages work effort. A negative income tax would be simpler to implement and could be set up to encourage work effort. Income-maintenance programs are a short-run solution to the problem of poverty.**

Key Terms

Lorenz curve (p. 340)
wealth (p. 341)
human-capital investment (p. 344)
personal wealth (p. 345)
distributive justice (p. 347)

in-kind income (p. 350)
absolute poverty standard (p. 351)
relative poverty standard (p. 351)
negative income tax (NIT) (p. 353)

Questions and Problems

1. Identify the following statements as issues of normative or positive economics:
   a. It is not right to have 15 percent of the population living under conditions of poverty.
   b. If the income distribution is made more equal by redistributive taxes, there will be a tradeoff between equality and efficiency.

2. Draw a Lorenz curve for absolute equality. Draw a Lorenz curve for absolute inequality. Explain in words what the absolute-inequality Lorenz curve means.

3. "If all people were the same, the Lorenz curve would be a 45-degree line." Evaluate this statement.

4. "The fact that women earn on average seventy percent of what men earn proves beyond a shadow of a doubt that there is sex discrimination." Evaluate this statement.

5. There are two views of the causes of poverty. One view says that the poor are poor through no fault of their own. The other says that the poor are poor through choice. Give arguments for each position.

6. Does the "leaking bucket" analogy apply to Rawls' view of distributive justice as well as to the utilitarian view?

7. Contrast the utilitarian view of distributive justice with the Rawlsian view.

8. Explain why under a relative poverty standard poverty would be more difficult to eliminate.

9. Would the work incentives be greater with a 25 percent negative income tax (NIT) rate or a 50 percent NIT rate? Rework Exhibit 6 in the text to illustrate your answer.

10. Consider two hypothetical societies. One consists of 8 risk avoiders and 2 risk seekers. The other consists of 5 risk seekers and 5 risk avoiders. Which society would have a more equal distribution of income?

11. If society dictated that all blue-eyed males can only work as janitors, what would happen to the incomes of blue-eyed males?

12. Joe wants goods today; Bill is more willing to wait until tomorrow for goods. Which one would be more likely to invest in human capital?

13. The official U.S. poverty-income standard is adjusted upward each year to account for the general increase in prices. If a family's income just keeps up with the poverty income over the years, what is happening to its relative poverty position?

14. Explain why the market value of in-kind benefits provided to the poor may be a misleading measure of their impact on poverty.

15. Education is distributed among the population more equally than income. What does this tell us about education and inequality?

Doing Economics

Based on the sources of income differences discussed in the text, develop a list of possible reasons for income inequality (willingness to work, innate ability, level of education, luck, riskiness or unpleasantness of job, discrimination, etc.). Ask at least ten noneconomic students and at least ten people who are not students, faculty, or staff to rank the importance of these factors on a scale from 1 (not important) to 5 (very important). In addition, ask them whether they think that most income differences between people are "just" in an ethical sense. Which factors do students think are most important? Are their significant differences between the responses of students and nonstudents? Can you explain these?

Issues in Economics

P A R T F O U R

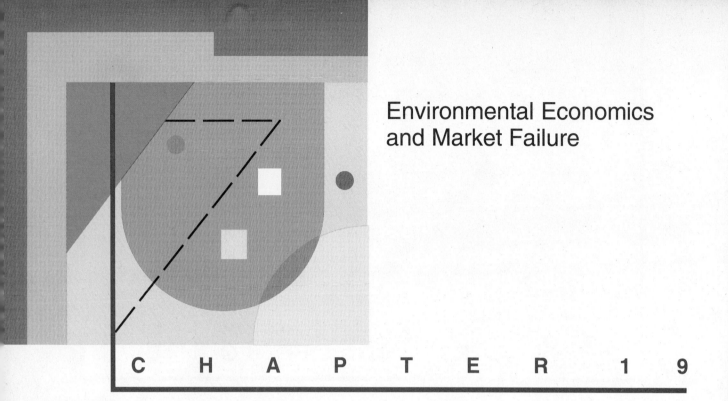

Environmental Economics and Market Failure

C H A P T E R   1 9

CHAPTER FOCUS   Everybody's business is frequently nobody's business. This chapter examines two types of market failure—externalities and public goods. Externalities are present when the person imposing costs on others (and society), does not have to weigh these costs in private cost/benefit calculations. Externalities include environmental pollution—the pollution of the air, the dumping of chemical wastes into rivers and the atmosphere, and the depletion of the ozone layer by the discharge of aerosol sprays.

People have strong views regarding the relationship between the economy and the environment. Many believe that news reports of oil spills, toxic waste dumping, and the killing of whales and dolphins indicate the failure of private economic decision-making. A more extreme conclusion, drawn from reports of global warming and a disappearing ozone layer, is that our lives or the lives of future generations are in danger. In both cases, people call for steps to be taken to preserve the environment. Perhaps it is necessary to return to a simpler life-style, with less production, fewer automobiles, and no aerosol spray cans.

Our knowledge is still insufficient to evaluate long-run environmental risks. Not knowing the risks, we must still select a course of action to ensure a reasonable environment for future generations.

After studying this chapter, you will be able to:

- Define externalities.
- Define the social optimum.
- List the three approaches to internalizing externalities.
- Determine optimal abatement expenditures.
- Differentiate between the regulatory approach and the incentive approach to environmental protection.

EXTERNALITIES AND MARKET FAILURE

When a factory dumps wastes into a lake, the people who use the lake for recreational purposes (swimming and boating) or economic production (fishing) will find that their level of satisfaction is directly reduced. The polluting factory does not pay a price for its dumping activities. Private markets do not necessarily penalize the factory for dumping waste. The waste-dumping factory may not be required to pay for the costs it imposes on the other parties. Pollution is an example of **market failure**.

> **Market failure** occurs when the price system fails to produce the quantity of a good that would be socially optimal.

Externalities are present whenever the actions of one agent have direct economic effects on other parties. Externalities represent one source of market failure, because they cause private parties (individuals and firms) to produce output levels that are different from the socially optimal level.

> **Externalities** exist when a producer or consumer does not bear the full marginal cost or enjoy the full marginal benefit of an economic action.

When externalities are present, market transactions between two parties have harmful or beneficial effects on third parties. The effects are *external to the price system and are not the outcome of mutual agreement* between all the interested parties.

Take the example of a factory that imposes external cleaning or health-care costs on the community by polluting its air or water. The unique feature of these costs is that they are not paid by the factory, but by economic agents external to the factory. These costs do not show up anywhere in the factory's accounting.

Externalities can benefit third parties as well. The person who pays for an education is not the only one who benefits from that education. Society benefits because education provides a common culture and language and encourages scientific progress.

External costs or external benefits cause **social costs** and **social benefits** to deviate from the private costs and benefits studied in earlier chapters. When externalities are present, private costs and benefits do not capture the full social costs or benefits of economic actions.

Ronald Harry Coase (1910–)

Ronald Coase founded the movement applying economics to the law. Born in England in 1910, he attended the London School of Economics and taught there from 1935 to 1951. Other teaching posts included the University of Buffalo (1951–1958), the University of Virginia (1958–1964), and finally the University of Chicago (1964–1982). He strongly believed that economics should always be discussed in the context of real-world problems. His famous contribution to economics, the paper, "The Problem of Social Cost," published in *Journal of Law and Economics* (October, 1960), is exceptional in modern economics because it uses no math. It is a fascinating blend of simple economics, real-world examples, and law.

Coase did not bow to conventional wisdom, and earned perhaps lasting fame by inspiring the Coase theorem. Before his work, economists followed A. C. Pigou (1877–1959), who argued that the party responsible for imposing external costs (such as polluters and smokers) should be the one restrained by government-imposed taxation. Coase challenged this view by showing that the damage could be dealt with more efficiently by the straightforward enforcement of property rights. He argued that as far as economic efficiency is concerned it does not make any difference whether the damaged party bribed the polluter or the polluter compensated the damaged party. In Coase's world, government action may only be needed if transaction costs are too high for private parties to carry out an agreement. To Coase government's main role is to enforce property rights, whether those rights belong to the polluting party or the damaged party.

Coase received the Nobel Prize in economics in 1991.

Social costs are the sum of private costs and external costs.

Social benefits are the sum of private benefits and external benefits.

Externalities are present when private costs or benefits deviate from social costs or benefits.

If there are no external costs or external benefits, private and social costs are the same and private and social benefits are the same. The polluting factory, however, imposes external costs on the community that do not enter into the factory's private costs. Hence, the factory's social cost exceeds its private cost by the amount of the external cost.

Externalities cause the economy to produce output levels either above or below the socially optimal levels. Private firms will produce "too much" of goods and services that are produced with significant external costs. Private firms will produce "too little" of goods and services that are produced with significant external benefits. The following discussion concerns social inefficiencies due to external costs.

If economic agents must pay for the costs imposed on others, they will take into account these costs in private cost/benefit calculations. In the late 1980s evidence accumulated that chlorofluorocarbons (CFBs), used in aerosol sprays such as deodorants, contribute to the depletion of the ozone layer that protects the earth from the sun's harmful ultraviolet rays. Only a handful of firms produce CFBs. In early 1988 the major producer ceased producing CFBs, largely to avoid the possibility of facing multi-billion dollar lawsuits.

An externality can be internalized in three ways:

1. by redefining property rights,
2. by making voluntary agreements, or
3. by taxing the party causing the externality.

Redefining Property Rights

A simple example of the effects of internalization would be the merger of two factories located on a river. Prior to the merger, the downstream factory has to pay water-purification costs because the upstream factory is polluting the water. After the merger, the external costs imposed on the downstream factory become *internal costs* to the merged firms. Pollution costs will now be considered in private cost/benefit calculations by both factories. The merging of two factories involved the redefining of **property rights**.

> **Property rights** specify who owns a resource and who has the right to use it.

When the two factories located on the same river merged, the owners of the downstream factory acquired property rights in the polluting factory. Poorly defined property rights are an important cause of externalities. When it is unclear to whom property rights belong—such as who owns the air people breathe, the fish in the seas, or the water of a river—externalities usually result.

If the property rights for a resource are held by the community, but each person has free access to the resource, the resource will likely be exploited and abused. Fishing businesses will overfish ocean waters; factories will overpollute the air.

If private property rights for the resource could be established, most externalities would disappear. If hunting land that had been commonly owned becomes privately owned, the private owner can charge hunters fees to hunt game on that land. The rational private owner would set fees high enough to prevent game from being depleted. The same principle could be applied more broadly. If one person in the community were somehow given ownership of the community's air, that person would have the legal right to charge the polluting factory for its use of the air. Every month, the polluting factory would get a bill from the owner of the community's air. If one country held the property rights to the ocean's fishing grounds, it could charge fishing businesses from all countries for their use of the ocean and could prevent the depletion of reserves of fish.

In many cases, it is not easy to eliminate externalities by changing property rights. When persons take private ownership of hunting land, it is relatively easy and inexpensive for them to erect fences, control access, and charge hunters appropriate fees. In other cases, it is difficult if not impossible to define and enforce private property rights.

Air pollution is an example of the problems caused by poorly defined property rights. The ownership rights to clean air are too poorly defined to allow an "owner" of clean air to sue polluters. Even if some entity could be assigned the ownership of air, the "owner" would have to know how much pollution each car or factory has emitted. The owner would then have to be in a position to collect a fee from each polluter equal to the marginal external cost, which the owner would have to be able to calculate. The amount of information the private "owner" of air would have to be able to collect to put appropriate private price tags on air is clearly excessive. A similar problem would face the person who had been assigned ownership of the ocean's fish. The difficulty of redefining private property rights in a meaningful way limits this approach to internalizing externalities.

Poorly defined property rights create externality problems.

Redefining property rights to internalize externalities is difficult because it is costly to define and enforce property rights.

Voluntary Agreements

Voluntary agreements between those that create the externality and affected third parties are a second means of internalizing externalities. The above example of a merger of two factories on a river illustrates how voluntary agreements internalize externalities. The two firms agreed to merge. Each firm had clear property rights to their own property, and the merger took place through the legal system. With well-defined property rights, voluntary agreements negotiated through the legal system can internalize external costs.

The proposition that voluntary agreements can handle some externality problems is called the *Coase theorem*, after Ronald H. Coase. (See Gallery of Economists.) Coase argued that external costs and benefits can be internalized by negotiations among affected parties. Coase gave the example of a rancher whose cattle occasionally stray onto a neighboring farm and damage the neighbor's crops. If the rancher were legally liable for the damage to the farmer, then private bargaining would result in a deal between the rancher and the farmer in which the farmer would be paid for the increased cost of growing crops imposed by the straying cattle. These extra costs would induce the rancher to reduce the size of the herd (or build better fences) and the potential externality would disappear.

Likewise, the externality could be internalized even if the rancher's cattle had the legal right to stray onto the farmer's land. The farmer in this case would make a deal in which the rancher would agree to reduce the size of the herd or build a fence in return for a cash payment from the farmer. Again, when a price tag is placed on the externality, it disappears. In either case, the same amounts of crops and cattle would be produced. The social effect is the same, but the income-distribution effects are quite different. In the first case, the rancher transfers income to the farmer. In the second case, the farmer transfers income to the rancher. The distribution of income depends on who has the property rights.

Whenever externalities are present, perfect competition does not lead to economic efficiency. The competitive firm produces too much output when it imposes external costs. The competitive firm produces that level of output at which marginal *private* costs and marginal *private* benefits are equal; it ignores the external costs of its actions. At the profit-maximizing level of output, marginal social costs *exceed* marginal social benefits. Society as a whole would be better off if the competitive firm reduced its output to the point where marginal social costs and marginal social benefits are equal. These propositions are illustrated in Exhibit 1, which shows the optimal level of output for a competitive firm when external costs are present.

> The Coase theorem says that externalities can be internalized by voluntary agreements.

> Externalities cause production to deviate from social efficiency.

INTERNALIZING EXTERNALITIES

If external costs are included in calculations of private gain, competitive economic decisions will push the economy to produce the social optimum of goods and services. **Internalization** occurs when private price tags are placed on externalities.

> **Internalization** is the process of putting private price tags on externalities.

Under what conditions can externalities be dealt with by means of voluntary agreements? The most important requirement is that the number of individuals involved in a voluntary agreement be small to keep bargaining costs down. The factory-merger example involved only two negotiating parties. If it had been

EXHIBIT 1 Perfect Competition with External Costs

When external costs are present, competitive firms produce too much output. They produce at the output level where marginal private costs equal price, not where marginal social costs equal price.

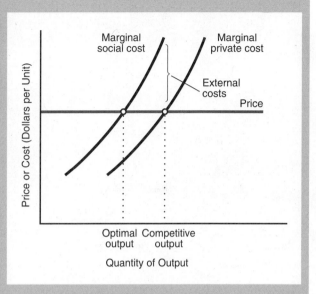

Government Action

necessary to merge not two but four factories located on the river, the agreement would have been more difficult to reach. If bargaining costs were high, the other downstream factories would have an incentive to sit on the sidelines and hope that the other downstream factories would arrange the reduction in pollution by the upstream factories.

Government Action

Governments can internalize externalities by imposing corrective taxes. Exhibit 1 demonstrates that competitive firms produce "too much" output when external costs are present. By considering only private marginal cost, the firm is led to produce at an output level above the social optimum.

Governments have the power to levy taxes on the production of goods and services, and these taxes become part of the private costs of the firm. If a tax equal to marginal external cost could be placed on the firms that cause external costs, the externality would be internalized. The firm would consider not only the private marginal cost but also the external marginal cost (which is paid in the form of a tax).

Exhibit 2 shows how this tax would be structured. Consider a competitive cotton farm; the pesticides it uses harm the environment. Thus, the marginal social cost, MSC, exceeds the firm's MC. Without government action, the firm will produce q_2 units where $MC = P$. The optimal level of output is only q_1 units. If a government follows the optimal policy, it would impose a tax of ab units in Exhibit 2. The firm must now take into account the costs imposed on others and will, accordingly, reduce production to the efficient level where marginal social costs equal marginal social benefits.

The use of taxes to internalize externalities is especially appropriate when private bargaining costs are high and voluntary agreements cannot be reached. When the government steps in with corrective taxes, the government in effect takes on the bargaining costs of the private parties. If the externality affects many people, it is cheaper to use collective or government action to internalize the externality. If

Government can internalize externalities by imposing a tax equal to the marginal external cost.

EXHIBIT 2 Internalizing Externalities with a Tax

A tax of *ab* per unit will cause the firm to produce where *MSC* = *P* instead of *MC* = *P*.

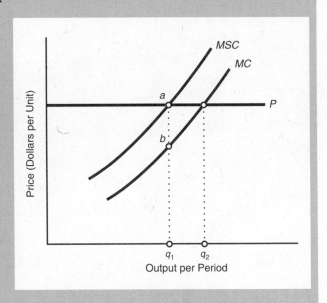

external costs are imposed on thousands of individuals, voluntary agreement among the affected parties is unlikely.

Externalities do not automatically require government action. Some externalities can be dealt with on a private basis through voluntary agreements among affected parties. In fact, in some cases private markets come up with inventive solutions to externalities. Other externalities impose costs that are too low to warrant government action. Both government action to correct externalities and externalities themselves can impose costs on individuals. Both the market mechanism and government action have advantages and disadvantages. There are, therefore, few hard-and-fast rules on whether the government or the market should solve the problem.

PUBLIC GOODS

One of the most important functions of government is to provide **public goods**. Competitive markets will fail to supply or will undersupply public goods because they are unprofitable. Thus, public goods and services are provided by the government. Goods and services such as public schools, public parks, public roads and bridges, national defense, police protection, or public health services are generally made available to the public at no explicit charge and are financed by taxes (although in some instances governments charge for government services, as in the case of postage or admission fees to public parks).

Public goods are goods or services with the following qualities:
1. the provision of the public good to one person also gives the good to everyone in the same neighborhood; and
2. no one in the neighborhood can be excluded from enjoying the benefits of the good or service.

Nonrivalry

If a dam is built that protects a particular geographic area from flooding, everyone who lives in the protected area benefits. Moreover, the fact that one person's house is protected by the dam does not reduce any other house's protection. Residents of the area are not *rivals* for flood protection. Similarly, viewers of television programs are not rivals. One person can view a program without affecting another viewer's enjoyment.

If the government builds an antimissile system that substantially reduces the likelihood of nuclear attack by a foreign nation, everyone in the protected geographical area benefits. The protection of one person's life and property does not reduce the protection enjoyed by others.

Public goods can be contrasted with ordinary private goods such as food and drink, cars, houses, shoes, dresses, and medical services. Different consumers are indeed "rivals" for private goods. A hamburger eaten by one person cannot be eaten by someone else; a house occupied by one family cannot be occupied by another.

Some goods can have public or private characteristics depending on the circumstances. For example, one person can enjoy an uncrowded movie without reducing another person's consumption, but a crowded movie or sporting event is like a private good because each additional spectator displaces another possible spectator. The problem of rationing the available supply of most private goods is solved by charging prices; those who consume the good place a higher value on it than those who do not consume the good.

Nonexclusion

The second characteristic of public goods is that people cannot be excluded from using them once they are provided. Excluding people from using the good (once it has been produced) is too costly. National defense and flood control are cases in point. Once a missile system has been put in place, it is not possible to exclude anyone in the protected area from being protected. Once a flood-control dam has been built, it is not possible to exclude homeowners in the protected area from benefiting.

In the case of private goods, it is easy to exclude people (who do not pay for the good) from using the good. The grocery store will not allow you to take out groceries that have not been paid for (and it has security personnel to back this up). The gas-station attendant will not pump gas for nonpayers.

It should be noted that goods can have both private- and public-good characteristics. Nonrival goods such as cable television or an uncrowded movie are provided as private goods because nonpayers can be excluded quite simply. In order to be a public good, the good must possess both characteristics of public goods. An uncrowded movie theater sells tickets on the private market—even though one person attending the movie does not prevent another person from enjoying the movie—because nonpayers can easily be prevented from viewing a movie.

Public goods are characterized by nonrivalry and nonexclusion.

Free Riders

A public good can be provided privately only if beneficiaries finance it with voluntary contributions. Since those who benefit from the good cannot be excluded from its use whether or not they are paying for it, people need not contribute. In the case of public goods, there will be a strong temptation not to pay. A person who enjoys the benefits of a good without paying is a **free rider**.

> A **free rider** is anyone who enjoys the benefits of a good or service without paying the cost.

When some of the beneficiaries act as free riders, the private revenues voluntarily contributed to pay for a public good will be less than the social benefits the good generates—in which case, the good will not be produced at all or will be underproduced by the private market. Public television is a case in point. Noncontributors cannot be prevented from viewing public-television programming. Despite frequent public appeals against free riding, few public television stations are self-supporting. Instead, they require government assistance to survive.

Free riding makes it difficult for private markets to provide public goods.

The free-rider problem confounds the production of public goods. Voluntary agreements will work if free riding is not excessive. Voluntary cooperation is more likely the smaller the group, the more often collective decisions are made, and the greater the gain from adopting cooperative behavior.

Examples of cooperative behavior abound. Some people make voluntary contributions to civic clubs for extra police protection; volunteers work to improve the community; private roads are built that connect several families to public roads. But if the group is large, if collective decisions are made infrequently, and if the individual gains little by cooperating, free riding will be more prevalent.

Example 1 classifies a number of goods as private or public goods.

EXTERNALITIES AND ENVIRONMENT

Externalities are present whenever social costs or benefits differ from private costs or benefits. When one firm imposes external costs on a second firm, when one neighbor's rundown house disrupts the enjoyment of the neighborhood by other home owners, you have an externality. Environmental pollution is a particularly important form of externality because it imposes external costs broadly on the community. Environmental pollution is a form of externality that is typically hard to deal with by redefining property rights and voluntary agreements. Property rights to the atmosphere, rivers, lakes, and oceans are difficult to define, and the number of people affected is large, making it difficult to negotiate agreements. Hence, in the area of environmental pollution government looms large.

Optimal Abatement

Modern production and consumption patterns impose significant **waste-disposal costs** on society. When firms produce goods and services, wastes in the form of air pollutants, toxic chemicals, solid wastes, and noise are created. Wastes are also created by modern consumption; we as consumers produce wastes (automobile exhausts, noise, solid wastes). Wastes must be disposed of either in the ground, in water, or in the air. (Someday, they may be disposed of in outer space.)

> **Waste-disposal costs** are the costs of disposing of the residual materials generated by production and consumption.

EXAMPLE 1

Classifying Selected Goods as Private Goods or Public Goods

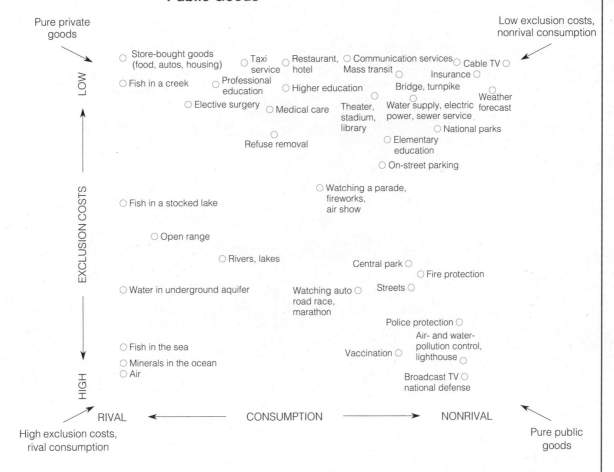

Pure private goods, in the upper left corner, are characterized by low exclusion costs (free riders can be excluded easily) and by rival consumption. Pure public goods, in the lower right corner, are characterized by high exclusion costs (free riding can't be prevented) and by nonrival consumption (one person's consumption of a good does not detract from another's consumption of it). Goods in the other two corners meet only one of the two characteristics of a public good. In the lower left corner, goods are characterized by high exclusion costs but rival consumption. In the upper right corner, goods are characterized by nonrival consumption but low exclusion costs.

SOURCE: E. S. Savas, *Privatizing the Public Sector* (Chatham, NJ: Chatham House Publishers, Inc., 1982), p. 34.

Waste-disposal costs are real opportunity costs. If public or private resources are devoted to pollution prevention (scrubbers on smokestacks, for example), these resources are not available for other uses. If individuals purchase unpolluted water to avoid drinking health-damaging polluted water, they also incur opportunity costs. If the health of individuals in the community deteriorates because of

EXHIBIT 3 Optimal Pollution Abatement

This figure shows how the optimal amount of pollution abatement is determined. The marginal-social-benefit curve is downward-sloping (people place a higher value on the first units of abatement). The marginal social cost of pollution abatement is assumed constant. The optimal amount of abatement is quantity *a* (where marginal social costs equal marginal social benefits). Point *b*, the total prohibition of pollution, is not optimal because the marginal social benefit (zero) is less than the marginal social cost.

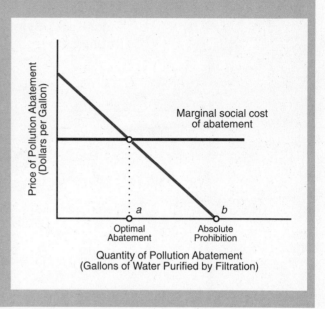

pollution from toxic-waste dumps, there are costs to the individual and community, be they explicit cash outlays or less visible opportunity costs.

Modern societies produce vast quantities of wastes, and each society must decide how much of its resources to devote to pollution abatement. Cost/benefit analysis provides, at least in principle, a practical guideline. Exhibit 3 shows the marginal social costs and marginal social benefits of different quantities of resources devoted to pollution abatement—in this case, the number of gallons of water purified through filtration procedures. For simplicity, we let the marginal social cost of each successive unit of abatement be constant. Marginal social benefits decline with more abatement because society values the first units of abatement more highly than subsequent units.

As Exhibit 3 shows, a choice must be made among the different amounts of pollution abatement. At one extreme, absolutely no resources are devoted to abatement. At the other extreme, resources are devoted to abatement to the point where additional expenditures on abatement yield no further marginal social benefit. The optimal level of abatement occurs when the marginal social cost of an extra unit of abatement equals the marginal social benefit. If additional abatement exceeds this optimal level, the extra benefits to society fall short of the extra opportunity costs to society.

Exhibit 3 demonstrates why society should not aim for the total elimination of pollution. To totally eliminate pollution, society would have to devote scarce resources to pollution abatement until the marginal social benefits are driven down to zero. The last dollar spent on pollution abatement yields zero benefits but has a positive marginal cost to society. The last dollar uses up scarce resources that could have been devoted to producing other things; yet it yields no marginal benefit to society.

The theoretical standard for evaluating pollution-abatement programs used in Exhibit 3 has a number of practical problems. First, it is very difficult to know the exact costs and benefits of various pollution-abatement activities. Some costs and benefits occur only over time. Measuring the full costs even at one point in time is

Regulation or Markets to Protect the Environment?

Throughout the world, societies rely on government action to deal with pollution. In the United States, a number of state, local, and federal agencies are involved in pollution control. The most important federal agency is the Environmental Protection Agency (EPA), which, since 1970, has been charged with regulating pollution activities, acting through the states and through its own authority. The EPA derives its authority through a number of congressional acts (the Clean Air Act, the Water Pollution Control Act, the National Environmental Policy Act, the Toxic Substances Control Act, and many other environmental acts).

The Regulatory Approach

To enforce federal environmental laws, the EPA usually follows a *regulatory approach*. The EPA specifies what each individual waste discharger must do with respect to air, water, and noise pollution. The EPA sets ceilings on the amounts of pollutants that can be discharged and requires that the discharger meet these ceilings by a specified date using the best practical (or best available) pollution-control technology. The EPA issues permits to each pollution source, and the permit specifies how much of each pollutant can be discharged and a time schedule for pollution reduction.

Aside from enforcing its directives, the most basic problem facing the EPA is to decide how much pollution to allow. Environmental laws are not always specific. Cost/benefit analysis shows that the absolute prohibition of pollution discharges is not a reasonable social goal. This policy would cause all pollution-abatement activities to be carried out to levels where marginal social costs far outweigh marginal social benefits. The resource costs to society of this action would be prohibitive.

Devising direct controls that lead to optimal abatement policies is difficult. The EPA sets discharge limits without reference to the marginal costs and benefits of its actions. Yet there is a growing realization that environmental policies (which are already costly) require a balancing of costs and benefits. For this reason, the EPA has experimented with economic-incentive-based environmental policies.

Market Solutions

Exhibit 2 demonstrated that governments could internalize externalities by imposing per-unit taxes or charges equal to marginal external costs. This principle applies to optimal pollution abatement. The government could impose fees—called *effluent charges*—for the discharge of pollutants that equal the marginal external cost of the pollutant. Such effluent charges would cause the polluting firm to consider the external costs of pollution in its private economic calculations. Establishing optimal effluent charges is difficult because estimating the marginal external costs of each pollution-discharge activity is difficult.

The EPA has experimented with a number of "market solutions." In one program, firms or groups of firms are allowed to create pollution-abatement programs (which they presumably do at the least cost to themselves) subject to a total-emissions limit assigned to the plant or region. If several firms are involved, they are allowed to trade pollution rights among themselves and even to buy and sell rights to pollute. Another EPA program permits new pollution sources to operate if they are able to obtain an offset (a reduction in pollution discharges) from existing firms. (See Example 2.)

The basic notion behind these incentive schemes is that the costs of pollution abatement will be reduced if dischargers are allowed to make their own decisions. Firms that can reduce discharges cheaply will buy pollution rights from firms that can only reduce emissions expensively. Even if the end result is not an optimal balance of costs and benefits, at least the costs of pollution control will be reduced under such programs.

The market solution ensures that pollution abatement occur at a lower cost of society's resources. Hence, it is preferable to the regulatory approach.

EXAMPLE 2

Trading Pollution Rights

In December 1990, in an unprecedented arrangement, Metallized Paper Corporation of America bought pollution rights from USX's Clairton Works and from Papercraft Corporation in Allegheny County, Pennsylvania. Metallized Paper paid USX $75,000 for the right to emit 75 tons of pollution per year, purchased 32 tons from Papercraft, and received an additional 500-ton donation from USX. This sale of pollution rights was legal under the Federal Clean Air Act. Both USX and Papercraft Corporation possessed rights to emit a certain number of tons of pollutants into the environment up to a limit determined by the Environmental Protection Agency. By selling these rights, both agreed to cut back on their pollution emissions by the number of tons sold.

The sale was sanctioned by county and state officials, who had spent two years persuading Metallized Paper to locate in Allegheny County. Various environmental groups protested the sale because the company's plant would emit chemicals, known as volatile organic compounds, that contribute to the formation of ozone. State officials, however, defended their action on the grounds that the overall amount of pollution would not increase. Rights to pollute were merely traded from companies that could reduce their emissions cheaply to one that required significant expenditures to limit pollution.

SOURCE: "Trading of Pollution Rights Draws Fire," *Christian Science Monitor,* December 4, 1990.

difficult because of the large number of people and things that are affected to varying degrees. Second, waste-disposal problems involve complicated physical, biological, and chemical interactions with the total environment. A particular abatement procedure increasing water purity may shift discharges to the atmosphere. Third, there are income-distribution effects associated with pollution abatement. Someone in society must pay for pollution abatement. Who should receive the benefits and who should bear the costs of pollution abatement? Should private firms pay? Should only affected individuals pay? Should the general public pay?

Chapter Summary

**The most important point to learn from this chapter is:
Externalities may justify government action if private parties have difficulties placing price tags on external costs and benefits; the appropriate policy response for the government is to create a market for externalities either with taxes, subsidies, or privately priced permits.**

1. Market failure occurs when the price system fails to produce the socially optimal quantity of a good. Two examples of market failure are externalities and public goods. Externalities occur when marginal social costs (or benefits) do not equal marginal private costs (or benefits). Social efficiency requires that marginal social benefits and marginal social costs be equal, but private market participants equate marginal private benefits with marginal private costs. Externalities can be

internalized by redefining property rights, by making voluntary agreements, or by taxing or subsidizing the externality generator.

2. Pure public goods have two characteristics: First, the consumption of the good by one user does not reduce its consumption by others (nonrival consumption). Second, no one can in practice be prevented from using the good (nonexclusion).

3. Waste disposal costs arise because modern production and consumption require disposing of residual wastes such as air pollutants, toxic chemicals, and solid wastes. Pollution problems cannot easily be solved by redefining property rights or by voluntary agreement; government intervention is typically required.

> *Policy Focus:* **Policymakers must decide between a regulatory approach or a market approach to dealing with pollution. The market approach appears better because it allows pollution abatement to occur at a lower cost of society's resources.**

Key Terms

market failure (p. 361)
externalities (p. 361)
social costs (p. 361)
social benefits (p. 361)
property rights (p. 363)

internalization (p. 364)
public goods (p. 366)
free rider (p. 368)
waste-disposal costs (p. 368)

Questions and Problems

1. Factory A produces 1,000 tons of sulfuric acid. It costs A $10,000 to produce 1,000 tons. As a consequence of producing 1,000 tons of sulfuric acid, people in the community must increase their medical payments by $5,000; they lose $4,000 in wages by being sick; their dry-cleaning bills increase by $1,000. What are the private and social costs of the 1,000 tons of sulfuric acid?

2. Explain how the external costs calculated in the previous example might be internalized. Will this internalization be handled differently when there are three people hurt by the factory compared to when 300,000 people are hurt? In which case is government action more likely?

3. Almost everybody thinks we need national defense. Why is it, therefore, difficult to get people to pay voluntarily their share of national defense costs? Why is there no problem in getting people to pay for shoes?

4. If new cost-efficient technologies were developed that reduced the marginal costs of pollution abatement, what would happen to the optimal level of pollution abatement?

5. Does the pollution-trading concept used in recent years by the EPA solve the problem of choosing the optimal level of pollution?

6. Explain why economists do not favor the total elimination of pollution. Why would it not be efficient to totally eliminate pollution from our environment?

7. Discuss the two characteristics of public goods.

8. In 1986, it was proposed that a worldwide tax be placed on aerosol sprays to protect the world's ozone layer. At what rate should the tax be set?

9. In which case would it be easier to establish property rights? First, Farmer Jones wishes to keep stray cattle off his farmland. Second, Farmer Jones wishes to prevent the commercial jets landing at a nearby airport from disturbing his egg-laying chickens. Third, Farmer Jones wishes to keep Farmer Smith from depleting the stock of fish in a lake they share.

10. The 15th Annual Report of Council on Environmental Quality quoted a group of scientists who stressed the need to measure environmental quality accurately:

"Although ecologists measure numerous variables as indicators of change, many measurements are based on inadequately tested assumptions, and most have relatively poor precision with limited potential for improvement. The lack of precision and occasional controversy over the validity of an approach have lessened the effectiveness of ecological inputs to decision making."[*]

What does this mean for the application of economics to controlling externalities?

---

*T. Tietenberg, *Environmental and Natural Resource Economics,* 2nd ed. (Glenview, Ill.: Scott, Foresman and Company, 1988).

Doing Economics

Does anyone living near you do something on a regular basis that bothers you? Analyze the situation using the economics of externalities. Are property rights clearly defined? Could you resolve the situation individually via a market? If you could, but have not done so, why not? What authoritarian or regulatory resolution could be imposed? How would the other person in this situation answer these questions?

International Trade and Protection

C H A P T E R   2 0

CHAPTER FOCUS It pays for both individuals and countries to specialize in the goods and services they best produce. This chapter examines the reasons for and consequences of international trade, and the effects of tariffs and quotas on trade. We shall see that the gain from international trade consists more in its imports than its exports. Through international trade, as John Stuart Mill (1806–1873) said, "a country obtains things which it either could not have produced at all, or which it must have produced at a greater expense of capital and labor than the cost of the things which it exports to pay for them."

After studying this chapter, you will be able to:

- Understand how the law of comparative advantage guarantees that every country can gain from exporting and importing.

- Explain how countries can even export goods in which they have absolute cost disadvantages.

- Discuss the similarities and differences between tariffs, import quotas, and voluntary export restraints.

- Determine the relative costs and benefits of protecting a particular industry from international competition.

THE REASONS FOR INTERNATIONAL TRADE

International trade allows a country to specialize in the goods and services that it can produce at a relatively low cost and export those goods in return for imports whose domestic production is relatively costly. As a consequence, international trade enables a country—and the world—to consume and produce more than would be possible without trade. We shall later show that a country can benefit from trade even when it is more efficient (uses fewer resources) in the production of *all* goods than any other country. Adam Smith noted:

> *What is prudence in the conduct of every private family can scarce be folly in that of a great kingdom. If a foreign country can supply us with a commodity cheaper than we ourselves can make it, better buy it with some part of the produce of our industry employed in a way in which we have some advantage.*

Aside from the tangible benefit of increasing the world's output of goods and services, trade has intangible benefits as well. Trade offers diversity to our lives and work. The advantages of particular climates and lands are shared: the United States imports oil from the hot desert of Saudi Arabia to drive cars in cool comfort; Americans can enjoy coffee, bananas, and spices without living in the tropics; and we can have the economy and durability of Japanese cars without driving in hectic Tokyo. Thus, international (and interregional) trade enables us to enjoy a more diverse menu of goods and services than would be possible without trade. World trade also encourages the diffusion of knowledge and culture because trade serves as a point of contact between people of different lands.

THE UNITED STATES IN WORLD TRADE

The Volume of U.S. Trade

The world's largest exporting countries are Germany and the United States. Exhibit 1 shows the merchandise exports of West Germany, the United States, Japan, France, the United Kingdom, Italy, Canada, and the Netherlands. These countries account for about half of world trade. Because of its size and diversity, the United States is less dependent on trade than any of the other seven countries, as the lower U.S. ratio of exports to GDP demonstrates.

GALLERY OF ECONOMISTS

David Ricardo (1772–1823)

Born in London in 1772, David Ricardo made a fortune by the time he was 25, retired, became one of the world's greatest economists, and then entered politics. Starting as a stockbroker he soon became a multimillionaire even by today's standards. Wealth gave him the leisure to study economics, mathematics, chemistry, mineralogy, and geology. At the age of 27 he borrowed a copy of Adam Smith's *Wealth of Nations*, and the rest is history. Today we have the Ricardian theory of trade, the Ricardian theory of value, the Ricardian theory of distribution, and the Ricardian equivalence theorem. Perhaps no other economist is honored by so many theorems. This is all the more remarkable because he was an active economist for only fourteen years.

Ricardo had the rare ability to switch from the abstract to the concrete. He could speculate in corn, or foreign exchange, or wheat, and make a handsome profit; he would then turn his enormous analytical skills to the mechanisms determining the price of corn or the price of foreign exchange. In his practical life, he concentrated on day-to-day movements in prices. In his scholarly investigations, he thought in terms of the long run—years or even decades.

Ricardo's most important work was his classic *Principles of Political Economy and Taxation*, published in 1817. Among its many insights, Ricardo's law of comparative advantage stands out as perhaps the most enduring. Because foreign wages need not be the same as domestic wages, Ricardo pointed out, "the labour of 100 Englishmen cannot be given for that of 80 Englishmen, but the produce of the labour of 100 Englishmen may be given for the produce of the labour of 80 Portuguese, 60 Russians, or 120 East Indians."

U.S. Exports and Imports

Exhibit 2 shows the principal commodity exports and imports of the United States in 1992. About 8 percent of American exports consist of agricultural goods, such as wheat, soybeans, corn, cotton, and tobacco. Chemicals, business machines and computers, and aircraft make up about 16 percent of total merchandise exports. Consumer products and automobiles dominate American imports. The American propensity to drive foreign cars, wear clothes made in Taiwan or shoes made in Italy or Brazil, and watch Japanese TV sets shows up in the heavy imports of consumer goods and automotive vehicles. These aggregate statistics hide the fact that the United States is almost entirely dependent on foreign suppliers for bananas, cocoa, coffee, diamonds, manganese, cobalt, nickel, natural rubber, tea, tin, natural silk, and spices.

Exhibit 3 shows how the U.S. involvement in foreign trade has increased from 1960 to 1992. In 1960, the United States exported about 4 percent of GDP, and imports were only 3 percent of GDP. In 1992, imports had grown to about 11.2 percent of GDP, and exports had risen to about 10.7 percent of GDP. The much-discussed U.S. merchandise trade deficit shows up clearly for recent years. Notice that up until the 1970s the U.S. had a merchandise trade surplus.

THE LAW OF COMPARATIVE ADVANTAGE

In Chapter 2 we saw how the **law of comparative advantage** could be used to explain the benefits people enjoy from specialization. Individuals are made better

EXHIBIT 1 Size of Exports in Eight Major Countries, 1990

Country	Exports as Percent of GNP	Total Exports (billions of dollars)
West Germany	30	398
United States	7	393
Japan	10	287
France	20	210
United Kingdom	20	185
Italy	20	181
The Netherlands	50	131
Canada	21	127

SOURCE: *Statistical Abstract of the United States*, 1992, p. 848.

EXHIBIT 2 Principal Commodities of U.S. Merchandise Trade, 1992

Commodities	Quantity (billions of dollars)	Percentage of Total*
Exports		
Industrial machinery	137	31
Agricultural	36	8
Chemicals, bus. machines, and comp.	31	7
Civilian aircraft	38	9
Other exports	197	45
Total	439	100
Imports		
Consumer goods (nonauto)	123	23
Automotive vehicles	91	17
Petroleum	56	10
Metals	30	6
Coffee, cocoa, sugar	3	1
Other imports	233	44
Total	536	100

*Totals may not sum to 100 due to rounding.

SOURCE: U.S. Department of Commerce, *Survey of Current Business*, March 1993, Table 2.

off by specializing and engaging in trade with other people. The law of comparative advantage can also help explain the gains from international specialization. Interpersonal trade and international trade are very similar because many of the individual traits of persons and nations cannot be transferred to other persons and nations. David Ricardo (see Gallery of Economists) proved in 1817 that international specialization pays if each country devotes its resources to those activities in which it has a comparative advantage.

EXHIBIT 3 U.S. Merchandise Exports and Imports

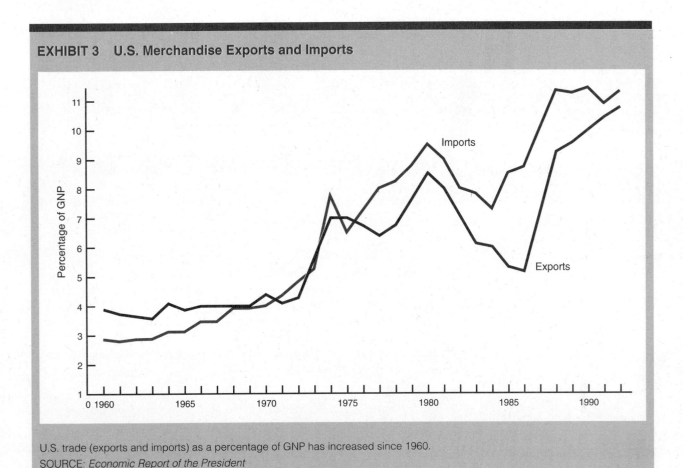

U.S. trade (exports and imports) as a percentage of GNP has increased since 1960.

SOURCE: *Economic Report of the President*

The **law of comparative advantage** states that people or countries specialize in those activities in which they have the greatest advantage or the least disadvantage compared to other people or countries.

Profound truths are sometimes difficult to discover; the real world is so complex it can hide its basic nature. Ricardo's genius was to provide a simplified model of trade without the irrelevant details that cloud our vision. He considered a hypothetical world with only two countries and only two goods. The two "countries" could be America and Europe; the two goods could be food and clothing. For the sake of simplicity, let us assume also that:

1. labor is the only productive factor, and there is only one type of labor;
2. labor cannot move between the two countries (this assumption reflects the relative international immobility of productive factors compared to goods;
3. the output from a unit of labor is constant (in other words, productivity is constant no matter how many units of output are produced);
4. laborers are indifferent between working in the food or clothing industries, provided only that wages are the same; and
5. there is no unemployment (each worker can produce food or clothing on his or her own without being attached to a firm that has capital).

Exhibit 4 shows the hypothetical output of food or clothing from one unit of labor in each of the two hypothetical countries. America can produce 6 units of

EXHIBIT 4   Hypothetical Food and Clothing Output from One Unit of Labor

Trade patterns depend on comparative, and not on absolute, advantages. In our hypothetical example, America is 6 times more efficient than Europe in food production and twice as efficient in clothing production. America has an absolute advantage in both food and clothing but has only a comparative advantage in food production. Europe has an absolute disadvantage in the production of both goods but has a comparative advantage in clothing production. Europe will export clothing to America in return for food, and both will gain by this pattern of trade.

Country	Units of Food Output from 1 Unit of Labor	Units of Clothing Output from 1 Unit of Labor
America	6	2
Europe	1	1

food with 1 unit of labor and can produce 2 units of clothing with 1 unit of labor. Europe can produce either a unit of food or a unit of clothing with 1 unit of labor. America is 6 times more efficient than Europe in food production (it produces 6 times as much with the same labor); America is only twice as efficient in clothing production (it produces twice as much with the same labor).

We have deliberately constructed a case where America has an **absolute advantage** over Europe in all lines of production.

> A country has an **absolute advantage** in the production of a good if it uses fewer resources to produce a unit of the good than any other country.

Even under these circumstances, however, both countries stand to benefit from specialization and trade according to comparative advantage, as demonstrated below.

The Case of Self-Sufficiency

Assume that each country in our hypothetical world is initially self-sufficient and must consume only what it produces at home.

America. A self-sufficient America must produce both food and clothing. American workers can produce 6 units of food or 2 units of clothing from a unit of labor (see Exhibit 4). Thus, in the marketplace, 6 units of food will have the same value as 2 units of clothing. In other words, 3 units of food (F) will have the same value as 1 unit of clothing (C), because these quantities use the same amount of labor. In opportunity-cost terms, to acquire 1 unit of clothing, a worker must sacrifice 3 units of food.

America's opportunity cost of 1 unit of clothing is 3 units of food:

$$3F = 1C.$$

Under conditions of self-sufficiency, the American price of a unit of clothing will be 3 times the price of a unit of food.

These same facts are shown in panel (a) of Exhibit 5. Panel (a) shows America's production-possibilities frontier. Labor is the only factor of production, and a total of 15 units of labor are assumed to be available to the American economy. America's production-possibilities frontier is a straight line because

a. America   **b. Europe**

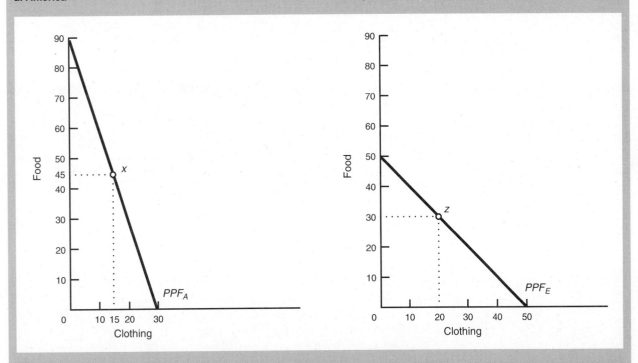

Panel (a) shows a hypothetical production-possibilities frontier for America. Based on the labor-productivity rates in Exhibit 4, if 15 units of labor are available and labor is the only factor of production, America could produce either 30 units of clothing, 90 units of food, or some mixture of the two—such as that combination represented by point x, where 45 units of food and 15 units of clothing are produced. Panel (b) shows a hypothetical PPF for Europe, where 50 units of labor are available. Europe could produce 50 units of clothing, 50 units of food, or a combination, such as that represented by point z, where 30 units of food and 20 units of clothing are produced.

opportunity costs are constant in our example. If everyone worked in clothing production, 30 (= 15 × 2) units of clothing could be produced. If everyone worked in food production, 90 (= 15 × 6) units of food could be produced. The economy would likely produce a mix of food and clothing to meet domestic consumption. Such a combination could be point x where 45 units of food and 15 units of clothing are produced and consumed in America. Without trade, America consumes 45F and 15C, the combination of which reflects America's preferences.

Europe.   In a self-sufficient Europe, workers can produce 1 unit of food or 1 unit of clothing with a unit of labor. A unit of clothing and a unit of food have the same labor costs and, hence, the same price. In other words, Europeans must give up 1 unit of food to get 1 unit of clothing.

Europe's opportunity cost of a unit of clothing is a unit of food:

$$1F = 1C.$$

Panel (b) of Exhibit 5 shows Europe's production-possibilities frontier. In our example, Europe is more populous than the United States; it has 50 units of labor available. Europe has a straight-line production-possibilities frontier as well and can produce either 50 units of food, 50 units of clothing, or some combination of the two. A likely situation would be for Europe to produce and consume at a point such as z, where 30 units of food and 20 units of clothing are produced. Without trade, Europe consumes $30F$ and $20C$, the combination that reflects Europe's preferences.

Without trade, each country must consume on its production-possibilities frontier. To produce (and consume) more requires either a larger labor force or an increase in the efficiency of labor.

The World.   If both Europe and America were self-sufficient, the total amount of food and clothing produced would be the amount produced by America ($45F$ and $15C$ plus the amount produced by Europe ($30F$ and $20C$). Thus, the total amount of food produced would be 75 units ($45F + 30F$), and the total amount of clothing produced would be 35 units ($15C + 20C$).

The Case of International Trade

If trade opened between Europe and America (as described in Exhibit 4), an American trader would find that 1 unit of clothing sells for 1 unit of food in Europe but sells for 3 units of food in America. If the trader applies 1 unit of labor in American food production and ships the resulting 6 units of food to Europe, he or she can obtain 6 units of clothing instead of only 2 by producing it at home! It makes no difference that clothing production is half as efficient in Europe. What matters is that in Europe food and clothing use the same amount of labor, and so food and clothing sell for the same price in Europe.

Americans would soon discover that clothing could be brought more cheaply in Europe than at home. Soon the law of supply and demand would do its work. Americans would stop producing clothing to concentrate on food production and would begin to demand European clothing. This increased demand would drive up the price of European clothing. Europe would presumably shift from food production to clothing production; eventually the pressure of American demand would lead Europe to specialize completely in clothing production.

The end result would be that Americans would get clothing more cheaply (at less than $3F$ for $1C$) than before trade; Europeans would receive a higher price for their clothing (at more than $1F$ for $1C$).

In making trade decisions, each country needs to know how much clothing is worth in terms of food, or the **terms of trade**.

> The **terms of trade** is the rate at which two products can be exchanged for each other between countries.

The terms of trade between Europe and America will settle some place between America's and Europe's opportunity costs. If America's opportunity cost of 1 unit of cloth is 3 units of food, and Europe's opportunity cost of 1 unit of cloth is 1 unit of food, the terms of trade will settle between $1C = 3F$ and $1C = 1F$. Europe is willing to sell 1 unit of cloth for at least 1 unit of food; America is willing to pay no more than 3 units of food for 1 unit of cloth.

The cheap imports of clothing from Europe will drive down the price of clothing in America. When Europe exports clothing to America, the European price of clothing will rise.

Although the final equilibrium terms of trade cannot be determined without knowing each country's preferences, one can determine that the final terms of trade will be somewhere between $3F$ and $1F$ for $1C$. If the world terms of trade at which both Europe and America can trade are set by the market at $2F = 1C$, Americans would no longer get only 2 units of clothing for 1 unit of labor but could produce 6 units of food and trade that food for 3 units of clothing (because $2F = 1C$) in Europe. Europeans would no longer have to work so hard to get a unit of food. They could produce 1 unit of clothing and trade that clothing for 2 units of food instead of getting only 1 unit of food for the hour of work.

When the terms of trade in the world are $2F = 1C$, Americans will devote all their labor to food production, and Europeans will devote all their labor to clothing production. Each country completely specializes because we made the simplifying assumption of constant rather than increasing costs of production. With increasing opportunity costs, America would likely produce some cloth and Europe some food because as each country specialized their costs of production would become more similar.

THE GAINS FROM TRADE

When American workers are specialized in food production and European workers are specialized in clothing production, the gains to each may be measured by their sacrifices before and after trade. Americans before trade sacrificed 3 units of food for 1 unit of clothing. After trade, Americans need sacrifice only 2 units of food for a unit of clothing (with terms of trade $2F = 1C$). Europeans before trade sacrificed 1 unit of clothing for 1 unit of food. After trade, Europeans need sacrifice only half a unit of clothing (because clothing sells for twice as much as food after trade).

The gains from trade are shown more dramatically in Exhibit 6. Before trade, America is at point x in panel (a), and Europe is at point z in panel (b). When trade opens up at the terms of trade $2F = 1C$, America moves its production to point p_A (specialization in food production), as the arrows show. Thus, America increases its food production from 45 units to 90 units. America can now trade each unit of food for half a unit of clothing. America trades 40 units of food for 20 units of clothing. Now America consumes at point c_A, with consumption at 50 units of food and 20 units of clothing. Trade enables America to consume above its production-possibilities frontier. In this example, trade shifts consumption from x to c_A. The dotted line shows the consumption possibilities available to Americans when $2F = 1C$ in the world market.

Europe's story is told in panel (b) of Exhibit 6. Europe shifts production from z, where $30F$ and $20C$ are produced, to point p_E, where 50 units of clothing are produced. The terms of trade are $2F = 1C$; when Europe trades 20 units of clothing for 40 units of food, Europe's consumption shifts from z to c_e—which is above the original production-possibilities frontier. Europe is also better off. The dotted line in Exhibit 6 shows the consumption possibilities available to Europeans when $2F = 1C$ in the world market.

In this simple world, the benefits of trade are dramatic. Everybody is made better off; nobody is hurt by trade. In effect, trade has the same effect on consumption as an increase in national resources or an improvement in efficiency of resource use. As a consequence of trade, countries are able to consume beyond their original production-possibilities frontiers. (See Example 1.)

In the real world, imports of goods from abroad displace the domestic production of competing goods, and in the process some people may find that their income falls. Because the Ricardian model assumes only one factor of production, the model simply cannot account for changes in the distribution of income. The

The law of comparative advantage guarantees that the most productive countries can gain from imports and that the least productive countries will be able to export something.

EXHIBIT 6   The Effects of Trade

a. America

b. Europe

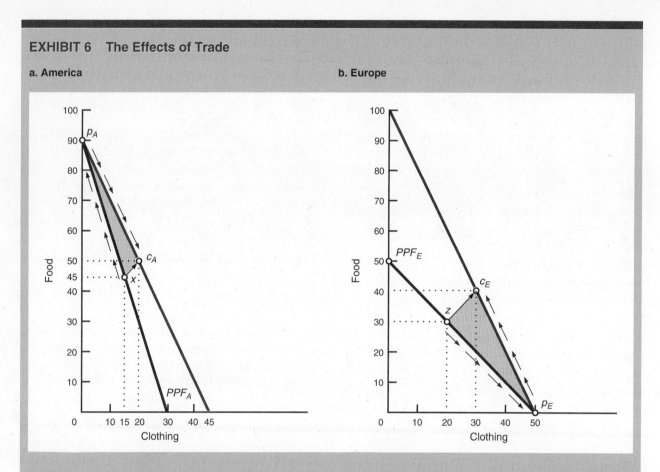

As shown in panel (a), before trade America produces and consumes at point x. When trade opens up at the terms of $2F = 1C$ (where F = units of food and C = units of clothing), America produces at p_A, specializing in food production, and trades 40 units of food for 20 units of clothing. America, therefore, consumes at point c_A, where it consumes 50 units of food and 20 units of clothing. Trade shifts American consumption from x to c_A. As shown in panel (b), before trade Europe produces and consumes at point z. When trade opens up, Europe shifts production to p_E, specializing in clothing production, and trades 20 units of clothing for 40 units of food. Europe, therefore, shifts consumption from z to point c_E, where 30 units of clothing and 40 units of food are consumed. The arrows pointing up in panel (a) and down in panel (b) show the effects of trade on domestic production, and the arrows pointing down in panel (a) and up in panel (b) show the effects of trade on domestic consumption. Both countries consume somewhere on the red line above their original production-possibilities frontiers.

model does demonstrate that in a world with many factors and shifts in distribution of income, trade increases average real income. Although trade makes the *average* person better off, some people are made even better off than the average while others are made worse off.

PROTECTIONISM

The American dairy industry contends that imported cheese and ice cream hurt its business. Americans love dairy products, but the U.S. government loves the dairy industry even more. Thus, cheese and ice cream imports are severely limited. This happens in other industries. Why?

When each country specializes and trades according to comparative advantage, each country can consume more than would be possible if it had to produce

EXAMPLE 1

U.S. Comparative Advantage

According to Ricardian theory, every country has a comparative advantage in something. But what determines comparative advantage in the real world? A country tends to export those goods that intensively use the productive factors the country has in abundance. For instance, if labor is plentiful relative to land or capital, a country's wages will be lower than wages in countries with abundant land or capital. Even if technical know-how were the same across countries, labor-cheap countries would have a comparative advantage in the production of labor-intensive goods. While the Ricardian theory assumes only one factor and takes cost differences as given, in the real world comparative advantage is the consequence of differences in the relative abundance of different factors.

The United States abounds in highly skilled technical labor and has a comparative advantage in manufactured goods that require intensive investment in research and development (R&D) such as the laser optical computer shown in the photograph. Industries with relatively high R&D expenditures contribute most to American export sales. Chemicals, nonelectrical or electrical machinery, aircraft, and professional and scientific instruments are the major R&D-intensive industries. These industries generate a surplus of exports over imports. The manufacturing industries that are not in this category—like textiles or paper products or food manufacturers—generate a trade deficit (a surplus of imports over exports).

The products of R&D industries tend to be new products, which are nonstandardized and not well suited to simple, repetitive mass-production techniques. The production processes for these products—such as hand-held calculators—become more standardized each year. The longer a product remains on the market, the easier it is for it to become standardized and the less need there is for highly trained workers. When new goods become old goods, other countries can gain a comparative advantage over the United States. The United States then moves on to the next new product generated with its giant research establishment and abundant supply of engineers, scientists, and skilled labor in order to fulfill its comparative advantage. The U.S. comparative advantage in manufacturing is in new products and processes.

at home everything that it consumed. As shown earlier, with **free trade** a country can consume above its production-possibilities frontier.

> **Free trade** is international trade unimpeded by artificial barriers such as tariffs (import taxes) or import quotas.

Is it to a country's advantage to adopt complete free trade or is it to a country's advantage to interpose some trade barriers between it and the rest of the world?

TRADE BARRIERS

Tariffs

An import **tariff** raises the price paid by domestic consumers as well as the price received by domestic producers of similar or identical products.

> A **tariff** is a tax levied on imports.

A tariff on clothing from Taiwan will raise the prices paid by American consumers of clothing imports and the prices charged by American clothing producers.

Suppose a country levies a $1 tariff on imported shoes that cost $10 in the foreign market. If domestic and foreign shoes are the same, both imported and domestically produced shoes will sell for $11 in the home market. Because consumers will pay more for shoes than otherwise, the tariff discourages shoe consumption. Because the domestic producer of shoes will be able to charge more for shoes, the tariff encourages domestic production. The $1 tariff discourages shoe imports and foreign shoe production.

The same result (of discouraging shoe consumption and encouraging domestic production) could also be accomplished by taxing domestic consumption of shoes by $1 and giving every domestic firm a $1 subsidy per pair of shoes produced.

Import Quotas

An **import quota** sets the number of units of a particular product that can be imported into the country during a specified period of time. U.S. import quotas on imported steel, for example, might specify the number of tons of steel of a specified grade that can be imported into the United States in a particular year.

> An **import quota** is a quantitative imitation on the amount of imports of a specific product during a given period.

Generally speaking, importers of products that fall under quota restrictions must obtain an import license to import the good. By limiting the number of licenses issued to the number specified by the quota, the quantity of imports cannot exceed the maximum quota limit.

Import licenses can be distributed in a variety of ways. One option is for import licenses to be auctioned off by the government in a free and fair market. If import licenses are scarce (more importers want licenses than are available), they will sell for a price that reflects their scarcity. In such a case, an import license is similar to a tariff: it restricts imports and raises revenue for the government.

Import licenses may also be handed out on a first-come-first-served basis, on the basis of favoritism, or according to the amount of past imports by the importer. When import quotas are not auctioned off, the potential revenue that the government could collect goes to the lucky few importers who get the scarce import licenses. For this reason, some importers, especially those who are likely to obtain import licenses, prefer import quotas to tariffs. Instead of the government collecting the revenue, the importers can cash in on the scarcity value of the import licenses. The license permits them to buy a product cheaply in the world market and then to sell it at a handsome profit in the home market. For example, in late 1993, world sugar prices were about $0.10 a pound. The U.S. sugar quota keeps domestic sugar prices at about $0.20 a pound. The importers collect the difference! American consumers pay higher prices, and the government gains no revenues.

Voluntary Export Restraints

A **voluntary export restraint** is a popular trade barrier in use by the United States.

> A **voluntary export restraint** is an agreement between two governments in which the exporting country voluntarily limits the export of a certain product to the importing country.

The U.S. government has negotiated a number of voluntary export restraints with foreign governments that limit the foreign country's volume of commodity exports to the U.S. market. Unlike tariffs or import quotas, voluntary export restraints do not generate any revenue for the importing country or its government. Instead, foreign exporters or the foreign government collect the scarcity value of the right to export to the huge American market.

Voluntary export restrictions are particularly widespread in textiles. An agreement among 29 countries restricts trade in textiles. The importing country induces the exporting country to impose export quotas under the threat of imposing tariff or import quotas. Under these quota agreements, not all those who wish to export textiles to the United States can do so. First, they must acquire scarce export licenses. The privilege to export textiles to the United States is a property right that can be bought and sold in several Asian countries. The voluntary export quotas imposed by Japan on automobile exports to the United States is another example. When the U.S. threatened to impose an import quota, the Japanese government ordered its auto companies to voluntarily limit exports to the United States to about 1.8 million units a year from 1981 to 1985. In 1985, the "voluntary" export limit was raised to 2.3 million units per year. A Brookings Institution study concluded that before the export limit was raised the Japanese-American curb boosted average car prices by about $2,500.

Like import tariffs, import quotas and voluntary export restraints limit the quantity of foreign goods available in the domestic market. Such nontariff barriers raise the price paid by domestic consumers and the price that can be charged by domestic producers on their import-competing products. Domestic producers benefit from quotas by being able to charge higher prices. The importer who receives a license to buy cheap imports gains, or, if licenses are auctioned, the government gains some revenues. The loser from quotas is the consumer, who pays higher prices.

Other Nontariff Barriers

The importance of nontariff barriers in world trade has grown in the last decade. It has been estimated that nearly 50 percent of world trade is conducted under some sort of nontariff barrier. Import and voluntary export quotas are not the only nontariff barriers. Three other major impediments to trade are *government procurement practices, technical standards*, and *domestic-content rules*. Governments tend to give preferential treatment to domestic producers when they purchase goods and services. Further, the free flow of products can be impeded by technical standards that imported products must meet. For example, imported cars must pass American pollution-control and safety standards; imported foods and drugs must meet U.S. food and drug standards. American autoworker unions have proposed domestic-content rules, which would require domestic automakers to use American-made parts for a certain fraction of a car's cost. Recent talks among the major trading nations indicate a desire to limit such nontariff barriers, but no agreements have been forthcoming on limiting import quotas or voluntary export restraints.

Tariffs and nontariff barriers raises costs to consumers and protect the domestic producers of import-competing products. The following discussion of the economics of protection applies to tariffs, but tariff and nontariff barriers have similar effects.

THE CASE AGAINST PROTECTION

Economists' enthusiasm for free trade has remained steadfast for more than two hundred years because it is easy to demonstrate that the benefits of protection are outweighed by the costs.

Measuring Benefits and Costs

According to the law of comparative advantage, specialization benefits the country as a whole, while tariffs or quotas eliminate or reduce those gains from specialization. The argument for free trade presented thus far has rested on the rather simple Ricardian model which, for simplicity, ruled out the existence of different types of land, labor, and capital. In the real world, when trade opens, some people are hurt. The import of Japanese cars keeps domestic car prices lower than otherwise, which keeps car buyers happy but certainly hurts domestic auto producers. The export of American wheat keeps domestic prices of bread higher than otherwise but makes wheat farmers happy. The law of comparative advantage, however, guarantees that the *net* advantages are on the side of trade rather than protection.

Exhibit 7 shows why consumers benefit from lower prices. If the price of a video game is $36, the demand curve in Exhibit 7 shows that 6,000 games are demanded. If the price of the game were to fall to $24, about 9,000 games would be demanded. The gain to consumers of the lower price is the area $G + H$. The people who would have bought 6,000 units at $36 have to pay only $24 and, therefore, save $12 per unit. Their gain is $12 × 6,000, or $72,000 (area G). When the price is $24, new customers come into the market who buy 3,000 additional video games. The average new customer would have been willing to pay $30 (the average of $36 and $24). Since new customers are paying only $24 per game, their gain is $6 × 3,000, or $18,000 (area H). Thus, if the price falls from $36 to $24 per game, consumers gain $G + H$. Conversely, if the price rises from $24 to $36, consumers lose $G + H$.

The demand curve in Exhibit 7 showed how consumers benefit from lower

EXHIBIT 7 Consumer Benefits from Lower Prices

When the price falls from $36 to $24 per video game, consumers benefit by the area $G + H$. Those who would buy 6,000 units at $36 each (point *a*) benefit by area G because they save $12 per unit. Those new customers who buy the 3,000 additional units when the price is $24 (point *b*) benefit by area H.

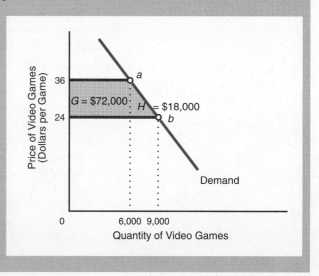

prices. Similarly, the supply curve in Exhibit 8 can show how producers benefit from higher prices. If the price of a ton of coal is $140, Exhibit 8 shows that at that price 9 million tons of coal will be supplied. If the price of coal were $200, 12 million tons would be supplied. The gain to producers from raising the price from $140 to $200 is the area $J + K$. Coal producers who would have suppled 9 million tons at a price of $140 receive $200 per ton (a $60 gain on each of the 9 million tons). Their gain is $60 × 9 million, or $540 million (area J). When the price rises to $200 per ton, 3 million additional tons are produced. The average producer of this new coal would have been willing to receive $170 (the average of $200 and $140) for a ton of coal. Because the new suppliers are in fact receiving $200, their gain is $30 × 3 million, or $90 million (area K). Thus, if the price of a ton of coal rises from $140 to $200, producers gain $J + K$. Conversely, if the price falls from $200 to $140, producers lose $J + K$.

Why Tariffs Impose Net Costs

Exhibit 9 shows the supply and demand conditions in a country whose imports of a particular good are so small relative to the world supply that the world price (p_w) is taken as given. The amount imported by this country will not affect the world price.

With a zero tariff, consumers can purchase all they want at the prevailing world price, p_w. According to Exhibit 9, the quantity represented by the distance between q_1 and q_4 would be imported because this quantity is the difference between the quantity demanded at p_w and the quantity supplied by domestic producers.

When a tariff (t) is imposed, the price rises to $p_w + t$; the new domestic price equals the world price plus the tariff rate. The country now imports only that quantity represented by the distance between q_2 and q_3.

The tariff benefits domestic producers of the competitive product by the area N. The government (or public) benefits by area T, which equals the revenue from the tariff (the tariff rate times the quantity of imports). The loss to consumers from the increase in price is the sum of areas $N + R + T + V$. If the gains (area $N + T$)

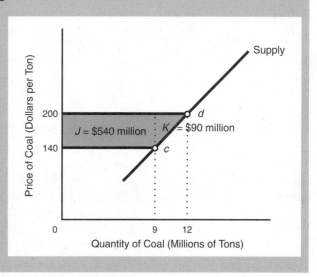

EXHIBIT 8   Producer Benefits from Higher Prices

When the price rises from $140 to $200, producers benefit by the area $J + K$. Those who would sell 9 million tons at $140 per ton (point c) benefit by area J. Those new suppliers who sell 3 million additional tons when the price is $200 per ton (point d) benefit by area K.

EXHIBIT 9   The Effects of a Tariff

Before the tariff, the price of the product is p_w. The tariff raises the price to $p_w + t$, that is, the world price plus the amount of the duty. Consumers lose area $N + R + T + V$. Producers gain area N. The government gains the tariff revenue of area T, which equals the tariff per unit times the quantity of imports. The net loss is area $R + V$. The tariff lowers imports from $(q_4 - q_1)$ to $(q_3 - q_2)$.

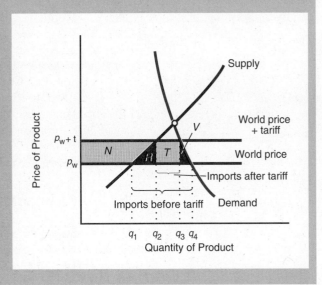

are subtracted from the losses (area $N + R + T + V$), the tariff imposes a net loss to the country of area $R + V$.

The bottom line is that protection imposes costs on society that are greater than the benefits received by the individual industries being protected. Trade barriers raise prices and lead to economic inefficiency (shifting resources from efficient to less efficient industries). One way to look at the costs of protection is to examine the cost of maintaining a job through protection. A trade barrier increases the number of jobs available in the protected industry (but not necessarily in the economy). Example 2 estimates the annual costs to consumers per job protected by different trade barriers. In general, the cost per job is more than twice as much as the average earnings in that job. In other words, if trade barriers save a $20,000-a-year job, that job costs the rest of the community more than $40,000.

Such losses may be an underestimate, according to economists Gordon Tullock and Anne Krueger. Tullock and Krueger argue that because producers have an incentive to expend resources to get the tariff passed, the import-competing industry may form a committee, lobby Congress, or advertise the plight of its industry. When the color-TV industry was hurt by imports, the industry formed COMPACT (the Committee to Preserve American Color Television). Such expenditures reduce gains to protected producers and, thus, further increase the costs of protection.

The Explanation for Tariffs

Since exports of things must pay for the imports of things, restricting imports will ultimately restrict exports.

The exports of goods, services, and securities must equal the imports of goods, services, and securities. If the United States, or any country, restricts imports, it necessarily restricts exports. In other words, subsidizing import-competing industries by means of tariff or nontariff barriers penalizes a whole host of unseen export industries. Imports can be more visible than exports.

If tariffs impose a cost on the community, why do they exist? Why would a representative democracy, which is supposed to represent consumer interests, establish trade barriers?

EXAMPLE 2

Measuring the Costs of Protection

The accompanying table shows the annual cost to consumers for each job protected in a few selected industries. Trade barriers protect jobs in particular industries at the cost of higher prices for consumers. What is the ratio of annual costs to benefits? The table shows that the ratio of cost to benefits ranges from 10 for citizens band transceivers to 3.6 for autos. In other words, the trade barrier for citizens band transceivers costs consumers $85,539 for each $8,500 job saved! The trade barrier for autos costs consumers $85,400 for each $23,566 job saved. Thus, the hidden costs of protection far exceed the visible benefits.

Product and Restriction	Number of Jobs Protected	Average Earnings	Cost per Job	Ratio of Cost to Earnings
Citizens band transceivers (tariffs, 1978–81)	587	$ 8,500	$85,539	10.1
Apparel (tariffs, 1977–81)	116,188	6,669	45,549	6.8
Footwear* (tariffs and quotas, 1977)	21,000	8,340	77,714	9.3
Carbon steel* (tariffs and quotas, 1977)	20,000	24,329	85,272	3.5
Autos* (proposed local content law, 1986–91)	58,000	23,566	85,400	3.6

*In 1980 dollars.

SOURCE: Keith E. Maskus, "Rising Protectionism and U.S. International Trade Policy," Federal Reserve Bank of Kansas City, *Economic Review* (July/August 1984), pp. 3–17.

Tariffs are explained by the fact that the costs they impose are highly diffused among millions of people, while the (smaller) benefits are concentrated among specific sectors of the economy associated with the protected industry. The costs imposed on the community are large in total but so small per person that it is not worth the trouble to any one person to join a committee to fight tariffs on each and every imported good, while the benefits to protected sectors are well worth the costs of lobbying. For example, assume people devote about 0.5 percent of all consumption to sugar (in all its various forms). A trade barrier that raises the price of sugar by 50 percent helps domestic sugar producers enormously, but it raises the cost of living to consumers by only 0.25 percent (50 percent of 0.5 percent). To the consumer, this cost is just too small to worry about. The costs of fighting against each request for protection are prohibitive.

The benefits of protection are relatively small but concentrated on the few, while the costs are relatively large but diffused among the many.

U.S. TRADE POLICIES

The tariff history of the United States is shown in Exhibit 10, which shows that tariffs have fluctuated up and down with the ebb and flow of protectionism in the U.S. Congress. In modern times, tariffs hit their peak with the infamous Smoot-Hawley Tariff of 1930. Economists were so appalled by the prospect of this tariff bill that in a rare show of agreement, 1,028 of them signed a petition asking

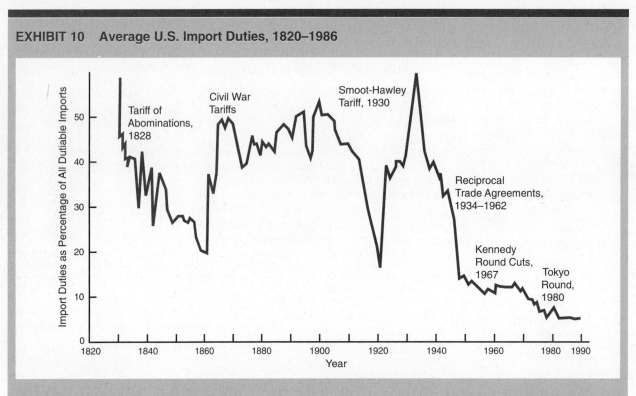

EXHIBIT 10 Average U.S. Import Duties, 1820–1986

Tariff of
Abominations,
1828

Civil War
Tariffs

Smoot-Hawley
Tariff, 1930

Reciprocal
Trade Agreements,
1934–1962

Kennedy
Round Cuts,
1967

Tokyo
Round,
1980

Import Duties as Percentage of All Dutiable Imports

Year

As attitudes toward free trade and protectionism have fluctuated in the United States, average tariff rates have also fluctuated but have shown a distinct downward trend.

SOURCES: *Historical Statistics of the United States; Statistical Abstract of the United States*

President Hoover to veto the bill. Because politics tends to override economics in tariff legislation, the bill was signed.

The Trade-Agreements Program and GATT

The Smoot-Hawley tariff, like most of the preceding 18 tariff acts stretching back to 1779, was the result of political *logrolling* in the U.S. Congress. Logrolling occurs when some politicians trade their own votes on issues of minor concern to their constituents in return for other politicians' votes on issues of greater concern to their constituents. Tariffs, historically, are the best example of the sacrifice of general interests for special interests.

Having established the highest tariff rates in U.S. history, the Smoot-Hawley Act triggered angry reactions overseas, as predicted by economists. As one nation after another erected trade barriers, the volume of world trade declined more than it would have due to the Great Depression. The export markets of the United States shrank at the time of a very deep domestic depression.

In order to secure a larger market for U.S. exports, Congress amended the Tariff Act of 1930 with the Reciprocal Trade Agreements Act of 1934. The President was authorized to negotiate reciprocal agreements that promised to lower U.S. trade barriers or tariffs in return for similar concessions abroad. The fact that Congress did not have to approve the tariff cuts marked a significant change in the power of special interests to influence U.S. tariff policy.

The trade-agreements program has been broadened under successive exten-

Free Trade

The law of comparative advantage has a clear policy implication: A country can gain from free trade even if its trading partners have import restrictions. Why? Trade pays because goods can be purchased more cheaply abroad than they can be produced at home as measured by opportunity costs.

There is perhaps no clearer example of the benefits of international trade than a comparison of less-developed countries that have encouraged trade and those that do not.

In 1960, India, South Korea, and Thailand were at about the same stage of development—extreme poverty. South Korea and Thailand embarked on a course that encouraged expanded international trade, whereas India looked inward and emphasized the protection of domestic industries from cheaper foreign imports. The consequences could not be more dramatic. By 1990, South Korea's per capita income was over seven times that of India, and Thailand's per capita income was over four times that of India.

Experiences like these can be multiplied many times. Free-trade success stories like Hong Kong, Singapore, and Taiwan have ushered in the Pacific century. Many countries—even India—are now jumping on the free-trade bandwagon. Mexico once banned many imports and levied tariffs above 100 percent on some goods. Beginning in 1986 Mexico unilaterally opened its markets to foreign goods. Mexico sought a free-trade agreement with the United States. In 1992, Canada, Mexico, and the Bush administration signed a free-trade agreement (which must be approved under the Clinton administration).

Many studies have shown that the per-capita incomes of free-trade countries grow at about 1 percent more per year than the per-capita incomes of protectionist countries over several decades. Moreover, the gains come quickly. One study of 30 episodes of trade liberalization found that within just one year, the growth rate of GDP increased by an average of about 1 percent.

Trade pays not only because of the gains from increased specialization, but also because it forces innovation and speeds the diffusion of technology. For example, the competition from Japanese cars almost certainly improved the quality of the cars produced by Ford and Chrysler.

In the face of all of this evidence, there are still a few calls for managed trade over free trade. Presumably, managed trade would mean that trade policy might be used to pry open foreign markets or to promote selected domestic industries. The evidence is not clear on this issue. When we argue that "free" trade is better than "protection," we are simply saying that countries that have "freer" trade do much better than those countries that have more protection. That is all we know. We do not know whether a little bit more or little bit less free trade is beneficial. The difficulty with such attempts to manage trade is that it bolsters the case of special-interest groups trying to protect their own industries.

sions and modifications. The Trade Expansion Act of 1962 gave the president the power to reduce tariffs by up to 50 percent and to remove duties of less than 5 percent. Under the authority of this act, the United States engaged in multilateral negotiations, known as the Kennedy Round, which resulted in an average reduction of 35 percent on industrial tariff rates. The Trade Reform Act of 1974 allowed the president to reduce tariffs by up to 60 percent and to eliminate duties of less than 5 percent. This act resulted in the Tokyo Round (1980) of multilateral reductions, in which the United States agreed to cut tariffs on industrial goods by 31 percent, the European Community agreed to cut tariffs by 27 percent, and

Japan agreed to cut tariffs by 28 percent. The Trade and Tariff Act of 1984 authorized the president to enter into a new round of multilateral reductions in trade barriers (called the Uruguay Round).

Clearly, the trade-agreements program has been an enormous success. In 1932, the average tariff rate was about 59 percent; today the average tariff rate is about 5 percent. The trade-agreement obligations of the United States and other countries are carried out under the General Agreement on Tariffs and Trade (GATT), established in 1948. All of the major countries belong to GATT, and members are responsible for about 85 percent of world trade. GATT is an agreement that spells out rules on the conduct of trade and procedures to settle trade disputes. GATT is also the forum in which international tariff negotiations take place.

Chapter Summary

The most important point to learn from this chapter is: Every country gains by exporting those goods in which their advantages are the greatest, or their disadvantages are the smallest, and by importing those goods in which their advantages are the smallest, or their disadvantages are the greatest.

1. The United States and Germany are the world's largest exporting countries, but trade as a percentage of GDP is smaller in the United States.

2. In a simple two-country, two-good world, even if one country has an absolute advantage in both goods, both countries can still gain by specialization and trade. If the two countries were denied the opportunity to trade, they would have to use domestic production to meet domestic consumption. With trade, specialization allows them to consume beyond their domestic production-possibilities frontiers by producing at home and then trading the product in which the country has comparative advantage. Countries will specialize in those products whose domestic opportunity costs are low relative to their opportunity costs in the other countries. Through trade, countries are able to exchange goods at more favorable terms than those dictated by domestic opportunity costs.

3. The major trade barriers are tariffs, import quotas, voluntary export restraints, and other nontariff barriers. A *tariff* is a tax levied on imports. It raises both the price paid by the domestic consumer and the price received by the domestic producer of the import-competing product. *Import quotas* limit the amount of imports of specified products. They raise the prices paid by domestic consumers and the prices received by domestic producers of import-competing products. Quotas are normally regulated by import licenses. If import licenses are sold to importers, the government receives their scarcity value. If they are not sold, private importers benefit from their scarcity value. *Voluntary export restraints* direct governments to restrict their exports to another country.

4. The basic argument against protection is that the costs of protection outweigh the benefits of protection. The loss to consumers from a tariff is greater than the gain to the protected producers.

5. The politics of tariffs explains why tariffs are passed. Although the costs of tariffs are large in total, these costs are small per person. Special-interest groups, therefore, lobby and spend funds to obtain tariff protection.

6. U.S. trade policies have changed over the years. The Smoot-Hawley tariff of 1930 caused a further restriction of trade during the Great Depression by setting very high

tariff rates. Since then, legislation has been passed that allows the U.S. president to negotiate tariff reductions.

> *Policy Focus:* **Free trade pays such obvious dividends that more and more countries are liberalizing their trade. The evidence for managed trade is not compelling.**

Key Terms

law of comparative advantage (p. 377)
absolute advantage (p. 380)
terms of trade (p. 382)
free trade (p. 385)

tariff (p. 385)
import quota (p. 386)
voluntary export restraint (p. 386)

Questions and Problems

1. Name the three largest exporting countries in the world.

2. Suppose that 1 unit of labor in Asia can be used to produce 10 units of food or 5 units of clothing. Also suppose that 1 unit of labor in South America can be used to produce 4 units of food or 1 unit of clothing.
   a. Which country has an absolute advantage in food? In clothing?
   b. What is the relative cost of producing food in Asia? In South America?
   c. Which country will export food? Clothing?
   d. Draw the production-possibilities frontier for each country if Asia has 10 units of labor and South America has 20 units of labor.
   e. What is the range for the final terms of trade between the two countries?
   f. If the final terms of trade are 3 units of food for 1 unit of clothing, compute the wage in Asia and the wage in South America, assuming that a unit of food costs $40 and a unit of clothing costs $120.

3. What happens to the answers to parts (a), (b), and (c) of question 2 when the South American productivity figures are changed so that 1 unit of labor is used to produce either 40 units of food or 10 units of clothing?

4. What are the differences and similarities between an import duty and an import quota?

5. What is the difference between an import quota and a voluntary export restraint.

6. Economists agree that tariffs hurt the countries that impose them. Yet nearly all countries impose tariffs. Is something wrong with the economists' argument?

7. Assume a country can export all the wheat it wants at the world price of $5 per bushel. Using an analysis parallel to the discussion of Exhibit 9 in the text, show the impact of imposing a $1-per-bushel export tariff on every bushel exported. Does the benefit to consumers and government exceed the cost to producers of wheat? (*Hint:* An export tariff means that if a foreigner purchases wheat, he or she must pay the domestic price plus the $1 export duty.)

8. A country imports shoes. The world price of shoes is $20 a pair. Show that a tariff of $5 per pair will impose larger costs on shoe consumers than the sum of the benefits to domestic shoe producers and the total tariff revenue from shoe imports.

Doing Economics

Consider the economy of your home state. What are its major exports? How does its comparative advantage in these products come about? (*Hint:* Think about the conditions or factors of production that are abundant. Is labor cheap or expensive? Are there raw materials present

that are important? Is climate or proximity to ports important?) Are there any industries that seem to defy the law of comparative advantage? Why do you think they are present?

GLOSSARY

absolute advantage is possessed by a country in the production of a good if it uses fewer resources to produce a unit of the good than any other country **(2)**.

absolute poverty standard establishes a specific income level for a given-sized household below which the household is judged to be living in a state of poverty **(18)**.

accounting cost see **explicit cost**.

agent is a party that acts for, on behalf of, or as a representative of a principal **(7)**.

antitrust legislation is the legislation that controls market structure and conduct **(12)**.

average cost see **long-run average cost _(LRAC)_**.

average fixed cost _(AFC)_ is fixed cost divided by output:
$$AFC = FC \div Q \qquad (8).$$

average total cost _(ATC)_ is total cost divided by output, or the sum of average variable cost and average fixed cost:
$$ATC = TC \div Q = AVC + AFC \qquad (8).$$

average variable cost _(AVC)_ is variable cost divided by output:
$$AVC = VC \div Q \qquad (8).$$

bankrupt the condition of a corporation that cannot pay its bills or its interest obligations **(7A)**.

bargaining see **collective bargaining**.

behavior see **monopoly-profit-seeking behavior, opportunistic behavior**.

benefits see **social benefits**.

bonds are obligations that bind the corporation to pay a fixed sum of money (the principal) at maturity and also to pay a fixed sum of money annually until the maturity date. This fixed annual payment is called _interest,_ or the _coupon payment_ **(7A)**.

budget line is all the combinations of goods the consumer is able to buy given a certain income and set prices. The budget line shows the consumption possibilities available to the consumer **(6A)**.

capital good see **rate of return on capital**.

capitalism is an economic system characterized by private ownership of the factors of production, market allocation of resources, the use of economic incentives, and decentralized decision making **(1)**.

cartel is an arrangement that allows the participating firms to operate the industry as a shared monopoly. In effect, the participating firms coordinate their output and pricing decisions to yield that industry price and output combination that would have prevailed had this industry been a pure monopoly with each firm as a branch of one giant firm **(11)**.

cash market see **spot (cash) market**.

**ceteris paribus** is an assumption that considers the effects of change in one factor assuming that all other relevant factors remain the same **(1)**.

circular-flow diagram summarizes the flows of goods and services from producers to households and the flows of the factors of production from households to business firms **(2)**.

clearing price see **equilibrium (market-clearing) price**.

collective bargaining is the process whereby the union bargains with management as the representative of all union employees **(16)**.

comparative advantage see **law of comparative advantage**.

compensating wage differentials are the higher rewards (wages or fringe benefits) that must be paid workers to compensate them for undesirable job characteristics **(15)**.

competition see **nonprice competition, perfect competition**.

competitive market see **perfectly competitive market**.

complements are two goods related in such a way that the demand for one rises of the price of the other falls (or the demand for one falls if the price of the other rises) **(3)**.

concentration ratio is the percentage of industry sales (or output, or labor force, or assets) accounted for by the x largest firms **(11)**.

conglomerate merger occurs when one company takes over another company in a different line of business **(12)**.

conscious parallelism is the process through which the actions of producers can be coordinated within certain ranges without formal or even informal agreements. All oligopolists use their understanding of the industry to make their own decisions and may anticipate the behavior of other oligopolists **(11)**.

constant-cost industry is relatively small and, hence, can expand or contract without significantly affecting the terms at which factors of production used in the industry are purchased. The long-run industry supply curve for a constant-cost industry is horizontal **(9)**.

constant returns to scale are present when a given percent change in inputs results in the same percent change in output (8).

consumer equilibrium occurs when the consumer has spent all income and marginal utilities per dollar are equal on each good purchased $(MU_A/P_A = MU_B/P_B)$. At this point, the consumer is not inclined to change purchases unless some other factor (such as prices, income, or preferences) changes (6).

contrived scarcity is the production of less than the economically efficient quantity of a good by a monopoly (10).

corporation is a form of business enterprise that is owned by a number of stockholders. The corporation has the legal status of a fictional individual and is authorized by law to act as a single person. The stockholders elect a board of directors that appoints the management of the corporation, usually headed by a president. Management is charged with the actual operation of the corporation (7).

cost see **average variable cost (AVC), average total cost (ATC), average fixed cost (AFC), explicit cost, implicit cost, information cost, long-run average cost (LRAC), opportunity cost, transaction cost.**

cost industry see **constant-cost industry, increasing-cost industry.**

costs see **fixed costs (FC), social costs, transaction cost, variable costs (VC), waste-disposal costs.**

craft union is a union that represents workers of a single occupation (16).

credit markets are markets for borrowing and lending funds (17).

cross-piece elasticity of demand (E_{xy}) is the percentage change in demand of the first product *(x)* divided by the percentage change in the price of the related product *(y)* (5).

demand curve or **schedule** for a good shows the various quantities demanded at different prices, holding other factors constant, over a specified time period (3); see also **kinked-demand curve, market-demand curve.**

demanded see **quantity demanded.**

dependent variable is the variable that changes as a result of a change in the value of another variable (1A).

derived demand is the demand for a factor of production that results (is derived) from the demand for the goods and services a factor of production helps produce (14).

diagram see **circular-flow diagram, scatter diagram.**

differentials see **compensating wage differentials.**

dilemma see **prisoners' dilemma game.**

diminishing marginal rate of substitution see **law of diminishing marginal rate of substitution.**

diminishing returns see **law of diminishing returns.**

direct relationship see **positive relationship.**

discrimination see **price discrimination.**

diseconomies of scale are present when a given percentage change in inputs leads to a smaller percentage change in output (8).

disposal costs see **waste-disposal costs.**

distortion see **growth distortion, inflation distortion.**

distribution of income see **functional distribution of income, personal distribution of income.**

distributive justice is present when society's resources are distributed fairly among the members of society (18).

earnings (P/E) ratio see **price/earnings (P/E) ratio.**

earnings per share (EPS) is the annual profit of the corporation divided by the number of shares outstanding (7A).

economic efficiency is present when society's resources are so organized that it is impossible to make everyone better off by *any* reallocation of resources; in other words, making one person better off must be at the expense of someone else (10).

economic problem is how to allocate scarce resources among competing ends (2).

economic profits are the excess of revenues over total opportunity costs (8).

economic rent is the excess of the payment to the factor over its opportunity cost (17); see also **pure economic rent.**

economic system is the set of organizational arrangements and institutions that are established to solve the economic problem (1,18).

economics is the study of how *scarce resources* are *allocated* among *competing ends* (1).

economies of scale are present in the production process when large output volumes can be produced at a lower cost per unit than small output volumes (2); are present when a given percentage change in input leads to a larger percentage change in output (8).

effect see **income effect, interest-rate effect, real-balance effect, substitution effect.**

efficiency results when no resources are unemployed and when no resources are misallocated (1).

efficient stock market hypothesis states that stock prices are determined by the information currently available on the present and future earnings of corporations. Changes in stock prices are due to changes in the information available on present and future earnings of corporations (7A).

elastic demand see **perfectly elastic demand.**

elasticity of demand see **cross-price elasticity of demand (E_{xy}), income elasticity of demand (E_i), price elasticity of demand (E_d).**

elasticity of supply see **price elasticity of supply (E_s).**

elastic supply see **perfectly elastic supply.**

employee association is an organization that represents employees in a particular profession (16).

employment trade-off see **wage/employment trade-off.**

entrepreneur organizes, manages, and assumes the risk for an enterprise (7).

equilibrium (market-clearing) price of a good or service is that price at which the amount people are prepared to buy equals the amount offered for sale (2); the price at which the quantity demanded by consumers equals the quantity supplied by producers (3).

equilibrium price of a good or service is that price at which the amount of the good people are prepared to buy equals the amount offered for sale (2).

exchange see **foreign exchange.**

exhaustive expenditures are government purchases of goods and services that divert real economic resources from the private sector, making them no longer available for private use (4).

expenditures see **exhaustive expenditures.**

explicit cost (also called an *accounting cost*) is incurred when an actual payment is made (8).

externalities are present when private parties do not bear the full marginal cost or enjoy the full marginal benefit of an economic action. A part of the costs (or benefits) is borne by third parties (4;19).

factors of production are the resources used to produce goods and services; they can be divided into three categories—land, labor, and capital (1).

fixed cost see **average fixed cost** *(AFC)*.

fixed costs *(FC)* are those costs that do not vary with output **(8)**.

flow diagram see **circular-flow diagram**.

free rider is anyone who enjoys the benefits of a good or service without paying the cost **(6)**.

free trade is international trade unimpeded by artificial barriers, such as tariffs (import taxes) or import quotas **(20)**.

functional distribution of income is the distribution of income among the four broad classes of productive factors—land, labor, capital, and entrepreneurship **(14)**.

futures market is one where a buyer and seller agree now on the price of a commodity to be delivered at some specified date in the future **(13)**.

goods see **inferior goods, normal goods, public goods**.

government debt is the cumulated sum of outstanding IOUs that the government unit owes it creditors **(4)**.

government deficit is an excess of government outlays over government revenues **(4)**.

government surplus is an excess of government revenues over government outlays **(4)**.

groups see **noncompeting groups**.

growth distortion is the measurement of changes in a variable over time that does not reflect the concurrent change in other relevant variables with which the variable should be compared, such as population size **(1A)**.

horizontal merger is a merger of two firms in the same line of business (such as an insurance company merging with another insurance company or a shoe manufacturer merging with another shoe manufacturer **(12)**.

household production is work in the home, including such activities as meal preparation, do-it-yourself repair, child rearing, and cleaning **(15)**.

human capital investment is the expenditure of resources on schooling, health, and training **(18)**.

immediate run is a period of time so short that the quantity supplied cannot be changed at all. In the immediate run—sometimes called the *momentary period* or *market period*—supply curves are perfectly inelastic **(5)**.

implicit cost is incurred when an alternative is sacrificed but no actual payment appears to be made **(8)**.

import quota is a quantitative limitation on the amount of imports of a specific product during a given period **(16)**.

incidence of a tax is the actual distribution of the burden of tax payment **(4)**.

income see **functional distribution of income, in-kind income, national income, personal income, personal disposable income, personal distribution of income**.

income effect is the change in the quantity of X demanded that is attributable to the welfare change that accompanies the price change **(6)**.

income elasticity of demand *(E_i)* is the percentage change in the demand for a product divided by the percentage change in income *holding all prices fixed* **(5)**.

income tax see **negative income tax** *(NIT)*.

increasing-cost industry is one in which, when the industry expands, the factor prices of resources used in the industry are bid up. As the number of firms in the industry contracts, the prices of these factors fall. Hence, the long-run industry supply curve for an increasing-cost industry is upward-sloping **(9)**.

independent variable is the variable that causes the change in the value of the dependent variable **(1A)**.

index see **stock-price index**.

indifference curve shows all the alternative combinations of two goods that yield the same total satisfaction to a particular consumer and among which the consumer is indifferent **(6A)**.

industrial union is a union that represents employees of an industry or a firm regardless of their specific occupation **(16)**.

industry see **constant-cost industry, increasing-cost industry**.

industry-supply curve see **long-run industry-supply curve**.

inelastic demand see **perfectly inelastic demand**.

inelastic supply see **perfectly inelastic supply**.

inferior goods are those for which demand falls as income increases, holding all prices constant **(3)**.

inflation distortion is the measurement of the dollar value of a variable over time without adjustment for the inflation rate over that period **(1A)**.

information cost is the cost of acquiring information on prices, product qualities, and product performance **(2)**.

in-kind income consists primarily of benefits—such as free public education, school-lunch programs, public housing, or food stamps—for which the recipient is not required to pay **(18)**.

interest is the price of credit. Interest is set where the amount businesses wish to invest is balanced with the amount people are prepared to save **(17)**.

interest rate measures the yearly cost of borrowing as a percent of the amount loaned **(17)**.

intermediaries buy in order to sell again or simply to bring together a buyer and a seller **(7)**.

internalization is the process of putting private price tags on externalities **(19)**.

inverse relationship see **negative (or inverse) relationship**.

kinked-demand curve results when other firms match a firm's price decreases but don't match the firm's price increases **(11)**.

labor shortage occurs when the number of workers firms wish to hire at the prevailing wage rate exceeds the number willing to work at that wage rate **(15)**.

labor surplus occurs when the number of workers willing to work at the prevailing wage rate exceeds the number firms wish to employ at that wage rate **(15)**.

labor union is a collective organization of workers and employees whose objective is to improve conditions of pay and work **(16)**.

lag see **effectiveness lag, recognition lag, regulatory lag**.

law of comparative advantage states that it is better for people to specialize in those activities in which their advantages over other people are greatest or in which their disadvantages compared to others are the smallest **(2;20)**.

law of demand states that there is a negative (or inverse) relationship between the price of a good and the quantity demanded, holding other factors constant **(3)**.

law of diminishing marginal rate of substitution is that as more of one good (A) is consumed, the amount of the other good (B) that the consumer is willing to sacrifice for one more unit of good A declines **(6A)**.

law of diminishing marginal utility states that as more of a good or service is consumed during any given time period, its marginal utility declines, holding the consumption of everything else constant **(6)**.

law of diminishing returns states that as ever larger quantities of a variable factor are combined with fixed amounts of the firm's other factors, the marginal physical product of the variable factor will eventually decline **(8)**.

law of increasing costs states that as more of a particular commodity is produced, its opportunity cost per unit will increase **(1)**.

law of scarcity states that the wants of every society exceed its ability to satisfy those wants **(1)**.

leader see **price leader**.

leisure is time spent in any activity other than work in the labor force or work in the home **(15)**.

line see **budget line**.

long run is a period of time long enough for new firms to enter the market, for old firms to disappear, and for existing plants to be expanded. In the long run, firms have more flexibility in adjusting to price changes **(5)**; a period of time long enough to vary all inputs **(18)**.

long-run average cost (LRAC) consists of the minimum average cost for each level of output when all factor inputs are variable and when factor prices and the state of technology are fixed **(8)**.

long-run industry-supply curve shows the quantities that the industry is prepared to supply at different prices *after* the entry or exit of firms is completed **(9)**.

Lorenz curve shows the percentage of all income earned by households at successive income levels. The cumulative share of households (ranked from lowest to highest incomes) is plotted on the horizontal axis of the Lorenz curve, and the cumulative share of income earned by the cumulative percent of households is plotted on the vertical axis **(1)**.

luxuries are those products that have an income elasticity of demand greater than 1 **(5)**.

macroeconomics is the study of the economy in the large. Rather than dealing with individual markets and individual consumers and producers, macroeconomics examines the economy as a whole **(1)**.

marginal analysis aids decision making by examining the consequences of making relatively small changes from the current state of affairs **(4)**.

marginal cost (MC) is the addition to total cost (or equivalently to variable cost) of producing one more unit of output:

$$MC = \frac{\Delta TC}{\Delta Q} = \frac{\Delta VC}{\Delta Q} \qquad \textbf{(8)}.$$

marginal factor cost (MFC) is the extra cost to the firm of using one more unit of a factor of production **(14)**.

marginal physical product (MPP) of a factor of production is the increase in output per period that results from increasing the factor by one unit, holding all other inputs and the level of technology fixed **(8)**.

marginal-productivity theory of income distribution states that the functional distribution of income between land, labor, and capital is determined by the relative marginal revenue product of that factor **(14)**.

marginal rate of substitution (MRS) is how much of one good a person is just willing to give up to acquire one unit of another **(6A)**; see also **law of diminishing marginal rate of substitution**.

marginal revenue (MR) is the increase in total revenue

(TR) that results from each one-unit increase in the amount of output:

$$MC = \frac{\Delta TR}{\Delta Q}$$

(9); the additional revenue raised per unit increase in quantity sold **(10)**.

marginal revenue curve shows how much marginal revenue is at each level of output **(10)**.

marginal revenue product (MRP) of any factor of production is the extra revenue generated by increasing the factor by one unit **(14)**.

marginal utility (MU) of any good or service is the increase in utility that a consumer experiences when consumption of that good or service (and that good or service alone) is increased by one unit. In general,

$$MU = \frac{\Delta TU}{\Delta Q},$$

where *TU* is total utility and *Q* is the quantity of the good **(6)**.

marginal utility per dollar is the ratio *MU/P* and indicates the increase in utility from another dollar spent on the good **(6)**.

market is an established arrangement by which buyers and sellers come together to exchange particular goods or services **(3)**; see also **auction market, futures market, perfectly competitive market, spot (cash) market**.

market-clearing price see **equilibrium price**.

market-demand curve is the demand curve of all persons participating in the market for that particular product **(3)**; the total quantities demanded by all consumers in the market at each price. It is the horizontal summation of all individual demand curves in that market **(6)**.

market failure occurs when the price system fails to produce the quantity of a good that would be socially optimal **(19)**.

market period see **immediate run**.

markets see **credit markets**.

market socialism is an economic system characterized by state ownership of the factors of production, the use of primarily economic incentives, market allocation of resources, and decentralized decision making **(20)**.

market test is the process that ensures that goods and services in the private sector yield a benefit equal to or greater than their cost **(4)**.

maximization see **profit maximization**.

maximization rule see **profit-maximization rule**.

merger see **conglomerate merger, horizontal merger, vertical merger**.

microeconomics studies the economic decision making of firms and individuals in markets; it is the study of the economy of the small **(1)**.

midpoints formula for determining the elasticity of demand *(E_d)* for a given segment of the demand curve is:

$$E_d = \frac{\text{Percent Change in Quantity Demanded}}{\text{Percent Change in Price}}$$
$$= \frac{\dfrac{\text{Change in Quantity Demanded}}{\text{Average of Two Quantities}}}{\div \dfrac{\text{Change in price}}{\text{Average of Two Prices}}} \qquad \textbf{(5)}.$$

momentary period see **immediate run**.

money is anything that is widely accepted in exchange for goods and services **(2)**.

money price is a price expressed in monetary units (such as dollars, francs, etc.) **(2)**.

monopolistic competition has four characteristics:

1. the number of sellers is large enough so that each seller acts independently of the other;
2. the product is differentiated from seller to seller;
3. there is free entry into and exit from the industry;
4. sellers are price makers (11).

monopoly see **pure monopoly**.

monopoly-profit-seeking behavior is the activity of anyone trying to achieve or maintain a monopoly in order to gain the monopoly profits (10).

monopsony is a market in which buyers can affect the price of the product by altering the quantities they purchase. A *pure monopsony* is a market with only one buyer (14).

mutual interdependence is a characteristic of an industry in which the actions of one firm will affect other firms in the industry and in which these interrelationships will be recognized (11).

necessities are those products that have an income elasticity of demand less than 1 (5).

negative income tax (NIT) would supplement incomes by giving recipients who earn less than the *break-even income* an amount equal to a minimum acceptable income and subtracting a given percentage of each extra dollar the family earns on its own (18).

negative (or inverse) relationship exists between two variables if an increase in the value of one variable is associated with a *reduction* in the value of the other variable (1A).

net worth see **wealth**.

NIT see **negative income tax**.

noncompeting groups are groups of people who are differentiated by natural ability and abilities acquired through education, training, and experience to the extent that one group does not compete with another for jobs (15).

nonprice competition is the attempt to attract customers through improvements in product quality or service that shift the firm's demand curve to the right (11).

normal goods are those for which demand increases when income increases, holding all prices constant (3).

normal profit requires zero economic profit or accounting profit equal to a normal competitive return on the resources used in the firm (9).

normative economics is the study of *what ought to be* in the economy (1).

oligopoly is an industry characterized by a recognized mutual interdependence, moderate to high barriers to entry, a relatively small number of firms in the industry, and price making (firms are able to exercise varying degrees of control over price) (11).

opportunist behavior occurs when the agent is able to formally fulfill a contract while engaging in behavior that is not in the interests of the principal (7).

opportunity cost of a particular action is the loss of the next best alternative (1); the value of the next best forgone alternative (8).

parallelism see **conscious parallelism**.

parity see **purchasing-power parity (PPP)**.

partnership is a business enterprise that is owned by two or more people (called partners), who make all the business decisions, who share the profits of the business, and who bear the financial responsibility for any losses (7).

payments see **balance of payments, transfer payments**.

P/E ratio see **price/earnings (P/E) ratio**.

perfect competition is true of an industry in which
1. there is a large number of buyers and sellers in the market.
2. each buyer and seller has perfect information about prices and product.
3. the product being sold is homogeneous; that is, it is not possible (or even worthwhile) to distinguish the product of one firm from that of other firms.
4. there are no barriers to entry into or exit from the market; there is freedom of entry and exit.
5. all firms are price takers: no single seller is large enough to exert any control over the product price, so each seller accepts the market price as given (9).

perfectly competitive market has the following characteristics:
1. The product's price is uniform throughout the market.
2. Buyers and sellers have perfect information about price and the product's quality.
3. There are a large number of buyers and sellers.
4. No single buyer or seller purchases or sells enough to change the price (3).

perfectly elastic demand is illustrated by a horizontal demand curve, in which case quantity demanded is most responsive to price (5).

perfectly elastic supply is demonstrated by a horizontal supply curve; quantity supplied is most responsive to price (5).

perfectly inelastic demand is illustrated by a vertical demand curve, in which case quantity demanded is least responsive to price (5).

perfectly inelastic supply is demonstrated by a vertical supply curve; quantity supplied is least responsive to price (5).

personal distribution of income is the distribution of income among households, or how much income one family earns from the factors of production it owns relative to other families (14).

personal wealth (or net worth) is the value of one's total assets minus one's liabilities (18).

positive economics is the study of *what is* in the economy (1).

positive (or direct) relationship exists between two variables if an increase in the value of one variable is associated with an *increase* in the value of the other variable (1A).

poverty standard see **absolute poverty standard, relative poverty standard**.

PPF see **production-possibilities frontier (PPF)**.

preferences are a person's evaluations of goods and services independent of budget and price considerations (6).

present value (PV) of money to be received in the future is the most anyone would pay today in order to receive the money in the future. The present value is sometimes called the *discounted value* because it is smaller than the amount to be received in the future (7A).

price see **equilibrium price, money price, relative price**.

price discrimination exists when the same product or service is sold at different prices to different buyers (10).

price/earnings (P/E) ratio is the stock price divided by the earnings per share (7A).

price elasticity of demand (E_d) is the percentage change in the quantity demanded divided by the percentage change in price (5); see also **cross-price elasticity of demand (E_{xy})**.

price elasticity of supply (E_s) is defined as the percentage change in the quantity supplied divided by the percentage change in price **(5)**.

price leader is a firm whose price changes are consistently imitated by other firms in the industry **(11)**.

price maker is a firm with the ability to control to some degree the price of the good or service it sells **(10)**; in a factor market is a buyer of inputs whose purchases are large enough to affect the price of the input **(14)**.

price-seeking behavior see **monopoly-profit-seeking behavior**.

price system coordinates economic decisions by allowing people with property rights to resources to trade freely, buying and selling at whatever relative prices emerge in the market-place **(2)**.

price taker is a seller that does not have the ability to control the price of the good it sells **(9)**; in a factor market a buyer of an input whose purchases are not large enough to affect the price of the input. The price-taking firm must accept the market price as given **(15)**.

principal is a party that has controlling authority and that engages an agent to act subject to the principal's control and instruction **(7)**.

principal/agent problem exists between the firm and any of its employees when the firm (as a principal) and the employee (as an agent) have different goals and objectives for the employee's behavior **(15)**.

principle of substitution states that practically no good is irreplaceable in meeting *demand* (the amount of a good people are prepared to buy). Users are able to substitute one product for another to satisfy demand **(2)**.

prisoners' dilemma game is a game with 2 players in which both players benefit from cooperating, but in which each player has an incentive to cheat on the agreement **(11)**.

problem see **economic problem, principal/agent problem**.

production-possibilities frontier *(PPF)* shows the combinations of goods that can be produced when the factors of production are utilized to their full potential. It reveals the economic choices open to society **(1)**.

profit see **normal profit**.

profit maximization is the search by firms for the product quality, output, and price that give the firm the highest possible profits **(7)**.

profit-maximization rule is that a firm will maximize profits by producing that level of output at which marginal revenue *(MR)* equals marginal cost *(MC)* (This rule applies to all firms, be they perfectly competitive or monopolistic.) **(9)**.

profits see **economic profits**.

progressive tax is one where the higher the income, the larger the percentage of income paid as taxes **(4)**.

property rights are the rights of an owner to use and exchange property **(2)**.

proportional tax is one where each taxpaying unit pays the same percentage of income as taxes **(4)**.

proprietorship see **sole proprietorship**.

public goods have two properties: (1) no one can be excluded from using the good once it is provided; and (2) the use of the good by one person does not detract from the use by another person (that is, consumption is nonrival) **(4,19)**.

purchasing-power parity *(PPP)* exists between two currencies when changes in the exchange rate reflect only relative changes in the price levels of the two countries **(17)**.

pure economic rent is the price paid to a productive factor that is completely inelastic in supply. Land is the classic example of such a factor **(17)**.

pure monopoly exists 1) when there is one seller in the market for some good or service that has no close substitutes, 2) when the seller has considerable control over price, and 3) when barriers to entry protect the seller from competition **(10)**.

quantity demanded is the amount of a good or service consumers are prepared to buy at a given price (during a specified time period), holding other factors constant **(3)**.

quantity supplied of a good or service is the amount of the good or service offered for sale at a given price, holding other factors constant **(3)**.

rate see **interest rate, law of diminishing marginal rate of substitution, real interest rate**.

rate of return on capital measures the annual return of the capital investment as a percentage of the investment cost **(17)**.

rate regulation is government control of the prices (rates) that regulated enterprises are allowed to charge **(12)**.

ratio see **concentration ratio, price/earnings** *(P/E)* **ratio**.

regressive tax is one where the higher the income, the smaller the percentage of income paid as taxes **(4)**.

regulatory lag occurs when government regulators adjust rates some time after operating costs and the rate base have increased **(12)**.

relationship see **direct relationship, negative (or inverse) relationship, positive relationship**.

relative price is price expressed in terms of other commodities **(2)**.

relative poverty standard defines the poor in terms of the income of others **(18)**.

rent see **economic rent, pure economic rent**.

returns see **law of diminishing returns**.

returns to scale see **constant returns to scale**.

rider see **free rider**.

rule see **least-cost rule, profit-maximization rule, shutdown rule**.

rule of reason stated that monopolies were in violation of the Sherman Act if they engaged in unfair or illegal business practices. Being a monopoly in and of itself was not considered a violation of the Sherman Act according to this rule **(12)**.

run see **immediate run, long run, short run**.

scale see **constant returns to scale, diseconomies of scale, economies of scale**.

scarcity exists when the goods and services that people want exceeds the ability of the economy to produce those goods and services **(1)**; see also **contrived scarcity**.

scatter diagram consists of a number of separate points, each of which plots the value of one variable (measured along the horizontal axis) against a value of another variable (measured along the vertical axis) for a specific time interval **(1A)**.

share see **earnings per share** *(EPS)*.

shortage results if at the current price the quantity demanded exceeds the quantity supplied; the price is too low to equate the quantity demanded with the quantity supplied (3); see also **labor shortage**.

short run is a period of time long enough for existing firms to produce more goods but not long enough for existing firms to expand their capacity or for new firms to enter the market. Thus, output can be varied but only within the limits of existing plant capacity (5); a period of time so short that the existing plant and equipment cannot be varied; such inputs are fixed in supply. Additional output can be produced only by expanding the variable inputs of labor and raw materials (8).

shutdown rule states that if the firm's revenues at all output levels are less than variable costs, it minimizes its losses by shutting down. If there is at least one output level at which revenues exceed variable costs, the firm should not shut down (9).

slope of a straight line is the ratio of the rise (or fall) in Y (measured on the vertical axis) over the run in X (measured on the horizontal axis) (1A).

social benefits are private benefits plus external benefits (19).

social costs are private costs plus external costs (19).

social efficiency occurs when the economy produces all those goods and services whose marginal social benefits equal their marginal social costs (19).

socialism is an economic system in which land and capital are owned by the state and the use of these resources is determined by the state (1).

sole proprietorship is a form of business that is owned by one individual who makes all the business decisions, receives the profits that the business earns, and bears the financial responsibility for losses (7).

speculators are those who buy or sell in the hope of *profiting* from market fluctuations (13).

spot (cash) market is an arrangement where buyers and sellers agree now about payment and delivery of the product now (13).

standard see **absolute poverty standard, relative poverty standard**.

stock each share of stock represents the ownership of $1/n$ percent of the corporation, where n is the number of shares outstanding. Owners of shares can vote on corporate matters and receive dividends proportional to their share holdings (7A).

stock exchange is a market in which shares of stock of corporations are bought and sold and in which the prices of shares of stock are determined (7A).

stock-price index (such as the Dow Jones Industrial Average, the Standard & Poors Index, and the New York Stock Exchange Index) measures the general movements of stock prices (7A).

strike occurs when all unionized employees cease to work until management agrees to specific union demands (16).

substitutes are two goods for which the demand for one rises when the price of the other rises (or if the demand for one falls when the price of the other falls) (3).

substitution see **import substitution, law of diminishing marginal rate of substitution, principle of substitution**.

substitution effect is the change in quantity of X demanded that occurs when the price of X changes and the consumer is compensated to keep utility or welfare constant (6).

supply curve or **schedule** of a particular good or service shows the various quantities supplied at different prices, holding other factors constant, during a particular time period (3); see also **long-run industry-supply curve**.

surplus results if at the current price the quantity supplied exceeds the quantity demanded; the price is too high to equate the quantity demanded with quantity supplied (3); see also **full-employment surplus, government surplus, labor surplus**.

surplus value is the value of any labor over and above the amount of labor the worker would have to provide to meet subsistence needs (18,33).

taker see **price taker**.

tangent is a straight line that touches the curve at only one point (1A).

tariff is a tax levied on imports (16).

tax see **incidence of a tax, progressive tax, proportional tax, regressive tax**.

terms of trade is the rate at which two products can be exchanged for each other between countries (16).

total costs *(TC)* are fixed costs plus variable costs: $TC = VC + FC$ (8); see also **average total cost (ATC)**.

total revenue *(TR)* of sellers in a market is equal to the price of the commodity times the quantity sold: $TR = P \times Q$ (5).

total revenue test is:
1. If price and total revenue move in different directions, $E_d > 1$ *(demand is elastic)*.
2. If price and total revenue move in the same direction, $E_d < 1$ (demand is inelastic).
3. If total revenue does not change when price changes, $E_d = 1$ (demand is unitary elastic) (5).

total utility is the amount of satisfaction (utility) obtained from consuming a particular quantity of a good or service. It is the sum of the marginal utilities of each successive unit of consumption (6).

trade-off see **wage/employment trade-off**.

transaction cost is the cost associated with bringing together buyers and sellers (2).

transfer payments transfer income from one individual or organization to another (4).

union see **craft union, industrial union, labor union**.

utility is the satisfaction that a person enjoys from consuming goods and services (6); see also **law of diminishing marginal utility, total utility**.

value see **present value *(PV)***.

variable see **dependent variable, independent variable**.

variable costs *(VC)* are those that do vary with output (8); see also **average variable cost (AVC)**.

vertical merger is a merger of two firms that are part of the same materials, production, or distribution network (such as a personal-computer manufacturer merging with a retail computer-distribution chain or a machinery manufacturer merging with a machinery-parts supplier) (12).

voluntary export restraint is an agreement between two governments in which the exporting country voluntarily limits the export of a certain product to the importing country (20).

wage differentials see **compensating wage differentials**.

wage/employment trade-off confronts any labor union

that faces a downward-sloping demand curve: higher wages can be obtained only by sacrificing the number of jobs; lower unemployment can be obtained only by sacrificing higher wages **(16)**.

waste-disposal costs are the costs of disposing of the wastes created by economic activity **(19)**.

wealth (or net worth) is the value of one's total assets minus one's liabilities **(18)**.

PHOTO CREDITS

Page numbers in italics indicate exhibits.

TABLE 2
Unemployment and Wages

Year or Month	Unemployment Rate, all Workers	Males 16–19 Years	Males 20 Years and Over	Females 16–19 Years	Females 20 Years and Over	Both Sexes 16–19 Years	White	Black and Other	Experienced Wage and Salary Workers	Married Men, Spouse Present	Women who Maintain Families	Avg Weekly Hours Manufacturing Total	Avg Hourly Earnings Total Private Current Dollars	1982 Dollars	Manufacturing
1948	—	9.8	3.2	8.3	3.6	9.2	3.5	5.9	4.3	—	—	—	—	—	—
1949	—	14.3	5.4	12.3	5.3	13.4	5.6	8.9	6.8	3.5	—	—	—	—	—
1950	5.2	12.7	4.7	11.4	5.1	12.2	4.9	9.0	6.0	4.6	—	—	—	—	—
1951	3.2	8.1	2.5	8.3	4.0	8.2	3.1	5.3	3.7	1.5	—	—	—	—	—
1952	2.9	8.9	2.4	8.0	3.2	8.5	2.8	5.4	3.4	1.4	—	—	—	—	—
1953	2.8	7.9	2.5	7.2	2.9	7.6	2.7	4.5	3.2	1.7	—	—	—	—	—
1954	5.4	13.5	4.9	11.4	5.5	12.6	5.0	9.9	6.2	4.0	—	—	—	—	—
1955	4.3	11.6	3.8	10.2	4.4	11.0	3.9	8.7	4.8	2.6	—	40.7	$1.71	$6.15	$1.85
1956	4.0	11.1	3.4	11.2	4.2	11.1	3.6	8.3	4.4	2.3	—	40.4	1.80	6.38	1.95
1957	4.2	12.4	3.6	10.6	4.1	11.6	3.8	7.9	4.6	2.8	—	39.8	1.89	6.47	2.04
1958	6.6	17.1	6.2	14.3	6.1	15.9	6.1	12.6	7.3	5.1	—	39.2	1.95	6.50	2.10
1959	5.3	15.3	4.7	13.5	5.2	14.6	4.8	10.7	5.7	3.6	—	40.3	2.02	6.69	2.19
1960	5.4	15.3	4.7	13.9	5.1	14.7	5.0	10.2	5.7	3.7	—	39.7	2.09	6.79	2.26
1961	6.5	17.1	5.7	16.3	6.3	16.8	6.0	12.4	6.8	4.6	—	39.8	2.14	6.88	2.32
1962	5.4	14.7	4.6	14.6	5.4	14.7	4.9	10.9	5.6	3.6	—	40.4	2.22	7.07	2.39
1963	5.5	17.2	4.5	17.2	5.4	17.2	5.0	10.8	5.6	3.4	—	40.5	2.28	7.17	2.45
1964	5.0	15.8	3.9	16.6	5.2	16.2	4.6	9.6	5.0	2.8	—	40.7	2.36	7.33	2.53
1965	4.4	14.1	3.2	15.7	4.5	14.8	4.1	8.1	4.3	2.4	—	41.2	2.46	7.52	2.61
1966	3.7	11.7	2.5	14.1	3.8	12.8	3.4	7.3	3.5	1.9	—	41.4	2.56	7.62	2.71
1967	3.7	12.3	2.3	13.5	4.2	12.9	3.4	7.4	3.6	1.8	4.9	40.6	2.68	7.72	2.82
1968	3.5	11.6	2.2	14.0	3.8	12.7	3.2	6.7	3.4	1.6	4.4	40.7	2.85	7.89	3.01
1969	3.4	11.4	2.1	13.3	3.7	12.2	3.1	6.4	3.3	1.5	4.4	40.6	3.04	7.98	3.19
1970	4.8	15.0	3.5	15.6	4.8	15.3	4.5	8.2	4.8	2.6	5.4	39.8	3.23	8.03	3.35
1971	5.8	16.6	4.4	17.2	5.7	16.9	5.4	9.9	5.7	3.2	7.3	39.9	3.45	8.21	3.57
1972	5.5	15.9	4.0	16.7	5.4	16.2	5.1	10.0	5.3	2.8	7.2	40.5	3.70	8.53	3.82
1973	4.8	13.9	3.3	15.3	4.9	14.5	4.3	9.0	4.5	2.3	7.1	40.7	3.94	8.55	4.09
1974	5.5	15.6	3.8	16.6	5.5	16.0	5.0	9.9	5.3	2.7	7.0	40.0	4.24	8.28	4.42
1975	8.3	20.1	6.8	19.7	8.0	19.9	7.8	13.8	8.2	5.1	10.0	39.5	4.53	8.12	4.83
1976	7.6	19.2	5.9	18.7	7.4	19.0	7.0	13.1	7.3	4.2	10.1	40.1	4.86	8.24	5.22
1977	6.9	17.3	5.2	18.3	7.0	17.8	6.2	13.1	6.6	3.6	9.4	40.3	5.25	8.36	5.68
1978	6.0	15.8	4.3	17.1	6.0	16.4	5.2	11.9	5.6	2.8	8.5	40.4	5.69	8.40	6.17
1979	5.8	15.9	4.2	16.4	5.7	16.1	5.1	11.3	5.5	2.8	8.3	40.2	6.16	8.17	6.70
1980	7.0	18.3	5.9	17.2	6.4	17.8	6.3	13.1	6.9	4.2	9.2	39.7	6.66	7.78	7.27
1981	7.5	20.1	6.3	19.0	6.8	19.6	6.7	14.2	7.3	4.3	10.4	39.8	7.25	7.69	7.99
1982	9.5	24.4	8.8	21.9	8.3	23.2	8.6	17.3	9.3	6.5	11.7	38.9	7.68	7.68	8.49
1983	9.5	23.3	8.9	21.3	8.1	22.4	8.4	17.8	9.2	6.5	12.2	40.1	8.02	7.79	8.83
1984	7.4	19.6	6.6	18.0	6.8	18.9	6.5	14.4	7.1	4.6	10.3	40.7	8.32	7.80	9.19
1985	7.1	19.5	6.2	17.6	6.6	18.6	6.2	13.7	6.8	4.3	10.4	40.5	8.57	7.77	9.54
1986	6.9	19.0	6.1	17.6	6.2	18.3	6.0	13.1	6.6	4.4	9.8	40.7	8.76	7.81	9.73
1987	6.1	17.8	5.4	15.9	5.4	16.9	5.3	11.6	5.8	3.9	9.2	41.0	8.98	7.73	9.91
1988	5.4	16.0	4.8	14.4	4.9	15.3	4.7	10.4	5.2	3.3	8.1	41.1	9.28	7.69	10.19
1989	5.2	15.9	4.5	14.0	4.7	15.0	4.5	10.0	5.0	3.0	8.1	41.0	9.66	7.64	10.48
1990	5.4	16.3	4.9	14.7	4.8	15.5	4.7	10.1	5.3	3.4	8.2	40.8	10.02	7.53	10.83
1991	6.6	19.8	6.3	17.4	5.7	18.6	6.0	11.1	6.5	4.4	9.1	40.7	10.34	7.46	11.18
1992	7.4	21.5	7.0	18.5	6.3	20.0	6.5	12.7	7.1	5.0	9.9	41.0	10.59	—	11.45

Source: *Economic Report of the President*, 1993